Beginning
PHP6, Apache, MySQL® Web Development

(continued)

Beginning
PHP6, Apache, MySQL® Web Development

Beginning
PHP6, Apache, MySQL® Web Development

Timothy Boronczyk

Elizabeth Naramore

Jason Gerner

Yann Le Scouarnec

Jeremy Stolz

Michael K. Glass

WILEY

Wiley Publishing, Inc.

Beginning PHP6, Apache, MySQL® Web Development

Published by
Wiley Publishing, Inc.
10475 Crosspoint Boulevard
Indianapolis, IN 46256
www.wiley.com

Copyright © 2009 by Wiley Publishing, Inc., Indianapolis, Indiana

Published simultaneously in Canada

ISBN: 978-0-470-39114-3

Manufactured in the United States of America

10 9 8 7 6 5 4 3 2

Library of Congress Cataloging-in-Publication Data.

Beginning PHP6, Apache, MySQL web development / Timothy Boronczyk . . . [et al.].
    p. cm.
   Includes index.
   ISBN 978-0-470-39114-3 (paper/website)
    1. Web sites—Design.   2. Apache (Computer file : Apache Group)   3. PHP (Computer program language)   4. MySQL (Electronic resource)   I. Boronczyk, Tim, 1979-
TK5105.888.B426   2009
006.7'8—dc22

2008047012

About the Authors

Timothy Boronczyk is a native of Syracuse, New York, where he works as a programmer by day and a freelance developer, writer, and technical editor by night. He has been involved in web design since 1998, and over the years has written several articles on PHP programming and various design topics, as well as the book *PHP and MySQL: Create-Modify-Reuse* (Wrox). Timothy holds a degree in software application programming, is a Zend Certified Engineer, and recently started his first business venture, Salt City Tech (www.saltcitytech.com). In his spare time, he enjoys photography, hanging out with friends, and sleeping with his feet hanging off the end of his bed. He's easily distracted by shiny objects.

Elizabeth Naramore graduated from Miami University (Ohio) with a degree in organizational behavior and has been a web developer since 1997. Her main focus is in e-commerce, but she develops sites across numerous industries. She is currently a moderator at PHPBuilder.com, an online help center for PHP. She lives in Cincinnati, Ohio, with her husband and two children, and looks forward to someday returning to Miami U. to get her masters in computer science.

Jason "Goldbug" Gerner currently spends his days working as a web developer in Cincinnati and burns free time complaining about lack of support for web standards and abusing XML. He can often be found lurking in the PHPBuilder.com discussion forums, waiting to chime in with nagging comments about CSS or code efficiency.

Yann "Bunkermaster" Le Scouarnec is the senior developer for Jolt Online Gaming, a British gaming company. He is a moderator at PHPBuilder.com and a developer of open source PHP software for the gaming community. He has also worked for major software corporations as a software quality expert.

Jeremy "Stolzyboy" Stolz is a web developer at J&M Companies, Inc. (www.jmcompanies.com), a print company in Fargo, North Dakota. Jeremy is primarily a PHP/MySQL developer, but he has also worked with many other languages. When not working, he frequents the Internet and tries to keep his programming skills sharp and up to date. He is a contributor to and moderator at PHPBuilder.com.

Michael "BuzzLY" Glass has been a gladiator in the software/Web site development arena for more than eight years. He has more than ten years of commercial programming experience with a wide variety of technologies, including PHP, Java, Lotus Domino, and Vignette StoryServer. He divides his time between computer programming, playing pool in the APA, and running his web site at www.ultimatespin.com. You can usually find him slinking around on the PHPBuilder.com forums, where he is a moderator with the nickname BuzzLY.

Credits

Acquisitions Editor
Jenny Watson

Development Editor
Adaobi Obi Tulton

Technical Editor
Robert Shimonski

Production Editor
Kathleen Wisor

Copy Editor
Foxxe Editorial Services

Editorial Manager
Mary Beth Wakefield

Production Manager
Tim Tate

Vice President and Executive Group Publisher
Richard Swadley

Vice President and Executive Publisher
Barry Pruett

Associate Publisher
Jim Minatel

Project Coordinator, Cover
Lynsey Stanford

Proofreader
Jen Larsen, Word One

Indexer
Robert Swanson

Acknowledgments

Thanks to my husband and soul mate, who continues to be supportive of everything I do, and who inspires me to always do a little better. Thanks to my children, who make me understand the importance of looking outside the box and keeping my sense of humor, and who make me proud to be a mom. Also, thank you to Debra for always keeping us on track, and for having faith in us.

— *Elizabeth Naramore*

I thank all the innocent bystanders who got pushed around because of this project: Debra and Nancy, who were patient enough not to have homicidal thoughts; and my wife and kids, who barely saw me for six months.

— *Yann Le Scouarnec*

I'd like to thank my wife, my baby daughter, and the rest of my family for being patient with me while I was working on this project.

— *Jeremy Stolz*

Thanks, Staci, for putting up with long and late hours at the computer. Elizabeth and Jason, it wouldn't have been the same project without you two. And thanks to my code testers at www.ultimatespin.com: Spidon, Kaine, Garmy, Spidermanalf, Ping, Webhead, and FancyDan. You guys rock!

To Donna and Gerry, who have influenced my life more than they can ever know, and who have taught me the importance of finishing what you've started.

— *Michael Glass*

Beginning
PHP6, Apache, MySQL® Web Development

Contents

Contents

Contents

Contents

Contents

Contents

Introduction

Welcome to *Beginning PHP6, Apache, MySQL Web Development*, your new trusty resource for assistance in creating your own dynamic web sites. There are a lot of technologies available that can be used to deliver great web sites, and we're glad you chose the Apache/MySQL/PHP (sometimes referred to simply as AMP) approach. You may or may not have had a taste of these three components in the past, but either way we're confident that you will be impressed with the power that lies within them. With this guide by your side, you'll soon learn why this combination is rapidly becoming the most popular way to develop dynamic web sites!

Apache, MySQL and PHP are each complex in and of themselves, and it's impossible for this book to cover every advanced detail of all three. The purpose of this book is to give you the best possible foundation for understanding how each of the core components work separately and together, which will enable you to take full advantage of all that they have to offer. Where we cannot discuss some of the advanced topics, either because it would lead us off on a tangent and cause us to lose focus or because of the space constraints of print media, we provide plenty of direction to authoritative resources you can go to for more information. We show you the tip of the iceberg and provide you with the tools to explore it to its greatest depths. When you've finished reading this book, you'll have a thorough understanding of the core concepts you need to be an effective developer using Apache, MySQL, and PHP, and hopefully a burning desire to continue learning and growing as a developer.

Who's This Book For?

We assume that anyone reading this book has some experience with web site development concepts and a basic working knowledge of HTML and CSS. Knowledge of other programming languages besides PHP is not a prerequisite for this book, but certainly any programming experience you have will help you understand and apply the concepts we present.

This book is geared toward the "newbie" to Apache, MySQL, and PHP, and we've done our best to distill many of the core concepts and code snippets down to their most basic levels. You will find more complex and perhaps more efficient ways of accomplishing the same tasks we present in this book as your knowledge, comfort level, and experience increase. When that happens, you can congratulate yourself and know that you have come over to the "dark side" to join us as Apache, MySQL, and PHP enthusiasts!

What's Covered in the Book

A variety of topics are covered in this book:

- ❑ Installation and configuration of Apache, MySQL, and PHP.
- ❑ Basic introduction to each component and how they interact with one another.

- ❑ Gathering information from and interacting with your web site visitors.

- ❑ How to avoid errors and how to handle them when they inevitably occur.

- ❑ Creating, altering and working with image files.

- ❑ Handling user registration and logins.

- ❑ E-mailing and setting up e-mail lists.

- ❑ Building a content management system.

- ❑ Enhancing your web site by adding e-commerce capabilities.

- ❑ Incorporating a discussion forum into your site.

- ❑ Monitoring the health of your web site through the use of activity logs and error logs.

- ❑ Selecting a third-party web hosting provider.

- ❑ Finding the text editor that's right for you.

- ❑ Using multiple interfaces to connect to MySQL from PHP.

As you read through the chapters in this book and learn about each of these topics, you will be creating two complete web sites. The first is a movie review site that displays information about films and their respective reviews. This project will cover the basics, such as writing PHP code, creating a MySQL database, filling the database with data and showing specific information to your visitors based on what they want to see.

The second project is a comic book fan web site. This site will be developed in the latter part of the book and will incorporate some of the more complex topics of working with Apache, MySQL and PHP. You will create a truly interactive web site where your visitors can interact with you and with other members of the site.

We take you step by step through the development of each of these sites, and you will continually build upon them as new concepts are introduced. Note, however, that each of the chapters in this book has been designed as a standalone chapter, so that if you are not particularly interested in reading a specific topic then you are free to move on to another.

If you thought the days of the "pop quiz" were over, think again! We have provided handy exercises at the end of most of the chapters to test your knowledge of discussed topic and challenge you to think one step further. We've provided answers to these exercises in Appendix A.

As any programmer knows, software is constantly being improved and debugged, and while we used the latest and greatest versions of Apache, MySQL, and PHP at the time of publishing, chances are those versions won't be around for long. It is important for you to visit the source web sites for each component to get the most updated versions and recent release notes. We recommend that you always use the most recent stable releases when developing web sites using Apache, MySQL, and PHP. Using older software versions or versions that have not been fully tested by the developers can be dangerous to your application and leave bugs in your code.

The most recent stable versions that were in effect at the time of this book's writing were:

- ❑ **PHP:** Version 6.0.0
- ❑ **Apache:** Version 2.2.9
- ❑ **MySQL:** Version 5.0.67

Future editions of this book will address changes and improvements in these programs as they become available.

What You Need to Use This Book

This book is designed to be multiplatform and we cover topics and issues for both Windows-based and Linux-based machines. You will need Apache, MySQL and PHP to do the exercises in this book. All three are open source programs, so you can download and use them free of charge. We have provided instructions for downloading and installing all three components in Chapter 1 and Appendix I.

You will also need a text editor to enter your code. Many editors are available that you can use, and some of the more popular ones are compared in Appendix F. Finally, you'll need a web browser, such as Mozilla Firefox, Internet Explorer, Google Chrome, Apple Safari or Opera to view your web pages.

Conventions

To help you follow along and get the most from the text, we've used a number of conventions throughout the book.

Try It Out

The *Try It Out* is an exercise you should work through, following the text in the book.

1. They usually consist of a set of steps.

2. Each step has a number.

3. Follow the steps through with your copy of the database.

How It Works

After each *Try It Out*, the code you've typed will be explained in detail.

> **Boxes like this one hold important, not-to-be forgotten information that is directly relevant to the surrounding text.**

Tips, hints, tricks, and asides to the current discussion are offset and placed in italics like this.

As for styles in the text:

❑   We *highlight* important words when we introduce them

❑   We show filenames, URLs, and code within the text like this: `www.example.com`

❑   We present code in two different ways:

```
In code examples we highlight new and important code with a gray background.
The highlighting is not used for code that's less important in the present
context, or that has been shown before.
```

Source Code

As you work through the examples in this book, you may choose either to type in all the code manually or to use the source code files that accompany the book. All of the source code used in this book is available for download at `www.wrox.com`. Once at the site, simply locate the book's title (either by using the Search box or by using one of the title lists) and click the Download Code link on the book's detail page to obtain all the source code for the book.

> *Because many books have similar titles, you may find it easiest to search by ISBN; for this book the ISBN is 987-0-4703-9114-3.*

Alternatively, you can go to the main Wrox code download page at `www.wrox.com/WileyCDA/Section/id-105127.html` to see the code available for this book and all other Wrox books.

Once you download the code, just uncompress it with your favorite compression utility.

Errata

We make every effort to ensure that there are no errors in the text or in the code. However, no one is perfect and mistakes do occur. If you find an error in one of our books, such as a spelling mistake or faulty piece of code, we would be very grateful for your feedback. By sending in errata, you may save another reader hours of frustration and at the same time you will be helping us provide even higher-quality information.

To find the errata page for this book, go to `www.wrox.com` and locate the title using the Search box or one of the title lists. Then, click the Book Errata link on the book details page. On this page you can view all errata that has been submitted for this book and posted by Wrox editors. A complete book list including links to each book's errata is also available at `www.wrox.com/WileyCDA/Section/id-105077.html`.

If you don't spot "your" error on the Book Errata page, go to `www.wrox.com/WileyCDA/Section/id-106036.html` and complete the form there to send us the error you have found. We'll check the information and, if appropriate, post a message to the book's errata page and fix the problem in subsequent editions of the book.

p2p.wrox.com

For author and peer discussion, join the P2P forums at p2p.wrox.com. The forums are a web-based system for you to post messages relating to Wrox books and related technologies and interact with other readers and technology users. The forums offer a subscription feature to e-mail you topics of interest of your choosing when new posts are made to the forums. Wrox authors, editors, other industry experts, and your fellow readers are present on these forums.

At p2p.wrox.com you will find a number of different forums that will help you not only as you read this book but also as you develop your own applications. You can read messages in the forums without joining P2P, but you must join in order to post your own messages. To join the forums, just follow these steps:

1. Go to p2p.wrox.com, and click the Register Now link.

2. Read the terms of use and click Agree.

3. Provide the required information to join as well as any optional information you wish to provide and click Submit.

4. You will receive an e-mail with information describing how to verify your account and complete the joining process.

Once you join, you can post new messages and respond to messages other users post. You can read messages at any time on the Web. If you would like to have new messages from a particular forum e-mailed to you, click the Subscribe to this Forum icon by the forum name in the forum listing.

For more information about how to use Wrox P2P, be sure to read the P2P FAQs for answers to questions about how the forum software works as well as many common questions specific to P2P and Wrox books. To read the FAQs, click the FAQ link on any P2P page.

Part I
Movie Review Web Site

Configuring Your Installation

We assume that since you've spent your hard-earned money to purchase this book, you undoubtedly know the enormous benefits of using Apache, MySQL, and PHP (AMP) together to create and deliver dynamic web sites. But just in case you found this book on your desk one Monday morning with a sticky note from your boss reading "Learn this!," this chapter looks at what makes the "AMP" combination so popular. This chapter also walks you through installing and configuring all three components of the AMP platform on Windows (installation and configuration for Linux-based platforms can be found in Appendix I).

Projects in This Book

You will develop two complete web sites and a few "side projects" over the course of this book:

❑ **Movie Review web site:** By developing this site, you will be introduced to the necessary skills to write a PHP program, work with variables and include files, and use data from MySQL. Using PHP and MySQL together makes your site truly dynamic as pages are created on the fly for your visitors. You will also get experience in validating user input while working on this site.

❑ **Comic Book Fan web site:** While creating this web site, you'll learn how to build and normalize databases from scratch, manipulate images and send e-mails from PHP. You'll also learn about authenticating users, managing content through a Content Management System, creating a mailing list, setting up an e-commerce section and developing and customizing a discussion forum.

This book also covers how to learn about your visitors through the use of log files and how to troubleshoot common mistakes or problems you will undoubtedly encounter while programming. The appendixes in this book will provide you with the necessary reference materials you'll need to assist you in your web development journey once you complete the book and propose tools to help make you a more efficient coder. After reading this book, you will be able to create a well-designed, dynamic web site using freely available tools.

A Brief Introduction to Apache, MySQL, PHP, and Open Source

There are many open source projects from address books to full-fledged operating systems. Apache, MySQL, and PHP are all open source projects that can be installed on a wide variety of platforms. They are most popular on Linux (giving the acronym "LAMP") although Windows-based Apache, MySQL and PHP installations are becoming increasingly popular, especially for developers.

The open source movement is a collaboration of some of the finest minds in programming and development, which make up the open source community. The open source movement is defined by the efforts of the community to make for easier development and standardization of systems, applications and/or programs. By allowing the open exchange of source code and other information, programmers from all over the world contribute to making truly powerful and efficient pieces of software usable by everyone. This is the opposite of the closed source model, which is more commonly referred to as "proprietary." Bugs get fixed, improvements are made, and a good software program can becomes a great program through the contributions of many people to publicly available source codes.

A Brief History of Open Source Initiatives

The term *open source* was coined in 1998 after Netscape decided to publish the source code for its popular Navigator browser. This announcement prompted a small group of software developers who had been long-time supporters of the soon-to-be open source ideology to formally develop the Open Source Initiative (OSI) and the Open Source Definition. An excerpt taken from the OSI's web site (www.opensource.org) briefly defines the organization's objectives:

> *The OSI is a non-profit corporation formed to educate about and advocate for the benefits of open source and to build bridges among different constituencies in the open-source community. [. . .] One of our most important activities is as a standards body, maintaining the Open Source Definition for the good of the community.*

Although the OSI's ideology was initially promoted in the hacker community, a global base of programmers began to offer suggestions and supply fixes to improve Netscape's performance upon Netscape's release of the browser's source code. The OSI's mission was off and running and the mainstream computing world began to embrace the idea.

Linux was the first operating system that could be considered open source (although BSD distributed from the University of California Berkeley in 1989 was a close runner-up), and many programs followed soon thereafter. Large software corporations such as Corel began to offer versions of their programs that worked on Linux machines. People soon had entire open source systems, from the operating system right up to the applications they used every day.

Although there are now numerous classifications of OSI open source licenses, any software that bears the OSI certification seal can be considered open source because it has passed the Open Source Definition test. These programs are available from a multitude of web sites; the most popular is www.sourceforge.net, which houses more than 175,000 open source projects!

Why Open Source Rocks

Open source programs are very cool because:

- ❑ **Open source programs are free:** The greatest thing about open source software is that its source code is free of charge and widely available to the general public. This makes it easy for software developers and programmers to volunteer their time to improve existing software and create new programs. Open source software cannot, by definition, require any sort of licensing or sales fees that restrict access to its source code.

- ❑ **Open source programs are cross-platform and "technology-neutral":** By requiring open source software to be non–platform specific, the open source community has ensured that the programs are usable by virtually everyone. According to the Open Source Definition provided by the OSI at http://opensource.org/docs/definition.php, open source programs must not be dependent on any "individual technology or style of interface" and must be "technology-neutral." As long as the software can run on more than one operating system, it meets that criteria.

- ❑ **Open source programs must not restrict other software:** This means that if an open source program is distributed along with other programs, those other programs are free to be open source or proprietary in nature. This gives software developers maximum control and flexibility.

- ❑ **Open source programs embrace diversity:** The diversity of minds and cultures simply produce a better result. For this reason, open source programs cannot discriminate against any person or group, nor can they discriminate against any field of endeavor. For example, a program designed for use in the medical profession cannot be limited to that profession if someone in another field wants to take the program's source code and modify it to fit his or her needs.

For a complete list of criteria a piece of software must meet before it can be considered "open source," or for more information about the OSI and the open source community, visit the OSI web site at www.opensource.org.

How the AMP Pieces Work Together

Now that you've learned about some of the spirit and history of open source, it's important to understand the role Apache, MySQL and PHP play in creating your web site.

Imagine for a moment that your dynamic web site is like a fancy restaurant. Hungry diners come to your place and each one wants something different and specific. They don't worry so much about how the food is prepared so long as it looks great and tastes delicious. Unlike a buffet spread where everything is laid out and your patrons just pick and choose from what's available, a nice restaurant encourages interaction between the patron and waiter and complete customization of any meal to meet any specific dietary needs. Similarly, your web site shouldn't be a static page with little interaction from its visitors; it should be a dynamic site where visitors can choose what they want to see.

Continuing with this scenario, you can characterize the components of the AMP platform as follows:

❑ **PHP:** Whatever people ask for, your highly trained master of culinary arts, the chef, prepares it without complaint. She is quick, flexible, and able to prepare a multitude of different types of foods. PHP acts in much the same way as it mixes and matches dynamic information to meet the request for fresh web pages.

❑ **MySQL:** Every chef has a well-stocked stockroom of ingredients. In this case, the ingredients used by PHP are records of information stored in MySQL's databases.

❑ **Apache:** This is the waiter. He gets requests from the patron and relays them back to the kitchen with specific instructions about how the meal should be prepared. Then he serves the meal once it is complete.

When a patron (web site visitor) comes to your restaurant (web site), he or she sits down and orders a meal with specific requirements (requests a particular page or resource), such as a steak served medium well. The waiter (Apache) takes those specific requirements back to the kitchen and passes them off to the chef (PHP). The chef then goes to the stockroom (MySQL) to retrieve the ingredients (data) to prepare the meal and presents the final dish (web page) back to the waiter, who in turn serves it to the patron exactly the way he or she ordered it.

You can choose to install one, two or all three of the AMP components based on your specific needs. Each is a powerful application in its own right. But the reason the Apache, MySQL, and PHP combination has become so popular is that they work incredibly well together. We obviously recommend that you install all three. You can even benefit from installing them on your development system that is separate from your hosting server. This way, you can develop and test your site in the comfort of your own workspace without having to upload scripts up to the hosting server to test every little change. It also gives you a safe environment to test your code without breaking a live web site.

Installing Apache, MySQL, and PHP on Windows

After following these instructions, you will have successfully installed Apache, MySQL, and PHP on your Windows system. We cover installing them on Windows XP– and Windows Vista–based systems. You should review each component's web site if you want more detailed installation instructions or information on other supported platforms.

❑ **Apache:** `http://httpd.apache.org/docs/2.2/platform/windows.html`

❑ **MySQL:** `http://dev.mysql.com/doc/refman/5.1/en/windows-installation.html`

❑ **PHP:** `www.php.net/install.windows`

Installing Apache

As your web server, Apache's main job is to listen to any incoming requests from a browser and return an appropriate response. Apache is quite powerful and can accomplish virtually any task that you as a webmaster require.

According to the Netcraft web site (www.netcraft.com), Apache is running over 83.5 million Internet servers, more than Microsoft, Sun ONE, and Zeus combined at the time of this writing. Its flexibility, power, and, of course, price make it a popular choice. It can be used to host a web site for the general public, a company-wide intranet or for simply testing your pages before they are uploaded to a secure server on another machine.

Follow these steps to download and install Apache on your Windows machine (installation instructions can be found in Appendix I):

1. Go to www.apache.org, and click the HTTP Server link in the Apache Projects list. The Apache Software Foundation offers many different software packages, though the HTTP Server is the only one we are concerned with.

2. Click the Download link under the most recent version of Apache.

3. Click the Win 32 Binary (MSI Installer) link to download the installation package. Whether you choose the download without mod_ssl or the one that includes OpenSLL depends on your local laws, needs and personal preferences. We do not use any of the functionality offered by mod_ssl in this book, so if you want to lean towards the safe side feel free to download the package without mod_ssl.

If you experience problems downloading this file, you can try downloading from a different mirror site. Select an available mirror from the drop-down box near the top of the download page.

4. You should be able to double-click the MSI file to initiate the installation wizard for Apache once it has finished downloading, but you may experience some issues depending on what security policies Windows has in effect. We recommend running the installer with administrative privileges from within a console window.

To open a console as an Administrator in Windows XP, navigate through Start ⇨ All Programs ⇨ Accessories, right-click on Command Prompt and select the Run As option. In Windows Vista, navigate through Start ⇨ All Programs ⇨ Accessories, right-click on Command Prompt, and select the Run as Administrator option.

5. Use the cd command to navigate to where you downloaded the installer file, and then run the installer using msiexec -i. The Installation Wizard will open.

```
cd C:\Users\Timothy\Downloads\
msiexec -i apache_2.2.9-win32-x86-no_ssl-r2.msi
```

6. After accepting the installation agreement, you will see a screen that is equivalent to a readme.txt file — it gives basic information about the Apache software and where to go to find more information. We highly recommend that you read this.

7. Enter the following information on the Server Information screen:

❏ Domain name: For example, example.com

❏ Server name: For example, www.example.com

❏ Net administrator's e-mail address

❏ Whether to install Apache for all users or only the current user.

We recommend the default option, which is to install Apache for all users on port 80 as a service.

8. At the Setup Type screen, the Typical installation option is recommended for beginners and will suffice for most of your needs. If you have special circumstances or are an advanced user, feel free to chose the Custom setup option.

9. You can specify which directory Apache will be installed in on the Destination Folder screen. Again, we recommend the default (`C:\Program Files\Apache Software Foundation\Apache2.2`), although you may want to change this depending on your needs and your system's configuration.

10. How long it takes for Apache to be installed on your system depends on many factors, but typically it shouldn't take longer than a couple minutes. The wizard will tell you when it has finished, and you can click the Finish button to close the window.

11. To close the console window from which you launched the installation file, you can either click the X in the window's top-right corner or enter `exit` at the prompt.

12. Next, bring up the System Properties window. In Windows XP, this is done by right-clicking on the My Computer icon on your desktop and selecting Properties. In Windows Vista, this is done by right-clicking on the Computer icon on your desktop, selecting Properties, and then selecting Advanced System Settings.

13. Select the Advanced tab, and then click the Environment Variables button. Select PATH from the System variables section and then Edit. Add the path to Apache's `bin` directory to the end of the existing list (`C:\Program Files\Apache Software Foundation\Apache2.2\bin` by default). This will allow you to run Apache's utilities from the command line without having to explicitly type the full path each time.

Starting and Stopping Apache

Apache runs as a service waiting for web requests and handling them in the background; you don't interact with it on the desktop like other applications. Instead, you set Apache's options with its configuration file. There are three ways to start and stop the server:

❑ **Windows Service Manager:** Go to Start ⇨ Control Panel ⇨ Administrative Tools, and click on the Services icon. Alternatively, you can go to Start ⇨ Run and execute `services.msc`. If you installed Apache as a Windows service for all users (the suggested installation type), then you will see its entry in the listing of services. Just highlight the entry and click the desired action (start, stop or restart).

❑ **The `net` command:** The `net` command is used to monitor network related services. Open up a command window that has administrative privileges, and type `net start apache2.2` to start Apache and `net stop apache2.2` to stop Apache.

❑ **Apache Service Monitor:** The Apache Service Monitor is installed by default with Apache and typically can be found running in your system tray. If it's not there, then you can find it by going to Start ⇨ All Programs ⇨ Apache HTTP Server 2.2 ⇨ Monitor Apache Servers. Just highlight the server's entry and click the desired action button (start, stop or restart).

Apache only reads its main configuration file once when it starts up, so you will need to restart Apache any time you make changes to its configuration file for those changes to be active.

Testing Your Installation

To test the installation of your Apache server, open a web browser and type the following URL:

```
http://localhost/
```

If the installation was successful then you will see an Apache "success" page in your browser. If not, check your error log by opening the `error.log` file, which you can find in the `logs` subdirectory of Apache's installation directory (`C:\Program Files\Apache Software Foundation\Apache2.2\logs` by default). By searching through the log file, you can find issues, or maybe an indication of where your installation may have experienced a problem. For a more in-depth discussion of logs, please refer to Chapter 17.

If you had installation problems, note that you might experience some errors such "no services installed" if Apache is trying to share port 80 with another web server or application, such as a locally installed firewall application. To fix this, you can tell Apache to use a different port. Open your `httpd.conf` file in the `conf` subdirectory (`C:\Program Files\Apache Software Foundation\Apache2.2\conf` by default) and locate the following lines:

```
# Listen: Allows you to bind Apache to specific IP addresses and/or
# ports, instead of the default. See also the <VirtualHost>
# directive.
#
# Change this to Listen on specific IP addresses as shown below to
# prevent Apache from glomming onto all bound IP addresses (0.0.0.0)
#
#Listen 12.34.56.78:80
Listen 80
```

Change the last line of this block to read:

```
Listen 8080
```

Then, locate the following lines:

```
# ServerName gives the name and port that the server uses to identify itself.
# This can often be determined automatically, but we recommend you specify
# it explicitly to prevent problems during startup.
#
# If this is not set to valid DNS name for your host, server-generated
# redirections will not work. See also the UseCanonicalName directive.
#
# If your host doesn't have a registered DNS name, enter its IP address here.
# You will have to access it by its address anyway, and this will make
# redirections work in a sensible way.
#
ServerName www.example.com:80
```

Change the last line of this section to the following:

```
ServerName www.example.com:8080
```

Now restart Apache and retest the installation with the following:

```
http://localhost:8080/
```

If you are still experiencing problems, the Apache Foundation has provided a nifty document about some other issues that may arise during installation. You can view it by going to `http://httpd .apache.org/docs/2.2/platform/windows.html`.

Installing PHP

PHP is a server-side scripting language that allows your web site to be truly dynamic. PHP stands for *PHP: Hypertext Preprocessor* (and, yes, we're aware PHP is a "recursive acronym" — probably meant to confuse the masses). Its flexibility and relatively small learning curve (especially for programmers who have a background in other programming languages like C, Java and Perl) make it one of the most popular scripting languages used today. PHP's popularity continues to increase as businesses and individuals everywhere embrace it as an alternative to Microsoft's ASP.NET languages. According to Netcraft, PHP code can be found running on approximately 21 million web sites.

There are several different installation methods for PHP, though we strongly recommend you follow the manual installation process. At the time of publication, the automated installer is not complete, secure or intended for use on live servers. Follow these steps to install PHP on your system:

1. Go to the PHP web site at `www.php.net`.

2. Click on the Download link to go to the site's downloads page.

3. Scroll down to the Windows Binary section, and click on the appropriate link to download the latest PHP .zip package.

4. Click any of the mirror sites to begin the download. If you have difficulties downloading from one mirror, then try a different mirror that may be closer to you.

5. Once the Zip file has been downloaded, extract its contents using any standard unzip program and save it to the directory of your choice. We recommend a directory named `C:\PHP`.

    Both Windows XP and Windows Vista have built-in capabilities to extract files from Zip archives. If you are on a different version of Windows or prefer to use a dedicated compression tool, we recommend 7-Zip available at `www.7-zip.org`. It is a free application that can work with many different compression formats, including Zip.

6. It is advised to run PHP with a `php.ini` file. By default, the PHP installation provides two copies of the file with common configuration values: `php.ini-dist` and `php.ini-recommended`. Rename the configuration file of your choice to `php.ini`.

    The `php.ini-dist` file is meant to be used for development purposes while `php.ini-recommended` has additional security measures and should be used when your site goes live. Depending on your reason for using PHP, choose the `php.ini` file that best suits your needs. For the purposes of this book, we are going to be using the `php.ini-dist`. Feel free to switch to the `php.ini-recommended` file as your default once you are more familiar with how PHP behaves.

7. Bring up the System Properties window. In Windows XP, this is done by right-clicking on the My Computer icon on your desktop and selecting Properties. In Windows Vista, this is done by right-clicking on the Computer icon on your desktop, selecting Properties and then Advanced System Settings.

8. Select the Advanced tab, and then click the Environment Variables button. Add the directory to which you extracted PHP to your System's PATH variable (C:\PHP in our configuration). Also create a new System variable PHPRC with the same directory as its value. This allows other applications (such as Apache) to find PHP without your having to copy files into your System directory.

Configuring PHP to Use MySQL

MySQL support was included in earlier versions of PHP by default, but starting with PHP version 5 you now have to specifically enable this. For PHP to play nice with MySQL, you need to make two changes to your php.ini file. Open the file using your text editor and locate the following lines:

```
; Directory in which the loadable extensions (modules) reside.
extension_dir = "./"
```

Change the line to:

```
extension_dir = "C:\PHP\ext"
```

Then locate the following line:

```
;extension=php_mysql.dll
```

The semicolon is what denotes a comment within this file and will be ignored. Simply remove the semicolon at the beginning of the line to uncomment it:

```
extension=php_mysql.dll
```

Finally, copy the file libmysql.dll from your C:\PHP directory into your C:\Windows\System32 or C:\WINNT\System32 directory.

Configuring Apache to Use PHP

Now that both Apache and PHP are installed, there are a few more customizable options that need to be adjusted. To configure Apache to recognize a PHP file as one that needs to be parsed with the PHP engine, you need to first locate the following lines in your httpd.conf file:

```
# AddType allows you to add to or override the MIME configuration
# file specified in TypesConfig for specific file types.
#
#AddType application/x-gzip .tgz
#
# AddEncoding allows you to have certain browsers uncompress
# information on the fly. Note: Not all browsers support this.
#
#AddEncoding x-compress .Z
#AddEncoding x-gzip .gz .tgz
#
# If the AddEncoding directives above are commented-out, then you
# probably should define those extensions to indicate media types:
#
AddType application/x-compress .Z
AddType application/x-gzip .gz .tgz
```

Then add the following lines:

```
AddType application/x-httpd-php .php
AddType application/x-httpd-php-source .phps
PHPIniDir "C:\PHP"
```

If you installed PHP in a location other than the recommended C:\PHP, then make sure your path matches the location of the directory.

Next, you need to add the PHP module into your httpd.conf program so that Apache can properly coordinate with PHP to serve the dynamically generated pages PHP will produce. In your configuration file, locate the following lines:

```
# Dynamic Shared Object (DSO) Support
#
# To be able to use the functionality of a module which was built as a DSO you
# have to place corresponding 'LoadModule' lines at this location so the
# directives contained in it are actually available _before_ they are used.
# Statically compiled modules (those listed by 'httpd -l') do not need
# to be loaded here.
#
# Example:
# LoadModule foo_module modules/mod_foo.so
#
LoadModule actions_module modules/mod_actions.so
LoadModule alias_module modules/mod_alias.so
LoadModule asis_module modules/mod_asis.so
LoadModule auth_basic_module modules/mod_auth_basic.so
#LoadModule auth_digest_module modules/mod_auth_digest.so
...
#LoadModule usertrack_module modules/mod_usertrack.so
#LoadModule version_module modules/mod_version.so
#LoadModule vhost_alias_module modules/mod_vhost_alias.so
```

Add the following line:

```
LoadModule php6_module "C:\PHP\php6apache2_2.dll"
```

Again, make sure your path matches the location of the php6apache2_2.dll file if you did not install PHP in the recommended directory.

Oh, and remember to restart Apache after you've saved your modifications to httpd.conf or else Apache will not be aware of your changes!

Testing the Configuration

To ensure that both PHP and Apache have been configured to work together, let's write a short test program. Open notepad and type the following program:

```
<html>
 <head>
  <title>PHP Testing</title>
 </head>
 <body>
<?php
echo "<p>If you see this then we did it right!</p>";
?>
 </body>
 </html>
```

Save this file as `test.php` in Apache's `htdocs` directory. By default it is at `C:\Program Files\Apache Software Foundation\Apache2.2\htdocs`. Then, open your web browser and visit `http://localhost/test.php`. You should see the screen shown in Figure 1-1.

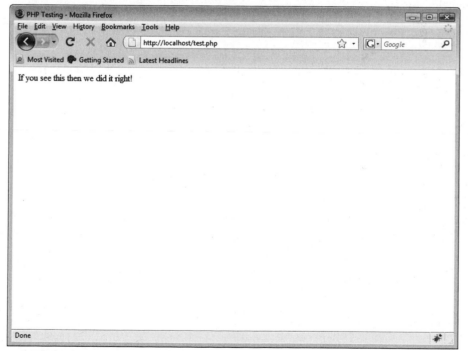

Figure 1-1

Installing MySQL

Another open source favorite, MySQL, is the database construct that enables PHP and Apache to work together to access and display data in a readable format to a browser. It is a Structured Query Language (SQL) server designed for heavy loads and processing of complex queries. As a relational database system, MySQL allows many different tables to be joined together for maximum efficiency and speed.

MySQL is the perfect choice for providing data via the Internet because of its ability to handle heavy loads, its advanced security measures and (depending on who you ask) it's easier to manage than some of the other open source database servers available. Follow these steps to install MySQL on your Windows system:

1. Go to the MySQL web site at www.mysql.com, and click the Developer Zone tab. Then, click the Downloads link on the navigation bar just under the tabs.

2. Scroll down and click on the link for the latest General Availability version of MySQL.

3. Scroll down to the Windows section of the downloadable files and click Pick a Mirror next to the Windows Essentials package.

4. Select the download from a nearby mirror and the download will begin.

5. As was with Apache, you should be able to double-click the MSI file to initiate the Installation Wizard, but you may experience some issues depending on what security policies Windows has in effect. We recommend running the installer with administrative privileges from within a console window.

   To open a console as an Administrator in Windows XP, navigate through Start ⇨ All Programs ⇨ Accessories, right-click on Command Prompt, and select the Run As option. In Windows Vista, navigate through Start ⇨ All Programs ⇨ Accessories, right-click on Command Prompt, and select the Run as administrator option.

6. Use the cd command to navigate to where you downloaded the installer file, and then run the installer using msiexec -i. The Installation Wizard will open.

   ```
   cd C:\Users\Timothy\Downloads\
   msiexec -i mysql-essential-5.1.26-rc-win32.msi
   ```

7. At the Setup Type screen, the Typical installation option is recommended for beginners and will suffice for most of your needs. If you have special circumstances or are an advanced user, feel free to choose the Complete or Custom setup options instead.

8. How long it takes for MySQL to be installed on your system depends on many factors, but the installation should proceed quickly and shouldn't take longer than a couple of minutes. After the wizard has finished installing the appropriate files, its final screen will simply indicate the installation is complete. Click Finish to end the wizard.

9. To close the console window from which you launched the installation file, you can either click the X in the window's top-right corner or enter exit at the prompt.

Configuring MySQL

The MySQL Server Instance Configuration Wizard is used on Windows to install MySQL as a service and establish a basic configuration. Go to Start ⇨ All Programs ⇨ MySQL ⇨ MySQL Server Instance Configuration Wizard to launch the utility.

You can choose either a Detailed Configuration or Standard Configuration, and we recommend the Standard Configuration option unless you are an advanced user.

We also recommend you check the option to include the bin directory in Window's PATH variable. This will allow you to run MySQL's utilities from the command line without having to explicitly type the full path each time and without having to manually configure the PATH variable as you did with Apache and PHP.

Last, we recommend you specify a password for MySQL's root user so your installation isn't left vulnerable to unauthorized access.

The Configuration Wizard will prepare a basic configuration file at `C:\Program Files\MySQL\MySQL Server 5.1\my.ini` by default and install MySQL as a windows service. You can fine-tune your installation by modifying the directives in `my.ini`. MySQL only reads this file once when it starts up, so you will need to restart MySQL any time you make changes to it for them to be active.

Starting and Stopping MySQL

Like Apache, MySQL runs as a background service without much interaction on the desktop. You can start and stop the server in one of two ways:

- ❑ **Windows Service Manager:** Go to Start ⇨ Control Panel ⇨ Administrative Tools, and click on the Services icon. Alternatively, you can go to Start ⇨ Run and execute `services.msc`. Highlight the MySQL entry, and click the desired action (start, stop, or restart).
- ❑ **The `net` command:** Open up a command window that has administrative privileges, and type `net start mysql` to start MySQL and `net stop mysql` to stop MySQL.

Testing Your Installation

As with the other applications, it's a good idea to test your MySQL installation. MySQL comes with a command-line client that you can use to connect to the MySQL server that is running and execute queries against your databases. Go to a command line and run:

```
mysql.exe -u root -p test
```

MySQL should prompt you for a password, and you need to enter whatever you set it as for the root user when you configured the MySQL installation.

The `-u` option provides the username that you're using to connect to MySQL, in this case `root`, and `-p` tells MySQL to prompt you for the password. `test` is the name of the database you will be using. The `test` database is installed by default.

The prompt will change to `mysql` ⇨ and whatever you enter will be sent to the MySQL server. See what database tables have been set up by default. Type the following:

```
SHOW DATABASES;
```

You should see three existing databases, `information_schema`, `mysql` and `test`. To see what tables there are in the `mysql` database, type the following:

```
SHOW TABLES FROM mysql;
```

To exit the MySQL client, type `exit`.

Setting Up Dedicated MySQL User Accounts

Malicious hackers can be quite crafty in the ways in which they break into your system, especially if you are directly connected to the Internet. MySQL allows you to pick and choose what user is allowed to perform what function based on the privileges that you establish. All user privilege information is stored in a database called `mysql`.

If you're the only one accessing the MySQL database, you may not have to worry about adding users. You have already used MySQL's root account to verify you can communicate with the running instance of the MySQL server. However, use of the root account should be limited for administrative tasks only. What if you have, say, an Aunt Edna who is going to help you out by inputting some backlogged information? You want her to be able to go into the tables and look at things, and even insert some information. But you probably don't want her to be able to delete your entire database. By restricting her privileges as a user, you help to protect your data.

Connect to MySQL using the MySQL command-line client as the `root` user as previously discussed. Then follow these steps:

1. If you would like to see all the privileges that can be assigned, you can type the following:

```
SHOW COLUMNS FROM user FROM mysql;
```

2. You only want to look at what users are already there, so type the following:

```
SELECT user, host FROM mysql.user;
```

You should see what is depicted in Figure 1-2.

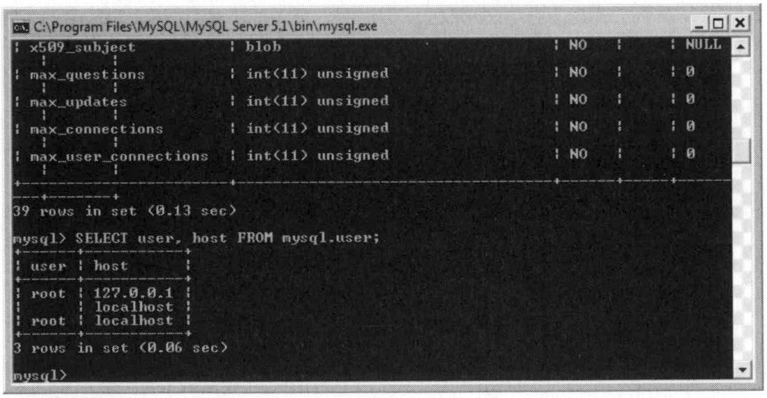

Figure 1-2

3. Because you want to set up a secure service, you want to remove the blank user for the `localhost` host. Type the following:

```
DELETE FROM mysql.user WHERE Host="localhost" AND User="";
```

You will get a response from MySQL that states:

```
Query OK, 1 row affected (0.02 sec)
```

Note the time it takes to process the query may differ based on the speed of your computer, but the important thing here is that you see "Query OK."

4. Now you're going to GRANT Aunt Edna some privileges as a new user, so type the following:

```
GRANT SELECT,INSERT,UPDATE ON *.*
TO edna@localhost
IDENTIFIED BY "ednapass";
```

You'll notice how the prompt changed to -> on the second line. MySQL will not run the query until it encounters the terminating semicolon. This allows you to enter longer queries on multiple lines.

You have now established edna as a valid user will be allowed access to your MySQL system provided two things:

❑ She attempts her connection from the localhost — not a different connection from a remote computer.

❑ She supplies the correct password: ednapass.

Your Aunt Edna will now be allowed to select information from the database, insert new information in the database, and update old information in the database. By giving her access to all the tables in the database (via the use of ON *.*), you have allowed her to modify any table in existence.

As you become more familiar with working with tables and MySQL commands, modifying privileges or user information will become easier for you because the information is all stored in a table (just like everything else in MySQL).

A complete list of privileges that you can grant is available at the MySQL web site, http://dev.mysql.com/doc/refman/5.1/en/privileges-provided.html.

Where to Go for Help and Other Valuable Resources

Although we've certainly tried to make this as easy as possible for you, there are so many different variables in computers and their setups that it is virtually impossible to cover every possible situation. Anyone who works with computers on a regular basis is surely aware that, while in theory everything seems relatively simple, things don't always go as planned (or as you think they should). To your advantage, there are several avenues for help should you find yourself in a difficult situation.

Help within the Programs

Before getting online and searching for help, you can try looking for answers to your problems within the programs themselves.

In Apache, the manual was installed with the standard installation and can be accessed in `C:\Program Files\Apache Software Foundation\Apache2.2\manual`. A check of your error log will be most helpful as well (`C:\Program Files\Apache Software Foundation\Apache2.2\logs\error.log`).

With the MySQL client, you can see some information and command-line arguments by typing the following at your command prompt:

```
mysql.exe --help
```

This provides a multitude of commands that will help you find what you need, or at the very least, a valuable "cheat sheet" for administering your MySQL server. In addition, this will allow you to see the current settings for your server at a glance, so you can potentially troubleshoot any problem spots.

Source Web Sites

You undoubtedly know where to find these by now, but just in case, the web sites associated with each of our three components have incredibly detailed information to help you work out any issues or report any bugs you may find:

- ❑ For Apache questions and information: www.apache.org
- ❑ For PHP questions and information: www.php.net
- ❑ For MySQL questions and information: www.mysql.com

Summary

By now, you should have an idea of what AMP is and how it fits into the world of open source software. You know that the abbreviation AMP refers to Apache, MySQL, and PHP, all of which work together to help you develop dynamic web sites.

Now you've installed, configured and tested the installation for Apache, MySQL, and PHP, you should be ready to start making a web site! You'll get your hands dirty in the next chapter starting with lessons on PHP code and the creation of your movie review web site.

Creating PHP Pages Using PHP6

This chapter discusses the basics of PHP and starts you on your way to creating your first complete web site. The site will feature movie reviews, and your visitors will be able to find information about a particular movie after you complete your web site. Perhaps more importantly, you will be well on your way to being able to program in PHP.

This chapter covers the following basic PHP commands and structures:

- ❏ Using echo to display text
- ❏ Constants and variables
- ❏ Using a URL to pass variable values
- ❏ Sessions and cookies
- ❏ HTML forms
- ❏ if/else statements
- ❏ Includes
- ❏ Functions
- ❏ Arrays and foreach
- ❏ while and do/while
- ❏ Using classes and methods with object-oriented programming (OOP)

By the end of this chapter, if you actually try all the "Try It Out" exercises, you will have created a simple login form, given your users the option to either see a review of your favorite movie or see a list of your top favorite movies, and offered them a numbered list of the movies based on how many they want to see. You can even alphabetize the list for them, if you so desire.

Overview of PHP Structure and Syntax

PHP programs are written using a text editor, such as Notepad, Simple Text, or vi, just like HTML pages. However, unlike HTML, PHP files end with a `.php` extension. This extension signifies to the server that it needs to parse the PHP code before sending the resulting HTML code to the viewer's web browser.

In a five-star restaurant, patrons see just a plate full of beautiful food served up just for them. They don't see where the food comes from, nor how it was prepared. In a similar fashion, PHP fits right into your HTML code and is invisible to the people visiting your site.

How PHP Fits with HTML

We assume that you know some HTML and CSS before you embark on your Apache, MySQL, and PHP journey, and you've undoubtedly seen how JavaScript code and other languages can be interspersed within the HTML markup in an HTML document. What makes PHP so different is that it not only allows HTML pages to be created on the fly, but it is invisible to your web site visitors. The only thing they see when they view the source of your code is the resulting HTML output. In this respect, PHP gives you a bit more security by hiding your programming logic.

HTML can also be written inside the PHP code of your page, which allows you to format text while keeping blocks of code together. This will also help you write organized, efficient code, and the browser (and, more importantly, the person viewing the site) won't know the difference.

PHP can also be written as a standalone program with no HTML at all. This is helpful for storing your connection variables, redirecting your visitors to another page of your site, or performing other functions discussed in this book.

The Rules of PHP Syntax

One of the benefits of using PHP is that the language is relatively simple and straightforward. As with any computer language, there is usually more than one way to perform the same task. You can research different ways to make your code more efficient once you feel comfortable writing PHP programs. But for the sake of simplicity, we cover only the most common uses, rules, and functions of PHP.

First, you should always keep these two basic rules of PHP in mind:

❑ PHP code is denoted in the page with opening and closing tags, as follows:

```
<?php
?>
```

❑ Generally speaking, PHP statements end with a semicolon:

```
<?php
$num = 1 + 2;
echo $num;
?>
```

especially important when you are just starting out. When you become more experienced as a coder, you can condense the whitespace (spaces, tabs, and carriage returns).

What Makes a Great Program?

Truly professional code follows three general guidelines:

❏ **Consistency:** Blocks of well-written code always look the same, having the same indentation, syntax shortcuts, and consistent bracket placement and formatting styles throughout. The great thing about PHP is that it really doesn't care about tabs or indents, so you are free to create a style that is all your own and works best for you.

In addition, although there may be more than one possible syntax for accomplishing the same goal, good coders will be consistent with whichever method they choose. For example, the following two snippets of code mean the same thing, as far as PHP is concerned:

```php
<?php
if ($_POST['fname'] == 'Joe') {
    echo '<p>Hi ' . $_POST['fname'] . '</p>';
}
?>
```

```php
<?php
if($_POST['fname']=='Joe'){echo('<p>Hi ' . $_POST['fname'] . '</p>');}
?>
```

You should pick one style and stick with it throughout your program.

❏ **Frequent comments:** The more you use comments throughout your code, the better off you will be. Although it's not so important in smaller, simpler programs, as your programs become more and more complex, it will be hard for you to remember what you did, where you did it, and why you did it the way you did. Detailed comments act as a road map and can help you find your way. Also, if you are working on a collaborative project, using comments will help your fellow programmers follow your logic as well.

❏ **The use of line numbers:** Some text editors insert line numbers for you, while others do not. Text editors are discussed later in this chapter, but you should know that it is important to denote line numbers somehow in your code, if they are not provided for you, because PHP lets you know when your program generates errors, and it notifies you of the line number in which the error occurs. You can imagine how time-consuming and inefficient your debugging will be if you have to count lines manually every time you encounter an error.

Why Should You Care about What Your Code Looks Like?

It's important to follow good coding practices for three reasons:

❏ **For efficiency:** The easier your code is to read and follow, the easier it will be to keep track of where you are within your code, and the quicker it will be to pick up where you left off after a break.

You can add comments in your program by using double forward slashes (//) for one-line comments or /* to mark the start and */ to mark the end of a comment that may extend over several lines. You will see plenty of comments in code throughout this book.

And there you have it! Now you're an expert. Okay — there might be a few more things you need to learn, but this gets you started.

The Importance of Coding Practices

Before you jump in, you should realize how the structure of your code can affect your script. As far as the web server parsing the PHP code is concerned, the structure of your code really doesn't matter. Indentation doesn't matter, and, generally speaking, neither do carriage returns. This gives you freedom as a programmer to format your source code as you see fit. To the server, your code will show up as a continuous line, regardless of tabs, indents, and line returns. But to the human eye, how well your code is laid out can really make a difference.

Take a look at the following examples.

Example 1:

```php
<?php
//check to make sure the first name is equal to Joe before granting access
if ($_POST['fname'] == 'Joe') {
    echo '<p>Hi ' . $_POST['fname'] . '</p>';
} else {
    echo '<p>Your name isn\'t Joe so you cannot enter the web site.</p>';
}
?>
```

Example 2:

```php
<?php
  //check to make sure the first name is equal to Joe before granting a

  if ($_POST['fname'] == 'Joe')
    {
      echo '<p>';
      echo 'Hi ';
      echo $_POST['fname'];
      echo '</p>';
    }
  else
    {
      echo '<p>';
      echo 'Your name\'s not Joe so you cannot enter the web site!';
      echo '</p>';
    }
?>
```

You can see that although Example 2 involves more typing, it will be much easier to spot any syntax or locate a specific portion of the code for the purpose of troubleshooting problems. Th

❑ **For debugging:** Knowing where your problem lies is a major debugging tool. If comments are used correctly, you can easily follow your own logic, and if you have line numbers and consistent formatting, you can easily scan your document to pinpoint a trouble area.

❑ **For future expansions and modifications:** Using comments in your code is especially important for future changes because it's difficult to remember the logic behind code that was written years or even just months ago. Also, if you are working on code that involves a team, if everyone is using the same coding style, it will be much easier to make changes or additions to someone else's work down the road.

Okay, enough preaching about good code — let's get to it.

Creating Your First Program

You can't get much simpler than this first program, but try it out to get a feel for what the results look like. The PHP statement echo, seen in the example that follows, is one of the most commonly used PHP functions and one that you will undoubtedly become intimate with. It is used to send text (or variable values or a variety of other things) to the browser.

Try It Out   Using echo

Try using echo to see what results you achieve.

1. Enter the following program in your favorite text editor (Notepad, Simple Text, or whatever you choose), and save it as firstprog.php.

   Regardless of your editor, make sure you save it in a plaintext format to avoid parsing problems. If you're using Notepad, double-check to ensure that the file is not saved as firstprog.php.txt by default.

```
<html>
 <head>
  <title>My First PHP Program</title>
 </head>
 <body>
<?php
echo "I'm a lumberjack.";
?>
 </body>
</html>
```

2. Open this program using your browser. Your resulting screen should look like the one in Figure 2-1.

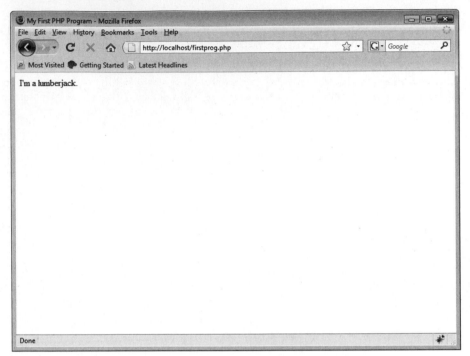

Figure 2-1

3. Now view the source of the HTML code, so you can see what happened with the PHP portions of the code. As you can see, the PHP portion of the code has vanished, leaving only the resulting HTML code.

4. Now add the following highlighted line to your script, so you can get a better feel for how your PHP code will be parsed:

```
<html>
 <head>
  <title>My First PHP Program</title>
 </head>
 <body>
<?php
echo "I'm a lumberjack.";
echo 'And I\'m okay.';
?>
 </body>
</html>
```

5. Save the revised file and open it in your browser. As you can see, the line runs together without a line break, even though you had your PHP code on two different lines, as shown in Figure 2-2.

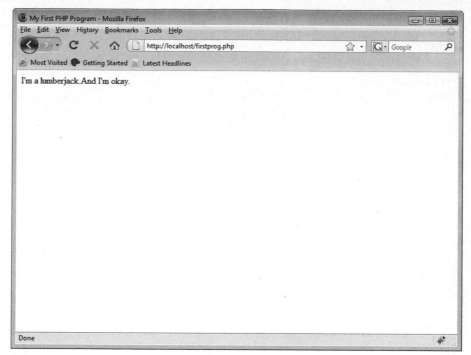

Figure 2-2

How It Works

When a browser calls a PHP program, it first searches through the entire code line by line to locate all PHP sections (those encased in the <?php and ?> tags), and it then processes them one at a time. To the server, all PHP code is treated as one line, which is why your two lines of code were shown as one continuous line on the screen. After the PHP code has been parsed accordingly, the server goes back and gobbles up the remaining HTML and spits it out to the browser, PHP sections included.

Also, you should have noticed that you used single quotation marks (') in your addition, which we did to highlight an important point. There are different ways to mark the start and end of a string of text, with the most common being the use of double quotation marks (") or single quotation marks. PHP treats single-quoted and double-quoted strings differently, which you will learn more about later, but choosing your quotes can be an important detail when you want to include a single quote/ apostrophe or double quotation marks in your text.

PHP can easily understand the following statement:

```
echo "I'm a lumberjack.";
```

The statement instructs PHP to output the sequence of characters I'm a lumberjack. to the browser. It knows where the start and end of the sequence is because the text is surrounded in double quotation marks.

While single quotation marks are an entirely valid way to delimit a string, PHP would become confused with the following statement:

```
echo 'I'm a lumberjack.';
```

In fact, PHP would display a scary error message:

```
Parse error: syntax error, unexpected T_STRING, expecting ',' or ';' in C:\
Program Files\Apache Software Foundation\Apache2.2\htdocs\firstprog.php on
line 7
```

The problem is the apostrophe in the word `I'm`. PHP thinks it matches the single quotation mark that started the string of text, making the text just `I`. The rest of the statement, `m a lumberjack.`, is unintelligible gibberish to PHP.

The same problem would happen if you were using double quotation marks and wrote a statement like:

```
echo "Joe says, "Hello World!"";
```

You can solve this dilemma simply by using single quotation marks to delimit the string:

```
echo 'Joe says, "Hello World!"';
```

Now it's quite clear to PHP what your intention is, and it can dutifully output `Joe says, "Hello World!"` to the browser.

Another way to address the problem is to escape any single quotes/apostrophes in your single-quoted strings and double quotes in double-quoted strings by using a backslash (\). Escaping lets PHP know it should ignore the special meaning of the character and treat it as if it were any other plain character in the string.

Feel free to experiment with different quotation marks and escaping. You'll see many different examples as you progress through this book.

Using HTML to Spice Up Your Pages

As you can see in the previous example, using PHP code to output plaintext results in rather bland pages. You can make them look more professional and less utilitarian by adding some HTML to your output. HTML can be inserted within your PHP block of code using the `echo` statement. In fact, anything you can code in HTML can be output from within a PHP section of code.

Integrating HTML with PHP

You will be better able to see how easily you can use HTML in the PHP program with the following practical example.

Try It Out   **Using PHP within HTML**

In this example, you'll use some PHP and HTML together.

1.   Modify the highlighted lines of `firstprog.php`:

```
<html>
 <head>
  <title>My First PHP Program</title>
 </head>
 <body>
<?php
   echo "<h1>I'm a lumberjack.</h1>";
   echo "<h2>And I'm okay.</h2>";
?>
 </body>
</html>
```

2.   Save your file, and reload the page. Your screen should now look something like the one in Figure 2-3.

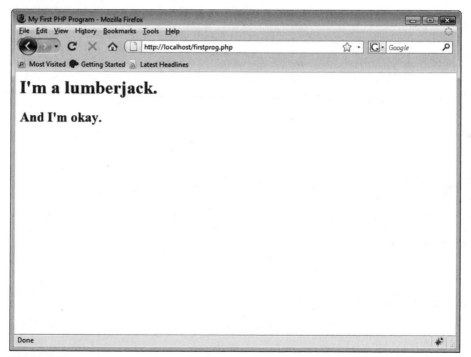

Figure 2-3

How It Works

The echo statement basically outputs whatever it's told to the browser, whether it be HTML code, variable values, or plaintext. We wanted to prove a point, and so here we simply chose to echo HTML code in this example.

```
echo "<h1>I'm a lumberjack.</h1>";
echo "<h2>And I'm okay.</h2>";
```

You can see that by inserting some HTML code within the PHP section of the program, you accomplish two things:

❑ You can improve the look of your site.

❑ You can keep PHP lines of code together without having to jump back and forth between HTML and PHP.

If you view the source of your HTML code, you will see the HTML code you inserted using the echo statement displayed just as you intended.

Considerations with HTML inside PHP

The following list discusses some pitfalls commonly seen with the practice of inserting HTML inside PHP:

❑ **You have to check for double quotation marks.** As you may have noted when you worked through the previous example, using the echo statement may involve the use of double quotation marks. Because HTML also uses double quotation marks, you can do one of two things to avoid problems:

   ❑ Escape your HTML double quotation marks with a backslash, as in the following:

   ```
   echo "<p style=\"font-size: 80%;\">";
   ```

   ❑ Use single quotation marks around your HTML. This can help improve the readability of your code if you have many quotes.

   ```
   echo '<p style="font-size: 80%;">';
   ```

❑ **Remember that you still have to follow PHP's rules, even though you're coding in HTML.** Sometimes when you begin to code in HTML within your PHP section, you can temporarily forget that you need to follow PHP guidelines and end your sentences with a semicolon, as well as close all quotes at the end of your echo statements.

❑ **Don't try to cram too much HTML into your PHP.** If you find yourself in the middle of a PHP portion of your program, and your HTML is becoming increasingly complex or lengthy, consider ending the PHP section and coding strictly in HTML. Consider the following examples:

❑   **Example 1:**

```php
<?php
    echo '<table style="font-family: Arial,sans-serif; font-size: 80%; ';
    echo 'width: 100%;">';
    echo '<tr>';
    echo '<td style="width: 50%;">';
    echo 'First Name:';
    echo '</td>';
    echo '<td style="width: 50%">';
    echo $_POST['fname'];
    echo '</td>';
    echo '</tr>';
    echo '</table>';
?>
```

❑   **Example 2:**

```php
<table style="font-family: Arial,sans-serif; font-size: 80%; width: 100%;">
 <tr>
  <td style="width: 50%;">
   First Name:
  </td>
  <td style="width: 50%">
<?php echo $_POST['fname'];?>
  </td>
 </tr>
</table>
```

Although we have not yet discussed variables, you can see in the first example that the only thing PHP was really needed for was to provide the value represented by $_POST['fname'] and display it on the screen. The rest of the related code was just to output HTML. In this instance, you're better off just staying in HTML and pulling out the PHP line when you need it, instead of coding all of the HTML inside PHP. It really doesn't matter to the server, but for human beings it makes for easier formatting, easier debugging, and less typing (which is always a good thing). In essence, it is up to you to balance your HTML with PHP and discover what works best for your coding style.

Using Constants and Variables to Add Functionality

We've covered the basics of using the echo function to display text the way you want it. Really, this works no differently from coding an HTML page. However, using constants and variables allows you to take advantage of the true power of PHP.

Overview of Constants

A constant is a placeholder for a value that you reference within your code that is formally defined before using it. When naming constants, remember they must begin with a letter or an underscore, and cannot begin with a number. Names are also case-sensitive, though typically they are named using all capital letters so you can easily identify them within your code.

You define a value assigned to a constant with the PHP function `define()`. Once you've defined a constant, it can't be changed or undefined.

Using Constants

In this exercise, you'll see how you can use constants in your program.

1. Open your text editor, and type the following program:

```html
<html>
 <head>
  <title>My Movie Site</title>
 </head>
 <body>
<?php
define ('FAVMOVIE', 'The Life of Brian');
echo 'My favorite movie is ';
echo FAVMOVIE;
?>
 </body>
</html>
```

2. Save this file as `moviesite.php`, and open it in your browser. You should see the text shown in Figure 2-4.

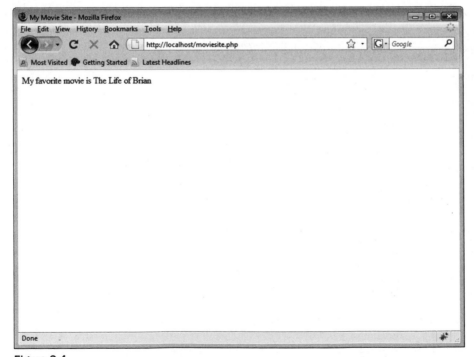

Figure 2-4

How It Works

By defining the constant known as FAVMOVIE, you have set the value as "The Life of Brian," which can be recalled and displayed later on. Although this constant can't be changed or reset throughout your script, it is available for use by any part of your script.

Overview of Variables

Unlike constants, variables are obviously meant to be variable — they are meant to change or be changed at some point in your program. Variables do not need to be defined or declared and can simply be assigned when needed. They act as a container that stores information for later use in your scripts, and the contents of them can be changed.

Variables are denoted with a dollar sign ($) and are case-sensitive (in other words, $dateEntered and $DateEntered are treated as different variables). The first letter of the variable name must be an underscore or letter, and cannot be a number.

Try It Out   **Using Variables**

In this exercise, you'll add variables to your existing script.

1.   Open your text editor, and make the following changes to your moviesite.php file (noted in highlighted lines):

```
<html>
 <head>
  <title>My Movie Site</title>
 </head>
 <body>
<?php
define('FAVMOVIE', 'The Life of Brian');
echo 'My favorite movie is ';
echo FAVMOVIE;
echo '<br/>';
$movierate = 5;
echo 'My movie rating for this movie is: ';
echo $movierate;
?>
 </body>
</html>
```

2.   Save the changes, and access the file in your browser. Your screen should now look like the one in Figure 2-5.

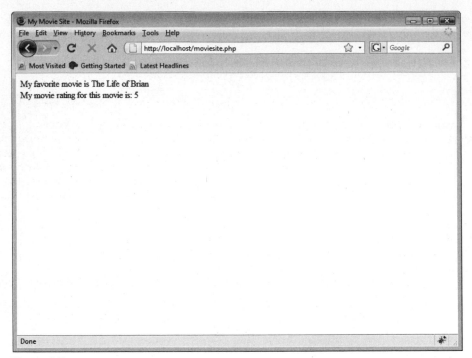

Figure 2-5

How It Works

The value 5 is assigned to the variable `movierate`. Numbers do not need to be quoted as strings do. In fact, the following would cause PHP to see the value of `movierate` as a string containing the character 5:

```
$movierate = '5';
```

Keeping this value as an integer makes it much easier to perform mathematical calculations on it later on, such as giving the viewer the average movie rate. For example:

```php
<?php
$bobsmovierate = 5;
$joesmovierate = 7;
$grahamsmovierate = 2;
$zabbysmovierate = 1;
$avgmovierate = (($bobsmovierate + $joesmovierate + $grahamsmovierate
              + $zabbysmovierate) / 4);
echo 'The average movie rating for this movie is: ';
echo $avgmovierate;
?>
```

PHP also has numerous built-in mathematical functions that you can use on variables that contain numbers, such as:

- ❏ `rand([$min, $max])`: Returns a random number.

- ❏ `ceil($value)`: Returns the next highest integer by rounding the value upwards.

- ❏ `floor($value)`: Returns the next lowest integer by rounding the value downwards.

- ❏ `number_format($number[,$decimal_places[,$decimal_point, $thousands_sep]])`: Formats the number based on the chosen number of decimal places, using the designated decimal point and thousands separator if they are provided. By default, PHP uses a period for the decimal point and a comma for the thousands separator, so if that's acceptable for you, you can leave off the optional parameters, as noted by the brackets above. If you would like to take out the comma, for example, you could type the following code:

```
$price = 12345.67;
number_format($price);              //returns 12,345.67
number_format($price, 2, '.', '');  //returns 12345.67
```

- ❏ `max($value1[, $value2[, $...]])`: Returns the largest value found in the set of supplied arguments.

- ❏ `min($value1[, $value2[, $...]])`: Returns the smallest value found in the set of supplied arguments.

For a listing of more useful functions that are available to you in PHP, please refer to Appendix C.

Passing Variables between Pages

Suppose your web site allows viewers to enter their name on the front page. You'd like to be able to greet the user by name on each page in your web site, but to do so you need some way to pass the value of the name variable from page to page. There are basically four ways to accomplish this task: pass the variables in the URL, through a session, via a cookie, or with an HTML form. The method you choose is based on the situation and what best fits your needs at the time.

Passing Variables through a URL

The first method of passing variables between pages is through the page's URL. You've undoubtedly seen URLs such as this:

```
http://www.mydomain.com/news/articles/showart.php?id=12345
```

This is an example of passing variable values through the URL. It requests that the article with the ID number of "12345" be chosen for the `showart.php` program. The text after the URL is called the *query string*.

You can also combine variables in a URL by using an ampersand (&), as in this example:

```
http://www.mydomain.com/news/articles/showart.php?id=12345&lang=en
```

This asks to retrieve the file with an ID of "12345" and the language presumably equal to "en," for English.

There are a few disadvantages to passing variables through a URL:

❑ Everyone can see the values of the variables, so passing sensitive information isn't really very secure using this method.

❑ The user can arbitrarily change the variable value in the URL and try different combinations, leaving your web site potentially open to showing something you'd rather not show.

❑ A user might also pull up inaccurate or old information using a saved URL with older variables embedded in it (from a bookmark, for example).

Variables that you pass around in this way are accessible in your PHP code through the special $_GET array. The variable name that appears in the URL is used as a key, so to retrieve the value of id you would reference $_GET['id'], or to retrieve the value of lang you would reference $_GET['lang'].

Try It Out   **Using URL Variables**

In this exercise, you'll modify your program to show the URL variables in action.

1.   Modify your moviesite.php file as follows (changes are highlighted):

```
<html>
 <head>
  <title>My Movie Site - <?php echo $_GET['favmovie']; ?></title>
 </head>
 <body>
<?php
//delete this line: define('FAVMOVIE', 'The Life of Brian');
echo 'My favorite movie is ';
echo $_GET['favmovie'];
echo '<br/>';
$movierate = 5;
echo 'My movie rating for this movie is: ';
echo $movierate;
?>
 </body>
</html>
```

2.   Save your moviesite.php file, and start a new document in your text editor.

3.   Type the following code:

```
<html>
 <head>
  <title>Find my Favorite Movie!</title>
 </head>
<body>
<?php
echo '<a href="moviesite.php?favmovie=Stripes">';
echo 'Click here to see information about my favorite movie!';
echo '</a>';
?>
 </body>
 </html>
```

4.   Save this file as movie1.php, and open it in your browser. Your screen should look like the one in Figure 2-6.

Figure 2-6

5.   Now click the link and see what you get (see Figure 2-7).

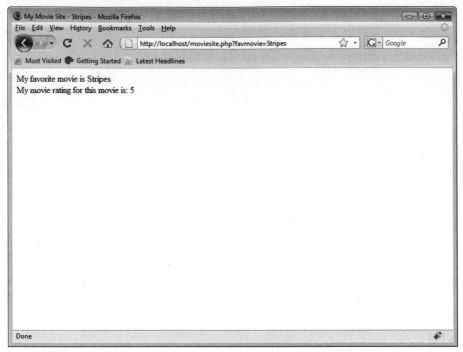

Figure 2-7

You see the value for $favmovie as "Stripes" in the URL, as shown in Figure 2-7, but it is also made available in the rest of the script by $_GET['favmovie'] and shows in the page's title and body text.

How It Works

Here are a few points to note about your program:

❑ As you can see from the "Title" section of your program, PHP code can be inserted in a straight line in the midst of your HTML code. This is helpful when you just need to insert one tidbit of information grabbed from PHP.

❑ You can also insert PHP information anywhere in your HTML program, including the title.

❑ If you do not reference the favmovie value using $_GET, but instead just use $favmovie, there is nothing shown for the value. If you have E_ALL turned on in your php.ini file, you will see the "undefined variable" error message. You did not need to do this when you referenced $movierate, though, as the value is kept within moviesite.php; you did not get the information from another page or source.

Special Characters in URLs

Passing variables through a URL poses an interesting problem if there are spaces, ampersands, or other special characters in the value of your variable. Luckily, substitutes exist for special characters that maintain the integrity of the variables' values. There is a special function called urlencode() to use when passing these values through a URL. If you wanted to change your favorite movie from "Stripes" to "Life of Brian," you would use `urlencode()` to encode the value and insert the proper HTML special characters.

To try this out, perform these steps:

1. Make the following highlighted changes to your `movie1.php` file:

```
<html>
 <head>
  <title>Find my Favorite Movie!</title>
 </head>
 <body>
<?php
//add this line:
$myfavmovie = urlencode('Life of Brian');

//change this line:
echo "<a href=\"moviesite.php?favmovie=$myfavmovie\">";
echo 'Click here to see information about my favorite movie!';
echo '</a>';
?>
 </body>
</html>
```

2. Save the file, and open it again in your browser. Clicking the link now displays the page shown in Figure 2-8.

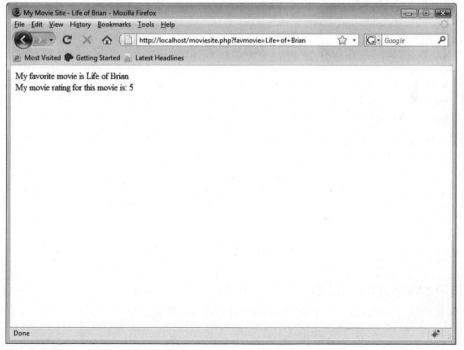

Figure 2-8

Passing Variables with Sessions

As we mentioned before, passing a value through a URL is fine if the information is not of a particularly sensitive nature, or if it is relatively static and there is no danger of a user pulling up old information from a previously saved page. If you are transmitting information such as usernames or passwords, however, or personal information such as addresses and phone numbers, better methods exist for passing the information while keeping it private, such as using cookies. You'll learn more about cookies in Chapter 12.

A *session* is basically a temporary set of variables that exists only until the browser has shut down. Examples of session information include a session ID and whether or not an authorized person has logged in to the site. This information is stored temporarily for your PHP programs to refer back to whenever needed.

Every session is assigned a unique session ID, which keeps all the current information together. Your session ID can either be passed through the URL or through the use of cookies. Although it is preferable for security reasons to pass the session ID through a cookie so that it is hidden from the human eye, if cookies are not enabled then the backup method is through the URL.

This setting is determined in your `php.ini` file. If you would like to force the user to pass variables through cookies (instead of allowing a backup plan), you would set the following line:

```
session.use_only_cookies = 1
```

Also, make sure before using sessions that your `php.ini` file has been modified to show a valid path for `session.save_path`, as described in Chapter 1.

Then all you need to do to begin a session in PHP is call the function `session_start()`. But first, you need to decide what information will be stored in your session. Anything that has been stored in a database can be retrieved and stored temporarily along with your session information. Usually, it is information such as username and login information, but it can also be preferences that have been set at some point by the user. A session identifier will also be stored in the session array of variables.

Try It Out   Passing the Visitor's Username

Suppose you want to pass your visitor's username, and whether or not he or she has authentically logged in to the site between the first page and the second page. This functionality will be discussed more in Chapter 12, but for now we'll whip together a quick sample to highlight passing the visitor's username in a session variable.

Follow these steps:

1. Change your `movie1.php` file to include the following highlighted lines.

```php
<?php
session_start();
$_SESSION['username'] = 'Joe12345';
$_SESSION['authuser'] = 1;
?>
<html>
```

```
 <head>
  <title>Find my Favorite Movie!</title>
 </head>
 <body>
<?php
$myfavmovie = urlencode('Life of Brian');
echo "<a href=\"moviesite.php?favmovie=$myfavmovie\">";
echo 'Click here to see information about my favorite movie!';
echo '</a>';
?>
 </body>
</html>
```

2. Now save your movie1.php file.

3. Open moviesite.php to make the following highlighted changes:

```
<?php
session_start();

//check to see if user has logged in with a valid password
if ($_SESSION['authuser'] != 1) {
    echo 'Sorry, but you don\'t have permission to view this page!';
    exit();
}
?>
<html>
 <head>
  <title>My Movie Site - <?php echo $_GET['favmovie']; ?></title>
 </head>
 <body>
<?php
echo 'Welcome to our site, ';
echo $_SESSION['username'];
echo '! <br/>';
echo 'My favorite movie is ';
echo $_GET['favmovie'];
echo '<br/>';
$movierate = 5;
echo 'My movie rating for this movie is: ';
echo $movierate;
?>
 </body>
</html>
```

4. Click the link in movie1.php, and you should see the text for moviesite.php shown in Figure 2-9.

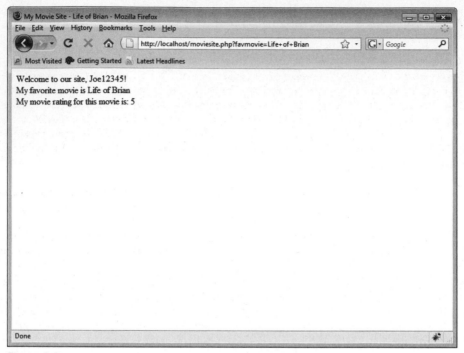

Figure 2-9

How It Works

Here are a few important things to note about this procedure:

❑ All PHP session information is at the top of the page, before any HTML code is used. This is very important! If there is even a leading space before the PHP code at the top of the page, you will receive an error such as:

```
Warning: session_start(): Cannot send session cache limiter - headers already
sent(output started at C:\Program Files\Apache Software Foundation\Apache2.2\
htdocs\moviesite.php:1) in C:\Program Files\Apache Software Foundation\
Apache2.2\htdocs\moviesite.php on line 2
```

❑ Some other situations also will give you the "headers already sent" error, which we discuss in Chapter 18.

❑ Refer to the session variables using syntax $_SESSION['varname']. If you don't, then the variables will contain empty values, and you may receive a warning message.

❑ You must use the function session_start() before you send any output to the browser and before you use any session variables. It's best to place session_start() at the beginning of your script.

Passing Variables with Cookies

Cookies are tiny bits of information stored on your web site visitor's computer. There appears to be some sort of paranoia about using cookies. In theory, cookies can be intercepted to gain information such as a person's IP address and operating system, but cookies are primarily used for storing information only. A few ad campaigns have developed technology to use cookies to track your browsing habits, and many people see this as an invasion of privacy, so some people choose to disable this feature in their web browsers. Also, because cookies are stored in a commonly named directory, anyone with access to someone else's computer (either via a hack or physical location) can potentially open cookie files and glean information about the owner. Because of these possibilities, it's not a good idea to store any private information on a computer.

> *For more information on cookies and the potential security risks (however minute), you are encouraged to visit the W3 Security FAQ web site at* www.w3.org/Security/faq/wwwsf2.html#CLT-Q10.

Because your visitors may either have cookies turned off or may physically delete cookies from their computers, relying on cookie information probably isn't the best idea from a web development standpoint.

So why do developers use cookies, anyway? The advantage of storing information in a cookie versus a session is longevity. Sessions alone can't store information for more than the length of time the browser window is open. Like the elusive and mean-spirited video game that loses all high scores once it's unplugged, a session loses all information once a browser closes. Cookies, on the other hand, can live on a person's computer for as long as the developer has decided is long enough, and then they automatically expire. It is because of this longevity that cookies are fabulous for storing information such as a visitor's username or language preferences. These are the pieces of information that users won't have to retype every time they visit your site, and if for some reason someone did get wind of the information, it wouldn't be the end of the world.

We mentioned earlier that sessions alone can't store information for very long. However, you can alter this limitation if you use sessions in conjunction with cookies. If your sessions are passing variables using cookies, you *can* set the life of these cookies to longer than the life of the browser, using the session.cookie_lifetime configuration in your php.ini file. Keep in mind, however, that not only will the session information be stored on the person's computer, but the Session ID also will be stored, and that can cause you problems later on.

To set a cookie, you use the appropriately named setcookie() function. When setting a cookie, you can determine the following information set along with it:

- ❏ Cookie name (this is mandatory).
- ❏ Value of the cookie (such as the person's username).
- ❏ Time in seconds when the cookie will expire. (This time is based on a UNIX timestamp, but you can set it using the syntax time()+60*60*24*365, which keeps the cookie alive for a year. This is optional, but if it is not set, then the cookie will expire when the browser is closed.)
- ❏ Path (the directory where the cookie will be saved — the default is usually sufficient; this is optional).
- ❏ Domain (domains that may access this cookie — this is optional).
- ❏ Whether a cookie must have a secure HTTPS connection to be set (defaults to 0; to enable this feature, set this to 1).

You make each of these settings as follows:

```
setcookie($name[, $value[, $expire[, $path[, $domain[, $secure]]]]])
```

As you can probably guess by now, those values will be referenced in the script as
`$_COOKIE['cookiename']`.

Try It Out   **Setting a Cookie**

In this exercise, you'll have the web site set a cookie on Joe's machine so that he (theoretically) doesn't
have to type his username (Joe12345) every time he comes back to visit. To do this, follow these steps:

1. Modify your `movie1.php` file as shown:

```php
<?php
setcookie('username', 'Joe', time() + 60);
session_start();
//delete this line: $_SESSION['username'] = 'Joe12345';
$_SESSION['authuser'] = 1;
?>
<html>
 <head>
  <title>Find my Favorite Movie!</title>
 </head>
 <body>
<?php
$myfavmovie = urlencode('Life of Brian');
echo "<a href=\"moviesite.php?favmovie=$myfavmovie\">";
echo 'Click here to see information about my favorite movie!';
echo '</a>';
?>
 </body>
</html>
```

2. Save the file.

3. Make the following changes to your `moviesite.php` file:

```php
<?php
session_start();

//check to see if user has logged in with a valid password
if ($_SESSION['authuser'] != 1) {
    echo 'Sorry, but you don\'t have permission to view this page!';
    exit();
}
?>
<html>
 <head>
  <title>My Movie Site - <?php echo $_GET['favmovie']; ?></title>
 </head>
```

```
<body>
<?php
echo 'Welcome to our site, ';
echo $_COOKIE['username'];
echo '! <br/>';
echo 'My favorite movie is ';
echo $_GET['favmovie'];
echo '<br/>';
$movierate=5;
echo 'My movie rating for this movie is: ';
echo $movierate;
?>
 </body>
</html>
```

4.   Save the file.

5.   Close out your browser window and open a new window (in case you have any session information from the previous example lingering about). Then open the movie1.php file. Click the link, and your screen should look like the one in Figure 2-10.

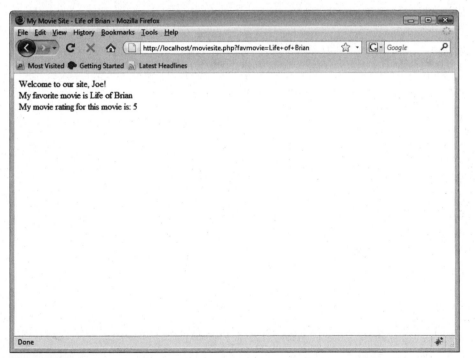

Figure 2-10

How It Works

If you didn't notice, you changed the username from Joe12345 when you were using sessions, to Joe when you were using cookies. This was to double-check that the information was coming from the cookie, and not the session. When using cookies, remember the following:

❑ Like sessions, cookies must be placed at the very top of the page, before your first <html> line. Otherwise, you get a "headers already sent" error.

❑ The expire time for the cookie was set to 60 seconds so you could play with and test your cookies without having to wait around for them to expire. For a normal application storing usernames, it would be logical to set this higher.

❑ Unlike sessions, cookie information can't be accessed in the current page where the cookies have been set. You have to move on to the next page for the cookie to be set and accessible to your program.

Passing Information with Forms

Up until now, you've passed information among pages successfully, but you've been the one to supply all the information. Although it would be a great world if you really knew that much about your web site visitors, it might get a little labor-intensive on your part. What do you say to letting your users supply you with information for a change?

If you've never filled out a form online, then you have probably been living in a cave somewhere with no Internet access. Forms are the great Venus flytraps, just lying in wait to gobble up useful information from web site visitors. Forms allow your web site to be truly interactive; they take data from the user and send it off somewhere to be massaged, manipulated, and perhaps stored, and then some result is sent back to the user. You'll have the chance to work more with forms in Chapter 5, but we will briefly touch on them here to make sure you have a basic understanding of how they work.

Fast Primer on Forms

In case you are a bit rusty on the syntax of forms, or if you just need a quick reference, here is a down-and-dirty discussion of forms. Forms are coded in HTML and stay in HTML. A form is made up of four parts:

❑ **Opening tag line:** Indicated by <form>. This tag line must include an action attribute and a method attribute. An action gives the form a URL or path to another program that will take the data included in the form and carry it from there. A method (GET or POST) tells the form how the data is to be carried. (POST is generally the preferred method; it's more secure because it doesn't pass its information along in the URL.)

❑ **Content of the form, including input fields:** Input fields are the areas where the user types in the information (or selects it in the case of a check box or radio button). An input field must include a type and name attribute, but can include other attributes such as maxlength. The type of an input field can be one of many different selections, the most common being:

   ❑ **Text:** Used for collecting from 2 characters up to 2,000 characters. The parameter used to limit the number of accepted characters for a particular input field is maxlength. To collect large amounts of input (such as comments), the input field textarea is recommended over text.

❏ **Check box:** Used to allow users to make a selection from a list of choices; also permits users to make more than one choice. Individual choices must be indicated with a `value` attribute.

❏ **Radio:** Also known as radio buttons. Used for allowing users to choose from a list, but radio buttons permit only one choice. Individual choices must be indicated with a `value` attribute.

❏ **Select:** Also known as drop-down boxes. Used for allowing users to choose from a list of choices. Individual choices are indicated with an `option/value` pair.

❏ **Password:** Hides what the user is typing behind asterisks, but does not compromise the value of the variable.

The name of the input field will also do double duty as your variable name in your PHP program. To avoid issues with PHP parsing, you should name your input fields according to the PHP variable naming guidelines covered earlier in this chapter.

❏ **Action button(s) or images, typically submit/clear or a user-defined button, technically considered input types as well:** These are indicated with the input types `submit`, `reset`, and `image` for user-created buttons.

❏ **Closing tag line:** Indicated with a `</form>` tag.

Got it? Good! Now let's move on.

Try It Out   Using Forms to Get Information

Because your program is slowly increasing in size, for this exercise, we suggest you switch to a text editor that will add line numbers to your document. If you are using a text editor that inserts these line numbers already, you do not need to worry about adding these in. Otherwise, you may want to add periodic line numbers as comments to help you keep track. In addition to adding line numbers to your program, you are also going to insert comments to help you keep track of what is going on.

Here's how to use forms to get information from visitors:

1. Open your `movie1.php` file and make the following changes:

```php
<?php
//delete this line: setcookie('username', 'Joe', time() + 60);
session_start();
$_SESSION['username'] = $_POST['user'];
$_SESSION['userpass'] = $_POST['pass'];
$_SESSION['authuser'] = 0;

//Check username and password information
if (($_SESSION['username'] == 'Joe') and
    ($_SESSION['userpass'] == '12345')) {
    $_SESSION['authuser'] = 1;
} else {
    echo 'Sorry, but you don\'t have permission to view this page!';
    exit();
}
?>
```

```
<html>
 <head>
  <title>Find my Favorite Movie!</title>
 </head>
 <body>
<?php
$myfavmovie = urlencode('Life of Brian');
echo "<a href=\"moviesite.php?favmovie=$myfavmovie\">";
echo "Click here to see information about my favorite movie!";
echo "</a>";
?>
 </body>
</html>
```

2. Now make these changes to your `moviesite.php` file:

```
<?php
session_start();

//check to see if user has logged in with a valid password
if ($_SESSION['authuser'] !=1 ) {
    echo 'Sorry, but you don\'t have permission to view this page!';
    exit();
}
?>
<html>
 <head>
  <title>My Movie Site - <?php echo $_GET['favmovie']; ?></title>
 </head>
 <body>
<?php
echo 'Welcome to our site, ';
//delete this line: echo $_COOKIE['username'];
echo $_SESSION['username'];
echo '! <br/>';
echo 'My favorite movie is ';
echo $_GET['favmovie'];
echo '<br/>';
$movierate = 5;
echo 'My movie rating for this movie is: ';
echo $movierate;
?>
 </body>
</html>
```

3. Start a new file:

```
<?php
session_unset();
?>
<html>
 <head>
  <title>Please Log In</title>
 </head>
```

```
<body>
 <form method="post" action="movie1.php">
  <p>Enter your username:
   <input type="text" name="user"/>
  </p>
  <p>Enter your password:
   <input type="password" name="pass"/>
  </p>
  <p>
   <input type="submit" name="submit" value="Submit"/>
  </p>
 </form>
</body>
</html>
```

4. Save this file as `login.php`.

5. Load the `login.php` file into your browser. Your screen will look like the one shown in Figure 2-11.

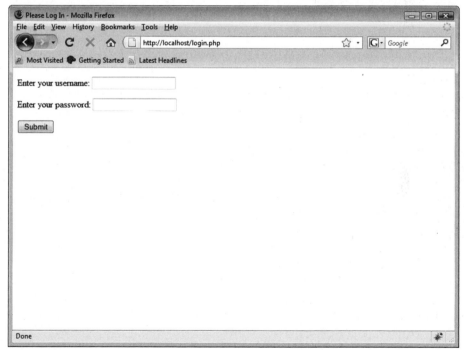

Figure 2-11

6. Log in with the username Joe12345 and the password 12345. The username is wrong, so if the authorization script works, your screen should look like the one shown in Figure 2-12.

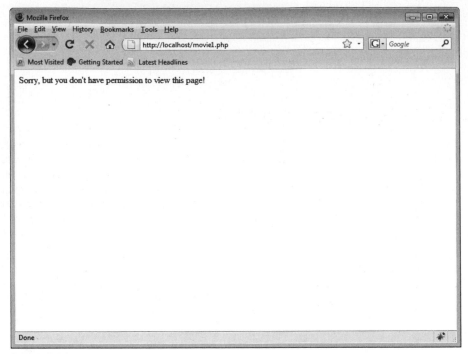

Figure 2-12

Now try logging in with the correct username (Joe) and password (12345). Your movie1.php site should load as it did before, and the link should take you to the moviesite.php page.

How It Works

In login.php, you first release any variables from sessions that may be lingering around, with the command session_unset(). Then you ask for two variables from the user: username and password (variable names user and pass, respectively). These are submitted to movie1.php (the "action" in the form) via the POST method (the "method" in the form). This is why you have to refer to them using the $_POST syntax at the beginning of movie1.php.

The file movie1.php actually accomplishes several things:

❑ It starts the session and, by default, registers the variables. Values are set based on the information sent from the form in login.php.

❑ It checks to see if the username and password are acceptable. In real life, you would match this information to a database for authentication and verification.

❑ It sets the authuser to 1 if the acceptable username/password combination has been supplied, which grants the user permission to then proceed to other pages in the site, such as moviesite.php.

❑ If the username/password combination is not acceptable, a tactful error message is displayed to the user.

Because the information is passed on to `moviesite.php` as before, the only thing `moviesite.php` has to check is that the user is authorized through the `authuser` variable.

Using if/else Arguments

You've seen now that you can assign many different values to variables. At some point in the course of your script, you're going to want to take specific actions based on the value of a variable. For example, consider a `$password` variable. If users suppy the correct password, you'll want to grant them access to the site. If a user enters an incorrect password, you might want to ask him or her to try again or maybe lock the user out. You can use the `if` statement to dictate the action your script takes based on the value of a variable. And if you add the `else` statement to an `if`, you open up a whole range of possible actions.

Using if Statements

The syntax for a basic `if` statement is as follows:

```
if (condition) action to be taken if true;
```

As in this example:

```
if ($stockmarket > 10000) echo 'Hooray! Time to Party!';
```

If the action to take is longer than a simple statement that will easily fit on one line, you must use brackets (`{}`) to enclose your action section:

```
if ($stockmarket > 10000) {
    echo 'Hooray! Time to Party!';
    $mood = 'happy';
    $retirement = 'potentially obtainable';
}
```

It is often advised to use brackets whether they are technically required or not, just so you don't add lines later and forget to add the brackets as well. Sometimes this can save you a lot of grief.

Operators

The operators used to compare two values are similar to those comparison operators you likely encountered in elementary-school math. A list of these operators follows. Please note that these are only for use within the `if` statement itself, and are not to be used when assigning values to variables.

Operator	Appropriate Syntax
equal to	==
not equal to	!= or <>
greater than	>
less than	<
greater than or equal to	>=
less than or equal to	<=
equal to, AND data types match (both are integers, or both are strings)	===
not equal to, OR the data types are not the same	!==

Make sure you don't confuse the = operator with the == or === operator. The = operator is used to assign values to variables. The == and === operators test for equality.

Special Syntax Considerations

You should pay special attention to the use of semicolons in if statements. Semicolons are required in individual lines within the if statement, but not at the end of the if statement itself. Also, take special note of the use of the double equals sign when comparing values. This takes some getting used to and can slip you up if you're not careful.

The way you indent your lines does not matter to PHP, but it does to the human eye. If possible, try to keep your indenting consistent and easy to read.

Try It Out   Using if

This exercise will start you off with a brief script to illustrate if by itself.

1. Open your text editor, and type the following program:

```
<html>
 <head>
  <title>How many days in this month?</title>
 </head>
 <body>
<?php
date_default_timezone_set('America/New_York');
$month = date('n');
if ($month ==  1) { echo '31'; }
if ($month ==  2) { echo '28 (unless it\'s a leap year)'; }
if ($month ==  3) { echo '31'; }
if ($month ==  4) { echo '30'; }
if ($month ==  5) { echo '31'; }
if ($month ==  6) { echo '30'; }
```

```
if ($month ==  7) { echo '31'; }
if ($month ==  8) { echo '31'; }
if ($month ==  9) { echo '30'; }
if ($month == 10) { echo '31'; }
if ($month == 11) { echo '30'; }
if ($month == 12) { echo '31'; }
?>
 </body>
</html>
```

2. Save this as `date.php`, and open it in your browser.

The result should display the number of days in the current month.

How It Works

The script gets the value for variable `$month` by tapping into one of PHP's numerous built-in date functions; `date('n')` returns a value equal to the numerical equivalent of the month as set in your server, such as 1 for January, 2 for February, and so on. (We talk more about `date()` in Appendix C.)

Then the script tests the `if` statements for each potential value for `$month` until it gets the right answer. If the first `if` statement is false, the program immediately goes to the next line and executes it. When it gets to the right month, it carries out the rest of the statement in the line and then goes to the next line and executes it as well. It does not stop once it comes across a true statement, but continues as if nothing has happened.

Using if and else Together

Using `if` by itself is fine and dandy in some cases, but there are other times when the `if/else` combination is more appropriate. For example, suppose you usually want to show a certain message on your site, but you have a holiday message you'd like shown for the month of December. Or suppose that on your movie review site, you want to show an abbreviated version of a movie review for those who haven't yet seen the movie. It's these "either/or" cases where you need to whip out the all-powerful `if/else` combination.

Try It Out   Using if and else

Let's keep with the date theme and let the user know whether or not the current year is a leap year. Follow these steps to accomplish this:

1. Open your text editor, and enter the following code:

```
<html>
 <head>
  <title>Is it a leap year?</title>
 </head>
 <body>
<?php
date_default_timezone_set('America/New_York');
$leapyear = date('L');
```

```
if ($leapyear == 1) {
    echo 'Hooray! It\'s a leap year!';
}
else {
    echo 'Aww, sorry, mate. No leap year this year.';
}
?>
 </body>
</html>
```

2. Save this file as `leapyear.php`, and open it in your browser.

You should now see a statement based on whether or not the current year is a leap year.

How It Works

Suppose the year is 2003. That's not a leap year, so the value of `$leapyear` would be 0. When the script reads the `if` statement, the condition is false, so the script skips down to the next line, the `else` statement, and then executes the code it finds there. This is basically the same as when `if` is used alone. Now, however, suppose the year is 2004. That is a leap year, so the code in the `if` statement is executed. When that's done, the script skips the `else` statement and continues on with the script.

The `if` and `else` statements can be very helpful in controlling the flow and resulting output of your scripts. With them, you can tailor your site accordingly, with basically unlimited possibilities. You can display different messages based on a person's age (if users are over 18, they see one message; if they are under 18, they see another one). You can display a message if it's Tuesday versus if it's Wednesday. You can display a "good morning," "good afternoon," or "good evening" message based on the time of day. You can also place `if` statements within other `if` statements so that your script checks for the day of the week, and if it's a certain day, it checks for the time and displays a message, such as "It's Friday afternoon — the weekend's almost here!"

Using Includes for Efficient Code

Are you getting sick of typing the same things over and over again? The makers of PHP have blessed us frustrated developers with a little time-saving device called *includes*, which save you from reentering frequently used text over and over.

Suppose that you want to type the same message on every page of your site. Perhaps it is your company's name and address, or maybe today's date. If you are coding each page of your site from scratch, this is not very efficient, for a couple of reasons:

❑ You are typing the same information over and over again, which is never good.

❑ In the case of an update or a change, you have to make the change in every single page of your site. Again, this is redundant and time-consuming, and it increases the chances for human errors.

A solution to this problem is to use an include. *Includes* are PHP files that get pulled into other PHP files. You take commonly used information and put it in a separate file. For example, if you have a set of defined variables that need to be referenced in every page on your site, you could define them once in a single PHP script. Then, on each of your pages where you want the variables to appear, you use an `include` statement that specifies the file that defines the variables. When your script is parsed, the parser inserts the code from the include file into your page, just as if you'd typed it there yourself. The final output is then sent to the browser.

Includes can really use any extension, and some people use `.inc` to remind themselves the file should be included into other script files. However, you should still use the `.php` extension. The file extension should commonly hint at the type of file, and it is indeed PHP code, after all. But why would you consider naming a file anything other than PHP? If you are storing potentially sensitive information (for example, server variables such as passwords), then giving the file a `.php` extension makes sure it is never accessible to anyone directly, because the information is parsed before it is sent to the browser. If you keep your project well organized, then you shouldn't have any difficulty remembering that a file is an include.

You can add an include in any other file, and if you place the `include` statement in an `if` statement, you can control when the include is inserted.

Try It Out   Adding a Welcome Message

Suppose you want every page in the movie review site to show a welcome message and perhaps today's date. You want to create a file that includes this information, so follow these steps:

1. Open your text editor, and type the following:

```
<div style="text-align: center">
 <p>Welcome to my movie review site!<br/>
<?php
date_default_timezone_set('America/New_York');
echo 'Today is ';
echo date('F d');
echo ', ';
echo date('Y');
?>
 <br/>
</div>
```

2. Save this file as `header.php`.

3. To include this file in the three existing movie web site files, add the following line, immediately after the `<body>` tag, to `login.php`, `movie1.php`, and `moviesite.php`:

```
<?php include 'header.php'; ?>
```

4. Save your files.

5. Take a look at the files again. If you open `login.php`, you should see the screen shown in Figure 2-13.

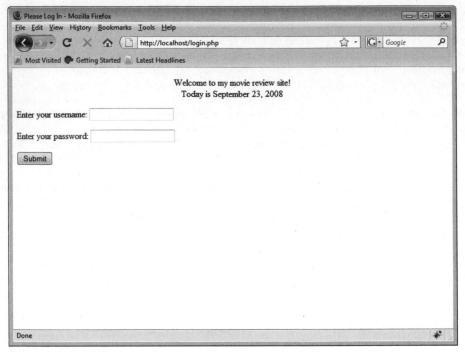

Figure 2-13

You will see the same two lines on every page where you have included the `header.php` file.

How It Works

When PHP comes across an `include` line in a script, it stops working on the current program and immediately shoots on over to whatever file it's told to include. The server parses that second file and carries the results back to the original file, where the parsing continues from where it left off.

Suppose you decided you didn't want dates to be shown with leading zeros. Luckily, PHP has a solution for that when formatting the date function. Make the following change to your `header.php` file and see what happens:

```
<div style="text-align: center">
 <p>Welcome to my movie review site!<br/>';
<?php
date_default_timezone_set('America/New_York');
echo 'Today is ';
echo date('F j');
echo ', ';
echo date('Y');
?>
 </p>
</div>
```

Your problem is fixed ... but the best thing is that it's fixed in all the pages in your site in one fell swoop, thanks to the magic of includes.

Using Functions for Efficient Code

As with includes, functions make your code (and your typing) more efficient and easier to debug. *Functions* are blocks of code that can be called from anywhere in your program. They enable you to execute lines of code without having to retype them every time you want to use them. Functions can help set or update variables. You can also set a function to execute only if a certain criterion has been fulfilled.

Functions are miniprograms within themselves. They don't know about any other variables around them unless you let the other variables outside the function come in through a door called *global*. You use the `global $varname` command to make an outside variable's value accessible to the function. This does *not* apply to any values assigned to any variables that are global by default, such as `$_POST`, `$_GET`, and so on.

Your function can be located anywhere within your script and can be called from anywhere within your script. Therefore, you can list all your commonly used functions at the top of your program, and they can all be kept together for easier debugging. Better yet, you can put all your functions in a file and *include* them in your programs. Now you're rolling!

> *PHP provides you with a comprehensive set of built-in functions (which you can find in Appendix C), but sometimes you need to create your own customized functions.*

Try It Out   **Working with Functions**

This exercise demonstrates functions in action by adding a list of favorite movies to your movie reviews site.

1. Open your `movie1.php` page, and modify it as shown in the highlighted text:

```php
<?php
session_start();
$_SESSION['username'] = $_POST['user'];
$_SESSION['userpass'] = $_POST['pass'];
$_SESSION['authuser'] = 0;

//Check username and password information
if (($_SESSION['username'] == 'Joe') and
    ($_SESSION['userpass'] == '12345')) {
    $_SESSION['authuser'] = 1;
} else {
    echo 'Sorry, but you don\'t have permission to view this page!';
    exit();
}
?>
<html>
 <head>
  <title>Find my Favorite Movie!</title>
 </head>
 <body>
<?php include 'header.php'; ?>
<?php
$myfavmovie = urlencode('Life of Brian');
echo "<a href=\"moviesite.php?favmovie=$myfavmovie\">";
echo "Click here to see information about my favorite movie!";
```

```php
echo "</a>";
?>
```

```html
  <br/>
  <a href="moviesite.php?movienum=5">Click here
   to see my top 5 movies.</a>
  <br/>
  <a href="moviesite.php?movienum=10">Click here
   to see my top 10 movies.</a>
 </body>
</html>
```

2. Now modify `moviesite.php` as shown:

```php
<?php
session_start();

//check to see if user has logged in with a valid password
if ($_SESSION['authuser'] !=1 ) {
    echo "Sorry, but you don't have permission to view this page!";
    exit();
}
?>
<html>
 <head>
  <title>
<?php
if (isset($_GET['favmovie'])) {
    echo ' - ';
    echo $_GET['favmovie'];
}
?>
  </title>
 </head>
 <body>
<?php include 'header.php'; ?>
<?php
function listmovies_1() {
    echo '1. Life of Brian<br/>';
    echo '2. Stripes<br/>';
    echo '3. Office Space<br/>';
    echo '4. The Holy Grail<br/>';
    echo '5. Matrix<br/>';
}

function listmovies_2() {
    echo '6. Terminator 2<br/>';
    echo '7. Star Trek IV<br/>';
    echo '8. Close Encounters of the Third Kind<br/>';
    echo '9. Sixteen Candles<br/>';
    echo '10. Caddyshack<br/>';
}

if (isset($_GET['favmovie'])) {
    echo 'Welcome to our site, ';
```

```
        echo $_SESSION['username'];
        echo '! <br/>';
        echo 'My favorite movie is ';
        echo $_GET['favmovie'];
        echo '<br/>';
        $movierate = 5;
        echo 'My movie rating for this movie is: ';
        echo $movierate;
    } else {
        echo 'My top ';
        echo $_GET['movienum'];
        echo ' movies are:';
        echo '<br/>';

        listmovies_1();
        if ($_GET['movienum'] == 10) {
            listmovies_2();
        }
    }
?>
  </body>
</html>
```

3. Now you must go through the `login.php` file before you can see your changes. Log in as Joe and use the password 12345. Your `movie1.php` page should look like the one in Figure 2-14.

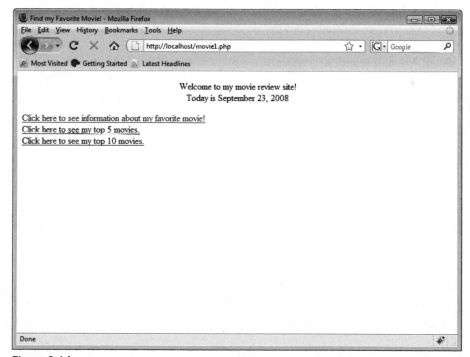

Figure 2-14

4. Click the "5 movies" link. Your screen should look like Figure 2-15.

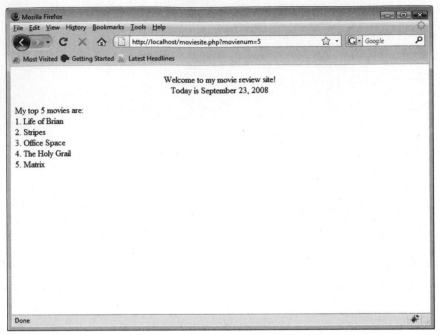

Figure 2-15

5.   Go back and click the "top 10" link; your screen will look like the one in Figure 2-16.

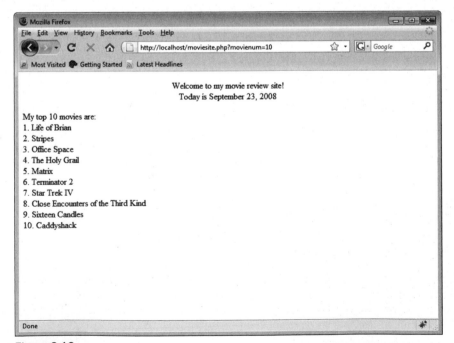

Figure 2-16

How It Works

This has been a rudimentary look at how to use functions, but you can see how they work. The `movie1.php` page gave users the option of looking at 5 or 10 of your favorite movies. Whichever link they choose sets the value for `$movienum`.

In addition, `moviesite.php` accomplishes several other tasks:

❑ It sets up the functions `listmovies_1()` and `listmovies_2()`, which prints a portion of the total top 10 list.

❑ You also added this line:

```
if (isset($_GET['favmovie'])) {
```

The `isset` function checks to see if a variable has been set yet (this doesn't check the value, just whether or not it has been used). You didn't want to show users the information about your favorite movie if they didn't click on the link to see it, so you used `if/else` to take it right out of there. If the variable `favmovie` has not yet been set, the program jumps on down to the `else` portion.

❑ The script performs another `if` statement to check the value of `movienum` to run the correct corresponding functions.

❑ It also references the `movienum` variable for the title of the list, so the program displays the correct number of movies in the list.

As you get more advanced in your PHP programming skills, you might store a list of all your favorite movies in a database and reference them that way, changing your `listmovies()` function to list only one movie at a time and running the function `listmovies()` a number of times. You could also give your users the option of choosing how many movies they want displayed, perhaps through a drop-down box or radio buttons. That would be your new `movienum` variable.

All about Arrays

You've learned about variables and how they are used, but what if you need to have more than one value assigned to that variable? That, my friend, is a good old-fashioned array. *Arrays* are nothing more than lists of information mapped with keys and stored under one variable name. For example, you can store a person's name and address or a list of states in one variable.

Arrays can be a hard thing to wrap your brain around, so let's take a visual approach. Say you see a man sitting at a table at a local restaurant. He has several characteristics that are unique to him, such as first name, last name, and age. You could easily store this pertinent information in three variables: `$firstname`, `$lastname`, and `$age`.

Now, suppose his wife sits down to join him. How can you store her information? If you use the same variable names, how will you know which is her information and which is her husband's? This is where arrays come in. You can store all of his information under one variable, and all of her information under another.

If you put all the information in a chart, it would look like this:

	First Name	Last Name	Age
Husband	Albert	Einstein	129
Wife	Mileva	Einstein	128

An array is just a row of information, and its keys are the column headers. *Keys* are identifiers that help keep the information organized and easy to access. In this instance, you wouldn't know what each of those variables represented if you didn't have column headers. Now let's see how you can use arrays in PHP syntax.

Array Syntax

With an array, you can store multiple pieces of related information under one variable name, like this:

```php
<?php
$husband = array('firstname' =>'Albert',
                 'lastname'  =>'Einstein',
                 'age'       =>'129');

echo $husband['firstname'];
?>
```

Notice how you use => instead of = when assigning values to keys of arrays. All of Albert's information is stored in the variable name husband. By using the key "firstname" you can retrieve his first name. Likewise, "lastname" will retrieve his last name, and "age" his age.

You don't have to store all the values at the same time, though, as in the previous example. Instead, you can assign each member of the array directly, referencing its key in the following manner:

```php
<?php
$husband['firstname'] = 'Albert';
$husband['lastname']  = 'Einstein';
$husband['age']       = 129;
?>
```

This has the same effect as our first example. And if this looks familiar to you already, great! It should! Those special variables we discussed earlier, like $_GET, $_POST, $_COOKIE, and $_SESSION, are arrays!

You can also have arrays within arrays (also known as *multidimensional arrays*). In the earlier example, you had two people sitting at one table. What if you pulled up another table and added a few more people to the mix? How in the heck would you store everyone's information and keep it all separate and organized? Like this!

```php
<?php
$table[1] = array('husband' => array('firstname' => 'Albert',
                                      'lastname'  => 'Einstein',
                                      'age'       => 129),
```

```
                         'wife'     => array('firstname' => 'Mileva',
                                             'lastname'  => 'Einstein',
                                             'age'       => 128));

    // do the same for each table in your restaurant
    ?>
```

Then if someone asks you, "Hey, what are the first names of the couple sitting at table one?" you can easily print the information with a few simple `echo` statements:

```
<?php
echo $table[1]['husband']['firstname'];
echo ' and ';
echo $table[1]['wife']['firstname'];
?>
```

This script would produce the output "Albert and Mileva."

If you want to simply store a list and not worry about the particular order, or what each value should be mapped to (such as a list of states or flavors of ice cream), you don't need to explicitly name the keys; PHP can automatically assign numeric keys with integers starting with 0. This would be set up as follows:

```
<?php
$flavors[] = 'blue raspberry';
$flavors[] = 'root beer';
$flavors[] = 'pineapple';
?>
```

These would then be referenced like this:

```
<?php
echo $flavors[0]; //outputs "blue raspberry"
echo $flavors[1]; //outputs "root beer"
echo $flavors[2]; //outputs "pineapple"
?>
```

Sorting Arrays

A common task you may find yourself doing with arrays is sorting their values. PHP provides many functions that making sorting array values easy. Here are just a few common array-sorting functions, although you will find a more extensive list in Appendix C.

❑   `sort($array)`: Sorts an array in ascending value order

❑   `rsort($array)`: Sorts an array in descending value order

❑   `asort($array)`: Sorts an array in ascending value order while maintaining the key/value relationship

❑   `arsort($array)`: Sorts an array in descending value order while maintaining the key/value relationship

Try It Out   Sorting Arrays

Before we go further, let's do a quick test on sorting arrays, so you can see how the array acts when it is sorted. Type the following program in your text editor, and call it `sorting.php`.

```php
<?php
$flavors[] = 'blue raspberry';
$flavors[] = 'root beer';
$flavors[] = 'pineapple';

sort($flavors);
print_r($flavors);
?>
```

How It Works

Notice anything weird in the preceding code? Yes, we've introduced a new function: `print_r()`. This simply prints out information about a variable so that people can read it. It is frequently used to check array values, specifically. The output would look like that in Figure 2-17.

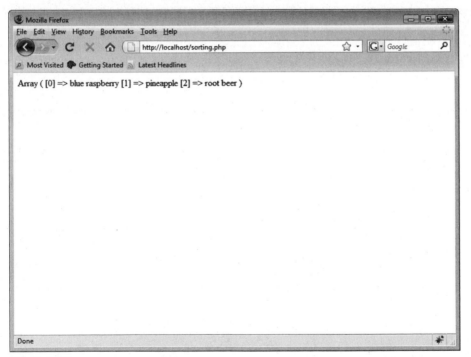

Array ([0] => blue raspberry [1] => pineapple [2] => root beer)

Figure 2-17

You can see that the `sort()` function has done what it's supposed to, and sorted the values in ascending alphabetical order. You can also see the keys that have been automatically assigned to each value (and reassigned by `sort()` in this case).

foreach Constructs

PHP also provides a `foreach` command that applies a set of statements for each value in an array. What an appropriate name, eh?

Your syntax for the `foreach` command looks like this:

```php
<?php
$flavors[] = 'blue raspberry';
$flavors[] = 'root beer';
$flavors[] = 'pineapple';

echo 'My favorite flavors are:<br/>';
foreach ($flavors as $current_flavor) {
    //these lines will execute as long as there are more values in $flavors
    echo $current_flavor  '<br/> ';
}
?>
```

This produces a list of each of the flavors in whatever order they appear in your array.

When PHP is processing your array, it keeps track of what key it's on by using an internal array *pointer*. When your `foreach` construct is called, the pointer is ready and waiting patiently at the first key/value in the array. At the end of the loop, the pointer has moved down through the list and remains at the end, or the last key/value in the array.

Try It Out   Adding Arrays

In this exercise, you'll see what happens when you add arrays to the `moviesite.php` file. You'll also sort them and use the `foreach` construct.

1.   Make the following highlighted changes to the `moviesite.php` file:

```php
<?php
session_start();

//check to see if user has logged in with a valid password
if ($_SESSION['authuser'] !=1 ) {
    echo "Sorry, but you don't have permission to view this page!";
    exit();
}
?>
<html>
 <head>
  <title>My Movie Site
<?php
if (isset($_GET['favmovie'])) {
    echo ' - ';
    echo $_GET['favmovie'];
}
?>
  </title>
```

```php
 </head>
 <body>
<?php include 'header.php'; ?>
<?php
$favmovies = array('Life of Brian',
                   'Stripes',
                   'Office Space',
                   'The Holy Grail',
                   'Matrix',
                   'Terminator 2',
                   'Star Trek IV',
                   'Close Encounters of the Third Kind',
                   'Sixteen Candles',
                   'Caddyshack');

//delete these lines:
function listmovies_1() {
    echo '1. Life of Brian<br/>';
    echo '2. Stripes<br/>';
    echo '3. Office Space<br/>';
    echo '4. The Holy Grail<br/>';
    echo '5. Matrix<br/>';
}

function listmovies_2() {
    echo '6. Terminator 2<br/>';
    echo '7. Star Trek IV<br/>';
    echo '8. Close Encounters of the Third Kind<br/>';
    echo '9. Sixteen Candles<br/>';
    echo '10. Caddyshack<br/>';
}
//end of deleted lines

if (isset($_GET['favmovie'])) {
    echo 'Welcome to our site, ';
    echo $_SESSION['username'];
    echo '! <br/>';
    echo 'My favorite movie is ';
    echo $_GET['favmovie'];
    echo '<br/>';
    $movierate = 5;
    echo 'My movie rating for this movie is: ';
    echo $movierate;
} else {
    echo 'My top 10 favorite movies are:<br/>';

    if (isset($_GET['sorted'])) {
        sort($favmovies);
    }

    echo '<ol>';
    foreach ($favmovies as $movie) {
        echo '<li>';
        echo $movie;
```

```
            echo '</li>';
    }
    echo '</ol>';

    // delete these lines:
    echo 'My top ';
    echo $_GET['movienum'];
    echo ' movies are:';
    echo '<br/>';

    listmovies_1();
    if ($_GET['movienum'] == 10) {
        listmovies_2();
    }
    // end of deleted lines
}
?>
 </body>
</html>
```

2. Then change `movie1.php` as shown here:

```
<?php
session_start();
$_SESSION['username'] = $_POST['user'];
$_SESSION['userpass'] = $_POST['pass'];
$_SESSION['authuser'] = 0;

//Check username and password information
if (($_SESSION['username'] == 'Joe') and
    ($_SESSION['userpass'] == '12345')) {
    $_SESSION['authuser'] = 1;
} else {
    echo 'Sorry, but you don\'t have permission to view this page!';
    exit();
}
?>
<html>
 <head>
  <title>Find my Favorite Movie!</title>
 </head>
 <body>
<?php include 'header.php'; ?>
<?php
$myfavmovie = urlencode('Life of Brian');
echo "<a href=\"moviesite.php?favmovie=$myfavmovie\">";
echo "Click here to see information about my favorite movie!";
echo "</a>";
?>
  <br/>
  <!-- delete these lines
```

```
  <a href="moviesite.php?movienum=5">Click here
    to see my top 5 movies.</a>
  <br/>
  <a href="moviesite.php?movienum=10">Click here
    to see my top 10 movies.</a>
  end of deleted lines -->
```

```
  <a href="moviesite.php">Click here to see my
    10 movies.</a>
  <br/>
  <a href="moviesite.php?sorted=true">Click here
    to see my top 10 movies sorted alphabetically.</a>
```

```
  </body>
  </html>
```

3.   Now log in with the `login.php` file (log in as Joe with password 12345), and when you get the choice, click the link that lists the top 10 movies. You should see something like Figure 2-18.

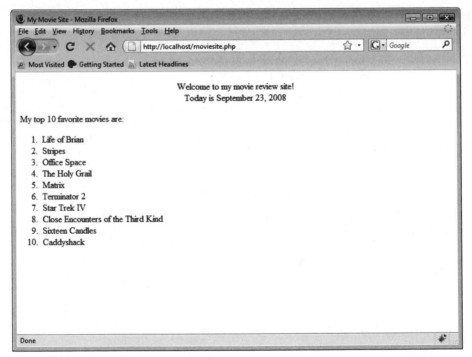

Figure 2-18

4.   Go back to `movie1.php`, and this time click the link that lists the movies sorted in alphabetical order. This time, you should see something like Figure 2-19.

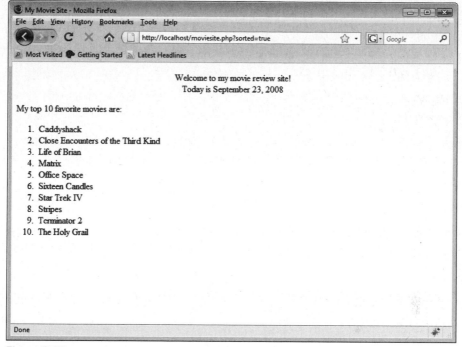

Figure 2-19

How It Works

You first put the movie list in one variable, $favmovies, with the array function. Then you were able to list the movies individually, using the foreach construct in moviesite.php. You also added a link that would allow users to show the list sorted alphabetically, by adding a variable named $_GET[sorted]. When this variable was set to true, the sort() function executed, and you passed that true variable through the URL in the link.

You may have noticed a shortcoming in the program . . . okay, you may have noticed many shortcomings, but one in particular stands out. You can no longer control how many movies are shown in your list. You are stuck with showing the total number of movies in the array. There's a way to fix that, which is what we'll talk about next.

While You're Here . . .

You've seen that foreach will take an action on each element of an array until it reaches the end, but you can also take an action on just some of the elements in an array, with the while statement. A while statement tells the server to execute a series of statements repeatedly as long as a given condition is true.

Here's an example of how you would use the while command. This code simply counts from 1 to 5 and prints each number on a separate line. First a variable $num is set to 0. This variable is then increased by 1 each time through the loop. The while checks to see that the value of $num is less than 5. After five times through the loop, the value of $num is 6, so the loop ends.

```php
<?php
$num = 0;
while ($num < 5) {
    $num = $num + 1;
    echo $num;
    echo '<br/>';
}
?>
```

The following code does the same thing, but it uses a do/while loop instead. This code works exactly the same way, except that the condition is checked at the end of the loop. With a while loop, it is possible for the condition to be false and the associated code never to execute. But with the check at the end, as with a do/while loop, then the commands inside the loop will always be executed at least once.

```php
<?php
$num = 0;
do {
    $num = $num + 1;
    echo $num;
    echo '<br/>';
} while ($num < 5);
?>
```

Try It Out **Using the while Function**

This exercise allows users to tell you how many movies they want to see, and enables you to number the list as you did before, using the while function.

1. Make the following changes to your movie1.php program:

```php
<?php
session_start();
$_SESSION['username'] = $_POST['user'];
$_SESSION['userpass'] = $_POST['pass'];
$_SESSION['authuser'] = 0;

//Check username and password information
if (($_SESSION['username'] == 'Joe') and
    ($_SESSION['userpass'] == '12345')) {
    $_SESSION['authuser'] = 1;
} else {
    echo 'Sorry, but you don\'t have permission to view this page!';
    exit();
}
?>
<html>
 <head>
  <title>Find my Favorite Movie!</title>
 </head>
 <body>
<?php include 'header.php'; ?>
<?php
$myfavmovie = urlencode('Life of Brian');
echo "<a href=\"moviesite.php?favmovie=$myfavmovie\">";
```

```
echo "Click here to see information about my favorite movie!";
echo "</a>";
?>
  <br/>
  <!-- delete these lines
  <a href="moviesite.php?">Click here to see my top
   10 movies.</a>
  <br/>
  <a href="moviesite.php?sorted=true">Click here
   to see my top 10 movies sorted alphabetically.</a>
   end deleted lines -->

  <br/>
  Or choose how many movies you would like to see:
  <br/>
  <form method="post" action="moviesite.php">
   <p>Enter number of movies (up to 10):
    <input type="text" name="num" maxlength="2" size="2"/>
    <br/>
    Check to sort them alphabetically:
    <input type="checkbox" name="sorted" />
   </p>
   <input type="submit" name="submit" value="Submit"/>
  </form>

  </body>
</html>
```

2. Make the following changes to moviesite.php:

```
<?php
session_start();

//check to see if user has logged in with a valid password
if ($_SESSION['authuser'] !=1 ) {
    echo "Sorry, but you don't have permission to view this page!";
    exit();
}
?>
<html>
 <head>
  <title>My Movie Site
<?php
if (isset($_GET['favmovie'])) {
    echo ' - ';
    echo $_GET['favmovie'];
}
?>
  </title>
 </head>
 <body>
<?php include 'header.php'; ?>
<?php
```

```php
$favmovies = array('Life of Brian',
                   'Stripes',
                   'Office Space',
                   'The Holy Grail',
                   'Matrix',
                   'Terminator 2',
                   'Star Trek IV',
                   'Close Encounters of the Third Kind',
                   'Sixteen Candles',
                   'Caddyshack');

if (isset($_GET['favmovie'])) {
    echo 'Welcome to our site, ';
    echo $_SESSION['username'];
    echo '! <br/>';
    echo 'My favorite movie is ';
    echo $_GET['favmovie'];
    echo '<br/>';
    $movierate = 5;
    echo 'My movie rating for this movie is: ';
    echo $movierate;
} else {
    echo 'My top ' . $_POST['num'] . ' favorite movies';

    if (isset($_POST['sorted'])) {
        sort($favmovies);
        echo ' (sorted alphabetically) ';
    }
    echo 'are:<br/>';

    // delete these lines
    echo '<ol>';
    foreach ($favmovies as $movie) {
        echo '<li>';
        echo $movie;
        echo '</li>';
    }
    echo '</ol>';
    // end of deleted lines

    $numlist = 0;
    echo '<ol>';
    while ($numlist < $_POST['num']) {
        echo '<li>';
        echo $favmovies[$numlist];
        echo '</li>';
        $numlist = $numlist + 1;
    }
    echo '</ol>';
}
?>
  </body>
</html>
```

70

3.   Now play around with your new `movie1.php` and `moviesite.php` files. `movie1.php` will look like Figure 2-20. Depending on how many movies you chose to show, and if they should be sorted alphabetically or not, `moviesite.php` may look like Figure 2-21.

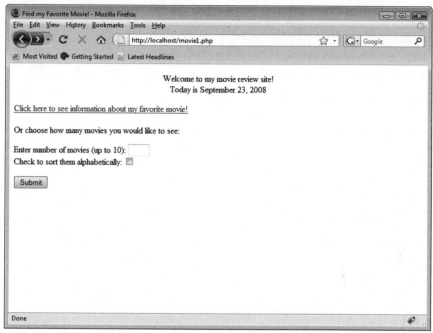

Figure 2-20

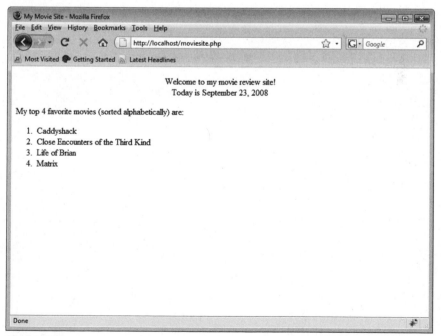

Figure 2-21

How It Works

Your code should show a list of the top movies based on how many you, as the user, chose to see and whether or not you wanted them listed alphabetically.

You'll notice several things in the code:

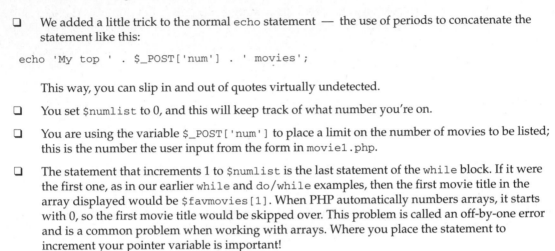

- ❏ We added a little trick to the normal `echo` statement — the use of periods to concatenate the statement like this:

  ```
  echo 'My top ' . $_POST['num'] . ' movies';
  ```

  This way, you can slip in and out of quotes virtually undetected.

- ❏ You set `$numlist` to 0, and this will keep track of what number you're on.

- ❏ You are using the variable `$_POST['num']` to place a limit on the number of movies to be listed; this is the number the user input from the form in `movie1.php`.

- ❏ The statement that increments 1 to `$numlist` is the last statement of the `while` block. If it were the first one, as in our earlier `while` and `do/while` examples, then the first movie title in the array displayed would be `$favmovies[1]`. When PHP automatically numbers arrays, it starts with 0, so the first movie title would be skipped over. This problem is called an off-by-one error and is a common problem when working with arrays. Where you place the statement to increment your pointer variable is important!

Now see, that wasn't so hard, was it? You're really cooking now!

Alternate Syntax for PHP

As a programmer, it's always great when you can find a quicker and easier way to make something happen. We have included some useful shortcuts or alternate syntax for tasks you are already familiar with.

Alternates to the echo Command

You already got a taste of `print_r()`, but you can also use the `print` command to display text or variable values in your page. The difference between `echo` and `print` is that when you use `print`, a value of 1 or 0 will also be returned upon the success or failure of the `print` command. In other words, you would be able to tell if something didn't print using the `print` command, whereas `echo` just does what it's told without letting you know whether or not it worked properly. For all other intents and purposes, the two are the same.

Alternates to Logical Operators

You may remember that and and or are obvious logical operators you use when comparing two expressions, but there are other ways to express these operators:

❑ && can be used in place of and, the only difference being the order in which the operator is evaluated during a mathematical function.

❑ || can be used in place of or, the only difference being the order in which the operator is evaluated during a mathematical function.

Alternates to Double Quotes: Using heredoc

Besides using double quotation marks to block off a value, you can also use the heredoc syntax:

```
$value = <<<ABC
This is the text that will be included in the value variable.
ABC;
```

This is especially helpful if you have double quotes and single quotes within a block of text, such as:

```
$value = <<<ABC
Last time I checked, I was 6'-5" tall.
ABC;
```

This keeps you from having to escape those characters out, and keeps things much simpler. Your ABC syntax can consist of any characters, just as long as they match. There is one caveat, though . . . you need to make sure there are no extra spaces after the first ABC (the marker needs to be the last thing on its line) or before the last ABC (that marker must be the first thing on its line). PHP will give you an error if either marker isn't in the appropriate position.

Alternates to Incrementing/Decrementing Values

You can have variable values incremented or decremented automatically, like this:

Syntax Shortcut	What It Does to the Value
++$value	Increases by one, and returns the incremented value
$value++	Returns the value, then increases by one
--$value	Decreases by one, and returns the decremented value
$value--	Returns the value, then decreases by one
$value = $value + 1	Increases the value by one
$value += 1	Increases the value by one

OOP Dreams

Object-oriented Programming (OOP) focuses on building programs from a set of "smart" or "self-aware" custom data types. The ability to design code modularly hopefully helps save you time, reduces stress and makes it easier to reuse your code or share it with others. Here, we'll take a quick run through the syntax that is associated with OOP in PHP. As a beginner, you won't really need to delve into the world of OOP (we do that in later chapters of this book), but it's important for you to understand the most basic concepts behind OOP.

First, imagine a box. It can be any type of box you want — a small jewelry box, a large wooden crate, plastic, tall and thin, short and wide . . . you get the idea.

Next, imagine yourself placing something inside the box. Again, it can be whatever you choose — a rock, a million dollars, a younger sibling . . .

Finally, close it up nice and tight — seal it with packing tape, nails, iron chains, encase it in concrete . . .

Now, wouldn't it be convenient if you could walk up to this box and ask it to tell you what's inside it, instead of having to go through all the trouble of opening it up again to look? With OOP, you can! Here's how this might appear as code:

```php
<?php
$mybox = new Box('Jack');
echo $mybox->get_what_is_inside();
?>
```

The variable $mybox stores a reference to a special "self-aware" box (also known as an object) built by new. You might find it helpful to think of new as a small engineering and construction team that's part of PHP and just loves to build new objects! Jack is placed inside the Box as it is being built. Later, when you want to ask the box its contents, you apply the special get_whats_inside() function against the object's reference.

Of course, the code won't run. new doesn't know how to construct Box yet, and PHP doesn't know what the function get_what_is_inside() is supposed to do. There must be a Box definition.

Classes

A class is a representation of an abstract data type. In layman's terms, it's the blueprint new will use to construct the object. A class provides the variable and function definitions that enable the box to be self-aware. With such a blueprint, new can build an object exactly to your specifications. Here's the class definition for Box:

```php
<?php
class Box
{
    private $what_is_inside;

    public function __construct($contents) {
        $this->what_is_inside = $contents;
    }

    public function get_whats_inside() {
```

```
            return $this->what_is_inside;
        }
    }
?>
```

A class's definition begins with the keyword class followed by whatever name you assign to it, and its variables and methods within braces. By observing the definition above, you'll notice it contains the variable $what_is_inside, which is used to remember the contents, and two functions: __construct()and get_what_is_inside().

When the box springs into existence, PHP will look for and execute the __construct() function automatically. Known as a constructor, its purpose is to initialize the object's internal variables.

The special variable $this is used to tell Box that $what_is_inside is a variable that belongs to the scope of the whole Box class, and not the functions themselves. The $contents variable, on the other hand, only exists within the scope of the constructor. $this->what_is_inside then is essentially a variable defined as part of the overall class and is available within any of its functions.

With a definition in place, new can create a Box object, the __construct()function will automatically be called with Jack passed in. The constructor accepts the value and uses it to initialize $what_is_inside, an internal variable that is accessible to functions that make up the class. The function get_what_is_ inside()then retrieves the stored value from the class's $what_is_inside variable.

Congratulations on your nice, new, shiny Jack-in-the-Box!

Properties and Methods

We've been using the terms variable and function when talking about $what_is_inside and get_ what_is_inside()because they are words you're already familiar with. While these terms are not necessarily incorrect, the more appropriate names in OOP parlance are *property* and *method*.

Variables that are defined as part of the class's definition and that are accessible in its functions are known as *properties*. They maintain the object's state and other attribute information.

Functions defined in a class are known as *methods*. They act as a method for communicating with and manipulating the data within the object. Methods provide the object with a standard interface that anyone can use.

The visibility of the properties and methods of a class can be set as public or private. Those that are marked with the private keyword are only accessible from within the class itself. Those marked with the public keyword, on the other hand, are accessible from both inside and outside the class.

Why Use OOP?

Using OOP has a few benefits over simply including a file with functions in it. First, with OOP, you can easily keep bits of related information together and perform complex tasks with that data. Objects wrap up not only the functions but the data the functions manipulate as well. Second, you can process the data an unlimited number of times without worrying about variables being overwritten. Third, you can have multiple copies of the same class running at the same time, without the internal variables being corrupted or overwritten.

75

OOP is an advanced concept, which is why we won't use it until later on in this book. For now, we've kept it simple to let you digest the basics.

Summary

Although we've covered many different topics in this chapter, our goal was to give you enough ammunition to get started on your own web site. Our hope is that you are beginning to realize the power of PHP and how easy it is to jump in and get started. As we talk about database connectivity in Chapter 3, you will start to see how PHP can work with a database to give you a very impressive site.

PHP is straightforward, powerful, and flexible. There are numerous built-in functions that can save you hours of work (date() for example, which takes one line to show the current date). You can find a helpful list of PHP functions in Appendix C; browse that list to find bits and pieces you can use in your own site development.

Exercises

To build your skills even further, here is an exercise you can use to test yourself. The answers are provided in Appendix A, but keep in mind that there is always more than one way to accomplish a given task, so if you choose to do things a different way, and the results are displayed the way you want, more power to you.

Try modifying your PHP files in the following ways:

1. Go back to your date.php file, and, instead of displaying only the number of days in the current month, add a few lines that say:

   The month is _____.

   There are _____ days in this month.

   There are _____ months left in the current year.

2. On your movie web site, write a file that displays the following line at the bottom center of every page of your site, with a link to your e-mail address.

   This site developed by: <u>ENTER YOUR NAME HERE</u>.

3. Write a program that displays a different message based on the time of day. For example, have the site display "Good Morning!" if it is accessed in the morning.

4. Write a program that formats a block of text (to be input by the user) based on preferences chosen by the user. Give your user options for color of text, font choice, and size. Display the output on a new page.

5. In the program you created in step 4, allow your users the option of saving the information for the next time they visit. If they choose "yes," save the information in a cookie.

6. Using functions, write a program that keeps track of how many times a visitor has loaded the page.

Using PHP with MySQL

So now that you've done some really cool stuff with PHP in Chapter 2, such as using includes and functions, it's time to make your web site truly dynamic and show users some real data. You may or may not have had experience with using or configuring databases before, so we'll take a look at what MySQL is and how PHP can tap into it. We will also show you what a MySQL database looks like in terms of the different tables and fields, and give you some quickie shortcuts to make your life much easier. (You can thank us later for those.)

By the end of this chapter, you will be able to:

❑   Understand what a MySQL database is.

❑   View data contained in the MySQL database.

❑   Connect to the database from your web site.

❑   Pull specific information out of the database, right from your web site.

❑   Use third-party software to easily manage tables.

❑   Use the source web site to troubleshoot problems you may encounter.

Although some of this information is expanded upon in later chapters, this chapter lays the groundwork for the more complex issues.

Overview of MySQL Structure and Syntax

Databases are stores of information. They allow one to easily record and then access large amounts of information for a wide variety of purposes. Because pretty much any type of data can be stored in a database, they can be found in use literally everywhere. Databases store names and addresses, medical records, police reports, sale transactions, information about music and video collections, and more! In the web sites you create as you work through this book, you will be storing information pertinent to the movie review site (such as movie titles and years of release) and comic book fan information (such as a list of authentic users/comic book fans and their passwords) in a MySQL database.

MySQL commands can be issued through the command prompt, as you did in Chapter 1 when you were installing it and granting permissions to users, or through PHP. We primarily use PHP to issue commands in this book, and we will discuss this shortly.

MySQL Structure

In a nonrelational database system, all information is stored in one big area, which sometimes makes it more difficult and cumbersome to extract only the data you want. But MySQL is a relational database system, which allows you to separate information into *tables*, or groups of pertinent information. Each table consists of separate *fields*, which represent each bit of information. For example, one field could contain a customer's first name, and another field could contain his or her last name. Fields can hold different types of data, such as text, numbers, dates, and so on.

If you are familiar with spreadsheet programs such as Microsoft Excel and OpenOffice.org Calc, you may find it helpful to think of a table as akin to a spreadsheet. Each spreadsheet acts as a table, with each row comprising one record and each column a different field. As the spreadsheet workbook is a collection of related spreadsheets, a database is a collection of related tables.

You create database tables based on what type of information you want to store in them. The separate tables of MySQL are then linked together with some common denominator, where the values of the common field are the same.

For an example of this structure, imagine a table that includes a customer's name, address, and ID number, and another table that includes the customer's ID number and the past orders the customer has placed. The common field is the customer's ID number, and the information stored in the two separate tables would be linked together via fields where the ID number is the same. This enables you to see all the information related to this customer at one time.

Let's take a look at the ways in which you can tailor database tables to fit your needs.

Field Types

When you create a table initially, you need to tell the MySQL database what types of information will be stored in each field. The different types of fields and some examples are listed in the table that follows.

MySQL Field Type	Description	Example
char(length)	Any character-based data can be stored in this field, but the field will have a fixed length denoted by the value in the parentheses.	Customer's State field always has two characters and would use char(2).
varchar(length)	Any character-based data can be in this field, and the data can vary in length from 0 up to 255 characters. The maximum length of the field is denoted in parentheses.	Customer's Address field has letters and numbers and varies in length.

use text type if you want to allow for entries greater than 255 characters e.g. a "Comments" field.

MySQL Field Type	Description	Example
int(length)	Integers that can range from −2,147,483,648 to +2,147,483,647 can be stored in this field. The length parameter limits the number of digits that can be shown, not the value. Mathematical functions can be performed on data in this field.	Quantity of a product on hand.
int(length) unsigned	Positive integers (and zero) up to 4,294,967,295 can be in this field. The length parameter limits the number of digits that can be displayed. Mathematical functions can be performed on data in this field.	Customer ID (if entirely numerical).
text	Any character-based data can be in this field, with a maximum size of 65,536 characters.	Comments field that allows longer text to be stored without limiting the field to 255 characters.
decimal(length,dec)	Numeric field that can store decimals. The length parameter limits the number of digits that can be displayed, and the dec parameter limits the number of decimal places that can be stored.	Prices. For example, a price field that would store prices up to 999.99 would be defined as decimal(5,2).
enum("option1", "option2", ...)	Allows only certain values to be stored in this field, such as "true" and "false," or a list of states. 65,535 different options are allowed.	Gender field for your users will have a value of either "male" or "female."
date	Stores a date in YYYY-MM-DD format.	Date of an order, a birthday, or the date a user joined as a registered user.
time	Stores time in hh:mm:ss format.	Time a news article was added to the web site.
datetime	Multipurpose field that stores both the date and time together as YYYY-MM-DD hh:mm:ss.	Last date and time a user visited your web page.

(handwritten margin notes: "Note the difference", "Good", "different from time stamp?")

Although the preceding field types should suffice for most of your needs, the table that follows lists some perhaps less-often-used types.

MySQL Field Type	Description
year(length)	Stores a year. By default, the year is four digits, though it is possible to specify a two-digit format by using the length parameter.
tinyint(length)	Numeric field that stores integers from -128 to 127. (Adding the unsigned parameter allows storage of 0 to 255.)
smallint(length)	Numeric field that stores integers from -32,768 to 32,767. (Adding the unsigned parameter allows storage of 0 to 65,535.)
mediumint(length)	Numeric field that stores integers from -8,388,608 to 8,388,607. (Adding the unsigned parameter allows storage of 0 to 16,777,215.)
bigint(length)	Numeric field that stores integers from −9,223,372,036,854,775,808 to 9,223,372,036,854,775,807. (Adding the unsigned parameter allows storage of 0 to 18,446,744,073,709,551,615.)
tinytext	Allows storage of up to 255 characters.
mediumtext	Allows storage of up to 1,677,215 characters.
longtext	Allows storage of up to 4,294,967,295 characters.
blob	Equal to a text field, except that it is case-sensitive when sorting and comparing. Stores up to 65,535 characters. blob and its derivatives (which follow) are generally used to store binary data.
tinyblob	Equal to the tinytext field, except that it is case-sensitive when sorting and comparing; see blob, above.
mediumblob	Equal to the mediumtext field, except that it is case-sensitive when sorting and comparing; see blob, above.
longblob	Equal to the longtext field, except that it is case-sensitive when sorting and comparing; see blob, above.

[handwritten note: std. text field allows up to 65,536]

Believe it or not, even more data types are supported by MySQL! You can find a complete list of them in Appendix D.

Choosing the Right Field Type

Although you won't actually be creating a database from scratch just yet, you should know how to figure out what field type will best serve your needs. We've put together a list of questions about fields that you can ask yourself before your database tables have been created. As you answer each of these questions, keep in mind the potential values that could exist for the particular field you're setting up.

First, ask yourself: Will the field contain both letters and numbers?

- ❑ If the answer is "yes," consider `char`, `varchar`, `text`, `tinytext`, `mediumtext`, `longtext`, `blob`, `tinyblob`, `mediumblob`, and `longblob`. Then ask yourself: How many characters will need to be stored? Will it vary from entry to entry?

  - ❑ **0–255 characters, variable length:** Use `varchar` if you want to delete any trailing spaces, or if you want to set a default value. Use `tinytext` if you don't care about trailing spaces or a default value, or if your text does not need to be case-sensitive. Use `tinyblob` if you don't care about trailing spaces or a default value, but your text does need to be case-sensitive.

  - ❑ **256–65,536 characters:** Use `text` if your text does not need to be case-sensitive in searches, sorts, or comparisons. Use `blob` if your text is case-sensitive.

  - ❑ **65,537–1,677,215 characters:** Use `mediumtext` if your text does not need to be case-sensitive; use `mediumblob` if your text is case-sensitive.

  - ❑ **1,677,216–4,294,967,295 characters:** Use `longtext` if your text does not need to be case-sensitive; use `longblob` if your text is case-sensitive.

- ❑ If the answer is "Yes, it may contain letters or numbers, but it must be one of a finite number of values," use `enum`.

- ❑ If the answer is "No, it will consist of dates and/or times only," use `timestamp` if you need to store the time and date when the information was entered or updated. If you need to store only the date, use `date`. If you need to store both the date and time, use `datetime`. If you need only the year, use `year`.

- ❑ If the answer is "No, it will consist only of numbers, and mathematical functions will be performed on this field," use one of the following, depending on the size of the number:

  - ❑ Integers from −127 to 127, use `tinyint`.
  - ❑ Integers from −32,768 to 32,767, use `smallint`.
  - ❑ Integers from −8,388,608 to 8,388,607, use `mediumint`.
  - ❑ Integers from −2,147,483,648 to 2,147,483,647, use `int`.
  - ❑ Integers from −9,223,372,036,854,775,808 to 9,223,372,036,854,775,807, use `bigint`.
  - ❑ Integers from 0 to 255, use `tinyint` unsigned.
  - ❑ Integers from 0 to 65,535, use `smallint` unsigned.
  - ❑ Integers from 0 to 16,777,215, use `mediumint` unsigned.
  - ❑ Integers from 0 to 4,294,967,295, use `int` unsigned.
  - ❑ Integers from 0 to 18,446,744,073,709,551,615, use `bigint` unsigned.
  - ❑ Decimals with fixed decimal places, use `dec`.

- ❑ If the answer is "No, it will consist of only numbers, but mathematical functions will not be performed on this field," use the preceding guidelines for text/number mix in the field.

If your field requirements do not fall into any of these categories, check Appendix D for a complete list of all available field types. You can also check the documentation at the MySQL web site (www.mysql.com) if you are still unsure about what type of field you need.

null/not null   *Not Null requires data to be input*

Your MySQL server also wants to know whether or not the field can be empty. You establish this with the null or not null option. null tells MySQL that it is okay if nothing is stored in the field, and not null tells MySQL to require *something*, *anything*, to be stored there. Be careful, though. The number zero is different from a null entry. A zero may be nothing in terms of quantity, but it *is* something in terms of data.

Important

If a field has been defined as not null and nothing is entered by the user, MySQL will enter a 0 in the field instead of producing an error. It is for this reason that you should not rely on MySQL to check data for accuracy, and instead put checks into place using PHP. We talk more about data validation in Chapter 8.

Indexes

MySQL uses *indexes* to speed up the process of searching for a particular row of information. Here's how indexes work: Imagine you have a room full of stacks upon stacks of receipts of everything you have ever bought in your life. Then you find you have to return some zippered parachute pants you bought in 1984, but unfortunately you need the receipt. So you start sifting through the massive stacks of papers. Lo and behold, five days later, you find the receipt in the last pile in the room. After cursing to yourself that perhaps you should get a little more organized, you realize you could at least group them by year of purchase. And then you start getting *really* organized and group them further into categories, such as apparel, 8-track tapes, and so on. So the next time you need to return something you purchased many years ago, you can at least jump to the correct pile and even know what category to look in. It all makes sense, right?

Now imagine that your data is stored all willy-nilly in rows within your table. Every time you want to search for something, you have to start at the first record and make your way down through all the rows until you find what you are looking for. What if you have 10,000 rows, and the one you happen to be looking for is at the very end? Pull up your chair and take your shoes off because it could be a while.

By using a special internal filing system, MySQL can jump to the approximate location of your data much more quickly. It does this through the use of indexes, also known as *keys*. In the receipt example, you decided to group your receipts by year. So if your receipts were stored in a database, an index entry would be "year." As you continue to further group your receipts, another index would be created for "category."

MySQL requires at least one index on every table so that it has something to go by. Normally, you would use a *primary key*, or unique identifier that helps keep the data separate. This field must be NOT NULL and/or UNIQUE; an example would be a customer ID number to keep each of your customers separate. As an example, you could easily have two different customers with the name John Smith, so you need a way to tell the difference. In the receipts table example, you could create a primary key and assign each receipt its own identifying number so you can tell each receipt apart.

When the unique parameter is turned on, MySQL makes sure that absolutely no duplicates exist for a particular field. This is typically used for only the primary key in your table, but it can be used with any field. For example, what if you ran a contest in which only the first person from every state who visited would be allowed to join your web site? You could use the unique parameter; then, anyone from a state whose slot has already been filled will get an error message when he or she tries to insert data into your website.

Auto-Increment

Say you have a field that you want to automatically increase by one whenever a new record is added. This can be a quite useful function when assigning ID numbers. You don't have to worry about what the last ID number was; the field automatically keeps track for you, and you can be sure each new record will be given a new, unique value.

You can designate a field to be auto-incremented by simply adding the `auto_increment` command when setting up your table. You can also determine what the first number in the count will be, if you don't want it to be 1. You will see this in action later in the chapter.

Other Parameters

You can make other specifications when creating your database, but those are for more advanced MySQL users. For a complete list of these parameters, we encourage you to visit the MySQL web site, `www.mysql.com`.

Types of MySQL Tables and Storage Engines

Now that you understand some of the general features of tables, you should know that there are two different types of tables: transaction-safe tables (TSTs) and non–transaction-safe tables (NTSTs). Transaction-safe tables allow lost data to be recovered, or perform a rollback of data to revert changes recently made. Non–transaction-safe tables are much faster and require much less memory to process updates, but changes are permanent with no real way to roll back changes if something goes wrong.

MySQL has many different storage engines available to store and retrieve data, but the five most common are:

- ❏ MyISAM
- ❏ MERGE
- ❏ MEMORY
- ❏ InnoDB
- ❏ BDB

If you're curious about other storage engines, issue the command SHOW ENGINES to MySQL to see which ones are available in your installation, and then read about them at `www.mysql.com`.

MyISAM

This is the default storage engine and will usually be sufficient for the average user's needs. It supports all the field types, parameters, and functions we've talked about so far. It supports non–transaction-safe tables. If you're a long-time MySQL user, this table replaces the older ISAM engine from long ago.

MERGE

This storage engine can manipulate several identical MyISAM tables as one entity. It supports non–transaction-safe tables.

MEMORY

These are mostly used for temporary tables because of their incredible speed, but they don't support a lot of the common features of the MyISAM table, such as `auto_increment` and `blob/text` columns. This type should be used in unique circumstances only. You might use it, for example, if you were working with user logs and you wanted to store the information in a temporary table to massage the data, but you didn't necessarily need to keep the data long-term. The tables are stored in memory and are lost if power to the server is cut. This storage engine supports non–transaction-safe tables.

InnoDB

This type supports transaction-safe tables. It is meant for extremely large and frequently accessed applications. It features a row-locking mechanism to prevent different users from attempting to make changes to a row or add the same row to the table. According to the MySQL web site, one instance of this type of table has been shown to support 800 inserts and updates per second — not too shabby! You can also learn more about InnoDB at its own web site: `www.innodb.com`.

BDB

BDB, or BerkeleyDB, is another type of table that supports transaction-safe tables. It is actually its own entity that works closely with the MySQL server and can be downloaded from `www.oracle.com/database/berkeley-db/index.html`. Like InnoDB tables, it is meant to support very large applications with literally thousands of users attempting to insert and update the same data at the same time.

MySQL Syntax and Commands

Although it is quite possible to access MySQL directly through a shell command prompt, we are going to access it through PHP for the purposes of this book. Regardless of the mode by which the MySQL server gets its information and requests, the syntax is the same.

Typically, you keep the MySQL commands in all caps, although this is not necessary. The purpose of this is to help keep the MySQL syntax separate from the variables and table or database names.

Common commands you will be using in this book include:

- ❏ CREATE: Creates new databases and tables
- ❏ ALTER: Modifies existing tables
- ❏ SELECT: Chooses the data you want
- ❏ DELETE: Erases the data from your table
- ❏ DESCRIBE: Lets you know the structure and specifics of the table
- ❏ INSERT INTO tablename VALUES: Puts values into the table
- ❏ UPDATE: Lets you modify data already in a table
- ❏ DROP: Deletes an entire table or database

How PHP Fits with MySQL

Since the onset of PHP6, you need to take a few extra steps to convince PHP and MySQL to play well with each other. Before your MySQL functions will be recognizable, make sure to enable MySQL in your php.ini file, which we covered in Chapter 1.

You can use MySQL commands within PHP code almost as seamlessly as you do with HTML. Numerous PHP functions work specifically with MySQL to make your life easier; you can find a comprehensive list in Appendix C.

Some of the more commonly used functions are:

- ❏ mysql_connect([$host[, $username[, $password]]]): Connects to the MySQL server and returns a resource which is used to reference the connection.

- ❏ mysql_select_db($database[, $resource]): Equivalent to the MySQL command USE and sets the active database.

- ❏ mysql_query($query[, $resource]): Used to send any MySQL command to the database server. In the case of SELECT queries, a reference to the result set will be returned.

- ❏ mysql_fetch_array($result): Return a row of data from the query's result set as an associative array, numeric array or both.

- ❏ mysql_fetch_assoc($result): Return a row of data from the query's result set as an associative array.

- ❏ mysql_error([$resource]): Shows the error message generated by the previous query.

You will become very familiar with these commands and many more.

You can send any MySQL command to the server through PHP, using the mysql_query command, as shown in the following example. You do this by sending the straight text through PHP, either through a variable or through the mysql_query command directly, like this:

```
$results = mysql_query('SELECT * FROM TABLE');
```

But one could argue it is better to do it in two steps, like this:

```
$query = 'SELECT * FROM TABLE';
$results = mysql_query($query);
```

This way you can print out the value of $query for debugging purposes if there is a problem. Either way, the results of the query are put into a temporary array stored as $results, which you'll learn more about later.

Connecting to the MySQL Server

Before you can do anything with MySQL, you must first connect to the MySQL server using your specific connection values. Connection variables consist of the following parameters:

❑ **Hostname:** In our case, this is `localhost` because everything has been installed locally. You will need to change this to whatever host is acting as your MySQL server, if MySQL is not on the same server.

❑ **Username and password:** We're going to use a new username that we created for use with the examples throughout the rest of the book. Refer to the instructions in Chapter 1 on how to create a new user, and then create a user named `bp6am` with the password `bp6ampass`.

You issue this connection command with the PHP function called `mysql_connect()`. As with all of your PHP/MySQL statements, you can either put the information into variables or leave it as text in your MySQL query.

Here's how you would do it with variables:

```
$host = 'localhost';
$user = 'bp6am';
$pass = 'bp6ampass';
$db = mysql_connect($host, $user, $pass);
```

The following statement has the same effect:

```
$db = mysql_connect('localhost', 'bp6am', 'bp6ampass');
```

For the most part, your specific needs and the way you are designing your table will dictate what piece of code you use. Most people use the first method for security's sake and put the variables in a different file. Then they include them wherever they need to make a connection to the database.

Looking at a Ready-Made Database

Create the database that you will be using for your movie site. It consists of three tables:

❑ A `movie` table, which stores the names of the movies and information about them

❑ A `movietype` table, which stores the different categories of movies

❑ A `people` table, which stores the names of the actors and directors in the movies

The typical syntax for a CREATE command is as follows:

```
CREATE TABLE [IF NOT EXISTS] tablename (
    fieldname definition,
    ...
    [key definitions]
)
table options
```

The typical syntax for an INSERT command is as follows:

```
INSERT INTO tablename
    (field names...)
VALUES
    (field values...)
```

You can set a few extra parameters for both commands, which you can learn more about in MySQL's documentation at www.mysql.com.

Try It Out   Creating a Database

In this exercise, you'll create the database and tables that will be used in the next several chapters of the book.

1. Open your editor, and type the following code. This creates your database and the tables you need to hold the data.

```php
<?php
//connect to MySQL
$db = mysql_connect('localhost', 'bp6am', 'bp6ampass') or
    die ('Unable to connect. Check your connection parameters.');

//create the main database if it doesn't already exist
$query = 'CREATE DATABASE IF NOT EXISTS moviesite';
mysql_query($query, $db) or die(mysql_error($db));

//make sure our recently created database is the active one
mysql_select_db('moviesite', $db) or die(mysql_error($db));

//create the movie table
$query = 'CREATE TABLE movie (
        movie_id        INTEGER UNSIGNED  NOT NULL AUTO_INCREMENT,
        movie_name      VARCHAR(255)      NOT NULL,
        movie_type      TINYINT           NOT NULL DEFAULT 0,
        movie_year      SMALLINT UNSIGNED NOT NULL DEFAULT 0,
        movie_leadactor INTEGER UNSIGNED  NOT NULL DEFAULT 0,
        movie_director  INTEGER UNSIGNED  NOT NULL DEFAULT 0,

        PRIMARY KEY (movie_id),
        KEY movie_type (movie_type, movie_year)
    )
    ENGINE=MyISAM';
mysql_query($query, $db) or die (mysql_error($db));

//create the movietype table
$query = 'CREATE TABLE movietype (
        movietype_id    TINYINT UNSIGNED NOT NULL AUTO_INCREMENT,
        movietype_label VARCHAR(100)      NOT NULL,
        PRIMARY KEY (movietype_id)
    )
```

```
      ENGINE=MyISAM';
mysql_query($query, $db) or die(mysql_error($db));

//create the people table
$query = 'CREATE TABLE people (
        people_id            INTEGER UNSIGNED     NOT NULL AUTO_INCREMENT,
        people_fullname   VARCHAR(255)         NOT NULL,
        people_isactor    TINYINT(1) UNSIGNED NOT NULL DEFAULT 0,
        people_isdirector TINYINT(1) UNSIGNED NOT NULL DEFAULT 0,

        PRIMARY KEY (people_id)
    )
    ENGINE=MyISAM';
mysql_query($query, $db) or die(mysql_error($db));

echo 'Movie database successfully created!';
?>
```

2. Save this file as db_ch03-1.php.

3. Create a new file, and name it db_ch03-2.php. This is the file that will populate the database:

```
<?php
// connect to MySQL
$db = mysql_connect('localhost', 'bp6am', 'bp6ampass') or
    die ('Unable to connect. Check your connection parameters.');

//make sure you're using the correct database
mysql_select_db('moviesite', $db) or die(mysql_error($db));

// insert data into the movie table
$query = 'INSERT INTO movie
        (movie_id, movie_name, movie_type, movie_year, movie_leadactor,
        movie_director)
    VALUES
        (1, "Bruce Almighty", 5, 2003, 1, 2),
        (2, "Office Space", 5, 1999, 5, 6),
        (3, "Grand Canyon", 2, 1991, 4, 3)';
mysql_query($query, $db) or die(mysql_error($db));

// insert data into the movietype table
$query = 'INSERT INTO movietype
        (movietype_id, movietype_label)
    VALUES
        (1,"Sci Fi"),
        (2, "Drama"),
        (3, "Adventure"),
        (4, "War"),
        (5, "Comedy"),
        (6, "Horror"),
        (7, "Action"),
        (8, "Kids")';
mysql_query($query, $db) or die(mysql_error($db));
```

```
// insert data into the people table
$query  = 'INSERT INTO people
        (people_id, people_fullname, people_isactor, people_isdirector)
    VALUES
        (1, "Jim Carrey", 1, 0),
        (2, "Tom Shadyac", 0, 1),
        (3, "Lawrence Kasdan", 0, 1),
        (4, "Kevin Kline", 1, 0),
        (5, "Ron Livingston", 1, 0),
        (6, "Mike Judge", 0, 1)';
mysql_query($query, $db) or die(mysql_error($db));

echo 'Data inserted successfully!';
?>
```

4. First, run `db_ch03-1.php` from your browser; then, run `db_ch03-2.php`.

How It Works

We hope you didn't have too many errors when running the previous files, and that you saw the two success statements. Although we tried to insert useful comments throughout the code, let's dissect everything one step at a time.

First, you connected to the MySQL server so that you could begin sending MySQL commands and working with the database and tables. You also wanted to be told if there was an error, and you wanted your program to immediately stop running if there was one. You did this in the first few lines of code:

```
// connect to MySQL
$db = mysql_connect('localhost', 'bp6am', 'bp6ampass') or
    die ('Unable to connect. Check your connection parameters.');
```

Then you actually created the database itself. If for some reason the database could not be created, you told the server to stop running and show you what the problem was:

```
//create the main database if it doesn't already exist
$query = 'CREATE DATABASE IF NOT EXISTS moviesite';
mysql_query($query, $db) or die(mysql_error($db));
```

You also made sure to select your database, so the server would know which database you would be working with next:

```
//make sure our recently created database is the active one
mysql_select_db('moviesite', $db) or die(mysql_error($db));
```

Then you began making your individual tables, starting with the movie table. You defined the individual field names and set up their parameters with the following SQL:

```
CREATE TABLE movie (
    movie_id        INTEGER UNSIGNED  NOT NULL AUTO_INCREMENT,
    movie_name      VARCHAR(255)      NOT NULL,
    movie_type      TINYINT           NOT NULL DEFAULT 0,
    movie_year      SMALLINT UNSIGNED NOT NULL DEFAULT 0,
    movie_leadactor INTEGER UNSIGNED  NOT NULL DEFAULT 0,
```

```
        movie_director   INTEGER UNSIGNED  NOT NULL DEFAULT 0,

        PRIMARY KEY (movie_id),
        KEY movie_type (movie_type, movie_year)
)
ENGINE=MyISAM
```

Once you had your MySQL statement ready to go, you just had to send it to the server with the `mysql_query()` function. Again, you told the server to stop executing the program and let you know what the error was, if there was one:

```
mysql_query($query, $db) or die (mysql_error($db));
```

You also created the `movietype` and `people` tables in much the same way.

You assume that everything was successful if your program runs all the way to the end, so you output a success statement, just to let yourself know:

```
echo 'Movie database successfully created!';
```

With your `moviedata.php` file, you populated the tables with information. First you had to connect to the MySQL server and select the database.

```
//connect to MySQL
$db = mysql_connect('localhost', 'bp6am', 'bp6ampass') or
    die ('Unable to connect. Check your connection parameters.');

//make sure you're using the correct database
mysql_select_db('moviesite', $db) or die(mysql_error($db));
```

Then you began by inserting data into the `movie` table. You first listed the columns you would be accessing, and you then listed the values for each record, as in the following SQL:

```
INSERT INTO movie
    (movie_id, movie_name, movie_type, movie_year, movie_leadactor,
     movie_director)
VALUES
    (1, "Bruce Almighty", 5, 2003, 1, 2),
    (2, "Office Space", 5, 1999, 5, 6),
    (3, "Grand Canyon", 2, 1991, 4, 3)
```

You did the same for the other two tables, `movietype` and `people`.

Then, because you instructed your program to die if there were any errors, you echoed a success statement to let yourself know that the entire program executed without errors:

```
echo 'Data inserted successfully!';
```

Querying the Database

Now that you have some data in the database, you probably want to retrieve it. You use the SELECT statement to choose data that fits your criteria.

Typical syntax for this command is as follows:

```
SELECT [field names]
AS [alias]
FROM [tablename]
WHERE [criteria]
ORDER BY [fieldname to sort on] [ASC|DESC]
LIMIT [offset, maxrows]
```

You can set numerous other parameters, but these are the most commonly used:

❑   SELECT [field names]: First decide what specific field names you want to retrieve. If you want to see them all, you can use * in place of the field names.

❑   AS: You use alias field names so that you can reference them later as different names. An example would be:

```
SELECT movie_name, movie_year AS relase_year FROM movie
```

❑   FROM: You need to name the table or tables from which you are pulling the data.

❑   WHERE: List your criteria for filtering out the data, as described in the following section.

❑   ORDER BY: Use this parameter if you want the data sorted on a particular field. The results are returned in ascending order by default, though you can explicitly request ascending order with ASC. If you want the results returned in descending order, use DESC.

❑   LIMIT: This enables you to limit the number of results returned and offset the first record returned to whatever number you choose. An example would be:

```
LIMIT 9, 10
```

This would show records 10 through 19. This is a useful feature for pagination (showing only a certain number of records on a page and then allowing the user to click a Next page link to see more).

For a complete reference, we refer you to the official documentation at www.mysql.com.

WHERE, oh WHERE

The beast clause called WHERE deserves its own little section because it's really the meat of the query. (No offense to the other clauses, but they are pretty much no brainers.) WHERE is like a cool big brother who can really do some interesting stuff. While SELECT tells MySQL which fields you want to see, WHERE tells it which records you want to see. It is used as follows:

```
// retrieves all information about all customers
SELECT * FROM customers;

// retrieves all information about male customers
SELECT * FROM customers WHERE gender = "Male"
```

Let's look at the WHERE clause in a little more detail:

❑ **Comparison operators** are the heart of a WHERE clause and include the following:

    ❑   = is used to test if two values are equal

    ❑   != is used to test if two values are not equal

    ❑   < is used to test if one value is less than the second

    ❑   <= is used to test if one value is less than or equal to the second

    ❑   > is used to test if one value is greater than the second

    ❑   >= is used to test if one value is greater than or equal to the second

    ❑   LIKE lets you compare text and allows you to use % and _ as wildcards. Wildcards allow you to search even if you know a piece of what's in the field but don't know the entire value, or you don't want an exact match. For example:

```
SELECT * FROM products WHERE description LIKE "%shirt%"
```

    ❑   The WHERE clause in this query matches any records that have the text pattern "shirt" in the description column, such as "t-shirt," "blue shirts," or "no shirt, no shoes, no service." Without the % wildcard, you would have those products that have a description of just "shirt" returned, and nothing else.

❑ **Logical operators** such as AND, NOT, OR, and XOR are also accepted in the WHERE clause:

```
SELECT * FROM products WHERE description LIKE "%shirt%" AND price <= 24.95
```

This gives you all the products that have the word or text pattern of "shirt" in the description and that have a price of less than or equal to $24.95.

Now that you understand how a SELECT query is written, let's look at it in action, shall we?

Try It Out   **Using the SELECT Query**

In this exercise, you'll create a short script that demonstrates how the SELECT query works.

1. Open your text editor, and type this code:

```php
<?php
$db = mysql_connect('localhost', 'bp6am', 'bp6ampass') or
    die ('Unable to connect. Check your connection parameters.');
mysql_select_db('moviesite', $db) or die(mysql_error($db));

// select the movie titles and their genre after 1990
$query = 'SELECT
        movie_name, movie_type
    FROM
        movie
    WHERE
```

```
         movie_year > 1990
     ORDER BY
         movie_type';
$result = mysql_query($query, $db) or die(mysql_error($db));

// show the results
while ($row = mysql_fetch_array($result)) {
    extract($row);
    echo $movie_name . ' - ' . $movie_type . '<br/>';
}
?>
```

2.   Save this file as `select1.php`, and then run it from your browser.

How It Works

You should see the screen shown in Figure 3-1 after running `select1.php`.

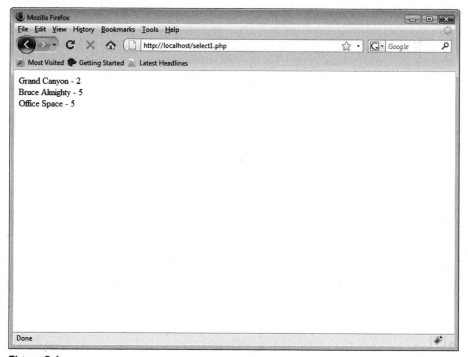

Figure 3-1

First you had to connect to the MySQL server and the specific database. Then you planned out your query and assigned it to the `$query` variable.

You wanted to choose only the `movie_name` and `movie_type` fields from the `movie` table because you don't care about seeing the rest of the information contained in the table at this time. If you had wanted to retrieve everything, you simply could have written:

```
SELECT
    movie_id, movie_name, movie_type, movie_year, movie_leadactor, movie_
director
FROM
    movie
```

or even:

```
SELECT * FROM movie
```

The `WHERE` condition in your query limited the results to only movies filmed after 1990. You also asked the server to sort the results by movie type, with the `ORDER` clause.

Then you issued the query to the MySQL server and stored the response in a variable, `$result`.

```
$result = mysql_query($query, $db) or die(mysql_error($db));
```

Then, you looped through the results with a while loop:

```
while ($row = mysql_fetch_array($result)) {
    extract($row);
    echo $movie_name . ' - ' . $movie_type . '<br/>';
}
```

You retrieved the row's data as an array named `$row` for each row in the returned result set, using the `mysql_fetch_array()` function. You then extracted all the variables in `$row`, using the `extract()` function to find variables with the same name as the array's keys; echoed out what you needed; and then went on to the next row of results from your query. When there were no more rows that matched your criteria, the `while` loop ended.

Pretty easy, eh? Let's try using the `foreach` loop instead of the `while` function, and see how it works.

Working with PHP and Arrays of Data: foreach

The `foreach` loop is similar to the `while` loop, if you're using `while` to loop through a list of results from your query. Its purpose is to apply a block of statements to every row in your results set. It is used in this way:

```
foreach ($row as $value) {
    echo $value;
    echo '<br>';
}
```

The preceding code would take all the variables in the `$row` array and list each value, with a line break in between them. You can see this in action in Chapters 4 and 5 and get a better idea of how it can be used.

Try It Out   **Using foreach**

This exercise contrasts foreach with the while you used in the previous exercise.

1.   In your select1.php file, make the following highlighted changes:

```php
<?php
$db = mysql_connect('localhost', 'bp6am', 'bp6ampass') or
    die ('Unable to connect. Check your connection parameters.');
mysql_select_db('moviesite', $db) or die(mysql_error($db));

// select the movie titles and their genre after 1990
$query = 'SELECT
        movie_name, movie_type
    FROM
        movie
    WHERE
        movie_year > 1990
    ORDER BY
        movie_type';
$result = mysql_query($query, $db) or die(mysql_error($db));

// show the results
while ($row = mysql_fetch_assoc($result)) {
    foreach ($row as $value) {
        echo $value . ' ';
    }
    echo '<br/>';
}
?>
```

How It Works

You should see the same results as before, except that there is now no dash between the elements. Pretty sneaky, huh? mysql_fetch_array actually returns two sets of arrays (one with associative indices, one with numerical indices), so you see duplicate values if you use foreach without first isolating one of the arrays. You can do this by using either mysql_fetch_array($result, MYSQL_ASSOC) or mysql_fetch_assoc($result) to perform the same thing and return only one of the arrays. You still need to use the while function to proceed through the selected rows one at a time, but you can see that using foreach applies the same sets of commands to each value in the array, regardless of their contents.

Sometimes you will need to have more control over a specific value, and therefore you can't apply the same formatting rules to each value in the array, but the foreach function can also come in handy when using formatting functions, such as creating tables. In the following exercise, you'll create another version of the select1.php program that illustrates this.

Using foreach to Create a Table

In this exercise, you'll use `foreach` to apply some formatting rules to the results of your query.

1. Open your text editor, and enter the following script:

```php
<?php
$db = mysql_connect('localhost', 'bp6am', 'bp6ampass') or
    die ('Unable to connect. Check your connection parameters.');
mysql_select_db('moviesite', $db) or die(mysql_error($db));

// select the movie titles and their genre after 1990
$query = 'SELECT
        movie_name, movie_type
    FROM
        movie
    WHERE
        movie_year > 1990
    ORDER BY
        movie_type';
$result = mysql_query($query, $db) or die(mysql_error($db));

// show the results
echo '<table border="1">';
while ($row = mysql_fetch_assoc($result)) {
    echo '<tr>';
    foreach ($row as $value) {
        echo '<td>' . $value . '</td>';
    }
    echo '</tr>';
}
echo '</table>';
?>
```

2. Save this script as `select2.php`, and then open it in your browser. You should see something like Figure 3-2.

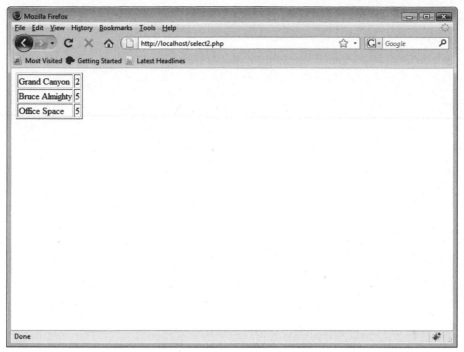

Figure 3-2

How It Works

You used the mysql_query() function and while loop to retrieve your desired records and fields. Then for each value you retrieved, you placed it in a separate table cell, using a foreach loop.

You can see that this script would easily output a long string of array variables with a few lines of code, whereas if you had to echo out each separate variable with the accompanying HTML code, this script would be quite lengthy.

A Tale of Two Tables

The preceding code is all nice and neat and pretty, but it doesn't do you a whole lot of good if you don't have a secret decoder ring to tell you what those cryptic "movie type" numbers correspond to in plain English. That information is all stored in a separate table, the movietype table. So how do you get this information?

You can get information from more than one table in two ways:

❑ Reference the individual tables in your query and link them temporarily through a common field.

❑ Formally JOIN the individual tables in your query.

Let's try out these methods and then talk about each of them in more detail.

Referencing Two Tables

You can distinguish between two tables in your database by referencing them in the SELECT statement, as follows:

```
// retrieves customers' names from customers table and order_total from
// orders table where the cust_ID field in the customers table equals the
// cust_ID field in the orders table.

SELECT
    customers.name, orders.order_total
FROM
    customers, orders
WHERE
    customers.cust_ID = orders.cust_ID
```

If a customer's ID is 123, you will see all the order_totals for all the orders for that specific customer, enabling you to determine all the money customer 123 has spent at your store.

Although you are linking the two tables through the cust_ID field, the names do not have to be the same. You can compare any two field names from any two tables. An example would be:

```
// retrieves customers' names from customers table and order_total from
// orders table where the email field in the customers table equals the
// shiptoemail field in the orders table.
SELECT
    customers.name, orders.order_total
FROM
    customers, orders
WHERE
    customers.email = orders.shiptoemail
```

This would link your tables through the email and shiptoemail fields from different tables.

Try It Out   **Referencing Individual Tables**

This exercise will show you how to reference multiple tables in your query.

1. Change your select2.php program as shown here (changes are highlighted):

```
<?php
$db = mysql_connect('localhost', 'bp6am', 'bp6ampass') or
    die ('Unable to connect. Check your connection parameters.');
mysql_select_db('moviesite', $db) or die(mysql_error($db));

// select the movie titles and their genre after 1990
$query = 'SELECT
        movie.movie_name, movietype.movietype_label
    FROM
        movie, movietype
    WHERE
```

```
            movie.movie_type = movietype.movietype_id AND
            movie_year > 1990
        ORDER BY
            movie_type';
$result = mysql_query($query, $db) or die(mysql_error($db));

// show the results
echo '<table border="1">';
while ($row = mysql_fetch_assoc($result)) {
    echo '<tr>';
    foreach ($row as $value) {
        echo '<td>' . $value . '</td>';
    }
    echo '</tr>';
}
echo '</table>';
?>
```

2.   Save your script and run it. Your screen should look something like Figure 3-3.

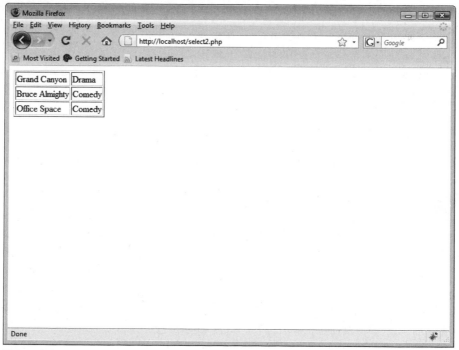

Figure 3-3

How It Works

Now you can see a table with the movie names and actual words for the type of movie, instead of your cryptic code, as was the case in Figure 3-2. The common fields were linked in the WHERE portion of the statement. ID numbers from the two different tables (fieldname movie_type in the movie table and fieldname movietype_id in the movietype table) represented the same thing, so that's where you linked them together.

Joining Two Tables

In life as in code, regardless of the circumstances under which two things join together, it is rarely a simple thing. More often than not, it comes with conditions and consequences.

In the world of MySQL, joins are also complex things. We will discuss joins in greater detail in Chapter 10; meanwhile, we walk you through a very simple and commonly used join so you can get a taste of what joining is all about. The JOIN function gives you greater control over how your database tables relate to and connect with each other, but it also requires a greater understanding of relational databases (another topic covered in Chapter 10).

Try It Out Joining Two Tables

In this exercise, you'll link the two tables with a JOIN.

1. Make the following highlighted changes to select2.php:

```php
<?php
$db = mysql_connect('localhost', 'bp6am', 'bp6ampass') or
    die ('Unable to connect. Check your connection parameters.');
mysql_select_db('moviesite', $db) or die(mysql_error($db));

// select the movie titles and their genre after 1990
$query = 'SELECT
        movie_name, movietype_label
    FROM
        movie LEFT JOIN movietype ON movie_type = movietype_id
    WHERE
        movie.movie_type = movietype.movietype_id AND
        movie_year > 1990
    ORDER BY
        movie_type';
$result = mysql_query($query, $db) or die(mysql_error($db));

// show the results
echo '<table border="1">';
```

```
while ($row = mysql_fetch_assoc($result)) {
    echo '<tr>';
    foreach ($row as $value) {
        echo '<td>' . $value . '</td>';
    }
    echo '</tr>';
}
echo '</table>';
?>
```

2. Save the script, and open it in your browser.

How It Works

You should see the same result as in the previous example. As you can see, you simply listed all the fields you wanted to see, regardless of the table they were in (MySQL will find them as long as the table name is referenced there somewhere). You did this in the first line of the SELECT statement:

```
SELECT movie_name, movietype_label
```

Then you told MySQL what tables you wanted to access and what type of join should be used to bring them together, in these statements:

```
FROM
    movie LEFT JOIN movietype
```

You used the LEFT join statement in this case. Although there are other things that go along with this, the LEFT join, in layman's terms, simply means that the second table (movietype in the example) is dependent on the first table (movie). You are getting the main information from movie and looking up a bit of information from movietype.

You then told the server which field to use to join them together, with:

```
ON movie_type = movietype_id
```

Again, you don't need to clarify which table is being used, but if you have overlapping field names across tables, you can add this if you like to avoid confusion.

You kept your condition about only showing the movies that were made after 1990, and sorted them by numerical movie type with these lines:

```
WHERE
    movie.movie_type = movietype.movietype_id AND
    movie_year > 1990
ORDER BY
    movie_type
```

And the rest of the code is the same. See, joining wasn't that bad, was it?

Helpful Tips and Suggestions

We all get into a little trouble now and then. Instead of sitting in the corner and sucking your thumb, or banging your head in frustration against your keyboard, relax! We are here to help.

Documentation

The folks at MySQL have provided wonderfully thorough documentation covering more than you ever wanted to know about its capabilities, quirks, and plans for the future. We have stated this time and time again, but the official web site really can provide you with the most up-to-date and accurate information.

You can search the documentation, or even add your own comments if you've discovered something especially helpful that might help out other developers just like you. Because this is all open source, you really do get a community feeling when you read through the documentation.

Once again, you can find the manual at www.mysql.com.

Using MySQL Query Browser

Now that you've been given the task of learning MySQL and PHP on your own from scratch, we're going to let you in on a dirty little secret called MySQL Query Browser. MySQL Query Browser is another wonderful open source project that enables you to access your MySQL databases through a GUI desktop application. It's easy to install and manage, and it makes administering your tables and data a breeze. It does have some limitations, but for the most part it will make you a lot more efficient.

With this software, you can easily do the following:

- ❏ Drop and create databases
- ❏ Create, edit, and delete tables
- ❏ Create, edit, and delete fields
- ❏ Enter any MySQL statements
- ❏ View and print table structure
- ❏ Generate PHP code
- ❏ View data in table format

You can download the software by visiting http://dev.mysql.com/downloads/gui-tools/5.0.html. MySQL Query Browser is part of the MySQL Tools package. Figure 3-4 shows what MySQL Query Browser looks like.

Figure 3-4

Summary

We've covered some pretty fundamental programming concepts in this chapter, and we'll delve more into them in future chapters. But for now you should have a pretty good handle on the basics.

You should have a good understanding of databases and tables, and know how to insert data and retrieve stored information from those tables. You should also have a good understanding of how MySQL works with PHP to make dynamic pages in your web site.

In the next few chapters, you will build on this knowledge to create more complex applications.

Exercises

We have started you on the MySQL/PHP journey, and in the next few chapters we take you places you've never dreamed of. To fine-tune your skills, here are a few exercises to make sure you really know your stuff:

1. Create a PHP program that prints the lead actor and director for each movie in the database.

2. Pick only comedies from the movie table, and show the movie name and the year it was produced. Sort the list alphabetically.

3. Show each movie in the database on its own page, and give the user links in a "page 1, page 2, page 3"–type navigation system. Hint: Use LIMIT to control which movie is on which page.

Using Tables to Display Data

Now that you can successfully marry PHP and MySQL to produce dynamic pages, what happens when you have rows and rows of data that you need to display? You need to have some mechanism for your viewers to easily read the data, and it needs to be presented in a nice, neat, organized fashion. The easiest way to do this is to use tables.

This chapter covers the following:

❏ Creating a table to hold the data from the database.

❏ Creating column headings automatically.

❏ Populating the table with the results of a basic MySQL query.

❏ Populating the table with the results of more complex MySQL queries.

❏ Making the output user-friendly.

Creating a Table

Before you can list your data, you need to set up the structure, column headings, and format of your HTML table. This way, your data has some place to go! The skeleton of this table gives you the blueprint for how your data will be laid out once it is retrieved from the database.

Try It Out   **Building a Table**

In this exercise, you'll define the table headings for your table and then fill it with data.

1.   Open your favorite text/HTML editor, and enter the following code:

```
<div style="text-align: center;">
 <h2>Movie Review Database</h2>
 <table border="1" cellpadding="2" cellspacing="2"
  style="width: 70%; margin-left: auto; margin-right: auto;">
 <tr>
  <th>Movie Title</th>
  <th>Year of Release</th>
  <th>Movie Director</th>
  <th>Movie Lead Actor</th>
  <th>Movie Type</th>
 </tr>
 </table>
</div>
```

2.   Save this file as `table1.php`, and upload it to your Web server.

3.   Load your favorite browser and view the page that you have just uploaded. Your table should look like the one in Figure 4-1.

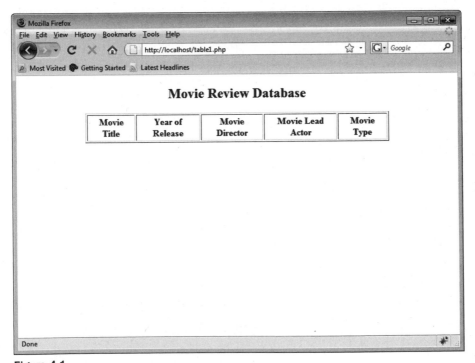

Figure 4-1

4. Open the file `table1.php` in your editor again, and add the code to connect to the database at the top. We used the database created in Chapter 3 for the purposes of the example here. Remember to substitute your own values for the server name, username, password, and database name in the given example, if necessary.

```php
<?php
//connect to MySQL
$db = mysql_connect('localhost', 'bp6am', 'bp6ampass') or
    die ('Unable to connect. Check your connection parameters.');

// make sure you're using the right database
mysql_select_db('moviesite', $db) or die(mysql_error($db));
?>
```

```html
<div style="text-align: center;">
 <h2>Movie Review Database</h2>
 <table border="1" cellpadding="2" cellspacing="2"
  style="width: 70%; margin-left: auto; margin-right: auto;">
  <tr>
   <th>Movie Title</th>
   <th>Year of Release</th>
   <th>Movie Director</th>
   <th>Movie Lead Actor</th>
   <th>Movie Type</th>
  </tr>
 </table>
</div>
```

5. Run a SQL query against the database and get the results. And while you are at it, count how many records were returned from the query.

```php
<?php
//connect to MySQL
$db = mysql_connect('localhost', 'bp6am', 'bp6ampass') or
    die ('Unable to connect. Check your connection parameters.');

// make sure you're using the right database
mysql_select_db('moviesite', $db) or die(mysql_error($db));
```

```php
// retrieve information
$query = 'SELECT
        movie_name, movie_year, movie_director, movie_leadactor,
        movie_type
    FROM
        movie
    ORDER BY
        movie_name ASC,
        movie_year DESC';
$result = mysql_query($query, $db) or die(mysql_error($db));

// determine number of rows in returned result
$num_movies = mysql_num_rows($result);
```

```
?>
<div style="text-align: center;">
 <h2>Movie Review Database</h2>
 <table border="1" cellpadding="2" cellspacing="2"
  style="width: 70%; margin-left: auto; margin-right: auto;">
  <tr>
   <th>Movie Title</th>
   <th>Year of Release</th>
   <th>Movie Director</th>
   <th>Movie Lead Actor</th>
   <th>Movie Type</th>
  </tr>
 </table>
</div>
```

6. After the closing `tr` tag but before the closing `table` tag in the original HTML, enter a `while` loop to process through the retrieved records. Then, output the number of movie records after the closing `table` tag.

```
<?php
//connect to MySQL
$db = mysql_connect('localhost', 'bp6am', 'bp6ampass') or
     die ('Unable to connect. Check your connection parameters.');

// make sure you're using the right database
mysql_select_db('moviesite', $db) or die(mysql_error($db));

// retrieve information
$query = 'SELECT
        movie_name, movie_year, movie_director, movie_leadactor,
        movie_type
     FROM
        movie
     ORDER BY
        movie_name ASC,
        movie_year DESC';
$result = mysql_query($query, $db) or die(mysql_error($db));

// determine number of rows in returned result
$num_movies = mysql_num_rows($result);
?>
<div style="text-align: center;">
 <h2>Movie Review Database</h2>
 <table border="1" cellpadding="2" cellspacing="2"
  style="width: 70%; margin-left: auto; margin-right: auto;">
  <tr>
   <th>Movie Title</th>
   <th>Year of Release</th>
   <th>Movie Director</th>
   <th>Movie Lead Actor</th>
   <th>Movie Type</th>
  </tr>
```

```php
<?php
// loop through the results
while ($row = mysql_fetch_assoc($result)) {
    extract($row);
    echo '<tr>';
    echo '<td>' . $movie_name . '</td>';
    echo '<td>' . $movie_year . '</td>';
    echo '<td>' . $movie_director . '</td>';
    echo '<td>' . $movie_leadactor . '</td>';
    echo '<td>' . $movie_type . '</td>';
    echo '</tr>';
}
?>
  </table>
<p><?php echo $num_movies; ?> Movies</p>
</div>
```

7. Open the page in your web browser; it should look like Figure 4-2.

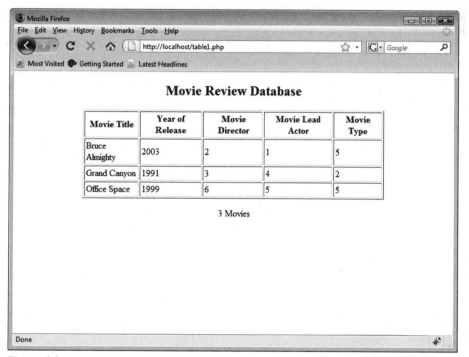

Figure 4-2

How It Works

The preceding code does quite a lot of work for you, so let's look at it in more detail.

First a connection to the database is established, and then you select the movies database. Next, you issue a query to the database to retrieve the name, release year, and lead actor of some movies. The `mysql_num_rows()` function takes the result reference and returns the number of total matching records MySQL found.

The `while` statement loops through the records that have been returned. It executes the block of code that is between the braces for each record. Don't worry; PHP is smart enough to know how many records there are and what record number it is currently on, in this case, so there is no danger of having the wrong values assigned to a record.

The first line in the `while` loop uses the `extract()` function to create variables with the same name as the field names and populates them with their values from the current record. The next seven lines then simply output the values with a little HTML mixed in for good measure.

Wait a Minute

So far we've used `echo` to output content from within PHP mode (between the `<?php` and `?>` tags). Larger chunks of HTML code are outside the tags and are output to the browser immediately, without being parsed by PHP. The script drops in and out of PHP mode, bouncing back and forth between HTML and PHP code. Some will argue this is the optimal way of doing things, while others will argue it's confusing and makes things more difficult to maintain. So, let's take another look at `heredoc` syntax.

Try It Out   **Putting It All Together**

Copy the `table1.php` file to `table2.php`, and follow these steps.

1. Replace the HTML code responsible for the table's column headers with a `heredoc` statement saved to a `$table` variable:

```
$table = <<<ENDHTML
<div style="text-align: center;">
 <h2>Movie Review Database</h2>
 <table border="1" cellpadding="2" cellspacing="2"
  style="width: 70%; margin-left: auto; margin-right: auto;">
  <tr>
   <th>Movie Title</th>
   <th>Year of Release</th>
   <th>Movie Director</th>
   <th>Movie Lead Actor</th>
   <th>Movie Type</th>
  </tr>
ENDHTML;
```

2.   Replace the echo statements within the `while` loop with a `heredoc` statement, appending it to the `$table` variable:

```
$table .= <<<ENDHTML
<tr>
 <td>$movie_name</td>
 <td>$movie_year</td>
 <td>$movie_director</td>
 <td>$movie_leadactor</td>
 <td>$movie_type</td>
</tr>
ENDHTML;
```

Note the use of . = instead of just the = sign. This is important because it appends the `heredoc` block to the existing content already stored in `$table`. If you just used =, the content would be replaced, which is not what you want to happen.

3.   Replace the HTML code for the closing of the `table` and `echo` statement that outputs the number of movies returned with a `heredoc` statement appended to `$table`.

```
$table .= <<<ENDHTML
 </table>
<p>$num_movies Movies</p>
</div>
ENDHTML;
```

Here is what the code in `table2.php` should look like now:

```php
<?php
//connect to MySQL
$db = mysql_connect('localhost', 'bp6am', 'bp6ampass') or
    die ('Unable to connect. Check your connection parameters.');

// make sure you're using the right database
mysql_select_db('moviesite', $db) or die(mysql_error($db));

// retrieve information
$query = 'SELECT
        movie_name, movie_year, movie_director, movie_leadactor,
        movie_type
    FROM
        movie
    ORDER BY
        movie_name ASC,
        movie_year DESC';
$result = mysql_query($query, $db) or die(mysql_error($db));

// determine number of rows in returned result
$num_movies = mysql_num_rows($result);
```

```php
$table = <<<ENDHTML
<div style="text-align: center;">
 <h2>Movie Review Database</h2>
 <table border="1" cellpadding="2" cellspacing="2"
  style="width: 70%; margin-left: auto; margin-right: auto;">
  <tr>
   <th>Movie Title</th>
   <th>Year of Release</th>
   <th>Movie Director</th>
   <th>Movie Lead Actor</th>
   <th>Movie Type</th>
  </tr>
ENDHTML;
```

```php
// loop through the results
while ($row = mysql_fetch_assoc($result)) {
    extract($row);
    $table .= <<<ENDHTML
    <tr>
     <td>$movie_name</td>
     <td>$movie_year</td>
     <td>$movie_director</td>
     <td>$movie_leadactor</td>
     <td>$movie_type</td>
    </tr>
ENDHTML;

}
```

```php
$table .= <<<ENDHTML
 </table>
<p>$num_movies Movies</p>
</div>
ENDHTML;
?>
```

4. Save `table2.php`, and open it in your web browser. You'll notice there's no output! That's because you haven't instructed PHP to echo back the contents of `$table`.

5. Add an `echo` statement at the end of the file. Save and view the page again. It should now look the same as before, as in Figure 4-2.

```php
echo $table;
```

How It Works

At first there was no output when you viewed the page in your web browser, because the information was collected in the `$table` variable and not sent out to the browser. The `echo` statement you added at the end of the code then output it. Voilà! The table is now visible on the page!

As you keep adding text to `$table`, you need to make sure you use `.=` instead of just `=` when assigning it. The `.=` appends content after whatever is already stored in the variable, whereas `=` would just replace the existing value.

As you may recall from our earlier discussion regarding using `heredoc`, in Chapter 2, you can change `ENDHTML` to whatever you'd like, but the beginning and ending tags must match. For example, this will work fine:

```
$table =<<<HAHAHA
    // code here
HAHAHA;
```

But, this will not work:

```
$table =<<<HAHAHA
    // code here
BOOHOO;
```

You will receive an error such as the one shown in Figure 4-3.

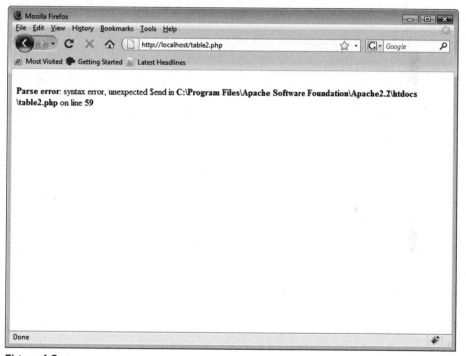

Figure 4-3

Note that there must be *no* spaces after the `<<<ENDHTML` and the `ENDHTML;` flags. In addition, there can be no leading space, indentation, or any other characters on the `heredoc` closing tag line (semicolons are permissible). You'll receive an error if there is even one space. (You can potentially spend *hours* trying to fix an error as a result of having a single space after these tags!) Always remember to delete all spaces after these tags.

Also, `heredoc` syntax can be used in other places, instead of just with `echo` or `print`. It is used to assign large blocks of content to a variable, so it could also be used to assign a SQL query statement to a variable. For example:

```
$query = <<<ENDSQL
SELECT
    movie_name, movie_year, movie_director, movie_leadactor
    movie_type
FROM
    movie
ORDER BY
    movie_name ASC,
    movie_year DESC
ENDSQL;
```

The table may look pretty, but, as in Chapter 3, it doesn't do users much good if they don't have their secret decoder ring to decipher which actors and directors were associated with your movies. You need to link your tables to pull in this information.

Improving Your Table

In this exercise, you'll link the tables together so you can output meaningful data.

1. Modify your `table2.php` file as shown in the highlighted text:

```php
<?php
// take in the id of a director and return his/her full name
function get_director($director_id) {

    global $db;

    $query = 'SELECT
                people_fullname
        FROM
                people
        WHERE
                people_id = ' . $director_id;
    $result = mysql_query($query, $db) or die(mysql_error($db));

    $row = mysql_fetch_assoc($result);
    extract($row);

    return $people_fullname;
}

// take in the id of a lead actor and return his/her full name
function get_leadactor($leadactor_id) {

    global $db;

    $query = 'SELECT
```

```
            people_fullname
        FROM
            people
        WHERE
            people_id = ' . $leadactor_id;
    $result = mysql_query($query, $db) or die(mysql_error($db));

    $row = mysql_fetch_assoc($result);
    extract($row);

    return $people_fullname;
}

// take in the id of a movie type and return the meaningful textual
// description
function get_movietype($type_id) {

    global $db;

    $query = 'SELECT
            movietype_label
      FROM
          movietype
      WHERE
          movietype_id = ' . $type_id;
    $result = mysql_query($query, $db) or die(mysql_error($db));

    $row = mysql_fetch_assoc($result);
    extract($row);

    return $movietype_label;
}
```

```
//connect to MySQL
$db = mysql_connect('localhost', 'bp6am', 'bp6ampass') or
    die ('Unable to connect. Check your connection parameters.');

// make sure you're using the right database
mysql_select_db('moviesite', $db) or die(mysql_error($db));

// retrieve information
$query = 'SELECT
        movie_name, movie_year, movie_director, movie_leadactor,
        movie_type
    FROM
        movie
    ORDER BY
        movie_name ASC,
        movie_year DESC';
$result = mysql_query($query, $db) or die(mysql_error($db));

// determine number of rows in returned result
$num_movies = mysql_num_rows($result);

$table = <<<ENDHTML
```

```
<div style="text-align: center;">
 <h2>Movie Review Database</h2>
 <table border="1" cellpadding="2" cellspacing="2"
  style="width: 70%; margin-left: auto; margin-right: auto;">
  <tr>
   <th>Movie Title</th>
   <th>Year of Release</th>
   <th>Movie Director</th>
   <th>Movie Lead Actor</th>
   <th>Movie Type</th>
  </tr>
ENDHTML;

// loop through the results
while ($row = mysql_fetch_assoc($result)) {
    extract($row);
    $director = get_director($movie_director);
    $leadactor = get_leadactor($movie_leadactor);
    $movietype = get_movietype($movie_type);

    $table .= <<<ENDHTML
    <tr>
     <td>$movie_name</td>
     <td>$movie_year</td>
     <td>$director</td>
     <td>$leadactor</td>
     <td>$movietype</td>
    </tr>
ENDHTML;
}

$table .= <<<ENDHTML
 </table>
<p>$num_movies Movies</p>
</div>
ENDHTML;

echo $table;
?>
```

2. Save your file, and reload it in your browser. Your screen should now look like Figure 4-4.

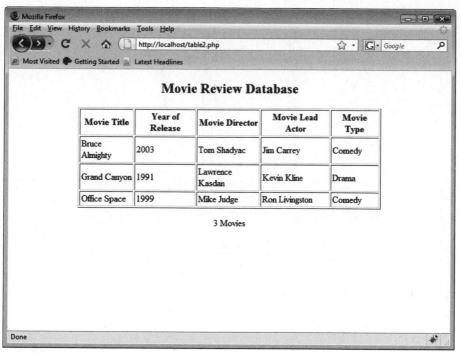

Figure 4-4

How It Works

With the custom functions `get_director()`, `get_leadactor()`, and `get_movietype()` added, the script requests that specific information be retrieved from the server for each separate row in the table. This enables you to pull the information you want without muddling up your original query with a `LEFT JOIN`.

Congratulations! You have successfully developed a powerful script that will query a database and put its contents into an HTML table. Give yourself a pat on the back. But like all good explorers, onward we must go.

Who's the Master?

Now let's build on the good work that you've done so far and add more information and functionality to your table. Implementing master and child relationships on your site can allow your users to click on a movie title in your table for more information about the movie. Of course, these would all be dynamically generated, so let's find out how to do such a cool thing and exactly what master/child relationships mean.

Try It Out   **Adding Links to the Table**

The steps in this section will enable you to load extra information, depending on the movie that you click. This requires you to do the following:

1.   Open `table2.php` and edit the query that retrieves the movie information to retrieve the movie_id field as well as the ones it's already fetching.

```
// retrieve information
$query = 'SELECT
        movie_id, movie_name, movie_year, movie_director,
        movie_leadactor, movie_type
    FROM
        movie
    ORDER BY
        movie_name ASC,
        movie_year DESC';
```

2.   Edit the `heredoc` that generates the table's rows so the movie's title is a hyperlink.

```
$table .= <<<ENDINFO
<tr>
    <td><a href="movie_details.php?movie_id=$movie_id">$movie_name</a></td>
    <td>$movie_year</td>
    <td>$director</td>
    <td>$leadactor</td>
    <td>$movietype</td>
</tr>
ENDINFO;
```

3.   Save the file as `table3.php`, and open the page with your browser. Your screen should look like Figure 4-5.

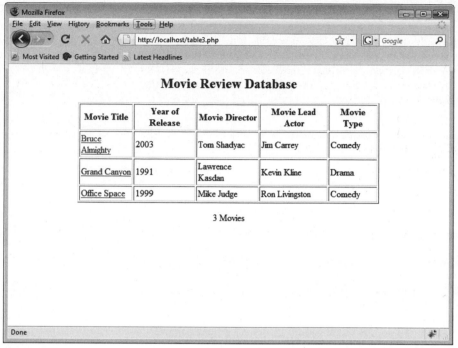

Figure 4-5

How It Works

You should notice a slight change between Figure 4-4 (`table2.php`) and Figure 4-5 (`table3.php`). You now have links to more detailed information about each movie for your visitor to click.

The first change made in the previous section altered the MySQL query to include the `$movie_id` field. The second change created the HTML code that produces a hyperlink on the movie name. If you'd like, you can also add a nice little touch with the inclusion of tooltips for each of the movies in the list. This is done by adding a `title` attribute to the a element. Unfortunately, some web browsers don't support this (apologies to those of you who have such browsers).

For a discussion on the use of alt and title attributes for tooltips, see `http://developer.mozilla` `.org/en/docs/Defining_Cross-Browser_Tooltips`.

```
<a href="movie_details.php?movie_id=$movie_id"
  title="Click here to find out more about $movie_name">$movie_name</a>
```

So now that the changes have been made, what do they actually do? Place your mouse over some hyperlinks, and, if you view your status bar, you'll see that each link is unique and is created dynamically. This page is known as the *master page*, and the page that we are going to link to is known as the *child page*.

Before you can go any further, you need to add some data to your existing database that you can use for your movie details. If you recall from Chapter 3, you currently have the movie name, director, lead actor, type, and year of release for each movie. Let's also add the running time, how much the movie made, and how much it cost to produce.

Try It Out   Adding Data to the Table

In this exercise, you'll add some additional data about each movie to the database.

1. Open your text editor, and type the following code:

```php
<?php
$db = mysql_connect('localhost', 'bp6am', 'bp6ampass') or
    die ('Unable to connect. Check your connection parameters.');
mysql_select_db('moviesite', $db) or die(mysql_error($db));

//alter the movie table to include running time, cost and takings fields
$query = 'ALTER TABLE movie ADD COLUMN (
    movie_running_time TINYINT UNSIGNED NULL,
    movie_cost         DECIMAL(4,1)      NULL,
    movie_takings      DECIMAL(4,1)      NULL)';
mysql_query($query, $db) or die (mysql_error($db));

//insert new data into the movie table for each movie
$query = 'UPDATE movie SET
        movie_running_time = 101,
        movie_cost = 81,
        movie_takings = 242.6
    WHERE
        movie_id = 1';
mysql_query($query, $db) or die(mysql_error($db));

$query = 'UPDATE movie SET
        movie_running_time = 89,
        movie_cost = 10,
        movie_takings = 10.8
    WHERE
        movie_id = 2';
mysql_query($query, $db) or die(mysql_error($db));

$query = 'UPDATE movie SET
        movie_running_time = 134,
        movie_cost = NULL,
        movie_takings = 33.2
    WHERE
        movie_id = 3';
mysql_query($query, $db) or die(mysql_error($db));

echo 'Movie database successfully updated!';
?>
```

2. Save this file as db_ch04-1.php, and then open it in your browser. You should see the success messages as the information is entered into the database.

How It Works

First, the script used the ALTER TABLE command to add the appropriate fields to the existing movie table, and then it used the UPDATE command to insert the new data into those fields. If you aren't familiar with these commands, you should consider reviewing Chapter 3 again.

Now that you have the data in place, you need to create a new page that you'll use to display the extra movie information (movie_details.php).

Try It Out   **Displaying Movie Details**

In this exercise, you'll create a new page to display the data you added in the previous exercise.

1. Open your text editor, and type the following program:

```php
<?php
// take in the id of a director and return his/her full name
function get_director($director_id) {

    global $db;

    $query = 'SELECT
            people_fullname
        FROM
            people
        WHERE
            people_id = ' . $director_id;
    $result = mysql_query($query, $db) or die(mysql_error($db));

    $row = mysql_fetch_assoc($result);
    extract($row);

    return $people_fullname;
}

// take in the id of a lead actor and return his/her full name
function get_leadactor($leadactor_id) {

    global $db;

    $query = 'SELECT
            people_fullname
        FROM
            people
        WHERE
            people_id = ' . $leadactor_id;
    $result = mysql_query($query, $db) or die(mysql_error($db));

    $row = mysql_fetch_assoc($result);
    extract($row);
```

```php
        return $people_fullname;
}

// take in the id of a movie type and return the meaningful textual
// description
function get_movietype($type_id) {

    global $db;

    $query = 'SELECT
            movietype_label
        FROM
            movietype
        WHERE
            movietype_id = ' . $type_id;
    $result = mysql_query($query, $db) or die(mysql_error($db));

    $row = mysql_fetch_assoc($result);
    extract($row);

    return $movietype_label;
}

// function to calculate if a movie made a profit, loss or just broke even
function calculate_differences($takings, $cost) {

    $difference = $takings - $cost;

    if ($difference < 0) {
        $color = 'red';
        $difference = '$' . abs($difference) . ' million';
    } elseif ($difference > 0) {
        $color ='green';
        $difference = '$' . $difference . ' million';
    } else {
        $color = 'blue';
        $difference = 'broke even';
    }

    return '<span style="color:' . $color . ';">' . $difference . '</span>';
}

//connect to MySQL
$db = mysql_connect('localhost', 'bp6am', 'bp6ampass') or
    die ('Unable to connect. Check your connection parameters.');
mysql_select_db('moviesite', $db) or die(mysql_error($db));

// retrieve information
$query = 'SELECT
        movie_name, movie_year, movie_director, movie_leadactor,
        movie_type, movie_running_time, movie_cost, movie_takings
    FROM
        movie
    WHERE
```

```
         movie_id = ' . $_GET['movie_id'];
$result = mysql_query($query, $db) or die(mysql_error($db));

$row = mysql_fetch_assoc($result);
$movie_name         = $row['movie_name'];
$movie_director     = get_director($row['movie_director']);
$movie_leadactor    = get_leadactor($row['movie_leadactor']);
$movie_year         = $row['movie_year'];
$movie_running_time = $row['movie_running_time'] .' mins';
$movie_takings      = $row['movie_takings'] . ' million';
$movie_cost         = $row['movie_cost'] . ' million';
$movie_health       = calculate_differences($row['movie_takings'],
                        $row['movie_cost']);

// display the information
echo <<<ENDHTML
<html>
 <head>
  <title>Details and Reviews for: $movie_name</title>
 </head>
 <body>
  <div style="text-align: center;">
   <h2>$movie_name</h2>
   <h3><em>Details</em></h3>
   <table cellpadding="2" cellspacing="2"
    style="width: 70%; margin-left: auto; margin-right: auto;">
    <tr>
     <td><strong>Title</strong></strong></td>
     <td>$movie_name</td>
     <td><strong>Release Year</strong></strong></td>
     <td>$movie_year</td>
    </tr><tr>
     <td><strong>Movie Director</strong></td>
     <td>$movie_director</td>
     <td><strong>Cost</strong></td>
     <td>$$movie_cost<td/>
    </tr><tr>
     <td><strong>Lead Actor</strong></td>
     <td>$movie_leadactor</td>
     <td><strong>Takings</strong></td>
     <td>$$movie_takings<td/>
    </tr><tr>
     <td><strong>Running Time</strong></td>
     <td>$movie_running_time</td>
     <td><strong>Health</strong></td>
     <td>$movie_health<td/>
    </tr>
   </table></div>
 </body>
</html>
ENDHTML;
?>
```

2. Save it as `movie_details.php`, and upload it to the web server.

3. Open `table3.php` in your browser, and click on one of the movie links. It will open `movie_details.php`, and you will see something like Figure 4-6.

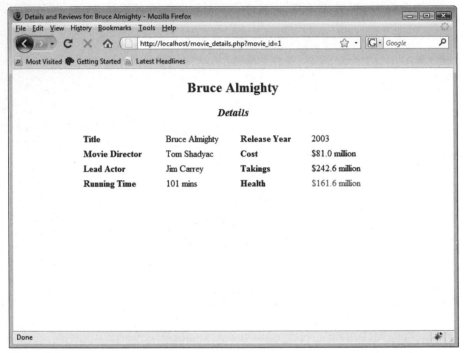

Figure 4-6

How It Works

Three of the four custom functions at the start of the script should be familiar to you: `get_director()`, `get_leadactor()`, and `get_movietype()`. Each accepts an id key and translates it into the corresponding human-friendly value by performing a database lookup in the appropriate table. In effect, you can think of functions as tiny custom programs that exist within a larger script — they take in some information, process it, and return some result.

The fourth custom function, `calculate_differences()`, generates an HTML string to show whether a movie made a profit, lost money, or broke even. It accepts the movie's takings and the production cost, then subtracts the cost from the takings to find the difference. An `if` statement is used to further refine the output. If the movie lost money, then the difference will be negative, so the first block of code sets the color to red and trims the leading negative sign by converting the difference to its absolute value with `abs()`. If the difference is positive, then the movie made money, and the amount will be set in green. The final clause sets the color blue in case the movie broke even financially.

The script connects to the database and retrieves the movie information from the movie table. The `WHERE` clause of the query will make sure that this information is for the requested movie, because it compares the `movie_id` field with the value passed in to this script through the URL. You'll notice,

124

though, that this time you didn't use `extract()` to retrieve the field information after the query. Instead, you're assigning them directly from the `$row` array into variables of their own. This is because you're not using the values as they are, but rather appending 'mins' to the running time and 'million' to the amounts.

Then the `calculate_differences()` function is called, and the returned HTML code is saved as `$movie_health`. After that, the information is displayed back to the user in an HTML-formatted table, using `echo` and `heredoc` syntax.

A Lasting Relationship

What if you wanted to find all the reviews for a particular movie? As it stands, you'd need to create a new SQL query in the `movies_details.php` page and execute it when the page loaded, which would make a total of two SQL queries in one page. It would work, but it would not be very efficient. (We're all efficient coders, aren't we?) This also results in unnecessary code.

It's time to answer the question: What's a relationship?

A *relationship* is a way of joining tables so that you can access the data in all those tables. The benefit of MySQL is that it is a relational database and, as such, supports the creation of relationships between tables. When used correctly (this can take a bit of time to get your head around), relationships can be very, very powerful and can be used to retrieve data from many, many tables in one SQL query.

The best way to demonstrate this is to build upon what you have done so far, so let's do it.

Try It Out   Creating and Filling a Movie Review Table

Before you can access movie reviews in your movie review table, you need to create the table and then fill it with data.

1.   Open your text editor, and type the following code:

```php
<?php
$db = mysql_connect('localhost', 'bp6am', 'bp6ampass') or
    die ('Unable to connect. Check your connection parameters.');
mysql_select_db('moviesite', $db) or die(mysql_error($db));

//create the reviews table
$query = 'CREATE TABLE reviews (
        review_movie_id INTEGER UNSIGNED NOT NULL,
        review_date     DATE           NOT NULL,
        reviewer_name   VARCHAR(255)   NOT NULL,
        review_comment  VARCHAR(255)   NOT NULL,
        review_rating   TINYINT UNSIGNED NOT NULL  DEFAULT 0,

        KEY (review_movie_id)
    )
    ENGINE=MyISAM';
```

```
mysql_query($query, $db) or die (mysql_error($db));

//insert new data into the reviews table
$query = <<<ENDSQL
INSERT INTO reviews
    (review_movie_id, review_date, reviewer_name, review_comment,
        review_rating)
VALUES
    (1, "2008-09-23", "John Doe", "I thought this was a great movie
        Even though my girlfriend made me see it against my will.", 4),
    (1, "2008-09-23", "Billy Bob", "I liked Eraserhead better.", 2),
    (1, "2008-09-28", "Peppermint Patty", "I wish I'd have seen it
        sooner!", 5),
    (2, "2008-09-23", "Marvin Martian", "This is my favorite movie. I
        didn't wear my flair to the movie but I loved it anyway.", 5),
    (3, "2008-09-23", "George B.", "I liked this movie, even though I
        Thought it was an informational video from my travel agent.", 3)
ENDSQL;
mysql_query($query, $db) or die(mysql_error($db));

echo 'Movie database successfully updated!';
?>
```

2. Save this file as db_ch04-2.php, and open it in your browser. Your reviews table has now been created as well as populated.

How It Works

By now you should be familiar with creating tables using MySQL and PHP, so this should be pretty self-explanatory. If you're having trouble, you might want to go back and review the relevant sections in Chapter 3.

Try It Out   **Displaying the Reviews**

In this example, you're going to link two tables (movies and reviews) and show the reviews for a particular movie. This requires a lot of changes to the movie_details.php page, so you would be best served by making a backup copy of the file, as you can't ever be too careful. If you make any mistakes, then you can always revert back to your original version. To display the reviews, follow these steps:

1. Add this code to the top of movie_details.php:

```
// function to generate ratings
function generate_ratings($rating) {
    $movie_rating = '';
    for ($i = 0; $i < $rating; $i++) {
        $movie_rating .= '<img src="star.png" alt="star"/>';
    }
    return $movie_rating;
}
```

2. Now split the tail end of the `heredoc` block that outputs the movie's information so that there are two:

```
      <td><strong>Health</strong></td>
      <td>$movie_health<td/>
    </tr>
  </table>
ENDHTML;


echo <<<ENDHTML
  </div>
 </body>
</html>
ENDHTML;
```

3. Add this code between the two `heredoc` blocks to fill the break you just made:

```
// retrieve reviews for this movie
$query = 'SELECT
        review_movie_id, review_date, reviewer_name, review_comment,
        review_rating
    FROM
        reviews
    WHERE
        review_movie_id = ' . $_GET['movie_id'] . '
    ORDER BY
        review_date DESC';

$result = mysql_query($query, $db) or die(mysql_error($db));

// display the reviews
echo <<< ENDHTML
  <h3><em>Reviews</em></h3>
  <table cellpadding="2" cellspacing="2"
    style="width: 90%; margin-left: auto; margin-right: auto;">
    <tr>
      <th style="width: 7em;">Date</th>
      <th style="width: 10em;">Reviewer</th>
      <th>Comments</th>
      <th style="width: 5em;">Rating</th>
    </tr>
ENDHTML;

while ($row = mysql_fetch_assoc($result)) {
    $date = $row['review_date'];
    $name = $row['reviewer_name'];
    $comment = $row['review_comment'];
    $rating = generate_ratings($row['review_rating']);
```

```
    echo <<<ENDHTML
    <tr>
      <td style="vertical-align:top; text-align: center;">$date</td>
      <td style="vertical-align:top;">$name</td>
      <td style="vertical-align:top;">$comment</td>
      <td style="vertical-align:top;">$rating</td>
    </tr>
ENDHTML;
}
```

4. Save the file as `movie_details.php` (overwriting the existing one — we hope you have made a backup copy, as suggested).

5. Upload the file to your web server, load `table3.php`, and click a movie.

You'll see something similar to Figure 4-7.

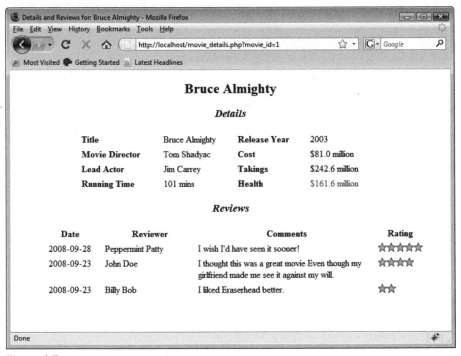

Figure 4-7

How It Works

The `generate_ratings()` function is fairly straightforward. You send it the value that is in the ratings field for a movie, and it creates an HTML string of rating images for that movie and returns it. Notice that you are using `. =` to ensure that movies with a rating of more than 1 will get additional images added to the single rating image.

By splitting the `heredoc` block into two sections, you made room to insert the HTML code that displays the reviews without breaking your page layout. The first portion displays the opening HTML tags and the details table, while the second portion displays the closing tags for the page.

The MySQL query retrieves all the reviews for the movie with the appropriate `review_movie_id`. The ORDER BY phrase of the query instructs MySQL to sort the results first in chronologically descending order. After that, the fields are extracted from the result set and displayed as a row in the table.

You've made quite a few changes in this section. But, as you can see, the changes have been well worth it. Now you know how to use MySQL to create relationships between tables. You successfully retrieved all the reviews from the review table, depending on the `movie_id` variable. You also looked at using the `$_GET` superglobal array to pass values from one page to another.

Summary

You've learned how to work with HTML tables to display your data, how to pull data from more than one database table and have it displayed seamlessly with data from another table, and how to create dynamic pages that display detailed information about the rows in your database. You can also include images to graphically display data to your web site visitors, as with this chapter's example of using rating stars.

So far, you've hard-coded all the additions to the database yourself, which isn't very dynamic. In Chapter 6, we'll teach you how to let the user add items to the database and edit them. But first, you need to know how to use forms with PHP, which is the subject of our next chapter.

Exercises

1. Add an entry in the top table of your `movie_details.php` file that shows the average rating given by reviewers.

2. Change each column heading of the reviews table in your `movie_details.php` to a link that allows the user to sort by that column (i.e., the user would click on "Date" to sort all the reviews by date).

3. Alternate the background colors of each row in the review table of your `movie_details.php` file to make them easier to read. Hint: odd-numbered rows would have a background of one color, even-numbered rows would have a background of another color.

Form Elements: Letting the User Work with Data

An interactive web site requires user input, which is generally gathered through forms. As in the paper-based world, the user fills in a form and submits its content for processing. In a web application, the processing isn't performed by a sentient being; rather, it is performed by a PHP script. Thus, the script requires some sort of coded intelligence.

When you fill in a paper form, you generally use a means to deliver its content (the postal service is one example) to a known address (such as a mail-order bookstore). The same logic applies to online forms. The data from an HTML form is sent to a specific location and processed.

The form element is rather simple in HTML. It states where and how it will send the contents of the elements it contains once submitted. It is after that point that PHP comes into play. PHP uses a set of simple yet powerful expressions that, when combined, provide you with the means to do virtually anything you want. The PHP script receives the data from the form and uses it to perform an action such as updating the contents of a database, sending an e-mail, testing the data format, and so on.

In this chapter, you begin to build a simple application that allows you to add, edit, or delete members of a data set (in this instance, the data will be movies, actors, and directors). This chapter welcomes you into a world of PHP/MySQL interaction by covering the following:

❑   Creating forms using buttons, text boxes, and other form elements.

❑   Creating PHP scripts to process HTML forms.

❑   Passing hidden information to the form-processing script via hidden form controls and a URL query string.

Your First Form

As a wise man once said, "Every journey starts with a single step." To start this particular journey, you will focus on a very simple form. It will include only a text field and a submit button. The processing script will display only the value entered in the text field.

Say My Name

In this exercise, you are going to get PHP to respond to a name entered in a form. This is a simple variation of the commonly used "hello world" program, allowing you to take your first step into interactivity.

1. Create `form1.html` with your favorite text editor.

2. Enter the following code:

```html
<html>
 <head>
  <title>Say My Name</title>
 </head>
 <body>
  <form action="formprocess1.php" method="post">
   <table>
    <tr>
     <td>Name</td>
     <td><input type="text" name="name" /></td>
    </tr><tr>
     <td colspan="2" style="text-align: center;">
      <input type="submit" name="submit" value="Submit" /></td>
    </tr>
   </table>
  </form>
 </body>
</html>
```

3. Create another empty file named `formprocess1.php`, and enter the following code:

```html
<html>
 <head>
  <title>Say My Name</title>
 </head>
 <body>
<?php
echo '<h1>Hello ' . $_POST['name'] . '!</h1>';
?>
  <pre>
<strong>DEBUG:</strong>
<?php
print_r($_POST);
?>
  </pre>
 </body>
</html>
```

4. Open `form1.html` in your browser.

5. Type your name in the name text box (as shown in Figure 5-1), and click the Submit button.

Figure 5-1

You can see two distinct parts on the resulting page: the "Hello Test" portion and the DEBUG part shown in Figure 5-2.

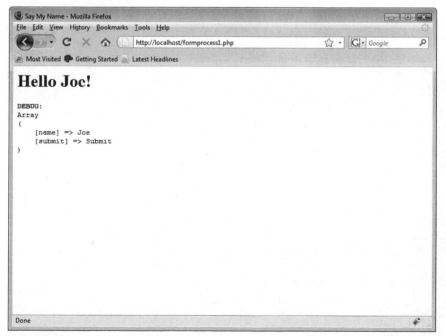

Figure 5-2

Congratulations, you just coded your first form-processing script.

How It Works

As with any good recipe, it's an excellent idea to start working on forms by understanding the ingredients you will be using. You'll need some background information about HTML form elements and a few PHP functions to familiarize yourself with forms.

Let's start with the HTML form itself.

You can find HTML references at the World Wide Web Consortium web site at www.w3.org/MarkUp.

FORM Element

First, we'll introduce the first HTML element you'll need: form. It delimits the form's area in the page and holds the fields you want your web site users to fill in.

```
<form action="formprocess1.php" method="post">
<!--form controls go here-->
</form>
```

Notice that the form element has an ending tag and two attributes. The first attribute (action) is the recipient page address (the form-processing script). The second attribute (method) is the way in which you will send the data to the recipient. You may recall that there are two separate ways of sending a form to its processing script: the POST and the GET methods.

The POST method takes the data from the form fields and sends it through an HTTP header. In this case, the data cannot be seen in the URL. The GET method gets the data from the form fields, encodes it, and appends it to the destination URL.

INPUT Element

The second new HTML element included here is input. This is the basis of most forms and can be used in many different ways to gather many different types of information. In this case, you use two different types of input: the text and submit types.

Here's the input text type:

```
<input type="text" name="name" />
```

The input text type is a standard single-line text box. As with all form controls, it needs a name so that the processing script can access its content using the following syntax:

```
<?php
echo $_POST['name']; // will display the value typed in
?>
```

And here's the input submit type:

```
<input type="submit" name="submit" value="Submit" />
```

As its name cleverly hints, the submit element displays a button that causes the browser to submit the form when it is pressed. The button's text is set through the value attribute. As mentioned for the text input, this form control needs a name for a processing reference.

Processing the Form

In this little script, you may have noticed a few new functions and some new syntax, and you are probably curious about them.

The first form-processing script is an interactive variation of the famous "hello world," but in this case it displays "hello" and the name you type in the text box. To make this happen, you need to print the value of the text field you filled in on the form. You know the echo command, so let's move on to the other piece, $_POST['name'].

The $_POST global array contains all form data submitted with the POST method. The array index of the field is its name. In a moment, you'll see how to check the content of your $_POST array using the print_r() function.

```php
<?php
echo '<h1>Hello ' . $_POST['name'] . '!</h1>';?>
```

In this example, $_POST['name'] displays what you entered in the name field.

You might wonder what print_r($_POST) does. It simply dumps the whole contents of the super global $_POST array to the output. This is a great way to debug your forms. The $_POST array, as with all arrays, has case-sensitive indexes. Use this tip to check for case and display the state of your objects when building a script.

When receiving the submitted form information, PHP sets the $_POST array with the data that the form sends. As with any array, you can directly access any of the indexes by name. In this instance, you can clearly see that the name index contains the value Joe. This trick works for all forms, even the most complicated ones.

Let's move on to see how you can use more HTML elements during form input to interact with the user.

Driving the User Input

The form in this example allows you to lead the user to choose values from a set of values you provide. Defining a value set is done through the use of specific HTML elements, such as list boxes, radio buttons, and check boxes.

Two kinds of predefined user input are in HTML forms. The first kind allows you to choose one item from the available options; the second allows the user to choose multiple items. Drop-down list boxes and radio buttons allow for one selection only. Check boxes and multiline list boxes provide for multiple choices.

Limiting the Input Choice

Let's start with the simple type of input. Follow these steps to create a single-selection list:

1. Create a text file named `form2.html`, and open it in your favorite text editor.

2. Enter the following code:

```html
<html>
 <head>
  <title>Greetings Earthling</title>
 </head>
 <body>
  <form action="formprocess2.php" method="post">
   <table>
    <tr>
     <td>Name</td>
     <td><input type="text" name="name" /></td>
    </tr><tr>
     <td>Greetings</td>
     <td>
      <select name="greeting">
       <option value="Hello">Hello</option>
       <option value="Hola">Hola</option>
       <option value="Bonjour">Bonjour</option>
      </select>
     </td>
    </tr><tr>
     <td> </td>
     <td>
      <input type="checkbox" name="debug" checked="checked"/>
      Display Debug info
     </td>
    </tr><tr>
     <td colspan="2" style="text-align: center">
      <input type="submit" name="submit" value="Submit" />
     </td>
    </tr>
   </table>
  </form>
 </body>
</html>
```

3. Create another empty file named `formprocess2.php`, and enter the following code:

```html
<html>
 <head>
  <title>Greetings Earthling</title>
 </head>
 <body>
<?php
```

```
echo '<h1>' . $_POST['greeting'] . ' ' . $_POST['name'] . '!</h1>';

if (isset($_POST['debug'])) {
    echo '<pre><strong>DEBUG:</strong>' . "\n";
    print_r($_POST);
    echo '</pre>';
}
?>
 </body>
</html>
```

4. Save `formprocess2.php`.

5. Call the page from your browser. As you can see from the resulting page, as displayed in Figure 5-3, the form got a bit more complicated.

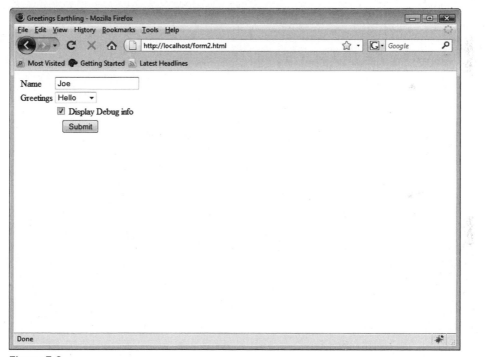

Figure 5-3

6. Enter your name, and click the Submit button. The display page that appears, shown in Figure 5-4, is rather simple; it holds only debug information and a greeting.

137

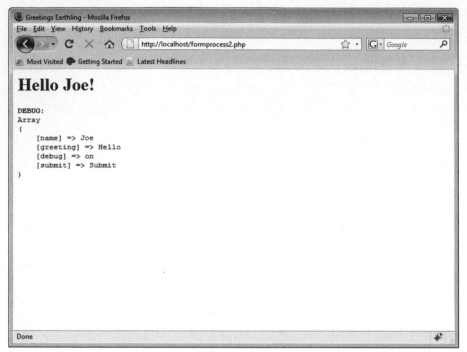

Figure 5-4

How It Works

As you see, this code uses logic similar to that in `formprocess1.php`. Two fields have been added (a drop-down list box and a check box).

`formprocess2.php` does the same thing as `formprocess1.php`, but with an added twist. It displays the debugging information only if the debug check box is selected, and greets you using any of the drop-down list choices in the subsections that follow.

The check box can represent only two possibilities: When checked, it passes the value `on` to the `$_POST` array, but otherwise it isn't sent by the browser at all. This is a great way to represent Boolean typed data.

The `SELECT` element (also known as a list) allows you to display a fixed list of choices from which the user has to choose an element. The item selected won't be sent as displayed but will be sent as its value. In this example, the value and its display are identical, but in a database-driven system, you would probably see record IDs as the values and their text labels as list choices. A good example is a product number and its name.

Be sure to set the value part of the OPTION items when using lists. If these are not set, the list looks the same but is totally useless because all choices will send the same null value.

One Form, Multiple Processing

Forms always react in a predefined way based on how you code your processing script to handle the data that the user sends to the system. You can create a single form with more than one defined action by using different submit buttons.

Try It Out   Radio Button, Multiline List Boxes

In the following example, you create a form that prepares a search and creates a movie/actor/director interface.

1. Create a text file named form3.php, and open it in your text editor. Then type the following code:

```
<html>
 <head>
  <title>Add/Search Entry</title>
  <style type="text/css">
  <!--
td {vertical-align: top;}
  -->
  </style>
 </head>
 <body>
  <form action="formprocess3.php" method="post">
   <table>
    <tr>
     <td>Name</td>
     <td><input type="text" name="name"/></td>
    </tr><tr>
     <td>Movie Type</td>
     <td>
      <select name="movie_type">
       <option value="">Select a movie type...</option>
       <option value="Action">Action</option>
       <option value="Drama">Drama</option>
       <option value="Comedy">Comedy</option>
       <option value="Sci-Fi">Sci-Fi</option>
       <option value="War">War</option>
       <option value="Other">Other...</option>
      </select>
     </td>
    </tr><tr>
     <td>Item Type</td>
     <td>
      <input type="radio" name="type" value="movie" checked="checked" />
Movie<br/>
      <input type="radio" name="type" value="actor" /> Actor<br/>
```

139

```
          <input type="radio" name="type" value="director"/> Director<br/>
        </td>
      </tr><tr>
      <td> </td>
      <td><input type="checkbox" name="debug" checked="checked" />
       Display Debug info
      </td>
      </tr><tr>
      <td colspan="2" style="text-align: center;">
        <input type="submit" name="submit" value="Search" />
        <input type="submit" name="submit" value="Add" />
      </td>
      </tr>
    </table>
  </form>
 </body>
</html>
```

2. Create another file named `formprocess3.php`, and enter the following code:

```php
<?php
if ($_POST['type'] == 'movie' && $_POST['movie_type'] == '') {
    header('Location: form3.php');
}
?>
<html>
 <head>
  <title><?php echo $_POST['submit'] . ' ' . $_POST['type'] . ': ' .
    $_POST['name']; ?></title>
 </head>
 <body>
<?php
if (isset($_POST['debug'])) {
    echo '<pre>';
    print_r($_POST);
    echo '</pre>';
}

$name = ucfirst($_POST['name']);
if ($_POST['type'] == 'movie')
{
    $foo = $_POST['movie_type'] . ' ' . $_POST['type'];
} else {
    $foo = $_POST['type'];
}

echo '<p>You are ' . $_POST['submit'] . 'ing ';
echo ($_POST['submit'] == 'Search') ? 'for ' : '';
echo 'a ' . $foo . ' named ' . $name . '</p>';
?>
 </body>
</html>
```

3. Start your browser and open `form3.php`. The form shown in Figure 5-5 appears. Notice that the form has two submit buttons. One is labeled Search, the other Add.

Figure 5-5

4. Type **Kevin Kline** in the Name field.

5. Leave `Movie Type` as is; then, move on to the `Item Type` field, which you'll set to Actor.

6. Clear the Display Debug info check box if you like; then, click the Search button. The results appear, as shown in Figure 5-6.

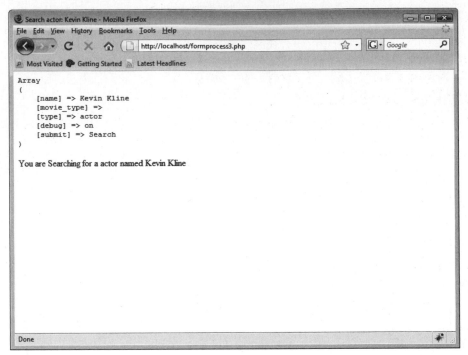

Figure 5-6

7. Now play around a bit with the form. Look at the output and how it changes when you modify the data.

How It Works

You just coded a simple form with two possible actions. Depending on the button you click and the data you choose to enter, this code outputs different information.

What's new in the form page itself? A group of radio buttons and a new submit button have been added. Let's have a closer look at these.

Radio INPUT Element

The radio button is a very simple element. By default, if no radio button is specified as CHECKED, no default choice is made. Always remember that choosing the default value is a very important part of building a form. Users often leave defaults in forms, and in that case, if you do not set a default value, you will not receive any information for that field when the form is submitted.

```
<input type="radio" name="type" value="movie" checked="checked" /> Movie<br/>
<input type="radio" name="type" value="actor" /> Actor<br/>
<input type="radio" name="type" value="director"/> Director<br/>
```

For multiple radio buttons to be linked together to form a group and be processed as a single form element, they need to share the same name and supply different values (quite obviously). In the preceding code, the name is always `type`. This tells the browser that the radio buttons are linked together and that selecting one of them will clear the others.

Multiple Submit Buttons

As with radio buttons, the submit buttons share the same name but supply different values. Clicking one of these buttons will cause the browser to submit the form. As you can see in the DEBUG block, the submit button sends its own information to the script. By reading this value, the script allows you to have multiple submit buttons for the same form, and performs different processing actions depending on which one was clicked.

```
<input type="submit" name="submit" value="Search" />
<input type="submit" name="submit" value="Add" />
```

Basic Input Testing

Now let's move our attention to the processing script, to see what's new in there.

The following code checks that the item type is `movie`, and if it is, it checks that the user has selected a valid movie type from the list. If he or she has not, then the visitor is redirected to the form page.

The test is an `if` comparison that makes use of the `&&` operator (the Boolean And operator). You can think of this in simple Monopoly game parlance: if the item type is movie *and* the movie type is not specified, then you go back to square one without passing go, and you do not collect $200. Otherwise, the script can continue processing.

```
if ($_POST['type'] == 'movie' && $_POST['movie_type'] == '') {
    header('Location: form3.php');
}
```

The header function allows you to send a raw HTTP header. This can be quite handy when dealing with implementing access restrictions and when redirecting users to other scripts. In this instance, it redirects the user to the `form3.php` page.

> *PHP will automatically send some HTTP headers before it sends any output to the browser. This is important to keep in mind, because once sent, HTTP headers cannot be sent again. If you use the* `header()` *function after output has already been sent (either by an* echo *or* print *statement, HTML, whitespace, etc.), then you will receive a warning resembling the following:*

```
Warning: Cannot modify header information - headers already sent by (output
started at C:\Program Files\Apache Software Foundation\Apache2.2\htdocs\
formprocess3.php:2) in C:\Program Files\Apache Software Foundation\Apache2.2\
htdocs\formprocess3.php on line 4
```

Here are two examples of problem code:

```
<?php
header('Location: form3.php');
?>
```

This code will fail because there is an empty line before the opening `<?php` *tag. The whitespace will be sent as output before the* `header()` *function is called.*

```
<?php
echo 'foobar';
header('Location: form3.php');
?>
```

This code will fail because the `echo` *statement will output "foobar" before the* `header()` *function is called.*

To avoid this problem, you might want to consider using output buffering functions or setting a few special directives in your `php.ini` *file. But output buffering is an advanced concept, and there's no guarantee other servers will have the same* `ini` *values as yours when you try to run your code on them. Ultimately, the best solution is to be aware of this issue and make sure you keep your code clean and organized.*

Ternary Operator

If PHP makes it past the `if` statement with header redirect, then the rest of the page can be generated. The script goes on to output HTML and construct the rest of the page. Everything is pretty straightforward and isn't anything we haven't looked at earlier, except the `ucase()` function and the ternary operator. `ucase()` is a function that returns a string with the first character capitalized. But the ternary comparison operation `?:` is much more interesting because it acts as a handy shortcut for an `if-else` construct. The ternary operator is not PHP-specific; many other languages have it as well.

To be honest, I remember when I first saw the `?:` operator, and thought to myself, "Wow . . . that's too strange. I'm never going to use that! I'll just stick with using `if-else`." But as I saw it more and started using it, I realized how useful it is for writing short, clear code, especially when validating input data. The form of the operator is this:

```
[expression] ? [execute if TRUE] : [execute if FALSE];
```

The expression to the left of the `?` is evaluated. If it is found to be true, then the first action (between the `?` and `:`) is performed. Otherwise, if it is found to be false, then the second action (after the `:`) is performed. This is handy with `echo` statements and assigning variables. The line that uses the ternary operator in `formprocess3.php` is:

```
echo ($_POST['submit'] == 'Search') ? 'for ' : '';
```

If the user clicks the Search submit button, then the condition will evaluate true, and "for " will be applied back to `echo`. If the user clicks the Add submit button, then the condition will be false, and an empty string will be passed back to echo. The following `if-else` statement effectively accomplishes the same thing:

```php
if ($_POST['submit'] == 'Search') {
    echo 'for ';
} else {
    echo '';
}
```

The ternary operator is a great way to apply a quick true/false filter of sorts. But don't be tempted to use it as a full-fledged `if-else` statement, especially with nesting, because then your code becomes exponentially more difficult to read and maintain. Consider this example:

```php
<?php
$num = 42;
if ($num < 0) {
    $value = 'The value is negative.';
} else {
    if ($num > 0) {
    $value = 'The value is positive.';
    } else {
    $value = 'The value is zero.';
    }
}
?>
```

This is much easier to read and understand, and consequently to maintain, than if it were compressed into two ternary operators:

```php
<?php
$num = 42;
echo 'The value is ';
echo ($num < 0) ? 'negative.' : ($num > 0) ? 'positive.' : 'zero.';
?>
```

So what's the bottom line? Use syntactical shortcuts and conveniences that are available to you, if they make your life easier and your code more concise, but don't go overboard — and keep readability and maintainability in mind as well.

Linking Forms Together

Now that you know most of the form elements, let's create a skeleton for the movie application. The system will add new items or search for existing ones. Database interaction has been touched upon earlier and will be explored more in Chapter 6, but for now you'll just build the forms and output the results to the browser.

Bonding It All Together

In this exercise, you'll create several new scripts that work together to simulate allowing the user to add information to the database.

1.   Create a file named `form4.php`, and enter the following code:

```
<html>
 <head>
  <title>Multipurpose Form</title>
  <style type="text/css">
  <!--
td {vertical-align: top;}
  -->
  </style>
 </head>
 <body>
  <form action="form4a.php" method="post">
   <table>
    <tr>
     <td>Name</td>
     <td><input type="text" name="name" /></td>
    </tr><tr>
     <td>Item Type</td>
     <td>
      <input type="radio" name="type" value="movie" checked="checked" />
Movie<br/>
      <input type="radio" name="type" value="actor" /> Actor<br/>
      <input type="radio" name="type" value="director"/> Director<br/>
     </td>
    </tr><tr>
     <td>Movie Type<br/><small>(if applicable)</small></td>
     <td>
      <select name="movie_type">
       <option value="">Select a movie type...</option>
       <option value="Action">Action</option>
       <option value="Drama">Drama</option>
       <option value="Comedy">Comedy</option>
       <option value="Sci-Fi">Sci-Fi</option>
       <option value="War">War</option>
       <option value="Other">Other...</option>
      </select>
     </td>
    </tr><tr>
     <td> </td>
     <td><input type="checkbox" name="debug" checked="checked" />
      Display Debug info
     </td>
    </tr><tr>
     <td colspan="2" style="text-align: center;">
      <input type="submit" name="submit" value="Search" />
      <input type="submit" name="submit" value="Add" />
     </td>
    </tr>
```

```
      </table>
     </form>
   </body>
 </html>
```

2. Create a new file called `form4a.php`, and enter the following code:

```php
<?php
// Make sure the user selected a movie type if they're adding a
// movie. If not, then send them back to the first form.
if ($_POST['submit'] == 'Add') {
    if ($_POST['type'] == 'movie' && $_POST['movie_type'] == '') {
        header('Location: form4.php');
    }
}
?>
<html>
 <head>
  <title>Multipurpose Form</title>
  <style type="text/css">
  <!--
td {vertical-align: top;}
  -->
  </style>
 </head>
 <body>
<?php
// Show a form to collect more information if the user is adding something
if ($_POST['submit'] == 'Add') {
    echo '<h1>Add ' . ucfirst($_POST['type']) . '</h1>';
?>
  <form action="form4b.php" method="post">
   <input type="hidden" name="type" value="<?php echo $_POST['type']; ?>"/>
   <table>
    <tr>
     <td>Name</td>
     <td>
      <?php echo $_POST['name']; ?>
      <input type="hidden" name="name" value="<?php echo $_POST['name']; ?>"/>
     </td>
    </tr>
<?php
    if ($_POST['type'] == 'movie') {
?>
    <tr>
     <td>Movie Type</td>
     <td>
      <?php echo $_POST['movie_type']; ?>
      <input type="hidden" name="movie_type"
       value="<?php echo $_POST['movie_type']; ?>"/>
     </td>
    </tr><tr>
     <td>Year</td>
     <td><input type="text" name="year" /></td>
```

```
      </tr><tr>
       <td>Movie Description</td>
<?php
     } else {
         echo '<tr><td>Biography</td>';
     }
?>
       <td><textarea name="extra" rows="5" cols="60"></textarea></td>
       </tr><tr>
         <td colspan="2" style="text-align: center;">
<?php
if (isset($_POST['debug'])) {
     echo '<input type="hidden" name="debug" value="on" />';
}
?>
         <input type="submit" name="submit" value="Add" />
         </td>
       </tr>
      </table>
     </form>
<?php
// The user is just searching for something
} else if ($_POST['submit'] == 'Search') {
     echo '<h1>Search for ' . ucfirst($_POST['type']) . '</h1>';
     echo '<p>Searching for ' . $_POST['name'] . '...</p>';
}

if (isset($_POST['debug'])) {
     echo '<pre>';
     print_r($_POST);
     echo '</pre>';
}
?>
     </body>
</html>
```

3. Create another new file named form4b.php, in which you will add this code:

```
<html>
 <head>
  <title>Multipurpose Form</title>
  <style type="text/css">
  <!--
td {vertical-align: top;}
  -->
  </style>
 </head>
 <body>
<?php
if ($_POST['type'] == 'movie') {
    echo '<h1>New ' . ucfirst($_POST['movie_type']) . ': ';
} else {
    echo '<h1>New ' . ucfirst($_POST['type']) . ': ';
}
```

```
echo $_POST['name'] . '</h1>';

echo '<table>';
if ($_POST['type'] == 'movie') {
    echo '<tr>';
    echo '<td>Year</td>';
    echo '<td>' . $_POST['year'] . '</td>';
    echo '</tr><tr>';
    echo '<td>Movie Description</td>';
} else {
    echo '<tr><td>Biography</td>';
}
echo '<td>' . nl2br($_POST['extra']) . '</td>';
echo '</tr>';
echo '</table>';

if (isset($_POST['debug'])) {
    echo '<pre>';
    print_r($_POST);
    echo '</pre>';
}
?>
 </body>
</html>
```

4. Open `form4.php` in your web browser. The new form is displayed, shown in Figure 5-7, which prompts the visitor for more details.

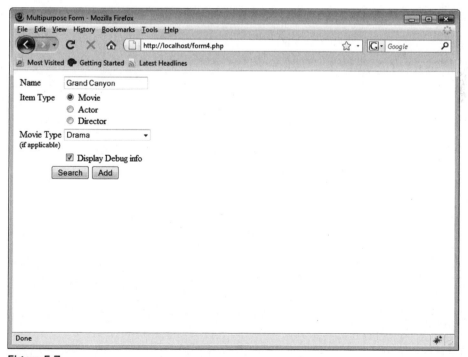

Figure 5-7

5. Enter the name of the movie you want to add: Grand Canyon.

6. Click the Add button; this takes you to the add form shown in Figure 5-8.

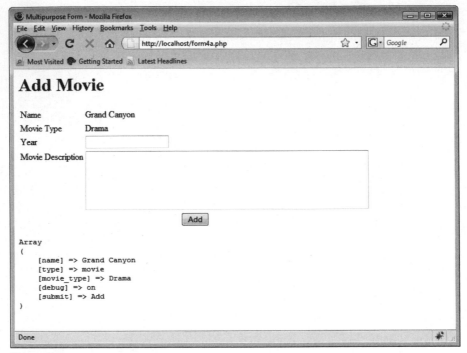

Figure 5-8

7. Enter a date for the year the movie was made: 1991.

8. Select Drama in the Movie type list.

9. Type a quick movie description, making sure you enter multiple lines and press the Enter key between them.

10. Click the Add button, and see how the information is displayed (see Figure 5-9).

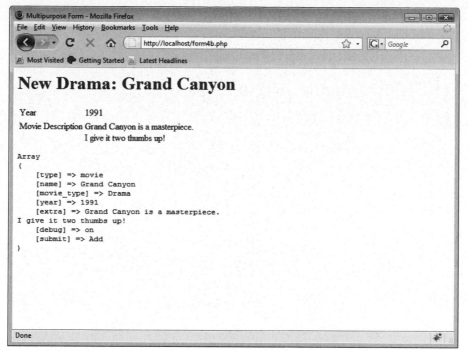

Figure 5-9

How It Works

This set of scripts is designed around a simple idea: passing data through multiple scripts from form to form. The key to this has been input elements with their type attribute set to hidden. These fields are not displayed by the browser to the user, but their values are submitted with the rest of the form fields' data. This is but one way to pass data between forms, though it is very common.

Summary

You've learned a lot of about forms in this chapter. Forms are composed of fields. Each field type has a specific purpose and allows a certain data type to be entered. Text fields can be used to enter text or numeric data. Lists can be used to enter any type of data and have a limited set of possible values. Lists are a good way to drive user input when multiple choices are available. Check boxes are good for true or false values.

Exercises

See how you might accomplish the following:

1. Create a form and a processing page that let you choose a rating (stars, thumbs up, number from 1 to 5, whatever), and provide comments for a movie.

2. Create a form with several text input boxes that allow you to populate the options of a select field on a subsequent page.

3. Create a calculator form that takes two numbers and calculates their sum.

Letting the User Edit the Database

Retrieving data from a database is all well and good when you've first fed the database some data. But databases don't generate their own content, and only a few get fed data by other systems, such as integrated systems. What this means is that you have to feed your system with data that comes from PHP. For our purposes here, and from what you've seen in previous chapters, all interaction with the database uses SQL. You already know the basic SQL syntax to put your own data in a table and retrieve it for users to see. But now, let's look at the other side of the equation — data processing.

This chapter covers database editing, including:

❑   Adding entries, which is quite simple — but you will find that adding entries in a relational database is yet another exercise.

❑   Deleting entries without corrupting the database structure and referential integrity.

❑   Modifying entries to replace some existing fields with new content in an existing record.

Preparing the Battlefield

We'll continue to use the moviesite database from the previous chapters here. First you'll start by creating the administrative page that lists the movies and people in your database and provides links for you to manage them. Then you will create the auxiliary pages that will let you add and delete movie records.

Setting Up the Environment

First, you need a start page. Follow these steps to create one:

1. Create a file named `admin.php`, and enter the following code:

```php
<?php
$db = mysql_connect('localhost', 'bp6am', 'bp6ampass') or
    die ('Unable to connect. Check your connection parameters.');
mysql_select_db('moviesite', $db) or die(mysql_error($db));
?>
<html>
 <head>
  <title>Movie database</title>
  <style type="text/css">
   th { background-color: #999;}
   .odd_row { background-color: #EEE; }
   .even_row { background-color: #FFF; }
  </style>
 </head>
 <body>
 <table style="width:100%;">
  <tr>
   <th colspan="2">Movies <a href="movie.php?action=add">[ADD]</a></th>
  </tr>
<?php
$query = 'SELECT * FROM movie';
$result = mysql_query($query, $db) or die (mysql_error($db));

$odd = true;
while ($row = mysql_fetch_assoc($result)) {
    echo ($odd == true) ? '<tr class="odd_row">' : '<tr class="even_row">';
    $odd = !$odd;
    echo '<td style="width:75%;">';
    echo $row['movie_name'];
    echo '</td><td>';
    echo ' <a href="movie.php?action=edit&id=' . $row['movie_id'] . '">
[EDIT]</a>';
    echo ' <a href="delete.php?type=movie&id=' . $row['movie_id'] . '">
[DELETE]</a>';
    echo '</td></tr>';
}
?>
  <tr>
   <th colspan="2">People <a href="people.php?action=add"> [ADD]</a></th>
  </tr>
<?php
$query = 'SELECT * FROM people';
$result = mysql_query($query, $db) or die (mysql_error($db));
```

```
$odd = true;
while ($row = mysql_fetch_assoc($result)) {
    echo ($odd == true) ? '<tr class="odd_row">' : '<tr class="even_row">';
    $odd = !$odd;
    echo '<td style="width: 25%;">';
    echo $row['people_fullname'];
    echo '</td><td>';
    echo ' <a href="people.php?action=edit&id=' . $row['people_id'] .
        '"> [EDIT]</a>';
    echo ' <a href="delete.php?type=people&id=' . $row['people_id'] .
        '"> [DELETE]</a>';
    echo '</td></tr>';
}
?>
  </table>
 </body>
</html>
```

2. Now open the file in your browser. You will see the page as shown in Figure 6-1.

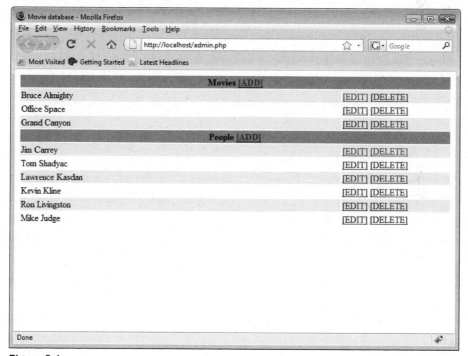

Figure 6-1

All links are broken at the moment, but do not worry; that's perfectly normal, because you haven't yet created the other pages.

How It Works

You must always have a central administration interface that allows you to perform actions on the data and easily see the content. This script provides that admin interface. It shows you all the data and allows you to manage everything in sight. So how does it do it?

As in Chapter 4, here, you connect to the database and display its contents. The code generates an HTML `table` that holds the name of each movie and person, along with ADD, EDIT, and DELETE links.

Odd and even rows of the table appear in different colors, as a visual cue that helps line up the entry with the EDIT and DELETE links. Before the start of each `while` loop that is responsible for listing the results of the database query, the variable `$odd` is set to `true`. How the `tr` tag is generated upon each iteration depends on the value of `$odd`, and then the value of `$odd` is toggled in preparation for the next iteration of the loop.

Inserting a Record in a Relational Database

Databases often hold more than just one table. All those tables can be totally independent, but that would be like using your car to store things in the trunk, but never to drive around in. Usually the tables are related to one another in some manner.

In old systems in which relational databases didn't exist, every row held all the information possible. Imagine your system running with only one table holding all the information for your application. Your `movie` table, for example, would store all the data about the actors and the directors and the movie types. Each record would have all this information specified. Now suppose that one day you were to decide that a movie category should be changed from "action" to "adventure." You would then have to go through all the records in the table records to change the movie type label. The possibility for mistakes is exponentially greater as well!

This is not the case in modern relational database management systems (RDBMS); you can create a `movietype` table storing a reference of all the possible movie types, and then link movies to the relevant movie type. To link different tables, you use a primary key/foreign key pair.

A primary key is a value or set of values that can be used to uniquely identify each record in a table. The primary key of the `movietype` table is the numeric identification of each type of movie stored in the `movietype_id` field. For example, in your database, the id 1 references comedy. The foreign key is a value in another table that can be used to reference back to the primary key. The reference in the `movie` table is to the `movietype` primary key.

In the following exercise, you use PHP and SQL to insert a movie in your database. This movie is of a known movie type from the `movietype` reference table.

Try It Out   **Inserting a Movie with Known Movie Type and People**

This time, let's do something a bit more complicated. You'll be able to add a movie to the system while specifying an existing movie type and existing actor and director.

1.   Create a new empty file with your text editor, and enter the following code. Save it as `movie.php`.

```php
<?php
$db = mysql_connect('localhost', 'bp6am', 'bp6ampass') or
    die ('Unable to connect. Check your connection parameters.');
mysql_select_db('moviesite', $db) or die(mysql_error($db));
?>
<html>
 <head>
  <title>Add Movie</title>
 </head>
  <body>
   <form action="commit.php?action=add&type=movie" method="post">
    <table>
     <tr>
      <td>Movie Name</td>
      <td><input type="text" name="movie_name"/></td>
     </tr><tr>
      <td>Movie Type</td>
      <td><select name="movie_type">
<?php
// select the movie type information
$query = 'SELECT
        movietype_id, movietype_label
    FROM
        movietype
    ORDER BY
        movietype_label';
$result = mysql_query($query, $db) or die(mysql_error($db));

// populate the select options with the results
while ($row = mysql_fetch_assoc($result)) {
    foreach ($row as $value) {
        echo '<option value="' . $row['movietype_id'] . '">';
        echo $row['movietype_label'] . '</option>';
    }
}
?>
      </select></td>
     </tr><tr>
      <td>Movie Year</td>
      <td><select name="movie_year">
```

```php
<?php
// populate the select options with years
for ($yr = date("Y"); $yr >= 1970; $yr--) {
    echo '<option value="' . $yr . '">' . $yr . '</option>';
}
?>
      </select></td>
    </tr><tr>
     <td>Lead Actor</td>
     <td><select name="movie_leadactor">
<?php
// select actor records
$query = 'SELECT
        people_id, people_fullname
    FROM
        people
    WHERE
        people_isactor = 1
    ORDER BY
        people_fullname';
$result = mysql_query($query, $db) or die(mysql_error($db));

// populate the select options with the results
while ($row = mysql_fetch_assoc($result)) {
    foreach ($row as $value) {
        echo '<option value="' . $row['people_id'] . '">';
        echo $row['people_fullname'] . '</option>';
    }
}
?>
      </select></td>
    </tr><tr>
     <td>Director</td>
     <td><select name="movie_director">
<?php
// select director records
$query = 'SELECT
        people_id, people_fullname
    FROM
        people
    WHERE
        people_isdirector = 1
    ORDER BY
        people_fullname';
$result = mysql_query($query, $db) or die(mysql_error($db));

// populate the select options with the results
while ($row = mysql_fetch_assoc($result)) {
    foreach ($row as $value) {
        echo '<option value="' . $row['people_id'] . '">';
```

```
            echo $row['people_fullname'] . '</option>';
        }
    }
    ?>
        </select></td>
      </tr><tr>
       <td colspan="2" style="text-align: center;">
        <input type="submit" name="submit" value="Add" />
       </td>
      </tr>
     </table>
    </form>
   </body>
</html>
```

2. Create a new empty file named `commit.php`, and enter the following code:

```php
<?php
$db = mysql_connect('localhost', 'bp6am', 'bp6ampass') or
    die ('Unable to connect. Check your connection parameters.');
mysql_select_db('moviesite', $db) or die(mysql_error($db));
?>
<html>
 <head>
  <title>Commit</title>
 </head>
 <body>
<?php
switch ($_GET['action']) {
case 'add':
    switch ($_GET['type']) {
    case 'movie':
        $query = 'INSERT INTO
            movie
                (movie_name, movie_year, movie_type, movie_leadactor,
                movie_director)
            VALUES
                ("' . $_POST['movie_name'] . '",
                ' . $_POST['movie_year'] . ',
                ' . $_POST['movie_type'] . ',
                ' . $_POST['movie_leadactor'] . ',
                ' . $_POST['movie_director'] . ')';
        break;
    }
    break;
```

```
    }

    if (isset($query)) {
        $result = mysql_query($query, $db) or die(mysql_error($db));
    }
    ?>
    <p>Done!</p>
    </body>
</html>
```

3. Open your browser on the `admin.php` page, and click the ADD link in the movie table's header. You should see on the screen the form in which you can enter movie information.

4. Add a movie named "Test" with a random movie type, actor, and director, as shown in Figure 6-2.

Figure 6-2

5. Click the Add button, and you will see the confirmation message shown in Figure 6-3.

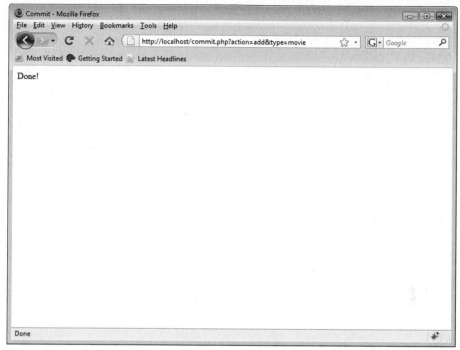

Figure 6-3

How It Works

HTML forms allow you to drive the way users enter the data. Once submitted, the form sends the server information that PHP can use to generate and run the SQL INSERT statement.

As you see in the movie insertion form in movie.php, you have four select boxes and a text field. The text field content is left to your discretion, but the select boxes are quite directive and only allow you to chose a predetermined value.

To generate the list of movie types, you simply query the database, retrieve the records and display the types, and reference their primary key as the item value. Each known movie type will have an item in the select box.

Back in Chapter 2, you were introduced to the while loop and the foreach loop. The year list is a selection of years from 1970 to the current year, and is generated with a new type of loop, the for loop.

When using these types of loops, you should know that for loops will offer a more restricted way of setting up code for repetitive execution. They begin with the keyword for and then a set of three statements: first a variable set to an initial value to be used as the loop's counter, then a conditional statement, and finally the increment in which the counter value is adjusted after each execution of the loop. The code block that gets executed is bracketed and follows the `for` statement, following this syntax:

```
for (initialize; condition; increment) {
    // code
}
```

The initial value of `$yr` is set to the current year with the help of the `date()` function. The condition is set so the loop will continue executing as long as the value `$yr` is greater than or equal to 1970. Each time the loop executes, the value of `$yr` is reduced by 1. The code that is repeatedly executed uses the value of `$yr` to place the years into the select's items.

`for` loops are more restricted than the other loops, in that the variable is intended only to act as a counter mechanism. It wouldn't be good practice to change its value within the code block! This is compared to the `do-while` and `while` loops, where the value is intentionally changed in the code block to affect the loop's behavior.

The same steps followed to generate the movie type listing are followed for the actor and director select fields. A query is sent to the database, the results are retrieved, and the person is displayed with the primary key as the item value. The only difference between the queries is the `WHERE` clause that filters the retrieved results to first just the actors and then just the directors.

Now that your form is ready, you need to have a script that uses this data to create records. This is the purpose of `commit.php`. As you can see, the `switch` statement using the `$_GET['action']` value is totally useless for now, but in the next exercises you will add a lot of code to the `movie.php` script so you can use it to edit the movies. Then `commit.php`'s `switch` will be more important.

Deleting a Record

Deleting records is easy (perhaps a bit too easy at times). Deleting always means losing data, so be especially careful when doing so. To delete a record you need to point to the record through a set of conditions in a `WHERE` statement. Once this statement is executed, there is no turning back. Records are deleted without hope of return; that's why we advise caution when using the `DELETE` statement. MySQL deletes everything that matches the query, and forgetting one little thing in your `WHERE` clause could have disastrous consequences.

Because deleting records is irrevocable, you may find it beneficial to make sure your `WHERE` clause causes the correct records to be selected first. You can use MySQL's command-line program, first discussed in Chapter 1, to issue a `SELECT` statement and then review the result set that is returned. Then, when you are certain the correct records are selected, you can prepare your `DELETE` statement.

Try It Out   **Deleting a Single Record**

Before asking PHP to delete anything though MySQL, let's first try it ourselves to familiarize ourselves with the DELETE statement.

1. Open a console window and connect to the MySQL server with the command-line program, as in Chapter 1:

```
"C:\Program Files\MySQL\MySQL Server 5.0\bin\mysql.exe" -u root -p
```

2. Select the movies database by entering the following:

```
USE movies;
```

3. Test the WHERE clause using a SELECT statement:

```
SELECT * FROM movie WHERE movie_id = 4;
```

4. Verify the WHERE clause is correct by examining the returned results to see that it is indeed the record you wish to delete.

5. Delete the record by using a DELETE statement:

```
DELETE FROM movie WHERE movie_id = 4;
```

6. See that the record was deleted by reissuing the SELECT statement:

```
SELECT * FROM movie WHERE movie_id = 4;
```

How It Works

The DELETE SQL statement is very simple to use. The most important aspect is to make sure you have the proper selection of records with the WHERE clause in your query.

As you know, a database often holds related records in different tables. Deleting some records without considering their relations introduces you to chaos and heavy manual database tweaking. MySQL unfortunately doesn't manage relations for you, and thus will not automatically preserve referential integrity.

To avoid that problem, you can use a more elaborate form of the DELETE statement, the *Cascade Delete*, as discussed in the following section.

Cascade Delete

Now that you know how to use DELETE, you will implement it to delete a known person from your application's database. Because you store references to known people in the movie table, you will need to update the movie table content so you don't reference deleted people. (The update-specific exercises come next in this chapter.) Deleting the person only would be like throwing away your car keys and expecting your parking spot to be empty. You need to make sure no reference to a deleted record is left in the remaining data.

Follow these steps to implement the Cascade Delete:

1. Create a new text file named delete.php, and enter the following code:

```php
<?php
$db = mysql_connect('localhost', 'bp6am', 'bp6ampass') or
    die ('Unable to connect. Check your connection parameters.');
mysql_select_db('moviesite', $db) or die(mysql_error($db));

if (!isset($_GET['do']) || $_GET['do'] != 1) {
    switch ($_GET['type']) {
    case 'movie':
        echo 'Are you sure you want to delete this movie?<br/>';
        break;
    case 'people':
        echo 'Are you sure you want to delete this person?<br/>';
        break;
    }
    echo '<a href="' . $_SERVER['REQUEST_URI'] . '&do=1">yes</a> ';
    echo 'or <a href="admin.php">no</a>';
} else {
    switch ($_GET['type']) {
    case 'people':
        $query = 'UPDATE movie SET
                movie_leadactor = 0
            WHERE
                movie_leadactor = ' . $_GET['id'];
        $result = mysql_query($query, $db) or die(mysql_error($db));

        $query = 'DELETE FROM people
            WHERE
                people_id = ' . $_GET['id'];
        $result = mysql_query($query, $db) or die(mysql_error($db));
?>
<p style="text-align: center;">Your person has been deleted.
<a href="movie_index.php">Return to Index</a></p>
<?php
        break;
    case 'movie':
        $query = 'DELETE FROM movie
            WHERE
                movie_id = ' . $_GET['id'];
        $result = mysql_query($query, $db) or die(mysql_error($db));
?>
<p style="text-align: center;">Your movie has been deleted.
```

```
<a href="movie_index.php">Return to Index</a></p>
<?php
        break;
    }
}
?>
```

2.   Open `admin.php` in your browser again, and note the DELETE links next to each movie or person.

3.   Try deleting the test movie you added in the previous exercise by clicking the DELETE link next to its name. You will be asked for confirmation, as in Figure 6-4.

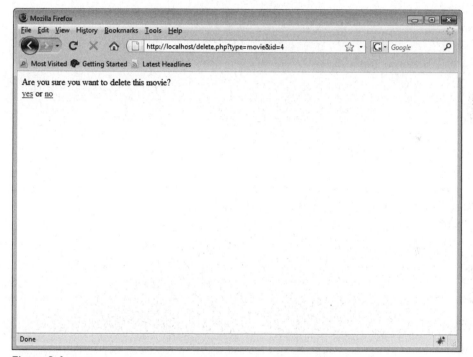

Figure 6-4

4.   Click the "yes" link to confirm the deletion, and wait for the confirmation message, shown in Figure 6-5.

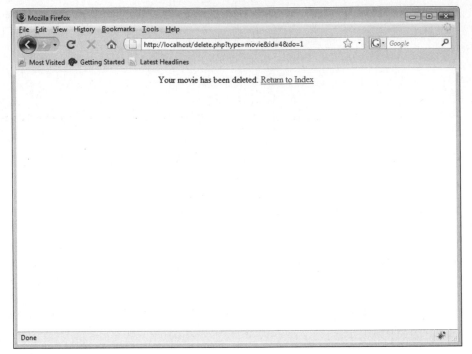

Figure 6-5

How It Works

First, you need to understand that in a relational database you cannot delete records and just forget about them. Deleting data must be considered carefully. For example, if you delete a person from the people table, this prevents you from finding a potential reference to that person in the movie table. If you delete Jim Carrey from the people table, who will *Bruce Almighty*'s lead actor be? If you don't do anything, Jim Carrey's id will remain in the record, and you will have a corrupted database. You don't want that, do you? The answer is: Certainly not! The solution to this problem is to make sure that you always have the round peg (a foreign key) in the round hole (a record). The script runs in two modes, with the help of an if statement. First, when it is called by following the link from admin.php, the query string is simply the record type (either a movie or person) and the record's id. A parameter named do does not appear. This triggers the first block of code of the if construct to be executed by PHP:

```
switch ($_GET['type']) {
case 'movie':
    echo 'Are you sure you want to delete this movie?<br/>';
    break;
case 'people':
    echo 'Are you sure you want to delete this person?<br/>';
    break;
}
echo '<a href="' . $_SERVER['REQUEST_URI'] . '&do=1">yes</a> ';
echo 'or <a href="admin.php">no</a>';
```

A `switch` statement is used to display the correct prompt, depending on the `type` submitted, and then links are generated to confirm the delete process or to cancel it. The link to confirm the process directs you back to the current page with the same URL parameters, but also appends `do`.

The second time the script is called, the `do` parameter is set, and so the next block of the `if` structure is executed, and again a `switch` statement is used to act appropriately, depending on the type of record to be deleted.

Because we want to preserve the integrity of the database, the `movie` table must be updated first, before deleting a record from the `person` table:

```
$query = 'UPDATE movie SET
        movie_leadactor = 0
    WHERE
        movie_leadactor = ' . $_GET['id'];
$result = mysql_query($query, $db) or die(mysql_error($db));

$query = 'DELETE FROM people
    WHERE
        people_id = ' . $_GET['id'];
$result = mysql_query($query, $db) or die(mysql_error($db));
```

The `UPDATE` statement works in a very simple way. It sets the fields specified to the new value specified in all records, meeting the requirements of the `WHERE` statement. You might wonder what would happen if someone were to forget the `WHERE` part. Well, curiosity is a fine quality: This would update *all* records in the table, which is probably not something you want to do in real life.

Editing Data in a Record

Having data in the database is all well and good, but data has a mind of its own and tends to want to be updated. To update data, you need to identify the data to update and present the system user with a nice interface to do so. Using the same interface as was used to create the data is often a good practice.

Try It Out   Editing a Movie

In this exercise, you create a script that enables you to edit a movie. You will build on the existing `movie.php` script you created earlier.

1. Open `movie.php` in your text editor and modify the code as follows:

```
<?php
$db = mysql_connect('localhost', 'bp6am', 'bp6ampass') or
    die ('Unable to connect. Check your connection parameters.');
mysql_select_db('moviesite', $db) or die(mysql_error($db));
```

```php
if ($_GET['action'] == 'edit') {
    //retrieve the record's information
    $query = 'SELECT
            movie_name, movie_type, movie_year, movie_leadactor, movie_director
        FROM
            movie
        WHERE
            movie_id = ' . $_GET['id'];
    $result = mysql_query($query, $db) or die(mysql_error($db));
    extract(mysql_fetch_assoc($result));
} else {
    //set values to blank
    $movie_name = '';
    $movie_type = 0;
    $movie_year = date('Y');
    $movie_leadactor = 0;
    $movie_director = 0;
}
?>
<html>
 <head>
  <title><?php echo ucfirst($_GET['action']); ?> Movie</title>
 </head>
 <body>
  <form action="commit.php?action=<?php echo $_GET['action']; ?>&type=movie"
   method="post">
   <table>
    <tr>
     <td>Movie Name</td>
     <td><input type="text" name="movie_name"
      value="<?php echo $movie_name; ?>"/></td>
    </tr><tr>
     <td>Movie Type</td>
     <td><select name="movie_type">
<?php
// select the movie type information
$query = 'SELECT
        movietype_id, movietype_label
    FROM
        movietype
    ORDER BY
        movietype_label';
$result = mysql_query($query, $db) or die(mysql_error($db));

// populate the select options with the results
while ($row = mysql_fetch_assoc($result)) {
    foreach ($row as $value) {
        if ($row['movietype_id'] == $movie_type) {
            echo '<option value="' . $row['movietype_id'] .
                '" selected="selected">';
        } else {
            echo '<option value="' . $row['movietype_id'] . '">';
        }
        echo $row['movietype_label'] . '</option>';
```

```
        }
    }
?>
        </select></td>
    </tr><tr>
     <td>Movie Year</td>
     <td><select name="movie_year">
<?php
// populate the select options with years
for ($yr = date("Y"); $yr >= 1970; $yr--) {
    if ($yr == $movie_year) {
        echo '<option value="' . $yr . '" selected="selected">' . $yr .
            '</option>';
    } else {
        echo '<option value="' . $yr . '">' . $yr . '</option>';
    }
}
?>
        </select></td>
    </tr><tr>
     <td>Lead Actor</td>
     <td><select name="movie_leadactor">
<?php
// select actor records
$query = 'SELECT
        people_id, people_fullname
    FROM
        people
    WHERE
        people_isactor = 1
    ORDER BY
        people_fullname';
$result = mysql_query($query, $db) or die(mysql_error($db));

// populate the select options with the results
while ($row = mysql_fetch_assoc($result)) {
    foreach ($row as $value) {
        if ($row['people_id'] == $movie_leadactor) {
            echo '<option value="' . $row['people_id'] .
                '" selected="selected">';
        } else {
            echo '<option value="' . $row['people_id'] . '">';
        }
        echo $row['people_fullname'] . '</option>';
    }
}
?>
        </select></td>
    </tr><tr>
     <td>Director</td>
     <td><select name="movie_director">
<?php
// select director records
$query = 'SELECT
```

```
        people_id, people_fullname
    FROM
        people
    WHERE
        people_isdirector = 1
    ORDER BY
        people_fullname';
$result = mysql_query($query, $db) or die(mysql_error($db));

// populate the select options with the results
while ($row = mysql_fetch_assoc($result)) {
    foreach ($row as $value) {
        if ($row['people_id'] == $movie_director) {
            echo '<option value="' . $row['people_id'] .
                '" selected="selected">';
        } else {
            echo '<option value="' . $row['people_id'] . '">';
        }
        echo $row['people_fullname'] . '</option>';
    }
}
?>
    </select></td>
  </tr><tr>
    <td colspan="2" style="text-align: center;">
<?php
if ($_GET['action'] == 'edit') {
    echo '<input type="hidden" value="' . $_GET['id'] . '" name="movie_id" />';
}
?>
      <input type="submit" name="submit"
       value="<?php echo ucfirst($_GET['action']); ?>" />
    </td>
   </tr>
  </table>
 </form>
 </body>
</html>
```

2. Open the `commit.php` script and edit its content to match this new code:

```
<?php
$db = mysql_connect('localhost', 'bp6am', 'bp6ampass') or
    die ('Unable to connect. Check your connection parameters.');
mysql_select_db('moviesite', $db) or die(mysql_error($db));
?>
<html>
 <head>
  <title>Commit</title>
 </head>
 <body>
<?php
switch ($_GET['action']) {
```

```
case 'add':
    switch ($_GET['type']) {
    case 'movie':
        $query = 'INSERT INTO
            movie
                (movie_name, movie_year, movie_type, movie_leadactor,
                movie_director)
            VALUES
                ("' . $_POST['movie_name'] . '",
                 ' . $_POST['movie_year'] . ',
                 ' . $_POST['movie_type'] . ',
                 ' . $_POST['movie_leadactor'] . ',
                 ' . $_POST['movie_director'] . ')';
        break;
    }
    break;
case 'edit':
    switch ($_GET['type']) {
    case 'movie':
        $query = 'UPDATE movie SET
                movie_name = "' . $_POST['movie_name'] . '",
                movie_year = ' . $_POST['movie_year'] . ',
                movie_type = ' . $_POST['movie_type'] . ',
                movie_leadactor = ' . $_POST['movie_leadactor'] . ',
                movie_director = ' . $_POST['movie_director'] . '
            WHERE
                movie_id = ' . $_POST['movie_id'];
        break;
    }
    break;
}

if (isset($query)) {
    $result = mysql_query($query, $db) or die(mysql_error($db));
}
?>
  <p>Done!</p>
 </body>
</html>
```

3. Now open your browser and go to the admin.php page.

4. Try clicking the EDIT link next to the *Bruce Almighty* movie, change a few boxes and the movie name, and press the Edit button in the form, as shown in Figure 6-6.

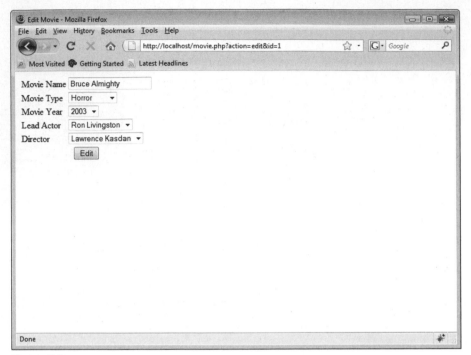

Figure 6-6

5. Edit the *Bruce Almighty* entry again with the procedure in step 4, and fix it so it's back to its own old self.

Now the EDIT links for movies actually do something!

You see that the script loads the stored values and allows you to edit the data easily. Play around a bit, and get a feel for the way it all works.

How It Works

The `commit.php` code is very much the same as what you saw already, with the exception of a new branch of code in the `switch` statement that handles updating the record in the database with the incoming values. But there is an interesting twist in `movie.php`, so let's look at it a bit more closely.

First, look at the `if` statement at the start of the script. You defined its branches on a query string parameter named `action`. If the action is `edit`, you query the database for a record corresponding to the id specified in the `id` query string parameter and set some variables. These variables are set to void if `action` is not `edit`.

```php
if ($_GET['action'] == 'edit') {
    //retrieve the record's information
    $query = 'SELECT
            movie_name, movie_type, movie_year, movie_leadactor, movie_
director
        FROM
            movie
        WHERE
            movie_id = ' . $_GET['id'];

    $result = mysql_query($query, $db) or die(mysql_error($db));
    extract(mysql_fetch_assoc($result));
} else {
    //set values to blank
    $movie_name = '';
    $movie_type = 0;
    $movie_year = date('Y');
    $movie_leadactor = 0;
    $movie_director = 0;
}
```

The variables set in the preceding code are used to set the default value of the form fields. Each field has a known value if you are editing a record, and has a blank value if you are creating a new record.

```php
<td><input type="text" name="movie_name"
 value="<?php echo $movie_name; ?>"/></td>
```

In this example, the movie_name field takes the $movie_name variable's content as its default value. This allows you to reload the form with data from the record to edit it.

Editing a text field is pretty straightforward, but setting the value in a list is another story. You can't just display the list and hope the user will reset the value to the original when he or she edits the record. You need to reload the whole list and make the previously set value appear as the default in the list, so the user can just skip it if he or she doesn't want to edit it.

How do you do this? The script holds the solution:

```php
<td>Movie Type</td>
<td><select name="movie_type">
<?php
// select the movie type information
$query = 'SELECT
        movietype_id, movietype_label
    FROM
        movietype
    ORDER BY
        movietype_label';

$result = mysql_query($query, $db) or die(mysql_error($db));

// populate the select options with the results
while ($row = mysql_fetch_assoc($result)) {
    foreach ($row as $value) {
```

```
             if ($row['movietype_id'] == $movie_type) {
                 echo '<option value="' . $row['movietype_id'] .
                     '" selected="selected">';
             } else {
                 echo '<option value="' . $row['movietype_id'] . '">';
             }
             echo $row['movietype_label'] . '</option>';
         }
     }
     ?>
       </select></td>
```

You load the list as you would have done if adding a record, but you compare the current value in the `foreach` iteration to the default value. If they are identical, add a simple `selected="selected"` flag to the option value. This sets the default list value to the current value in the table.

Summary

As you've learned in this chapter, there are three basic actions in modifying the content of a database:

❑   Insert

❑   Delete

❑   Update

These actions are performed by the database itself through SQL queries that PHP executes on MySQL. Read up on the SQL statements used in this chapter to get a good feel for how far they can take you, and at what level you feel confident using these commands.

And finally, always remember that testing your query alone in MySQL's command-line client or in a program such as MySQL Query Browser can save you a lot of time debugging it before you incorporate it into your PHP script.

Exercise

It may seem as if we're about to take it easy on you, with only one exercise, but don't be fooled! This single exercise covers a lot of what we mentioned in this chapter.

1.   Create the edit/delete code for the `people` table. Use the movie code as an example.

Manipulating and Creating Images with PHP

Now that you've been rocking and rolling with manipulating and displaying data using PHP, why stop there? Did you know that PHP can also manipulate and create images on the fly? It can, with a little help from the GD library. GD loosely stands for "Graphics Draw," but the industry generally refers to it in short as the GD library.

This chapter covers the following:

- ❑ Enabling your PHP setup to use the GD library.
- ❑ Allowing your users to upload their own images.
- ❑ Retrieving information about an image, such as size or file type.
- ❑ Creating a new image.
- ❑ Copying an image or a portion of an image.
- ❑ Creating thumbnails (smaller versions of images).
- ❑ Creating black-and-white versions of images.
- ❑ Adding watermarks and captions to images.

Working with the GD Library

GD is written in C++ and allows for the manipulation of certain image types. Because PHP can't automatically process images with its core built-in functions, you need to make sure you have the GD library and extension enabled. Fortunately, a bundled version comes with all recent versions of PHP. While we recommend you use the bundled version included with PHP, if for some reason you don't have the bundled version, then you can find an external version of the library at http://www.libgd.org/releases/.

What File Types Can I Use with GD & PHP?

GD itself can work with a multitude of image formats. When you use it from within PHP you can find out information about any GIF, JPG, PNG, SWF, SWC, PSD, TIFF, BMP, IFF, JP2, JPX, JB2, JPC, XBM, or WBMP image file. You can also create and manipulate images in GIF, JPG, PNG, WBMP, and XBM image formats. With the help of GD, you can use PHP to draw shapes such as squares, polygons, and ellipses, as well as overlay text.

> *Depending on your version of GD, GIF support may or may not be enabled. You can tell if GIF support is enabled with the use of the* `gd_info` *function described in the Try It Out section "Testing Your GD Installation," which follows.*

Enabling GD in PHP

If you are using a shared web host, there's a good chance they have already enabled GD on their installation of PHP. If you are running your own server, then you will probably need to enable it yourself. Enabling it yourself is not very difficult.

In Windows, first make sure the `php_gd.dll` file is in the ext folder within the PHP installation's directory. For example, if you installed PHP to `C:\PHP`, then the folder you need to look in is `C:\PHP\ext`. Then, find the following line in your `php.ini` file:

```
;extension=php_gd2.dll
```

Remove the leading semicolon to uncomment it. Save the change, and restart Apache for it to take effect.

In Linux, things are a bit trickier but still not overly difficult. You need to recompile PHP with the `--with-gd` configure option to enable GD. The steps necessary to compiling PHP on Linux are outlined in Appendix I. Once you have GD enabled, let's test it!

Try It Out   **Testing Your GD Installation**

You should first make sure everything is working properly, before you delve further into using GD:

1. Open your editor, and enter the following code:

```
<?php
echo '<pre>';
print_r(gd_info());
echo '</pre>';
?>
```

2. Save this file as `gdtest.php`.

3. Open the file in your web browser. You should see a page that looks like the one shown in Figure 7-1.

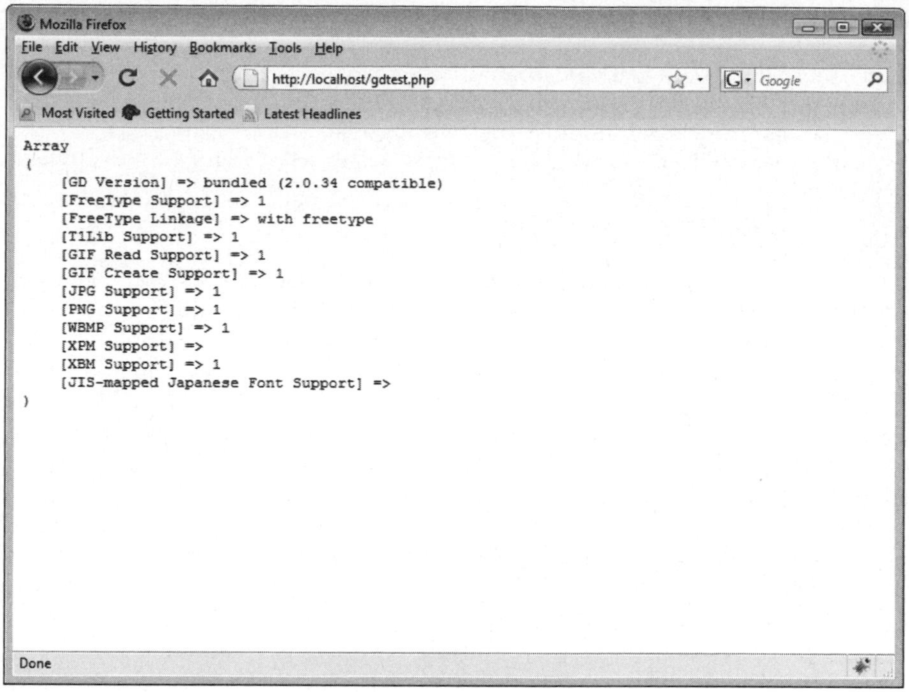

Figure 7-1

How It Works

The gd_info() function is quite useful because it tells you what version of GD is available to PHP and what capabilities it affords you. Its purpose is to put all the information about the GD version into an array that you can then view. This not only serves as a test to make sure that GD and PHP are playing nice with each other, but it lets you see what your capabilities and limitations are for using the GD functions in PHP. For the purposes of the examples in this chapter, you will need to have JPG, GIF, and PNG support. If your version of GD doesn't support any of these image types, you will need to upgrade. You can find full upgrade instructions and source files at www.libgd.org.

Now that you know that your GD library is working correctly, and which image types are supported in your installation, let's move along.

Allowing Users to Upload Images

Suppose you wanted to add a little spice to your movie review site, and you thought it would be a good idea to let users upload pictures of themselves dressed as their favorite movie actors in their favorite roles. In the rest of this chapter, you will create this look-alike photo gallery.

There is some debate about whether or not actual images can be efficiently stored in a database using the `blob` MySQL column type. Our personal preference is not to store the actual image, but to store only information about the image, and if needed, a link to the image. The images themselves are then stored in a regular directory in the filesystem. With that being said, let's create a table in your movie review database that will store the links to the images your users upload.

Try It Out   **Creating the Image Table**

First, you need to create a table that will hold information about your images. You are going to store basic information about each image, such as the user's name and the title of the image. Then, you need to design an HTML form to give your users the ability to submit an image for display. The form will collect some basic information about the image, and then accept the users' upload of the file directly from the comfort of their own browser, without the aid of any special file-transfer software.

1. Create a directory to hold the uploaded images. In this exercise, the images will be stored in a directory named `images`.

2. After the directory is in place, you can create a new table in the `moviesite` database. Open your text editor, and type the following:

```php
<?php
$db = mysql_connect('localhost', 'bp6am', 'bp6ampass') or
    die ('Unable to connect. Check your connection parameters.');
mysql_select_db('moviesite', $db) or die(mysql_error($db));

//create the images table
$query = 'CREATE TABLE images (
        image_id        INTEGER      NOT NULL AUTO_INCREMENT,
        image_caption   VARCHAR(255) NOT NULL,
        image_username  VARCHAR(255) NOT NULL,
        image_filename  VARCHAR(255) NOT NULL DEFAULT "",
        image_date      DATE         NOT NULL,
        PRIMARY KEY (image_id)
    )
    ENGINE=MyISAM';
mysql_query($query, $db) or die (mysql_error($db));

echo 'Images table successfully created.';
?>
```

3. Save this file as `db_ch07-1.php`. Open this file in your browser, and you should see the message "Images table successfully created."

4. Now open your editor, and type the following code to create the HTML form:

```html
<html>
 <head>
  <title>Upload your pic to our site!</title>
  <style type="text/css">
  <!--
td {vertical-align: top;}
```

```
   -->
  </style>
 </head>
 <body>
  <form action="check_image.php" method="post" enctype="multipart/form-data">
   <table>
    <tr>
     <td>Your Username</td>
     <td><input type="text" name="username" /></td>
    </tr>
     <td>Upload Image*</td>
     <td><input type="file" name="uploadfile" /></td>
    </tr><tr>
     <td colspan="2">
      <small><em>* Acceptable image formats include: GIF, JPG/JPEG and PNG.
       </em></small>
     </td>
    </tr><tr>
     <td>Image Caption<br/>
     </td>
     <td><input type="text" name="caption" /></td>
    </tr><tr>
     <td colspan="2" style="text-align: center">
      <input type="submit" name="submit" value="Upload"/>
     </td>
    </tr>
   </table>
  </form>
 </body>
</html>
```

5.   Save this file as `upload_image.html`.

6.   Create a new file in your editor by typing the following code:

```php
<?php
$db = mysql_connect('localhost', 'bp6am', 'bp6ampass') or
    die ('Unable to connect. Check your connection parameters.');
mysql_select_db('moviesite', $db) or die(mysql_error($db));

//change this path to match your images directory
$dir ='C:/Program Files/Apache Software Foundation/Apache2.2/htdocs/images';

//make sure the uploaded file transfer was successful
if ($_FILES['uploadfile']['error'] != UPLOAD_ERR_OK) {
    switch ($_FILES['uploadfile']['error']) {
    case UPLOAD_ERR_INI_SIZE:
        die('The uploaded file exceeds the upload_max_filesize directive ' .
            'in php.ini.');
        break;
    case UPLOAD_ERR_FORM_SIZE:
        die('The uploaded file exceeds the MAX_FILE_SIZE directive that ' .
            'was specified in the HTML form.');
        break;
```

```php
        case UPLOAD_ERR_PARTIAL:
            die('The uploaded file was only partially uploaded.');
            break;
        case UPLOAD_ERR_NO_FILE:
            die('No file was uploaded.');
            break;
        case UPLOAD_ERR_NO_TMP_DIR:
            die('The server is missing a temporary folder.');
            break;
        case UPLOAD_ERR_CANT_WRITE:
            die('The server failed to write the uploaded file to disk.');
            break;
        case UPLOAD_ERR_EXTENSION:
            die('File upload stopped by extension.');
            break;
    }
}

//get info about the image being uploaded
$image_caption = $_POST['caption'];
$image_username = $_POST['username'];
$image_date = date('Y-m-d');
list($width, $height, $type, $attr) =
    getimagesize($_FILES['uploadfile']['tmp_name']);

// make sure the uploaded file is really a supported image
switch ($type) {
case IMAGETYPE_GIF:
    $image = imagecreatefromgif($_FILES['uploadfile']['tmp_name']) or
        die('The file you uploaded was not a supported filetype.');
    $ext = '.gif';
    break;
case IMAGETYPE_JPEG:
    $image = imagecreatefromjpeg($_FILES['uploadfile']['tmp_name']) or
        die('The file you uploaded was not a supported filetype.');
    $ext = '.jpg';
    break;
case IMAGETYPE_PNG:
    $image = imagecreatefrompng($_FILES['uploadfile']['tmp_name']) or
        die('The file you uploaded was not a supported filetype.');
    $ext = '.png';
    break;
default:
    die('The file you uploaded was not a supported filetype.');
}

//insert information into image table
$query = 'INSERT INTO images
    (image_caption, image_username, image_date)
VALUES
```

```
            ("' . $image_caption . '", "' . $image_username . '", "' . $image_date .
            '")';
$result = mysql_query($query, $db) or die (mysql_error($db));

//retrieve the image_id that MySQL generated automatically when we inserted
//the new record
$last_id = mysql_insert_id();

//because the id is unique, we can use it as the image name as well to make
//sure we don't overwrite another image that already exists
$imagename = $last_id . $ext;

// update the image table now that the final filename is known.
$query = 'UPDATE images
    SET image_filename = "' . $imagename . '"
    WHERE image_id = ' . $last_id;
$result = mysql_query($query, $db) or die (mysql_error($db));

//save the image to its final destination
switch ($type) {
case IMAGETYPE_GIF:
    imagegif($image, $dir . '/' . $imagename);
    break;
case IMAGETYPE_JPEG:
    imagejpeg($image, $dir . '/' . $imagename, 100);
    break;
case IMAGETYPE_PNG:
    imagepng($image, $dir . '/' . $imagename);
    break;
}
imagedestroy($image);
?>
<html>
 <head>
  <title>Here is your pic!</title>
 </head>
 <body>
  <h1>So how does it feel to be famous?</h1>
  <p>Here is the picture you just uploaded to our servers:</p>
   <img src="images/<?php echo $imagename; ?>" style="float:left;">
  <table>
   <tr><td>Image Saved as: </td><td><?php echo $imagename; ?></td></tr>
   <tr><td>Image Type: </td><td><?php echo $ext; ?></td></tr>
   <tr><td>Height: </td><td><?php echo $height; ?></td></tr>
   <tr><td>Width: </td><td><?php echo $width; ?></td></tr>
   <tr><td>Upload Date: </td><td><?php echo $image_date; ?></td></tr>
  </table>
 </body>
</html>
```

7. Save this file as `check_image.php`.

8. Now open `upload_image.html` in your browser. The page will load, and your screen should look like Figure 7-2.

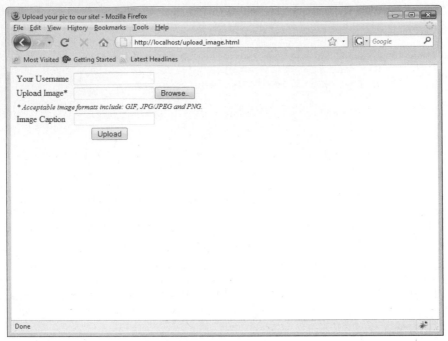

Figure 7-2

9. Upload your image. Your page should now look something like Figure 7-3.

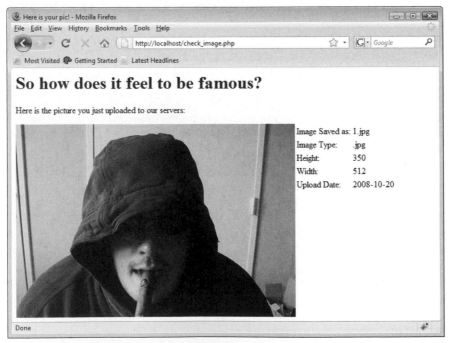

Figure 7-3

How It Works

In `upload_image.html`, you have given the HTML form the ability to accept files simply by doing two things. The first is using the `file` type `input` element. The input element now displays a Browse button next to the text area, which allows a visitor to surf his or her local disk and populate the field with the file's path. The second is specifying the form's `enctype` attribute to `multipart/form-data`. Providing this attribute is necessary for the file to transfer correctly.

```
<form action="check_image.php" method="post" enctype="multipart/form-data">
...
    <td>Upload Image*</td>
    <td><input type="file" name="uploadfile" /></td>
...
```

Keep in mind that the form element's method attribute should be set to `post` as well. Some browsers support the `put` method for transfers as well, and if you need to use this, then you'll want to read the PHP manual at `http://www.php.net/manual/en/features.file-upload.put-method.php`. Either way, image transfers will not work with `get`.

There is much more going on in `check_image.php`. A cursory overview shows that the script first connects to MySQL and selects the `moviesite` database. It makes sure a file was uploaded correctly and that it is one of the allowed file types. It then stores the picture's information into the database. Finally, the script saves a copy of the uploaded image to its permanent location in the filesystem and outputs a summary back to the visitor. If the process breaks down at any point for any reason (the user doesn't upload a file, or the file is an invalid file type for example), then PHP stops its processing and displays an error message.

You can use several different methodologies when dealing with images. For example, if you think you will have numerous files for each user, you can create a directory for each user and store each image within it. On the other hand, a single directory for storing the images might be a better choice if you are planning to allow only one image file to be uploaded. In this instance, you are keeping all the image files in one directory just for the sake of simplicity. Regardless of the structure you choose, you must apply some checks for duplicate filenames, so files that have already been uploaded aren't overwritten. In this case, you renamed each incoming file the same name as the unique ID assigned to it. This ensures that each file will have its own unique name and you won't have any problems if two users upload a file with the same name.

PHP stores information about recently uploaded files in the `$_FILES` array. The array has multiple levels, and the first key is the name you assigned to the form's image field. So, because the field's definition in `upload_image.html` was this:

```
<input type="file" name="uploadfile" />
```

then information about the file will be available in `createimages.php` in `$_FILES['uploadfile']`. This way, you can access the correct file if you have been allowing multiple images to be uploaded. For example, let's say you were working with a form that had the following:

```
<input type="file" name="uploadfile1" /><br/>
<input type="file" name="uploadfile2" /><br/>
<input type="file" name="uploadfile3" />
```

You would then have `$_FILES['uploadfile1']`, `$_FILES['uploadfile2']`, and `$_FILES['uploadfile3']`.

The next level of the $_FILES array is information about the uploaded file. Possible keys are:

- ❏ name: References the name of the file as it was on the user's local machine.
- ❏ type: Stores the file's MIME type as provided by the browser.
- ❏ size: The size of the uploaded file in bytes.
- ❏ tmp_name: The name of the uploaded file on the server.
- ❏ error: The error code associated with the file transfer.

The file is transferred from the visitor's computer up to the server and is stored as a temporary file. The temporary file is deleted after the receiving script finishes executing. This is very important to remember because if you do not somehow move the temporary file to a more permanent location in the filesystem in the processing script, then the uploaded file will be lost forever. The name key holds the name of the original file on the local machine. The tmp_name key holds the name of the temporary copy of the file on the server.

The type key holds the MIME type of the uploaded file, for example image/jpg or image/gif. But this value is set by the browser and may not be correct. So while it's provided to you for convenience, you must also realize that PHP doesn't check the value for accuracy, and you mustn't depend too much on it. A malicious user could fake the type value and cause you headaches.

The size key holds the size of the uploaded file. The file size is represented in bytes, so a 15K file would have a value here of 15,360.

The error key holds the error code associated with the file upload. It holds a numeric value, but PHP also has predefined constants to represent the value, and using these constants makes your script easier to read and manage. These constants are:

- ❏ UPLOAD_ERR_OK: The file uploaded successfully and there is no error.
- ❏ UPLOAD_ERR_INI: The size of the uploaded file exceeds the upload_max_filesize directive set in php.ini.
- ❏ UPLOAD_ERR_FORM_SIZE: The size of the uploaded file exceeded the MAX_FILE_SIZE directive set in the HTML form.
- ❏ UPLOAD_ERR_PARTIAL: The file was only partially uploaded and is not complete.
- ❏ UPLOAD_ERR_NO_FILE: The user did not upload a file.
- ❏ UPLOAD_ERR_NO_TMP_DIR: The temporary directory on the server to which the file is initially uploaded is missing.
- ❏ UPLOAD_ERR_CANT_WRITE: The temporary directory exists on the server, but PHP cannot write to it.
- ❏ UPLOAD_ERR_EXTENSION: The file upload was stopped by a PHP extension.

There are a handful of places where you can provide restrictions on file uploading, and they are related to UPLOAD_ERR_INI, UPLOAD_ERR_FORM_SIZE, and UPLOAD_ERR_EXTENSION.

The UPLOAD_ERR_INI value is returned when the size of the uploaded file exceeds the upload_max_filesize directive set in the php.ini configuration file. By default, this directive is set to 2 megabytes:

```
upload_max_filesize = 2M
```

Depending on the type and size of files your PHP application is designed to transfer, you may want to change this value, especially for pictures, as the resolution of digital cameras keep increasing. If you do change this, then you should also look at the post_max_size directive in php.ini. While upload_max_filesize limits the size of a file upload, post_max_size limits the size of an entire post transaction. An uploaded file is only part of the form data that gets posted by upload_image .html, so if upload_max_filesize is set larger than upload_post_max_size, then the upload transfer could still fail. Between these two directives, you can impose a hard limit on the maximum amount of data that can be received by PHP.

The UPLOAD_ERR_FORM_SIZE value is returned when the uploaded file exceeds the size set by a special hidden field in the HTML form. Here is the form from upload_image.html, with the added hidden field labeled MAX_FILE_SIZE:

```html
<form action="check_image.php" method="post" enctype="multipart/form-data">
  <table>
   <tr>
    <td>Your Username</td>
    <td><input type="text" name="username" /></td>
   </tr>
    <td>Upload Image*</td>
    <td>
     <input type="hidden" name="MAX_FILE_SIZE"  value="262144"/>
     <input type="file" name="uploadfile" />
    </td>
   </tr><tr>
    <td colspan="2">
     <small><em>* Acceptable image formats include: GIF, JPG/JPEG and PNG.
       </em></small>
    </td>
   </tr><tr>
    <td>Image Caption<br/>
    </td>
    <td><input type="text" name="caption" /></td>
   </tr><tr>
    <td colspan="2" style="text-align: center">
     <input type="submit" value="Submit"/>
    </td>
   </tr>
  </table>
</form>
```

MAX_FILE_SIZE should appear before the file input field. It does not set a hard limit, as the php.ini directives do, because someone could modify the field's value before posting the form's data, but it is still useful as a convenience. The idea is that the server can stop receiving the file once this limit is reached, and PHP can start formulating its response once it has decided the size is greater than what is allowed. The user doesn't have to wait for the entire file to upload just to see a "file is too large" error. I tend to avoid using MAX_FILE_SIZE because there is some debate over the ultimate usefulness of

`MAX_FILE_SIZE`, based on browser support and the fact that it only imposes a soft limit. But feel free to experiment with it and formulate your own usage preference.

After the script sees that the file upload was successful, the `getimagesize()` function is used to retrieve some information about it (we've always thought that perhaps the function would be better named `getimageinfo()` because it returns more than just the image's size, but we digress . . .). It returns an array with 5 elements:

- ❑ **0:** The image's width measured in pixels.
- ❑ **1:** The image's height measured in pixels.
- ❑ **2:** A numeric value identifying the file's image type.
- ❑ **3:** A string like `height="yyy" width="xxx"` that can be used to include in an HTML `img` tag.
- ❑ **4:** A string corresponding to the MIME type of the image.

While integers are efficient for computers to work with, they aren't always easier for human beings to work with or remember. So PHP offers predefined constants that match up with the numeric value identifying the file's image type returned by index 2. They are:

- ❑ `IMAGETYPE_GIF`: Returned for GIF images (MIME type `image/gif`).
- ❑ `IMAGETYPE_JPEG`: Returned for JPEG files (MIME type `image/jpeg`).
- ❑ `IMAGETYPE_PNG`: Returned for PNG files (MIME type `image/png`).
- ❑ `IMAGETYPE_SWF`: Returned for SWF files (MIME type `application/x-shockwave-flash`).
- ❑ `IMAGETYPE_PSD`: Returned for Photoshop format files (MIME type `image/psd`).
- ❑ `IMAGETYPE_BMP`: Returned for bitmap files (MIME type `image/bmp`).
- ❑ `IMAGETYPE_TIFF_II`: Returned for TIFF files using little-endian/Intel byte order encoding (MIME type `image/tiff`).
- ❑ `IMAGETYPE_TIFF_MM`: Returned for TIFF files using big-endian/Motorola byte order encoding (MIME type `image/tiff`).
- ❑ `IMAGETYPE_JPC`: Returned for JPEG2000 code stream files (MIME type `application/octet-stream`).
- ❑ `IMAGETYPE_JP2`: Returned for JPEG2000 JP2 files (MIME type `image/jp2`).
- ❑ `IMAGETYPE_JPX`: Returned for JPEG2000 JPX files (MIME type `application/octet-stream`).
- ❑ `IMAGETYPE_JB2`: Returned for JBIG2 bitmap files (MIME type `application/octet-stream`).
- ❑ `IMAGETYPE_SWC`: Returned for Flash Component Distribution files (MIME type `application/x-shockwave-flash`).
- ❑ `IMAGETYPE_IFF`: Returned for Amiga bitmap files (MIME type `image/iff`).
- ❑ `IMAGETYPE_WBMP`: Returned for Wireless Bitmap files (MIME type `image/vnd.wap.wbmp`).
- ❑ `IMAGETYPE_XBM`: Returned for X Bitmap graphic files (MIME type `image/xbm`).
- ❑ `IMAGETYPE_ICO`: Returned for icon files (MIME type `image/vnd.microsoft.icon`).

Note that WBMP is not the same type of file as a Windows bitmap (BMP). WBMP files are Wireless Bitmap files, used in Palm Pilots and other compact wireless devices. The PHP/GD combo does not provide for direct manipulation of BMP files. If you need to work with BMP files, you may want to take a look at the ImageCreateFromBMP and ImageBMP library classes at www.jpexs.com/php.html or use the imagick PECL extension at http://pecl.php.net/package/imagick.

After the script determines the type of image that was uploaded, it reads the file into memory. The `imagecreatefrom*()` function opens an image file and returns a resource handle so you can work with it. Remember that the file is first uploaded to a temporary location, and it is then your responsibility as a programmer to move it to a more permanent location before it is lost forever. Typically, you would use the `move_uploaded_file()` for this. The first parameter to `move_uploaded_files()` is the temporary filename, and the second is the permanent location, like this:

```
move_uploaded_file($_FILES['upload_file']['tmp_name'],
    $dir . '/' . $_FILES['upload_file']['name']);
```

And in most cases this is fine. However, as an extra precaution, we have chosen to load the image file into memory using the correct function and then rewrite it out to a new file at the target location in the `images` directory. This acts as an extra check to make sure the uploaded image is a valid image file of the type it's claimed to be, because the `imagecreatefrom*()` function will fail if the format is invalid.

At the same time, you assign the file extension based on the file type, since you will need to have that information available when you resave your file. If the uploaded file doesn't match any of your cases, the default is applied. The default action is that the reader will see the "The file you uploaded was not a supported filetype." message. This all helps you to filter out unacceptable file types, non-image files, or corrupted files that have been uploaded.

Assuming everything is going smoothly, you can then insert the information in the table, with the following lines:

```
//insert info into image table
$query = 'INSERT INTO images
    (image_caption, image_username, image_date)
VALUES
    ("' . $image_caption . '", "' . $image_username . '", "'
. $image_date . '")';

$result = mysql_query($query, $db) or die (mysql_error($db));

//retrieve the image_id that MySQL generated automatically when we inserted
//the new record
$last_id = mysql_insert_id();

//because the id is unique, we can use it as the image name as well to make
//sure we don't overwrite another image that already exists
$imagename = $last_id . $ext;

// update the image table now that the final filename is known.
$query = 'UPDATE images
    SET image_filename = "' . $imagename . '"
    WHERE image_id = ' . $last_id;

$result = mysql_query($query, $db) or die (mysql_error($db));
```

Initially, you do not know what the name of the file will be as it is saved on disk, because the filename is based on the image record's primary key, which is automatically assigned by MySQL. Therefore, the first query inserts the information that you do know — the image's caption, the user's username, and the current date. Once the record is created, you use the `mysql_insert_id()` function to find out what value MySQL assigned as the key. That knowledge then allows you to update the record and set the image's filename correctly.

You then write the image file to the images directory, with the following code:

```
// save the image to its final destination
switch ($type) {
case IMAGETYPE_GIF:
    imagegif($image, $dir . '/' . $imagename);
    break;
case IMAGETYPE_JPEG:
    imagegif($image, $dir . '/' . $imagename, 100);
    break;
case IMAGETYPE_PNG:
    imagepng($image, $dir . '/' . $imagename);
    break;
}
imagedestroy($image);
```

Here, each of the functions `imagegif()`, `imagejpeg()`, and `imagepng()` writes the image data accessible by the `$image` resource to the specified filename. The `imagejpeg()` function also accepts an optional third parameter, which affects the image quality of the file because of compression. A value of 100 means you desire 100% quality with minimal compression, whereas 0 would give the least visual quality, but the highest image compression would be used, for a smaller file size on disk.

The `imagedestroy()` function simply takes the `$image` resource and frees the memory used to load the original image. PHP will automatically clean up used memory and open resources when the execution of your script has completed, but still it's considered a good practice to explicitly write this code in yourself.

Finally, in the HTML portion of the script, you simply spit the picture back out to the user, so he or she can see that the image was successfully uploaded.

Converting Image File Types

Is issuing the second query to the database to update the filename really necessary? Not really, but we set up the initial database code and PHP script to bring us to this point. PHP can use GD to convert image types from one format to another quite easily. If you were to allow image uploads in GIF, JPEG, or PNG formats but save them to the images directory as JPEG images, then you would no longer need the `filename` column in the database table, and you could streamline the `check_image.php` script.

Try It Out   **Streamlining the Process**

Let's make a few changes that not only highlight how to convert between image types but also will streamline our code.

1.   Open your text editor, and enter the following code:

```php
<?php
$db = mysql_connect('localhost', 'bp6am', 'bp6ampass') or
    die ('Unable to connect. Check your connection parameters.');
mysql_select_db('moviesite', $db) or die(mysql_error($db));

//create the images table
$query = 'ALTER TABLE images DROP COLUMN image_filename';

mysql_query($query, $db) or die (mysql_error($db));

echo 'Images table successfully updated.';
?>
```

2.   Save your work as db_ch07-2.php. Open the file in a web browser now, and you see a message that the images table was successfully modified.

3.   Make the following changes to the code in check_image.php (as highlighted):

```php
<?php
$db = mysql_connect('localhost', 'bp6am', 'bp6ampass') or
    die ('Unable to connect. Check your connection parameters.');
mysql_select_db('moviesite', $db) or die(mysql_error($db));

//change this path to match your images directory
$dir ='C:/Program Files/Apache Software Foundation/Apache2.2/htdocs/images';

//make sure the uploaded file transfer was successful
if ($_FILES['uploadfile']['error'] != UPLOAD_ERR_OK) {
    switch ($_FILES['uploadfile']['error']) {
    case UPLOAD_ERR_INI_SIZE:
        die('The uploaded file exceeds the upload_max_filesize directive ' .
            'in php.ini.');
        break;
    case UPLOAD_ERR_FORM_SIZE:
        die('The uploaded file exceeds the MAX_FILE_SIZE directive that ' .
            'was specified in the HTML form.');
        break;
    case UPLOAD_ERR_PARTIAL:
        die('The uploaded file was only partially uploaded.');
        break;
    case UPLOAD_ERR_NO_FILE:
        die('No file was uploaded.');
        break;
    case UPLOAD_ERR_NO_TMP_DIR:
        die('The server is missing a temporary folder.');
        break;
```

```
        case UPLOAD_ERR_CANT_WRITE:
            die('The server failed to write the uploaded file to disk.');
            break;
        case UPLOAD_ERR_EXTENSION:
            die('File upload stopped by extension.');
            break;
    }
}

//get info about the image being uploaded
$image_caption = $_POST['caption'];
$image_username = $_POST['username'];
$image_date = date('Y-m-d');
list($width, $height, $type, $attr) =
    getimagesize($_FILES['uploadfile']['tmp_name']);

// make sure the uploaded file is really a supported image
```

```
// delete these lines
switch ($type) {
case IMAGETYPE_GIF:
    $image = imagecreatefromgif($_FILES['uploadfile']['tmp_name']) or
        die('The file you uploaded was not a supported filetype.');
    $ext = '.gif';
    break;
case IMAGETYPE_JPEG:
    $image = imagecreatefromjpeg($_FILES['uploadfile']['tmp_name']) or
        die('The file you uploaded was not a supported filetype.');
    $ext = '.jpg';
    break;
case IMAGETYPE_PNG:
    $image = imagecreatefrompng($_FILES['uploadfile']['tmp_name']) or
        die('The file you uploaded was not a supported filetype.');
    $ext = '.png';
    break;
default:
    die('The file you uploaded was not a supported filetype.');
}
// end deleted lines
```

```
$error = 'The file you uploaded was not a supported filetype.';
switch ($type) {
case IMAGETYPE_GIF:
    $image = imagecreatefromgif($_FILES['uploadfile']['tmp_name']) or
        die($error);
    break;
case IMAGETYPE_JPEG:
    $image = imagecreatefromjpeg($_FILES['uploadfile']['tmp_name']) or
        die($error);
    break;
case IMAGETYPE_PNG:
    $image = imagecreatefrompng($_FILES['uploadfile']['tmp_name']) or
```

```
            die($error);
        break;
default:
        die($error);
    }

//insert information into image table
$query = 'INSERT INTO images
        (image_caption, image_username, image_date)
VALUES
        ("' . $image_caption . '", "' . $image_username . '", "' . $image_date .
        '")';
$result = mysql_query($query, $db) or die (mysql_error($db));

//retrieve the image_id that MySQL generated automatically when we inserted
//the new record
$last_id = mysql_insert_id();

// delete these lines

//because the id is unique, we can use it as the image name as well to make
//sure we don't overwrite another image that already exists
$imagename = $last_id . $ext;

// update the image table now that the final filename is known.
$query = 'UPDATE images
        SET image_filename = "' $imagename . '"
        WHERE image_id = ' . $last_id;
$result = mysql_query($query, $db) or die (mysql_error($db));

//save the image to its final destination
switch ($type) {
case IMAGETYPE_GIF:
        imagegif($image, $dir . '/' . $imagename);
        break;
case IMAGETYPE_JPEG:
        imagejpeg($image, $dir . '/' . $imagename, 100);
        break;
case IMAGETYPE_PNG:
        imagepng($image, $dir . '/' . $imagename);
        break;
}
// end of deleted lines

// save the image to its final destination
$imagename = $last_id . '.jpg';
imagejpeg($image, $dir . '/' . $imagename);
imagedestroy($image);
?>
<html>
 <head>
  <title>Here is your pic!</title>
```

```
  </head>
  <body>
    <h1>So how does it feel to be famous?</h1>
    <p>Here is the picture you just uploaded to our servers:</p>
     <img src="images/<?php echo $imagename; ?>" style="float:left;">
    <table>
      <tr><td>Image Saved as: </td><td><?php echo $imagename; ?></td></tr>
  <!-- delete this line
      <tr><td>Image Type: </td><td><?php echo $ext; ?></td></tr>
  -->
      <tr><td>Height: </td><td><?php echo $height; ?></td></tr>
      <tr><td>Width: </td><td><?php echo $width; ?></td></tr>
      <tr><td>Upload Date: </td><td><?php echo $image_date; ?></td></tr>
    </table>
  </body>
</html>
```

4. If you save the file, and then load `upload_image.html` in your browser and upload your picture, you will notice you get basically the same results, even though the processing has been streamlined.

How It Works

We no longer need to distinguish the file type once the image has been loaded into memory with the appropriate `createimagefrom*()` function, so the `switch` block that opens the file and stores the extension to `$ext` has been rewritten. And later, because the `imagegif()` and `imagepng()` functions take the image in memory at `$image` and save it out as a GIF or PNG image respectively, that `switch` block is deleted. The image is saved to the `images` directory as a JPEG, using the `imagejpeg()` function, regardless of what format the uploaded image was in originally. Now you can reference all the images later on in your application, in the same way, no matter what valid format was uploaded.

Special Effects

Now that you've got a directory full of images, what comes next? Playing with them, of course! What if you wanted to allow your users to make their images black and white, blur the image, or apply some other effect? Let's add that option to your `showimage` page, so your users can choose whether or not they want to see their image in grayscale. You will be using the `imagefilter()` function, which can do many things, only one of which is to convert the image to grayscale.

This function can also make a negative of your image, alter the brightness or contrast of your image, and emboss, blur, smooth, detect edges within, and colorize your image. Whew! It's a pretty powerful function, and one you want to remember. You can find complete syntax for using this function and the filter types at `www.php.net/imagefilter`.

Using Filters

In this exercise, you'll add the ability for users to apply a filter to their images, using the
`imagefilter()` function to your site. You'll give users the option to show their image as a negative
image, in black and white, blurred, and embossed.

1. Open `check_image.php`, and make the following highlighted changes:

```
<?php
$db = mysql_connect('localhost', 'bp6am', 'bp6ampass') or
    die ('Unable to connect. Check your connection parameters.');
mysql_select_db('moviesite', $db) or die(mysql_error($db));

//change this path to match your images directory
$dir ='C:/Program Files/Apache Software Foundation/Apache2.2/htdocs/images';

// handle the uploaded image
if ($_POST['submit'] == 'Upload') {

    //make sure the uploaded file transfer was successful
    if ($_FILES['uploadfile']['error'] != UPLOAD_ERR_OK) {
        switch ($_FILES['uploadfile']['error']) {
        case UPLOAD_ERR_INI_SIZE:
            die('The uploaded file exceeds the upload_max_filesize directive ' .
                'in php.ini.');
            break;
        case UPLOAD_ERR_FORM_SIZE:
            die('The uploaded file exceeds the MAX_FILE_SIZE directive that ' .
                'was specified in the HTML form.');
            break;
        case UPLOAD_ERR_PARTIAL:
            die('The uploaded file was only partially uploaded.');
            break;
        case UPLOAD_ERR_NO_FILE:
            die('No file was uploaded.');
            break;
        case UPLOAD_ERR_NO_TMP_DIR:
            die('The server is missing a temporary folder.');
            break;
        case UPLOAD_ERR_CANT_WRITE:
            die('The server failed to write the uploaded file to disk.');
            break;
        case UPLOAD_ERR_EXTENSION:
            die('File upload stopped by extension.');
            break;
        }
    }

    //get info about the image being uploaded
    $image_caption = $_POST['caption'];
    $image_username = $_POST['username'];
    $image_date = date('Y-m-d');
    list($width, $height, $type, $attr) =
```

```php
        getimagesize($_FILES['uploadfile']['tmp_name']);

    // make sure the uploaded file is really a supported image
    $error = 'The file you uploaded was not a supported filetype.';
    switch ($type) {
    case IMAGETYPE_GIF:
        $image = imagecreatefromgif($_FILES['uploadfile']['tmp_name']) or
            die($error);
        break;
    case IMAGETYPE_JPEG:
        $image = imagecreatefromjpeg($_FILES['uploadfile']['tmp_name']) or
            die($error);
        break;
    case IMAGETYPE_PNG:
        $image = imagecreatefrompng($_FILES['uploadfile']['tmp_name']) or
            die($error);
        break;
    default:
        die($error);
    }

    //insert information into image table
    $query = 'INSERT INTO images
        (image_caption, image_username, image_date)
    VALUES
        ("' . $image_caption . '", "' . $image_username . '", "' . $image_date .
        '")';
    $result = mysql_query($query, $db) or die (mysql_error($db));

    //retrieve the image_id that MySQL generated automatically when we inserted
    //the new record
    $last_id = mysql_insert_id();

    // delete these lines

    // save the image to its final destination
    $imagename = $last_id . '.jpg';
    imagejpeg($image, $dir . '/' . $imagename);
    imagedestroy($image);
    // end deleted lines

    $image_id = $last_id;
    imagejpeg($image, $dir . '/' . $image_id  . '.jpg');
    imagedestroy($image);
} else {
    // retrieve image information
    $query = 'SELECT
        image_id, image_caption, image_username, image_date
    FROM
        images
    WHERE
        image_id = ' . $_POST['id'];
    $result = mysql_query($query, $db) or die (mysql_error($db));
    extract(mysql_fetch_assoc($result));

    list($width, $height, $type, $attr) = getimagesize($dir . '/' .
```

```php
$image_id .
        '.jpg');
}

if ($_POST['submit'] == 'Save') {
    // make sure the requested image is valid
    if (isset($_POST['id']) && ctype_digit($_POST['id']) &&
        file_exists($dir . '/' . $_POST['id'] . '.jpg')) {
        $image = imagecreatefromjpeg($dir . '/' . $_POST['id'] . '.jpg');
    } else {
        die('invalid image specified');
    }

    // apply the filter
    $effect = (isset($_POST['effect'])) ? $_POST['effect'] : -1;
    switch ($effect) {
    case IMG_FILTER_NEGATE:
        imagefilter($image, IMG_FILTER_NEGATE);
        break;
    case IMG_FILTER_GRAYSCALE:
        imagefilter($image, IMG_FILTER_GRAYSCALE);
        break;
    case IMG_FILTER_EMBOSS:
        imagefilter($image, IMG_FILTER_EMBOSS);
        break;
    case IMG_FILTER_GAUSSIAN_BLUR:
        imagefilter($image, IMG_FILTER_GAUSSIAN_BLUR);
        break;
    }

    // save the image with the filter applied
    imagejpeg($image, $dir . '/' . $_POST['id'] . '.jpg', 100);
?>
<html>
 <head>
  <title>Here is your pic!</title>
 </head>
 <body>
  <h1>Your image has been saved!</h1>
  <img src="images/<?php echo $_POST['id']; ?>.jpg" />
 </body>
</html>
<?php
} else {
?>
<html>
 <head>
  <title>Here is your pic!</title>
 </head>
 <body>
  <h1>So how does it feel to be famous?</h1>
  <p>Here is the picture you just uploaded to our servers:</p>
<!-- delete this line
    <img src="images/<?php echo $imagename; ?>" style="float:left;">
```

```
    -->

<?php
    if ($_POST['submit'] == 'Upload') {
        $imagename = 'images/' . $image_id . '.jpg';
    }
    else {
        $imagename = 'image_effect.php?id=' . $image_id . '&e=' .
            $_POST['effect'];
    }
?>
    <img src="<?php echo $imagename; ?>" style="float:left;">
  <table>
<!-- delete this line
    <tr><td>Image Saved as: </td><td><?php echo $imagename; ?></td></tr>
-->
    <tr><td>Image Saved as: </td><td><?php echo $image_id . '.jpg';
?></td></tr>

    <tr><td>Height: </td><td><?php echo $height; ?></td></tr>
    <tr><td>Width: </td><td><?php echo $width; ?></td></tr>
    <tr><td>Upload Date: </td><td><?php echo $image_date; ?></td></tr>
  </table>
  <p>You may apply a special effect to your image from the list of options
below.
Note: saving an image with any of the filters applied  <em>cannot be
undone</em>.</p>
  <form action="<?php echo $_SERVER['PHP_SELF']; ?>" method="post">
  <div>
    <input type="hidden" name="id" value="<?php echo $image_id;?>"/>
    <select name="effect">
     <option value="-1">None</option>
<?php
    echo '<option value="' . IMG_FILTER_GRAYSCALE . '"';
    if (isset($_POST['effect']) && $_POST['effect'] == IMG_FILTER_GRAYSCALE) {
        echo ' selected="selected"';
    }
    echo '>Black and White</option>';

    echo '<option value="' . IMG_FILTER_GAUSSIAN_BLUR . '"';
    if (isset($_POST['effect']) && $_POST['effect'] ==
        IMG_FILTER_GAUSSIAN_BLUR) {
        echo ' selected="selected"';
    }
    echo '>Blur</option>';

    echo '<option value="' . IMG_FILTER_EMBOSS . '"';
    if (isset($_POST['effect']) && $_POST['effect'] == IMG_FILTER_EMBOSS) {
        echo ' selected="selected"';
    }
    echo '>Emboss</option>';

    echo '<option value="' . IMG_FILTER_NEGATE . '"';
    if (isset($_POST['effect']) && $_POST['effect'] == IMG_FILTER_NEGATE) {
        echo ' selected="selected"';
```

```
        }
        echo '>Negative</option>';
    ?>
        </select>
        <input type="submit" value="Preview" name="submit" />
        <br/><br/>
        <input type="submit" value="Save" name="submit" />
    </div>
  </form>
 </body>
</html>
<?php
}
?>
```

2.   Next, you want to create a new file that will show the image with the appropriate filter
      applied to it. Open your browser, and type the following, saving it as `image_effect.php`:

```php
<?php
//change this path to match your images directory
$dir ='C:/Program Files/Apache Software Foundation/Apache2.2/htdocs/images';

// make sure the requested image is valid
if (isset($_GET['id']) && ctype_digit($_GET['id']) && file_exists($dir . '/'.
    $_GET['id'] . '.jpg')) {
    $image = imagecreatefromjpeg($dir . '/' . $_GET['id'] . '.jpg');
} else {
    die('invalid image specified');
}

// apply the filter
$effect = (isset($_GET['e'])) ? $_GET['e'] : -1;
switch ($effect) {
case IMG_FILTER_NEGATE:
    imagefilter($image, IMG_FILTER_NEGATE);
    break;
case IMG_FILTER_GRAYSCALE:
    imagefilter($image, IMG_FILTER_GRAYSCALE);
    break;
case IMG_FILTER_EMBOSS:
    imagefilter($image, IMG_FILTER_EMBOSS);
    break;
case IMG_FILTER_GAUSSIAN_BLUR:
    imagefilter($image, IMG_FILTER_GAUSSIAN_BLUR);
    break;
}

// show the image
header('Content-Type: image/jpeg');
imagejpeg($image, '', 100);
?>
```

3. Now, try this out. Go to `upload_image.html` and upload another image. Your page will now look something like Figure 7-4.

Figure 7-4

4. Select a filter from the drop-down list, and press Preview. Your page will now resemble Figure 7-5.

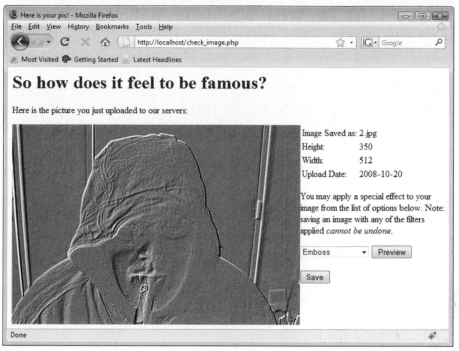

Figure 7-5

5. Click the Save button, and your page will resemble Figure 7-6.

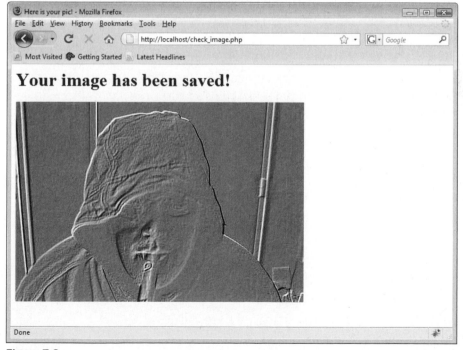

Figure 7-6

How It Works

The new file and the changes you made in check_image.php allow a user to apply a filter to his or her image once it's been uploaded, and to preview the effect before saving it permanently. The code in check_image.php has been restructured with a handful of if statements that check the value of $_POST['submit'] and act accordingly, to facilitate this flow. The new check_effect.php script provides the mechanism by which the filters can be previewed without losing the original image.

The magic happens with check_effect.php, which is referenced from check_image.php to show the filter's preview. Its call is written as an img tag, and the image's id and the selected filter are passed in the file's query string.

```php
<?php
if ($_POST['submit'] == 'Upload') {
    $imagename = 'images/' . $image_id  . '.jpg';
} else {
    $imagename = 'image_effect.php?id=' . $image_id  . '&e=' .
        $_POST['effect'];
}
?>
<img src="<?php echo $imagename; ?>" style="float:left;">
```

The image is read into memory, and the appropriate filter is applied using the imagefilter() function within the following switch code:

```php
switch ($effect) {
case IMG_FILTER_NEGATE:
    imagefilter($image, IMG_FILTER_NEGATE);
    break;
case IMG_FILTER_GRAYSCALE:
    imagefilter($image, IMG_FILTER_GRAYSCALE);
    break;
case IMG_FILTER_EMBOSS:
    imagefilter($image, IMG_FILTER_EMBOSS);
    break;
case IMG_FILTER_GAUSSIAN_BLUR:
    imagefilter($image, IMG_FILTER_GAUSSIAN_BLUR);
    break;
}
```

After the function applies the filter against the image in memory, the picture is then flushed out to the browser. It is important that the second parameter to the imagejpeg() function in check_effect.php be blank so the image isn't saved to disk, or else the original image might be overwritten. This will let the user test other effects before saving the one he or she likes best.

```php
header('Content-Type: image/jpeg');
imagejpeg($image, '', 100);
```

A similar course of action is followed in `check_image.php`, though at this point you do want the original image to be overwritten, after the changes have been approved. Here the filename is provided to `imagejpeg()`.

```
imagejpeg($image, $dir . '/' . $_POST['id'] . '.jpg', 100);
```

The user is presented with four different effects in the script, but this is only a subset of built-in effects `imagefilter()` knows about. In fact, there are 11 different filters available, defined by these predefined constants:

- ❑ `IMG_FILTER_BRIGHTNESS` changes the brightness of the image.

- ❑ `IMG_FILTER_COLORIZE` colorizes the image.

- ❑ `IMG_FILTER_CONTRAST` changes the contrast of the image.

- ❑ `IMG_FILTER_EDGEDETECT` sharpens the edges found in the image.

- ❑ `IMG_FILTER_EMBOSS` embosses the image.

- ❑ `IMG_FILTER_GAUSSIAN_BLUR` blurs the image using the Gaussian blur method.

- ❑ `IMG_FILTER_GRAYSCALE` converts the image into grayscale.

- ❑ `IMG_FILTER_MEAN_REMOVAL` uses mean removal to achieve a patchy effect.

- ❑ `IMG_FILTER_NEGATE` reverses all colors in the image.

- ❑ `IMG_FILTER_SELECTIVE_BLUR` blurs the image using the selective blur method.

- ❑ `IMG_FILTER_SMOOTH` smooths the image.

Some of these filters will require third and sometimes even fourth, fifth, and sixth parameters to be passed to `imagefilter()`, specifically `IMG_FILTER_BRIGHTNESS`, `IMG_FILTER_COLORIZE`, `IMG_FILTER_CONTRAST`, and `IMG_FILTER_SMOOTH`. The extra argument provides additional information for the filter to be applied correctly. Specifically, `IMG_FILTER_BRIGHTNESS` uses an argument to set the desired level of brightness, `IMG_FILTER_CONTRAST` uses it to set the desired level of contrast, and `IMG_FILTER_SMOOTH` uses it to set the desired level of smoothing. This value can range from 0 to 100. `IMG_FILTER_BRIGHTNESS` and `IMG_FILTER_COLORIZE` may even be given a negative value, depending on the direction of the adjustment.

`IMG_FILTER_COLORIZE` uses the extra information to specify the color applied to the image. Each argument is the color's component in the order of red, blue, green, and an alpha channel. The range for each color component is 0 to 255, or 0x00 to 0xFF if you are using hexadecimal notation, and 0 to 100 for the alpha channel.

These basic filters can be combined to achieve different effects. For example, you see that `IMG_FILTER_GRAYSCALE` and `IMG_FILTER_COLORIZE` allow you to adjust color information in an image, but what if you wanted to apply a sepia tone? Such an effect simulates the faded brownish color of some early photographs, but there is no prebuilt feature available with the GD extension. You can first strip out the unnecessary color information and then colorize your image with a brownish/ tan color:

```php
<?php
//change this path to match your images directory
$dir ='C:/Program Files/Apache Software Foundation/Apache2.2/htdocs/images';

$image = imagecreatefromjpeg($dir . '/1.jpg');

// strip the color information so it is black and white
imagefilter($image, IMG_FILTER_GRAYSCALE);

// apply a brownish hue
imagefilter($image, IMG_FILTER_COLORIZE, 0xFF, 0xB9, 0x80, 30);

// output the image
header('Content-Type: image/jpeg');
imagejpeg($image, '', 100);
?>
```

Adding Captions

A special group of functions allows you to add captions or a copyright notice or other text to your images. PHP/GD is relatively advanced in allowing you to control the size and type of font that is used, even allowing you to load your own font on demand. You're absolutely encouraged to experiment with all the cool font functions available to you, but we will try to keep it simple here to get you started.

Try It Out   Embedding Text in Images

You will be modifying the `check_image.php` and `check_effect.php` files to show captions along with the images, but these will be minor changes.

1. Open the `check_image.php` file, and make the following highlighted changes:

```php
<?php
//connect to MySQL
$db = mysql_connect('localhost', 'bp6am', 'bp6ampass') or
    die ('Unable to connect. Check your connection parameters.');
mysql_select_db('moviesite', $db) or die(mysql_error($db));

//change this path to match your images directory
$dir ='C:/Program Files/Apache Software Foundation/Apache2.2/htdocs/images';

//change this path to match your fonts directory and the desired font
putenv('GDFONTPATH=' . 'C:/Windows/Fonts');
```

202

```
$font = 'arial';

// handle the uploaded image
if ($_POST['submit'] == 'Upload') {

    //make sure the uploaded file transfer was successful
    if ($_FILES['uploadfile']['error'] != UPLOAD_ERR_OK)
    {
        switch ($_FILES['uploadfile']['error']) {
        case UPLOAD_ERR_INI_SIZE:
            die('The uploaded file exceeds the upload_max_filesize directive ' .
                'in php.ini.');
            break;
        case UPLOAD_ERR_FORM_SIZE:
            die('The uploaded file exceeds the MAX_FILE_SIZE directive that ' .
                'was specified in the HTML form.');
            break;
        case UPLOAD_ERR_PARTIAL:
            die('The uploaded file was only partially uploaded.');
            break;
        case UPLOAD_ERR_NO_FILE:
            die('No file was uploaded.');
            break;
        case UPLOAD_ERR_NO_TMP_DIR:
            die('The server is missing a temporary folder.');
            break;
        case UPLOAD_ERR_CANT_WRITE:
            die('The server failed to write the uploaded file to disk.');
            break;
        case UPLOAD_ERR_EXTENSION:
            die('File upload stopped by extension.');
            break;
        }
    }

    //get info about the image being uploaded
    $image_caption = $_POST['caption'];
    $image_username = $_POST['username'];
    $image_date = @date('Y-m-d');
    list($width, $height, $type, $attr) =
        getimagesize($_FILES['uploadfile']['tmp_name']);

    // make sure the uploaded file is really a supported image
    $error = 'The file you uploaded was not a supported filetype.';
    switch ($type) {
    case IMAGETYPE_GIF:
        $image = imagecreatefromgif($_FILES['uploadfile']['tmp_name']) or
            die($error);
        break;
    case IMAGETYPE_JPEG:
        $image = imagecreatefromjpeg($_FILES['uploadfile']['tmp_name']) or
            die($error);
        break;
    case IMAGETYPE_PNG:
```

```
        $image = imagecreatefrompng($_FILES['uploadfile']['tmp_name']) or
            die($error);
        break;
    default:
        die($error);
    }

    //insert information into image table
    $query = 'INSERT INTO images
        (image_caption, image_username, image_date)
    VALUES
        ("' . $image_caption . '", "' . $image_username . '", "'
. $image_date .'")';

    $result = mysql_query($query, $db) or die (mysql_error($db));

    //retrieve the image_id that MySQL generated automatically when we
inserted
    //the new record
    $last_id = mysql_insert_id();

    // save the image to its final destination
    $image_id = $last_id;
    imagejpeg($image, $dir . '/' . $image_id  . '.jpg');
    imagedestroy($image);

} else {
    // retrieve image information
    $query = 'SELECT
        image_id, image_caption, image_username, image_date
    FROM
        images
    WHERE
        image_id = ' . $_POST['id'];
    $result = mysql_query($query, $db) or die (mysql_error($db));
    extract(mysql_fetch_assoc($result));

    list($width, $height, $type, $attr) = getimagesize($dir . '/' . $image_id .
        '.jpg');
}

if ($_POST['submit'] == 'Save') {
    // make sure the requested image is valid
    if (isset($_POST['id']) && ctype_digit($_POST['id']) &&
        file_exists($dir . '/' . $_POST['id'] . '.jpg')) {
        $image = imagecreatefromjpeg($dir . '/' . $_POST['id'] . '.jpg');
    } else {
        die('invalid image specified');
    }

    // apply the filter
    $effect = (isset($_POST['effect'])) ? $_POST['effect'] : -1;
    switch ($effect) {
```

```php
        case IMG_FILTER_NEGATE:
            imagefilter($image, IMG_FILTER_NEGATE);
            break;
        case IMG_FILTER_GRAYSCALE:
            imagefilter($image, IMG_FILTER_GRAYSCALE);
            break;
        case IMG_FILTER_EMBOSS:
            imagefilter($image, IMG_FILTER_EMBOSS);
            break;
        case IMG_FILTER_GAUSSIAN_BLUR:
            imagefilter($image, IMG_FILTER_GAUSSIAN_BLUR);
            break;
    }

    // add the caption if requested
    if (isset($_POST['emb_caption'])) {
        imagettftext($image, 12, 0, 20, 20, 0, $font, $image_caption);
    }

    // save the image with the filter applied
    imagejpeg($image, $dir . '/' . $_POST['id'] . '.jpg', 100);
?>
<html>
 <head>
  <title>Here is your pic!</title>
 </head>
 <body>
  <h1>Your image has been saved!</h1>
  <img src="images/<?php echo $_POST['id']; ?>.jpg" />
 </body>
</html>
<?php
} else {
?>
<html>
 <head>
  <title>Here is your pic!</title>
 </head>
 <body>
  <h1>So how does it feel to be famous?</h1>
  <p>Here is the picture you just uploaded to our servers:</p>
<?php
    if ($_POST['submit'] == 'Upload') {
        $imagename = 'images/' . $image_id . '.jpg';
    } else {
        $imagename = 'image_effect.php?id=' . $image_id . '&e=' .
            $_POST['effect'];

        if (isset($_POST['emb_caption'])) {
            $imagename .= '&capt=' . urlencode($image_caption);
        }
    }
?>
    <img src="<?php echo $imagename; ?>" style="float:left;">
```

```php
<table>
 <tr><td>Image Saved as: </td><td><?php echo $image_id . '.jpg'; ?></td></tr>
 <tr><td>Height: </td><td><?php echo $height; ?></td></tr>
 <tr><td>Width: </td><td><?php echo $width; ?></td></tr>
 <tr><td>Upload Date: </td><td><?php echo $image_date; ?></td></tr>
</table>
 <p>You may apply special options to your image below. Note: saving an image
with any of the options applied  <em>cannot be undone</em>.</p>
  <form action="<?php echo $_SERVER['PHP_SELF']; ?>" method="post">
   <div>
    <input type="hidden" name="id" value="<?php echo $image_id;?>"/>
    Filter: <select name="effect">
     <option value="-1">None</option>
<?php
    echo '<option value="' . IMG_FILTER_GRAYSCALE . '"';
    if (isset($_POST['effect']) && $_POST['effect'] == IMG_FILTER_GRAYSCALE)
{
        echo ' selected="selected"';
    }
    echo '>Black and White</option>';

    echo '<option value="' . IMG_FILTER_GAUSSIAN_BLUR . '"';
    if (isset($_POST['effect']) && $_POST['effect'] ==
        IMG_FILTER_GAUSSIAN_BLUR) {
        echo ' selected="selected"';
    }
    echo '>Blur</option>';

    echo '<option value="' . IMG_FILTER_EMBOSS . '"';
    if (isset($_POST['effect']) && $_POST['effect'] == IMG_FILTER_EMBOSS) {
        echo ' selected="selected"';
    }
    echo '>Emboss</option>';

    echo '<option value="' . IMG_FILTER_NEGATE . '"';
    if (isset($_POST['effect']) && $_POST['effect'] == IMG_FILTER_NEGATE) {
        echo ' selected="selected"';
    }
    echo '>Negative</option>';
?>
    </select>
    <br/><br/>
<?php
    echo '<input type="checkbox" name="emb_caption"';
    if (isset($_POST['emb_caption'])) {
        echo ' checked="checked"';
    }
    echo '>Embed caption in image?';
?>
    <br/><br/>
    <input type="submit" value="Preview" name="submit" />
    <input type="submit" value="Save" name="submit" />
   </div>
```

```
      </form>
    </body>
  </html>
  <?php
  }
  ?>
```

2. The Arial font is used in this exercise, but you should use a font that is installed on your
    server. If you attempt to run the following script with a font that is not installed on the server,
    you will get an error. Add the following highlighted lines to your image_effect.php file:

```php
<?php
//change this path to match your images directory
$dir ='C:/Program Files/Apache Software Foundation/Apache2.2/htdocs/images';

//change this path to match your fonts directory and the desired font
putenv('GDFONTPATH=' . 'C:/Windows/Fonts');
$font = 'arial';

// make sure the requested image is valid
if (isset($_GET['id']) && ctype_digit($_GET['id']) && file_exists($dir . '/' .
    $_GET['id'] . '.jpg')) {
    $image = imagecreatefromjpeg($dir . '/' . $_GET['id'] . '.jpg');
} else {
    die('invalid image specified');
}

// apply the filter
$effect = (isset($_GET['e'])) ? $_GET['e'] : -1;
switch ($effect) {
case IMG_FILTER_NEGATE:
    imagefilter($image, IMG_FILTER_NEGATE);
    break;
case IMG_FILTER_GRAYSCALE:
    imagefilter($image, IMG_FILTER_GRAYSCALE);
    break;
case IMG_FILTER_EMBOSS:
    imagefilter($image, IMG_FILTER_EMBOSS);
    break;
case IMG_FILTER_GAUSSIAN_BLUR:
    imagefilter($image, IMG_FILTER_GAUSSIAN_BLUR);
    break;
}

// add the caption if requested
if (isset($_GET['capt'])) {
    imagettftext($image, 12, 0, 20, 20, 0, $font, $_GET['capt']);
}

// show the image
header('Content-Type: image/jpeg');
imagejpeg($image, '', 100);
?>
```

3. Now go back and try out the new option. You should see something similar to Figure 7-7.

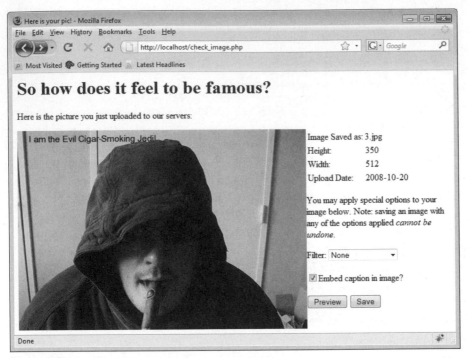

Figure 7-7

You can see how easy it is to automatically overlay text on to your images. Let's break it down.

How It Works

First, you added a line specifying the font path the GD library will use when searching for the specified font, and then you provided the name of the particular font you want to use. Alternatively, you could have just assigned the entire path and filename of the font to the `$font` variable. Next, the "Embed caption in image?" option was added to your form in `check_image.php`. When processing the workflow, the script sees if the option is checked and either passes the caption along to `image_effect.php` in the URL string or uses the `imagettftext()` function after the preview has been approved. Finally, you added the lines referencing the desired font and a call to `imagettftext()` to the `image_effect.php` script as well.

The `imagettftext()` function is only one of the many text/string functions available in PHP/GD. The function accepts eight values, in this order:

1. The image reference on which the text is placed (`$image` in this example).

2. The font size of the text measured in points (12 in this example).

3. The rotation of the text in degrees (0 in this example because the text is not rotated).

4. The x-coordinate for the starting position of the text, with 0 being the leftmost boundary of the image (20 in this example).

5. The y-coordinate for the starting position of the text's baseline, with 0 being the upper boundary of the image (20 in this example).

6. The color of the text, using the color index (0, or black, in this example).

7. The name of the font file you want to reference (`arial.ttf` in this example).

8. The string of text to be shown (the contents of the `$image_caption` variable in this example).

When the font's name does not start with a leading / then .ttf will be appended to it, and the path specified by the GDFONT environment variable will be searched for it. The scripts here are using the `arial.ttf` font located in the `C:\Windows\Fonts` directory. If you wanted to use a font file that was stored in the local project directory, then you would need to set the value of GDFONT accordingly, for example:

```
putenv('GDFONTPATH=' . realpath('.'));
```

The text string is treated as a UTF-8 encoded string. Although named entities such as `&copy;` or `&delta;` aren't understood by `imagettftext()`, you can use a character's hexadecimal format, such as `&#xA9;` and `&#x394;`. If a character is not supported by the font, then GD will substitute a small empty rectangle in its place.

Adding Watermarks and Merging Images

Because you are showing these images on the Movie Review Site, make your logo show up lightly behind each image that is hosted by you, as a watermark. You can do this with your own logo to protect any copyrighted images, just as easily as we did the overlaying text.

In this section, you will actually be merging two images (your source image and your logo image) to create the desired effect. For reference, the logo file used here as a sample is a transparent PNG file and is shown in Figure 7-8.

Figure 7-8

Merging Two Images

To merge the two images, again you will change the check_image.php file and your image_effect .php file.

1. Add the following three sections to your check_image.php file, in the same areas as before with the embedded caption code:

```
...
    // add the caption if requested
    if (isset($_POST['emb_caption'])) {
        imagettftext($image, 12, 0, 20, 20, 0, $fntdir . '/' . 'arial.ttf',
            $image_caption);
    }
    //add the logo watermark if requested
    if (isset($_POST['emb_logo'])) {
        // determine x and y position to center watermark
        list($wmk_width, $wmk_height) = getimagesize('images/logo.png');
        $x = ($width - $wmk_width) / 2;
        $y = ($height - $wmk_height) / 2;

        $wmk = imagecreatefrompng('images/logo.png');
        imagecopymerge($image, $wmk, $x, $y, 0, 0, $wmk_width, $wmk_height,
20);
        imagedestroy($wmk);
    }
...
        if (isset($_POST['emb_caption'])) {
            $imagename .= '&capt=' . urlencode($image_caption);
        }
        if (isset($_POST['emb_logo'])) {
            $imagename .= '&logo=1';
        }
...
<?php
    echo '<input type="checkbox" name="emb_caption"';
    if (isset($_POST['emb_caption'])) {
        echo ' checked="checked"';
    }
    echo '>Embed caption in image?';
    echo '<br/><br/><input type="checkbox" name="emb_logo"';
    if (isset($_POST['emb_logo'])) {
        echo ' checked="checked"';
    }
    echo '>Embed watermarked logo in image?';
?>
...
```

2. Add the following line to your `image_effect.php` file, as before:

```
...
// add the caption if requested
if (isset($_GET['capt'])) {
    imagettftext($image, 12, 0, 20, 20, 0, $font, $_GET['capt']);
}
```

```
//add the logo watermark if requested
if (isset($_GET['logo'])) {
    // determine x and y position to center watermark
    list($width, $height) = getimagesize($dir . '/' . $_GET['id'] . '.jpg');
    list($wmk_width, $wmk_height) = getimagesize('images/logo.png');
    $x = ($width - $wmk_width) / 2;
    $y = ($height - $wmk_height) / 2;

    $wmk = imagecreatefrompng('images/logo.png');
    imagecopymerge($image, $wmk, $x, $y, 0, 0, $wmk_width, $wmk_height, 20);
    imagedestroy($wmk);
}
```

```
// show the image
header('Content-Type: image/jpeg');
imagejpeg($image, '', 100);
?>
```

3. Go ahead and try it out! Your screen should resemble that in Figure 7-9.

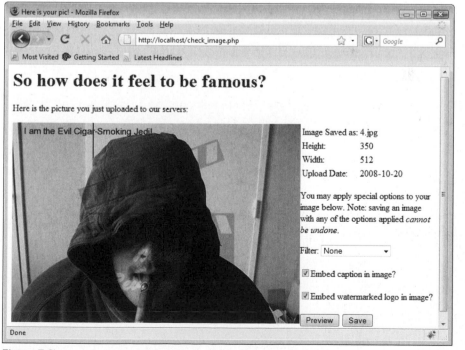

Figure 7-9

How It Works

You have simply added another option for your users, and you did it using the `imagecopymerge()` function. Note that before you could merge the two images, you had to make the second image "GD friendly" by creating a duplicate copy. Because your image was a PNG image, you used the `imagecreatefrompng()` function.

The nine arguments for the `imagecopymerge()` function are as follows, in this order:

1. The resource of the destination image (`$image` in this example, since the `$image` file is the one you are making all the changes to and the one that will be shown at the end of your script).

2. The resource of the second image, or source image (`$wmk` in this example).

3. The x-coordinate on the destination image (0 represents the leftmost boundary).

4. The y-coordinate on the destination image (0 represents the uppermost boundary).

5. The x-coordinate on the second image to start copying from (0 in this example, because you want the whole image).

6. The y-coordinate on the second image to start copying from (0 in this example, because you want the whole image).

7. The width of the portion of the second image to be merged (`$wmk_width` in this example, representing as much of the second image as will fit on the destination image).

8. The height of the portion of the second image to be merged (`$wmk_height` in this example, representing as much of the second image as will fit on the destination image).

9. The percent of transparency of the two images to be merged, with 100 being equal to the second image completely opaque, and 0 completely transparent.

We hope you're still with us, because there is one more thing we would like to do.

Creating Thumbnails

Of course, showing your users' images at full size is fine, if they want to see them up close. However, that format is not too conducive to showing a photo gallery or list of many photos on a page. This section discusses how you can automatically create a thumbnail of each of your uploaded files that will be used for just that purpose — a photo gallery of all your photos.

Creating Thumbnails

You want to automatically create a thumbnail version of all the images that are uploaded by the users, so you will be modifying check_image.php and including this function.

1. Create a subdirectory of your images folder to house the thumbnails. For this example, we created C:\Program Files\Apache Software Foundation\Apache2.2\htdocs\images\thumbs. Make sure your directory has write permissions.

2. Modify your check_image.php file by adding the two new sections of code that follow:

```
...
//change this path to match your images directory
$dir ='C:/Program Files/Apache Software Foundation/Apache2.2/htdocs/images';

//change this path to match your thumbnail directory
$thumbdir = $dir . '/thumbs';
...
    // save the image with the filter applied
    imagejpeg($image, $dir . '/' . $_POST['id'] . '.jpg', 100);

    //set the dimensions for the thumbnail
    $thumb_width = $width * 0.10;
    $thumb_height = $height * 0.10;

    //create the thumbnail
    $thumb = imagecreatetruecolor($thumb_width, $thumb_height);
    imagecopyresampled($thumb, $image, 0, 0, 0, 0, $thumb_width,
$thumb_height,
        $width, $height);
    imagejpeg($thumb, $dir . '/' . $_POST['id'] . '.jpg', 100);
    imagedestroy($thumb);
?>
<html>
 <head>
  <title>Here is your pic!</title>
 </head>
 <body>
  <h1>Your image has been saved!</h1>
  <img src="images/<?php echo $_POST['id']; ?>.jpg" />
 </body>
</html>
```

3. Now you're going to create `gallery.php`, which will act as your photo gallery to display the thumbnail images. Type the following in your editor:

```php
<?php
//connect to MySQL
$db = mysql_connect('localhost', 'bp6am', 'bp6ampass') or
    die ('Unable to connect. Check your connection parameters.');
mysql_select_db('moviesite', $db) or die(mysql_error($db));

//change this path to match your images directory
$dir ='images';

//change this path to match your thumbnail directory
$thumbdir = $dir . '/thumbs';
?>
<html>
 <head>
  <title>Welcome to our Photo Gallery</title>
  <style type="text/css">
   th { background-color: #999;}
   .odd_row { background-color: #EEE; }
   .even_row { background-color: #FFF; }
  </style>
 </head>
 <body>
  <p>Click on any image to see it full sized.</p>
  <table style="width:100%;">
   <tr>
    <th>Image</th>
    <th>Caption</th>
    <th>Uploaded By</th>
    <th>Date Uploaded</th>
   </tr>
<?php
//get the thumbs
$result = mysql_query('SELECT * FROM images') or die(mysql_error());

$odd = true;
while ($rows = mysql_fetch_array($result)) {
    echo ($odd == true) ? '<tr class="odd_row">' : '<tr class="even_row">';
    $odd = !$odd;
    extract($rows);
    echo '<td><a href="' . $dir . '/' . $image_id . '.jpg">';
    echo '<img src="' . $thumbdir . '/' . $image_id . '.jpg">';
    echo '</a></td>';
    echo '<td>' . $image_caption . '</td>';
    echo '<td>' . $image_username . '</td>';
    echo '<td>' . $image_date . '</td>';
    echo '</tr>';
}
?>
  </table>
 </body>
</html>
```

4. Now upload some images, using your `upload_image.html` page. When you have a few, go to `gallery.php` in your browser and see what you have. Your screen should look something like Figure 7-10.

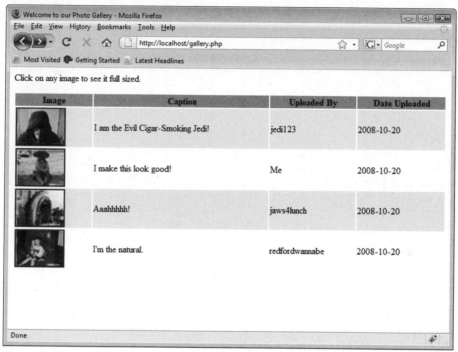

Figure 7-10

Ok, so it's not pretty, and it's mostly utilitarian in appearance. The important thing is that it works! You can add the bells and whistles later; we just want to make sure you can make a thumbnail.

How It Works

The actual thumbnail itself is created in your `check_image.php` file, so let's take a look at that first. You first give your thumbnail its own directory, and you're using the same naming scheme, for simplicity's sake. Then the following lines complete the task of making the thumbnail for you:

```
//set the dimensions for the thumbnail
$thumb_width = $width * 0.10;
$thumb_height = $height * 0.10;

//create the thumbnail
$thumb = imagecreatetruecolor($thumb_width, $thumb_height);
imagecopyresampled($thumb, $image, 0, 0, 0, 0, $thumb_width, $thumb_height,
    $width, $height);
imagejpeg($thumb, $dir . '/' . $_POST['id'] . '.jpg', 100);
imagedestroy($thumb);
```

The size of the thumbnails is set equal to 10% of the size of the original picture. By using percentages instead of hard integers, you ensure that the proportions are kept equal and no skewing of your image occurs. Of course, you can make this smaller or larger depending on your users' preferences and the typical dimensions of the file uploads. Or you can do some math to determine appropriate hard integers based on the percentages and a maximum ceiling value. We just kept it simple.

The process then creates a blank image in memory based on the smaller dimensions for the thumbnail and copies the source image onto it. The newly created thumbnail is then saved in the proper location, with the same name as the full-size image. Easy as pie, right?

Summary

This chapter covered a lot, and yet it only scratches the surface of image manipulation using the GD extension. You have seen how you can upload images, resize them, change their coloring, create an automatic thumbnail, create new images, and merge two images together.

You used a form to get the image from the user and implemented appropriate checks to make sure the uploaded file was indeed an image of the correct format. Not all forms are so straightforward to check, though. In the next chapter, you'll learn how to check that users enter information in your form in the proper format, and how to give them appropriate feedback when they don't.

Exercises

1. Create a site called "A Virtual Vacation." Offer different backgrounds that people can superimpose photos of themselves on, and let them send virtual postcards to their friends and family.

2. Have a page on your site with funny photographs or cartoons, and allow your users to write the caption for them. Place the text in a speech bubble that is appropriately sized, based on the length of the caption they submit.

3. Create a page for kids where they can choose different heads, bodies, and tails from animals and put them together to make a new creation and a new image. Or, create a virtual paper doll site where kids can place different outfits on a model and then save the images they create.

Validating User Input

If you plan to accept user input on your site, you have to be prepared for mistakes. Incorrect input could be simple human error or a deliberate attempt to circumvent the purpose (or security) of your web application. The most common human errors include basic typographical errors and format errors — such as showing a year as two digits when a full four-digit year was requested or needed. Erroneous input sent deliberately could be from a user who doesn't want to provide his or her e-mail address, or from an attacker intentionally trying to corrupt your database with polluted values. No matter what the source, your script needs to be able to handle incorrect input. There are many ways to do so, but perhaps the most popular is to identify the bad data and return the user to the form with an appropriate error message. This chapter covers user input validation, including:

❑ Validating simple string values.

❑ Validating integer values.

❑ Validating formatted text input.

Users Are Users Are Users . . .

Let's start by considering this example: You work in a bank. You are developing a new system to allow the employees to start the workflow of updating customer account information on the company intranet. You use your well-known MM-DD-YYYY format for the date. It all works quite well when testing, but when it's put in production, your users say it doesn't work. Why? Because all your banking systems use the ISO 8601 YYYY-MM-DD date format (a standard used in many systems because the date can be sorted alphabetically). Your users are confused between the two different formats and input wrong information to the system. If the data is in the wrong format, you can end up with a corrupted database or trigger errors in your application.

You can avoid this by using well-known formats and *validating* the user input. When you expect an integer value, for example, you can check that it is an integer before you try to use it. It's a simple enough rule, and you'll learn how to do it later in this chapter.

Incorporating Validation into the Movie Site

To really understand the role of user input and validation, you need to see it in action. So, first you need to add a few fields to the `movie` table in your beloved movie database.

The movie application provides a lot of opportunities to check for user input. You will need to add a few features to the application, however, to provide more case studies. It will also help you to review what you learned in the previous chapters.

Try It Out   Adapting Your Script to the User Input

You must first add two new columns to the `movie` table. You've done this several times already, so it should be a simple process.

1. Open a text editor, and enter this code:

```php
<?php
$db = mysql_connect('localhost', 'bp6am', 'bp6ampass') or
    die ('Unable to connect. Check your connection parameters.');
mysql_select_db('moviesite', $db) or die(mysql_error($db));

//alter the movie table to include release and rating
$query = 'ALTER TABLE movie ADD COLUMN (
    movie_release INTEGER UNSIGNED DEFAULT 0,
    movie_rating  TINYINT UNSIGNED DEFAULT 5)';
mysql_query($query, $db) or die(mysql_error($db));

echo 'Movie database successfully updated!';
?>
```

2. Save the file as `db_ch08.php`.

3. Open the page in your web browser. You should see the message "Movie database successfully updated!"

How It Works

You've added two fields — `movie_release` and `movie_rating` — at the end of the `movies` table. The `movie_release` field allows you to store a timestamp for the movie's release date. The `movie_rating` field allows you to give the movie a rating when viewing it. If this rating goes from 0 to 10, then 5 would be a neutral rating.

Forgot Something?

Sometimes, when a user enters data in a form, he or she forgets to fill in a field. When this happens, the system has to react so that the insertion of the invalid or incomplete data will not corrupt the database. In some cases, these errors are made on purpose. An attacker may try to inject erroneous tracking information to corrupt your statistics, or attempt to try to find holes in your application. This is more common than you may think, so it is very important to design and test your system so it can react to such errors — whether benign or malicious — to protect your data.

Try It Out   **Adapting Your Script to the User Input**

In this exercise, you'll be making sure that the script can react appropriately when the user fails to enter data in all the fields.

1. Open the code file `movie.php` you wrote in Chapter 6, and modify it as shown in the highlighted lines:

```php
<?php
$db = mysql_connect('localhost', 'bp6am', 'bp6ampass') or
    die ('Unable to connect. Check your connection parameters.');
mysql_select_db('moviesite', $db) or die(mysql_error($db));

if ($_GET['action'] == 'edit') {
    //retrieve the record's information
    $query = 'SELECT
            movie_name, movie_type, movie_year, movie_leadactor, movie_
director
        FROM
            movie
        WHERE
            movie_id = ' . $_GET['id'];
    $result = mysql_query($query, $db) or die(mysql_error($db));
    extract(mysql_fetch_assoc($result));
} else {
    //set values to blank
    $movie_name = '';
    $movie_type = 0;
    $movie_year = date('Y');
    $movie_leadactor = 0;
    $movie_director = 0;
}
?>
<html>
 <head>
  <title><?php echo ucfirst($_GET['action']); ?> Movie</title>
  <style type="text/css">
<!--
#error { background-color: #600; border: 1px solid #FF0; color: #FFF;
 text-align: center; margin: 10px; padding: 10px; }
-->
  </style>
 </head>
 <body>
<?php
if (isset($_GET['error']) && $_GET['error'] != '') {
    echo '<div id="error">' . $_GET['error'] . '</div>';
}
?>
```

```php
  <form action="commit.php?action=<?php echo $_GET['action']; ?>&type=movie"
   method="post">
   <table>
    <tr>
     <td>Movie Name</td>
     <td><input type="text" name="movie_name"
      value="<?php echo $movie_name; ?>"/></td>
    </tr><tr>
     <td>Movie Type</td>
     <td><select name="movie_type">
<?php
// select the movie type information
$query = 'SELECT
        movietype_id, movietype_label
    FROM
        movietype
    ORDER BY
        movietype_label';
$result = mysql_query($query, $db) or die(mysql_error($db));

// populate the select options with the results
while ($row = mysql_fetch_assoc($result)) {
    foreach ($row as $value) {
        if ($row['movietype_id'] == $movie_type) {
            echo '<option value="' . $row['movietype_id'] .
                '" selected="selected">';
        } else {
            echo '<option value="' . $row['movietype_id'] . '">';
        }
        echo $row['movietype_label'] . '</option>';
    }
}
?>
     </select></td>
    </tr><tr>
     <td>Movie Year</td>
     <td><select name="movie_year">
<?php
// populate the select options with years
for ($yr = date("Y"); $yr >= 1970; $yr--) {
    if ($yr == $movie_year) {
        echo '<option value="' . $yr . '" selected="selected">' . $yr .
            '</option>';
    } else {
        echo '<option value="' . $yr . '">' . $yr . '</option>';
    }
}
?>
     </select></td>
    </tr><tr>
     <td>Lead Actor</td>
     <td><select name="movie_leadactor">
<?php
// select actor records
$query = 'SELECT
        people_id, people_fullname
```

```php
    FROM
        people
    WHERE
        people_isactor = 1
    ORDER BY
        people_fullname';
$result = mysql_query($query, $db) or die(mysql_error($db));

// populate the select options with the results
while ($row = mysql_fetch_assoc($result)) {
    foreach ($row as $value) {
        if ($row['people_id'] == $movie_leadactor) {
            echo '<option value="' . $row['people_id'] .
                '" selected="selected">';
        } else {
            echo '<option value="' . $row['people_id'] . '">';
        }
        echo $row['people_fullname'] . '</option>';
    }
}
?>
      </select></td>
    </tr><tr>
     <td>Director</td>
     <td><select name="movie_director">
<?php
// select director records
$query = 'SELECT
        people_id, people_fullname
    FROM
        people
    WHERE
        people_isdirector = 1
    ORDER BY
        people_fullname';
$result = mysql_query($query, $db) or die(mysql_error($db));

// populate the select options with the results
while ($row = mysql_fetch_assoc($result)) {
    foreach ($row as $value) {
        if ($row['people_id'] == $movie_director) {
            echo '<option value="' . $row['people_id'] .
                '" selected="selected">';
        } else {
            echo '<option value="' . $row['people_id'] . '">';
        }
        echo $row['people_fullname'] . '</option>';
    }
}
?>
      </select></td>
    </tr><tr>
     <td colspan="2" style="text-align: center;">
<?php
if ($_GET['action'] == 'edit') {
```

```
      echo '<input type="hidden" value="' . $_GET['id'] . '" name="movie_id" />';
}
?>
        <input type="submit" name="submit"
          value="<?php echo ucfirst($_GET['action']); ?>" />
      </td>
    </tr>
   </table>
  </form>
 </body>
</html>
```

2. Open the commit.php script, and modify it as shown in the highlighted lines:

```
<?php
$db = mysql_connect('localhost', 'bp6am', 'bp6ampass') or
     die ('Unable to connect. Check your connection parameters.');
mysql_select_db('moviesite', $db) or die(mysql_error($db));

// Delete these lines
?>
<html>
 <head>
  <title>Commit</title>
 </head>
 <body>
<?php
// End deleted lines
switch ($_GET['action']) {
case 'add':
    switch ($_GET['type']) {
    case 'movie':
        $error = array();
        $movie_name = isset($_POST['movie_name']) ?
            trim($_POST['movie_name']) : '';
        if (empty($movie_name)) {
            $error[] = urlencode('Please enter a movie name.');
        }
        $movie_type = isset($_POST['movie_type']) ?
            trim($_POST['movie_type']) : '';
        if (empty($movie_type)) {
            $error[] = urlencode('Please select a movie type.');
        }
        $movie_year = isset($_POST['movie_year']) ?
            trim($_POST['movie_year']) : '';
        if (empty($movie_year)) {
            $error[] = urlencode('Please select a movie year.');
        }
        $movie_leadactor = isset($_POST['movie_leadactor']) ?
            trim($_POST['movie_leadactor']) : '';
        if (empty($movie_leadactor)) {
            $error[] = urlencode('Please select a lead actor.');
        }
        $movie_director = isset($_POST['movie_director']) ?
```

```
                trim($_POST['movie_director']) : '';
        if (empty($movie_director)) {
            $error[] = urlencode('Please select a director.');
        }
        if (empty($error)) {
            $query = 'INSERT INTO
                movie
                    (movie_name, movie_year, movie_type, movie_leadactor,
                    movie_director)
                VALUES
                    ("' . $movie_name . '",
                    ' . $movie_year . ',
                    ' . $movie_type . ',
                    ' . $movie_leadactor . ',
                    ' . $movie_director . ')';
        } else {
          header('Location:movie.php?action=add' .
              '&error=' . join($error, urlencode('<br/>')));
        }
```

```
// Delete these lines
        $query = 'INSERT INTO
            movie
                (movie_name, movie_year, movie_type, movie_leadactor,
                movie_director)
            VALUES
                ("' . $_POST['movie_name'] . '",
                ' . $_POST['movie_year'] . ',
                ' . $_POST['movie_type'] . ',
                ' . $_POST['movie_leadactor'] . ',
                ' . $_POST['movie_director'] . ')';
// End deleted lines
        break;
    }
    break;
case 'edit':
    switch ($_GET['type']) {
    case 'movie':
```

```
        $error = array();
        $movie_name = isset($_POST['movie_name']) ?
            trim($_POST['movie_name']) : '';
        if (empty($movie_name)) {
            $error[] = urlencode('Please enter a movie name.');
        }
        $movie_type = isset($_POST['movie_type']) ?
            trim($_POST['movie_type']) : '';
        if (empty($movie_type)) {
            $error[] = urlencode('Please select a movie type.');
        }
        $movie_year = isset($_POST['movie_year']) ?
            trim($_POST['movie_year']) : '';
        if (empty($movie_year)) {
            $error[] = urlencode('Please select a movie year.');
        }
        $movie_leadactor = isset($_POST['movie_leadactor']) ?
```

```
                    trim($_POST['movie_leadactor']) : '';
            if (empty($movie_leadactor)) {
                $error[] = urlencode('Please select a lead actor.');
            }
            $movie_director = isset($_POST['movie_director']) ?
                    trim($_POST['movie_director']) : '';
            if (empty($movie_director)) {
                $error[] = urlencode('Please select a director.');
            }
            if (empty($error)) {
                $query = 'UPDATE
                        movie
                    SET
                        movie_name = "' . $movie_name . '",
                        movie_year = ' . $movie_year . ',
                        movie_type = ' . $movie_type . ',
                        movie_leadactor = ' . $movie_leadactor . ',
                        movie_director = ' . $movie_director . '
                    WHERE
                        movie_id = ' . $_POST['movie_id'];
            } else {
                header('Location:movie.php?action=edit&id=' . $_POST['movie_id'] .
                    '&error=' . join($error, urlencode('<br/>')));
            }
```

```
// Delete these lines
        $query = 'UPDATE
                movie
            SET
                movie_name = "' . $_POST['movie_name'] . '",
                movie_year = ' . $_POST['movie_year'] . ',
                movie_type = ' . $_POST['movie_type'] . ',
                movie_leadactor = ' . $_POST['movie_leadactor'] . ',
                movie_director = ' . $_POST['movie_director'] . '
            WHERE
                movie_id = ' . $_POST['movie_id'];
// End deleted lines
        break;
    }
    break;
}

if (isset($query)) {
    $result = mysql_query($query, $db) or die(mysql_error($db));
}
?>
```

```html
<html>
 <head>
  <title>Commit</title>
 </head>
 <body>
  <p>Done!</p>
 </body>
</html>
```

3. Now open your browser and load `admin.php`, and then click the link to add a movie. You will be taken to the `movie.php` script you've just updated. Try adding a movie with no name, and notice the error message stating the mistake made in filling in the form, as shown in Figure 8-1.

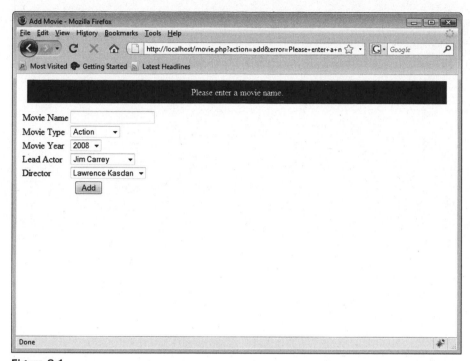

Figure 8-1

How It Works

When the form passes information to the `commit.php` script, the data has to be verified. In this case, you use a simple verification method: The `isset()` function returns `true` if the variable has been set, and `false` if not. To ensure that the user did not submit the form with a blank field or a simple space in the movie name field, you use `trim()` on the field's content to eliminate any space leading or trailing the string and to compare the value to a null string. (Some people like to trigger errors in web sites by entering erroneous input; don't make their job easy.)

At the same time, if an error is detected, you add a message to the `$error` variable that collects all the error messages. The error messages are URL encoded before being added because they will be passed on the URL string. They should be encoded to ensure that they will be passed back to the `movie.php` script correctly without being corrupted. (See `urlencode` and `urldecode` functions in the manual; for more information, check the PHP web site at `www.php.net/url`.)

```
$error = array();
$movie_name = (isset($_POST['movie_name']) ?
    trim($_POST['movie_name']) : '';
if (empty($movie_name)) {
    $error[] = urlencode('Please enter a movie name.');
}
```

225

Once you are sure that an error has occurred, you redirect the user back to the form with an error message stating the problem. When redirecting the user back to the form, the system needs to display the error message.

```
if (isset($_GET['error']) && $_GET['error'] != '') {
    echo '<div id="error">' . $_GET['error'] . '</div>';
}
```

This displays a rather colorful message that your user will not miss.

Checking for Format Errors

Checking for errors in dates or other formatted data is a requirement in most systems because users can't always be guided in their input. You should always check the data that the user enters, if you require a specific format or set of values.

At this point, you need the feared and powerful *regular expressions*. Regular expressions allow you to define a pattern and check to see if it can be applied to your data. They're very useful to check for dates, Social Security numbers, and any data that has to respect a predefined set of format requirements. (It helps to be sure to always indicate the format in the source field.)

Try It Out   Checking Dates and Numbers

In this exercise, you'll change a few pages so that you can check the format of the dates the user enters.

1.   Open the well-known `movie.php` file, and modify it as follows:

```
<?php
    $db = mysql_connect('localhost', 'bp6am', 'bp6ampass') or
        die ('Unable to connect. Check your connection parameters.');
    mysql_select_db('moviesite', $db) or die(mysql_error($db));

    if ($_GET['action'] == 'edit') {
        //retrieve the record's information
        $query = 'SELECT
                movie_name, movie_type, movie_year, movie_leadactor, movie_director,
                movie_release, movie_rating
            FROM
                movie
            WHERE
                movie_id = ' . $_GET['id'];
        $result = mysql_query($query, $db) or die(mysql_error($db));
        extract(mysql_fetch_assoc($result));
    } else {
        //set values to blank
        $movie_name = '';
```

```php
        $movie_type = 0;
        $movie_year = date('Y');
        $movie_leadactor = 0;
        $movie_director = 0;
        $movie_release = time();
        $movie_rating = 5;
}
?>
<html>
 <head>
  <title><?php echo ucfirst($_GET['action']); ?> Movie</title>
  <style type="text/css">
<!--
#error { background-color: #600; border: 1px solid #FF0; color: #FFF;
 text-align: center; margin: 10px; padding: 10px; }
-->
  </style>
 </head>
 <body>
<?php
if (isset($_GET['error']) && $_GET['error'] != '') {
    echo '<div id="error">' . $_GET['error'] . '</div>';
}
?>
  <form action="commit.php?action=<?php echo $_GET['action']; ?>&type=movie"
   method="post">
   <table>
    <tr>
     <td>Movie Name</td>
     <td><input type="text" name="movie_name"
      value="<?php echo $movie_name; ?>"/></td>
    </tr><tr>
     <td>Movie Type</td>
     <td><select name="movie_type">
<?php
// select the movie type information
$query = 'SELECT
        movietype_id, movietype_label
    FROM
        movietype
    ORDER BY
        movietype_label';
$result = mysql_query($query, $db) or die(mysql_error($db));

// populate the select options with the results
while ($row = mysql_fetch_assoc($result)) {
    foreach ($row as $value) {
        if ($row['movietype_id'] == $movie_type) {
            echo '<option value="' . $row['movietype_id'] .
                '" selected="selected">';
        } else {
            echo '<option value="' . $row['movietype_id'] . '">';
        }
        echo $row['movietype_label'] . '</option>';
```

```php
        }
    }
?>
      </select></td>
    </tr><tr>
     <td>Movie Year</td>
     <td><select name="movie_year">
<?php
// populate the select options with years
for ($yr = date("Y"); $yr >= 1970; $yr--) {
    if ($yr == $movie_year) {
        echo '<option value="' . $yr . '" selected="selected">' . $yr .
            '</option>';
    } else {
        echo '<option value="' . $yr . '">' . $yr . '</option>';
    }
}
?>
      </select></td>
    </tr><tr>
     <td>Lead Actor</td>
     <td><select name="movie_leadactor">
<?php
// select actor records
$query = 'SELECT
        people_id, people_fullname
    FROM
        people
    WHERE
        people_isactor = 1
    ORDER BY
        people_fullname';
$result = mysql_query($query, $db) or die(mysql_error($db));

// populate the select options with the results
while ($row = mysql_fetch_assoc($result)) {
    foreach ($row as $value) {
        if ($row['people_id'] == $movie_leadactor) {
            echo '<option value="' . $row['people_id'] .
                '" selected="selected">';
        } else {
            echo '<option value="' . $row['people_id'] . '">';
        }
        echo $row['people_fullname'] . '</option>';
    }
}
?>
      </select></td>
    </tr><tr>
     <td>Director</td>
     <td><select name="movie_director">
<?php
// select director records
$query = 'SELECT
```

```
            people_id, people_fullname
    FROM
            people
    WHERE
            people_isdirector = 1
    ORDER BY
            people_fullname';
$result = mysql_query($query, $db) or die(mysql_error($db));

// populate the select options with the results
while ($row = mysql_fetch_assoc($result)) {
    foreach ($row as $value) {
        if ($row['people_id'] == $movie_director) {
            echo '<option value="' . $row['people_id'] .
                '" selected="selected">';
        } else {
            echo '<option value="' . $row['people_id'] . '">';
        }
        echo $row['people_fullname'] . '</option>';
    }
}
?>
    </select></td>
  </tr><tr>
    <td>Movie Release Date<br/>
    <small>(dd-mm-yyyy)</small></td>
    <td><input type="text" name="movie_release"
    value="<?php echo date('d-m-Y', $movie_release); ?>"/></td>
  </tr><tr>
    <td>Movie Rating<br/>
    <small>(from 0 to 10)</small></td>
    <td><input type="text" name="movie_rating"
    value="<?php echo $movie_rating; ?>"/></td>
  </tr><tr>
    <td colspan="2" style="text-align: center;">
<?php
if ($_GET['action'] == 'edit') {
    echo '<input type="hidden" value="' . $_GET['id'] . '" name="movie_id" />';
}
?>
    <input type="submit" name="submit"
     value="<?php echo ucfirst($_GET['action']); ?>" />
    </td>
  </tr>
  </table>
 </form>
 </body>
</html>
```

2. Navigate to `movie.php` in a browser again, and note the two new fields that have been added, as shown in Figure 8-2.

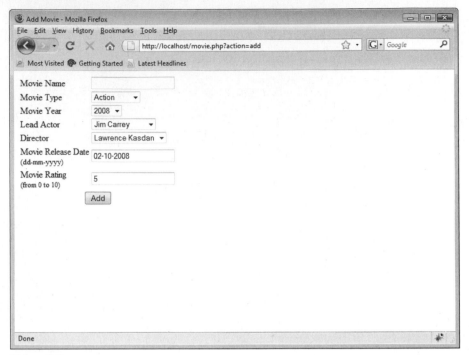

Figure 8-2

3.   Now open `commit.php`, and modify it as follows (modifications are highlighted):

```php
<?php
$db = mysql_connect('localhost', 'bp6am', 'bp6ampass') or
    die ('Unable to connect. Check your connection parameters.');
mysql_select_db('moviesite', $db) or die(mysql_error($db));

switch ($_GET['action']) {
case 'add':
    switch ($_GET['type']) {
    case 'movie':
        $error = array();
        $movie_name = isset($_POST['movie_name']) ?
            trim($_POST['movie_name']) : '';
        if (empty($movie_name)) {
            $error[] = urlencode('Please enter a movie name.');
        }
        $movie_type = isset($_POST['movie_type']) ?
            trim($_POST['movie_type']) : '';
        if (empty($movie_type)) {
            $error[] = urlencode('Please select a movie type.');
        }
        $movie_year = isset($_POST['movie_year']) ?
            trim($_POST['movie_year']) : '';
```

```
        if (empty($movie_year)) {
            $error[] = urlencode('Please select a movie year.');
        }
        $movie_leadactor = isset($_POST['movie_leadactor']) ?
            trim($_POST['movie_leadactor']) : '';
        if (empty($movie_leadactor)) {
            $error[] = urlencode('Please select a lead actor.');
        }
        $movie_director = isset($_POST['movie_director']) ?
            trim($_POST['movie_director']) : '';
        if (empty($movie_director)) {
            $error[] = urlencode('Please select a director.');
        }
        $movie_release = isset($_POST['movie_release']) ?
            trim($_POST['movie_release']) : '';
        if (!preg_match('|^\d{2}-\d{2}-\d{4}$|', $movie_release)) {
            $error[] = urlencode('Please enter a date in dd-mm-yyyy format.');
        } else {
            list($day, $month, $year) = explode('-', $movie_release);
            if (!checkdate($month, $day, $year)) {
                $error[] = urlencode('Please enter a valid date.');
            } else {
                $movie_release = mktime(0, 0, 0, $month, $day, $year);
            }
        }
        $movie_rating = isset($_POST['movie_rating']) ?
            trim($_POST['movie_rating']) : '';
        if (!is_numeric($movie_rating)) {
            $error[] = urlencode('Please enter a numeric rating.');
        } else if ($movie_rating < 0 || $movie_rating > 10) {
            $error[] = urlencode('Please enter a rating between 0 and 10.');
        }
        if (empty($error)) {
            $query = 'INSERT INTO
                movie
                    (movie_name, movie_year, movie_type, movie_leadactor,
                    movie_director, movie_release, movie_rating)
                VALUES
                    ("' . $movie_name . '",
                    ' . $movie_year . ',
                    ' . $movie_type . ',
                    ' . $movie_leadactor . ',
                    ' . $movie_director . ',
                    ' . $movie_release . ',
                    ' . $movie_rating . ')';
```

```
          } else {
              header('Location:movie.php?action=add' .
                  '&error=' . join($error, urlencode('<br/>')));
          }
          break;
    }
    break;
case 'edit':
    switch ($_GET['type']) {
    case 'movie':
        $error = array();
        $movie_name = isset($_POST['movie_name']) ?
            trim($_POST['movie_name']) : '';
        if (empty($movie_name)) {
            $error[] = urlencode('Please enter a movie name.');
        }
        $movie_type = isset($_POST['movie_type']) ?
            trim($_POST['movie_type']) : '';
        if (empty($movie_type)) {
            $error[] = urlencode('Please select a movie type.');
        }
        $movie_year = isset($_POST['movie_year']) ?
            trim($_POST['movie_year']) : '';
        if (empty($movie_year)) {
            $error[] = urlencode('Please select a movie year.');
        }
        $movie_leadactor = isset($_POST['movie_leadactor']) ?
            trim($_POST['movie_leadactor']) : '';
        if (empty($movie_leadactor)) {
            $error[] = urlencode('Please select a lead actor.');
        }
        $movie_director = isset($_POST['movie_director']) ?
            trim($_POST['movie_director']) : '';
        if (empty($movie_director)) {
            $error[] = urlencode('Please select a director.');
        }
        $movie_release = isset($_POST['movie_release']) ?
            trim($_POST['movie_release']) : '';
        if (!preg_match('|^\d{2}-\d{2}-\d{4}$|', $movie_release)) {
            $error[] = urlencode('Please enter a date in dd-mm-yyyy format.');
        } else {
            list($day, $month, $year) = explode('-', $movie_release);
            if (!checkdate($month, $day, $year)) {
                $error[] = urlencode('Please enter a valid date.');
            } else {
                $movie_release = mktime(0, 0, 0, $month, $day, $year);
            }
        }
        $movie_rating = isset($_POST['movie_rating']) ?
            trim($_POST['movie_rating']) : '';
```

```
            if (!is_numeric($movie_rating)) {
                $error[] = urlencode('Please enter a numeric rating.');
            } else if ($movie_rating < 0 || $movie_rating > 10) {
                $error[] = urlencode('Please enter a rating between 0 and 10.');
            }

        if (empty($error)) {
            $query = 'UPDATE
                    movie
                SET
                    movie_name = "' . $movie_name . '",
                    movie_year = ' . $movie_year . ',
                    movie_type = ' . $movie_type . ',
                    movie_leadactor = ' . $movie_leadactor . ',
                    movie_director = ' . $movie_director . ',
                    movie_release = ' . $movie_release . ',
                    movie_rating = ' . $movie_rating . '
                WHERE
                    movie_id = ' . $_POST['movie_id'];
        } else {
            header('Location:movie.php?action=edit&id=' . $_POST['movie_id'] .
                '&error=' . join($error, urlencode('<br/>')));
        }
        break;
    }
    break;
}

if (isset($query)) {
    $result = mysql_query($query, $db) or die(mysql_error($db));
}
?>
?>
<html>
 <head>
  <title>Commit</title>
 </head>
 <body>
  <p>Done!</p>
 </body>
</html>
```

4. Attempt to add a new movie, and try entering 2009-20-01 in the release date field. You will be brought back to the form with a nice, yet very explicit, message telling you that the date format is invalid, as shown in Figure 8-3.

Figure 8-3

5. Try entering letters in the rating field. This field could easily have been a drop-down, but it is a text field for the purposes of our exercise. The value will be refused, as shown in Figure 8-4.

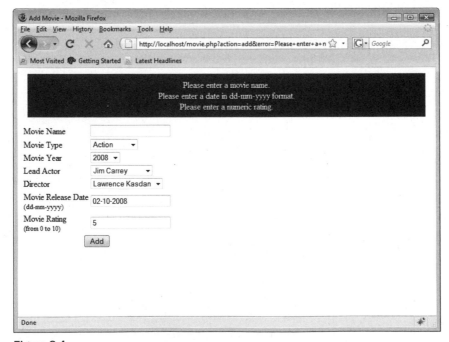

Figure 8-4

How It Works

First, let's look into the type-validating functions. In the `commit.php` code, you use the `is_numeric()` function. This function returns a Boolean TRUE if the value is indeed numeric, and FALSE if not. More of these validating functions are available, including:

- ❏ `is_array()`: Checks if the variable holds an array.
- ❏ `is_binary()`: Checks if the variable holds a native binary string.
- ❏ `is_bool()`: Checks for Boolean-type values (TRUE, FALSE, 0, or 1).
- ❏ `is_callable()`: Checks if the variable's value can be called as a function.
- ❏ `is_float()`: Checks if the variable holds a decimal value.
- ❏ `is_int()`: Checks if the variable holds an integer value.
- ❏ `is_null()`: Checks if the variable's value is null.
- ❏ `is_numeric()`: Checks if the variable holds a number or numeric string.
- ❏ `is_object()`: Checks if the variable stores an object.
- ❏ `is_resource()`: Checks to see if the variable is a resource.
- ❏ `is_string()`: Checks to see if the value is a string.
- ❏ `is_unicode()`: Checks to see if the value is a Unicode string.

In this instance, the use of `is_numeric` allows you to make sure that the user has entered a numeric value.

```
if (!is_numeric($movie_rating)) {
    $error[]= 'Please enter a numeric rating.';
} else
if ($movie_rating < 0 || $movie_rating > 10) {
    $error[]= 'Please enter a rating between 0 and 10.';

    }
}
```

The code first cleans up the value of leading and trailing spaces with the `trim()` function (always try to be prepared for typos and mishaps) and then tests to see if the value is numeric. If it's not, the error message queue is fed; if it is, the code tests the value to see if it is between 0 and 10. If the value is not between 0 and 10, the code adds an error message to the error message queue.

The `is_*` set of functions is great for determining the nature of a variable's contents, which is important in a dynamically typed language like PHP. For example, a variable could hold an integer one minute and a connection resource to a database the next. But another set of functions is the `ctype_*` functions, which can be used to further analyze the contents of numbers and strings. They are used to check whether the character or string falls within a certain class of characters. Sometimes `ctype_*` functions are preferred over `is_*` because the ctype extension uses a native C library behind the scenes, which can make it faster. Keep in mind ctype only checks the contents of alphanumeric strings, not arrays types, objects, or resources. For those, you must use the appropriate `is_*` function. The `ctype_*` functions are:

- ❏ `ctype_alnum()`: Checks if the value is made up of alphanumeric characters.

- ❏ `ctype_alpha()`: Checks if the value is all alphabetic characters.

- ❏ `ctype_cntrl()`: Checks if the value is control characters.

- ❏ `ctype_digit()`: Checks if the value is numeric characters.

- ❏ `ctype_graph()`: Checks if the value is made up of printable characters, except space.

- ❏ `ctype_lower()`: Checks if the string is all lowercase characters.

- ❏ `ctype_print()`: Checks if the string is all printable characters.

- ❏ `ctype_punct()`: Checks for any printable character that is not whitespace or an alphanumeric character.

- ❏ `ctype_space()`: Checks for whitespace characters.

- ❏ `ctype_upper()`: Checks for uppercase characters.

- ❏ `ctype_xdigit()`: Checks for characters representing a hexadecimal digit.

For more information on the `is_*` and `ctype_*` family of functions, see the documentation at `php.net/variables` and `php.net/ctype`, respectively.

The date validation is almost as simple to understand, if you know a little bit about regular expressions. Here's a closer look at it:

```
$movie_release = isset($_POST['movie_release']) ?
    trim($_POST['movie_release']) : '';
if (!preg_match('|^\d{2}-\d{2}-\d{4}$|', $movie_release)) {
    $error[] = urlencode('Please enter a date in dd-mm-yyyy format.');
} else {
    list($day, $month, $year) = explode('-', $movie_release);
    if (!checkdate($month, $day, $year)) {
        $error[] = urlencode('Please enter a valid date.');
    } else {
        $movie_release = mktime(0, 0, 0, $month, $day, $year);
    }
}
```

As you saw in this chapter's first exercise, you use the `trim()` function to clear all leading and trailing spaces in the received string, to make sure your user entered something other than just a space.

The next statement contains two conditions. The first condition tests for a regular expression match, using `preg_match()`. What is a regular expression, you may ask? A regular expression is a concise notation to describe patterns in strings. They can be a bit difficult to grasp at first because they are so cryptic, but they are very effective and powerful. Let's take a closer look at the regular expression `|^\d{2}-\d{2}-\d{4}$|`.

The pipe characters that start and end the expression are not properly part of the expression itself, but mark its beginning and end. In fact, it isn't required to use the pipe character, as the expression could be delimited with / or even @. It is a matter of preference, but try to use a marker character that doesn't appear in the regular expression, to avoid confusion, and make sure that you use the same character, whatever one you do choose, to mark both the beginning and end.

The \d is shorthand notation to match any digit. Alternately, you could have used [0-9] or [0123456789] to mean the same thing. As you can see, three sets of numbers are described in the regular expression pattern, one each for the day, the month, and the year.

The {2} and {4} specify the number of times the character class should match. Because the day and month value should be two digits, {2} is applied to their \d. Otherwise, just one digit would be matched. The year is expected to be four consecutive digits, so {4} is applied for its \d. By using repeating specifiers, you make your expression cleaner and easier to follow. \d\d-\d\d-\d\d\d\d (or even [0123456789][0123456789]-[0123456789][0123456789]-[0123456789][0123456789] [0123456789][0123456789]) is equally valid, but more difficult to maintain later on.

The ^ character anchors the pattern to match at the beginning of the string, and $ anchors the pattern to the end of the string. Including these in the regular expression pattern makes sure it only matches a value like 05-07-2008, and not ABC05-07-2008123.

So let's reiterate the pattern in English: The matching must begin at the start of the input string (^), and the pattern consists of one digit (\d) followed by a second digit ({2}), followed by a literal dash (-), followed again by one digit (\d) followed by a second digit ({2}), followed by a literal dash (-), followed by four digits (\d{4}), at which point the regular expression engine must be at the end of the input string ($). See, that wasn't too bad, was it?

There is, of course, a lot more to regular expressions than what we just discussed here. Here is a brief listing of the more common matching mechanisms you may encounter:

❑   ^ anchors the pattern match to the beginning of the line.

❑ $ anchors the pattern match to the end of the line.

❑   . matches any character except a newline.

❑   - means a range of characters, when used within a character class.

❑   [ ] marks a class of characters.

❑   [^] negates the class of characters.

❑   ? matches the character, class, or subpattern 0 or 1 times.

❑   + matches the character, class, or subpattern 1 or more times.

❑   * matches the character, class, or subpattern 0 or any number of times.

❑   {n} matches the character, class, or subpattern n times.

❑   {n,m} matches the character, class, or subpattern at least n times, at most m times.

❑   \d is shorthand notation for [0-9].

❑   \D is shorthand notation for [^0-9] (any character that is not a digit).

❑   \s is shorthand notation that matches any whitespace character.

❑   \S is shorthand notation that matches any non-whitespace character.

❑   \w is shorthand notation that matches any word character.

❑   \W is shorthand notation that matches any nonword character.

For more information on the syntax used in regular expressions, see the PHP manual page at http://www.php.net/manual/en/regexp.reference.php. And if you really want enough in-depth information on regular expressions to make your head explode, consider picking up a copy of the excellently written book *Mastering Regular Expressions*, by Jeffrey Friedl (http://oreilly.com/catalog/9780596528126/) from your local library.

Honestly, regular expressions are not that difficult, but they seem to be at first because they are so concise they are cryptic. But they really are very, very powerful tools for matching patterns. You'll see more regular expressions in Chapter 16.

Once you have verified that the date passed in by the user is in the appropriate format, you can change it into a timestamp, using the mktime() function, which allows you to create a timestamp from chunks of dates. It is also a very useful function for manipulating dates.

```
list($day, $month, $year) = explode('-', $movie_release);
if (!checkdate($month, $day, $year)) {
    $error[] = urlencode('Please enter a valid date.');
} else {
    $movie_release = mktime(0, 0, 0, $month, $day, $year);
}
```

The explode() function splits the date string on the dashes and returns an array, which is grabbed and placed into the $day, $month, and $year variables with list. With the individual components of the date available, it is verified as a valid date or not, with the checkdate() function. If the values make up a valid date, then checkdate() will return true; otherwise, it will return false. It is better to use checkdate() than to try to verify the date manually, because it takes leap years into account. And yes, you do want to check the date, even after the regular expression, because something like 99-99-9999 would pass the expression but be a very obviously erroneous date.

Summary

Validating user data is all about being prepared for the worst. Users make mistakes — that's the nature of users. Most errors are unintentional, but some are made intentionally to break your application and deny the service to others. It happens every day. As a developer, you must build into the application the ability to deal with user input errors.

Functions that can inspect the contents of a variable can help you meet most user input validation challenges. Learning how to use PHP's built-in functions — such as the `empty()`, `checkdate()`, `is_*`, and `ctype_*` functions — properly is often the key to successful validation in an interactive system.

Sometimes, more functionality is needed. This is when you will find yourself using regular expressions. As you learned in this chapter, regular expressions form a concise pattern-matching language. With them, you can write a pattern and compare any text against it. They can be a bit difficult to grasp at first because they are so cryptic, but they are very effective and powerful.

Exercises

1. Add validation to the code that adds and edits people records.

2. Write and test a regular expression pattern to validate an e-mail address.

Handling and Avoiding Errors

You will probably be spending a fair amount of time contemplating errors in your code, as do most web developers. No matter how good you are, how well you code, how long you have been coding, or how hard you try, you will encounter times when you have errors in your code.

It is of the utmost importance that you know how to handle your errors and debug your own code. Being able to efficiently and properly debug your code is an invaluable time saver, and in web development, $time == $money!

Luckily, PHP provides you with many ways to isolate and resolve most, if not all, of these unwanted errors. PHP also allows you to capture the errors and create your own custom error functions or pages. These features are useful when debugging your code and when notifying your webmaster about errors that seem to be happening to your applications as users are running them. Not only can you use PHP code to trap errors and customize the error messages, you can use the Apache web server to help do this.

How the Apache Web Server Deals with Errors

Apache has a directive, the ErrorDocument, that you can configure in the httpd.conf file to create custom error pages with PHP, so visitors to your site do not see the default server-based error pages, which may not be as helpful or descriptive as customized error messages.

You have limitless possibilities when creating these custom messages. As with the PHP error-catching pages, you can have the ErrorDocument call PHP pages to do whatever you would like them to do — from simply displaying a friendly error message to the user, to e-mailing a system administrator to notify him or her of the failure.

Unlike PHP error pages, the Apache ErrorDocument pages are used more for instances of missing pages (that is, a Page Not Found error or Forbidden Access error pages and other requests of that sort). So, if someone visits your site and runs into the Page Not Found error page, the script will e-mail the administrator, who can in turn check to see whether this was a valid request and there is something wrong with the page or server, or whether someone was just looking for the wrong pages, or if this was a malicious user trying to sniff around where he or she wasn't supposed to be.

Apache's ErrorDocument Directive

Error handling is an invaluable resource and a must have for web developers, to keep their sites up and running with the fewest end-user problems or complaints. If you rely solely on people contacting you to tell you about errors on your site, it is difficult to have a smoothly running server. Allowing the server to do this for you will greatly increase your success at running a smooth server. This section first looks at Apache's ErrorDocument method of error handling.

Try It Out   Using Apache's ErrorDocument Method

First of all, you need to make some changes to the `httpd.conf` file to allow you to create a custom error page. Apache is usually set up by default to go to its own internal error pages, but you don't want that. You want Apache to go to your custom error page, no matter what error has occurred.

To do this, you change the default settings to your own specific settings by following these steps:

1.   Open up your `httpd.conf` file, and you will find some lines that look like this:

```
#
# Customizable error responses come in three flavors:
# 1) plain text 2) local redirects 3) external redirects
#
# Some examples:
#ErrorDocument 500 "The server made a boo boo."
#ErrorDocument 404 /missing.html
#ErrorDocument 404 "/cgi-bin/missing_handler.pl"
#ErrorDocument 402 http://www.example.com/subscription_info.html
#
```

2.   Change that information to the following, and then restart Apache:

```
#
# Customizable error responses come in three flavors:
# 1) plain text 2) local redirects 3) external redirects
#
# Some examples:
ErrorDocument 400 /error.php?400
ErrorDocument 401 /error.php?401
ErrorDocument 403 /error.php?403
ErrorDocument 404 /error.php?404
ErrorDocument 500 /error.php?500
```

How It Works

You have just edited Apache's configuration file to help you with error handling. By using the `ErrorDocument` directive, you are able to send users to specific error pages, depending on what error the server has encountered. For example, if you receive a 404 error, the typical "Page Cannot Be Found" page, you can redirect it to a page you have created to look like your web site, while still getting the message through to the user that there has been a problem. You can do that with any and all error messages that the server can encounter.

Many `ErrorDocument` codes exist, but we will focus on the error messages you see typically in everyday web browsing:

- **400:** Bad Request
- **401:** Authorization Required
- **403:** Forbidden
- **404:** Not Found
- **500:** Internal Server Error

Numerous other error codes exist, of course. You can find a complete list at `http://rfc.net/rfc2616.html#p57`.

Although you are seeing just a few error codes in this exercise, you can catch others as well by simply adding another ErrorDocument to the `httpd.conf` file. For example, if you want to implement the 501 error code, you simply add `ErrorDocument 501 /error.php?501` to your code and add the error handling in the `error.php` page, which you'll see shortly.

Next, you'll see a simple way to show the user error messages, and then get into some more complex ways to notify the webmaster of errors occurring on the web site by using the `mail()` function, which you learned previously.

Try It Out   Displaying Custom Error Messages

To show the user error messages, follow these steps:

1. Open your text editor, and save a page called `error.php`.

2. Enter the following code:

```
<html>
 <head>
  <title>Beginning PHP6, Apache, MySQL Web Development Custom Error Page
</title>
 </head>
 <body>
<?php
switch ($_SERVER['QUERY_STRING']) {
case 400:
```

```
          echo '<h1>Bad Request</h1>';
          echo '<h2>Error Code 400</h2>';
          echo '<p>The browser has made a Bad Request.</p>';
          break;

   case 401:
          echo '<h1>Authorization Required</h1>';
          echo '<h2>Error Code 401</h2>';
          echo '<p>You have supplied the wrong information to access a secure ' .
              'resource.</p>';
          break;

     case 403:
          echo '<h1>Access Forbidden</h1>';
          echo '<h2>Error Code 403</h2>';
          echo '<p>You have been denied access to this resource.</p>';
          break;

     case 404:
          echo '<h1>Page Not Found</h1>';
          echo '<h2>Error Code 404</h2>';
          echo '<p>The page you are looking for cannot be found.</p>';
          break;

     case 500:
          echo '<h1>Internal Server Error</h1>';
          echo '<h2>Error Code 500</h2>';
          echo '<p>The server has encountered an internal error.</p>';
          break;

     default:
          echo '<h1>Error Page</h1>';
          echo '<p>This is a custom error page...</p>';
}

echo '<p><a href="mailto:sysadmin@example.com">Contact</a> the system ' .
     'administrator if you feel this to be in error.</p>';
?>
 </body>
</html>
```

3. Open your browser and type `http://localhost/nonexistent/page.html`, or any other page you know for certain doesn't reside on your server, into the address bar. You should see the Page Not Found message on the screen, similar to the message shown in Figure 9-1.

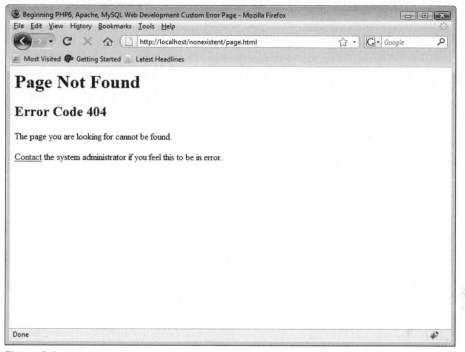

Figure 9-1

4. Another way to test or simulate the error messages, so that you can ensure you coded the page correctly, is to supply the page with the query string information via the browser. For example, to simulate an Internal Server Error error message, type `http://localhost/ error.php?500` into your address bar. The page will use the query string information and run the code just as if there were an Internal Server Error on one of your pages. The result will look pretty similar to the previous example, but will contain a different message. The Internal Server Error page will look like the one shown in Figure 9-2, displaying the Internal Server Error message on the screen.

Figure 9-2

How It Works

You have just created a simple error-handling PHP page. You created a PHP page that will handle the most common errors that servers encounter. By using the query string information along with the `switch()` statement, you are able to display custom error message pertinent to the error itself. This is useful if you don't want Apache to display its somewhat cryptic-looking error message to your users.

Apache's ErrorDocument: Advanced Custom Error Page

Up until this point, you've been showing the user a custom error message only. You can do countless other things, such as e-mailing the administrator or webmaster of the site, so he or she can look into the issue further should there be a problem with certain pages. This is a great way for you to keep track of your pages without having to check up on the server periodically. More than likely, if you haven't received any error e-mails, there haven't been problems with your server.

Try It Out **Creating an Error E-Mail**

In this exercise, you will create a script that generates an automatic e-mail that tells the administrator what time the error occurred, on what day, what the error was, what page generated the error, and what error message was displayed to the user who navigated to the page.

1. Open your `error.php` file, and add to it the code highlighted here:

```
<html>
 <head>
  <title>Beginning PHP6, Apache, MySQL Web Development Custom Error Page</title>
 </head>
 <body>
<?php
switch ($_SERVER['QUERY_STRING']) {
case 400:
    echo '<h1>Bad Request</h1>';
    echo '<h2>Error Code 400</h2>';
    echo '<p>The browser has made a Bad Request.</p>';
    break;

case 401:
    echo '<h1>Authorization Required</h1>';
    echo '<h2>Error Code 401</h2>';
    echo '<p>You have supplied the wrong information to access a secure ' .
        'resource.</p>';
    break;

  case 403:
    echo '<h1>Access Forbidden</h1>';
    echo '<h2>Error Code 403</h2>';
    echo '<p>You have been denied access to this resource.</p>';
    break;

  case 404:
    echo '<h1>Page Not Found</h1>';
    echo '<h2>Error Code 404</h2>';
    echo '<p>The page you are looking for cannot be found.</p>';
    break;

  case 500:
    echo '<h1>Internal Server Error</h1>';
    echo '<h2>Error Code 500</h2>';
    echo '<p>The server has encountered an internal error.</p>';
    break;

  default:
    echo '<h1>Error Page</h1>';
    echo '<p>This is a custom error page...</p>';
}
```

```
echo '<p><a href="mailto:sysadmin@example.com">Contact</a> the system ' .
    'administrator if you feel this to be in error.</p>';

$now = (isset($_SERVER['REQUEST_TIME'])) ? $_SERVER['REQUEST_TIME'] : time();
$page = (isset($_SERVER['REQUEST_URI'])) ? $_SERVER['REQUEST_URI'] :
'unknown';

$msg = wordwrap('A ' . $_SERVER['QUERY_STRING'] . ' error was encountered on ' .
    date('F d, Y', $now) . ' at ' . date('H:i:sa T', $now) . ' when a ' .
    'visitor attempted to view ' . $page . '.');

mail('admin@example.com', 'Error from Website', $msg);
?>
    </body>
</html>
```

How It Works

The output that you see in the browser will be the same as you saw before, but behind the scenes, the mail() function is used to send an e-mail to the administrator. The mail() function allows you to e-mail anyone you desire when an error occurs. You will learn about the mail() function in more detail in Chapter 11.

That's it! You just used Apache's ErrorDocument directive to help you maintain your server.

Error Handling and Creating Error-Handling Pages with PHP

This section looks at how you can troubleshoot your PHP scripts using simple, logical steps. But first, you need to understand what PHP does when it encounters an error and what it does with certain errors.

When a PHP script gets executed and encounters an error, it displays a message in the browser showing you what the error was. Depending on what type of error occurred, the script may not finish executing. You are likely to run into these sorts of errors when writing your own scripts. Don't feel ashamed if you receive errors; everybody makes errors when writing code, no matter what their level of expertise. Even though it is normal to receive errors during the development of your script, you don't want those errors (which are usually too complicated for the layperson to understand) popping up to end users, when your site has gone live. For this reason, it's important to know how to catch those unwanted errors and generate more user-friendly errors that let the user know that there will be a solution forthcoming.

Error Types in PHP

There are 13 predefined error constants that correspond to different types of errors in PHP. They are listed below, along with the E_ALL option. Each of these can be called by either an integer value or a named constant, but because the integer value they represent may change between different versions of PHP (as the value of E_ALL did in PHP 5.2), we recommend only using the constant name.

- ❏ E_ERROR: Fatal runtime errors that cannot be recovered from; the execution of the script is halted.

- ❏ E_WARNING: Nonfatal runtime errors.

- ❏ E_PARSE: Compile-time parse errors.

- ❏ E_NOTICE: Nonfatal runtime notices that indicate that the script encountered something that might be an error, but could also happen in the normal course of running a script.

- ❏ E_CORE_ERROR: Fatal errors that occur during PHP's initial startup; the execution of the script is halted.

- ❏ E_CORE_WARNING: Nonfatal errors that occur during PHP's initial startup.

- ❏ E_COMPILE_ERROR: Fatal compile-time errors; the execution of the script is halted.

- ❏ E_COMPILE_WARNING: Nonfatal compile-time errors.

- ❏ E_USER_ERROR: User-generated error messages (like E_ERROR, but instead generated by using the trigger_error() function); the execution of the script is halted.

- ❏ E_USER_WARNING: User-generated warning messages (like E_WARNING, but instead generated by using the trigger_error() function).

- ❏ E_USER_NOTICE: User-generated notice messages (like E_NOTICE, but instead generated by using the trigger_error() function).

- ❏ E_STRICT: Runtime notices that suggest changes to your code that would ensure the best interoperability and forward compatibility of your code.

- ❏ E_RECOVERABLE_ERROR: Catchable fatal errors that indicate that a probably dangerous error occurred, but did not leave the PHP's execution engine in an unstable state.

- ❏ E_ALL: All errors and warnings combined.

  Before version 6 of PHP, E_ALL *combined all errors and warnings except for* E_STRICT.

Typically, you don't have to worry about all of the error types; your main concern is with runtime errors such as notices, warnings, and errors, along with the user-generated equivalents. The simple, more trivial errors, such as warnings, aren't useful to users but can be helpful to you, since they notify you that you forgot to initialize a variable or something similar. Because initializing variables is purely for your benefit while you are coding to track down errors before your web site launch, it is of no use to display these errors to users once your site goes live. Your error-handling code helps resolve these cryptic errors, to offer helpful, user-friendly messages.

The three main types of errors discussed here are:

❑ **Fatal errors:** Fatal runtime errors. These indicate errors that the program can't recover from. Script execution is halted.

❑ **Warnings:** Runtime warnings (nonfatal errors). Script execution is not halted.

❑ **Notices:** Runtime notices. These indicate that the script has encountered something that could indicate an error, but that could also happen in the normal course of running the script.

Generating PHP Errors

Now let's generate some errors so that you can check out what you need to do to resolve them. Consider this code snippet, for example:

```php
<?php
//set string with "Wrox" spelled wrong
$string_variable = 'Worx books are awesome!';

//try to use str_replace to replace Worx with Wrox
//this will generate an E_WARNING
//because of wrong parameter count
str_replace('Worx', 'Wrox');
?>
```

If you run this snippet, you should see the following error:

```
Warning: Wrong parameter count for str_replace() in C:\Program Files\Apache
Software Foundation\Apache2.2\htdocs\warning_test.php on line 8.
```

The error occurred because `str_replace()` requires a third parameter for the function. The third parameter is the variable, `$string_variable`, or a string of text in which you want to search for the first parameter, "Worx," and replace it with "Wrox." Because this is a nonfatal error that does not halt script execution, you can still run code after the point where the error occurred. If you change the snippet to this:

```php
<?php
//set string with "Wrox" spelled wrong
$string_variable = 'Worx books are awesome!';

//try to use str_replace to replace Worx with Wrox
//this will generate an E_WARNING
//because of wrong parameter count
str_replace('Worx', 'Wrox');

//this is a non-fatal error, so the original
//variable should still show up after the warning
echo $string_variable;
?>
```

then the string will continue to execute after the error, and will produce the following output:

```
Warning: Wrong parameter count for str_replace() in C:\Program Files\Apache
Software Foundation\Apache2.2\htdocs\warning_test.php on line 8.
Worx books are great!
```

Next, we throw out a fatal error to show you how it produces different results when the error occurs. Let's create a fatal error by using the following code:

```php
<?php
//beginning of page
echo 'Beginning';

//we are going to make a call to
//a function that doesn't exist
//this will generate an E_ERROR
//and will halt script execution
//after the call of the function
fatalerror();

//end of page
echo 'End';
//won't be output due to the fatal error
?>
```

This produces the following output:

```
Beginning
Fatal error: Call to undefined function: fatalerror() in C:\Program Files\
Apache Software Foundation\Apache2.2\htdocs\error_test.php on line 10.
```

Notice that "Beginning" was output because it was before the function call, but "End" was not, because the fatal error halted the script execution. You can suppress the fatal error calls by putting an ampersand in front of the function call, like so: `@fatalerror()`. This suppresses the error, but the script still halts its execution.

> The default error reporting does not show E_NOTICE errors. However, you may want to show them during development. Enabling E_NOTICE errors for debugging can warn you about possible bugs or bad programming practices. For example, you might use something such as `$row[variable]`, but actually it is better to write this as `$row['variable']` because PHP will try to treat `variable` as a constant. If, however, it isn't a constant, PHP assumes it to be a string for the array. You can set error reporting by simply putting `error_reporting(number)` in your script, where `number` is the constant value shown earlier in the chapter.

If you don't know at what level your error reporting is set, you can simply call the `error_reporting()` function without any arguments, like this:

```php
<?php
echo error_reporting();
?>
```

By default, all error handling is handled by PHP's built-in error handler, which tells you the error and displays the message associated with that error. The message displays the error type, the error message, the filename, and the line number where the error occurred.

Usually, letting PHP generate its own errors is fine, but with complicated applications you may want to *catch* the errors so you can do something specific with an error, such as notifying an administrator so he or she can look into the problem further.

Try It Out   **Creating a Custom Error Handler**

You will now create a custom error handler to catch the errors and display a more friendly error message.

1. Open your text editor, and enter this code:

```php
<?php
function my_error_handler($e_type, $e_message, $e_file, $e_line) {
    echo '<h1>Oops!</h1>';
    echo '<p>Errors have occurred while executing this page. Contact the ' .
        '<a href="mailto:admin@example.com">administrator</a> to report
        it.</p>';
    echo '<hr/>';
    echo '<p><b>Error Type:</b> ' . $e_type . '<br/>';
    echo '<b>Error Message:</b> ' . $e_message . '<br/>';
    echo '<b>Filename:</b> ' . $e_file . '<br/>';
    echo '<b>Line Number:</b> ' . $e_line . '</p>';
}

//set the error handler to be used
set_error_handler('my_error_handler');

//set string with "Wrox" spelled wrong
$string_variable = 'Worx books are awesome!';

//try to use str_replace to replace Worx with Wrox
//this will generate an E_WARNING
//because of wrong parameter count
str_replace('Worx', 'Wrox');
?>
```

2. Save the file as custom_error.php, and open it in your browser. The output should look similar to that in Figure 9-3.

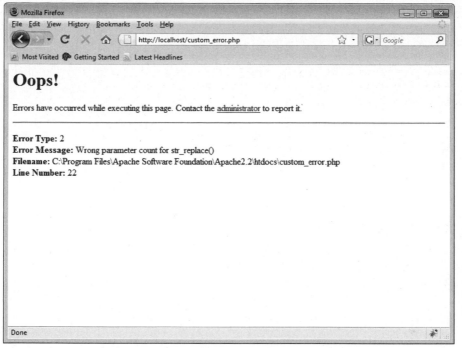

Figure 9-3

3. Because your error handler is user-defined, you can catch the errors, and you can recreate the error messages based on the error type. Edit the `custom_error.php` file like this:

```php
<?php
function my_error_handler($e_type, $e_message, $e_file, $e_line) {
// Delete these lines
    echo '<h1>Oops!</h1>';
    echo '<p>Errors have occurred while executing this page. Contact the ' .
        '<a href="mailto:admin@example.com">administrator</a> to report
it.</p>';
    echo '<hr/>';
    echo '<p><b>Error Type:</b> ' . $e_type . '<br/>';
    echo '<b>Error Message:</b> ' . $e_message . '<br/>';
    echo '<b>Filename:</b> ' . $e_file . '<br/>';
    echo '<b>Line Number:</b> ' . $e_line . '</p>';
// End deleted lines

    switch ($e_type) {
    case E_ERROR:
        echo '<h1>Fatal Error</h1>';
        echo '<p>A fatal error has occurred in ' . $e_file . ' at line ' .
            $e_line . '.<br/>' . $e_message . '.</p>';
        die();
        break;

    case E_WARNING:
        echo '<h1>Warning</h1>';
```

253

```
        echo '<p>A warning has occurred in ' . $e_file . ' at line ' . $e_line .
            '.<br/>' . $e_message . '.';
        break;

    case E_NOTICE:
        //don't show notice errors
        break;
    }
}

//set the error handler to be used
set_error_handler('my_error_handler');

//set string with "Wrox" spelled wrong
$string_variable = 'Worx books are awesome!';

//try to use str_replace to replace Worx with Wrox
//this will generate an E_WARNING
//because of wrong parameter count
str_replace('Worx', 'Wrox');
?>
```

4. Save the file, and load it in your browser. The results should look like Figure 9-4. One of the earlier code snippets you created produced a fatal error, which is why the E_ERROR case was called in the switch statement. This sort of handler is nice to use to trap any sort of error and perform different actions based on the error.

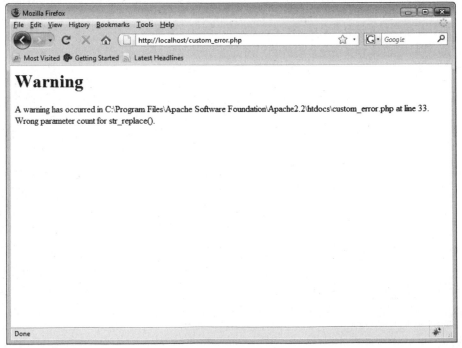

Figure 9-4

How It Works

Creating custom error message gives you nearly full control over your pages, regardless of success or failure when they are executed. What you have done is create a function called my_error_handler, which will catch the type of error, the error message, the file in which the error occurred, and the line in which the error occurred. By knowing those details, you can take whatever steps are necessary to ensure the success of your web site. The heart of the function's logic relies on a switch() construct, where you are able to display a certain error message, send specific error message e-mails, or do whatever else you may want, depending on which error was served up by Apache. For example, if you were to encounter an E_ERROR, the code would run the case E_ERROR: section of the switch(). Depending on which section of the switch() was used, you will see a different error message.

When trapping errors, you can display whatever you want to display, but you may not want the user to see the error message you created previously. You can create an error message that simply says there was an error on the page. Then you can apologize for the inconvenience and allow the user to go to another page. Finally, you can write the error message to a log file, write it to a database, or send it to the webmaster or administrator via e-mail, so that person can further review the error.

We personally prefer the e-mail method because it requires that the person be notified of the problem right away, and it doesn't require him or her to check the database or log files periodically. The only problem with this method occurs if there are a lot of requests to the page where the error is occurring; in that case the admin will be bombarded with e-mails. (Of course, this could light the proverbial fire under him or her to get the issue fixed!)

Try It Out   Creating a Full-Featured Error Page

For this exercise, you'll set up your full-featured error handler to do just what you want it to. You can then include this page in all your pages, so you can trap all the errors without using PHP's built-in handler.

1.   Open your text editor, and enter the following code:

```php
<?php
//create your error handler function
function my_error_handler($e_type, $e_message, $e_file, $e_line) {

    $msg = 'Errors have occurred while executing a page.' . "\n\n";
    $msg .= 'Error Type: ' . $e_type . "\n";
    $msg .= 'Error Message: ' . $e_message . "\n";
    $msg .= 'Filename: ' . $e_file . "\n";
    $msg .= 'Line Number: ' . $e_number . "\n";
    $msg = wordwrap($msg, 75);

    switch($error_type) {
    case E_ERROR:
        mail('admin@example.com', 'Fatal Error from Website', $msg);
        die();
        break;

    case E_WARNING:
        mail('admin@example.com', 'Warning from Website', $msg);
```

```
            break;
        }
    }

    //set error handling to 0 because we will handle all error reporting and
    //notify admin on warnings and fatal errors.
    error_reporting(0);

    //set the error handler to be used
    set_error_handler('my_error_handler');

    // Create the rest of your page here.
    ?>
```

2. Save the file as `feature_error.php`.

How It Works

Once you run this page, the code for the logic's actions is almost exactly the same, as far as the `switch()`. The only real difference is that it will be e-mailing the administrator, instead of merely displaying an error message to the user. It can still do that, but this example showed you the e-mail function instead of simply displaying a message to the users. Once you run this page and you receive an error, the script e-mails the admin with the error and some useful information about the user who visited the page that generated the error.

Other Methods of Error Handling

You've just seen some of what you can do with custom error messages, but there are other ways to deal with errors. *Exceptions* are a feature that enables your scripts to take specific actions based on the type of errors that you define. Other methods of error handling are more manual: inserting `echo` statements to check the value of your variables and watching to make sure your condition statements are being met properly. The PHP parser also provides some error messages for simple parse errors.

Exceptions

PHP5 introduced a new feature called exceptions. These are very similar to their counterparts in other languages, such as Java, so if you have done programming in another language, you may already be familiar with them. Exceptions handle unforeseen conditions in your web applications and provide you with an efficient way to handle errors that are encountered. PHP uses the `try/catch` method to handle exceptions.

Try It Out   **Experimenting with Exceptions**

In this exercise, you'll create a script that deliberately throws some exceptions, so you can see how they work.

1.   Create a PHP page with the following code:

```php
<?php
// $x = null;
// $x = 500;
$x = 1000;

try {
    if (is_null($x)) {
        throw new Exception('Value cannot be null.');
    }
    if ($x < 1000) {
        throw new Exception('Value cannot be less than 1000.');
    }

    echo 'Value passed validation.';
}
catch (Exception $e) {
    echo 'Validation failed. ' . $e->getMessage();
}
?>
```

2.   Save this code as `exceptions.php`, and then open it in your browser. You shouldn't see any errors.

3.   Comment out the line that sets `$x` to 1000, and remove the comment marks from the line that sets it to null.

4.   Save the file and run it again. Now you should see that the exception pertaining to the null value was thrown.

5.   Comment out the line that sets `$x` to a null value, and remove the comment marks from the one that sets it to 500.

6.   Save the file and run it again. Now you should see that the exception pertaining to value being less than 1000 was thrown.

How It Works

The usefulness of the `try` block is that all conditions in the `try` must be met, or the `catch` will be triggered. This is useful when you need to check many instances of different variables and situations, and you don't want to hop through that many `if/else` statements for your desired results. All you need is your trusty `if` statement and a thrown exception with an error message specific to the problem. If any `if` statement in the `try` block is true, the exception will be thrown and passed to the `catch` block. The `catch` block will then output the appropriate error message, depending on which exception was caught.

In the `catch` area, you can handle the error in any way you prefer. You may just want to tell the user about something, you may want to set some default variables, perform a combination of both, or do whatever you feel is needed at that point.

Another advantage to using exceptions is the way they propagate through nested functions and code. For example, if you have a function A that calls function B, which in turn calls function C, and an exception is thrown in function C without using `try{}`, the exception will stop processing the script immediately and bubble up through the call chain until a `catch` block is found.

If no `try{}...catch{}` block is found when traversing up the code, an error will be shown on the screen, indicating that an unhandled exception has occurred, like so:

```
Fatal error: Uncaught exception 'Exception' with message 'Value cannot be
null.' in C:\Program Files\Apache Software Foundation\Apache2.2\htdocs\
exceptions.php:8 Stack trace: #0 {main} thrown in C:\Program Files\Apache
Software Foundation\Apache2.2\htdocs\exceptions.php on line 8
```

Exceptions can also be rethrown, as follows:

```php
<?php
try {
    throw new Exception('This will be rethrown.');
}
catch (Exception $e) {
    throw $e;
}
?>
```

You can rethrow your exceptions in this way to deal with exceptions at different points in the code, or in one single place of your choosing.

All in all, exceptions act like an invisible "go to" that redirects the flow of your code to a specific location where you can handle the error. Using them can keep your code more organized and readable, because you don't have to mix error-handling code into your logic.

Not Meeting Conditions

Error trapping cannot catch all problems in your code. It will catch only problems related to PHP itself. Any problems you are having with conditions in your code will not be caught by simple error trapping. You'll have to do this manually, by using several different methods of troubleshooting in your code.

For example, say you are submitting a form and you are wondering why the condition isn't true when you are checking for submission. Suppose you have an input such as this:

```
<input type="submit" name="submit" value="Submit">
```

You are checking whether or not the submit button has been pressed, to see whether or not you should process the form information. You are probably doing a check similar to this:

```
if ($_POST['submit'] == 'submit') {
    //form has been submitted
} else {
    //form has not been submitted
}
```

See if you can figure out what is wrong with the code, causing you not to get the if statement. Here's a hint: The value of the submit button is Submit, not submit. To troubleshoot to see if your condition is working or not, you can simply put a line in your if statement such as this:

```
if ($_POST['submit'] == 'submit') {
    //form has been submitted
    echo 'In the if statement';
} else {
    //form has not been submitted
}
```

If you get into the if statement, the echoed line is output to the browser. If you don't change the lowercase "submit" to an uppercase "Submit," you don't see that echo in the browser, so you can then further investigate why you aren't getting into the if statement. Once you realize the error, you can change the case and test it again, and voilà, the line has been echoed.

You will find that you need to use this technique to establish where in your code actions are happening. Not only do you want to do this with if statements, but you will probably be using it to test for loops, while loops, foreach loops, do while loops, and many others, at other times when you are running conditions or expecting results, and you can't figure out why something isn't working.

Another common problem occurs when variables aren't being output. Most of the time, the variables are just fine, but the programmer can't figure out why they aren't being output. Again, the conditions aren't being met, and if a condition isn't met and the expected variables are in the condition, they obviously aren't going to be output. Many programmers run into this problem and have a hard time figuring it out. They tend to lay blame on the variables before checking to see whether or not their conditions have been met.

Sometimes the variables are the reason for the condition not being met, as shown in the previous paragraph. The programmer uses the wrong value to check the if statement, and the condition fails. The best thing for you to do in this situation is to troubleshoot. Throw in an echo here and an echo there to see where your problems are. You might even want to use print_r($_POST) to see what posted values are received. Don't give up at the first sign of defeat: You should exhaust all of your own programming resources before you go looking for help elsewhere.

Parse Errors

A parse error is another main error type. Parse errors occur when you forget a semicolon, when curly braces are mismatched, when square brackets aren't used properly, and so on. These parse errors usually don't have to do with a condition statement; they are mainly syntax errors that will cause the script to halt execution. Parse errors are worse than fatal errors because they won't even let the script run at all; they merely give you the error information.

Summary

You have read through a lot of useful information in this chapter. Learning from your own mistakes and errors will help you to be quicker at noticing small, trivial mistakes that are causing problems in your code. The single best action a programmer can learn is how to troubleshoot. Once you have that figured out, nothing can hold you back from creating seamless applications that will impress your clients — and yourself.

Exercises

Here are three short snippets of code to sift through. Try to spot the errors and figure out how to fix them. The answers are provided in Appendix A. Once you are finished, using what you have learned, create a little error-catching script to catch the errors.

1.

```php
<?php
$query = "SELECT * FROM table_name " .
         "WHERE name = '" . $_POST['name'] . "';"
$result = mysql_query($result)
  or die(mysql_error());
?>
```

2.

```php
<?php
if ($_POST['first_name'] = "Jethro") {
  echo "Your name is " . $_POST['first_name'];
}
?>
```

3.

```php
<?php
$full_name = $_POST['mrmiss'] ". " $_POST['first_name'] " " $_POST['last_name'];
?>
```

Part II
Comic Book Fan Site

Building Databases

You created a very nice movie review site by following along with the previous chapters, but now the handholding is over, my friend. It's time for us to push you out of the nest and let you begin to fly on your own. So, in this chapter, you will have the opportunity to create your own databases and your own web site.

We show you how to put together a comic book appreciation web site, but you can take the concepts we teach you and branch off to create that online auction or antique car site you have always dreamed about doing.

This chapter covers the basics of creating your own database. The topics discussed here include:

- ❑ Planning the design of your database.
- ❑ Database normalization.
- ❑ Creating your database.
- ❑ Creating and modifying tables in your database.
- ❑ Building web pages to access your data with PHP.

Getting Started

You have a great idea for a site, right? Excellent. But don't open up your PHP editor and start coding just yet! Believe it or not, many people approach the creation of a web site in just this way. You may be tempted to do this yourself. And while it is not impossible to create a good site by just diving into the code headfirst, you are seriously handicapping your chances for greatness, if you do it that way. Before you begin, you need a plan.

We're not going to tell you how to plan out an entire web site, complete with charts and maps and business models. That's not what this book is about. We are going to assume that you or somebody in your company has already learned that by reading other great books on business models, attending seminars, reading great articles on the web, and perhaps even hiring a business consultant to help with everything but building that dream site.

So we will assume you have a great idea for a web site *and* a plan. What do you suppose is the first step in creating a successful web application using PHP, Apache, and MySQL, after all that planning? We'll give you a clue: Look at the title of this chapter.

You need to build the database this site will be based on. Don't worry — one of the great things about relational database design is that you don't have to create *every* table your site will use. You can start with a few, and build upon them as time progresses. As long as you follow the basic principles of good database design, your database should be quite scalable and expand to any size.

Does this sound like a daunting task? Relax. You see, we know a secret that has been kept hidden like the magician's code: *Efficient database design is easy.* No, really, we promise! You see, most of us computer geeks like to seem invaluable and very intelligent, and it sounds quite impressive to most interviewers to see on a resume "Designed a comprehensive web site utilizing an RDBMS back end." But when you are done with this chapter, you will see how easy it really is and be able to put that on your own resume as well!

What Is a Relational Database?

Let's first cover a few basics of database design. A relational database is a collection of data organized in tables that can be used to create, retrieve, delete, and update that data in many different ways. This can be done without having to reorganize the tables themselves, especially if the data is organized efficiently.

Take a look at the first table that follows.

You can see that it contains a very simple collection of data, consisting of superheroes' aliases and real names, each assigned a superhero ID. Nothing too amazing, of course, but notice how the table relates to the league table that follows it. Each superhero has a League_ID that corresponds to an ID in the league table. Through this link, or *relationship*, you can see that Average Man is a member of the Dynamic Dudes League, because the ID in the league table matches his League_ID in the superhero table.

Superhero_ID	League_ID	Alias	Real_Name
1	2	Average Man	Jeff Smith
2	2	The Flea	Tom Jacobs
3	1	Albino Dude	George White
4	3	Amazing Woman	Mary Jones

League_ID	League_Name
1	Extraordinary People
2	Dynamic Dudes
3	Stupendous Seven
4	Justice Network

At first glance it may seem silly to create a table with one data column and an ID. Why not just put the league name in the superhero table? Imagine that you had a database of 10,000 superheroes, and 250 of them were in the Dynamic Dudes league. Now imagine that the Superhero Consortium decided to do a reorganization, and "Dynamic Dudes" was changed to the "Incredible Team." If the league name were in the superhero table, you would have to edit 250 records to change the value. And what if you missed one? You only have to change the name in one place if the leagues are in a separate, *related* table.

That relationship is the key to a relational database. And speaking of keys . . .

Keys

A *key* is a unique value that identifies each row within a table. It can be the value in a particular column or a collection of values across several columns. A key uniquely identifies each row within the table, because no two rows can have the same key. Each table is allowed to have one special key, called a *primary key*, that serves as a primary unique identifier for the table.

Most of the time, the primary key is a single column, but it is not uncommon to use more than one column to make up a primary key. The important distinction is that the primary key must be unique for each row. Because of that characteristic, you can use the key to identify a specific row of data.

The primary key must contain the following characteristics:

- ❑ It cannot be empty.

- ❑ It will never change in value. Therefore, a primary key cannot contain information that might change, such as part of a last name (for example, smith807).

- ❑ It must be unique. No two rows can contain the same primary key.

The League_ID column in the superhero table is also a key. It matches the primary key of the league table, but it is in a different, or *foreign*, table. For this reason, it is called a *foreign key*. Although it is not a requirement, many programmers will give the foreign key a name that identifies the table it refers to ("League") and some identifier that marks it as a key ("_ID"). This, along with the fact that keys are usually numeric, makes it fairly clear which column is the foreign key, if one exists in the table at all.

Keys do not have to be purely numeric. Other common values used as primary keys include Social Security numbers (which contain dashes) and usernames. Any value is valid as a primary key, as long as it is guaranteed to be unique for each individual record in the table and will not change over time.

Relationships

In order to be related, the two tables need a column they can use to tie them together. The superhero and league tables are related to each other by the League_ID column in the superhero table and the League_ID field in the league table. There is no explicit link created in the database; rather, you create the relationship by linking them with a SQL statement:

```
SELECT * FROM superhero, league WHERE superhero.League_ID = league.League_ID
```

In plain English, this statement tells the MySQL server to "select all records from the superhero table and the league table, and link the two tables by the superhero `League_ID` column and the league `League_ID` column."

There are three types of relationships: one-to-one (1:1), one-to-many (1:M), and many-to-many (M:N). The previous example is a one-to-many relationship. To figure out what type of relationship the tables have, ask yourself how many superheroes you can have in a league. The answer is more than one, or "many." How many leagues can a superhero belong to? The answer is "one." That is a one-to-many relationship. (Of course, in some universes, a superhero might belong to more than one league. But for this example, all of our superheroes will exhibit league loyalty.)

One-to-many is the most common database relationship. 1:1 relationships don't happen often, and a many-to-many relationship is actually two one-to-many relationships joined together with a "linking table." We will explore that further later in the chapter.

Although they are more rare, here's an example of a one-to-one (1:1) relationship. Say you have a link between a company and its main office address. Only one company can have that exact address. In many applications, however, the main office address is included in the company table, so no relationship is needed.

Referential Integrity

The concept of referential integrity may be a little lofty for a beginner book like this, but we think it is important to touch on this briefly. If your application has referential integrity, then when a record in a table refers to a record in another table (as the previous example did), the latter table will contain the corresponding record. If the record it references is deleted, then you have lost referential integrity.

This is not disastrous in many cases. You might have an article written by an author whose name no longer exists in the author table. You still want to keep the article, so losing the referential integrity between authors and articles is okay. However, if you have an order in your database that can't be related to a customer because the customer was deleted, then you might be hard-pressed to figure out where to send the product and whom to charge for it.

Ways exist to enforce referential integrity in a MySQL database, but these concepts and procedures are beyond the scope of this book. If you are interested in obtaining more information about referential integrity and foreign keys, visit `www.mysql.com/doc/en/InnoDB_foreign_key_constraints.html`.

Normalization

"Database normalization" is one of those big fancy terms that database administrators like to throw around, along with "Boyce-Codd Normal Form," "trivial functional dependency," and "Heisenberg compensator." The terms themselves aren't really important to know, to be able to design a good database, but the concepts are. We'll touch on normalization here.

For our purposes, we will define normalization as the process of organizing your database's table structure so that dependencies make sense, and there is no redundant data. In a moment, you are going to go through this process, because the best way to learn is to do!

Designing Your Database

It's time to design your application's database. This will be a relatively simple application, but it will help you learn important concepts, such as normalization, and expose you to various SQL commands. Typically, this is where you would go through a "Try It Out" section and learn "How It Works." When first designing a database, however, you do not need your computer. All you need is a pad of paper and a pencil. So, go get some paper and a pencil . . . we'll wait.

OK, let's draw some tables. The application you are going to design is a comic book character database. You will store a little bit of information about various characters, such as their alter egos, their real names, the powers they possess, and the locations of their secret lairs.

Creating the First Table

Before you open MySQL and start messing around with tables, you need to figure out how you are going to store all of the data. For simplicity, create one big table with all of the relevant data. You can draw it out on your piece of paper. Copy the information you see in the table that follows.

Name	Real Name	Power 1	Power 2	Power 3	Lair Address	City	State	Zip
Clean Freak	Carl Smith	Strength	X-ray vision	Flight	123 Poplar Avenue	Townsburg	OH	45293
Soap Stud	Efram Jones	Speed			123 Poplar Avenue	Townsburg	OH	45293
The Dustmite	Dustin Hare	Strength	Dirtiness	Laser vision	452 Elm Street #3D	Burgtown	OH	45201

Call this table "zero," because you're not even at the first step yet, and the data is just *ugly* from a relational database standpoint.

The first thing you should notice is that there are multiple power columns. What would you do if you had to add a character with more than three powers? You would have to create a new column, and that's not good. Instead, you should combine all the powers into one column, and then separate each power into its own separate row. The other columns are duplicated in these additional rows (so, Clean Freak would have three rows instead of one, each row including a different power in the power column, but the name, address, and so on would remain identical among the three listings). This concept is called *atomicity*. Each value (cell) is *atomic*, or has only one item of data.

You also should create a unique primary key for each character. Yes, you could use the character's name, but remember that a primary key should never be something that could change, and it must be unique. To handle this requirement, you'll create a Character ID column.

Because in this pass you have multiple rows with the same character, and the multiple rows are a result of the existence of multiple powers, you'll combine the Character ID column with the power column to create the primary key. When more than one column makes up the primary key, it is called a *composite primary key*. We'll mark the primary key columns with an asterisk (*) to highlight them for you.

Your table should look like the one that follows. Call this table "one" because it's your first pass at normalizing. (See, you are in the middle of a normalization process and didn't even realize it. We told you it wasn't difficult.)

Character Id*	Name	Real Name	Power*	Lair Address	City	State	Zip
1	Clean Freak	Carl Smith	Strength	123 Poplar Avenue	Townsburg	OH	45293
1	Clean Freak	Carl Smith	X-ray vision	123 Poplar Avenue	Townsburg	OH	45293
1	Clean Freak	Carl Smith	Flight	123 Poplar Avenue	Townsburg	OH	45293
2	Soap Stud	Efram Jones	Speed	123 Poplar Avenue	Townsburg	OH	45293
3	The Dustmite	Dustin Hare	Strength	452 Elm Street #3D	Burgtown	OH	45201
3	The Dustmite	Dustin Hare	Dirtiness	452 Elm Street #3D	Burgtown	OH	45201
3	The Dustmite	Dustin Hare	Laser vision	452 Elm Street #3D	Burgtown	OH	45201

Looking better, but there is still repeated data in there. In fact, the power column is what is causing the duplicate data. Separate out the power column, and use a foreign key to relate it to the original table. You will also further normalize the power table so that you get rid of duplicate data. This is pass number "two." See the three tables that follow.

Character Id*	Name	Real Name	Lair Address	City	State	Zip
1	Clean Freak	Carl Smith	123 Poplar Avenue	Townsburg	OH	45293
2	Soap Stud	Efram Jones	123 Poplar Avenue	Townsburg	OH	45293
3	The Dustmite	Dustin Hare	452 Elm Street #3D	Burgtown	OH	45201

Power_Id*	Power
1	Strength
2	X-ray vision
3	Flight
4	Speed
5	Dirtiness
6	Laser vision

Character_Id*	Power_Id*
1	1
1	2
1	3
2	4
3	1
3	5
3	6

As you can see, you have much less repeated data than you did before. The powers have been separated out, and a link table has been created to link each power to each appropriate character.

It may seem a bit nitpicky, but you still have some duplicate data that you can take care of in the character table. It is quite possible for more than one character to be in the same lair, as is the case with Clean Freak and Soap Stud. Create a lair table, and link it to the character table with keys. Also add a new column to the character table for good vs. evil alignment. See the two tables that follow.

Character_Id*	Lair_Id	Name	Real Name	Alignment
1	1	Clean Freak	Carl Smith	Good
2	1	Soap Stud	Efram Jones	Good
3	2	The Dustmite	Dustin Hare	Evil

Lair_Id*	Lair Address	City	State	Zip
1	123 Poplar Avenue	Townsburg	OH	45293
2	452 Elm Street #3D	Burgtown	OH	45201

We waited to add the alignment column to illustrate a point. If you are in the middle of the normalization process, and discover that there is some other data you need to add, it isn't difficult to do so. You could even add a completely new table if you needed to.

The city and state fields are not only duplicates, but also redundant data with the zip code (which is in itself a representation of the city/state). City and state are also not directly related to the lairs (because other lairs could exist in the same city). For these reasons, you will put city and state in a separate table.

Because the zip code is numeric, and a direct representation of city/state, you will make the zip column a primary key. This is pass "three," shown in the three tables that follow.

Character_Id*	Lair_Id	Name	Real Name	Alignment
1	1	Clean Freak	John Smith	Good
2	1	Soap Stud	Efram Jones	Good
3	2	The Dustmite	Dustin Hare	Evil

Lair_Id*	Zip_Id	Lair Address
1	45293	123 Poplar Avenue
2	45201	452 Elm Street #3D

Zip_Id*	City	State
45293	Townsburg	OH
45201	Burgtown	OH

You may have noticed that you have created a many-to-many (M:N) relationship between the characters and their powers (a character can have multiple powers, and many characters may have the same power). There are two tables with primary keys, and a linking table between them has two foreign keys, one for each of the tables. The combination of the foreign keys is a primary key for the char_power table. This enables the M:N relationship.

Just for fun, add a small table that links the superheroes to villains, and vice versa. This is another M:N relationship, because any superhero can have multiple villain enemies, and any villain can have multiple superhero enemies. Of course, you have the character table as one of the "many" sides of the equation — can you figure out which table to use for the other "many" side? If you said the character table, you are correct! This is just like the character-power relationship, but this time you reference the table to itself via a good_bad linking table. The hero_id and villain_id columns *each* link to the id column in the character table. Each column in the good_bad table is a foreign key, and both columns make up a composite primary key.

Hero_Id*	Villain_Id*
1	3
2	3

And just like that, you have created your database design. Congratulations! You now have a "map" that will help you create your database tables on the server. Not only that, but you just normalized your database design as well, by modifying your database table structure so that dependencies make sense, and there is no redundant data. In fact, you have actually gone through the proper normalization steps of First, Second, and Third Normal Form.

What's So Normal about These Forms?

Remember we told you to call the first table "zero"? That's called zero form.

It is basically the raw data, and is usually a very flat structure, with lots of repeated data. You see data like this sometimes when a small company keeps records of its customers in a spreadsheet.

The first pass through the table, which you called pass "one," was the first step of normalization, called First Normal Form, commonly abbreviated as 1NF. This step requires that you eliminate all repeating data in columns (which you did with the power column), create separate rows for each group of related data, and identify each record with a primary key. The first step satisfies the requirements of 1NF.

You can see where we're going with this, can't you? The Second Normal Form (2NF) requirements state that you must place subsets of data in multiple rows in separate tables. You did that by separating the power data into its own table. Second Normal Form also requires that you create a relationship with the original table by creating a foreign key. You did that in pass "two," when you satisfied the requirements for 2NF.

On your third pass, you removed all the columns not directly related to the primary key (city and state), and used the zip code as the foreign key to the new `city_state` table. Third Normal Form (3NF) is then satisfied. Congratulations! You normalized a database just like the pros do.

There are further requirements for database normalization, but Third Normal Form (3NF) is generally accepted as being good enough for most business applications. The next step is Boyce-Codd Normal Form (BCNF), followed by Fourth Normal Form (4NF) and Fifth Normal Form (5NF). In this case, the other forms don't apply — the database is as normalized as it needs to get. All tables are easily modifiable and updatable, without affecting data in the other tables.

> We know there are some database gurus out there who would tell you that in order to completely satisfy the forms of normalization, the alignment column should be put into its own table and linked with a foreign key as well. While that may be true in the strictest sense of the rules, we usually think of normalization as a guideline. In this case, we have only two values, good and evil. Those values will never change, and they will be the only values available to the user. Because of this, we can actually create a column with the ENUM datatype. Because the values good and evil will be hard-coded into the table definition, and we don't see a need ever to change the values in the future, there is no problem with keeping those values in the `char_main` table.

Standardization

When you are designing a new application, it is a very good idea to come up with *standards*, or design rules, that you adhere to in all cases. These can be extensive, such as the standards published by the W3C for HTML, XML, and other markup languages. They can also be very short, but very strict, such as the list of 10 standards brought down from a mountain by an old, bearded man long ago. For now, you'll just standardize your table structure. For this application, we came up with the following table standards:

❑ **Table names:** Table names should be descriptive, but relatively short. Table names will be in lowercase. They should describe what main function they serve, and which application they belong to. All six tables should start with comic_ to show that they belong to our comic book application. Many people prefer to list the name in a singular form.

❑ **Column names:** Table columns are similar to table names. All column names will be in lowercase. They will be kept short, but multiple words (such as lair and address) will be separated by an underscore (_) (e.g., lair_addr).

❑ **Primary keys:** Single primary keys will always be called tablename_id. Except in special cases, primary keys will be an integer datatype that is automatically incremented. If they consist of a single column, they will always be the first column of the table.

❑ **Foreign keys:** Foreign keys will end with _id. They will start with the table descriptor. For example, in the char_lair table, the foreign key for the char_zipcode table will be called zip_id.

Finalizing the Database Design

One other thing we like to do during the database design process is put the datatypes into the empty cells of each table. You can save these tables and easily refer to them when you are writing the SQL code. You may want to do this yourself (or just use the tables provided).

If you don't understand MySQL's datatypes, you can learn about them in Chapter 3, and datatypes are discussed in more detail a little later in this chapter as well. For now, just understand that datatypes are the type of data stored in each table column, such as INT (integer), VARCHAR (variable-length character string), CHAR (fixed-length character string), or ENUM (enumerated list). When appropriate, they are followed by the length in parentheses; for example, varchar(100) is a character column that can contain up to 100 characters.

Reduce the tables to two rows, one with column names, the other row blank. If you want, you can make a photocopy of your tables before erasing the data.

In keeping with the previously listed table standards, we arrive at the following tables. Yours should look very similar.

Character_Id*	Lair_Id	Name	Real_Name	Alignment
int	int	varchar(40)	varchar(80)	enum('good','evil')

Power_Id*	Power
int	varchar(40)

Character_Id*	Power_Id*
int	int

Lair_Id*	Zipcode_Id	Address
int	char(5)	varchar(40)

Zipcode_Id*	City	State
varchar(10)	varchar(40)	char(2)

Hero_Id*	Villain_Id*
int(11)	int(11)

We think it is about time you actually created these tables on the server. Ready? Let's create the database first, and then get going!

Creating a Database in MySQL

You can create a database in a number of ways. All require the execution of a SQL statement in one way or another, so let's look at that first:

```
CREATE DATABASE yourdatabase;
```

Were you expecting something more complicated? Well, an optional parameter is missing: IF NOT EXISTS. We're pretty sure you know whether or not it exists, but if it makes you feel better, you can certainly add it:

```
CREATE DATABASE IF NOT EXISTS yourdatabase;
```

To see a list of databases that already exist use:

```
SHOW DATABASES;
```

That's all there is to it. Think of the database as an empty shell. There is nothing special about it, really. The interesting stuff comes later, when you create tables and manipulate the data.

That said, you still have to figure out how you are going to execute a SQL statement. Here are a few suggestions:

❑ You can do this from the MySQL command prompt. It should only be done this way if you have access to the server on which MySQL is installed. If you are running your own server, or you have Telnet access to the server, this may be an option for you.

❑ If you are being hosted by an ISP, you may need to request that the ISP create a database for you. For example, on one author's site, the ISP has CPanel installed, and he simply clicks the module called *MySQL Databases*. From the next page, he simply types in the database he wants to create and clicks a button, and it's created for him.

   ISPs will usually give you this option because you have a limit in your contract on how many databases you are allowed to create. On one of our sites, for example, the limit is 10 databases.

❑ If you have PHPMyAdmin installed, you can run the SQL command from there. PHPMyAdmin is a PHP application that allows you to see your table structures and even browse data. It is also a dangerous tool, because you can easily drop tables or entire databases with the click of a button, so use it carefully.

❑ Another option is to run your SQL statement from a PHP file. Most likely, if you are hosted by an ISP, it won't allow the creation of databases in this manner. But almost any other SQL statement will work using this method. This is the way we've been running commands so far in the book, and will be running SQL commands through the rest of this chapter, as well.

Once you have determined how you are going to run that SQL command, go ahead and do it. Make sure you substitute your own database name for `yourdatabase`. Because you are going to develop a comic book appreciation web site, you could call it `comicsite`:

```
CREATE DATABASE IF NOT EXISTS comicbook_fansite;
```

Now that you have a design mapped out and a database created in MySQL, it is time to create some tables.

Try It Out   **Creating the Tables**

In this exercise, you'll create the file that will hold the hostname, username, password, and database values. Then you will create the database tables.

1. Open your favorite text editor, and enter the following code (making sure you use the proper values for your server):

```php
<?php
define('MYSQL_HOST','localhost');
define('MYSQL_USER','bp6am');
define('MYSQL_PASSWORD','bp6ampass');
define('MYSQL_DB','comicbook_fansite');
?>
```

2. Save the file as db.inc.php. This file will be included in each subsequent PHP file that needs to access the database, and provides the connection information. Keep it handy because you'll be using it in subsequent chapters as well.

3. Type the following code in your editor, and save it as db_ch10.php:

```php
<?php
require 'db.inc.php';

$db = mysql_connect(MYSQL_HOST, MYSQL_USER, MYSQL_PASSWORD) or
    die ('Unable to connect. Check your connection parameters.');
mysql_select_db(MYSQL_DB, $db) or die(mysql_error($db));

// create the comic_character table
$query = 'CREATE TABLE IF NOT EXISTS comic_character (
        character_id   INTEGER UNSIGNED       NOT NULL AUTO_INCREMENT,
        alias          VARCHAR(40)            NOT NULL DEFAULT "",
        real_name      VARCHAR(80)            NOT NULL DEFAULT "",
        lair_id        INTEGER UNSIGNED       NOT NULL DEFAULT 0,
        alignment      ENUM("good", "evil") NOT NULL DEFAULT "good",

        PRIMARY KEY (character_id)
    )
    ENGINE=MyISAM';
mysql_query($query, $db) or die (mysql_error($db));

// create the comic_power table
$query = 'CREATE TABLE IF NOT EXISTS comic_power (
        power_id  INTEGER UNSIGNED NOT NULL AUTO_INCREMENT,
        power     VARCHAR(40)      NOT NULL DEFAULT "",

        PRIMARY KEY (power_id)
    )
    ENGINE=MyISAM';
mysql_query($query, $db) or die (mysql_error($db));

// create the comic_character_power linking table
$query = 'CREATE TABLE IF NOT EXISTS comic_character_power (
        character_id  INTEGER UNSIGNED NOT NULL DEFAULT 0,
        power_id      INTEGER UNSIGNED NOT NULL DEFAULT 0,

        PRIMARY KEY (character_id, power_id)
    )
    ENGINE=MyISAM';
mysql_query($query, $db) or die (mysql_error($db));

// create the comic_lair table
$query = 'CREATE TABLE IF NOT EXISTS comic_lair (
        lair_id    INTEGER UNSIGNED NOT NULL AUTO_INCREMENT,
        zipcode_id CHAR(5)          NOT NULL DEFAULT "00000",
        address    VARCHAR(40)      NOT NULL DEFAULT "",

        PRIMARY KEY (lair_id)
    )
```

```
        ENGINE=MyISAM';
mysql_query($query, $db) or die (mysql_error($db));

// create the comic_zipcode table
$query = 'CREATE TABLE IF NOT EXISTS comic_zipcode (
        zipcode_id   CHAR(5)     NOT NULL DEFAULT "00000",
        city         VARCHAR(40) NOT NULL DEFAULT "",
        state        CHAR(2)     NOT NULL DEFAULT "",

        PRIMARY KEY (zipcode_id)
    )
    ENGINE=MyISAM';
mysql_query($query, $db) or die (mysql_error($db));

// create the comic_rivalry table
$query = 'CREATE TABLE IF NOT EXISTS comic_rivalry (
        hero_id      INTEGER UNSIGNED  NOT NULL DEFAULT 0,
        villain_id   INTEGER UNSIGNED  NOT NULL DEFAULT 0,

        PRIMARY KEY (hero_id, villain_id)
    )
    ENGINE=MyISAM';
mysql_query($query, $db) or die (mysql_error($db));

echo 'Done.';
?>
```

4. Run db_ch10.php by loading it in your browser. Assuming all goes well, you should see the message "Done" in your browser, and the database now should contain all six tables.

How It Works

Every PHP script that needs to access your database on the MySQL server will include db.inc.php. These constants will be used in your scripts to gain access to your database. By putting them here in one file, you can change the values any time you move servers, change the name of the database, or change your username or password, without having to explicitly edit every other code file. Any time you have information or code that will be used in more than one PHP script, you should include it in a separate file so you'll only need to make your changes in one location in the future.

```
define('MYSQL_HOST','localhost');
define('MYSQL_USER','bp6am');
define('MYSQL_PASS','bp6ampass');
define('MYSQL_DB','comicbook_fansite');
```

The db_ch10.php file is a one-time script: You should never have to run it again, unless you need to drop all of your tables and recreate them. Rather than explain all of the code in the page, we'll just look at one of the SQL statements:

```
CREATE TABLE IF NOT EXISTS comic_character (
    character_id  INTEGER UNSIGNED     NOT NULL AUTO_INCREMENT,
    alias         VARCHAR(40)          NOT NULL DEFAULT "",
    real_name     VARCHAR(80)          NOT NULL DEFAULT "",
    lair_id       INTEGER UNSIGNED     NOT NULL DEFAULT 0,
```

```
    alignment        ENUM("good", "evil") NOT NULL DEFAULT "good",

    PRIMARY KEY (character_id)
)
ENGINE=MyISAM
```

The syntax for creating a table in MySQL is the following:

```
CREATE [TEMPORARY] TABLE [IF NOT EXISTS] tbl_name
    [(create_definition,...)] [table_options] [select_statement]
```

Obviously, you are not using the TEMPORARY keyword, because you want this table to be permanent and exist after you close your connection with the database. You are using the IF NOT EXISTS keywords as a safety measure, in case this page were to be loaded twice. If you attempt to load the page again, MySQL will not attempt to recreate the tables and will not generate an error.

The table name in this case is comic_character. The columns the script creates are character_id, alias, real_name, lair_id, and alignment, which are the names we came up with earlier.

Let's look at each column:

- ❏ character_id INTEGER UNSIGNED NOT NULL AUTO_INCREMENT: The character_id column is set as an integer. An integer datatype can contain the values −2,147,483,648 to 2,147,483,648, but since you won't be storing negative values in the column, you make the definition UNSIGNED, which lets you store 0 to 4,294,967,295.

- ❏ NOT NULL will force a value into the column. With some exceptions, numeric columns will default to 0, and string columns will default to an empty string. Very rarely will you allow a column to carry a NULL value.

- ❏ AUTO_INCREMENT causes the column to increase the highest value in the table by 1 each time a record is added and store it in this column. A column designated as auto-incrementing does not have a default value.

- ❏ alias VARCHAR(40) NOT NULL DEFAULT "": The alias column is set as a VARCHAR datatype. By default, this datatype can hold up to 255 characters, but you are allotting 40 characters, which should be enough for any character name. A VARCHAR differs from a CHAR datatype by the way space is allotted for the column.

  A VARCHAR datatype occupies only the space it needs, whereas CHAR datatypes will always take up the space allotted to them when they are stored in the database. The only time you really need to use the CHAR datatype is for strings of known fixed length (such as the zipcode_id and state columns in the comic_zipcode table).

- ❏ real_name VARCHAR(80) NOT NULL DEFAULT "": This column is similar to alias. You are allotting 80 characters, which should be enough for your needs.

  Note that you did not separate the real_name column into first_name and last_name columns. You certainly could, if you wanted to do that, but in this small application it really isn't necessary. On the other hand, having separate columns for first and last name is almost a requirement in a company's human resources application, so that you can do things such as greet employees by their first names in a company memo.

❑ lair_id INTEGER UNSIGNED NOT NULL DEFAULT 0: The foreign key to the comic_lair table is also an integer with a default value of 0.

❑ alignment ENUM("good", "evil") NOT NULL DEFAULT "good": The alignment column can be one of two values: "good" or "evil." Because of this, you use an enum datatype, and default it to "good." (Everyone has some good in them, right?)

You now have a database. You have tables. If you just had a way to enter some data into your tables in your database, you'd have an application where your users would be able to store information about their favorite superheroes and villains. You need some sort of interface that they can use to create and edit data, which means you need to design some web pages for them.

Creating the Comic Character Application

It's back to the drawing board. Literally. Get away from your computer again, dig out that paper and pencil, and prepare to put together some ideas for a web application.

First of all, you need a page to display a list of comic book characters, along with some information about them. It doesn't need to include every detail about them (such as the location of their secret lair), but it should have enough data so that users can distinguish who they are and read a little bit of information about them.

You will list the following information:

❑ Character name (alias)

❑ Real name

❑ Alignment (good or evil)

❑ Powers

❑ Enemies

You also need a character input form. This form will serve two purposes. It will allow you to create a new character, in which case the form will load with blank fields and a create button, or it will allow you to edit an existing character, in which case it will load with the fields filled in and an update button. The form will also have a reset button to clear the new form or restore the edited form fields. A delete button should also be available, when editing an existing character, to allow the character's record to be deleted from the database.

The fields on your form will be as follows:

❑ Real name (text input)

❑ Character name/alias (text input)

❑ Powers (multiple select field)

❑   Lair address, city, state, and zip code (text inputs)

❑   Alignment (radio button: good/evil, default good)

❑   Enemies (multiple select field)

You also need a form for adding and deleting powers. This form will be relatively simple and will contain the following elements:

❑   A check box list of every power currently available

❑   A Delete Selected button

❑   A text field to enter a new power

❑   An Add Power button

You also need a PHP script that can handle all database inserts, deletes, and so on. This should simply do the required job and redirect the user to another page. This page handles *all* transactions for the character application (with redirect), including the following:

❑   Inserting a new character (character listing page)

❑   Editing an existing character (character listing page)

❑   Deleting a character (character listing page)

❑   Adding a new power (power editor page)

❑   Deleting a power (power editor page)

That's basically all there is to the application. Four pages (well, five if you count the db.inc.php file you created earlier) shouldn't be too difficult. You'll write them first, and we'll talk about how they work afterward.

Try It Out   Transaction Script

Some of these files are a bit long, but don't let that scare you. Most of the code consists of SQL statements, and they are explained clearly for you in the "How It Works" section that follows.

1.   Start with a transaction script. This code is the longest, but that's because it contains a lot of SQL statements. You know the drill . . . after entering it, save this one as char_transaction.php:

```php
<?php
require 'db.inc.php';

$db = mysql_connect(MYSQL_HOST, MYSQL_USER, MYSQL_PASSWORD) or
    die ('Unable to connect. Check your connection parameters.');
mysql_select_db(MYSQL_DB, $db) or die(mysql_error($db));

switch ($_POST['action']) {
```

```
case 'Add Character':

    // escape incoming values to protect database
    $alias = mysql_real_escape_string($_POST['alias'], $db);
    $real_name = mysql_real_escape_string($_POST['real_name'], $db);
    $address = mysql_real_escape_string($_POST['address'], $db);
    $city = mysql_real_escape_string($_POST['city'], $db);
    $state = mysql_real_escape_string($_POST['state'], $db);
    $zipcode_id = mysql_real_escape_string($_POST['zipcode_id'], $db);
    $alignment = ($_POST['alignment'] == 'good') ? 'good' : 'evil';

    // add character information into database tables
    $query = 'INSERT IGNORE INTO comic_zipcode
            (zipcode_id, city, state)
        VALUES
            ("' . $zipcode_id . '", "' . $city . '", "' . $state . '")';
    mysql_query($query, $db) or die (mysql_error($db));

    $query = 'INSERT INTO comic_lair
            (lair_id, zipcode_id, address)
        VALUES
            (NULL, "' . $zipcode_id . '", "' . $address . '")';
    mysql_query($query, $db) or die (mysql_error($db));

    // retrieve new lair_id generated by MySQL
    $lair_id = mysql_insert_id($db);
    $query = 'INSERT INTO comic_character
            (character_id, alias, real_name, lair_id, alignment)
        VALUES
            (NULL, "' . $alias . '", "' . $real_name . '", ' .
            $lair_id . ', "' . $alignment . '")';
    mysql_query($query, $db) or die (mysql_error($db));

    // retrieve new character_id generated by MySQL
    $character_id = mysql_insert_id($db);
    if (!empty($_POST['powers'])) {
        $values = array();
        foreach ($_POST['powers'] as $power_id) {
            $values[] = sprintf('(%d, %d)', $character_id, $power_id);
        }
        $query = 'INSERT IGNORE INTO comic_character_power
                (character_id, power_id)
            VALUES ' .
                implode(',', $values);
        mysql_query($query, $db) or die (mysql_error($db));
    }

    if (!empty($_POST['rivalries'])) {
        $values = array();
        foreach ($_POST['rivalries'] as $rival_id) {
            $values[] = sprintf('(%d, %d)', $character_id, $rival_id);
        }

        // alignment will affect column order
        $columns = ($alignment = 'good') ? '(hero_id, villain_id)' :
```

```
                        '(villain_id, hero_id)';

            $query = 'INSERT IGNORE INTO comic_rivalry
                    ' . $columns . '
                VALUES
                    ' . implode(',', $values);
            mysql_query($query, $db) or die (mysql_error($db));
        }

        $redirect = 'list_characters.php';
        break;

    case 'Delete Character':

        // make sure character_id is a number just to be safe
        $character_id = (int)$_POST['character_id'];

        // delete character information from tables
        $query = 'DELETE FROM c, l
            USING
                comic_character c, comic_lair l
            WHERE
                c.lair_id = l.lair_id AND
                c.character_id = ' . $character_id;
        mysql_query($query, $db) or die (mysql_error($db));

        $query = 'DELETE FROM comic_character_power
            WHERE
                character_id = ' . $character_id;
        mysql_query($query, $db) or die (mysql_error($db));

        $query = 'DELETE FROM comic_rivalry
            WHERE
                hero_id = ' . $character_id . ' OR villain_id = ' . $character_id;
        mysql_query($query, $db) or die (mysql_error($db));

        $redirect = 'list_characters.php';
        break;

    case 'Edit Character':

        // escape incoming values to protect database
        $character_id = (int)$_POST['character_id'];
        $alias = mysql_real_escape_string($_POST['alias'], $db);
        $real_name = mysql_real_escape_string($_POST['real_name'], $db);
        $address = mysql_real_escape_string($_POST['address'], $db);
        $city = mysql_real_escape_string($_POST['city'], $db);
        $state = mysql_real_escape_string($_POST['state'], $db);
        $zipcode_id = mysql_real_escape_string($_POST['zipcode_id'], $db);
        $alignment = ($_POST['alignment'] == 'good') ? 'good' : 'evil';

        // update existing character information in tables
        $query = 'INSERT IGNORE INTO comic_zipcode
                (zipcode_id, city, state)
```

```
        VALUES
            ("' . $zipcode_id . '", "' . $city . '", "' . $state . '")';
mysql_query($query, $db) or die (mysql_error($db));

$query = 'UPDATE comic_lair l, comic_character c
        SET
            l.zipcode_id = ' . $zipcode_id . ',
            l.address = "' . $address . '",
            c.real_name = "' . $real_name . '",
            c.alias = "' . $alias . '",
            c.alignment = "' . $alignment . '"
    WHERE
        c.character_id = ' . $character_id . ' AND
        c.lair_id = l.lair_id';
mysql_query($query, $db) or die (mysql_error($db));

$query = 'DELETE FROM comic_character_power
    WHERE
        character_id = ' . $character_id;
mysql_query($query, $db) or die (mysql_error($db));

if (!empty($_POST['powers'])) {
    $values = array();
    foreach ($_POST['powers'] as $power_id) {
        $values[] = sprintf('(%d, %d)', $character_id, $power_id);
    }
    $query = 'INSERT IGNORE INTO comic_character_power
            (character_id, power_id)
        VALUES
            ' . implode(',', $values);
    mysql_query($query, $db) or die (mysql_error($db));
}

$query = 'DELETE FROM comic_rivalry
    WHERE
        hero_id = ' . $character_id . ' OR villain_id = ' . $character_id;
mysql_query($query, $db) or die (mysql_error($db));

if (!empty($_POST['rivalries'])) {
    $values = array();
    foreach ($_POST['rivalries'] as $rival_id) {
        $values[] = sprintf('(%d, %d)', $character_id, $rival_id);
    }

    // alignment will affect column order
    $columns = ($alignment = 'good') ? '(hero_id, villain_id)' :
        '(villain_id, hero_id)';

    $query = 'INSERT IGNORE INTO comic_rivalry
            ' . $columns . '
        VALUES
            ' . implode(',', $values);

    mysql_query($query, $db) or die (mysql_error($db));
}
```

```
        $redirect = 'list_characters.php';
        break;

    case 'Delete Selected Powers':

        if (!empty($_POST['powers'])) {
            // escape incoming values to protect database-- they should be numeric
            // values, but just to be safe
            $powers = implode(',', $_POST['powers']);
            $powers = mysql_real_escape_string($powers, $db);

            // delete powers
            $query = 'DELETE FROM comic_power
                WHERE
                    power_id IN (' . $powers . ')';
            mysql_query($query, $db) or die (mysql_error($db));

            $query = 'DELETE FROM comic_character_power
                WHERE
                    power_id IN (' . $powers . ')';
            mysql_query($query, $db) or die (mysql_error($db));
        }

        $redirect = 'edit_power.php';
        break;

    case 'Add New Power':

        // trim and check power to prevent adding blank values
        $power = trim($_POST['new_power']);
        if ($power != '')
        {
            // escape incoming value
            $power = mysql_real_escape_string($power, $db);

            // create new power
            $query = 'INSERT IGNORE INTO comic_power
                    (power_id, power)
                VALUES
                    (NULL, "' . $power . '")';
            mysql_query($query, $db) or die (mysql_error($db));
        }

        $redirect = 'edit_power.php';
        break;

default:
    $redirect = 'list_characters.php';
}

header('Location: ' . $redirect);
?>
```

How It Works

You may have noticed that you're not loading a page in your browser to test the script, as you did in some of the previous exercises in the book. In fact, the script you just wrote has nothing to display — it only processes transactions and redirects the user. One tremendous advantage to using a transaction page in this manner is that the browser's history will have no memory of the transaction page once the browser arrives at the final destination page. The transaction page did not send any information to the browser other than the redirect. If the user refreshes his or her browser, it won't reexecute the transaction, making for a very clean application.

For example, say a user starts on the Character Database page that lists the characters and clicks the Edit Powers link. From the Edit Powers page, the user enters a power and clicks Add New Power. The user might do this five times to add five new powers, but, each time, the browser server submits the form to the transaction page, and the server redirects the user back to the power page. If the user then clicks the browser's Back button, the user is taken back to the Character Database page, as if he or she just came from there! This is almost intuitive to the average user and is the way applications should work.

It looks as if there is a lot happening on this page, but it's not that complicated. There are simply many different tasks that are performed by this page, depending on how the data got here. Let's take a closer look and see what makes it tick.

Remember that each button is named `action` and that each one has a different value. In the code that follows, you determine which button was clicked, and perform the appropriate action. For example, if the Delete Character button was clicked, you want to run the SQL commands only for removing character data.

```
switch ($_POST['action']) {
case 'Add Character':
    // ...
    break;

case 'Delete Character':
    // ...
    break;

case 'Edit Character':
    // ...
    break;

case 'Delete Selected Powers':
    // ...
    break;

case 'Add Character':
    // ...
    break;

default:
    // ...
}
```

The `switch` statement is a convenient and efficient way of providing a multiple choice of actions, all based on the possible values of the same variable or condition. It is easier to read than a complex if...else statement. The only "gotcha" you need to be aware of is to use `break` at the end of each `case` to prevent the rest of the code in the other `case` blocks from executing. Without the `break` keyword to tell PHP when to jump out of the `switch` statement, it will continue executing code in the other sections that follow, after the intended block is done.

The `INSERT` query that follows within the Add Character section is relatively simple. In plain English, it reads: "Insert the values `$zipcode_id`, `$city`, and `$state` into the columns `zipcode_id`, `city`, and `state` in the `comic_zipcode` table." The `IGNORE` keyword is a very cool option that allows you to do an insert without first using a `SELECT` query to see if the data is already in the table. In this case, you know there might already be a record for this zip code, so `IGNORE` tells the query "If you see this zip code in the table already, then don't do the `INSERT`."

```
$query = 'INSERT IGNORE INTO comic_zipcode
        (zipcode_id, city, state)
    VALUES
        ("' . $zipcode_id . '", "' . $city . '", "' . $state . '")';
mysql_query($query, $db) or die (mysql_error($db));
```

The `IGNORE` statement compares primary keys only. Therefore, even if another zip code is in the database with the same state, the `INSERT` still takes place. Thus, using `IGNORE` when inserting data into a table where the primary key is automatically incremented would have no effect at all, because the `INSERT` will *always* happen in that case. This might seem obvious to you, but just keep this in mind because with some more complex tables it may not be so intuitive.

In the `INSERT` that follows, you see the use of `NULL` as the first value. When you insert `NULL` into a column, MySQL does the following: If the column allows `NULL` values, then it accepts the `NULL` as is and inserts it; if it does not allow `NULL` (the column `lair_id` is set to `NOT NULL`), it will set the column to the default value. If a default value has not been determined, then the standard default for the datatype is inserted (i.e., an empty string for `VARCHAR`/`CHAR` types, 0 for `INTEGER` types, etc.). If the column is set to `AUTO_INCREMENT`, as is the case here, then the next highest available integer value for that column is inserted. This is exactly what you want to happen here because `lair_id` is the primary key, and new values must be unique.

```
$query = 'INSERT INTO comic_lair
        (lair_id, zipcode_id, address)
    VALUES
        (NULL, "' . $zipcode_id . '", "' . $address . '")';
mysql_query($query, $db) or die (mysql_error($db));
```

You also could have left out the `lair_id` field from the insert and inserted values into the `zip_id` and `lair_addr` columns only. MySQL treats ignored columns as if you had attempted to insert `NULL` into them. We like to specify every column when doing an insert, though. If you need to modify your SQL statement later, then having all the columns listed in the `INSERT` query can help you keep everything manageable.

Assuming the insert worked properly (`$result` returned `TRUE`), the `mysql_insert_id()` function will return the value of the last `AUTO_INCREMENT` from the last run query. This works only after running a query on a table with an `AUTO_INCREMENT` column. In this case, it returns the primary key value of the `lair_id` row you just inserted into the `comic_lair` table. You will need that value to insert into the `comic_character` table momentarily.

```
$lair_id = mysql_insert_id($db);
```

The connection variable is optional, but we think it's a good habit to always include it when calling `mysql_insert_id()`. If you omit it, then the function will use the most recently opened database connection. That's not a problem in a simple application like this one, but in a more complex application, where you might have multiple database connections open at the same time, it could get confusing.

Again, notice the use of NULL for the primary key and the use of `mysql_insert_id()` to return the primary key in the following:

```
$query = 'INSERT INTO comic_character
        (character_id, alias, real_name, lair_id, alignment)
    VALUES
        (NULL, "' . $alias . '", "' . $real_name . '", ' .
        $lair_id . ', "' . $alignment . '")';
mysql_query($query, $db) or die (mysql_error($db));

$character_id = mysql_insert_id($db);
```

Now comes the time to insert the character's powers into the database. At first, you could have used code similar to this to accomplish the task:

```
foreach ($_POST['powers'] as $power_id) {
    $query = 'INSERT IGNORE INTO comic_character_power
            (character_id, power_id)
        VALUES
            ' . $character_id . ', ' . (int) $_power_id;
    mysql_query($query, $db) or die (mysql_error($db));
}
```

You should always be interested in minimizing the number of times you run a query on the database. Each query takes precious time, which can add up noticeably in a complex application. The above code wouldn't be bad if only one or two powers were being associated with the character, but what if a really super-awesome character were created who had 20 powers? That would be 20 consecutively executed INSERT statements! At this point, you need to figure out how to insert all the powers with only one SQL command:

```
if (!empty($_POST['powers'])) {
    $values = array();
    foreach ($_POST['powers'] as $power_id) {
        $values[] = sprintf('(%d, %d)', $character_id, $power_id);
    }
    $query = 'INSERT IGNORE INTO comic_character_power
            (character_id, power_id)
        VALUES ' .
            implode(',', $values);
    mysql_query($query, $db) or die (mysql_error($db));
}
```

There are a couple of concerns here. First, if there is already a power for this user (there shouldn't be, because it's a new character, but still you should always be prepared), you don't need to insert the row. You already know how to take care of this by using the IGNORE keyword.

Second, you must insert multiple rows of data with only one query. This is easy enough; all you have to do is supply a comma-separated list of value grouping that matches up to the column grouping in the query. For example:

```
INSERT INTO table (col1, col2) VALUES (val1, val2), (val3, val4)
```

You accomplish this in the code by looping through the $_POST['powers'] array and putting the values for character ID and power ID into a new array. You then concatenate that array with a comma separator, and *voilà*! There are your multiple rows of data to insert.

You then do the same thing with the $_POST['rivalries'] array that you did with $_POST['powers']. This time, however, you insert data into the columns based on whether the character is good or evil. It doesn't really matter too much which column gets which ID, but for the most part you want good character IDs in the hero_id column and evil character IDs in the villain_id column.

```
if (!empty($_POST['rivalries'])) {
    $values = array();
    foreach ($_POST['rivalries'] as $rival_id) {
        $values[] = sprintf('(%d, %d)', $character_id, $rival_id);
    }

    $columns = ($alignment = 'good') ? '(hero_id, villain_id)' :
        '(villain_id, hero_id)';

    $query = 'INSERT IGNORE INTO comic_rivalry
            ' . $columns . '
        VALUES
            ' . implode(',', $values);
    mysql_query($query, $db) or die (mysql_error($db));
}
```

You have a little bit of referential integrity that you have to handle, beyond what MySQL is already handling for you, when it comes to the comic_rivalry table. Namely, you don't want to have a hero/villain_id combination to match up to a villain/hero_id combination. This isn't the end of the world for the purposes of a relational database, but for your purposes it is considered a duplication of data — something you don't want. You will handle this contingency when updating a character, but because this is a new character (with a brand new ID), you don't have to worry about that just yet.

Now that you're done inserting new character data, you set the page you are going to load next, and break out of the switch statement.

```
$redirect = 'list_characters.php';
break;
```

When deleting a character, you simply remove all instances of it from the relevant tables. To remove the data from the comic_lair table, you have to JOIN it to the comic_character table by matching up the lair IDs first. Then you delete all matching rows where the character ID matches.

```
$query = 'DELETE FROM c, l
    USING
        comic_character c, comic_lair l
    WHERE
        c.lair_id = l.lair_id AND
        c.character_id = ' . $character_id;
mysql_query($query, $db) or die (mysql_error($db));

$query = 'DELETE FROM comic_character_power
    WHERE
        character_id = ' . $character_id;
mysql_query($query, $db) or die (mysql_error($db));
```

Remembering that the comic_rivalry needs to maintain what we call "reverse" referential integrity (1, 3 matching 3, 1 for example), you remove all rows that contain the character's ID in either column:

```
$query = 'DELETE FROM comic_rivalry
    WHERE
        hero_id = ' . $character_id . ' OR villain_id = ' . $character_id;
mysql_query($query, $db) or die (mysql_error($db));
```

Updating a character is where things get interesting. First of all, you can simply do an INSERT IGNORE on the zip code table. If the address and zip code change, you don't really need to delete the old data because it might be used for other characters — it's perfectly fine to leave the old data alone. So, you just do an INSERT IGNORE as you did for a new character, and leave it at that.

```
$query = 'INSERT IGNORE INTO comic_zipcode
        (zipcode_id, city, state)
    VALUES
        ("' . $zipcode_id . '", "' . $city . '", "' . $state . '")';
mysql_query($query, $db) or die (mysql_error($db));
```

Here is the first UPDATE query, and incidentally it is the only one in the entire application. It is very similar to INSERT and SELECT queries, with the exception of the SET keyword. The SET keyword tells MySQL what columns to change and what values to set them to. The old values in the row are overwritten. This is a JOIN query because there is more than one table. The WHERE keyword specifies both the linking column (lair_id) and the condition that only rows for this character will be updated.

```
$query = 'UPDATE comic_lair l, comic_character c
    SET
        l.zipcode_id = ' . $zipcode_id . ',
        l.address = "' . $address . '",
        c.real_name = "' . $real_name . '",
        c.alias = "' . $alias . '",
        c.alignment = "' . $alignment . '"
    WHERE
        c.character_id = ' . $character_id . ' AND
        c.lair_id = l.lair_id';
mysql_query($query, $db) or die (mysql_error($db));
```

Because the comic_character_power table does not have an automatically incremented column as the primary key, you don't have to do an update on the table. An update is possible, but it is much easier to simply delete all the old links of character to power and insert new rows instead. In some cases, you may be deleting and inserting the same data (for instance, you might be adding `flight` as a power, but `invisibility` did not change; `invisibility` will still be deleted and reinserted). When updating data in an M:N relationship, you will usually simply delete the old data, and insert the updated/new data.

```
$query = 'DELETE FROM comic_character_power
    WHERE
        character_id = ' . $character_id;
mysql_query($query, $db) or die (mysql_error($db));

if (!empty($_POST['powers'])) {
    $values = array();
    foreach ($_POST['powers'] as $power_id) {
        $values[] = sprintf('(%d, %d)', $character_id, $power_id);
    }
    $query = 'INSERT IGNORE INTO comic_character_power
            (character_id, power_id)
        VALUES
            ' . implode(',', $values);
    mysql_query($query, $db) or die (mysql_error($db));
}
```

This brings you to the enemies data, where not only do you have to maintain referential integrity, but you also have to worry about updating rows where the ID can be present in either of the two linking columns. You must maintain the reverse referential integrity.

```
$query = 'DELETE FROM comic_rivalry
    WHERE
        hero_id = ' . $character_id . ' OR villain_id = ' . $character_id;
mysql_query($query, $db) or die (mysql_error($db));

if (!empty($_POST['rivalries'])) {
    $values = array();
    foreach ($_POST['rivalries'] as $rival_id) {
        $values[] = sprintf('(%d, %d)', $character_id, $rival_id);
    }

    $columns = ($alignment = 'good') ? '(hero_id, villain_id)' :
        '(villain_id, hero_id)';

    $query = 'INSERT IGNORE INTO comic_rivalry
            ' . $columns . '
        VALUES
            ' . implode(',', $values);

    mysql_query($query, $db) or die (mysql_error($db));
}
```

But how did you deal with referential integrity? It turns out that it takes care of itself when you follow the same method you employed when updating the `comic_character_power` table. By simply running the same DELETE query you ran when deleting a character and then immediately running the same INSERT query you ran when creating a new character, you ensure that only one set of rows exists to match up each character to his/her enemy. It's simple, it's elegant, and it works!

By this time, queries should seem quite familiar to you. The DELETE query is one of the simplest of the SQL statements. In these DELETE queries, you need to delete each power that was selected on the Edit Power page. You must do this not only in the comic_power table, but in the comic_character_ power table as well. (In this application, if a power is removed, then you remove that power from the characters as well.) To perform a DELETE on multiple rows, you use the IN keyword with which each ID in the supplied comma-separated list of power IDs is matched against the ID, and each matching row is deleted.

```
$query = 'DELETE FROM comic_power
    WHERE
        power_id IN (' . $powers . ')';
mysql_query($query, $db) or die (mysql_error($db));

$query = 'DELETE FROM comic_character_power
    WHERE
        power_id IN (' . $powers . ')';
mysql_query($query, $db) or die (mysql_error($db));
```

You first check to make sure a value was passed when adding a power (no need to run a query if there is nothing to add), and then attempt to insert the value into the power table. Once again, you use the IGNORE keyword in what follows, to avoid duplication of powers. We have already mentioned that you really use IGNORE only on tables that have a primary key that is not autogenerated, but there is an exception. IGNORE will not allow any duplicate data in any column that is designated as UNIQUE. In the comic_chararacter_power table, the power column is a UNIQUE column, so attempting to insert a duplicate value would result in an error. The IGNORE keyword prevents the insertion so you don't get an error returned. If the power already exists, then the script simply returns to the edit_power. php page and awaits further instructions.

```
$power = trim($_POST['new_power']);
if ($power != '')
{
    $power = mysql_real_escape_string($power, $db);

    $query = 'INSERT IGNORE INTO comic_power
            (power_id, power)
        VALUES
            (NULL, "' . $power . '")';
    mysql_query($query, $db) or die (mysql_error($db));
}
```

You should always have a default: option in your case statements. You don't need to do anything there, but it is good programming practice to include it. In this scenario, you are simply going to redirect the user back to the list_characters.php page.

```
default:
    $redirect = 'list_characters.php';
```

Finally, you reach the last command of char_transaction.php. To use the header() function, no data can have been sent to the client previously. If it has, you will get an error. In this case, char_transaction.php has no data sent to the client, so the header() function will work as advertised.

```
header('Location: ' . $redirect);
```

Each case sets a destination page after running its queries. This function will now send the user to that destination.

Try It Out   Editing Superhero Powers

The next page you're going to create is a script to allow you to create and modify superpowers.

1. Enter the following code in your editor, and save it as edit_power.php:

```
<html>
 <head>
  <title>Edit Powers</title>
  <style type="text/css">
   td { vertical-align: top; }
  </style>
 </head>
 <body>
  <img src="logo.jpg" alt="Comic Book Appreciation Site" style="float: left;" />
  <h1>Comic Book<br/>Appreciation</h1>
  <h2>Edit Character Powers</h2>
  <hr style="clear: both;"/>
  <form action="char_transaction.php" method="post">
   <div>
     <input type="text" name="new_power" size="20" maxlength="40" value="" />
     <input type="submit" name="action" value="Add New Power" />
   </div>
<?php
require 'db.inc.php';

$db = mysql_connect(MYSQL_HOST, MYSQL_USER, MYSQL_PASSWORD) or
    die ('Unable to connect. Check your connection parameters.');
mysql_select_db(MYSQL_DB, $db) or die(mysql_error($db));

$query = 'SELECT power_id, power FROM comic_power ORDER BY power ASC';
$result = mysql_query($query, $db) or die (mysql_error($db));

if (mysql_num_rows($result) > 0) {
    echo '<p><em>Deleting a power will remove its association with any ' .
         'characters as well-- select wisely!</em></p>';

    $num_powers = mysql_num_rows($result);
    $threshold = 5;
    $max_columns = 2;
```

```
        $num_columns = min($max_columns, ceil($num_powers/$threshold));
        $count_per_column = ceil($num_powers/$num_columns);

        $i = 0;
        echo '<table><tr><td>';
        while ($row = mysql_fetch_assoc($result)) {
            if (($i > 0) && ($i % $count_per_column == 0)) {
                echo '</td><td>';
            }
            echo '<input type="checkbox" name="powers[]" "value="' .
                $row['power_id'] . '" /> ';
            echo $row['power'] . '<br/>';
            $i++;
        }
        echo '</td></tr></table>';

        echo '<br/><input type="submit" name="action" ' .
            'value="Delete Selected Powers" />';
    } else {
        echo '<p><strong>No Powers entered...</strong></p>';
    }
    ?>
    </div>
    </form>
    <p><a href="list_characters.php">Return to Home Page</a></p>
    </body>
</html>
```

2. Load edit_power.php in your browser. When the page appears, it initially will be empty, as shown in Figure 10-1.

Figure 10-1

3. Enter an ultracool superpower such as *invisibility* or *x-ray vision* in the text box, and click Add New Power. Continue adding powers until you have at least six or seven. If you need help with power ideas, here are a few: *super strength, invisibility, x-ray vision, super speed, soccer mom, flexibility, flight, underwater breathing,* and *psychokinesis.* Moving on, you should now see the list of powers with check boxes next to them and a new button labeled "Delete Selected Powers." The screen should now resemble Figure 10-2.

Figure 10-2

4. Check the boxes next to one or two of the powers, and click Delete Selected Powers. They should go away.

How It Works

You will see this on every page, but we will mention it this one time only: You include the db.inc. php file that contains the constants used in the next couple of lines. By putting these constants in an included file, you can make any changes you may need in the future in one place. You use the require command instead of include. An included file will not stop the processing of the rest of the page, whereas a required file would immediately stop the processing if it is not found.

```
require 'db.inc.php';
```

Next, a connection to the server is made, and the appropriate database is selected. Notice the use of the constants you defined in db.inc.php:

```
$db = mysql_connect(MYSQL_HOST, MYSQL_USER, MYSQL_PASSWORD) or
    die ('Unable to connect. Check your connection parameters.');
mysql_select_db(MYSQL_DB, $db) or die(mysql_error($db));
```

What follows is a somewhat simple SQL select statement. It grabs the power_id and power columns from the comic_power table and sorts them alphabetically by power. This way, when you iterate through them later and put the data on the web page, they will be in an intelligible order.

```
$query = 'SELECT power_id, power FROM comic_power ORDER BY power ASC';
$result = mysql_query($query, $db) or die (mysql_error($db));
```

Now the script checks to make sure at least one row was returned. If so, it iterates through each row, building up the list of powers, using the power's ID as the check box's value.

```
while ($row = mysql_fetch_assoc($result)) {
    echo '<input type="checkbox" name="powers[]" "value="' .
        $row['power_id'] . '" /> ';
    echo $row['power'] . '<br/>';
}
```

Because the list of powers could get quite large, you might want to try to distribute them across multiple columns. If so, you would probably like to distribute them fairly evenly. The following lines of code do this for you.

First, you get a count of the number of powers, using mysql_num_rows(). Next, you set the threshold to 5 lines (after which a second column will be created), and a maximum number of columns (in this case, 3).

```
$num_powers = mysql_num_rows($result);
$threshold = 5;
$max_columns = 3;
```

Next, you determine how many columns to create. Assume there are 7 powers to display. First, you divide the count by the threshold (7 / 5), which gives you 1.4. Next, you use ceil() to round up to the nearest integer (ceil(1.4) = 2). Then you take the smaller of the two values (3 and 2), and store it in the $num_columns variable. In this example, $num_columns would equal 2.

To figure out how many powers go into each column, you divide the count by the number of columns, and round up to the nearest integer. In this case, ceil(7 / 2) = 4. So, you'll have two columns, with four values in each column (the last column will contain the remainder of powers, if there are fewer than four).

```
$num_columns = min($max_columns, ceil($num_powers/$threshold));
$count_per_column = ceil($num_powers/$num_columns);
```

Now you loop through each element of the result set. The counter $i will start at 0 and increment each time through the loop. In each loop, you add an output <input> tag to create the check box, using the power's ID as the value, and the power's name as the label. When the counter reaches a value that is evenly divisible by $count_per_column without a remainder, you close the table row and start a new one.

```
$i = 0;
echo '<table><tr><td>';
while ($row = mysql_fetch_assoc($result)) {
    if (($i > 0) && ($i % $count_per_column == 0)) {
        echo '</td><td>';
    }
    echo '<input type="checkbox" name="powers[]" "value="' .
        $row['power_id'] . '" /> ';
    echo $row['power'] . '<br/>';
    $i++;
}
echo '</td></tr></table>';
```

In this example, increments 0, 1, 2, and 3 end up in the first column. When $i reaches 4 (the value of $count_per_column), the script starts a new column. Feel free to play around with it by changing your $threshold and $max_columns values and adding a bunch of new power values, to see how these values interact when the table is built. For now, let's check out the rest of the code.

Continuing on for the rest of the if statement, if there is even one power, a row is created that contains a delete button. But if not, then the script creates a row that simply states that no powers have yet been entered.

```
    echo '<br/><input type="submit" name="action" ' .
        'value="Delete Selected Powers" />';
} else {
    echo '<p><strong>No Powers entered...</strong></p>';
}
```

Try It Out   **Managing the Characters**

The next file you're going to create will display a list of the characters in your database.

1. Enter the following code, and save it as list_characters.php:

```html
<html>
 <head>
  <title>Character Database</title>
  <style type="text/css">
   th { background-color: #999; }
   td { vertical-align: top; }
   .odd_row { background-color: #EEE; }
   .even_row { background-color: #FFF; }
  </style>
 </head>
 <body>
  <img src="logo.jpg" alt="Comic Book Appreciation Site" style="float: left;" />
  <h1>Comic Book<br/>Appreciation</h1>
  <h2>Character Database</h2>
  <hr style="clear: both;"/>
<?php
```

```php
require 'db.inc.php';

$db = mysql_connect(MYSQL_HOST, MYSQL_USER, MYSQL_PASSWORD) or
    die ('Unable to connect. Check your connection parameters.');
mysql_select_db(MYSQL_DB, $db) or die(mysql_error($db));

// determine sorting order of table
$order = array(1 => 'alias ASC',
               2 => 'real_name ASC',
               3 => 'alignment ASC, alias ASC');

$o = (isset($_GET['o']) && ctype_digit($_GET['o'])) ? $_GET['o'] : 1;
if (!in_array($o, array_keys($order))) {
    $o = 1;
}

// select list of characters for table
$query = 'SELECT
        character_id, alias, real_name, alignment
    FROM
        comic_character
    ORDER BY ' . $order[$o];
$result = mysql_query($query, $db) or die (mysql_error($db));

if (mysql_num_rows($result) > 0) {
    echo '<table>';
    echo '<tr><th><a href="' . $_SERVER['PHP_SELF'] . '?o=1">Alias</a></th>';
    echo '<th><a href="' . $_SERVER['PHP_SELF'] . '?o=2">Real Name</a></th>';
    echo '<th><a href="' . $_SERVER['PHP_SELF'] . '?o=3">Alignment</a></th>';
    echo '<th>Powers</th>';
    echo '<th>Enemies</th></tr>';

    $odd = true;    // alternate odd/even row styling
    while ($row = mysql_fetch_array($result)) {
        echo ($odd == true) ? '<tr class="odd_row">' : '<tr class="even_row">';
        $odd = !$odd;
        echo '<td><a href="edit_character.php?id=' . $row['character_id'] .
            '">' . $row['alias'] . '</a></td>';
        echo '<td>' . $row['real_name'] . '</td>';
        echo '<td>' . $row['alignment'] . '</td>';

        // select list of powers for this character
        $query2 = 'SELECT
                power
            FROM
                comic_power p
                JOIN comic_character_power cp
                    ON p.power_id = cp.power_id
            WHERE
                cp.character_id = ' . $row['character_id'] . '
            ORDER BY
                power ASC';
        $result2 = mysql_query($query2, $db) or die (mysql_error($db));

        if (mysql_num_rows($result2) > 0) {
```

```php
            $powers = array();
            while ($row2 = mysql_fetch_assoc($result2)) {
                $powers[] = $row2['power'];
            }
            echo '<td>' . implode(', ', $powers) . '</td>';
        } else {
            echo '<td>none</td>';
        }
        mysql_free_result($result2);

        // select list of rivalries for this character
        $query2 = 'SELECT
                c2.alias
            FROM
                comic_character c1
                JOIN comic_character c2
                JOIN comic_rivalry r
                    ON (c1.character_id = r.hero_id AND
                        c2.character_id = r.villain_id) OR
                       (c2.character_id = r.hero_id AND
                        c1.character_id = r.villain_id)
            WHERE
                c1.character_id = ' . $row['character_id'] . '
            ORDER BY
                c2.alias ASC';
        $result2 = mysql_query($query2, $db) or die (mysql_error($db));

        if (mysql_num_rows($result2) > 0) {
            $aliases = array();
            while ($row2 = mysql_fetch_assoc($result2)) {
                $aliases[] = $row2['alias'];
            }
            echo '<td>' . implode(', ', $aliases) . '</td>';
        } else {
            echo '<td>none</td>';
        }
        mysql_free_result($result2);
        echo '</tr>';
    }
    echo '</table>';

} else {
    echo '<p><strong>No Characters entered...</strong></p>';
}
?>
  <p><a href="edit_character.php">Add New Character</a></p>
  <p><a href="edit_power.php">Edit Powers</a></p>
 </body>
</html>
```

2. In the last file for this chapter, you'll create the ability to add and modify characters. Enter the next block of code, and save it as edit_character.php:

```php
<?php
require 'db.inc.php';

$db = mysql_connect(MYSQL_HOST, MYSQL_USER, MYSQL_PASSWORD) or
    die ('Unable to connect. Check your connection parameters.');
mysql_select_db(MYSQL_DB, $db) or die(mysql_error($db));

$action = 'Add';

$character = array('alias' => '',
                   'real_name' => '',
                   'alignment' => 'good',
                   'address' => '',
                   'city' => '',
                   'state' => '',
                   'zipcode_id' => '');
$character_powers = array();
$rivalries = array();

// validate incoming character id value
$character_id = (isset($_GET['id']) && ctype_digit($_GET['id'])) ?
    $_GET['id'] : 0;

// retrieve information about the requested character
if ($character_id != 0) {
    $query = 'SELECT
            c.alias, c.real_name, c.alignment,
            l.address, z.city, z.state, z.zipcode_id
        FROM
            comic_character c, comic_lair l, comic_zipcode z
        WHERE
            z.zipcode_id = l.zipcode_id AND
            c.lair_id = l.lair_id AND
            c.character_id = ' . $character_id;
    $result = mysql_query($query, $db) or die (mysql_error($db));

    if (mysql_num_rows($result) > 0) {
        $action = 'Edit';
        $character = mysql_fetch_assoc($result);
    }
    mysql_free_result($result);

    if ($action == 'Edit') {
        // get list of character's powers
        $query = 'SELECT
                power_id
            FROM
                comic_character_power
            WHERE character_id = ' . $character_id;
        $result = mysql_query($query, $db) or die (mysql_error($db));

        if (mysql_num_rows($result) > 0) {
```

```php
        while ($row = mysql_fetch_array($result)) {
            $character_powers[$row['power_id']] = true;
        }
    }
    mysql_free_result($result);

    // get list of character's rivalries
    $query = 'SELECT
            c2.character_id
        FROM
            comic_character c1
            JOIN comic_character c2
            JOIN comic_rivalry r
                ON (c1.character_id = r.hero_id AND
                    c2.character_id = r.villain_id) OR
                   (c2.character_id = r.hero_id AND
                    c1.character_id = r.villain_id)
        WHERE
            c1.character_id = ' . $character_id . '
        ORDER BY
            c2.alias ASC';
    $result = mysql_query($query, $db) or die (mysql_error($db));

    $rivalries = array();
    if (mysql_num_rows($result) > 0) {
        while ($row = mysql_fetch_array($result)) {
            $rivalries[$row['character_id']] = true;
        }
    }
    }
}
?>
<html>
 <head>
  <title><?php echo $action; ?> Character</title>
  <style type="text/css">
td { vertical-align: top; }
  </style>
 </head>
 <body>
  <img src="logo.jpg" alt="Comic Book Appreciation Site" style="float: left;" />
  <h1>Comic Book<br/>Appreciation</h1>
  <h2><?php echo $action; ?> Character</h2>
  <hr style="clear: both;"/>
  <form action="char_transaction.php" method="post">
   <table>
    <tr>
     <td>Character Name:</td>
     <td><input type="text" name="alias" size="40" maxlength="40"
       value="<?php echo $character['alias'];?>"></td>
    </tr><tr>
     <td>Real Name:</td>
     <td><input type="text" name="real_name" size="40" maxlength="80"
```

```php
                  value="<?php echo $character['real_name'];?>"></td>
      </tr><tr>
       <td>Powers:<br/><small><em>CTRL-click to select multiple powers
</em></small>
       </td>
       <td>
<?php
// retrieve and present the list of powers
$query = 'SELECT
        power_id, power
    FROM
        comic_power
    ORDER BY
        power ASC';
$result = mysql_query($query, $db) or die (mysql_error($db));

if (mysql_num_rows($result) > 0) {
    echo '<select multiple name="powers[]">';
    while ($row = mysql_fetch_array($result)) {
        if (isset($character_powers[$row['power_id']])) {
            echo '<option value="' . $row['power_id'] . '"
selected="selected">';
        } else {
            echo '<option value="' . $row['power_id'] . '">';
        }
        echo $row['power'] . '</option>';
    }
    echo '</select>';
} else {
    echo '<p><strong>No Powers entered...</strong></p>';
}
mysql_free_result($result);
?>
      </td>
    </tr><tr>
     <td rowspan="2">Lair Location:<br/><small><em>Address<br/>City, State,
      Zip Code</em></small></td>
     <td><input type="text" name="address" size="40" maxlength="40"
       value="<?php echo $character['address'];?>"></td>
    </tr><tr>
     <td><input type="text" name="city" size="23" maxlength="40"
       value="<?php echo $character['city'];?>">
      <input type="text" name="state" size="2" maxlength="2"
       value="<?php echo $character['state'];?>">
      <input type="text" name="zipcode_id" size="5" maxlength="5"
       value="<?php echo $character['zipcode_id'];?>"></td>
    </tr><tr>
     <td>Alignment:</td>
     <td><input type="radio" name="alignment" value="good"
       <?php echo ($character['alignment']=='good') ? 'checked="checked"' : '';
       ?>/> Good<br/>
```

```
              <input type="radio" name="alignment" value="evil"
                <?php echo ($character['alignment']=='evil') ? 'checked="checked"' : '';
                ?></> Evil
          </td>
      </tr><tr>
      </tr><tr>
        <td>Rivalries:<br/><small><em>CTRL-click to select multiple enemies</em>
          </small>
        </td>
        <td>
<?php
// retrieve and present the list of existing characters (excluding the
character
// being edited)
$query = 'SELECT
        character_id, alias
    FROM
        comic_character
    WHERE
        character_id != ' . $character_id . '
    ORDER BY
        alias ASC';
$result = mysql_query($query, $db) or die (mysql_error($db));

if (mysql_num_rows($result) > 0) {
    echo '<select multiple name="rivalries[]">';
    while ($row = mysql_fetch_array($result)) {
        if (isset($rivalries[$row['character_id']])) {
            echo '<option value="' . $row['character_id'] .
                '" selected="selected">';
        } else {
            echo '<option value="' . $row['character_id'] . '">';
        }
        echo $row['alias'] . '</option>';
    }
    echo '</select>';
} else {
    echo '<p><strong>No Characters entered...</strong></p>';
}
mysql_free_result($result);
?>
        </td>
    </tr><tr>
    <td colspan="2">
     <input type="submit" name="action"
      value="<?php echo $action; ?> Character" />
     <input type="reset" value="Reset">
<?php
```

```
if ($action == "Edit") {
    echo '<input type="submit" name="action" value="Delete Character" />';
    echo '<input type="hidden" name="character_id" value="' .
        $character_id . '" />';
}
?>
    </td>
    </tr>
  </table>
</form>
<p><a href="list_characters.php">Return to Home Page</a></p>
</body>
</html>
```

3. Open your browser and point it to the location of `list_characters.php`. This is your Character Database home page. It should look something like Figure 10-3. But because you don't currently have any characters to look at, let's move on.

Figure 10-3

4. Click the Add New Character link. A new page appears, ready for your data input, which should look like that in Figure 10-4. You will notice that the powers you entered are choices in the Powers field.

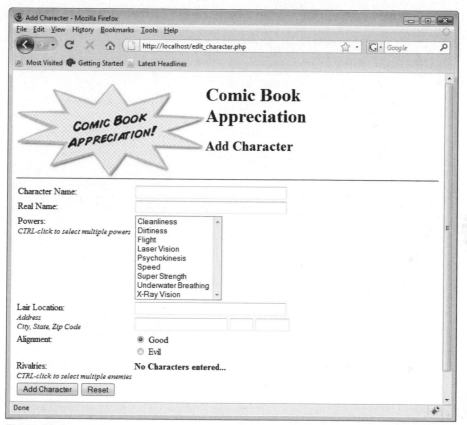

Figure 10-4

5. Enter the appropriate data for your character, and click Add Character. You should be taken back to the Character Database page, where you'll see the new character listed, as shown in Figure 10-5.

Figure 10-5

6. If you click New Character again, you now see an extra field for rivalries. You can select any previously created characters in the database as the current character's enemies.

7. From the home page, click one of your characters' names. The Edit Character page loads again, and the character's data will be automatically entered into the fields (see Figure 10-6). If you look at the URL for this page, you see ?id=# at the end, where # is the character's number.

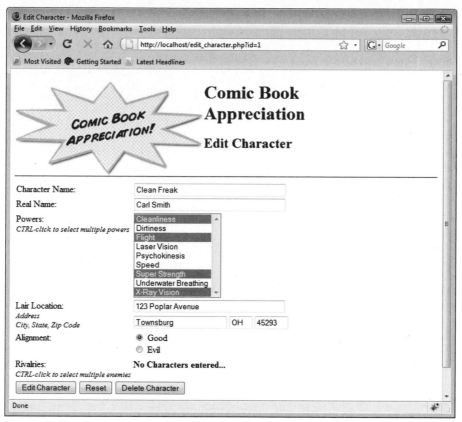

Figure 10-6

8. Change some of the data, and click Edit Character. You are taken back to the Character Database page, where you should immediately see the results of your changes. In fact, if you selected an enemy for this character, you should see the results change in the enemy's row as well.

How It Works

You created two different files in this exercise, so we're going to take them apart and look at them each individually here.

___

list_characters.php

The list_characters.php page has an optional parameter that can be passed: ?o=#, where # is 1, 2, or 3. This code retrieves that variable if it exists and converts it to the appropriate value if necessary to determine on which column the display should be sorted. If some smart-aleck types in an invalid value, or if no value is passed at all, then the script will default its value to 1.

```
$order = array(1 => 'alias ASC',
               2 => 'real_name ASC',
               3 => 'alignment ASC, alias ASC');

$o = (isset($_GET['o']) && ctype_digit($_GET['o'])) ? $_GET['o'] : 1;
if (!in_array($o, array_keys($order))) {
    $o = 1;
}
```

This value determines which column the character display will be sorted on: 1 is by alias, 2 is by real name, and 3 is first by alignment and then by alias. You will use the value $o as the key to your order array which will be appended to the appropriate SQL statement later.

You are going to build a table of characters in a moment. A SELECT query retrieves the list of characters sorted appropriately, and then the number of records is checked. If there are character records returned, then the table is constructed, but otherwise you want to display a "No Characters" message.

```
$query = 'SELECT
        character_id, alias, real_name, alignment
    FROM
        comic_character
    ORDER BY ' . $order[$o];
$result = mysql_query($query, $db) or die (mysql_error($db));

if (mysql_num_rows($result) > 0) {
    // ...
} else {
    echo '<p><strong>No Characters entered...</strong></p>';
}
```

The column headers for the Alias, Real Name, and Alignment columns are actually links back to the same page, but with different sort parameters appended to the address, so the viewer can sort the table to his or her heart's content by clicking on them.

```
echo '<tr><th><a href="' . $_SERVER['PHP_SELF'] . '?o=1">Alias</a></th>';
echo '<th><a href="' . $_SERVER['PHP_SELF'] . '?o=2">Real Name</a></th>';
echo '<th><a href="' . $_SERVER['PHP_SELF'] . '?o=3">Alignment</a></th>';
echo '<th>Powers</th>';
echo '<th>Enemies</th></tr>';
```

Each row is provided with an alternating odd/even class attribute, as you have done in several earlier chapters, so they can be colorized. Alternating the background color of the rows makes it easier for your users to read them. You also make the character's name a link to the edit_character.php page so that by clicking on it the user can edit the character's details.

```
$odd = true;
while ($row = mysql_fetch_array($result)) {
    echo ($odd == true) ? '<tr class="odd_row">' : '<tr class="even_row">';
    $odd = !$odd;
    echo '<td><a href="edit_character.php?id=' . $row['character_id'] .
        '">' . $row['alias'] . '</a></td>';
    echo '<td>' . $row['real_name'] . '</td>';
    echo '<td>' . $row['alignment'] . '</td>';
```

Next are two other SELECT statements to retrieve the appropriate data for the remaining columns: powers and rivalries. Because they are executed within a loop that is processing your first query's results, $query2, $result2 and $row2 variables are used, so you don't overwrite the first query's results that are still needed.

The first SELECT statement fetches the character's powers by JOINing the comic_power and comic_ character_power tables. If powers are returned, then they are listed in the table, but if no powers have been assigned to the character, then "none" is displayed.

```
$query2 = 'SELECT
        power
    FROM
        comic_power p
        JOIN comic_character_power cp
            ON p.power_id = cp.power_id
    WHERE
        cp.character_id = ' . $row['character_id'] . '
    ORDER BY
        power ASC';
$result2 = mysql_query($query2, $db) or die (mysql_error($db));

if (mysql_num_rows($result2) > 0) {
    $powers = array();
    while ($row2 = mysql_fetch_assoc($result2)) {
        $powers[] = $row2['power'];
    }
    echo '<td>' . implode(', ', $powers) . '</td>';
} else {
    echo '<td>none</td>';
}
mysql_free_result($result2);
```

The second SELECT statement fetches the character's rivals. This one is similar to the previous M:N query, with a couple of exceptions. First of all, you are linking the character table twice. You can see that you are creating two instances of that table, one for the hero character and one for the villain character. This distinction is very important.

The other exception is the ON statement. You have characters that you are attempting to link to other characters and enemies. Call them opponents, nemeses, or whatever. Typically, you expect good versus evil, and vice versa. However, you are allowing *any* character to be the enemy of *any other* character. That makes linking more interesting, because you are using a table a with a hero_id and villain_id. If you have two evil characters who are enemies to each other, which one gets stored in hero_id?

The answer is that it doesn't matter. What you want to do is to make sure that you not only don't have any duplicates in the comic_rivalry table, but also that you don't have what we call *reverse duplication*. In other words, if you have a row with hero_id=3 and villain_id=7, then hero_id=7 and villain_ id=3 must be considered a duplicate. There is no way to prevent that in MySQL using primary keys, so you must take care of that contingency in your code. You do that in a couple of places.

In this instance, you are combining two queries into one. The first one grabs all instances of each character where there character's ID is in the hero_id field, and his enemies' IDs are in the villain_id field. The second part of the ON statement reverses that and pulls all instances of each character where the character's ID is in the villain field, and his enemies' IDs are in the `hero_id` field. This does not prevent reverse duplication (that is handled elsewhere), but it does make sure you have grabbed every possible link to a character's enemy.

Again, if enemies are returned, then they are listed in the table. Otherwise, "none" is displayed.

```
$query2 = 'SELECT
        c2.alias
    FROM
        comic_character c1
        JOIN comic_character c2
        JOIN comic_rivalry r
            ON (c1.character_id = r.hero_id AND
                c2.character_id = r.villain_id) OR
               (c2.character_id = r.hero_id AND
                c1.character_id = r.villain_id)
    WHERE
        c1.character_id = ' . $row['character_id'] . '
    ORDER BY
        c2.alias ASC';
$result2 = mysql_query($query2, $db) or die (mysql_error($db));

if (mysql_num_rows($result2) > 0) {
    $aliases = array();
    while ($row2 = mysql_fetch_assoc($result2)) {
        $aliases[] = $row2['alias'];
    }
    echo '<td>' . implode(', ', $aliases) . '</td>';
} else {
    echo '<td>none</td>';
}
mysql_free_result($result2);
```

edit_character.php

This file does double duty so it's a little longer. But a lot of it is HTML, and much of what it does you have already done before, so this shouldn't be too difficult.

The default functionality of this page is Add Character mode. If there is a value in `$_GET['id']` other than 0, the script will pull the data and change the default values.

```
$action = 'Add';

$character = array('alias' => '',
                   'real_name' => '',
                   'alignment' => 'good',
                   'address' => '',
                   'city' => '',
                   'state' => '',
                   'zipcode_id' => '');
$character_powers = array();
$rivalries = array();

$character_id = (isset($_GET['id']) && ctype_digit($_GET['id'])) ?
```

```
        $_GET['id'] : 0;

if ($character_id != 0) {
    // ...
}
```

Next, the script gets the basic information about the character from the `comic_character`, `comic_lair`, and `comic_zipcode` tables.

```
$query = 'SELECT
        c.alias, c.real_name, c.alignment,
        l.address, z.city, z.state, z.zipcode_id
    FROM
        comic_character c, comic_lair l, comic_zipcode z
    WHERE
        z.zipcode_id = l.zipcode_id AND
        c.lair_id = l.lair_id AND
        c.character_id = ' . $character_id;
$result = mysql_query($query, $db) or die (mysql_error($db));

if (mysql_num_rows($result) > 0) {
    $action = 'Edit';
    $character = mysql_fetch_assoc($result);
}
mysql_free_result($result);
```

You may realize that the query is also a JOIN if you are an astute reader, although the JOIN keyword is not used. You can identify such a JOIN because there are two or more tables, and the WHERE clause matches columns from each of the tables. The JOIN in this case is implied, and ON has integrated into the WHERE clause.

It isn't until we are sure that a character with the provided ID really exists in the database that we switch the page's action to Edit mode, which acts as a failsafe if someone were to supply an invalid character ID. If the value of $action has been changed, then the script will continue retrieving the list of superpowers and rivals for the character.

```
if ($action == 'Edit') {
    $query = 'SELECT
            power_id
        FROM
            comic_character_power
        WHERE character_id = ' . $character_id;
    $result = mysql_query($query, $db) or die (mysql_error($db));

    if (mysql_num_rows($result) > 0) {
        while ($row = mysql_fetch_array($result)) {
            $character_powers[$row['power_id']] = true;
        }
    }
    mysql_free_result($result);

    $query = 'SELECT
            c2.character_id
```

```
        FROM
            comic_character c1
            JOIN comic_character c2
            JOIN comic_rivalry r
                ON (c1.character_id = r.hero_id AND
                    c2.character_id = r.villain_id) OR
                   (c2.character_id = r.hero_id AND
                    c1.character_id = r.villain_id)
        WHERE
            c1.character_id = ' . $character_id . '
        ORDER BY
            c2.alias ASC';
    $result = mysql_query($query, $db) or die (mysql_error($db));

    $rivalries = array();
    if (mysql_num_rows($result) > 0) {
        while ($row = mysql_fetch_array($result)) {
            $rivalries[$row['character_id']] = true;
        }
    }
}
```

The queries only retrieve the power IDs and rival IDs and store them in the appropriate array for later use. They will be used in the form's Powers and Rivalries fields so each assigned to the character will be automatically selected.

Note the similarity of the SQL statement that retrieves the list of rivalries to the one earlier in list_characters.php.

You next build the HTML form and insert the values into the appropriate places as defaults. This is how you fill in the fields with character data.

```
<td>Character Name:</td>
<td><input type="text" name="alias" size="40" maxlength="40"
    value="<?php echo $character['alias'];?>"></td>
```

When you build the Powers select field, the script loops through each power in the database and checks its ID against the list gathered earlier and stored in the $powers array. If that power's key exists in the $powers array, then the script sets the option element's selected attribute so that it will appear preselected in the form. In this way, the script builds a field of *all* powers where the character's chosen powers are selected in the list. Neat, huh?

```
        <td>Powers:<br/><small><em>CTRL-click to select multiple powers</em></小</small>
    </td>
    <td>
<?php
$query = 'SELECT
        power_id, power
    FROM
        comic_power
    ORDER BY
```

```
         power ASC';
$result = mysql_query($query, $db) or die (mysql_error($db));

if (mysql_num_rows($result) > 0) {
    echo '<select multiple name="powers[]">';
    while ($row = mysql_fetch_array($result)) {
        if (isset($character_powers[$row['power_id']])) {
            echo '<option value="' . $row['power_id'] . '"
selected="selected">';
        } else {
            echo '<option value="' . $row['power_id'] . '">';
        }
        echo $row['power'] . '</option>';
    }
    echo '</select>';
} else {
    echo '<p><strong>No Powers entered...</strong></p>';
}
mysql_free_result($result);
?>
    </td>
```

Note the [] in the select's name attribute. That is necessary for PHP to recognize the variable as an array when it gets posted to the char_transaction.php page. This is a requirement for any field that might post with multiple values.

Then the following code creates a set of radio buttons for "good" and "evil" Alignment. The character's alignment is preselected with the checked attribute.

```
<td>Alignment:</td>
<td><input type="radio" name="alignment" value="good"
  <?php echo ($character['alignment']=='good') ? 'checked="checked"' : '';
  ?></> Good<br/>
 <input type="radio" name="alignment" value="evil"
  <?php echo ($character['alignment']=='evil') ? 'checked="checked"' : '';
  ?></> Evil
</td>
```

Remember what you did with the Powers field? Ditto all of that for the Enemies field.

```
    <td>Rivalries:<br/><small><em>CTRL-click to select multiple enemies</em>
     </small>
    </td>
    <td>
<?php
$query = 'SELECT
        character_id, alias
    FROM
        comic_character
    WHERE
        character_id != ' . $character_id . '
    ORDER BY
```

```
        alias ASC';
$result = mysql_query($query, $db) or die (mysql_error($db));

if (mysql_num_rows($result) > 0) {
    echo '<select multiple name="rivalries[]">';
    while ($row = mysql_fetch_array($result)) {
        if (isset($rivalries[$row['character_id']])) {
            echo '<option value="' . $row['character_id'] .
                '" selected="selected">';
        } else {
            echo '<option value="' . $row['character_id'] . '">';
        }
        echo $row['alias'] . '</option>';
    }
    echo '</select>';
} else {
    echo '<p><strong>No Characters entered...</strong></p>';
}
mysql_free_result($result);
?>
    </td>
```

If the character entry form is in Edit mode, then the script will include a Delete Character button. The button won't appear in Add mode, since you can't delete a character you haven't created yet. Also, the character ID is not passed through any other form fields, so you create a hidden field to hold that information. You need that ID if you are going to update an existing character, right? Of course, if you are creating a new character, then the ID will be created for you when you insert all the appropriate data.

```
if ($action == "Edit") {
    echo '<input type="submit" name="action" value="Delete Character" />';
    echo '<input type="hidden" name="character_id" value="' .
        $character_id . '" />';
}
```

Summary

Whew! This chapter covered a lot of ground. You learned about how to plan the design of your application, including database design. You learned how to normalize your data so that it can easily be linked and manipulated without having redundant duplication. You created a brand-new database for your web site and started building your site by creating tables the application needed to access and update.

Congratulations! You've just created your first fully functioning web application with a relational database back end. (That's going to look *so* good on your resume.)

This chapter is only the beginning, however. With the knowledge you gained here, you can create almost any application you desire. Here are some examples of what you could do:

❑ **Content Management System (CMS):** Create a data entry system that will allow users and administrators to alter the content of the web site and your database without knowing any HTML.

❑ **Maintain a database of users visiting your site:** You can enable user authentication, e-mail your users to give them exciting news, sign them up for newsletters, and so on.

❑ **Create an online e-commerce site:** Create shopping carts where users can store the merchandise they will purchase. (This can be daunting — many choose to use a third-party shopping-cart application.)

❑ **Create an online discussion forum where your users can go to discuss how wonderful your site looks!**

These are just a few ideas. In fact, you are going to see how to do each of these things over the course of upcoming chapters. With a little imagination, you can come up with solutions to almost any problem you might face in building your site.

If any of the ideas presented in this chapter are difficult for you to grasp, that's okay — it is a large amount of new material crammed into only a few pages. We expected you to learn a lot, especially if you are a beginning programmer. The great thing about a book is that you can keep coming back! You will also be revisiting many of these concepts in later chapters. For example, in Chapter 16, where you learn to build your own forum, you will go through database normalization again, on a new set of databases. You will also have many more opportunities to create SQL queries, some familiar and some new.

For now, you have the basic knowledge for creating even the most complex sites. You have the first incarnation installed on your server. Take some time to play with your new toy.

Now all you need to do is let all of your friends and family know about your cool new site. If only you knew how to send e-mails using PHP. Well, we'll handle that in Chapter 11.

Exercises

See how you might accomplish the following tasks:

1. Add a "costume description" field to the character record, and provide a way to modify the costume description.

2. Modify the character listing to display the characters' locations alongside their powers.

Sending E-mail

So far, the chapters in this book have walked you through the creation of a comprehensive web site. You have designed your site so that users can add and modify data that is stored in databases. You have built dynamic pages for your users, ensuring that they have a rich and unique experience when they visit your web site. You are even displaying helpful error messages in case something goes wrong. But now it's time to get a little more interactive with your users, with e-mail. We are not talking about standard e-mail — we're talking about sending out e-mails using PHP.

Why would you want a server-side scripting language to send out e-mails? Perhaps you want to create a feedback form used for submitting information to an administrator's e-mail address, as introduced in Chapter 9. Maybe you want certain errors to be automatically e-mailed to the webmaster. Perhaps you would like to create an application that allows users to send their friends and family electronic postcards. (Nod your head in vigorous agreement to the latter, here, because that is exactly what you are going to do!)

Specifically, this chapter covers:

- ❑ Sending a basic e-mail
- ❑ Sending an HTML-formatted e-mail
- ❑ Using multipart messages
- ❑ Sending images
- ❑ Receiving confirmation

Setting Up PHP to Use E-mail

You need an e-mail server to be able to send e-mail with PHP. This chapter doesn't delve too deeply into the setup of an e-mail server for PHP, but here are the basics.

If you are working within a UNIX or Linux environment, then you will most likely have sendmail installed on your server, or it can be installed within minutes. If you are using a shared hosting service, then check with your provider to see if it uses sendmail or some equivalent.

If you are not using sendmail, or if you have Apache installed on a Windows server, then you have a couple of choices. You can use your existing SMTP (Simple Mail Transfer Protocol) service, or you can install an e-mail server such as Mailtraq on your computer. There are many online resources available to help you, if you have questions about setting up or using an e-mail server.

Once you have your e-mail server up and running, there are a couple of parameters you'll need to modify in your `php.ini` file. Of course, if you are using a hosting service, then your provider should already have these parameters set up.

❑ SMTP: Set this to the IP address or DNS name of your SMTP server. For example, if you have an e-mail server installed on the same server as your PHP server, you should be able to set SMTP to `localhost`.

❑ smtp_port: Set this to the port PHP uses to connect to the SMTP server.

❑ sendmail_from: The From address used by default by the PHP `mail()` command.

❑ sendmail_path: The path to the sendmail program. For most servers, this is `usr/sbin/sendmail`.

SMTP and smtp_port parameters apply to Windows only, while the sendmail_path parameter applies to UNIX/Linux only.

That's just about all there is to setting up PHP for e-mail. You will test to make sure it works correctly in the next section, "Sending an E-mail." You can find more information about setting up PHP for e-mail at `http://php.net/manual/en/ref.mail.php`.

Sending an E-mail

The actual method of sending an e-mail is quite simple. Of course, it can be made much more complex by sending HTML and images. However, you will start off with something simple.

Try It Out   **Sending a Simple E-mail**

This example is just about the simplest code you can write to send an e-mail. Of course, it's not very flexible, but it does demonstrate the `mail()` function quite well.

1. Start your editor, and enter the following code (make sure you put your own e-mail address in as the first parameter):

```php
<?php
mail('myaddress@example.com', 'Hello World',
    'Hi, world. Prepare for our arrival. We are starving!');
?>
```

2. Save the file as `firstmail.php`, and load it in your browser. You should see a blank page and receive an e-mail shortly at the address entered as the first parameter to `mail()`.

How It Works

Pretty cool, huh? That's all there is to it! The `mail()` function automatically sends an e-mail, using the following format:

```
mail(to_address, subject, message, headers, other_parameters)
```

If you want to send a message to multiple recipients, their addresses must be separated with a comma in the `to` parameter. For example:

```
mail('me@example.com, you@example.com', 'Hi', 'Whazzup?')
```

The parameters `headers` and `other_parameters` are optional. We will cover the `headers` parameter soon. The `other_parameters` are beyond the scope of this book, but if you want more information about the `mail()` function, point your browser to `php.net/manual/en/function.mail.php`.

You may have noticed when receiving this e-mail that there was no From address (or, maybe it was a bogus address). Ours says "www-data." In the next example, you'll see how to add a From: address to your e-mail, and you'll also collect information from the user before sending the e-mail.

Try It Out   **Collecting Data and Sending an E-mail**

In this exercise, you are going to create two web pages, `postcard.php` and `sendmail.php`. The file `postcard.php` will collect the data you are going to send. The file `sendmail.php` will actually send the message, using the data entered.

1. Start up your text editor, and enter the following code:

```html
<html>
 <head>
  <title>Enter E-mail Data</title>
 <style type="text/css">
```

```
  td { vertical-align: top; }
 </style>
</head>
<body>
 <form method="post" action="sendmail.php">
  <table>
   <tr>
    <td>To:</td>
    <td><input type="text" name="to_address" size="40"/></td>
   </tr><tr>
    <td>From:</td>
    <td><input type="text" name="from_address" size="40"/></td>
   </tr><tr>
    <td>Subject:</td>
    <td><input type="text" name="subject" size="40"/></td>
   </tr><tr>
    <td valign="top">Message:</td>
    <td>
     <textarea cols="60" rows="10"
      name="message">Enter your message here.</textarea>
    </td>
   </tr><tr>
    <td></td>
    <td>
     <input type="submit" value="Send"/>
     <input type="reset" value="Reset"/>
    </td>
   </tr>
  </table>
 </form>
</body>
</html>
```

2. Save the page as `postcard.php`. Note that `postcard.php` doesn't actually contain any PHP code in it. It simply collects the required data in an HTML form. You're giving it a `.php` extension because you will be adding PHP code to it later.

3. Start a new text document, and enter the following code:

```
<?php
$to_address = $_POST['to_address'];
$from_address = $_POST['from_address'];
$subject = $_POST['subject'];
$message = $_POST['message'];

$headers = 'From: ' . $from_address . "\r\n";
?>
<html>
 <head>
  <title>Mail Sent!</title>
 </head>
 <body>
<?php
$success = mail($to_address, $subject, $message, $headers);
```

```
if ($success) {
    echo '<h1>Congratulations!</h1>';
    echo '<p>The following message has been sent: <br/><br/>';
    echo '<b>To:</b> ' . $to_address . '<br/>';
    echo '<b>From:</b> ' . $from_address . '<br/>';
    echo '<b>Subject:</b> ' . $subject . '<br/>';
    echo '<b>Message:</b></p>';
    echo nl2br($message);
} else {
    echo '<p><strong>There was an error sending your message.</strong></p>';
}
?>
 </body>
</html>
```

4. Save this page as `sendmail.php`. This second page will take the values entered into the first page and send them in an e-mail.

5. Load up the first page, `postcard.php`, in your browser and enter some data. Make sure you use a valid e-mail address so that you can verify the e-mail's receipt. It should look something like Figure 11-1.

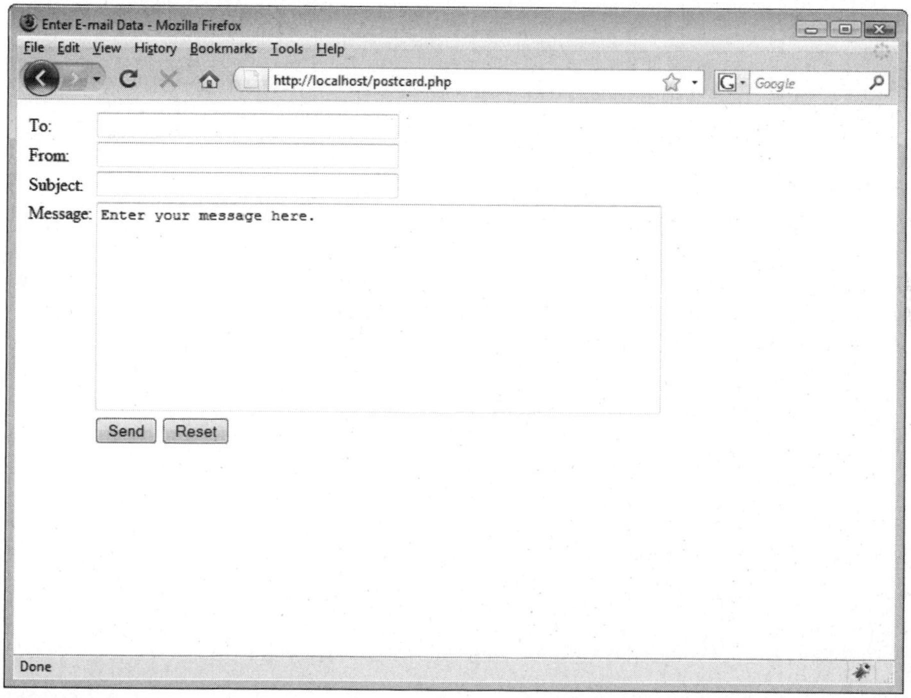

Figure 11-1

6. Click the Send button. A second page appears, similar to the one shown in Figure 11-2.

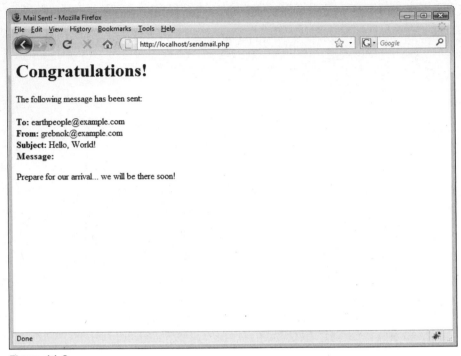

Figure 11-2

7. Open your e-mail client, and check your e-mail. You should find the e-mail message, as shown in Figure 11-3.

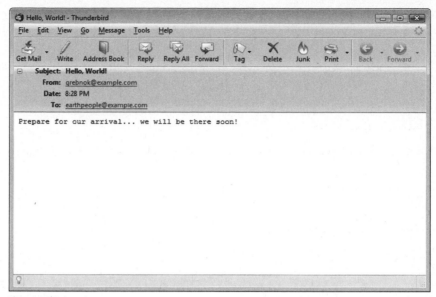

Figure 11-3

How It Works

Once you press the Send button on the form and submit its information, `sendmail.php` is loaded. The first step in your PHP code assigns all the fields from `postcard.php` to variables.

```
$to_address = $_POST['to_address'];
$from_address = $_POST['from_address'];
$subject = $_POST['subject'];
$message = $_POST['message'];
```

To specify from whom the e-mail is coming, you use the optional fourth parameter to the `mail()` function, `headers`. Headers are explained in more detail in the section "Sending HTML by Using Headers," later in this chapter.

```
$headers = 'From: ' . $from_address . "\r\n";
```

The `mail()` function returns a value of `true` if it is successful and `false` if it fails. You can use this return value to make your application a little more robust by showing an error message if the message cannot be sent:

```
$success = mail($to_address, $subject, $message, $headers);
if ($success) {
    echo '<h1>Congratulations!</h1>';
    echo '<p>The following message has been sent: <br/><br/>';
    echo '<b>To:</b> ' . $to_address . '<br/>';
    echo '<b>From:</b> ' . $from_address . '<br/>';
```

```
        echo '<b>Subject:</b> ' . $subject . '<br/>';
        echo '<b>Message:</b></p>';
        echo nl2br($message);
    } else {
        echo '<p><strong>There was an error sending your message.</strong></p>';
    }
```

Of course, you can modify this to handle errors more elegantly by using the knowledge you acquired in Chapter 9 to do so.

You have now created your first PHP e-mail application. Congratulations! (Call your mother! She'll be so proud. Or better yet, e-mail her!) But you'll probably soon get tired of plaintext e-mails. I'm sure you're chomping at the bit to create colorful, formatted e-mails. How else are you going to enable users to send some pretty postcards?

Dressing Up Your E-mails with HTML

Because you are creating a postcard application, sending plaintext e-mails just won't do. You want to dress them up a bit and make them look attractive, and you can do that with the addition of HyperText Markup Language, or HTML for short. In this section, we add HTML to your e-mail code to dress it up and make it more visually appealing.

Try It Out   **Sending HTML Code in an E-mail**

First, let's try a little experiment. This step isn't vital, but it will help illustrate a point about headers.

1. Go back to step 5 of the previous "Try It Out" section, and send another e-mail. This time, put some HTML in the message. An example would be:

```
<html>
<h1>Hello, World!</h1>
<p>Prepare for our arrival... we will be there soon!</p>
</html>
```

2. When you have filled out the form and clicked the Send button, check your e-mail again. It should look something like the e-mail shown in Figure 11-4.

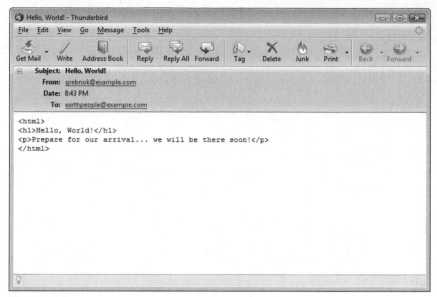

Figure 11-4

How It Works

Perhaps this heading should be "How It *Doesn't* Work." That's because your e-mail client does not know that it has received HTML. Why? Because you didn't tell it! In order for any HTML-capable client to display HTML, the client needs to be told that the incoming e-mail is going to have some HTML tags on it. Only then will it know how to properly display your message.

Try It Out   Sending HTML by Using Headers

You need a way for your e-mail to tell the client it contains HTML. This is accomplished by using headers. You already saw how to use headers to include a From: parameter. Now you are going to use a similar header to tell the client that the e-mail message contains HTML.

1. Edit your copy of sendmail.php in your text editor. Make the following highlighted modifications to the file:

```php
<?php
$to_address = $_POST['to_address'];
$from_address = $_POST['from_address'];
$subject = $_POST['subject'];
$message = $_POST['message'];

$headers = array();
```

```
$headers[] = 'MIME-Version: 1.0';
$headers[] = 'Content-type: text/html; charset=iso-8859-1';
$headers[] = 'Content-Transfer-Encoding: 7bit';
$headers[] = 'From: ' . $from_address;

?>
<html>
 <head>
  <title>Mail Sent!</title>
 </head>
 <body>
<?php
$success = mail($to_address, $subject, $message, join("\r\n", $headers));
if ($success) {
    echo '<h1>Congratulations!</h1>';
    echo '<p>The following message has been sent: <br/><br/>';
    echo '<b>To:</b> ' . $to_address . '<br/>';
    echo '<b>From:</b> ' . $from_address . '<br/>';
    echo '<b>Subject:</b> ' . $subject . '<br/>';
    echo '<b>Message:</b></p>';
    echo nl2br($message);
} else {
    echo '<p><strong>There was an error sending your message.</strong></p>';
}
?>
 </body>
</html>
```

2. Save the file.

3. Load `postcard.php` into your browser and fill in the fields. Be sure to include some HTML in the message field.

4. Click the Send button, and then open your e-mail client to see the new message, which will look something like Figure 11-5.

Figure 11-5

How It Works

You replaced the $headers variable with an array that stores multiple headers. This allows you to do many additional things with your e-mail, including sending HTML. This line is required in order to use extended MIME capabilities (such as HTML).

```
MIME-Version: 1.0
```

Note the \r\n. This is a carriage return and new line, which must be entered between each of the headers. UNIX sometimes allows just \n, but to be on the safe side, you should always use \r\n.

The following indicates that you will be using HTML in your message:

```
Content-type: text/html; charset=iso-8859-1
Content-Transfer-Encoding: 7bit
```

The headers are concatenated using the join() function with a carriage return and newline character (\r\n). The carriage return and newline combination must appear with each header, according to the specifications that describe the format of e-mails.

That's all there is to adding HTML to your messages. All you have to do is tell the e-mail client to expect HTML. Now you can get fancy and create e-mail with style sheets, images, and so on.

However, there is still a concern — what if you are using an e-mail program that does not accept or recognize HTML? You certainly want this application to be as user-friendly as possible, right? Not to worry — you'll take care of this with multipart (or mixed) messages.

Multipart Messages

You want to be able to send your postcards to anyone. However, some people don't have HTML capabilities in their e-mail client. Therefore, you will send your postcards using both plaintext and HTML.

Multipart Messages

You will use multipart messages to send messages with both plaintext and HTML. Here's how to do it:

1. Edit your copy of sendmail.php in your text editor. Make the following highlighted changes:

```php
<?php
<?php
$to_address = $_POST['to_address'];
$from_address = $_POST['from_address'];
$subject = $_POST['subject'];
$message = $_POST['message'];

$boundary = '==MP_Bound_xyccr948x==';

$headers = array();
$headers[] = 'MIME-Version: 1.0';
$headers[] = 'Content-type: multipart/alternative; boundary="' . $boundary . '"';
$headers[] = 'From: ' . $from_address;

$msg_body = 'This is a Multipart Message in MIME format.' . "\n";
$msg_body .= '--' . $boundary . "\n";
$msg_body .= 'Content-type: text/html; charset="iso-8859-1"' . "\n";
$msg_body .= 'Content-Transfer-Encoding: 7bit' . "\n\n";
$msg_body .= $message . "\n";
$msg_body .= '--' . $boundary . "\n";
$msg_body .= 'Content-type: text/plain; charset="iso-8859-1"' . "\n";
$msg_body .= 'Content-Transfer-Encoding: 7bit' . "\n\n";
$msg_body .= strip_tags($message) . "\n";
$msg_body .= '--' . $boundary . '--' . "\n";
?>
<html>
 <head>
  <title>Mail Sent!</title>
 </head>
 <body>
<?php
$success = mail($to_address, $subject, $msg_body, join("\r\n", $headers));
if ($success) {
    echo '<h1>Congratulations!</h1>';
    echo '<p>The following message has been sent: <br/><br/>';
    echo '<b>To:</b> ' . $to_address . '<br/>';
    echo '<b>From:</b> ' . $from_address . '<br/>';
    echo '<b>Subject:</b> ' . $subject . '<br/>';
```

```
        echo '<b>Message:</b></p>';
        echo nl2br($message);
    } else {
        echo '<p><strong>There was an error sending your message.</strong></p>';
    }
    ?>
     </body>
    </html>
```

How It Works

Multipart messages are not really that complicated. You must tell the e-mail client that data is coming in multiple parts — in this instance, plaintext and HTML. This is done in the header:

```
$headers[] = 'Content-type: multipart/alternative; boundary="' . $boundary . '"';
```

This tells the e-mail client to look for additional "Content-type" information in the message, which includes boundary information. The boundary is what separates the multiple parts of the message. It begins with two dashes (--) and goes at the beginning of the message, between the parts, and at the end. There is *no* significance to the content of this boundary. The key here is to make it as unique as possible, so that it most likely is not a value that would be repeated anywhere within the message. You can use symbols, numbers, and letters, in any combination. Many people choose to use rand() or md5() hash. The method you use is entirely up to you.

The following line simply tells older e-mail programs why they may not see the information they expected in their browser. It's not necessary, but it's user-friendly:

```
$msg_body = 'This is a Multipart Message in MIME format.' . "\n";
```

The HTML portion of your e-mail follows. Note the double dashes (--) in front of the boundary. Also note the use of two new lines (\r\n\r\n) on the Content-Transfer-Encoding line. Do not neglect those — the code will not work correctly without them.

```
$msg_body .= '--' . $boundary . "\n";
$msg_body .= 'Content-type: text/html; charset="iso-8859-1"' . "\n";
$msg_body .= 'Content-Transfer-Encoding: 7bit' . "\n\n";
$msg_body .= $message . "\n";
```

Next is the text portion of your e-mail. Note the similarity to the HTML portion. You do not need to include the same message body here. In fact, you would usually include an alternate message in text format.

```
$msg_body .= '--' . $boundary . "\n";
$msg_body .= 'Content-type: text/plain; charset="iso-8859-1"' . "\n";
$msg_body .= 'Content-Transfer-Encoding: 7bit' . "\n\n";
$msg_body .= strip_tags($message) . "\n";
```

This is the final boundary. Note the double dashes (--) at the end. This signifies that it's the end of the e-mail.

```
$msg_body .= '--' . $boundary . '--' . "\n";
```

Your boundary in this case was set by the following line:

```
$boundary = '==MP_Bound_xyccr948x==';
```

Storing Images

To create a postcard application, you need to have digital postcards available for the user to choose from. For the purposes of this example, you'll have four postcards. If you are ambitious, you can add more, and we hope that you will!

Try It Out   Storing Images

Let's add some nice postcards to the application, shall we?

1.   First, store your postcard images in a folder on your server. We have ours in the folder `postcards/`. Place them anywhere you like, but remember where they are.

2.   Start up your favorite editor, and enter the following code. Save it as `db_ch11-1.php`. Modify the code appropriately if you are using a different number of postcards, etc.

```php
<?php
require 'db.inc.php';

$db = mysql_connect(MYSQL_HOST, MYSQL_USER, MYSQL_PASSWORD) or
    die ('Unable to connect. Check your connection parameters.');
mysql_select_db(MYSQL_DB, $db) or die(mysql_error($db));

// create the postcard image table
$query = 'CREATE TABLE IF NOT EXISTS pc_image (
        image_id        INTEGER UNSIGNED NOT NULL AUTO_INCREMENT,
        image_url       VARCHAR(255)    NOT NULL DEFAULT "",
        description     VARCHAR(255)    NOT NULL DEFAULT "",

        PRIMARY KEY (image_id)
    )
    ENGINE=MyISAM';
mysql_query($query, $db) or die (mysql_error($db));

// change this path depending on your server
$images_path = 'http://localhost/postcards/';

//insert new data into the postcard image table
$query = 'INSERT IGNORE INTO pc_image
        (image_id, image_url, description)
    VALUES
```

```
        (1, "' . $images_path . 'punyearth.jpg", "Wish you were here"),
        (2, "' . $images_path . 'congrats.jpg", "Congratulations"),
        (3, "' . $images_path . 'visit.jpg", "We\'re coming to visit"),
        (4, "' . $images_path . 'sympathy.jpg", "Our Sympathies")';
mysql_query($query, $db) or die (mysql_error($db));

echo 'Success!';
?>
```

How It Works

First, the script connected to the server, using the correct username and password as listed in
db.inc.php. You wrote this file in Chapter 10, and it defines the constants you use to connect to the
MySQL database.

```
$db = mysql_connect(MYSQL_HOST, MYSQL_USER, MYSQL_PASSWORD) or
    die ('Unable to connect. Check your connection parameters.');
mysql_select_db(MYSQL_DB, $db) or die(mysql_error($db));
```

Next, you created the pc_image table in the database, containing three columns: image_id to store
the image's primary key value, image_url to store the location of the image file, and description to
store a brief description of the image.

```
$query = 'CREATE TABLE IF NOT EXISTS pc_image (
        image_id        INTEGER UNSIGNED NOT NULL AUTO_INCREMENT,
        image_url       VARCHAR(255)     NOT NULL DEFAULT "",
        description     VARCHAR(255)     NOT NULL DEFAULT "",

        PRIMARY KEY (image_id)
    )
    ENGINE=MyISAM';
mysql_query($query, $db) or die (mysql_error($db));
```

Next, you inserted references and descriptions of the images into the pc_image table. The beginning
of each path begins with $images_path, so you needed to change the value of this variable,
depending on your particular needs.

```
$images_path = 'http://localhost/postcards/';

$query = 'INSERT IGNORE INTO pc_image
        (image_id, image_url, description)
    VALUES
        (1, "' . $images_path . 'punyearth.jpg", "Wish you were here"),
        (2, "' . $images_path . 'congrats.jpg", "Congratulations"),
        (3, "' . $images_path . 'visit.jpg", "We\'re coming to visit"),
        (4, "' . $images_path . 'sympathy.jpg", "Our Sympathies")';
mysql_query($query, $db) or die (mysql_error($db));
```

Finally, "Success!" is displayed when the script reaches its end.

```
echo 'Success!';
```

Getting Confirmation

So far, you have a pretty good start to a postcard application. Any user can send a message to whomever he or she wants, and PHP takes care of mailing it. Unfortunately, there is still a small problem with the application.

As it stands right now, it is quite easy for the user to use any e-mail address in the From field.

This is a bad thing because nasty e-mails could be sent on someone else's behalf, and you don't want that. To prevent such maliciousness, you must first send a confirmation e-mail to the From address. Once you get the confirmation, you know the user entered a valid e-mail address, and you can go ahead and send the e-mail.

This act of achieving confirmation is the first step toward creating a workflow application. A workflow application requires input from various parties at different stages before it reaches its final destination.

To accommodate this workflow, your application must undergo a metamorphosis from what it was in the past. The `sendmail.php` script must be split into two separate processes such that, in between the two processes, you wait for confirmation.

To confirm an e-mail address, the postcard information needs to be temporarily stored in a table, to be retrieved later on, once confirmation has been established.

Try It Out   **Getting Confirmation**

In this exercise, you'll implement the confirmation e-mail into your application.

1. Open your editor, and create a new PHP file called `db_ch11-2.php`.

```php
<?php
require 'db.inc.php';

$db = mysql_connect(MYSQL_HOST, MYSQL_USER, MYSQL_PASSWORD) or
    die ('Unable to connect. Check your connection parameters.');
mysql_select_db(MYSQL_DB, $db) or die(mysql_error($db));

// create the confirmation table
$query = 'CREATE TABLE IF NOT EXISTS pc_confirmation (
        email_id    INTEGER UNSIGNED NOT NULL AUTO_INCREMENT,
        token       CHAR(32)        NOT NULL,
        to_email    VARCHAR(100)    NOT NULL,
        to_name     VARCHAR(50)     NOT NULL,
        from_name   VARCHAR(100)    NOT NULL,
        from_email  VARCHAR(50)     NOT NULL,
        subject     VARCHAR(255)    NOT NULL,
        postcard    VARCHAR(255)    NOT NULL,
```

```
            message        TEXT,

            PRIMARY KEY (email_id)
        )
      ENGINE=MyISAM';
  mysql_query($query, $db) or die (mysql_error($db));

  echo 'Success!';
  ?>
```

2. Run `db_ch10-2.php`, and you should see the success message displayed.

3. Open up `postcard.php` in your editor and replace its content with the following code:

```php
<?php
require 'db.inc.php';

$db = mysql_connect(MYSQL_HOST, MYSQL_USER, MYSQL_PASSWORD) or
    die ('Unable to connect. Check your connection parameters.');
mysql_select_db(MYSQL_DB, $db) or die(mysql_error($db));
?>
<html>
 <head>
  <title>Send Postcard</title>
  <script type="text/javascript">

window.onload = function() {
    // assign change_postcard_image to select field
    var s = document.getElementById('postcard_select');
    s.onchange = change_postcard_image;
}

function change_postcard_image() {
    var s = document.getElementById('postcard_select');
    var i = document.getElementById('postcard');
    var x = s.options.selectedIndex;

    // update image's src and alt attributes
    i.src = s.options[x].value;
    i.alt = s.options[x].text;
}
  </script>
 </head>
 <body>
  <h1>Send Postcard</h1>
  <form method="post" action="sendconfirm.php">
   <table>
    <tr>
     <td>Sender's Name:</td>
     <td><input type="text" name="from_name" size="40" /></td>
    </tr></tr>
     <td>Sender's E-mail:</td>
     <td><input type="text" name="from_email" size="40" /></td>
```

```
    </tr><tr>
     <td>Recipient's Name:</td>
     <td><input type="text" name="to_name" size="40" /></td>
    </tr></tr>
     <td>Recipient's E-mail:</td>
     <td><input type="text" name="to_email" size="40" /></td>
    </tr><tr>
     <td>Choose a Postcard:</td>
     <td><select id="postcard_select" name="postcard">
<?php
$query = 'SELECT image_url, description FROM pc_image ORDER BY description';
$result = mysql_query($query, $db) or die(mysql_error());

$row = mysql_fetch_assoc($result);
extract($row);

mysql_data_seek($result, 0);
while ($row = mysql_fetch_assoc($result)) {
    echo '<option value="' . $row['image_url'] . '">' . $row['description'] .
        '</option>';
}
mysql_free_result($result);
?>
     </select>
     </td>
    </tr><tr>
     <td colspan="2">
      <img id="postcard" src="<?php echo $image_url; ?>"
       alt="<?php echo $description; ?>" />
     </td>
    </tr><tr>
     <td>Subject:</td>
     <td><input type="text" name="subject" size="80" /></td>
    </tr><tr>
     <td colspan="2">
      <textarea cols="76" rows="12"
       name="message">Enter your message here</textarea>
     </td>
    </tr><tr>
     <td colspan="2">
      <input type="submit" value="Send" />
      <input type="reset" value="Reset the form" />
     </td>
    </tr>
   </table>
  </form>
 </body>
</html>
```

4. Next, write `sendconfirm.php`, the page that sends out the confirmation e-mail to the user.

```php
<?php
require 'db.inc.php';

$db = mysql_connect(MYSQL_HOST, MYSQL_USER, MYSQL_PASSWORD) or
    die ('Unable to connect. Check your connection parameters.');
mysql_select_db(MYSQL_DB, $db) or die(mysql_error($db));

$to_name = $_POST['to_name'];
$to_email = $_POST['to_email'];
$from_name = $_POST['from_name'];
$from_email = $_POST['from_email'];
$postcard = $_POST['postcard'];
$subject = $_POST['subject'];
$message = $_POST['message'];

$query = 'SELECT description FROM pc_image WHERE image_url = "' . $postcard . '"';
$result = mysql_query($query, $db) or die(mysql_error());

$description = '';
if (mysql_num_rows($result))
{
    $row = mysql_fetch_assoc($result);
    $description = $row['description'];
}
mysql_free_result($result);

$token = md5(time());

$query = 'INSERT INTO pc_confirmation
        (email_id, token, to_name, to_email, from_name, from_email, subject,
         postcard, message)
    VALUES
        (NULL, "' . $token . '",  "' . $to_name . '",  "' . $to_email . '",
         "' . $from_name . '",  "' . $from_email . '",   "' . $subject . '",
         "' . $postcard . '",  "' . $message . '")';
mysql_query($query, $db) or die(mysql_error());

$email_id = mysql_insert_id($db);

$headers = array();
$headers[] = 'MIME-Version: 1.0';
$headers[] = 'Content-type: text/html; charset="iso-8859-1"';
$headers[] = 'Content-Transfer-Encoding: 7bit';
$headers[] = 'From: no-reply@localhost';

$confirm_subject = 'Please confirm your postcard [' . $subject .']';

$confirm_message = '<html>';
$confirm_message .= '<p>Hello, ' . $from_name . '. Please click on the link ' .
    'below to confirm that you would like to send this postcard.</p>';
$confirm_message .= '<p><a href="http://localhost/confirm.php?id=' .
  $email_id . '&token=' . $token .'">Click here to confirm</a></p>';
```

```
$confirm_message .= '<hr />';
$confirm_message .= '<img src="' . $postcard . '" alt="' . $description .
    ' "/><br/>';
$confirm_message .= $message . '</html>';
?>
<html>
 <head>
  <title>Mail Sent!</title>
 </head>
 <body>
<?php
$success = mail($from_email, $confirm_subject, $confirm_message,
    join("\r\n", $headers));

if ($success) {
    echo '<h1>Pending Confirmation!</h1>';
    echo '<p>A confirmation e-mail has been sent to ' . $from_email . '. ' .
        'Open your e-mail and click on the link to confirm that you ' .
        'would like to send this postcard to ' . $to_name . '.</p>';
} else {
    echo '<p><strong>There was an error sending the confirmation.</strong></p>';
}
?>
 </body>
</html>
```

5.   Next is confirm.php. This file is loaded in the browser with an ID in the URL to designate
      which saved postcard is awaiting confirmation, and the script then sends the postcard to the
      intended recipient.

```
<?php
require 'db.inc.php';

$db = mysql_connect(MYSQL_HOST, MYSQL_USER, MYSQL_PASSWORD) or
    die ('Unable to connect. Check your connection parameters.');
mysql_select_db(MYSQL_DB, $db) or die(mysql_error($db));

$id = (isset($_GET['id'])) ? $_GET['id'] : 0;
$token = (isset($_GET['token'])) ? $_GET['token'] : '';

$query = 'SELECT email_id, token, to_name, to_email, from_name, from_email,
    subject, postcard, message FROM pc_confirmation WHERE
        token = "' . $token . '"';
$result = mysql_query($query, $db) or die(mysql_error());

if (mysql_num_rows($result) == 0) {
    echo '<p>Oops! Nothing to confirm.</p>';
        mysql_free_result($result);
    exit;
} else {
    $row = mysql_fetch_assoc($result);
        extract($row);
    mysql_free_result($result);
```

```
}

$boundary = '==MP_Bound_xyccr948x==';

$headers = array();
$headers[] = 'MIME-Version: 1.0';
$headers[] = 'Content-type: multipart/alternative; boundary="' . $boundary . '"';
$headers[] = 'From: ' . $from_email;

$postcard_message = '<html>';
$postcard_message .= '<p>Greetings, ' . $to_name . '! ';
$postcard_message .= $from_name . ' has sent you a postcard today.</p>';
$postcard_message .= '<p>Enjoy!</p>';
$postcard_message .= '<hr />';
$postcard_message .= '<img src="' . $postcard . '" alt="' . $description .
    ' "/><br/>';
$postcard_message .= $message;
$postcard_message .= '<hr/><p>You can also visit ' .
    '<a href="http://localhost/viewpostcard.php?id=' . $email_id . '&token=' .
    $token .'">http://localhost/viewpostcard.php?id=' . $email_id .
    '&token=' . $token .'</a> to view this postcard online.</p></html>';

$mail_message = 'This is a Multipart Message in MIME format' . "\n";
$mail_message .= '--' . $boundary . "\n";
$mail_message .= 'Content-type: text/html; charset="iso-8859-1"' . "\n";
$mail_message .= 'Content-Transfer-Encoding: 7bit' . "\n\n";
$mail_message .= $postcard_message . "\n";
$mail_message .= '--' . $boundary . "\n";
$mail_message .= 'Content-Type: text/plain; charset="iso-8859-1"' . "\n";
$mail_message .= 'Content-Transfer-Encoding: 7bit' . "\n\n";
$mail_message .= strip_tags($postcard_message) . "\n";
$mail_message .= '--' . $boundary . '--' . "\n";
?>
<html>
 <head>
  <title>Postcard Sent!</title>
 </head>
 <body>
<?php
$success = mail($to_email, $subject, $mail_message, join("\r\n", $headers));
if ($success) {
    echo '<h1>Congratulations!</h1>';
    echo '<p>The following postcard has been sent to ' . $to_name .
        ': <br/></p>';
    echo $postcard_message;
} else {
    echo '<p><strong>There was an error sending your message.</strong></p>';
}
?>
 </body>
</html>
```

6. Next, you'll create a form that allows a user to view the postcard. Call this one `viewpostcard.php`.

```php
<?php
require 'db.inc.php';

$db = mysql_connect(MYSQL_HOST, MYSQL_USER, MYSQL_PASSWORD) or
    die ('Unable to connect. Check your connection parameters.');
mysql_select_db(MYSQL_DB, $db) or die(mysql_error($db));

$id = (isset($_GET['id'])) ? $_GET['id'] : 0;
$token = (isset($_GET['token'])) ? $_GET['token'] : '';

$query = 'SELECT email_id, token, to_name, to_email, from_name, from_email,
    subject, postcard, message FROM pc_confirmation WHERE
        token = "' . $token . '"';
$result = mysql_query($query, $db) or die(mysql_error());

if (mysql_num_rows($result) == 0) {
    echo '<p>Oops! Nothing to view.</p>';
        mysql_free_result($result);
    exit;
} else {
    $row = mysql_fetch_assoc($result);
        extract($row);
    mysql_free_result($result);
}
?>
<html>
 <head>
  <title><?php echo $subject; ?></title>
 </head>
 <body>
<?php
echo '<img src="' . $postcard . '" alt="' . $description . ' "/><br/>';
echo $message;
?>
 </body>
</html>
```

7. Load `postcard.php` in your browser to verify that it works. The results should look similar to what's shown in Figure 11-6.

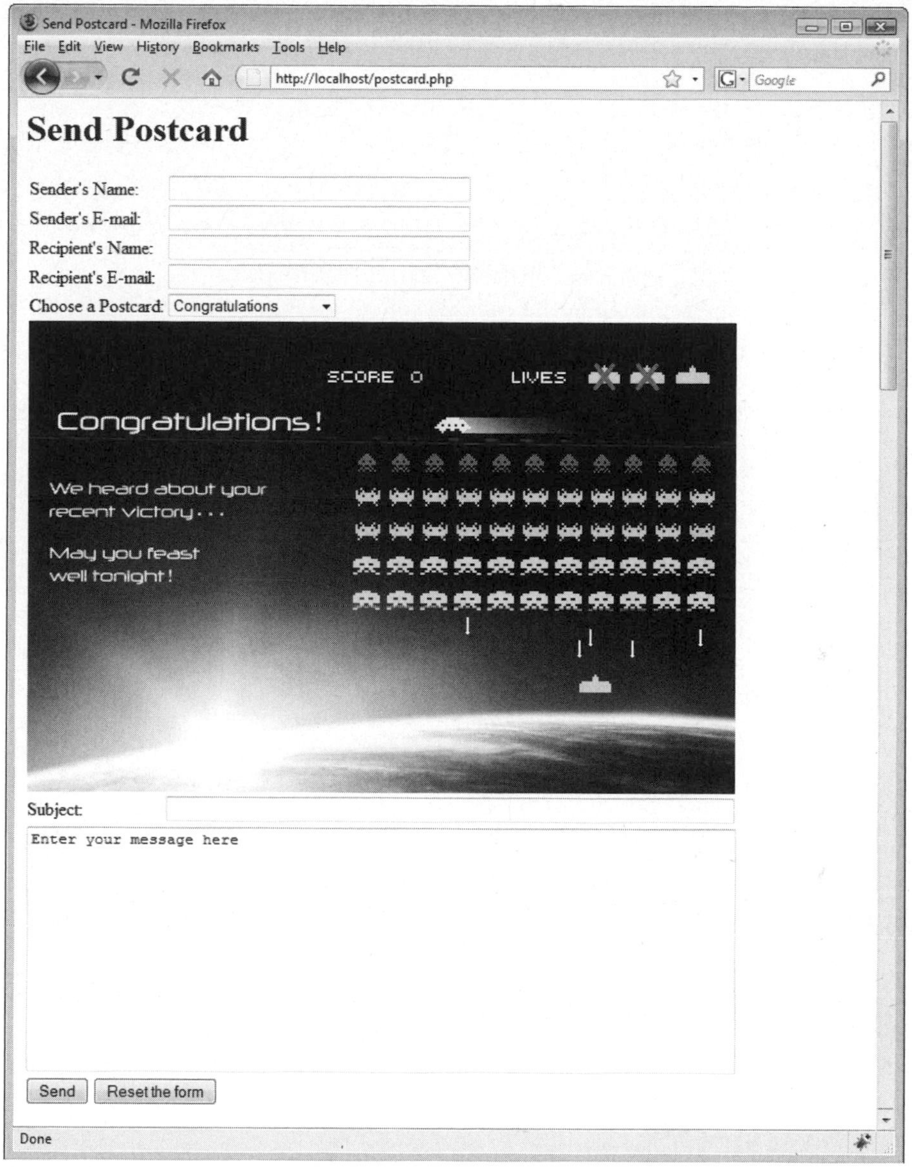
Send Postcard - Mozilla Firefox
File Edit View History Bookmarks Tools Help
http://localhost/postcard.php
Google
Send Postcard
Sender's Name:
Sender's E-mail:
Recipient's Name:
Recipient's E-mail:
Choose a Postcard:
Congratulations
SCORE 0
LIVES
Congratulations!
We heard about your recent victory...
May you feast well tonight!
Subject:
Enter your message here
Send
Reset the form
Done

Figure 11-6

8. Enter the appropriate information; remember to put in valid e-mail addresses in the Sender's E-mail and Recipient's E-mail fields.

9. In the Choose a Postcard field, select a postcard from the drop-down list, enter a message, and click the Send button. A screen similar to the one shown in Figure 11-7 loads.

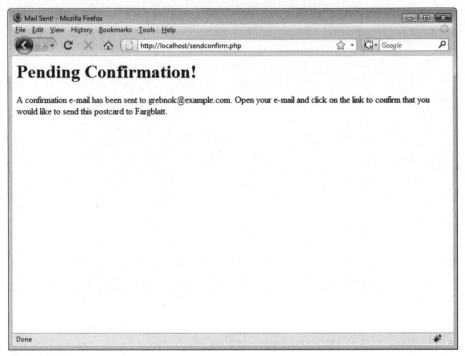

Figure 11-7

10. Check your e-mail. You should receive an e-mail that looks something like Figure 11-8.

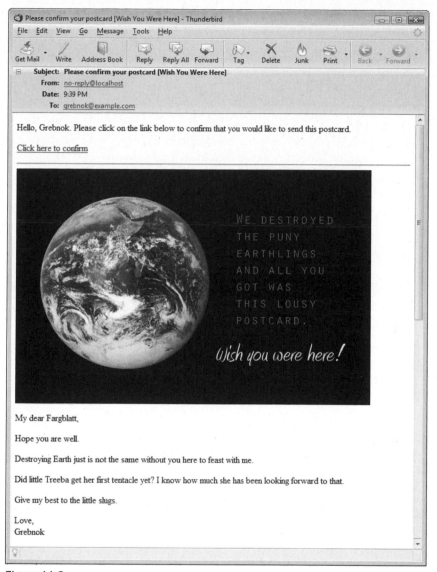

Figure 11-8

11. Click the link in the e-mail to confirm that you want to send the postcard.

12. Open the e-mail account this postcard was sent to (see Figure 11-9).

You did send it to an e-mail address you have access to, right? If you sent this to your little sister, we sure hope you didn't scare her!

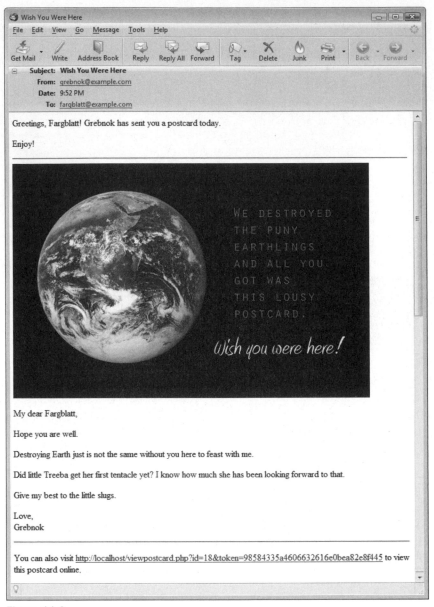

Figure 11-9

How It Works

Your application is getting more complex. However, it is still fairly basic in the functionality it offers. Here's what it does:

❑ The user loads `postcard.php` and fills out all the fields. He or she also selects a postcard to be sent. In the Sender's E-mail field, the user enters his or her e-mail address.

❑ After clicking Send, the user receives an e-mail showing what the postcard and message look like. A link is provided at the bottom of the e-mail for the user to click on, to confirm the postcard.

❑ Once the user clicks the confirmation link, the postcard is sent to the intended recipient.

Taking a closer look at the start of it, you see in postcard.php that you used a query to retrieve the list of images from the database. This is pretty straightforward and is something you've done several times already. But this time you used extract() on the first returned row and then reset the result list's internal pointer back to its beginning with mysql_data_seek(), before generating the options for the select element.

```
<select id="postcard_select" name="postcard">
<?php
$query = 'SELECT image_url, description FROM pc_image ORDER BY description';
$result = mysql_query($query, $db) or die(mysql_error());

$row = mysql_fetch_assoc($result);
extract($row);

mysql_data_seek($result, 0);
while ($row = mysql_fetch_assoc($result)) {
    echo '<option value="' . $row['image_url'] . '">' . $row['description'] .
        '</option>';
}
mysql_free_result($result);
?>
</select>
```

When the page first loads the select list, it shows its first option as the active postcard selection. The $image_url and $description variables populated by extract() are used as the initial values for the postcard's image element, so the two are initially in sync.

```
<img id="postcard" src="<?php echo $image_url; ?>"
 alt="<?php echo $description; ?>" />
```

Only the surface of using PHP, Apache, and MySQL has been scratched, but we're sure you will agree this book is large enough, and that if we were to start discussing the intricacies of JavaScript, then you might give yourself a hernia just trying to take it off the bookshelf! You're right, JavaScript is beyond the scope of this book. But because PHP code only runs on the server, not in the client's browser, it cannot be used to keep the displayed images in sync with each other once the page has been generated and sent off. Using JavaScript in this situation helps you reduce loading time and round trips to the server. The following lines of extra code written in JavaScript are included in the page:

```
<script type="text/javascript">

window.onload = function() {
    // assign change_postcard_image to select field
    var s = document.getElementById('postcard_select');
    s.onchange = change_postcard_image;
}

function change_postcard_image() {
    var s = document.getElementById('postcard_select');
```

```
        var i = document.getElementById('postcard');
        var x = s.options.selectedIndex;

        // update image's src and alt attributes
        i.src = s.options[x].value;
        i.alt = s.options[x].text;
    }
    </script>
```

If you want to know more about JavaScript, we recommend starting with *ppk on JavaScript*, by Peter-Paul Koch (New Riders, 2006).

Now you move on to `sendconfirm.php`. Much of it is similar to `sendmail.php`, so we'll just touch on the script's most important point. Before sending the confirmation e-mail, a token is generated and, together with the message, is stored in the `pc_confirmation` database table.

```
$token = md5(time());

$query = 'INSERT INTO pc_confirmation
        (email_id, token, to_name, to_email, from_name, from_email, subject,
          postcard, message)
    VALUES
        (NULL, "' . $token . '",  "' . $to_name . '",  "' . $to_email . '",
         "' . $from_name . '",  "' . $from_email . '",   "' . $subject . '",
         "' . $postcard . '",  "' . $message . '")';
mysql_query($query, $db) or die(mysql_error());
```

You used the `md5()` function to create the token. This returns a 128-bit "fingerprint," or "hash value," of the message passed to it. For example, the MD5 hash of "Hello World" is b10a8db164e0754105b7a99 be72e3fe5. The MD5 algorithm is designed as a one-way encryption of the data passed in to it, so it cannot be reversed to discover the original value. Using a one-way hash in this manner allows you to safely have the user click on a link in his or her e-mail to view the postcard. If you used a simple number or keyword, a malicious user could more easily guess the URL and ruin all your fun — guessing an MD5 hash would take too long to make it worthwhile for the hacker.

By passing in a time value, you can be fairly certain that the MD5 hash returned will be a unique value, which you use as a unique ID for the data. It is not 100 percent guaranteed to be unique, but because it is generated based on the current time in seconds and contains 32 alphanumeric characters, you can be reasonably sure it will be unique.

You should read RFC 1321 if you are interested in finding out more information about the MD5 hash. RFC 1321: "The MD5 Message-Digest Algorithm" is available online at `www.faqs.org/rfcs/rfc1321`.

`sendconfirm.php` sends an e-mail that includes a link to `confirm.php` and passes the message's ID and token in the URL string. The postcard data sits patiently until the sender receives the confirmation message and follows the link that will finally send the postcard to the intended recipient.

```
$confirm_message .= '<p><a href="http://localhost/confirm.php?id=' .
  $email_id . '&token=' . $token .'">Click here to confirm</a></p>';
```

When the sender receives the confirmation message, he or she clicks the link, and `confirm.php` is loaded in a web browser. The script takes in the message ID and unique validation token and uses them to retrieve the message from the database.

```
$id = (isset($_GET['id'])) ? $_GET['id'] : 0;
$token = (isset($_GET['token'])) ? $_GET['token'] : '';

$query = 'SELECT email_id, token, to_name, to_email, from_name, from_email,
    subject, postcard, message FROM pc_confirmation WHERE
token = "' . $token . '"';
$result = mysql_query($query, $db) or die(mysql_error());
```

The query will return all postcards that match your ID and token. Of course, there should always be just one match because $id is unique, even if, by some astronomical chance, $token is not.

Checking that `mysql_num_rows()` is not 0 (showing that the query matched no records) serves as a little extra insurance to make sure you don't try to send out a postcard if no postcard data exists. Of course, you'll probably think of a much more elegant error message than we've provided. In fact, this might even be a good place for the PHP `header()` function to redirect the user to a "more information" error page.

```
if (mysql_num_rows($result) == 0) {
    echo '<p>Oops! Nothing to confirm. Please contact your administrator.</p>';
        mysql_free_result($result);
    exit;
} else {
    $row = mysql_fetch_assoc($result);
        extract($row);
    mysql_free_result($result);
}
```

Creating a Reusable Mail Class

Now that you've seen how to perform basic e-mail functions using PHP, it's time to take what you've learned and make a nice reusable code component. PHP objects and classes were discussed briefly, earlier in this book, but you haven't done much with them. So, this code will be written as a class. The benefit to writing this as a class is that it will be self-contained to make reusability easier.

You are going to be creating a very handy file, class.SimpleMail.php. This file is going to contain a PHP class that will supplement PHP's simple mail() function. The class will encapsulate sending a multipart e-mail, which helps keep your source code cleaner when you use it.

1. Open your editor, and create a new PHP file called class.SimpleMail.php:

```php
<?php
class SimpleMail
{
    // class properties- parts of a message
    private $toAddress;
    private $CCAddress;
    private $BCCAddress;
    private $fromAddress;
    private $subject;
    private $sendText;
    private $textBody;
    private $sendHTML;
    private $HTMLBody;

    // initialize the message parts with blank or default values
    public function __construct() {
        $this->toAddress = '';
        $this->CCAddress = '';
        $this->BCCAddress = '';
        $this->fromAddress = '';
        $this->subject = '';
        $this->sendText = true;
        $this->textBody = '';
        $this->sendHTML = false;
        $this->HTMLBody = '';
    }

    // set TO address
    public function setToAddress($value) {
        $this->toAddress = $value;
    }

    // set CC address
    public function setCCAddress($value) {
        $this->CCAddress = $value;
    }

    // set BCC address
    public function setBCCAddress($value) {
        $this->BCCAddress = $value;
    }

    // set FROM address
    public function setFromAddress($value) {
```

```php
        $this->fromAddress = $value;
    }

    // set message subject
    public function setSubject($value) {
        $this->subject = $value;
    }

    // set whether to send email as text
    public function setSendText($value) {
        $this->sendText = $value;
    }

    // set text email message body
    public function setTextBody($value) {
        $this->sendText = true;
        $this->textBody = $value;
    }

    // set whether to send email as HTML
    public function setSendHTML($value) {
        $this->sendHTML = $value;
    }

    // set text HTML message body
    public function setHTMLBody($value) {
        $this->sendHTML = true;
        $this->HTMLBody = $value;
    }

    // send email
    public function send($to = null, $subject = null, $message = null,
        $headers = null) {

        $success = false;
        if (!is_null($to) && !is_null($subject) && !is_null($message)) {
            $success = mail($to, $subject, $message, $headers);
            return $success;
        } else {
            $headers = array();
            if (!empty($this->fromAddress)) {
                $headers[] = 'From: ' . $this->fromAddress;
            }

            if (!empty($this->CCAddress)) {
                $headers[] = 'CC: ' . $this->CCAddress;
            }

            if (!empty($this->BCCAddress)) {
                $headers[] = 'BCC: ' . $this->BCCAddress;
            }

            if ($this->sendText && !$this->sendHTML) {
                $message = $this->textBody;
```

```
        } elseif (!$this->sendText && $this->sendHTML) {
            $headers[] = 'MIME-Version: 1.0';
            $headers[] = 'Content-type: text/html; charset="iso-8859-1"';
            $headers[] = 'Content-Transfer-Encoding: 7bit';
            $message = $this->HTMLBody;
        } elseif ($this->sendText && $this->sendHTML) {
            $boundary = '==MP_Bound_xyccr948x==';
            $headers[] = 'MIME-Version: 1.0';
            $headers[] = 'Content-type: multipart/alternative; boundary="'
                . $boundary . '"';

            $message = 'This is a Multipart Message in MIME format.' . "\n";
            $message .= '--' . $boundary . "\n";
            $message .= 'Content-type: text/plain; charset="iso-8859-1"' .
                "\n";
            $message .= 'Content-Transfer-Encoding: 7bit' . "\n\n";
            $message .= $this->textBody  . "\n";
            $message .= '--' . $boundary . "\n";

            $message .= 'Content-type: text/html; charset="iso-8859-1"'
                . "\n";
            $message .= 'Content-Transfer-Encoding: 7bit' . "\n\n";
            $message .= $this->HTMLBody  . "\n";
            $message .= '--' . $boundary . '--';
        }

        $success = mail($this->toAddress, $this->subject, $message,
            join("\r\n", $headers));
        return $success;
    }
  }
}
?>
```

2. Next, create the file that will be used to demonstrate plaintext functionality, `mail_text.php`. Make sure you change the e-mail address to reflect the account to which you want to send the e-mail.

```
<?php
require 'class.SimpleMail.php';

$message = new SimpleMail();

$message->setToAddress('youremail@example.com');
$message->setSubject('Testing text email');
$message->setTextBody('This is a test using plain text email!');

if ($message->send()) {
    echo 'Text email sent successfully!';
} else {
    echo 'Sending of text email failed!';
}
?>
```

3. Now, create a file to send HTML-format e-mails. Remember to change the e-mail address, as you did in the previous step. Save this file as `mail_html.php`.

```php
<?php
require 'class.SimpleMail.php';

$message = new SimpleMail();

$message->setSendText(false);
$message->setToAddress('youremail@example.com');
$message->setSubject('Testing HTML Email');
$message->setHTMLBody('<html><p>This is a test using <b>HTML
    email</b>!</p></html>');

if ($message->send()) {
    echo 'HTML email sent successfully!';
} else {
    echo 'Sending of HTML email failed!';
}
?>
```

4. Next, create a file that will demonstrate multipart e-mails and the rest of the bells and whistles that make up the headers. Again, be sure to change the e-mail addresses appropriately. Save this file as `mail_multipart.php`.

```php
<?php
require 'class.SimpleMail.php';

$message = new SimpleMail();

$message->setToAddress('youremail@example.com');
$message->setFromAddress('myemail@example.com');
$message->setCCAddress('friend@example.com');
$message->setBCCAddress('secret@example.com');
$message->setSubject('Testing Multipart Email');
$message->setTextBody('This is the plain text portion of the email!');
$message->setHTMLBody('<html><p>This is the <b>HTML portion</b> of the
    email!</p></html>');

if ($message->send()) {
    echo 'Multi-part mail sent successfully!';
} else {
    echo 'Sending the multi-part mail failed!';
}
?>
```

5. Last, create a file to demonstrate the quick-message functionality in the `SimpleMail` class. Save this file as `mail_quick.php`.

```php
<?php
require 'class.SimpleMail.php';

$message = new SimpleMail();

if ($message->send('youremail@example.com', 'Testing Quick Email',
    'This is a quick test of SimpleMail->send().')) {
    echo 'Quick mail sent successfully!';
} else {
    echo 'Sending the quick mail failed!';
}
?>
```

Load up `mail_text.php`, `mail_html.php`, `mail_multipart.php`, and `mail_quick.php` in your browser. Assuming everything was typed carefully, all four "success" messages should appear, and you will have the matching e-mail messages in your inbox as proof.

How It Works

As you might have already discovered, using a PHP class for encapsulating functionality can be a great way to save coding time later on. Looking at `class.SimpleMail.php`, you start out by defining the class and its properties:

```php
<?php
class SimpleMail
{
    // class properties- parts of a message
    private $toAddress;
    private $CCAddress;
    private $BCCAddress;
    private $fromAddress;
    private $subject;
    private $sendText;
    private $textBody;
    private $sendHTML;
    private $HTMLBody;
```

Pretty straightforward so far. You'll notice the basic e-mail elements to, from, subject, and so on are listed as private members, which means that they are safe from accidentally being modified by code outside the class.

Next is the __construct() method. PHP calls this automatically when you create an instance of the class, and its purpose is to initialize any variables and resources the object will be using. Here the __construct() method sets initial values to the class's properties previously defined. Notice that when you are inside the class's definition and you want to reference one of the properties, you have to use the special syntax $this->.

```php
public function __construct() {
    $this->toAddress = '';
    $this->CCAddress = '';
    $this->BCCAddress = '';
    $this->fromAddress = '';
```

```
        $this->subject = '';
        $this->sendText = true;
        $this->textBody = '';
        $this->sendHTML = false;
        $this->HTMLBody = '';
    }
```

Because the properties were defined as private, you cannot assign values to them directly from outside the class. You need another way to assign them values. Here you use a set of *settor* methods. Each method takes in a value which is assigned to its corresponding property.

```
    public function setToAddress($value) {
        $this->toAddress = $value;
    }
```

Making an interface to set or get the values of an object's properties is considered good programming practice because it keeps things neatly encapsulated and helps preserve the state of the object's sensitive variables.

While the class does not have *gettor* methods used to retrieve the value of the property, you could very easily write them in yourself. A sample method to retrieve the `$toAddress` property would be:

```
    public function getToAddress() {
        return $this->toAddress;
    }
```

Finally the `send()` method is defined. You've given it four optional parameters that can be used when calling the method:

```
        public function send($to = null, $subject = null, $message = null,
            $headers = null) {
```

If at least the first three arguments are passed to `send()`, then the function will behave almost identically to the PHP built-in `mail()` function:

```
    $success = false;
    if (!is_null($to) && !is_null($subject) && !is_null($message)) {
        $success = mail($to, $subject, $message, $headers);
        return $success;
    } else {
    ...
```

You might be thinking, "Why bother with this when I can use the normal `mail()` function instead?" Truthfully, you very well could, in this example. However, the advantage here is that the PHP class can enhance the normal mail-sending process with custom error messages or fallback processes, and it will still be only one line in the calling script's code.

If fewer than three parameters are passed to the method, the normal send functionality begins, starting by setting the headers:

```
    $headers = array();
    if (!empty($this->fromAddress)) {
        $headers[] = 'From: ' . $this->fromAddress;
    }

    if (!empty($this->CCAddress)) {
```

```
        $headers[] = 'CC: ' . $this->CCAddress;
    }

    if (!empty($this->BCCAddress)) {
        $headers[] = 'BCC: ' . $this->BCCAddress;
    }
```

The $sendText and $sendHTML properties are checked to determine what format the e-mail should be sent in, starting with plaintext:

```
    if ($this->sendText && !$this->sendHTML) {
        $message = $this->textBody;
```

If the e-mail is specified as HTML-only, the headers and message body are set accordingly:

```
    } elseif (!$this->sendText && $this->sendHTML) {
        $headers[] = 'MIME-Version: 1.0';
        $headers[] = 'Content-type: text/html; charset="iso-8859-1"';
        $headers[] = 'Content-Transfer-Encoding: 7bit';
        $message = $this->HTMLBody;
```

In the case of multipart e-mails, the boundary tokens are set, and the e-mail message body is constructed with both the $textBody and $HTMLBody properties.

```
    } elseif ($this->sendText && $this->sendHTML) {

        $boundary = '==MP_Bound_xyccr948x==';
        $headers[] = 'MIME-Version: 1.0';
        $headers[] = 'Content-type: multipart/alternative; boundary="' .
            $boundary . '"';

        $message = 'This is a Multipart Message in MIME format.' . "\n";
        $message .= '--' . $boundary . "\n";
        $message .= 'Content-type: text/plain; charset="iso-8859-1"' . "\n";
        $message .= 'Content-Transfer-Encoding: 7bit' . "\n\n";
        $message .= $this->textBody . "\n";
        $message .= '--' . $boundary . "\n";

        $message .= 'Content-type: text/html; charset="iso-8859-1"' . "\n";
        $message .= 'Content-Transfer-Encoding: 7bit' . "\n\n";
        $message .= $this->HTMLBody . "\n";
        $message .= '--' . $boundary . '--';
    }
```

Finally, the send() method proceeds to send the e-mail after all the message and header construction is complete.

```
    $success = mail($this->toAddress, $this->subject, $message,
        join("\r\n", $headers));
    return $success;
```

Perhaps you have noticed that the methods are defined using the keyword `function`. That's because a method and function are practically the same thing. The difference is more in terminology; a method is a function that is defined as part of a class. You should also have noticed that the class's methods are declared as `public`. Unlike the properties, the methods are allowed to be accessed from outside the class.

The other scripts should be pretty straightforward. Starting in `mail_text.php`, you include your `SimpleMail` class, and create a new object instance of it:

```
require 'class.SimpleMail.php';

$message = new SimpleMail();
```

Next, the required properties are set:

```
$message->setToAddress('youremail@example.com');
$message->setSubject('Testing text email');
$message->setTextBody('This is a test using plain text email!');
```

And finally, the e-mail is sent, giving a success message:

```
if ($message->send()) {
    echo 'Text email sent successfully!';
} else {
    echo 'Sending of text email failed!';
}
```

When sending HTML-formatted e-mail, as in `mail_html.php`, you begin roughly the same way, including the `class.SimpleMail.php` file and creating a new instance of a `SimpleMail` object. It differs when you start setting the properties of the mail:

```
$message->setSendText(false);
$message->setToAddress('youremail@example.com');
$message->setSubject('Testing HTML Email');
$message->setHTMLBody('<html><p>This is a test using <b>HTML
    email</b>!</p></html>');
```

There are two things to take note of here. First, you're using the `setHTMLBody()` method instead of the `setTextBody()` message to provide your message. If you used the `setTextBody()` method instead of `setHTMLBody()`, then your e-mail would be empty! Second, you're explicitly turning off plaintext sending. If you didn't turn off plaintext sending, then the value for `$sendText` would be true (the default value), and the e-mail would be sent as multipart.

In the multipart example script, `mail_multipart.php`, you add extra header fields, such as `From`, `Cc`, and `Bcc`:

```
$message->setToAddress('youremail@example.com');
$message->setFromAddress('myemail@example.com');
$message->setCCAddress('friend@example.com');
$message->setBCCAddress('secret@example.com');
$message->setSubject('Testing Multipart Email');
$message->setTextBody('This is the plain text portion of the email!');
$message->setHTMLBody('<html><p>This is the <b>HTML portion</b> of the
    email!</p></html>');
```

No extra effort is needed to send a multipart message, other than specifying both a plaintext message and an HTML message. How simple is that?

In the final example, you use the basic emulation of PHP's `mail()` function that the class provides. Behold the short and sweet `mail_quick.php`:

```php
<?php
require 'class.SimpleMail.php';

$message = new SimpleMail();

if ($message->send('youremail@example.com', 'Testing Quick Email',
    'This is a quick test of SimpleMail->send().')) {
    echo 'Quick mail sent successfully!';
} else {
    echo 'Sending the quick mail failed!';
}
?>
```

All you had to do was include the class file and call the send method, using the three required parameters!

Summary

In this chapter, you've looked at PHP's `mail()` function and learned how to use it, by creating a postcard application. You may have seen similar applications at Hallmark's or Yahoo!'s web sites (`www.hallmark.com` and `www.yahoo.americangreetings.com`). Your application is not as complex as theirs, but with a little bit more work, it shouldn't be too difficult to offer your users some really terrific features.

You've also created a simple e-mail–sending PHP class that can be reused in applications that need basic e-mail functionality. Now you won't have to recode those messy multipart e-mail messages each time! Keep your eyes peeled in future chapters because it will be popping up from time to time to lend a hand.

The `mail()` function gives PHP the capability to communicate with the outside world, whether it be with users of the web site, web site or server administrators, or even another server. There are many opportunities to use `mail()`. A simple form on the web page that a user fills out to describe a technical problem can be immediately e-mailed to a tech support person, for example. Or the PHP server can send the web site administrator an e-mail any time a web page displays a fatal error. Complicated workflow applications can be created, such as content management applications.

You've experienced user interaction in this chapter by requiring that the user click a link in a confirmation e-mail before sending the postcard. In the next chapter, you'll take the interaction a step further, as you learn how to let the user create an account on your site. With this feature, you can keep track of your users and present custom information based on each user's preferences.

Exercises

See how you might accomplish the following tasks:

1. Create code to send a message to an e-mail account and blind carbon copy (BCC) yourself or another account.

2. Create a simple web form that e-mails comments or suggestions to an account of your choosing.

User Logins, Profiles, and Personalization

In this chapter, you'll learn how to implement user logins and profiles and how to personalize your web pages using PHP's session and cookie functions. You will create a useful login and personalization application that can easily be integrated into other applications you've created in this book thus far.

With Apache's support for additional per-directory configuration files and PHP's support for sessions, you can prevent hackers and the general public from stumbling onto your sensitive files. Session and cookie functions are probably two of the most important and useful functions you will encounter in the entire PHP programming language, because of the ability they give you to identify an individual viewing a page and restrict or grant access to certain content. You wouldn't want just anyone nosing about in your important files, and you certainly wouldn't want a malicious visitor changing information displayed on your web site in any way he or she desired.

Specifically, you learn how to do the following in this chapter:

- ❑ Restrict access to files and directories via htpasswd.

- ❑ Use PHP to accomplish the same functionality as with htpasswd, but with more control and flexibility.

- ❑ Store user and admin information in a database and utilize database-driven logins.

- ❑ Create a registration system with required and optional fields for users to sign up.

- ❑ Use cookies to preserve login information between sessions.

- ❑ Modify a navigation system depending on whether a user has logged in or not.

The Easiest Way to Protect Your Files

Using `htpasswd` is a simple and quick solution to restricting access to files or directory structures. Some web sites contain sensitive information that you don't want the public to access or view unrestrictedly. Or perhaps you have an administration section where administrators can change the content of the public site, such as a news or upcoming events section; you don't want everybody to have unauthorized access that enables them to change that content as well as see it.

Try It Out   **Creating htaccess and htpasswd Files**

In this exercise, you'll protect a folder so that a dialog box pops up requiring that a username and password be entered when a user visits any page in that directory.

Follow these steps:

1.   Create a new folder named `private` in your web directory.

2.   Open Apache's main configuration file, `httpd.conf`, and look for the following lines. By default, these lines are likely to be nested in the `<Directory>` section that configures your web root:

```
# AllowOverride controls what directives may be placed in .htaccess files.
# It can be "All", "None", or any combination of the keywords:
# Options FileInfo AuthConfig Limit
#
AllowOverride None
```

3.   To allow per-directory `.htaccess` support that will be used to configure your access restrictions, change the `AllowOverride` directive to look like this:

```
AllowOverride AuthConfig
```

4.   Save the configuration file, and restart Apache so it will recognize the change you made.

5.   Create a text file named `.htaccess` in the `private` directory that you want to restrict access to. Add to it the following lines:

```
AuthType Basic
AuthUserFile "C:\Program Files\Apache Software Foundation\Apache2.2\userauth"
AuthName "Restricted"
<LIMIT GET POST>
    require valid-user
</LIMIT>
```

Be sure to substitute the correct path for the `AuthUserFile` file if you set up Apache in a different directory, or if you are on Linux.

6. Open a command prompt, and type the following:

```
htpasswd -c "C:\Program Files\Apache Software Foundation\Apache2.2\
userauth" john
```

Again, be sure to substitute the correct path, depending on your needs.

7. When prompted to enter John's password, enter it as doe. You will then be required to reenter the password for confirmation.

8. Attempt to navigate to your protected directory with your web browser, and you should see a screen similar to Figure 12-1.

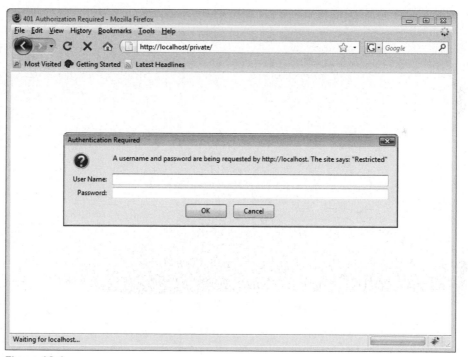

Figure 12-1

9. If you enter the correct username and password, you will be allowed to view the directory you are requesting, along with any file or folder that resides there. However, if you fail to enter the appropriate username and password three consecutive times, or press Cancel, then you will see a screen similar to that shown in Figure 12-2.

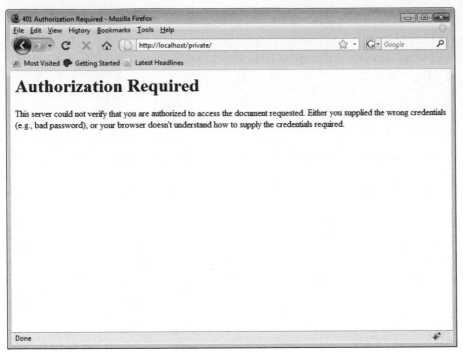

Figure 12-2

How It Works

When you request a page, Apache checks for any `.htaccess` files in every folder, from the web site's document root all the way down to the directory that has the file that you are requesting. Apache opens any `.htaccess` files it finds and interprets the configuration rules they contain. The directives you added to the `.htaccess` file in the private directory tell Apache to protect the directory and to give access only to valid users, as defined in the `userauth` file generated by `htpasswd`. No anonymous users will be allowed access.

```
AuthType Basic
AuthUserFile "C:\Program Files\Apache Software Foundation\Apache2.2\userauth"
AuthName "Restricted"
<LIMIT GET POST>
    require valid-user
</LIMIT>
```

Because no usernames or passwords are submitted with your initial request, Apache sends a message back to the browser requesting you to enter a username and password to access this section of the site. This is what triggers the browser to display a dialog box to submit the username and password. You are allowed access once these are accepted. Your web browser will remember to automatically submit the username and password when accessing the particular folder and throughout the directory tree for the rest of the browser session, so you don't have to keep supplying them over and over again for each page request.

There are, however, some problems and drawbacks to using `htpasswd`:

❑ The dialog box that pops up is often ugly.

❑ Your third-party hosting company may not allow the use of `.htaccess`.

❑ It's easier for a hacker to use brute force attacks with this type of authentication than when you use program-driven logins.

❑ It only restricts access to files; it does not modify the page's content depending on the user, to create a truly personal web site experience.

Luckily for you, you can use PHP to solve these problems.

Friendlier Logins Using PHP's Session and Cookie Functions

A *session* is information that persists on the server side between page requests when someone navigates around your web site. You can use session information to track a user throughout the site, and when this information is combined with user logins, you can set user preferences, identify privileges for different pages, and much more.

Cookies work in a similar fashion, although they are stored on a user's computer instead of the server. Because they are stored on a user's computer, the user is able to look at the cookie file and modify the information (or even delete it), if he or she chooses to do so. Cookies are somewhat less secure than sessions stored on the server.

The purpose of this chapter is not just to help you restrict access to certain files. PHP's session and cookie functions can be used to require that users of your site be authorized before they are allowed to use the pages to their full functionality, but the functions can also be used to customize the pages according to the users' preferences, for a truly personal browsing experience. You will see more of this later, but for now we'll start by showing you how to work with sessions.

Try It Out **Using PHP for Logins**

In this exercise, you'll use some code within PHP itself to authorize the user's username and password:

1. Open your text editor, and create a new PHP file with the following code. Save it as `secret.php`.

```php
<?php
include 'auth.inc.php';
?>
<html>
 <head>
  <title>Secret</title>
 </head>
 <body>
  <h1>You've found my secret!</h1>
 </body>
</html>
```

2. Start another PHP file using this code, and save it as `auth.inc.php`:

```php
<?php
// start or continue session
session_start();

if (!isset($_SESSION['logged']) || $_SESSION['logged'] != 1) {
    header('Refresh: 5; URL=login.php?redirect=' . $_SERVER['PHP_SELF']);
    echo '<p>You will be redirected to the login page in 5 seconds.</p>';
    echo '<p>If your browser doesn\'t redirect you properly automatically, ' .
        '<a href="login.php?redirect=' . $_SERVER['PHP_SELF'] .
        '">click here</a>.</p>';
    die();
}
?>
```

3. Create a third PHP file with the following code:

```php
<?php
session_start();

// filter incoming values
$username = (isset($_POST['username'])) ? trim($_POST['username']) : '';
$password = (isset($_POST['password'])) ? $_POST['password'] : '';
$redirect = (isset($_REQUEST['redirect'])) ? $_REQUEST['redirect'] :
'main.php';

if (isset($_POST['submit'])) {

    if (!isset($_SESSION['logged']) || $_SESSION['logged'] != 1) {

        if (!empty($_POST['username']) && $_POST['username'] == 'wroxbooks' &&
            !empty($_POST['password']) && $_POST['password'] == 'aregreat') {
```

```
                    $_SESSION['username'] = $username;
                    $_SESSION['logged'] = 1;
                    header ('Refresh: 5; URL=' . $redirect);
                    echo '<p>You will be redirected to your original page
                        request.</p>';
                    echo '<p>If your browser doesn\'t redirect you properly ' .
                        'automatically, <a href="' . $redirect . '">
                            click here</a>.</p>';
                    die();
            } else {
                // set these explicitly just to make sure
                $_SESSION['username'] = '';
                $_SESSION['logged'] = 0;

                $error = '<p><strong>You have supplied an invalid username
                    and/or ' .
                    'password!</strong> Please <a href="register.php">click here ' .
                    'to register</a> if you have not done so already.</p>';
            }
        }
}
?>
<html>
 <head>
  <title>Login</title>
 </head>
 <body>
<?php
if (isset($error)) {
    echo $error;
}
?>
  <form action="login.php" method="post">
   <table>
    <tr>
     <td>Username:</td>
     <td><input type="text" name="username" maxlength="20" size="20"
       value="<?php echo $username; ?>"/></td>
    </tr><tr>
     <td>Password:</td>
     <td><input type="password" name="password" maxlength="20" size="20"
       value="<?php echo $password; ?>"/></td>
    </tr><tr>
     <td> </td>
     <td>
      <input type="hidden" name="redirect" value="<?php echo $redirect ?>"/>
      <input type="submit" name="submit" value="Login"/>
    </tr>
   </table>
  </form>
 </body>
</html>
```

4. Save the file as `login.php`.

5. Navigate to the `secret.php` page you created. Because you haven't logged in yet, the `auth.inc.php` file you included redirects you to the `login.php` page, as shown in Figure 12-3.

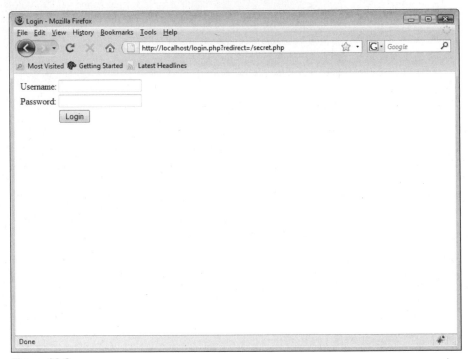

Figure 12-3

6. Try using incorrect login information so you can see how the page works. You will see a screen similar to the one shown in Figure 12-4.

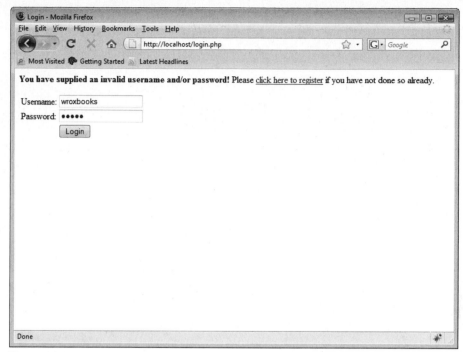

Figure 12-4

7. Now, input the correct information: `wroxbooks` for the username and `aregreat` for the password. You are redirected to the page you originally requested, because you supplied the correct information. You will see a screen similar to Figure 12-5.

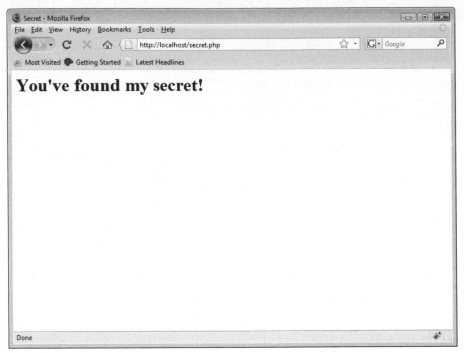

Figure 12-5

How It Works

The PHP pages you just created are used to authorize a user to view a certain page of your site. When you navigate to secret.php, the included auth.inc.php file checks to see if you have successfully started a session by logging in. If not, you are redirected to the login page. This is the magic line of code that does the checking:

```
if (!isset($_SESSION['logged']) || $_SESSION['logged'] != 1) {
```

The $_SESSION['logged'] is the variable you are checking for, and the value 1 is another way of checking for true.

Right now, you have a username and password hard-coded into your page. If you want numerous users, you would have to edit your page accordingly and add those values for those users.

```
if (!empty($_POST['username']) && $_POST['username'] == 'wroxbooks' &&
    !empty($_POST['password']) && $_POST['password'] == 'aregreat') {
```

This is a very useful way to protect your PHP files to limit use to logged-in users and administrators. However, there is one major drawback that you will resolve later when you integrate the database-driven system: Hard-coded usernames and passwords are only manageable when the number of users with login information is small. As the number of users grows, the credentials will become more cumbersome and unwieldy to manage.

In the next sections, you learn how you can use PHP in conjunction with MySQL to create user-driven login systems. You also learn how to allow for multiple administrators, multiple usernames and passwords, and privilege levels that can be managed with the MySQL database.

Using Database-Driven Information

Before you can use database-driven logins, you obviously need to have the appropriate tables set up. So first you will create the tables in your MySQL database. You will also add a few sample user accounts for testing purposes.

Try It Out   **Creating the Database Tables**

1.   Create a new PHP script with the following code:

```php
<?php
require 'db.inc.php';

$db = mysql_connect(MYSQL_HOST, MYSQL_USER, MYSQL_PASSWORD) or
    die ('Unable to connect. Check your connection parameters.');
mysql_select_db(MYSQL_DB, $db) or die(mysql_error($db));

// create the user table
$query = 'CREATE TABLE IF NOT EXISTS site_user (
        user_id     INTEGER     NOT NULL AUTO_INCREMENT,
        username    VARCHAR(20) NOT NULL,
        password    CHAR(41)    NOT NULL,

        PRIMARY KEY (user_id)
    )
    ENGINE=MyISAM';
mysql_query($query, $db) or die (mysql_error($db));

// create the user information table
$query = 'CREATE TABLE IF NOT EXISTS site_user_info (
        user_id     INTEGER     NOT NULL,
        first_name  VARCHAR(20) NOT NULL,
        last_name   VARCHAR(20) NOT NULL,
        email       VARCHAR(50) NOT NULL,
        city        VARCHAR(20),
        state       CHAR(2),
        hobbies     VARCHAR(255),

        FOREIGN KEY (user_id) REFERENCES site_user(user_id)
```

```
    )
      ENGINE=MyISAM';
mysql_query($query, $db) or die (mysql_error($db));

// populate the user table
$query = 'INSERT IGNORE INTO site_user
        (user_id, username, password)
    VALUES
        (1, "john", PASSWORD("secret")),
        (2, "sally", PASSWORD("password"))';
mysql_query($query, $db) or die (mysql_error($db));

// populate the user information table
$query = 'INSERT IGNORE INTO site_user_info
        (user_id, first_name, last_name, email, city, state, hobbies)
    VALUES
        (1, "John", "Doe", "jdoe@example.com", NULL, NULL, NULL),
        (2, "Sally", "Smith", "ssmith@example.com", NULL, NULL, NULL)';
mysql_query($query, $db) or die (mysql_error($db));

echo 'Success!';
?>
```

2. Save the file as db_ch12-1.php.

3. Open db_ch12-1.php in your web browser. PHP will execute the code to create the tables in your database and then show you the success message if everything goes correctly.

How It Works

First, you created an administration table named site user. This is where you can keep track of the administrators managing your system.

```
$query = 'CREATE TABLE IF NOT EXISTS site_user (
        user_id    INTEGER     NOT NULL AUTO_INCREMENT,
        username   VARCHAR(20) NOT NULL,
        password   CHAR(41)    NOT NULL,

        PRIMARY KEY (user_id)
    )
      ENGINE=MyISAM';
mysql_query($query, $db) or die (mysql_error($db));
```

Then, you created a second table named site_user_info to store additional information about your administrators, such as their names, where they are from, and their hobbies:

```
$query = 'CREATE TABLE IF NOT EXISTS site_user_info (
        user_id    INTEGER     NOT NULL,
        first_name VARCHAR(20) NOT NULL,
        last_name  VARCHAR(20) NOT NULL,
        email      VARCHAR(50) NOT NULL,
        city       VARCHAR(20),
```

```
          state         CHAR(2),
          hobbies       VARCHAR(255),

          FOREIGN KEY (user_id) REFERENCES site_user(user_id)
     )
     ENGINE=MyISAM';
mysql_query($query, $db) or die (mysql_error($db));
```

You then added a couple of administrators in your tables, so you can begin to create the registration portion of your PHP code to allow users to register and log in, and update their information or delete their accounts if needed.

```
$query = 'INSERT IGNORE INTO site_user
          (user_id, username, password)
     VALUES
          (1, "john", PASSWORD("secret")),
          (2, "sally", PASSWORD("password"))';
mysql_query($query, $db) or die (mysql_error($db));

$query = 'INSERT IGNORE INTO site_user_info
          (user_id, first_name, last_name, email, city, state, hobbies)
     VALUES
          (1, "John", "Doe", "jdoe@example.com", NULL, NULL, NULL),
          (2, "Sally", "Smith", "ssmith@example.com", NULL, NULL, NULL)';
mysql_query($query, $db) or die (mysql_error($db));
```

If you looked at the records stored in site_user after running db_ch12-1.php, you will have noticed what looks like gibberish stored in the password column. You aren't storing the user's actual password. Rather, you are storing a hash representation of it, by using MySQL's PASSWORD() function.

You can think of hashing as a form of one-way encryption. The algorithms that perform the hashing for you are quite complex, and guarantee that every time you hash the same value you will get the same gibberish-looking string as a result. If the input values are off, even ever so slightly, then the result will be wildly different. For example, when you hash the word "secret" with the PASSWORD() function, you get *14E65567ABDB5135D0CFD9A70B3032C179A49EE7. But if you hash "Secret" you get *0CD5E5F2DE02BE98C175EB67EB906B926F001B9B instead!

So how will you verify the user when he or she logs in to your web site and provides a username and password? Simple. Remember, the hash will always be the same for the same value. So all you need to do is take a provided password and hash it with PASSWORD(). Then, if that value matches the value stored in the database, you know the user entered the correct password. You will see this in action shortly.

It is a good idea to avoid storing the user's actual password, if you can. This way, if your database were to be compromised, the attacker would be faced with quite a task trying to figure out the users' passwords from the hash values. Unlike encryption, hashing is a one-direction-only process. That is, you cannot take a hash value and convert it back to the original value.

Once the user has been authenticated, you can again use sessions to track the user and provide access to sensitive sections of your web site. Let's continue forward in building the user login system.

Session Tracking with PHP and MySQL

In this exercise, you create a user login system that uses the database tables you created earlier. You will program it so that the user is required to input a username, password, first name, last name, and e-mail address. The other fields that will be stored in the site_user_info table will be optional.

1. First, create an index page that looks for login information, similar to the one in the previous example, but don't include an authorization page, so that you can show different content based on whether or not the user is logged in. This allows the user the chance to log in, if he or she wishes to. Call this page main.php, and use the following code to create it:

```php
<?php
session_start();
?>
<html>
 <head>
  <title>Main Page</title>
 </head>
 <body>
  <h1>Welcome to the home page!</h1>
<?php
if (isset($_SESSION['logged']) && $_SESSION['logged'] == 1) {
    // user is logged in
} else {
    // user is not logged in
}
?>
 </body>
</html>
```

2. Now, modify the main.php file as shown, so you can have different content show up, depending on whether or not a user is logged in. This first branch will be available when the user is logged in, and will contain links to the users' own personal area (which you create later), to allow them to update personal information or delete their account entirely. The second branch will simply contain some information about the benefits that registering provides and explain how to go about registering:

```php
<?php
session_start();
?>
<html>
 <head>
  <title>Main Page</title>
 </head>
 <body>
  <h1>Welcome to the home page!</h1>
<?php
if (isset($_SESSION['logged']) && $_SESSION['logged'] == 1) {
    // user is logged in
```

```
?>
    <p>Thank you for logging into our system, <b><?php
echo $_SESSION['username'];?>.</b></p>
    <p>You may now <a href="user_personal.php">click here</a> to go to your
own personal information area and update or remove your information should
you wish to do so.</p>
<?php
} else {
    // user is not logged in
?>
    <p>You are currently not logged in to our system. Once you log in,
you will have access to your personal area along with other user
information.</p>
    <p>If you have already registered, <a href="login.php">click
here</a> to log in. Or if you would like to create an account,
<a href="register.php">click here</a> to register.</p>
<?php
}
?>
 </body>
</html>
```

3. Create the registration page, making sure you include the optional fields, and that the username chosen by the user registering isn't the same as an existing username. Call it `register.php`. If users don't fill out some required fields, or use an already registered username, you will notify them and keep what has already been entered in the appropriate fields, so they don't have to reenter everything.

```php
<?php
session_start();

include 'db.inc.php';

$db = mysql_connect(MYSQL_HOST, MYSQL_USER, MYSQL_PASSWORD) or
    die ('Unable to connect. Check your connection parameters.');
mysql_select_db(MYSQL_DB, $db) or die(mysql_error($db));

$hobbies_list = array('Computers', 'Dancing', 'Exercise', 'Flying',
    'Golfing',
    'Hunting', 'Internet', 'Reading', 'Traveling', 'Other than listed');

// filter incoming values
$username = (isset($_POST['username'])) ? trim($_POST['username']) : '';
$password = (isset($_POST['password'])) ? $_POST['password'] : '';
$first_name = (isset($_POST['first_name'])) ? trim($_POST['first_name']) : '';
$last_name = (isset($_POST['last_name'])) ? trim($_POST['last_name']) : '';
$email = (isset($_POST['email'])) ? trim($_POST['email']) : '';
$city = (isset($_POST['city'])) ? trim($_POST['city']) : '';
$state = (isset($_POST['state'])) ? trim($_POST['state']) : '';
$hobbies = (isset($_POST['hobbies']) && is_array($_POST['hobbies'])) ?
```

```
        $_POST['hobbies'] : array();

 if (isset($_POST['submit']) && $_POST['submit'] == 'Register') {

     $errors = array();

     // make sure manditory fields have been entered
     if (empty($username)) {
         $errors[] = 'Username cannot be blank.';
     }

     // check if username already is registered
     $query = 'SELECT username FROM site_user WHERE username = "' .
         $username . '"';
     $result = mysql_query($query, $db) or die(mysql_error());
     if (mysql_num_rows($result) > 0) {
         $errors[] = 'Username ' . $username . ' is already registered.';
         $username = '';
     }
     mysql_free_result($result);

     if (empty($password)) {
         $errors[] = 'Password cannot be blank.';
     }
     if (empty($first_name)) {
         $errors[] = 'First name cannot be blank.';
     }
     if (empty($last_name)) {
         $errors[] = 'Last name cannot be blank.';
     }
     if (empty($email)) {
         $errors[] = 'Email address cannot be blank.';
     }

     if (count($errors) > 0) {
         echo '<p><strong style="color:#FF000;">Unable to process your ' .
             'registration.</strong></p>';
         echo '<p>Please fix the following:</p>';
         echo '<ul>';
         foreach ($errors as $error) {
             echo '<li>' . $error . '</li>';
         }
         echo '</ul>';
     } else {
         // No errors so enter the information into the database.

         $query = 'INSERT INTO site_user
                 (user_id, username, password)
             VALUES
                 (NULL, "' . mysql_real_escape_string($username, $db) . '", ' .
                 'PASSWORD("' . mysql_real_escape_string($password,
                     $db) . '"))';
```

```php
        $result = mysql_query($query, $db) or die(mysql_error());

        $user_id = mysql_insert_id($db);

        $query = 'INSERT INTO site_user_info
                (user_id, first_name, last_name, email, city, state, hobbies)
            VALUES
                (' . $user_id . ', ' .
                '"' . mysql_real_escape_string($first_name, $db)  . '", ' .
                '"' . mysql_real_escape_string($last_name, $db)   . '", ' .
                '"' . mysql_real_escape_string($email, $db)  . '", ' .
                '"' . mysql_real_escape_string($city, $db)  . '", ' .
                '"' . mysql_real_escape_string($state, $db)  . '", ' .
                '"' . mysql_real_escape_string(join(', ', $hobbies),
                  $db)  . '")';
        $result = mysql_query($query, $db) or die(mysql_error());

        $_SESSION['logged'] = 1;
        $_SESSION['username'] = $username;

        header('Refresh: 5; URL=main.php');
?>
<html>
 <head>
  <title>Register</title>
 </head>
 <body>
  <p><strong>Thank you <?php echo $username; ?> for registering!</strong></p>
  <p>Your registration is complete! You are being sent to the page you
requested. If your browser doesn't redirect properly after 5 seconds,
<a href="main.php">click here</a>.</p>
 </body>
</html>
<?php
        die();
    }
}
?>
<html>
 <head>
  <title>Register</title>
  <style type="text/css">
   td { vertical-align: top; }
  </style>
 </head>
 <body>
  <form action="register.php" method="post">
   <table>
    <tr>
     <td><label for="username">Username:</label></td>
     <td><input type="text" name="username" id="username" size="20"
       maxlength="20" value="<?php echo $username; ?>"/></td>
    </tr><tr>
     <td><label for="password">Password:</label></td>
     <td><input type="password" name="password" id="password" size="20"
```

```
                  maxlength="20" value="<?php echo $password; ?>"/></td>
       </tr><tr>
        <td><label for="email">Email:</label></td>
        <td><input type="text" name="email" id="email" size="20" maxlength="50"
          value="<?php echo $email; ?>"/></td>
       </tr><tr>
        <td><label for="first_name">First name:</label></td>
        <td><input type="text" name="first_name" id="first_name" size="20"
          maxlength="20" value="<?php echo $first_name; ?>"/></td>
       </tr><tr>
        <td><label for="last_name">Last name:</label></td>
        <td><input type="text" name="last_name" id="last_name" size="20"
          maxlength="20" value="<?php echo $last_name; ?>"/></td>
       </tr><tr>
        <td><label for="city">City:</label></td>
        <td><input type="text" name="city" id="city" size="20" maxlength="20"
          value="<?php echo $city; ?>"/></td>
       </tr><tr>
        <td><label for="state">State:</label></td>
        <td><input type="text" name="state" id="state" size="2" maxlength="2"
          value="<?php echo $state; ?>"/></td>
       </tr><tr>
        <td><label for="hobbies">Hobbies/Interests:</label></td>
        <td><select name="hobbies[]" id="hobbies" multiple="multiple">
<?php
foreach ($hobbies_list as $hobby)
{
    if (in_array($hobby, $hobbies)) {
        echo '<option value="' . $hobby . '" selected="selected">' . $hobby .
            '</option>';
    } else {
        echo '<option value="' . $hobby . '">' . $hobby . '</option>';
    }
}
?>
        </select></td>
       </tr><tr>
        <td> </td>
        <td><input type="submit" name="submit" value="Register"/></td>
       </tr>
      </table>
    </form>
   </body>
</html>
```

How It Works

The `register.php` script is the whole core of your registration system in one file: registration form, error handling, and placing the data into the database. The page allows users to enter different information for their accounts, and restricts users from using someone else's username for registration. Once users are registered, you can allow them to log in to the system and modify their account information as they see fit.

The `main.php` page checks whether or not a user is logged in. Again, the `$_SESSION['user_logged']` variable is being checked to see if users have already been logged in and are just revisiting some pages. They are shown different page content, depending on whether they are logged in or not.

Here's a quick recap of what you've done:

❏ You have an index page that checks whether or not a user is logged in.

❏ Based on that check, it either shows the user directions to log in or to register, to allow access to his or her personal information area.

❏ You have the registration area covered, along with the login process, and are keeping users tracked with their session information.

Try It Out   **Authorizing Users to Edit Their Accounts**

You will create the area where users are allowed to change their information or delete their account, but first you will need to slightly modify the authorization page, which checks whether or not users are logged in and redirects them accordingly. You also need to make some slight modifications to the login page:

1. Modify `auth.inc.php` with the highlighted changes:

```php
<?php
// start or continue session
session_start();

if (!isset($_SESSION['logged'])) {
    header('Refresh: 5; URL=login.php?redirect=' . $_SERVER['PHP_SELF']);
    echo '<p>You will be redirected to the login page in 5 seconds.</p>';
    echo '<p>If your browser doesn\'t redirect you properly automatically, ' .
        '<a href="login.php?redirect=' . $_SERVER['PHP_SELF'] .
        '">click here</a>.</p>';
    die();
}
?>
```

2. Update the `login.php` file to check the username and password against usernames and passwords stored in the MySQL database. The necessary changes are highlighted:

```php
<?php
session_start();

include 'db.inc.php';

$db = mysql_connect(MYSQL_HOST, MYSQL_USER, MYSQL_PASSWORD) or
    die ('Unable to connect. Check your connection parameters.');
mysql_select_db(MYSQL_DB, $db) or die(mysql_error($db));

// filter incoming values
$username = (isset($_POST['username'])) ? trim($_POST['username']) : '';
$password = (isset($_POST['password'])) ? $_POST['password'] : '';
```

```php
$redirect = (isset($_REQUEST['redirect'])) ? $_REQUEST['redirect'] :
    'main.php';

if (isset($_POST['submit'])) {
    $query = 'SELECT username FROM site_user WHERE ' .
            'username = "' . mysql_real_escape_string($username, $db) . '" AND ' .
            'password = PASSWORD("' . mysql_real_escape_string($password,
                $db) . '")';
    $result = mysql_query($query, $db) or die(mysql_error($db));
    if (mysql_num_rows($result) > 0) {
        $_SESSION['username'] = $username;
        $_SESSION['logged'] = 1;
        header ('Refresh: 5; URL=' . $redirect);
        echo '<p>You will be redirected to your original page request.</p>';
        echo '<p>If your browser doesn\'t redirect you properly
            automatically, ' .
                '<a href="' . $redirect . '">click here</a>.</p>';
        die();
    } else {
        $error = '<p><strong>You have supplied an invalid username and/or ' .
                'password!</strong> Please <a href="register.php">click here ' .
                'to register</a> if you have not done so already.</p>';
    }
}
?>
<html>
 <head>
  <title>Login</title>
 </head>
 <body>
<?php
if (isset($error)) {
    echo $error;
}
?>
   <form action="login.php" method="post">
    <table>
     <tr>
      <td>Username:</td>
      <td><input type="text" name="username" maxlength="20" size="20"
        value="<?php echo $username; ?>"/></td>
     </tr><tr>
      <td>Password:</td>
      <td><input type="password" name="password" maxlength="20" size="20"
        value="<?php echo $password; ?>"/></td>
     </tr><tr>
      <td> </td>
      <td>
       <input type="hidden" name="redirect" value="<?php echo $redirect ?>"/>
       <input type="submit" name="submit" value="Login"/>
     </tr>
    </table>
   </form>
 </body>
</html>
```

3. Create the `user_personal.php` page with the following code:

```php
<?php
include 'auth.inc.php';
include 'db.inc.php';

$db = mysql_connect(MYSQL_HOST, MYSQL_USER, MYSQL_PASSWORD) or
    die ('Unable to connect. Check your connection parameters.');
mysql_select_db(MYSQL_DB, $db) or die(mysql_error($db));
?>
<html>
 <head>
  <title>Personal Info</title>
 </head>
 <body>
  <h1>Welcome to your personal information area.</h1>
  <p>Here you can update your personal information, or delete your
    account.</p>
  <p>Your information as you currently have it is shown below.</p>
  <p><a href="main.php">Click here</a> to return to the home page.</p>
<?php
$query = 'SELECT
        username, first_name, last_name, city, state, email, hobbies
    FROM
        site_user u JOIN
        site_user_info i ON u.user_id = i.user_id
    WHERE
        username = "' . mysql_real_escape_string($_SESSION
          ['username'], $db) . '"';
$result = mysql_query($query, $db) or die(mysql_error($db));

$row = mysql_fetch_array($result);
extract($row);
mysql_free_result($result);
mysql_close($db);
?>
  <ul>
   <li>First Name: <?php echo $first_name; ?></li>
   <li>Last Name: <?php echo $last_name; ?></li>
   <li>City: <?php echo $city; ?></li>
   <li>State: <?php echo $state; ?></li>
   <li>Email: <?php echo $email; ?></li>
   <li>Hobbies/Interests: <?php echo $hobbies; ?></li>
  </ul>
  <p><a href="update_account.php">Update Account</a> |
   <a href="delete_account.php">Delete Account</a></p>
 </body>
</html>
```

How It Works

How it works isn't that much different from anything you've done so far in this book. You've made calls to the database, pulled information from it, and displayed the information. The only difference here is the use of the sessions, once again. The session is used to track users so they are not allowed to access someone else's account information.

You make a query that joins `site_user` and `site_user_info` to retrieve the account information, according to the user's supplied username that is stored in the session. This way, there is no confusion as to whose account the user should be in; that is, if the user was able to log in to the system, then the user was using his or her own account.

```
$query = 'SELECT
        username, first_name, last_name, city, state, email, hobbies
    FROM
        site_user u JOIN
        site_user_info i ON u.user_id = i.user_id
    WHERE
        username = "' . mysql_real_escape_string($_SESSION
['username'], $db) . '"';
$result = mysql_query($query, $db) or die(mysql_error($db));
```

Of course, this section is dependent on the login process. If users fail the login process, they won't be able to use this system to update or delete their account as they see fit.

Displaying, modifying, and deleting the information from MySQL is no different from what you have done thus far, but now you've used sessions for extra security.

Try It Out   **Editing User Accounts**

You may have noticed in the previous exercise that there are links to pages that you haven't created yet. Let's create them now. One page will allow logged-in users to update their accounts. The other will allow users to delete their accounts, upon confirming that that is their intention.

1.   Create the first page, `update_account.php`, with the following code:

```php
<?php
include 'auth.inc.php';
include 'db.inc.php';

$db = mysql_connect(MYSQL_HOST, MYSQL_USER, MYSQL_PASSWORD) or
    die ('Unable to connect. Check your connection parameters.');
mysql_select_db(MYSQL_DB, $db) or die(mysql_error($db));

$hobbies_list = array('Computers', 'Dancing', 'Exercise', 'Flying', 'Golfing',
    'Hunting', 'Internet', 'Reading', 'Traveling', 'Other than listed');

if (isset($_POST['submit']) && $_POST['submit'] == 'Update') {
    // filter incoming values
```

```php
$username = (isset($_POST['username'])) ? trim($_POST['username']) : '';
$user_id = (isset($_POST['user_id'])) ? $_POST['user_id'] : '';
$first_name = (isset($_POST['first_name'])) ? trim($_POST
   ['first_name']) : '';
$last_name = (isset($_POST['last_name'])) ? trim($_POST['last_name']) : '';
$email = (isset($_POST['email'])) ? trim($_POST['email']) : '';
$city = (isset($_POST['city'])) ? trim($_POST['city']) : '';
$state = (isset($_POST['state'])) ? trim($_POST['state']) : '';
$hobbies = (isset($_POST['hobbies']) && is_array($_POST['hobbies'])) ?
      $_POST['hobbies'] : array();

$errors = array();

// make sure the username and user_id is a valid pair (we don't
   want people to
// try and manipulate the form to hack someone else's account!)
   $query = 'SELECT username FROM site_user WHERE user_id =
' . (int)$user_id .
   ' AND username = "' . mysql_real_escape_string($_SESSION
      ['username'], $db) . '"';
$result = mysql_query($query, $db) or die(mysql_error());

if (mysql_num_rows($result) == 0) {
?>
<html>
 <head>
  <title>Update Account Info</title>
 </head>
 <body>
  <p><strong>Don't try to break out form!</strong></p>
 </body>
</html>
<?php
      mysql_free_result($result);
      mysql_close_db($db);
      die();
   }
   mysql_free_result($result);


   if (empty($first_name)) {
      $errors[] = 'First name cannot be blank.';
   }
   if (empty($last_name)) {
      $errors[] = 'Last name cannot be blank.';
   }
   if (empty($email)) {
      $errors[] = 'Email address cannot be blank.';
   }

   if (count($errors) > 0) {
      echo '<p><strong style="color:#FF000;">Unable to update your ' .
         'account information.</strong></p>';
      echo '<p>Please fix the following:</p>';
```

```php
            echo '<ul>';
            foreach ($errors as $error) {
                echo '<li>' . $error . '</li>';
            }
            echo '</ul>';
        } else {
            // No errors so enter the information into the database.

            $query = 'UPDATE site_user_info SET
                first_name = "' . mysql_real_escape_string($first_name, $db) . '",
                last_name = "' . mysql_real_escape_string($last_name, $db) . '",
                email = "' . mysql_real_escape_string($email, $db) . '",
                city = "' . mysql_real_escape_string($city, $db) . '",
                state = "' . mysql_real_escape_string($state, $db) . '",
                hobbies = "' . mysql_real_escape_string(join
                    (', ', $hobbies), $db) . '"
              WHERE
                user_id = ' . $user_id;
            mysql_query($query, $db) or die(mysql_error());
            mysql_close($db);
?>
<html>
 <head>
  <title>Update Account Info</title>
 </head>
 <body>
  <p><strong>Your account information has been updated.</strong></p>
  <p><a href="user_personal.php">Click here</a> to return to your
account.</a></p>
 </body>
</html>
<?php
        die();
    }
} else {
    $query = 'SELECT
        u.user_id, first_name, last_name, email, city, state, hobbies
          AS my_hobbies
        FROM
        site_user u JOIN site_user_info i ON u.user_id = i.user_id
        WHERE
        username = "' . mysql_real_escape_string($_SESSION['username'],
          $db) . '"';
    $result = mysql_query($query, $db) or die(mysql_error());
    $row = mysql_fetch_assoc($result);

    extract($row);
    $hobbies = explode(', ', $my_hobbies);

    mysql_free_result($result);
    mysql_close($db);
}
?>
```

```html
<html>
 <head>
  <title>Update Account Info</title>
  <style type="text/css">
   td { vertical-align: top; }
  </style>
  <script type="text/javascript">
   window.onload = function() {
      document.getElementById('cancel').onclick = goBack;
   }
   function goBack() {
      history.go(-1);
   }
  </script>
 </head>
<body>
  <h1>Update Account Information</h1>
  <form action="update_account.php" method="post">
   <table>
    <tr>
     <td>Username:</td>
     <td><input type="text" value="<?php echo $_SESSION['username']; ?>"
       disabled="disabled"/></td>
    </tr><tr>
     <td><label for="email">Email:</label></td>
     <td><input type="text" name="email" id="email" size="20" maxlength="50"
      value="<?php echo $email; ?>"/></td>
    </tr><tr>
     <td><label for="first_name">First name:</label></td>
     <td><input type="text" name="first_name" id="first_name" size="20"
       maxlength="20" value="<?php echo $first_name; ?>"/></td>
    </tr><tr>
     <td><label for="last_name">Last name:</label></td>
     <td><input type="text" name="last_name" id="last_name" size="20"
       maxlength="20" value="<?php echo $last_name; ?>"/></td>
    </tr><tr>
     <td><label for="city">City:</label></td>
     <td><input type="text" name="city" id="city" size="20" maxlength="20"
       value="<?php echo $city; ?>"/></td>
    </tr><tr>
     <td><label for="state">State:</label></td>
     <td><input type="text" name="state" id="state" size="2" maxlength="2"
       value="<?php echo $state; ?>"/></td>
    </tr><tr>
     <td><label for="hobbies">Hobbies/Interests:</label></td>
     <td><select name="hobbies[]" id="hobbies" multiple="multiple">
<?php
foreach ($hobbies_list as $hobby)
{
    if (in_array($hobby, $hobbies)) {
        echo '<option value="' . $hobby . '" selected="selected">' . $hobby .
            '</option>';
    } else {
```

```
            echo '<option value="' . $hobby . '">' . $hobby . '</option>';
      }
}
?>
      </select></td>
    </tr><tr>
     <td> </td>
     <td>
      <input type="hidden" name="user_id" value="<?php echo $user_id;?>"/>
      <input type="submit" name="submit" value="Update"/>
      <input type="button" id="cancel" value="Cancel"/>
    </tr>
   </table>
  </form>
 </body>
</html>
```

2. Create the next page and call it `delete_account.php`. It will allow users to delete their accounts. It contains the following code:

```php
<?php
include 'auth.inc.php';
include 'db.inc.php';

$db = mysql_connect(MYSQL_HOST, MYSQL_USER, MYSQL_PASSWORD) or
    die ('Unable to connect. Check your connection parameters.');
mysql_select_db(MYSQL_DB, $db) or die(mysql_error($db));

if (isset($_POST['submit']) && $_POST['submit'] == 'Yes') {
    $query = 'DELETE i FROM
            site_user u JOIN site_user_info i ON u.user_id = i.user_id
        WHERE u.username="' .
        mysql_real_escape_string($_SESSION['username'], $db) . '"';
    mysql_query($query, $db) or die(mysql_error($db));

    $query = 'DELETE FROM site_user WHERE username="' .
        mysql_real_escape_string($_SESSION['username'], $db) . '"';
    mysql_query($query, $db) or die(mysql_error($db));

    $_SESSION['logged'] = null;
    $_SESSION['username'] = null;
?>
<html>
 <head>
  <title>Delete Account</title>
 </head>
```

```
  <body>
   <p><strong>Your account has been deleted.</strong></p>
   <p><a href="main.php">Click here</a> to return to the homepage.</a></p>
  </body>
</html>
<?php
    mysql_close($db);
    die();
} else {
?>
<html>
 <head>
  <title>Delete Account</title>
  <script type="text/javascript">
   window.onload = function() {
       document.getElementById('cancel').onclick = goBack;
   }
   function goBack() {
       history.go(-1);
   }
  </script>
 </head>
 <body>
  <p>Are you sure you want to delete your account?</p>
  <p><strong>There is no way to retrieve your account once you
confirm!</strong></p>
  <form action="delete_account.php" method="post">
   <div>
    <input type="submit" name="submit" value="Yes"/>
    <input type="button" id="cancel" value=" No " onclick="history.go(-1);"/>
   </div>
  </form>
 </body>
</html>
<?php
}
?>
```

How It Works

Imagine new users coming to this section of the site for the first time. They navigate to the main.php page and initially see a screen similar to the one shown in Figure 12-6.

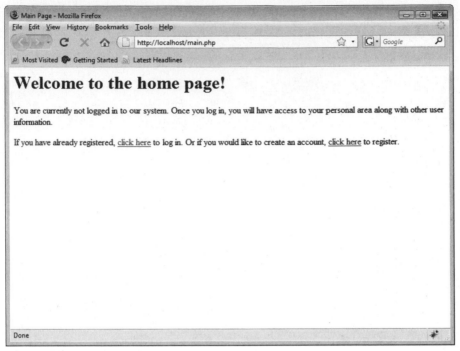

Figure 12-6

The users obviously haven't logged in yet, so they are not allowed to do anything else here. They are given the choice to log in if they have registered before, or they can register to activate an account.

Should the users decide to log in, they will be presented with the login form. Users will be required to supply the username and password they chose for themselves. The modifications you made to the login page result in two distinct differences from its previous incarnation. First, the authorization is coming from a MySQL database, rather than the hard-coding of the username and password combinations into the page itself. Second, if users don't enter the information correctly, they will be asked for the information again, but will have the option to register from that page, as well. This is shown in Figure 12-7.

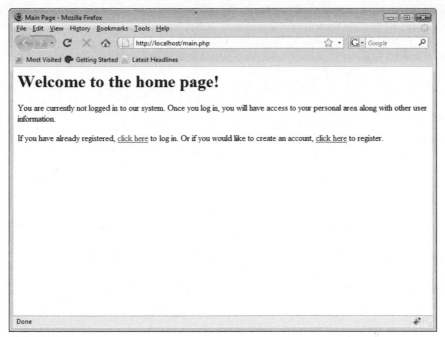

Figure 12-7

If a user chooses to register, he or she will see a page similar to the one in Figure 12-8.

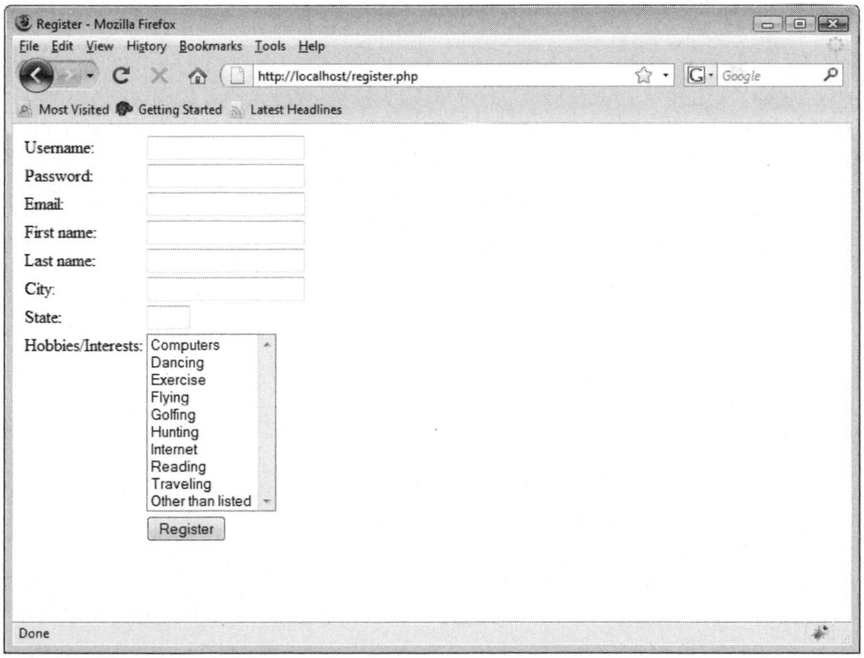

Figure 12-8

Now users can fill in their information and register to be users of this site. Once the user fills in the information and hits the Register button, the code checks whether or not the required fields have been filled out. If one (or more) of the required fields is not filled out, the form appears again, with the entered information still in the form and an error message stating what the problems were, as shown in Figure 12-9.

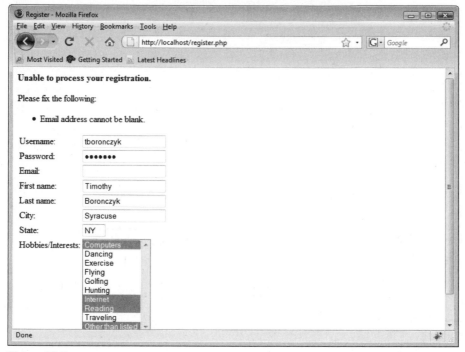

Figure 12-9

A check is also performed to see if the username entered has already been taken by someone else. Should that be the case, the form again retains any information that has been filled in, and an error message appears stating that the username is not available. The username field is blank so users know that they need to choose another username. This is shown in Figure 12-10.

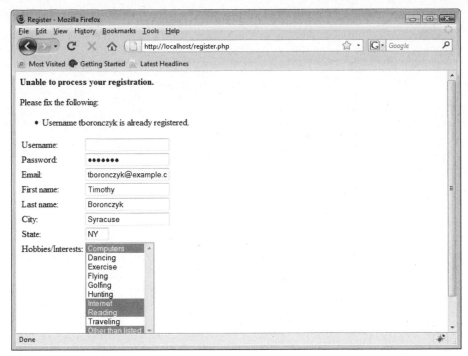

Figure 12-10

Once the registration is complete, the users are automatically logged in, and they will be redirected to the home page. After being redirected, the users can log in using the new account credentials that were just registered.

Once they are logged in, users are able to navigate to their own personal information pages, where they can update their information at any time. They are also allowed to delete their account from this location, if they so choose.

The beauty of sessions and keeping track of users is that you don't have to worry about passing information about the users with form data, or passing it through the query string or address bar. All the data is stored temporarily on the server where the web site resides. You also don't have to worry about people trying to put parameters into the address bar to fake the identity of another user. The session data is unavailable to users on the site, so only if they had access to the server itself would they be able to obtain the user-supplied data.

Now, you will look at the pages where the user's information is displayed, and where a user can update or delete his or her account. The display page simply displays the previously entered user information. The update page is also straightforward: It shows a form with the user's previously entered data and gives the user the ability to update it, if he or she wishes, or simply cancel the update and return to the previous screen. The delete page merely asks if the user is sure he or she wants to delete the account, and gives the option of returning to the previous screen. The user's information display page should look something like the one shown in Figure 12-11.

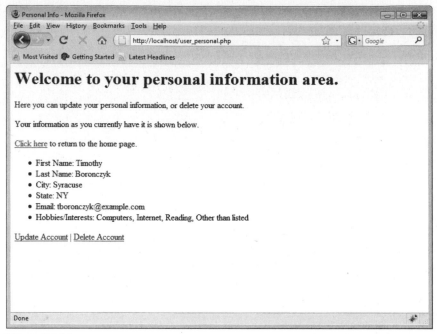

Figure 12-11

When users choose to update their accounts, they will see a screen similar to Figure 12-12.

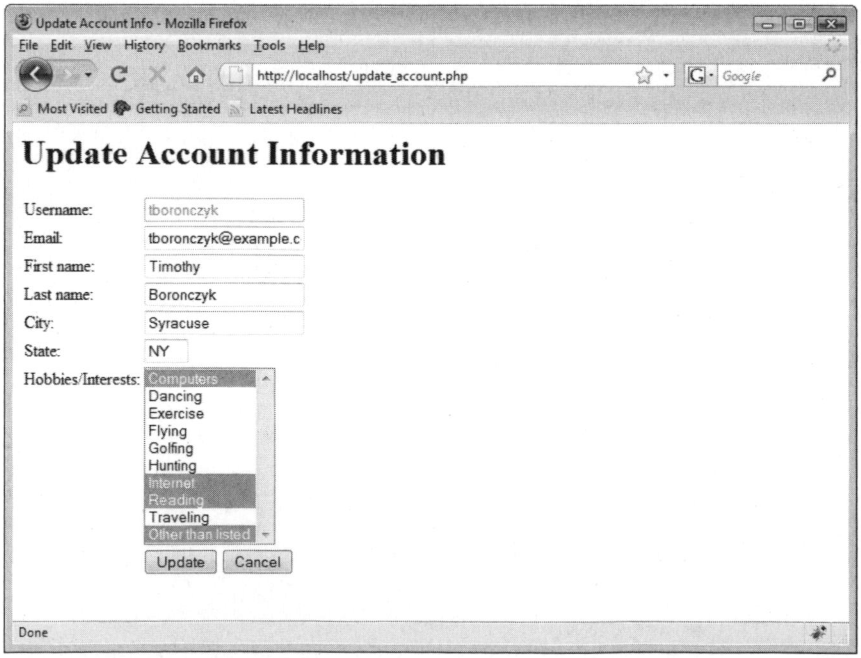

Figure 12-12

Should they update their information, users will be told that the information was indeed updated, and they can go back to their personal home page. That screen will look like the one in Figure 12-13.

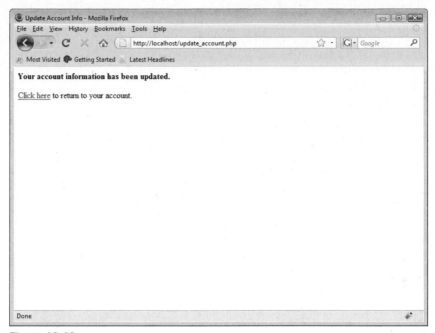

Figure 12-13

Finally, the delete page looks similar to the one shown in Figure 12-14. This appears once users choose the Delete Account link on the display page. From here, if users choose Yes, their account is deleted, their logged-in session will be destroyed, and they will be able to go back to the index page.

Figure 12-14

That's it for the user portion of the registration system. You'll create an administration section later in the chapter, where you can allow certain levels of admins to have different privileges from other users. But now, let's move on to a quick cookie example, which you can incorporate into the previous registration system.

Using Cookies in PHP

Cookies are used much like sessions, as explained previously. The main difference between sessions and cookies is that session information is stored on the server, and cookie information is stored on the user's computer. A benefit of cookies, though, is that you can control the amount of time the cookie is available, while sessions disappear when users close their browser.

A cookie is a small bit of information stored on a viewer's computer by his or her web browser, by request from a web page. The information is constantly passed in HTTP headers between the browser and web server; the browser sends the current cookie as part of its request to the server, and the server sends updates to the data back to the user as part of its response.

The size of a cookie depends on the browser, but in general it should not exceed 1K (1,024 bytes). The information can really be anything . . . it can be a name, the number of visits to the site, web-based shopping-cart information, personal viewing preferences, or anything else that can be used to help provide customized content to the user.

Try It Out   Cookie Tracking with PHP

Here's a quick example of how to use cookies in a page to see if the users have a corresponding cookie stored on their machines. Then, if you want, you can implement this into your login system, to allow persistent logins between single browser sessions. This is commonly known as a "remember me" option. You will be supplying the cookie's value through the code, but if you were to implement it, you could replace all the code you've done so far with cookies rather than sessions. You'll use four small pages for this example. We will give you all of them first and then explain how they work afterwards.

1. Create the first file, `cookies_set.php`:

```php
<?php
// Cookies may expire 30 days from now (given in seconds)
$expire = time() + (60 * 60 * 24 * 30);

setcookie('username', 'test_user', $expire);
setcookie('remember_me', 'yes', $expire);

header('Refresh: 5; URL=cookies_test.php');
?>
<html>
 <head>
  <title>Cookies Test (Set)</title>
 </head>
```

```
   <body>
    <h1>Setting Cookies</h1>
    <p>You will be redirected to the main test page in 5 seconds.</p>
    <p>If your browser doesn't redirect you automatically,
     <a href="cookies_test.php">click here</a>.</p>
   </body>
  </html>
```

2. Create the second file, `cookies_delete.php`:

```php
<?php
// Cookies expired sometime in the past
$expire = time() - 1000;

setcookie('username', null, $expire);
setcookie('remember_me', null, $expire);

header('Refresh: 5; URL=cookies_test.php');
?>
<html>
 <head>
  <title>Cookies Test (Delete)</title>
 </head>
 <body>
  <h1>Deleting Cookies</h1>
  <p>You will be redirected to the main test page in 5 seconds.</p>
  <p>If your browser doesn't redirect you automatically,
   <a href="cookies_test.php">click here</a>.</p>
 </body>
</html>
```

3. Create the third file, `cookies_view.php`:

```php
<html>
 <head>
  <title>Cookies Test (View)</title>
 </head>
 <body>
  <h1>These cookies are set</h1>
<?php
if (!empty($_COOKIE)) {
    echo '<pre>';
    print_r($_COOKIE);
    echo '</pre>';
} else {
    echo '<p>No cookies are set.</p>';
}
?>
  <p><a href="cookies_test.php">Back to main test page</a></p>
 </body>
</html>
```

4. Create the fourth file, `cookies_test.php`:

```html
<html>
 <head>
  <title>Cookies Test</title>
 </head>
 <body>
  <h1>This is the Cookies Test Page</h1>
  <p><a href="cookies_set.php">Set Cookies</a></p>
  <p><a href="cookies_view.php">View Cookies</a></p>
  <p><a href="cookies_Delete.php">Delete Cookies</a></p>
 </body>
</html>
```

How It Works

We ran through this cookie example to show you how you can keep persistent logins between single browser sessions. The `cookies_test.php` page is the starting navigation point, with options to set, view, and delete the cookies. It looks like the page shown in Figure 12-15.

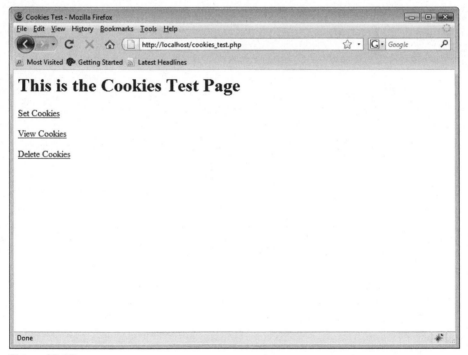

Figure 12-15

The Set Cookies link directs you to `cookies_set.php`, which does just what the name says: It sets cookie variables named `username` and `remember_me`, which are just hard-coded in this example. It then uses a header redirect to send you back to the main test page. Figure 12-16 shows `cookies_set.php` in action.

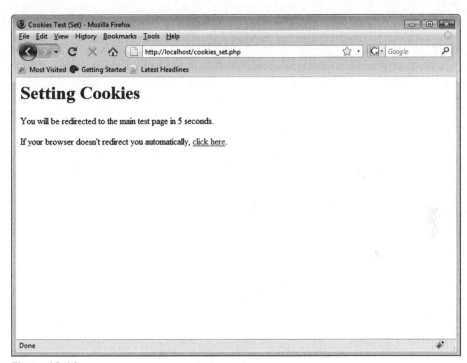

Figure 12-16

You can then navigate to `cookies_view.php`. This page checks to see if the cookie values are valid. If they are not, it says "No cookies are set," and you can try to set the cookies again. If the cookies were set successfully, then the screen will look like the one in Figure 12-17.

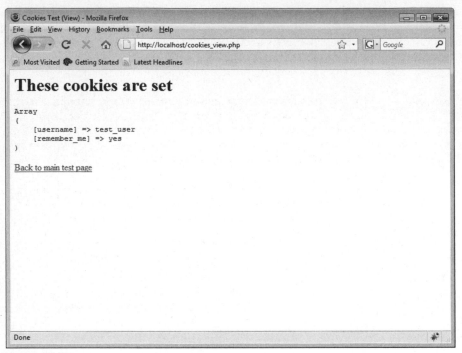

Figure 12-17

Try closing out your browser and then reopening it to visit `cookies_view.php` again. You'll see that the cookies are still active.

The cookies are set to expire 30 days from when they were set. If you want to delete them, you can visit the Delete Cookies link. It calls `cookies_delete.php`, which expires the cookies by setting their expiration date in the past and blanking out their values.

Remember that cookie information is exchanged within HTTP headers; cookies must be sent before the script generates any output.

If you look at the documentation for the `setcookie()` function, you will see that it can accept more arguments than what we've given it in this simple test. In addition to the information it stores, each cookie has a set of attributes: an expiration date, a valid domain, a valid domain path, and an optional security flag. These attributes help ensure that the browser sends the correct cookie when a request is made to a server.

The expiration time is used by the browser to determine when the cookie should be deleted. It is expressed as a UNIX timestamp plus the number of seconds before the cookie expires.

The valid domain is a partial or complete domain name to which the cookie will be sent. For example, if the value for the valid domain attribute is www.example.net, the client will send the cookie information every time the user visits the www.example.net subdomain. For the cookie to be accessible within all subdomains of example.net (such as www.example.net, mail.example.net, news.example.net, users.example.net, etc.), a leading dot should be used, as in .example.net.

The path attribute is used to identify sites within various paths in the same domain. For example, cookies with a path attribute of / will be accessible to both users.example.net/~joe and users.example.net/~sally. However, a cookie with a path attribute of /~tom will only be made available to users.example.net/~tom, not users.example.net/~sally. This is good to keep in mind if your site is on a shared server with the same domain name as other sites.

The security flag attribute restricts a browser from sending cookie information over unsecured connections. The default value is 0 and allows the cookie to be sent over any type of HTTP connection. It may be set to 1, which will only permit the cookie to be sent over a secure HTTP (HTTPS) connection that utilizes SSL (Secure Socket Layer).

Now that you have some cookie knowledge, you can use it in the login system if you want. When written and set appropriately, a cookie will only be sent to the appropriate web site. However, cookie information is still stored on the user's computer in a plaintext format and can be viewed by anyone with access to the local machine. Never use cookies to store sensitive information such as passwords and credit card information, and make sure that any major operation (such as changing a user's preferences or submitting/accessing credit card details) requires the user to enter his or her full password.

Administrator Registration

In this last portion of the chapter, you learn how logged-in admins can change information and delete information based on their access privileges. In this section, administrators are required to log in before they can view the users signed up in the user registration database. Once they are logged in, only certain privileged admins will be allowed to perform certain operations. For this example:

❑   Users with an admin privilege level of 0 are regular users.

❑   Users with an admin privilege level of 2 are allowed to update other user accounts, but not delete them.

❑   Users with an admin privilege level of 1 are allowed to update and delete other user accounts.

This would be useful if a user was, for some reason, unable to log in to the site, and the administrator needed to reset passwords, change usernames, and so on — but you don't want just any administrator to be allowed to do everything the main administrator does.

First, enter the code for all of the pages that are in the following steps. We will explain how they work afterwards.

1.   Create the first file, db_ch12-2.php:

```php
<?php
include 'db.inc.php';

$db = mysql_connect(MYSQL_HOST, MYSQL_USER, MYSQL_PASSWORD) or
    die ('Unable to connect. Check your connection parameters.');
mysql_select_db(MYSQL_DB, $db) or die(mysql_error($db));

// update the user table
$query = 'ALTER TABLE site_user
    ADD COLUMN admin_level TINYINT UNSIGNED NOT NULL DEFAULT 0
      AFTER password';
mysql_query($query, $db) or die (mysql_error($db));

// give one of our test accounts administrative privileges
$query = 'UPDATE site_user SET admin_level = 1 WHERE username = "john"';
mysql_query($query, $db) or die (mysql_error($db));

echo 'Success!';
?>
```

2.   Load db_ch12-2.php in your browser, and you should see the success message.

3.   Modify login.php as shown:

```php
<?php
session_start();

include 'db.inc.php';

$db = mysql_connect(MYSQL_HOST, MYSQL_USER, MYSQL_PASSWORD) or
    die ('Unable to connect. Check your connection parameters.');
mysql_select_db(MYSQL_DB, $db) or die(mysql_error($db));

// filter incoming values
$username = (isset($_POST['username'])) ? trim($_POST['username']) : '';
$password = (isset($_POST['password'])) ? $_POST['password'] : '';
$redirect = (isset($_REQUEST['redirect'])) ? $_REQUEST['redirect'] :
    'main.php';

if (isset($_POST['submit'])) {
    $query = 'SELECT admin_level FROM site_user WHERE ' .
        'username = "' . mysql_real_escape_string($username, $db)
          . '" AND ' .
        'password = PASSWORD("' . mysql_real_escape_string($password,
          $db) . '")';
```

```php
        $result = mysql_query($query, $db) or die(mysql_error($db));

        if (mysql_num_rows($result) > 0) {
            $row = mysql_fetch_assoc($result);
            $_SESSION['username'] = $username;
            $_SESSION['logged'] = 1;
            $_SESSION['admin_level'] = $row['admin_level'];
            header ('Refresh: 5; URL=' . $redirect);
            echo '<p>You will be redirected to your original page request.</p>';
            echo '<p>If your browser doesn\'t redirect you properly
              automatically, ' .
                 '<a href="' . $redirect . '">click here</a>.</p>';
            mysql_free_result($result);
            mysql_close($db);
            die();
        } else {
            // set these explicitly just to make sure
            $_SESSION['username'] = '';
            $_SESSION['logged'] = 0;
            $_SESSION['admin_level'] = 0;

            $error = '<p><strong>You have supplied an invalid username and/or ' .
                     'password!</strong> Please <a href="register.php">click here ' .
                     'to register</a> if you have not done so already.</p>';
        }
        mysql_free_result($result);
}
?>
<html>
 <head>
  <title>Login</title>
 </head>
 <body>
<?php
if (isset($error)) {
    echo $error;
}
?>
  <form action="login.php" method="post">
   <table>
    <tr>
     <td>Username:</td>
     <td><input type="text" name="username" maxlength="20" size="20"
       value="<?php echo $username; ?>"/></td>
    </tr><tr>
     <td>Password:</td>
     <td><input type="password" name="password" maxlength="20" size="20"
       value="<?php echo $password; ?>"/></td>
    </tr><tr>
     <td> </td>
     <td>
```

```
      <input type="hidden" name="redirect" value="<?php echo $redirect ?>"/>
      <input type="submit" name="submit" value="Login"/>
    </tr>
    </table>
   </form>
  </body>
</html>
<?php
mysql_close($db);
?>
```

4. Make these changes to `main.php`:

```php
<?php
session_start();
?>
<html>
 <head>
  <title>Logged In</title>
 </head>
 <body>
  <h1>Welcome to the home page!</h1>
<?php
if (isset($_SESSION['logged']) && $_SESSION['logged'] == 1) {
?>
   <p>Thank you for logging into our system, <b><?php
echo $_SESSION['username'];?>.</b></p>
   <p>You may now <a href="user_personal.php">click here</a> to go to your
own personal information area and update or remove your information should
you wish to do so.</p>
<?php
    if ($_SESSION['admin_level'] > 0) {
        echo '<p><a href="admin_area.php">Click here</a> to access your ' .
            'administrator tools.</p>';
    }
} else {
?>
   <p>You are currently not logged in to our system. Once you log in,
you will have access to your personal area along with other user
information.</p>
   <p>If you have already registered, <a href="login.php">click
here</a> to log in. Or if you would like to create an account,
<a href="register.php">click here</a> to register.</p>
<?php
}
?>
```

5. Create `admin_area.php` with the following code:

```php
<?php
include 'auth.inc.php';

if ($_SESSION['admin_level'] < 1) {
    header('Refresh: 5; URL=user_personal.php');
    echo '<p><strong></strong>You are not authorized for this page
      .</strong></p>';
    echo '<p>You are now being redirected to the main page.
      If your browser ' .
        'doesn\'t redirect you automatically, <a href="main.php">click ' .
        'here</a>.</p>';
    die();
}

include 'db.inc.php';

$db = mysql_connect(MYSQL_HOST, MYSQL_USER, MYSQL_PASSWORD) or
    die ('Unable to connect. Check your connection parameters.');
mysql_select_db(MYSQL_DB, $db) or die(mysql_error($db));
?>
<html>
 <head>
  <title>Administration Area</title>
  <style type="text/css">
   th { background-color: #999;}
   .odd_row { background-color: #EEE; }
   .even_row { background-color: #FFF; }
  </style>
 </head>
 <body>
  <h1>Welcome to the Administration area.</h1>
  <p>Here you can view and manage other users.</p>
  <p><a href="main.php">Click here</a> to return to the home page.</p>
  <table style="width:70%">
   <tr><th>Username</th><th>First Name</th><th>Last Name</th></tr>
<?php
$query = 'SELECT
        u.user_id, username, first_name, last_name
    FROM
        site_user u JOIN
        site_user_info i ON u.user_id = i.user_id
    ORDER BY
        username ASC';
$result = mysql_query($query, $db) or die(mysql_error($db));

$odd = true;
while ($row = mysql_fetch_array($result)) {
    echo ($odd == true) ? '<tr class="odd_row">' : '<tr class="even_row">';
    $odd = !$odd;
    echo '<td><a href="update_user.php?id=' . $row['user_id']. '">' .
        $row['username'] . '</a></td>';
```

```
        echo '<td>' . $row['first_name'] . '</td>';
        echo '<td>' . $row['last_name'] . '</td>';
        echo '</tr>';
}
mysql_free_result($result);
mysql_close($db);
?>
    </table>
  </body>
</html>
```

6. Create the file `update_user.php`:

```php
<?php
include 'auth.inc.php';

if ($_SESSION['admin_level'] < 1) {
    header('Refresh: 5; URL=user_personal.php');
    echo '<p><strong></strong>You are not authorized for this page
        .</strong></p>';
    echo '<p>You are now being redirected to the main page.
        If your browser ' .
            'doesn\'t redirect you automatically, <a href="main.php">click ' .
            'here</a>.</p>';
    die();
}

include 'db.inc.php';

$db = mysql_connect(MYSQL_HOST, MYSQL_USER, MYSQL_PASSWORD) or
    die ('Unable to connect. Check your connection parameters.');
mysql_select_db(MYSQL_DB, $db) or die(mysql_error($db));

$hobbies_list = array('Computers', 'Dancing', 'Exercise', 'Flying',
    'Golfing',
    'Hunting', 'Internet', 'Reading', 'Traveling', 'Other than listed');

if (isset($_POST['submit']) && $_POST['submit'] == 'Update') {
    // filter incoming values
    $username = (isset($_POST['username'])) ? trim($_POST['username']) : '';
    $user_id = (isset($_POST['user_id'])) ? $_POST['user_id'] : '';
    $password = (isset($_POST['password'])) ? $_POST['password'] : '';
    $first_name = (isset($_POST['first_name'])) ? trim($_POST
        ['first_name']) : '';
    $last_name = (isset($_POST['last_name'])) ? trim($_POST
        ['last_name']) : '';
    $email = (isset($_POST['email'])) ? trim($_POST['email']) : '';
    $city = (isset($_POST['city'])) ? trim($_POST['city']) : '';
    $state = (isset($_POST['state'])) ? trim($_POST['state']) : '';
    $hobbies = (isset($_POST['hobbies']) && is_array($_POST['hobbies'])) ?
        $_POST['hobbies'] : array();

    // delete user record
```

```php
    if (isset($_POST['delete'])) {
        $query = 'DELETE FROM site_user_info WHERE user_id = ' . $user_id;
        mysql_query($query, $db) or die(mysql_error());

        $query = 'DELETE FROM site_user WHERE user_id = ' . $user_id;
        mysql_query($query, $db) or die(mysql_error());
?>
<html>
 <head>
  <title>Update Account Info</title>
 </head>
 <body>
  <p><strong>The account has been deleted.</strong></p>
  <p><a href="admin_area.php">Click here</a> to return to the admin
    area.</a></p>
 </body>
</html>
<?php
        die();
    }

    $errors = array();
    if (empty($username)) {
        $errors[] = 'Username cannot be blank.';
    }

    // check if username already is registered
    $query = 'SELECT username FROM site_user WHERE username = "' .
        $username . '" AND user_id != ' . $user_id;
    $result = mysql_query($query, $db) or die(mysql_error());
    if (mysql_num_rows($result) > 0) {
        $errors[] = 'Username ' . $username . ' is already registered.';
        $username = '';
    }
    mysql_free_result($result);

    if (empty($first_name)) {
        $errors[] = 'First name cannot be blank.';
    }
    if (empty($last_name)) {
        $errors[] = 'Last name cannot be blank.';
    }
    if (empty($email)) {
        $errors[] = 'Email address cannot be blank.';
    }

    if (count($errors) > 0) {
        echo '<p><strong style="color:#FF000;">Unable to update the ' .
            'account information.</strong></p>';
        echo '<p>Please fix the following:</p>';
        echo '<ul>';
```

399

```
                foreach ($errors as $error) {
                    echo '<li>' . $error . '</li>';
                }
                echo '</ul>';
        } else {
            // No errors so enter the information into the database.

            if (!empty($password)) {
                $query = 'UPDATE site_user SET
                        password = PASSWORD("' .
                            mysql_real_escape_string($password, $db) . '")
                    WHERE
                        user_id = ' . $user_id;
                mysql_query($query, $db) or die(mysql_error());
            }

            $query = 'UPDATE site_user u, site_user_info SET
                username = "' . mysql_real_escape_string($username, $db) . '",
                first_name = "' . mysql_real_escape_string($first_name,
                    $db) . '",
                last_name = "' . mysql_real_escape_string($last_name, $db) . '",
                email = "' . mysql_real_escape_string($email, $db) . '",
                city = "' . mysql_real_escape_string($city, $db) . '",
                state = "' . mysql_real_escape_string($state, $db) . '",
                hobbies = "' . mysql_real_escape_string(join(', ', $hobbies),
                    $db) . '"
              WHERE
                u.user_id = ' . $user_id;
            mysql_query($query, $db) or die(mysql_error());
            mysql_close($db);
?>
<html>
 <head>
  <title>Update Account Info</title>
 </head>
 <body>
  <p><strong>The account information has been updated.</strong></p>
  <p><a href="admin_area.php">Click here</a> to return to the
    admin area.</a></p>
 </body>
</html>
<?php
        die();
    }
} else {

    $user_id = (isset($_GET['id'])) ? $_GET['id'] : 0;
    if ($user_id == 0) {
        header('Location: admin_area.php');
        die();
    }

    $query = 'SELECT
```

```
                username, first_name, last_name, email, city, state, hobbies
                    AS my_hobbies
             FROM
                site_user u JOIN site_user_info i ON u.user_id = i.user_id
             WHERE
                u.user_id = ' . $user_id;
        $result = mysql_query($query, $db) or die(mysql_error());

        if (mysql_num_rows($result) == 0)
        {
            header('Location: admin_area.php');
            die();
        }

        $row = mysql_fetch_assoc($result);
        extract($row);
        $password = '';
        $hobbies = explode(', ', $my_hobbies);

        mysql_free_result($result);
        mysql_close($db);
    }
?>
<html>
 <head>
  <title>Update Account Info</title>
  <style type="text/css">
   td { vertical-align: top; }
  </style>
  <script type="text/javascript">
   window.onload = function() {
       document.getElementById('cancel').onclick = goBack;
   }
   function goBack() {
       history.go(-1);
   }
  </script>
 </head>
<body>
  <h1>Update Account Information</h1>
  <form action="update_user.php" method="post">
   <table>
    <tr>
     <td><label for="username">Username:</label></td>
     <td><input type="text" name="username" id="username" size="20"
       maxlength="20" value="<?php echo $username ?>"/></td>
    </tr><tr>
     <td><label for="password">Password:</label></td>
     <td><input type="text" name="password" id="password" size="20"
       maxlength="20" value="<?php echo $password ?>"/>
     <small>(Leave blank if you're not changing the password.)</mall></td>
    </tr>
```

401

```
     <td><label for="email">Email:</label></td>
     <td><input type="text" name="email" id="email" size="20" maxlength="50"
       value="<?php echo $email; ?>"/></td>
   </tr><tr>
     <td><label for="first_name">First name:</label></td>
     <td><input type="text" name="first_name" id="first_name" size="20"
       maxlength="20" value="<?php echo $first_name; ?>"/></td>
   </tr><tr>
     <td><label for="last_name">Last name:</label></td>
     <td><input type="text" name="last_name" id="last_name" size="20"
       maxlength="20" value="<?php echo $last_name; ?>"/></td>
   </tr><tr>
     <td><label for="city">City:</label></td>
     <td><input type="text" name="city" id="city" size="20" maxlength="20"
       value="<?php echo $city; ?>"/></td>
   </tr><tr>
     <td><label for="state">State:</label></td>
     <td><input type="text" name="state" id="state" size="2" maxlength="2"
       value="<?php echo $state; ?>"/></td>
   </tr><tr>
     <td><label for="hobbies">Hobbies/Interests:</label></td>
     <td><select name="hobbies[]" id="hobbies" multiple="multiple">
<?php
foreach ($hobbies_list as $hobby)
{
    if (in_array($hobby, $hobbies)) {
        echo '<option value="' . $hobby . '" selected="selected">' . $hobby .
            '</option>';
    } else {
        echo '<option value="' . $hobby . '">' . $hobby . '</option>';
    }
}
?>
     </select></td>
<?php
if ($_SESSION['admin_level'] == 1) {
    echo '</tr><tr>';
    echo '<td> </td>';
    echo '<td><input type="checkbox" id="delete" name="delete"/>' .
        '<label for="delete">Delete</label></td>';
}
?>
   </tr><tr>
     <td> </td>
     <td>
      <input type="hidden" name="user_id" value="<?php echo $user_id;?>"/>
      <input type="submit" name="submit" value="Update"/>
      <input type="button" id="cancel" value="Cancel"/>
   </tr>
   </table>
  </form>
 </body>
</html>
```

How It Works

This whole section adds new functionality specifically for administrators only onto the existing code base. The purpose of db_ch12-2.php is to add a new column to the site_user table that tracks the privilege level of each user. It also explicitly sets privileges on your "john" user account, so you have a test scenario to work with.

```
$query = 'ALTER TABLE site_user
    ADD COLUMN admin_level TINYINT UNSIGNED NOT NULL DEFAULT 0 AFTER
      Password';
mysql_query($query, $db) or die (mysql_error($db));

$query = 'UPDATE site_user SET admin_level = 1 WHERE username = "john"';
mysql_query($query, $db) or die (mysql_error($db));
```

You made changes to main.php so that when the user logs in to the application and views his or her home page, the user will see a link to the administrator portion of the site if he or she has the appropriate privilege level.

```
if ($_SESSION['admin_level'] > 0) {
    echo '<p><a href="admin_area.php">Click here</a> to access your ' .
        'administrator tools.</p>';
}
```

The main.php page showing the administrator link looks like Figure 12-18.

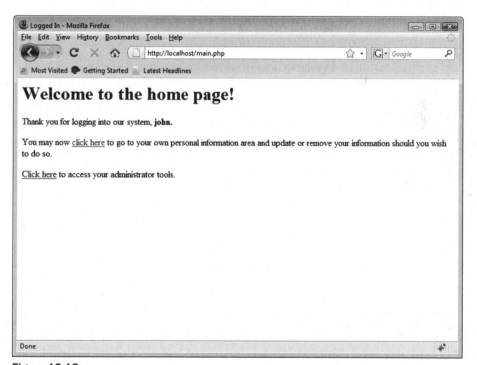

Figure 12-18

Clicking on the link to the administration section brings the user to the `admin_area.php` page, shown in Figure 12-19. It presents a list of accounts registered in the system for the user to manage.

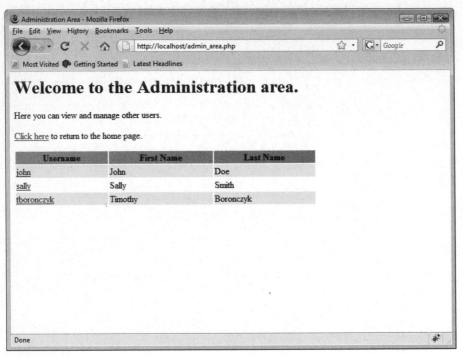

Figure 12-19

Depending on what link the administrator chooses, and whether he or she has a high enough admin level, the admin will be able to update or delete the user's account. This screen looks like Figure 12-20.

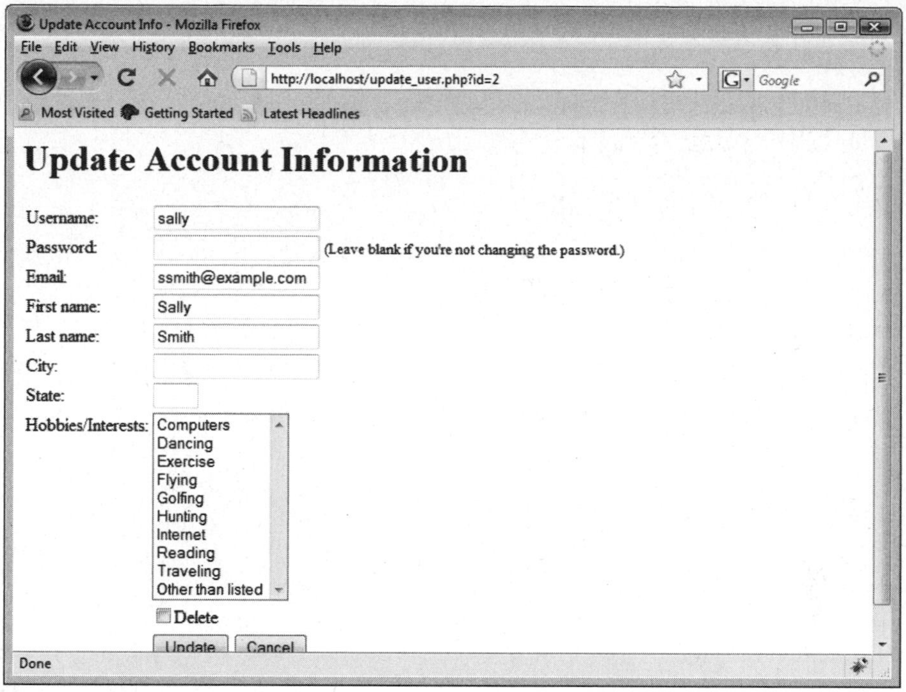

Figure 12-20

Summary

By now, you have a good understanding of the power of PHP and its session and cookie functions, along with MySQL and database-driven information. With these two powerful programs, along with Apache, you have some great tools to further your web development skill set. Just think about the possibilities you can explore with all you learned in this chapter:

❑ You can supplement Apache's configuration on a per-directory basis, and even restrict access to files/directories via htpasswd.

❑ You can use PHP to accomplish the same file restriction tasks as htpasswd, but with more control and functionality.

❑ You can store user and admin information in a database and make use of database-driven logins.

❑   You can create a registration system for users, with the required and optional fields.

❑   You can use cookies to retain login information between sessions.

❑   You can create a navigation system dependent on whether or not a user has logged in.

Exercises

Use these exercises to sharpen your PHP session- and cookie-handling skills.

1.   Create a hidden area that is only displayed to users who are logged in to your system.

2.   Use cookies to retain some information for 30 minutes, dependent on logged-in users.

3.   Create a system where only certain users have certain options, dependent on their user level.

Building a Content Management System

For whatever reason, people seem to get bored easily. One of your jobs as the administrator of a web site is not only to figure out how to get as many people to visit your site as possible, but to keep them coming *back*.

There are many different avenues for people to learn about your site, such as word of mouth, advertising, and search engines. To keep your users at your site, experts suggest making your site easy to navigate, making sure your pages load quickly, and giving users a personal experience. Getting your users to keep coming back as new ones learn about your site is how you grow your web site over time.

Fresh Content Is a Lot of Work

Take a moment and think about all the sites you visit on a frequent and regular basis. You know . . . the ones you have saved in your browser's bookmark list. What do most of those sites have in common?

Most likely, each site is periodically updated with new information. You might visit a news site each day to look up the weather in your area. Perhaps you are interested in your daily horoscope. Maybe you belong to an online message board and want to read the latest posts. In each case, the content gets updated on a regular basis — sometimes weekly, sometimes daily, and sometimes even hourly. Now, imagine how much work the web site developers have to do to update their content every day!

No matter what the purpose of your web site is, it probably contains lots of content — site news, images, user comments, and more. You don't want to have to maintain all that content by yourself, do you? Having the ability to offload some of that maintenance work on to others can sometimes make the difference between keeping or losing your sanity when things get hectic.

In theory, all a web site developer should ever have to do is maintain the site design and code — for instance, update some HTML, change a background color, fix a minor bug in the PHP code, and so on. The content should be completely separate from the design of the site so it can be maintained by other people. Because managing content is separate from design, the people that you assign the content management responsibilities to (er . . . we mean the kind people who are gracious enough to help you) don't have to know anything about web design!

Depending on the amount of content you have, entering it into your site will most likely take a lot of work. You need to come up with a way to organize it, categorize it, and push it to your web site. You may need a number of people, each assigned a certain role, working together to create the content and mold it into the appropriate form for presentation on the web site. Of course, you want this process to be efficient, so you definitely need to have the appropriate tools to do the job.

You Need a Content Management System

You've learned how to create your own databases and tables, and how to create web pages used to manage the information within them. You've also learned how to authenticate your users by making them log in to your web site. Armed with this knowledge, you could easily create an application to allow users to create new content (authors), edit that content (editors), and publish it. By assigning users to certain roles, you can manage who has access to certain functions within the site. In other words, you need a *system* in place to allow you to *manage* your web site *content* separately from the site design. You need a content management system (CMS).

There are many degrees of content management. On some sites, this might simply refer to a message board, where users sign up and then post messages to each other about their favorite color of lint. Other sites might have reporters in the field, writing news stories and sending them in to be published online. Still other sites might not only allow users to update content, but also allow administrators to change the layout of the site, including colors and images.

As you have no doubt figured out, the term *CMS* refers not only to the application used to manage content, but also to the people responsible for entering content and to the rules they must follow. It's up to you to find the people, but we'll help you establish the rules and develop the application. Are you ready? Great! Let's get started.

Laying Down the Rules

The CMS application you are going to build in this chapter will allow registered users to post articles. Those articles will be labeled as pending until a user with the proper permissions publishes them. Once an article is published, the content will show up as the newest article on the home page. Unregistered users will be able to read these articles, but they will not be able to post new ones. Registered users will also be able to post comments about the articles. When a visitor views a full article, all comments will be displayed below it.

This is a fairly typical set of rules for a web application such as this. There are pages for display (index, admin, pending articles, article review, and so on), editing (compose, user account, control panel), and transaction files (for users and articles). There are also some files used as includes (such as header and footer). Don't worry — some are only a few lines long. The whole application contains around 1,000 lines of code, which is pretty short by many application standards.

Preparing the Database

The first thing you're going to need to do is create the script that will set up your initial database structure. You'll be using the db.inc.php include file from previous chapters in establishing the connection to your database.

Try It Out   **Creating the Database Structure**

1. Place the following code in a file named db_ch13.php, and then load it in your browser. It will create your tables as well as insert an administrative user so that you can begin managing the site immediately.

```php
<?php
require 'db.inc.php';

$db = mysql_connect(MYSQL_HOST, MYSQL_USER, MYSQL_PASSWORD) or
    die ('Unable to connect. Check your connection parameters.');

mysql_select_db(MYSQL_DB, $db) or die(mysql_error($db));

$sql = 'CREATE TABLE IF NOT EXISTS cms_access_levels (
        access_level TINYINT UNSIGNED NOT NULL AUTO_INCREMENT,
        access_name  VARCHAR(50)      NOT NULL DEFAULT "",

        PRIMARY KEY (access_level)
    )
    ENGINE=MyISAM';
mysql_query($sql, $db) or die(mysql_error($db));

$sql = 'INSERT IGNORE INTO cms_access_levels
        (access_level, access_name)
    VALUES
        (1, "User"),
        (2, "Moderator"),
        (3, "Administrator")';
mysql_query($sql, $db) or die(mysql_error($db));

$sql = 'CREATE TABLE IF NOT EXISTS cms_users (
        user_id      INTEGER UNSIGNED NOT NULL AUTO_INCREMENT,
        email        VARCHAR(100)     NOT NULL UNIQUE,
        password     CHAR(41)         NOT NULL,
        name         VARCHAR(100)     NOT NULL,
        access_level TINYINT UNSIGNED NOT NULL DEFAULT 1,

        PRIMARY KEY (user_id)
    )
    ENGINE=MyISAM';
mysql_query($sql, $db) or die(mysql_error($db));

$sql = 'INSERT IGNORE INTO cms_users
        (user_id, email, password, name, access_level)
    VALUES
```

```
                (NULL, "admin@example.com", PASSWORD("secret"), "Administrator", 3)';
    mysql_query($sql, $db) or die(mysql_error($db));

    $sql = 'CREATE TABLE IF NOT EXISTS cms_articles (
            article_id    INTEGER UNSIGNED NOT NULL AUTO_INCREMENT,
            user_id       INTEGER UNSIGNED NOT NULL,
            is_published BOOLEAN          NOT NULL DEFAULT FALSE,
            submit_date  DATETIME         NOT NULL,
            publish_date DATETIME,
            title         VARCHAR(255)     NOT NULL,
            article_text MEDIUMTEXT,

            PRIMARY KEY (article_id),
            FOREIGN KEY (user_id) REFERENCES cms_users(user_id),
            INDEX (user_id, submit_date),
            FULLTEXT INDEX (title, article_text)
        )
        ENGINE=MyISAM';
    mysql_query($sql, $db) or die(mysql_error($db));

    $sql = 'CREATE TABLE IF NOT EXISTS cms_comments (
            comment_id    INTEGER UNSIGNED NOT NULL AUTO_INCREMENT,
            article_id    INTEGER UNSIGNED NOT NULL,
            user_id       INTEGER UNSIGNED NOT NULL,
            comment_date DATETIME         NOT NULL,
            comment_text MEDIUMTEXT,

            PRIMARY KEY (comment_id),
            FOREIGN KEY (article_id) REFERENCES cms_articles(article_id),
            FOREIGN KEY (user_id) REFERENCES cms_users(user_id)
        )
        ENGINE=MyISAM';
    mysql_query($sql, $db) or die(mysql_error($db));

    echo 'Success!';
    ?>
```

How It Works

In db_ch13.php, you create the table needed for access levels. All of the fields, their data types, and other parameters are defined in this SQL statement. You use IF NOT EXISTS so that the CREATE command does nothing if the table already exists.

```
    $sql = 'CREATE TABLE IF NOT EXISTS cms_access_levels (
            access_level TINYINT UNSIGNED NOT NULL AUTO_INCREMENT,
            access_name  VARCHAR(50)       NOT NULL DEFAULT "",

            PRIMARY KEY (access_level)
        )
        ENGINE=MyISAM';
    mysql_query($sql, $db) or die(mysql_error($db));
```

The next SQL statement inserts data into your newly created cms_access_levels table. These access levels are used throughout the CMS application to determine what functionality each user will have access to.

```
$sql = 'INSERT IGNORE INTO cms_access_levels
        (access_level, access_name)
    VALUES
        (1, "User"),
        (2, "Moderator"),
        (3, "Administrator")';
mysql_query($sql, $db) or die(mysql_error($db));
```

When creating the cms_users table, you use the UNIQUE keyword to add a constraint to ensure that each user's e-mail address is unique.

```
$sql = 'CREATE TABLE IF NOT EXISTS cms_users (
        user_id      INTEGER UNSIGNED NOT NULL AUTO_INCREMENT,
        email        VARCHAR(100)     NOT NULL UNIQUE,
        password     CHAR(41)         NOT NULL,
        name         VARCHAR(100)     NOT NULL,
        access_level TINYINT UNSIGNED NOT NULL DEFAULT 1,

        PRIMARY KEY (user_id)
)
ENGINE=MyISAM';
mysql_query($sql, $db) or die(mysql_error($db));
```

After you create the cms_users table, you insert one record so that you have an administrator account that is able to log in immediately. This account is given administrator privileges and allows you to administer the site as needed.

```
$sql = 'INSERT IGNORE INTO cms_users
        (user_id, email, password, name, access_level)
    VALUES
        (NULL, "admin@example.com", PASSWORD("secret"), "Administrator", 3)';
mysql_query($sql, $db) or die(mysql_error($db));
```

The cms_articles table will store the articles posted by the registered users of your site:

```
$sql = 'CREATE TABLE IF NOT EXISTS cms_articles (
        article_id   INTEGER UNSIGNED NOT NULL AUTO_INCREMENT,
        user_id      INTEGER UNSIGNED NOT NULL,
        is_published BOOLEAN          NOT NULL DEFAULT FALSE,
        submit_date  DATETIME         NOT NULL,
        publish_date DATETIME,
        title        VARCHAR(255)     NOT NULL,
        article_text MEDIUMTEXT,

        PRIMARY KEY (article_id),
        FOREIGN KEY (user_id) REFERENCES cms_users(user_id),
        INDEX (user_id, submit_date),
        FULLTEXT INDEX (title, article_text)
)
ENGINE=MyISAM';
mysql_query($sql, $db) or die(mysql_error($db));
```

You defined an index on the `user_id` and `submit_date` columns, using the `INDEX` keyword. Indexes let MySQL know that you will be searching for records using these columns specifically in your `WHERE` clause, and it will maintain a special index for the information so it can retrieve your results more quickly. Because you will be looking for articles by author and by date, these are the fields used to create the index.

You will also allow users of the CMS application to search for articles based on text that might be found in the article's title or body. To be able to perform such a search, you specified a `FULLTEXT INDEX` on the `title` and `article_text` columns. Again, this informs MySQL to track the data in the optimal manner for this application.

For more information on how MySQL uses indexes, visit `http://dev.mysql.com/doc/refman/5.1/en/mysql-indexes.html`.

Coding for Reusability

As you become a more seasoned programmer, you will notice oft-repeated bits of code in your applications. Instead of keying in the same code repeatedly (which can cause errors or be difficult to maintain in the future), you can place this code in separate files and then include the files in your scripts. In your CMS application, the same core functionality will be used on many different pages. It makes the most sense to write this code as functions or classes in a separate file and then include the file at the top of each script when the functionality is needed.

Try It Out   Creating Reusable Scripts

1. Enter the following code, and save it as `cms_output_functions.inc.php`. This file contains functions to generate different page elements throughout the CMS.

```php
<?php
// Return a string truncated to a maximum number of characters. If the string
// has been truncated, it will have $tail appended to the end.
function trim_body($text, $max_length = 500, $tail = '...') {
    $tail_len = strlen($tail);
    if (strlen($text) > $max_length) {
        $tmp_text = substr($text, 0, $max_length - $tail_len);
        if (substr($text, $max_length - $tail_len, 1) == ' ') {
            $text = $tmp_text;
        }
        else {
            $pos = strrpos($tmp_text, ' ');
            $text = substr($text, 0, $pos);
        }
        $text = $text . $tail;
    }
    return $text;
}
```

```php
// Display an article from the database.
function output_story($db, $article_id, $preview_only = FALSE) {
    if (empty($article_id)) {
        return;
    }
    $sql = 'SELECT
            name, is_published, title, article_text,
            UNIX_TIMESTAMP(submit_date) AS submit_date,
            UNIX_TIMESTAMP(publish_date) AS publish_date
        FROM
            cms_articles a JOIN cms_users u ON a.user_id = u.user_id
        WHERE
            article_id = ' . $article_id;
    $result = mysql_query($sql, $db) or die(mysql_error($db));

    if ($row = mysql_fetch_assoc($result)) {
        extract($row);
        echo '<h2>' . htmlspecialchars($title) . '</h2>';
        echo '<p>By: ' . htmlspecialchars($name) . '</p>';
        echo '<p>';
        if ($row['is_published']) {
            echo date('F j, Y', $publish_date);
        } else {
            echo 'Article is not yet published.';
        }
        echo '</p>';
        if ($preview_only) {
            echo '<p>' . nl2br(htmlspecialchars(trim_body($article_text))) .
'</p>';
            echo '<p><a href="cms_view_article.php?article_id=' . $article_id .
                '">Read Full Story</a></p>';
        } else {
            echo '<p>' . nl2br(htmlspecialchars($article_text)) . '</p>';
        }
    }
    mysql_free_result($result);
}

function show_comments($db, $article_id, $show_link = TRUE) {
    if (empty($article_id)) {
        return;
    }
    $sql = 'SELECT is_published FROM cms_articles WHERE article_id = ' .
        $article_id;
    $result = mysql_query($sql, $db) or die(mysql_error($db));
    $row = mysql_fetch_assoc($result);
    $is_published = $row['is_published'];
    mysql_free_result($result);

    $sql = 'SELECT
            comment_text, UNIX_TIMESTAMP(comment_date) AS comment_date,
            name, email
        FROM
```

```
                    cms_comments c LEFT OUTER JOIN cms_users u ON c.user_id = u.user_id
            WHERE
                    article_id = ' . $article_id . '
            ORDER BY
                    comment_date DESC';
        $result = mysql_query($sql, $db) or die(mysql_error($db));

        if ($show_link) {
            echo '<h3>' . mysql_num_rows($result) . ' Comments';
            if (isset($_SESSION['user_id']) and $is_published) {
                echo ' - <a href="cms_comment.php?article_id=' . $article_id .
                    '">Add one</a>';
            }
            echo '</h3>';
        }

        if (mysql_num_rows($result)) {
            echo '<div>';
            while ($row = mysql_fetch_array($result)) {
                extract($row);
                echo '<span>' . htmlspecialchars($name) . '</span>';
                echo '<span> (' . date('l F j, Y H:i', $comment_date) . ')
</span>';
                echo '<p>' . nl2br(htmlspecialchars($comment_text)) . '</p>';
            }
            echo '</div>';
        }
        echo '<br>';
        mysql_free_result($result);
}
?>
```

2. Three more files will be included in various scripts: `cms_header.inc.php`, `cms_footer` `.inc.php`, and `cms_http_functions.inc.php`. will contain the top and bottom portions of the page, and `cms_http.php` will contain a redirect function, which is used to send the user to another page. You'll enter those next.

Enter this code, and save it as `cms_header.inc.php`:

```
<?php session_start(); ?>
<html>
 <head>
  <title>CMS</title>
  <style type="text/css">
   td { vertical-align: top; }
  </style>
 </head>
 <body>
 <h1>Comic Book Appreciation</h1>
<?php
if (isset($_SESSION['name'])) {
    echo '<p>You are currently logged in as: ' . $_SESSION['name'] . ' </p>';
}
?>
```

```
    </div>
    <div id="navright">
     <form method="get" action="cms_search.php">
     <div>
      <label for="search">Search</label>
<?php
echo '<input type="text" id="search" name="search" ';
if (isset($_GET['keywords'])) {
    echo ' value="' . htmlspecialchars($_GET['keywords']) . '" ';
}
echo '/>';
?>
     <input type="submit" value="Search" />
     </div>
    </form>
   </div>
   <div id='navigation'>
    <a href="cms_index.php">Articles</a>
<?php
if (isset($_SESSION['user_id'])) {
    echo ' | <a href="cms_compose.php">Compose</a>';
    if ($_SESSION['access_level'] > 1) {
        echo ' | <a href="cms_pending.php">Review</a>';
    }
    if ($_SESSION['access_level'] > 2) {
        echo ' | <a href="cms_admin.php">Admin</a>';
    }
    echo ' | <a href="cms_cpanel.php">Control Panel</a>';
    echo ' | <a href="cms_transact_user.php?action=Logout">Logout</a>';
} else {
    echo ' | <a href="cms_login.php">Login</a>';
}
?>
  </div>
  <div id="articles">
```

3.   And now enter `cms_footer.inc.php`.

```
   </div>
  </body>
</html>
```

4.   Finally, enter `cms_http_functions.inc.php`.

```php
<?php
function redirect($url) {
    if (!headers_sent()) {
        header('Location: ' . $url);
    } else {
        die('Could not redirect; Output was already sent to the browser.');
    }
}
?>
```

How It Works

Many of the pages will require the same processing tasks to be performed repeatedly. This code has been written as reusable functions and placed in the `cms_output_functions.inc.php` file.

If an article is very long, you will want to show only a short excerpt. The function `trim_body()` takes in some text and returns a shortened (trimmed) version of it for display on a page. The first parameter, `$text`, is the text you want trimmed. The second parameter (`$max_length`) is the absolutely longest text string you want returned, expressed in number of characters. The default value is 500 characters, if a value is not specified. Finally, the third parameter (`$tail`) is the trailing characters to be placed at the end of trimmed text. It defaults to an ellipsis (`...`).

```php
function trim_body($text, $max_length = 500, $tail = '...') {
    $tail_len = strlen($tail);
    if (strlen($text) > $max_length) {
        $tmp_text = substr($text, 0, $max_length - $tail_len);
        if (substr($text, $max_length - $tail_len, 1) == ' ') {
            $text = $tmp_text;
        }
        else {
            $pos = strrpos($tmp_text, ' ');
            $text = substr($text, 0, $pos);
        }
        $text = $text . $tail;
    }
    return $text;
}
```

Your `trim_body()` function makes use of PHP's built-in `strlen()`, `substr()`, and `strrpos()` functions to perform some calculations on the incoming text and truncate it to the maximum number of characters. `strlen()` accepts a string and returns its length. `substr()` accepts a string, a starting offset, and optionally a length value and returns a substring starting at the offset. If no length parameter was passed, then `substr()` will return the characters up to the end of the string. `strrpos()` accepts a string and a character and searches for the character, starting from the end of the string, forwards up to the start of the string, then returns the position of the first occurrence it finds. `strrpos()` is a cousin of `strpos()`, which does the same, except that it starts searching from the beginning of the string.

Because the length of the trailing characters should count towards the maximum length of the string returned, you first determine the length of the trailing characters with `strlen()` and store that value to `$tail_len`. If the length of `$text` is greater than the requested maximum length, you chop the string down to size with `substr()`. In fact, if this were all it took to trim the body text, then you could have just used the `substr()` function in the first place, but there is still more processing that might need be done. You want to make sure you don't cut the string in the middle of a word! If the first character after where you cut the string isn't a space, then you can assume you've cut a word in half, and you need to find the last occurrence of a space (actually, this is the first space, if you're looking from the end of the string, which is why `strrpos()` is used). The position of the last space is then used to trim the string down a bit more, to remove the partial word.

The next function, `output_story()`, takes three arguments. The first argument, `$db`, is a resource to an open MySQL database connection. The second, `$article_id`, is the ID of the article you want to display from the table, and the last argument, `$preview_only`, indicates whether or not you want to trim the article using the `trim_body()` function you just created, to create a preview snippet. `output_story()` does not return a value; rather, it directly outputs the article to the browser.

```php
function output_story($db, $article_id, $preview_only = FALSE) {
    if (empty($article_id)) {
        return;
    }
    $sql = 'SELECT
            name, is_published, title, article_text,
            UNIX_TIMESTAMP(submit_date) AS submit_date,
            UNIX_TIMESTAMP(publish_date) AS publish_date
        FROM
            cms_articles a JOIN cms_users u ON a.user_id = u.user_id
        WHERE
            article_id = ' . $article_id;
    $result = mysql_query($sql, $db) or die(mysql_error($db));

    if ($row = mysql_fetch_assoc($result)) {
        extract($row);
        echo '<h2>' . htmlspecialchars($title) . '</h2>';
        echo '<p>By: ' . htmlspecialchars($name) . '</p>';
        echo '<p>';
        if ($row['is_published']) {
            echo date('F j, Y', $publish_date);
        } else {
            echo 'Article is not yet published.';
        }
        echo '</p>';
        if ($preview_only) {
            echo '<p>' . nl2br(htmlspecialchars(trim_body($article_text)))
. '</p>';
            echo '<p><a href="cms_view_article.php?article_id=' . $article_id .
                '">Read Full Story</a></p>';
        } else {
            echo '<p>' . nl2br(htmlspecialchars($article_text)) . '</p>';
        }
    }
    mysql_free_result($result);
}
```

The last function in `cms_output_functions.php` is `show_comments()`. Like the `output_story()` function before it, `show_comments()` accepts an open database connection and the article ID the comments are associated with. The third argument specifies whether or not to show a link to allow users to add their own comments.

```php
function show_comments($db, $article_id, $show_link = TRUE) {
    if (empty($article_id)) {
        return;
    }
    $sql = 'SELECT is_published FROM cms_articles WHERE article_id = ' .
        $article_id;
    $result = mysql_query($sql, $db) or die(mysql_error($db));
    $row = mysql_fetch_assoc($result);
    $is_published = $row['is_published'];
    mysql_free_result($result);

    $sql = 'SELECT
```

```
                    comment_text, UNIX_TIMESTAMP(comment_date) AS comment_date,
                    name, email
                FROM
                    cms_comments c LEFT OUTER JOIN cms_users u ON c.user_id = u.user_id
                WHERE
                    article_id = ' . $article_id . '
                ORDER BY
                    comment_date DESC';
        $result = mysql_query($sql, $db) or die(mysql_error($db));

        if ($show_link) {
            echo '<h3>' . mysql_num_rows($result) . ' Comments';
            if (isset($_SESSION['user_id']) and $is_published) {
                echo ' - <a href="cms_comment.php?article_id=' . $article_id .
                    '">Add one</a>';
            }
            echo '</h3>';
        }

        if (mysql_num_rows($result)) {
            echo '<div>';
            while ($row = mysql_fetch_array($result)) {
                extract($row);
                echo '<span>' . htmlspecialchars($name) . '</span>';
                echo '<span> (' . date('l F j, Y H:i', $comment_date)
. ')</span>';
                echo '<p>' . nl2br(htmlspecialchars($comment)) . '</p>';
            }
            echo '</div>';
        }
        echo '<br>';
        mysql_free_result($result);
    }
```

The `cms_output_functions.inc.php` file is included at the top of each script that requires one of its functions. If you want to add functionality to your CMS later and require the same processing code in several places, you should consider moving the logic into a function and placing it in `cms_output_functions.inc.php`.

Two additional files are included on every page that displays information back to the user's web browser: `cms_header.inc.php` and `cms_footer.inc.php`. Together they act as bookends of HTML code. `cms_header.inc.php` contains the top portion of an HTML document, while `cms_footer.inc.php` contains the bottom portion. While the contents of `cms_footer.inc.php` are rather unexciting, there is some session-related code in `cms_header.inc.php` worth reviewing. The very first line of `cms_header.inc.php` calls the `session_start()` function. As you undoubtedly remember from the last chapter, sessions allow you to store information for use later, in future pages of the visitor's viewing session. This makes sessions ideal for storing login data. By using `session_start()` at the beginning of your page, you gain the ability to set and retrieve `$_SESSION` variables.

Here's the first example of session variables. Once `session_start()` has been initialized, the variable `$_SESSION['name']` should be available to you, as long as the user has logged in. If `isset($_SESSION['name'])` returns TRUE, then you know the user is not logged in.

```
if (isset($_SESSION['name'])) {
    echo '<div id="logowelcome">You are currently logged in as: ' .
        $_SESSION['name'] . ' </div>';
}
```

In this CMS application, there are three values you will save as session variables: the user's name, login ID, and access level. You use these values to determine which menu items should be displayed. Here are the menu options and who should have access to them:

❑   **Article:** All users

❑   **Compose:** All logged-in users

❑   **Review:** All logged-in users with access level 2 or more

❑   **Admin:** All logged-in users with access level 3 or more

❑   **Control Panel:** All logged-in users

❑   **Logout:** All logged-in users

❑   **Login:** All users *not* logged in

You generate the menus by testing whether `$_SESSION['user_id']` has been set and the value of `$_SESSION['access_level']`.

```
    <div id='navigation'>
     <a href="cms_index.php">Articles</a>
<?php
if (isset($_SESSION['user_id'])) {
    echo ' | <a href="cms_compose.php">Compose</a>';
    if ($_SESSION['access_level'] > 1) {
        echo ' | <a href="cms_pending.php">Review</a>';
    }
    if ($_SESSION['access_level'] > 2) {
        echo ' | <a href="cms_admin.php">Admin</a>';
    }
    echo ' | <a href="cms_cpanel.php">Control Panel</a>';
    echo ' | <a href="cms_transact_user.php?action=Logout">Logout</a>';
} else {
    echo ' | <a href="cms_login.php">Login</a>';
}
?>
    </div>
```

Finally, you place the following function in `cms_http_functions.inc.php`, which is used to redirect a visitor to another page:

```
function redirect($url) {
    if (!headers_sent()) {
        header('Location: ' . $url);
    } else {
        die('Could not redirect; Output was already sent to the browser.');
    }
}
```

You may be wondering why we didn't include it in the `cms_output_functions.inc.php` file. We certainly could have, but we made the choice to separate it for two reasons. First, `cms_output_functions.inc.php` is for functions that are used when you want to output data to the visitor's web browser, either directly or indirectly (as in the case with `trim_body()`). The `cms_http_functions.inc.php` file is for browser-related functions; in this case, we have only one. Second, the `redirect()` function and the output functions are used at different times. By grouping functions with similar functionality, we minimize the size of included files.

Transaction Pages

So now you come to the tasty, gooey center of your application: the transaction pages. Well, perhaps tasty is an exaggeration, but data will be handled by one of the `cms_transact_user.php` or `cms_transact_article.php` scripts any time it is posted from a form. In the same spirit of using include files to contain reusable functions, keeping all your data-manipulation code in a centralized place, such as transaction files, can make future maintenance easier.

Try It Out   User Transactions

In your first transaction file, you're going to be creating the code that performs all user data manipulation, including login, account maintenance, and access control.

1. Enter this code, and save it as `cms_transact_user.php`:

```php
<?php
require_once 'db.inc.php';
require_once 'cms_http_functions.inc.php';

$db = mysql_connect(MYSQL_HOST, MYSQL_USER, MYSQL_PASSWORD) or
    die ('Unable to connect. Check your connection parameters.');

mysql_select_db(MYSQL_DB, $db) or die(mysql_error($db));

if (isset($_REQUEST['action'])) {

    switch ($_REQUEST['action']) {
    case 'Login':
        $email = (isset($_POST['email'])) ? $_POST['email'] : '';
        $password = (isset($_POST['password'])) ? $_POST['password'] : '';
        $sql = 'SELECT
                user_id, access_level, name
            FROM
                cms_users
            WHERE
                email = "' . mysql_real_escape_string($email, $db) . '" AND
                password = PASSWORD("' . mysql_real_escape_string($password,
                    $db) . '")';
```

```php
        $result = mysql_query($sql, $db) or die(mysql_error($db));
        if (mysql_num_rows($result) > 0) {
            $row = mysql_fetch_array($result);
            extract($row);
            session_start();
            $_SESSION['user_id'] = $user_id;
            $_SESSION['access_level'] = $access_level;
            $_SESSION['name'] = $name;
        }
        mysql_free_result($result);
        redirect('cms_index.php');
        break;

    case 'Logout':
        session_start();
        session_unset();
        session_destroy();
        redirect('cms_index.php');
        break;

    case 'Create Account':
        $name = (isset($_POST['name'])) ? $_POST['name'] : '';
        $email = (isset($_POST['email'])) ? $_POST['email'] : '';
        $password_1 = (isset($_POST['password_1'])) ? $_POST['password_1']
: '';

        $password_2 = (isset($_POST['password_2'])) ? $_POST['password_2']
: '';

        $password = ($password_1 == $password_2) ? $password_1 : '';
        if (!empty($name) && !empty($email) && !empty($password)) {
            $sql = 'INSERT INTO cms_users
                    (email, password, name)
                VALUES
                ("' . mysql_real_escape_string($email, $db) . '",
                PASSWORD("' . mysql_real_escape_string($password, $db) . '"),
                "' . mysql_real_escape_string($name, $db) . '")';
            mysql_query($sql, $db) or die(mysql_error($db));

            session_start();
            $_SESSION['user_id'] = mysql_insert_id($db);
            $_SESSION['access_level'] = 1;
            $_SESSION['name'] = $name;
        }
        redirect('cms_index.php');
        break;

    case 'Modify Account':
        $user_id = (isset($_POST['user_id'])) ? $_POST['user_id'] : '';
        $email = (isset($_POST['email'])) ? $_POST['email'] : '';
        $name = (isset($_POST['name'])) ? $_POST['name'] : '';
        $access_level = (isset($_POST['access_level'])) ?
$_POST['access_level']
            : '';
        if (!empty($user_id) && !empty($name) && !empty($email) &&
            !empty($access_level) && !empty($user_id)) {
```

```
                    $sql = 'UPDATE cms_users SET
                        email = "' . mysql_real_escape_string($email, $db) . '",
                        name = "' . mysql_real_escape_string($name, $db) . '",
                        access_level = "' . mysql_real_escape_string
($access_level,
                            $db) . '",
                    WHERE
                        user_id = ' . $user_id;
                mysql_query($sql, $db) or die(mysql_error($db));
            }
        redirect('cms_admin.php');
        break;

    case 'Send my reminder!':
        $email = (isset($_POST['email'])) ? $_POST['email'] : '';
        if (!empty($email)) {
            $sql = 'SELECT email FROM cms_users WHERE email="' .
                mysql_real_escape_string($email, $db) . '"';
            $result = mysql_query($sql, $db) or die(mysql_error($db));
            if (mysql_num_rows($result) > 0) {
                $password = strtoupper(substr(sha1(time()), rand(0, 32), 8));
                $subject = 'Comic site password reset';
                $body = 'Looks like you forgot your password, eh?
No worries. ' .
                        'We\'ve reset it for you!' . "\n\n";
                $body .= 'Your new password is: ' . $password;
                mail($email, $subject, $body);
            }
            mysql_free_result($result);
        }
        redirect('cms_login.php');
        break;

    case 'Change my info':
        session_start();
        $email = (isset($_POST['email'])) ? $_POST['email'] : '';
        $name = (isset($_POST['name'])) ? $_POST['name'] : '';
        if (!empty($name) && !empty($email) && !empty($_SESSION['user_id']))
        {
            $sql = 'UPDATE cms_users SET
                    email = "' . mysql_real_escape_string($email, $db) . '",
                    name = "' . mysql_real_escape_string($name, $db) . '",
                WHERE
                    user_id = ' . $_SESSION['user_id'];
            mysql_query($sql, $db) or die(mysql_error($db));
        }
        redirect('cms_cpanel.php');
        break;
    default:
        redirect('cms_index.php');
    }
} else {
    redirect('cms_index.php');
}
?>
```

How It Works

The application needs to access the database and to redirect users to various pages after completing transactions. You take care of the former by including db.inc.php, and the latter by including cms_http_functions.inc.php. Because transaction pages don't display anything on the screen, you don't need to include the cms_header.inc.php, cms_footer.inc.php, or cms_output_functions.inc.php files.

```
require_once 'db.inc.php';
require_once 'cms_http_functions.inc.php';
```

The $_REQUEST['action'] variable contains either the value of the button you clicked on the previous page, or a GET request in the URL (such as ?action=delete). If $_REQUEST['action'] is empty, then you don't do any transactions and simply redirect the user to the cms_index.php page:

```
if (isset($_REQUEST['action'])) {
    ...
} else {
    redirect('cms_index.php');
}
```

You use a switch statement because of the flexibility it gives you. If you expand the functionality of your CMS, you can end up having to add many more actions to cms_transact_user.php. With switch, it is a simple matter of adding a new case condition. You could certainly use a long chain of if/else statements instead of switch, but they can be cumbersome to work with and difficult to maintain over time.

```
switch ($_REQUEST['action']) {
    ...
default:
    redirect('cms_index.php');
}
```

The Login case handles user logins. Your e-mail and password are what you use to log in to the CMS. If both are not passed, the user will not be logged in. The address and password are filtered, and then the database is searched for a matching record in the cms_users table. If a match is found, then a session is started, and $_SESSION['user_id'], $_SESSION['name'], and $_SESSION['access_level'] are stored to log the user in.

```
case 'Login':
    $email = (isset($_POST['email'])) ? $_POST['email'] : '';
    $password = (isset($_POST['password'])) ? $_POST['password'] : '';

    $sql = 'SELECT
            user_id, access_level, name
        FROM
            cms_users
        WHERE
            email = "' . mysql_real_escape_string($email, $db) . '" AND
            password = PASSWORD("' . mysql_real_escape_string($password,
                $db) . '")';
    $result = mysql_query($sql, $db) or die(mysql_error($db));
    if (mysql_num_rows($result) > 0) {
```

```
            $row = mysql_fetch_array($result);
            extract($row);
            session_start();
            $_SESSION['user_id'] = $user_id;
            $_SESSION['access_level'] = $access_level;
            $_SESSION['name'] = $name;
        }
        mysql_free_result($result);
        redirect('cms_index.php');
        break;
```

Logging someone out is quite simple, really. If no session variables exist with the user ID, access level, and username, then the application knows the user is not logged in. All you need to do is purge the session variables. First you use `session_start()` to tell PHP you are accessing session variables. Then, you unset the session with `session_unset()`, which clears all the session variables, and finally you destroy the session with `session_destroy()`, which destroys all of the data registered to a session. All login data should be removed after calling both the `session_unset()` and `session_destroy()` functions.

```
    case 'Logout':
        session_start();
        session_unset();
        session_destroy();
        redirect('cms_index.php');
        break;
```

To create an account, all of the required fields must be filled in, and the two password fields must match (users are often required to enter their password twice when registering an account, to help prevent errors, and you will be implementing this in your CMS). After the incoming values are filtered, if everything is good, then you create the record in the cms_users table, automatically log the user in by setting $_SESSION['user_id'], $_SESSION['name'], and $_SESSION['access_level'], and redirect the user to cms_index.php.

```
    case 'Create Account':
        $name = (isset($_POST['name'])) ? $_POST['name'] : '';
        $email = (isset($_POST['email'])) ? $_POST['email'] : '';
        $password_1 = (isset($_POST['password_1'])) ? $_POST['password_1'] : '';
        $password_2 = (isset($_POST['password_2'])) ? $_POST['password_2'] : '';
        $password = ($password_1 == $password_2) ? $password_1 : '';
        if (!empty($name) && !empty($email) && !empty($password)) {
            $sql = 'INSERT INTO cms_users
                    (email, password, name)
                VALUES
                ("' . mysql_real_escape_string($email, $db) . '",
                PASSWORD("' . mysql_real_escape_string($password, $db) . '"),
                "' . mysql_real_escape_string($name, $db) . '")';
            mysql_query($sql, $db) or die(mysql_error($db));
            session_start();
            $_SESSION['user_id'] = mysql_insert_id($db);
            $_SESSION['access_level'] = 1;
            $_SESSION['name'] = $name;
        }
        redirect('cms_index.php');
        break;
```

When another user's account is modified by an administrator, all of the fields must have data. As long as they do, then the account is updated in the database, and the administrator is redirected to the `cms_admin.php` page:

```
case 'Modify Account':
    $user_id = (isset($_POST['user_id'])) ? $_POST['user_id'] : '';
    $email = (isset($_POST['email'])) ? $_POST['email'] : '';
    $name = (isset($_POST['name'])) ? $_POST['name'] : '';
    $access_level = (isset($_POST['access_level'])) ? $_POST['access_level']
        : '';
    if (!empty($user_id) && !empty($name) && !empty($email) &&
        !empty($access_level) && !empty($user_id)) {
        $sql = 'UPDATE cms_users SET
                email = "' . mysql_real_escape_string($email, $db) . '",
                name = "' . mysql_real_escape_string($name, $db) . '",
                access_level = "' . mysql_real_escape_string($access_level,
                    $db) . '",
            WHERE
                user_id = ' . $user_id;
        mysql_query($sql, $db) or die(mysql_error($db));
    }
    redirect('cms_admin.php');
    break;
```

If the user forgets his or her password, the user can have a new one generated and sent to the e-mail account registered in the system. Here, we suggest sending a simple plaintext e-mail, but there is no reason you can't take your wealth of knowledge from Chapter 11 and send HTML or multipart e-mail messages to your users.

You filter the incoming e-mail address and search for it in the database. If it can be found, then you know it is a registered address. Then you create a new random password, enter a subject and body for your e-mail message (including new password), and send the message on its merry way. You assume, of course, that the user will immediately open his or her e-mail to read the password, so you conveniently redirect the user to the login page.

```
case 'Send my reminder!':
    $email = (isset($_POST['email'])) ? $_POST['email'] : '';
    if (!empty($email)) {
        $sql = 'SELECT email FROM cms_users WHERE email="' .
            mysql_real_escape_string($email, $db) . '"';
        $result = mysql_query($sql, $db) or die(mysql_error($db));
        if (mysql_num_rows($result) > 0) {
            $password = strtoupper(substr(sha1(time()), rand(0, 32), 8));
            $subject = 'Comic site password reset';
            $body = 'Looks like you forgot your password, eh? No worries. ' .
                'We\'ve reset it for you!' . "\n\n";
            $body .= 'Your new password is: ' . $password;
            mail($email, $subject, $body);
        }
        mysql_free_result($result);
    }
    redirect('cms_login.php');
    break;
```

The following code may look *very* familiar. It is virtually identical to the previous Modify Account case, except that this time, the user is changing his or her own data. Because of this, the access level does not get updated.

```php
case 'Change my info':
    session_start();
    $email = (isset($_POST['email'])) ? $_POST['email'] : '';
    $name = (isset($_POST['name'])) ? $_POST['name'] : '';
    if (!empty($name) && !empty($email) && !empty($_SESSION['user_id']))
    {
        $sql = 'UPDATE cms_users SET
                email = "' . mysql_real_escape_string($email, $db) . '",
                name = "' . mysql_real_escape_string($name, $db) . '",
            WHERE
                user_id = ' . $_SESSION['user_id'];
        mysql_query($sql, $db) or die(mysql_error($db));
    }
    redirect('cms_cpanel.php');
    break;
```

Try It Out   Article Transactions

The previous transaction script wasn't so bad, was it? While it might seem like a lot of code, much of it is fairly simple and straightforward. You check some variables, execute some SQL queries, and then redirect the user. That's pretty much how most transactions work. Now, let's move on to the transaction file for working with articles and comments.

1.   Enter `cms_transact_article.php`:

```php
<?php
require_once 'db.inc.php';
require_once 'cms_http_functions.inc.php';

$db = mysql_connect(MYSQL_HOST, MYSQL_USER, MYSQL_PASSWORD) or
    die ('Unable to connect. Check your connection parameters.');

mysql_select_db(MYSQL_DB, $db) or die(mysql_error($db));

if (isset($_REQUEST['action'])) {

    switch ($_REQUEST['action']) {
    case 'Submit New Article':
        $title = (isset($_POST['title'])) ? $_POST['title'] : '';
        $article_text = (isset($_POST['article_text'])) ? $_POST['article
_text']
            : '';
        if (isset($_SESSION['user_id']) && !empty($title) &&
            !empty($article_text)) {
            $sql = 'INSERT INTO cms_articles
                    (user_id, submit_date, title, article_text)
```

```php
                VALUES
                    (' . $_SESSION['user_id'] . ',
                    "' . date('Y-m-d H:i:s') . '",
                    "' . mysql_real_escape_string($title, $db) . '",
                    "' . mysql_real_escape_string($article_text, $db) . '")';
            mysql_query($sql, $db) or die(mysql_error($db));
        }
        redirect('cms_index.php');
        break;

    case 'Edit':
        redirect('cms_compose.php?action=edit&article_id=' .
$_POST['article_id']);
        break;

    case 'Save Changes':
        $article_id = (isset($_POST['article_id'])) ? $_POST['article_id']
: '';

        $user_id = (isset($_POST['user_id'])) ? $_POST['user_id'] : '';
        $title = (isset($_POST['title'])) ? $_POST['title'] : '';
        $article_text = (isset($_POST['article_text'])) ?
$_POST['article_text']
            : '';
        if (!empty($article_id) && !empty($title) && !empty($article_text)) {
            $sql = 'UPDATE cms_articles SET
                    title = "' . mysql_real_escape_string($title, $db) . '",
                    article_text = "' . mysql_real_escape_string($article
_text,
                        $db) . '",
                    submit_date = "' . date('Y-m-d H:i:s') . '"
                WHERE
                    article_id = ' . $article_id;
            if (!empty($user_id)) {
                $sql .= ' AND user_id = ' . $user_id;
            }
            mysql_query($sql, $db) or die(mysql_error($db));
        }
        if (empty($user_id)) {
            redirect('cms_pending.php');
        } else {
            redirect('cms_cpanel.php');
        }
        break;

    case 'Publish':
        $article_id = (isset($_POST['article_id'])) ? $_POST['article_id']
: '';
        if (!empty($article_id)) {
            $sql = 'UPDATE cms_articles SET
                    is_published = TRUE,
                    publish_date = "' . date('Y-m-d H:i:s') . '"
                WHERE
                    article_id = ' . $article_id;
            mysql_query($sql, $db) or die(mysql_error($db));
        }
```

```php
            redirect('cms_pending.php');
            break;

    case 'Retract':
        $article_id = (isset($_POST['article_id'])) ? $_POST['article_id']
: '';
        if (!empty($article_id)) {
            $sql = 'UPDATE cms_articles SET
                    is_published = FALSE,
                    publish_date = "0000-00-00 00:00:00"
                WHERE
                    article_id = ' . $article_id;
            mysql_query($sql, $db) or die(mysql_error($db));
        }
        redirect('cms_pending.php');
        break;

    case 'Delete':
        $article_id = (isset($_POST['article_id'])) ? $_POST['article_id']
: '';
        if (!empty($article_id)) {
            $sql = 'DELETE a, c FROM
                    cms_articles a LEFT JOIN cms_comments c ON
                    a.article_id = c.article_id
                WHERE
                    a.article_id = ' . $article_id . ' AND
                    is_published = FALSE';
            mysql_query($sql, $db) or die(mysql_error($db));
        }
        redirect('cms_pending.php');
        break;

    case 'Submit Comment':
        $article_id = (isset($_POST['article_id'])) ? $_POST['article_id']
: '';
        $comment_text = (isset($_POST['comment_text'])) ?
            $_POST['comment_text'] : '';
        if (isset($_SESSION['user_id']) && !empty($article_id) &&
            !empty($comment_text)) {
            $sql = 'INSERT INTO cms_comments
                    (article_id, user_id, comment_date, comment_text)
                VALUES
                    (' . $article_id . ',
                    ' . $_SESSION['user_id'] . ',
                    "' . date('Y-m-d H:i:s') . '",
                    "' . mysql_real_escape_string($comment_text, $db)
. '")';
            mysql_query($sql, $db) or die(mysql_error($db));
        }
```

```
            redirect('cms_view_article.php?article_id=' . $article_id);
            break;

        default:
            redirect('cms_index.php');
    }
} else {
    redirect('cms_index.php');
}
?>
```

How It Works

As with `cms_transact_user.php`, you check the `$_REQUEST['action']` value in `cms_transact_article.php` to see if a button was pressed or an action was specified in the URL, and if so, then you act on it accordingly with the appropriate branch of a `switch` statement. The user is redirected to the main index page if no action was passed or if the action was not recognized by `cms_transact_article.php`.

```
if (isset($_REQUEST['action'])) {
    switch ($_REQUEST['action']) {
        ...
        default:
            redirect('cms_index.php');
    }
} else {
    redirect('cms_index.php');
}
```

Your first case handles the adding of a new article in the database. You first ensure that the title and article's body were both passed to the script and that the user is logged in (tested by the presence of the `$_SESSION['user_id']`). Then, you insert the article into the database, including the user's ID for the article's author and the date for its submission date.

```
case 'Submit New Article':
    $title = (isset($_POST['title'])) ? $_POST['title'] : '';
    $article_text = (isset($_POST['article_text'])) ? $_POST['article_text']
        : '';
    if (isset($_SESSION['user_id']) && !empty($title) &&
        !empty($article_text)) {
        $sql = 'INSERT INTO cms_articles
                (user_id, submit_date, title, article_text)
            VALUES
                (' . $_SESSION['user_id'] . ',
                "' . date('Y-m-d H:i:s') . '",
                "' . mysql_real_escape_string($title, $db) . '",
                "' . mysql_real_escape_string($article_text, $db) . '")';
        mysql_query($sql, $db) or die(mysql_error($db));
    }
    redirect('cms_index.php');
    break;
```

Handling the Edit case is simple. The `cms_compose.php` page will be set up to retrieve an article and preload it into the title and body fields, if the appropriate data is supplied in the URL. You simply need to append `action=edit and article_id=nn` to the address.

```
case 'Edit':
    redirect('cms_compose.php?action=edit&article_id=' . $_POST['article_
id']);
    break;
```

To save changes to an article, you take in and filter the article's ID, author's user ID, the article's title, and the body text. If the `$user_id` has a value, then you know a user is editing her or his own document, and you must add a condition to match the ID to the SQL statement. You then redirect the user either to the control panel, if the user is editing his or her own article, or to the review page, if the user is a moderator editing someone else's article.

```
case 'Save Changes':
    $article_id = (isset($_POST['article_id'])) ? $_POST['article_id'] : '';
    $user_id = (isset($_POST['user_id'])) ? $_POST['user_id'] : '';
    $title = (isset($_POST['title'])) ? $_POST['title'] : '';
    $article_text = (isset($_POST['article_text'])) ? $_POST['article_text']
        : '';
    if (!empty($article_id) && !empty($title) && !empty($article_text)) {
        $sql = 'UPDATE cms_articles SET
                title = "' . mysql_real_escape_string($title, $db) . '",
                article_text = "' . mysql_real_escape_string($article_text,
                    $db) . '",
                submit_date = "' . date('Y-m-d H:i:s') . '"
            WHERE
                article_id = ' . $article_id;
        if (!empty($user_id)) {
            $sql .= ' AND user_id = ' . $user_id;
        }
        mysql_query($sql, $db) or die(mysql_error($db));
    }
    if (empty($user_id)) {
        redirect('cms_pending.php');
    } else {
        redirect('cms_cpanel.php');
    }
    break;
```

In the Publish case, you accept in and filter the article's ID, and then modify its record in the database to set the status and publication date.

```
case 'Publish':
    $article_id = (isset($_POST['article_id'])) ? $_POST['article_id'] : '';
    if (!empty($article_id)) {
        $sql = 'UPDATE cms_articles SET
                is_published = TRUE,
                publish_date = "' . date('Y-m-d H:i:s') . '"
            WHERE
                article_id = ' . $article_id;
```

```
        mysql_query($sql, $db) or die(mysql_error($db));
    }
    redirect('cms_pending.php');
    break;
```

The Retract case is actually quite similar to the Publish case preceding it, only this time, after checking the article ID, you set is_published to false and clear out the publish_date field. Retracting an article in this case simply returns it to its prepublished state.

```
case 'Retract':
    $article_id = (isset($_POST['article_id'])) ? $_POST['article_id'] : '';
    if (!empty($article_id)) {
        $sql = 'UPDATE cms_articles SET
                is_published = FALSE,
                publish_date = "0000-00-00 00:00:00"
            WHERE
                article_id = ' . $article_id;
        mysql_query($sql, $db) or die(mysql_error($db));
    }
    redirect('cms_pending.php');
    break;
```

To delete an article, you check to see that an article ID was passed and then use it to delete the appropriate record. You use a JOIN in your query so you can delete any comments that have been made on the article as well.

```
case 'Delete':
    $article_id = (isset($_POST['article_id'])) ? $_POST['article_id'] : '';
    if (!empty($article_id)) {
        $sql = 'DELETE a, c FROM
                cms_articles a LEFT JOIN cms_comments c ON
                a.article_id = c.article_id
            WHERE
                a.article_id = ' . $article_id . ' AND
                is_published = FALSE';
        mysql_query($sql, $db) or die(mysql_error($db));
    }
    redirect('cms_pending.php');
    break;
```

The final case handles adding new comments. In the Submit Comment case, you insert the referenced article's ID, the user ID of the individual writing the comment, the date the comment was written, and finally the comment text itself. Afterwards, you redirect the user back to the article, so he or she can see the newly saved comment.

```
case 'Submit Comment':
    $article_id = (isset($_POST['article_id'])) ? $_POST['article_id'] : '';
    $comment_text = (isset($_POST['comment_text'])) ?
        $_POST['comment_text'] : '';
    if (isset($_SESSION['user_id']) && !empty($article_id) &&
        !empty($comment_text)) {
        $sql = 'INSERT INTO cms_comments
                (article_id, user_id, comment_date, comment_text)
```

```
            VALUES
                (' . $article_id . ',
                ' . $_SESSION['user_id'] . ',
                "' . date('Y-m-d H:i:s') . '",
                "' . mysql_real_escape_string($comment_text, $db) . '")';
        mysql_query($sql, $db) or die(mysql_error($db));
    }
    redirect('cms_view_article.php?article_id=' . $article_id);
    break;
```

User Interface

Whew! We hope you aren't getting bummed out that you've done all this coding and don't have anything to show in a browser yet! You've created your reusable functions and transaction pages, but haven't yet actually seen any real on-screen functionality. Well, now's your chance. In this section, we're going to be creating the scripts that make up the various user interface screens. Dust off your browser, and let's get started!

General Functionality

The first group of files you'll be creating here is going to provide general user access to the site. Scripts similar to these are found on many sites across the Internet, so you'll probably be familiar with their functionality.

Try It Out   **Main Index/Login Screen**

The first scripts you're going to code will deal with the action of a user visiting the site, logging in, requesting a new password and creating a new account.

1.   Create `cms_login.php`:

```php
<?php include 'cms_header.inc.php'; ?>
<h1>Member Login</h1>
<form method="post" action="cms_transact_user.php">
 <table>
  <tr>
   <td><label for="email">Email Address:</label></td>
   <td><input type="text" id="email" name="email" maxlength="100"/></td>
  </tr><tr>
   <td><label for="password">Password:</label></td>
   <td><input type="password" id="password" name="password" maxlength="20"/>
</td>
  </tr><tr>
   <td> </td>
   <td><input type="submit" name="action" value="Login"/></td>
```

```
      </tr>
    </table>
  </form>
  <p>Not a member yet? <a href="cms_user_account.php">Create a new account!
  </a></p>
  <p><a href="cms_forgot_password.php">Forgot your password?</a></p>
  <?php include 'cms_footer.inc.php'; ?>
```

2. Next, create `cms_forgot_password.php`:

```
<?php include 'cms_header.inc.php'; ?>
<h1>Email Password Reminder</h1>
<p>Forgot your password? Just enter your email address, and we'll email
you a new one!</p>
<form method="post" action="cms_transact_user.php">
  <div>
    <label for="email">Email Address:</label>
    <input type="text" id="email" name="email" maxlength="100"/>
    <input type="submit" name="action" value="Send my reminder!"/>
  </div>
</form>
<?php include 'cms_footer.inc.php'; ?>
```

3. Create `cms_index.php`:

```
<?php
require 'db.inc.php';
require 'cms_output_functions.inc.php';

$db = mysql_connect(MYSQL_HOST, MYSQL_USER, MYSQL_PASSWORD) or
    die ('Unable to connect. Check your connection parameters.');

mysql_select_db(MYSQL_DB, $db) or die(mysql_error($db));

include 'cms_header.inc.php';

$sql = 'SELECT
        article_id
    FROM
        cms_articles
    WHERE
        is_published = TRUE
    ORDER BY
        publish_date DESC';
$result = mysql_query($sql, $db);

if (mysql_num_rows($result) == 0) {
    echo '<p><strong>There are currently no articles to view.</strong></p>';
} else {
```

```
        while ($row = mysql_fetch_array($result)) {
            output_story($db, $row['article_id'], TRUE);
        }
    }
    mysql_free_result($result);

    include 'cms_footer.inc.php';
    ?>
```

4. Now load `cms_index.php` in your browser. Your screen should look like that in Figure 13-1.

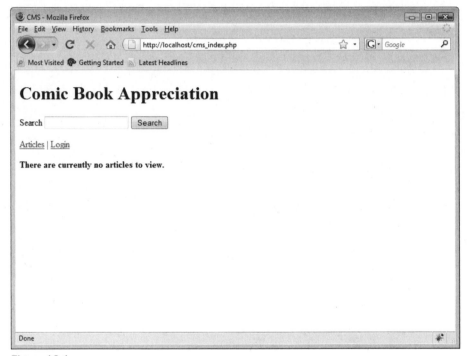

Figure 13-1

5. Click the Login link on the page, and `cms_login.php` will open up next in your browser (Figure 13-2). Enter the e-mail address and password you previously stored in the database with `db_ch13.php`, and click the Login button.

434

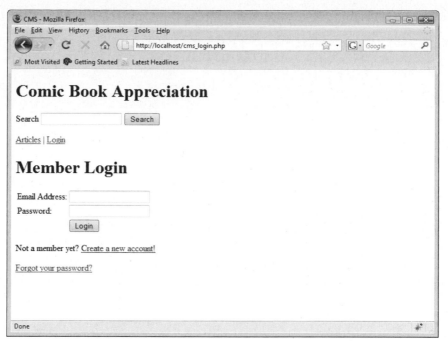

Figure 13-2

You should now see the `cms_index.php` page again, but this time you will see the new menu options that are available. This is shown in Figure 13-3.

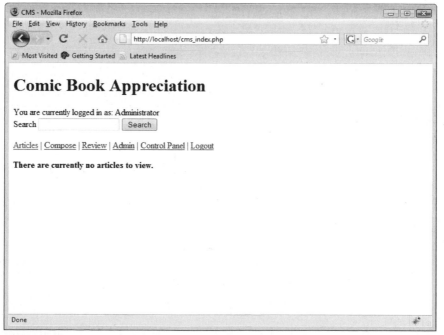

Figure 13-3

How It Works

cms_header.inc.php is included towards the top of cms_index.php to output the top portion of the HTML page.

```
include 'cms_header.inc.php';
```

The SQL statement retrieves all of the published articles in the cms_articles table and sorts them by publish_date, so the most recent articles are listed first.

```
$sql = 'SELECT
        article_id
    FROM
        cms_articles
    WHERE
        is_published = TRUE
    ORDER BY
        publish_date DESC';
$result = mysql_query($sql, $db);
```

If no articles are published, a message is output to inform the reader of this. Otherwise, if published articles are retrieved, then you loop through each record and display the article by calling output_story().

```
if (mysql_num_rows($result) == 0) {
    echo '<p><strong>There are currently no articles to view.</strong></p>';
} else {
    while ($row = mysql_fetch_array($result)) {
        output_story($db, $row['article_id'], TRUE);
    }
}
```

Finally, you output the bottom of the HTML content by including cms_footer.inc.php.

```
include 'cms_footer.inc.php';
```

The cms_login.php and cms_forgot_password.php files contain pretty much just the HTML code for their respective forms. Both include the cms_header.inc.php and cms_footer.inc.php scripts for the top and bottom portions of HTML code. The forms post their information to the cms_transact_user.php script, which performs the appropriate action on the data.

Try It Out   Account Creation

Now, the next thing you need to create is a script that will allow your CMS users to create new accounts for themselves. The processing logic has already been written in `cms_transact_user.php`, so that functionality will not appear explicitly in this script. However, the same form can be used to enter and later modify user information, so the code that you write will focus on providing that functionality.

1. Create this new file, and save it as `cms_user_account.php`:

```php
<?php
require 'db.inc.php';

$db = mysql_connect(MYSQL_HOST, MYSQL_USER, MYSQL_PASSWORD) or
    die ('Unable to connect. Check your connection parameters.');

mysql_select_db(MYSQL_DB, $db) or die(mysql_error($db));

$user_id = (isset($_GET['user_id']) && ctype_digit($_GET['user_id'])) ?
    $_GET['user_id'] : '';

if (empty($user_id)) {
    $name = '';
    $email = '';
    $access_level = '';
} else {
    $sql = 'SELECT
                name, email, access_level
            FROM
                cms_users
            WHERE
                user_id=' . $user_id;
    $result = mysql_query($sql, $db) or die(mysql_error($db));
    $row = mysql_fetch_array($result);
    extract($row);
    mysql_free_result($result);
}

include 'cms_header.inc.php';

if (empty($user_id)) {
    echo '<h1>Create Account</h1>';
} else {
    echo '<h1>Modify Account</h1>';
}
?>
<form method="post" action="cms_transact_user.php">
 <table>
  <tr>
   <td><label for="name">Full Name:</label></td>
   <td><input type="text" id="name" name="name" maxlength="100"
     value="<?php echo htmlspecialchars($name); ?>"/></td>
  </tr><tr>
   <td><label for="email">Email Address:</label></td>
```

```php
    <td><input type="text" id="email" name="email" maxlength="100"
      value="<?php echo htmlspecialchars($email); ?>"/></td>
  </tr>
<?php

if (isset($_SESSION['access_level']) && $_SESSION['access_level'] == 3)
{
    echo '<tr><td>Access Level</td><td>';

    $sql = 'SELECT
            access_level, access_name
        FROM
            cms_access_levels
        ORDER BY
            access_level DESC';
    $result = mysql_query($sql, $db) or die(mysql_error($db));

    while ($row = mysql_fetch_array($result)) {
        echo '<input type="radio" id="acl_' . $row['access_level'] .
            '" name="access_level" value="' . $row['access_level'] . '"';

        if ($row['access_level'] == $access_level) {
            echo ' checked="checked"';
        }
        echo '/> <label for="acl_' . $row['access_level'] . '">' .
            $row['access_name'] . '</label><br/>';
    }
    mysql_free_result($result);
    echo '</td></tr>';
}

if (empty($user_id)) {
?>
  <tr>
   <td><label for="password_1">Password:</label></td>
   <td><input type="password" id="password_1" name="password_1"
maxlength="50"/>
   </td>
  </tr><tr>
   <td><label for="password_2">Password (again):</label></td>
   <td><input type="password" id="password_2" name="password_2"
maxlength="50"/>
   </td>
  </tr><tr>
   <td> </td>
   <td>
    <input type="submit" name="action" value="Create Account"/>
   </td>
  </tr>
<?php
} else {
?>
```

```
   <tr>
    <td> </td>
    <td>
     <input type="hidden" name="user_id" value="<?php echo $user_id; ?>"/>
     <input type="submit" name="action" value="Modify Account"/>
    </td>
   </tr>
<?php
}
?>
 </table>
</form>
<?php
include 'cms_footer.inc.php';
?>
```

2. If you're still logged in to the CMS, click the Logout link.

3. Next, click Login, and then click "Create a new account!" You should see a screen similar to Figure 13-4.

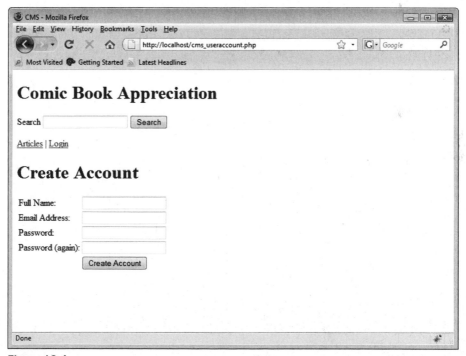

Figure 13-4

4. Enter data into each field, and click Create Account. For this example, enter the following:

- ❑ **Full Name:** George Test
- ❑ **E-mail Address:** gtest@example.com
- ❑ **Password:** phprocks
- ❑ **Password (again):** phprocks

Once you create a new user, you will be automatically logged in as that user. You should notice that you cannot see the Review or Admin menu items that were available to you when you previously logged in as Admin. Review is available to moderators or admins (levels 2 or 3) only, and Admin is available to admins only (level 3). Your initial account was created at level 3, but the account you just created defaulted to level 1 (User).

How It Works

You need to retrieve all of the data for this user, if a user ID has been passed. After filtering and assigning `$_GET['user_id']` to `$user_id`, you check to see if `$user_id` is empty. If it is, then you know you are displaying the form to create a new user account and initialize the variable used in the form's construction to empty values. If `$user_id` does contain a user's ID, you retrieve the information from the `cms_users` table.

```
$user_id = (isset($_GET['user_id']) && ctype_digit($_GET['user_id'])) ?
    $_GET['user_id'] : '';

if (empty($user_id)) {
    $name = '';
    $email = '';
    $access_level = '';
} else {
    $sql = 'SELECT
            name, email, access_level
        FROM
            cms_users
        WHERE
            user_id=' . $user_id;
    $result = mysql_query($sql, $db) or die(mysql_error($db));
    $row = mysql_fetch_array($result);
    extract($row);
    mysql_free_result($result);
}
```

If the `$user_id` has a value, then it means a user has been logged in, and this page contains the user's current data so she or he can modify the account. Otherwise, it's a new user who wants to create an account. The title needs to reflects this.

```
if (empty($user_id)) {
    echo '<h1>Create Account</h1>';
} else {
    echo '<h1>Modify Account</h1>';
}
```

The form posts its data to `cms_transact_user.php`. The first portion of the form's code is pretty much standard HTML code that displays the common fields with a small bit of PHP mixed in to safely output the contents of the variables that store the relevant field's value.

```
<form method="post" action="cms_transact_user.php">
 <table>
  <tr>
   <td><label for="name">Full Name:</label></td>
   <td><input type="text" id="name" name="name" maxlength="100"
     value="<?php echo htmlspecialchars($name); ?>"/></td>
  </tr><tr>
   <td><label for="email">Email Address:</label></td>
   <td><input type="text" id="email" name="email" maxlength="100"
     value="<?php echo htmlspecialchars($email); ?>"/></td>
  </tr>
```

If the user is logged in and editing his or her information, and if he or she has administrative privileges, then you generate a row in the table that allows the account's privileges to be changed. The list of privileges is retrieved from the `cms_access_levels table`, and each privilege is displayed as a radio button option on the form. While displaying the list, you also check to see if the particular privilege is held by the user, and if it is, then you set it to be checked by default.

```
if (isset($_SESSION['access_level']) && $_SESSION['access_level'] == 3)
{
    echo '<tr><td>Access Level</td><td>';

    $sql = 'SELECT
            access_level, access_name
        FROM
            cms_access_levels
        ORDER BY
            access_level DESC';
    $result = mysql_query($sql, $db) or die(mysql_error($db));

    while ($row = mysql_fetch_array($result)) {
        echo '<input type="radio" id="acl_' . $row['access_level'] .
            '" name="access_level" value="' . $row['access_level'] . '"';

        if ($row['access_level'] == $access_level) {
            echo ' checked="checked"';
        }
        echo '/> <label for="acl_' . $row['access_level'] . '">' .
            $row['access_name'] . '</label><br/>';
    }
    mysql_free_result($result);
    echo '</td></tr>';
}
```

What is displayed in the final portion of the form depends on whether the user is creating a new user account or updating his or her existing information. If the user is creating a new account, then the password fields are shown, and the submit button is given the value "Create Account." If the user is updating his or her information, then a hidden input field is output that contains the user_id, and the submit button is given the value "Modify Account." `cms_transact_user.php` will use the submit button's value to decide on the appropriate switch case to run when processing the form's posting.

```
if (empty($user_id)) {
?>
  <tr>
   <td><label for="password_1">Password:</label></td>
   <td><input type="password" id="password_1" name="password_1"
maxlength="50"/>
   </td>
  </tr><tr>
   <td><label for="password_2">Password (again):</label></td>
   <td><input type="password" id="password_2" name="password_2"
maxlength="50"/>
   </td>
  </tr><tr>
   <td> </td>
   <td>
    <input type="submit" name="action" value="Create Account"/>
   </td>
  </tr>
<?php
} else {
?>
  <tr>
   <td> </td>
   <td>
    <input type="hidden" name="user_id" value="<?php echo $user_id; ?>"/>
    <input type="submit" name="action" value="Modify Account"/>
   </td>
  </tr>
<?php
}
?>
```

Finally, you include `cms_footer.inc.php`, to close out the HTML neatly:

```
include 'cms_footer.inc.php';
```

User Management

So you may be wondering: If an administrative user can downgrade his or her privileges, how does the administrator create other administrators or moderators to help manage the site? The answer is within the script you are going to write next.

Administration Page

In this exercise, you'll create the pages necessary for administrators to manage the site's users.

1. Create `cms_admin.php`:

```php
<?php
require 'db.inc.php';
include 'cms_header.inc.php';

$db = mysql_connect(MYSQL_HOST, MYSQL_USER, MYSQL_PASSWORD) or
    die ('Unable to connect. Check your connection parameters.');

mysql_select_db(MYSQL_DB, $db) or die(mysql_error($db));

$sql = 'SELECT
        access_level, access_name
    FROM
        cms_access_levels
    ORDER BY
        access_name ASC';
$result = mysql_query($sql, $db) or die(mysql_error($db));

$privileges = array();
while ($row = mysql_fetch_assoc($result)) {
    $privileges[$row['access_level']] = $row['access_name'];
}
mysql_free_result($result);

echo '<h2>User Administration</h2>';

$limit = count($privileges);
for($i = 1; $i <= $limit; $i++) {
    echo '<h3>' . $privileges[$i] . '</h3>';
    $sql = 'SELECT
            user_id, name
        FROM
            cms_users
        WHERE
            access_level = ' . $i . '
        ORDER BY
            name ASC';
    $result = mysql_query($sql, $db) or die(mysql_error($db));

    if (mysql_num_rows($result) == 0) {
        echo '<p><strong>There are no ' . $privileges[$i] . ' accounts ' .
            'registered.</strong></p>';
    } else {
        echo '<ul>';
        while ($row = mysql_fetch_assoc($result)) {
            if ($_SESSION['user_id'] == $row['user_id']) {
                echo '<li>' . htmlspecialchars($row['name']) . '</li>';
```

```
            } else {
                echo '<li><a href="cms_user_account.php?user_id=' .
                    $row['user_id'] . '">' . htmlspecialchars($row['name']) .
                    '</a></li>';
            }
        }
        echo '</ul>';
    }
    mysql_free_result($result);
}

require 'cms_footer.inc.php';
?>
```

2. Go ahead and log out, and then log back in using your admin account. When you are logged
    in, click the Admin link. You should see a screen similar to Figure 13-5.

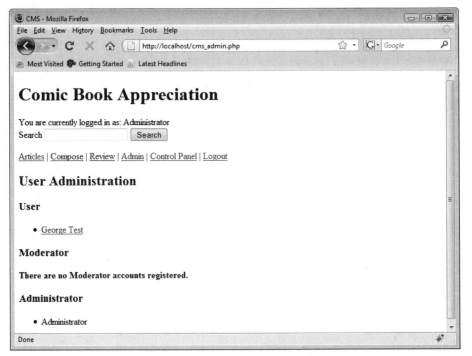

Figure 13-5

You should see George Test under the User heading. You will notice your administrator name
under Administrator, but it is not a link. You can alter your own account from your Control
Panel page.

3. Click the user listed under User. You should see a page similar to that in Figure 13-6. Notice that you can change the user's name and password. Also notice the Access Level option. You can set any user to be a User, Moderator, or Admin. User is the default for new users.

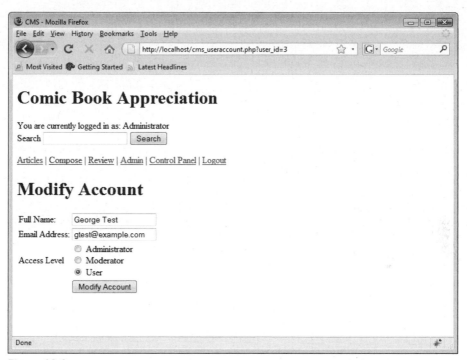

Figure 13-6

How It Works

Towards the start of the script, you query the database to retrieve the list of permissions from `cms_access_levels`. The name of each permission is stored in `$privileges`, an array that uses the `access_level`'s numeric ID as its index. You also fetch the number of records with the `mysql_num_rows()` function and store it in `$limit` for later use.

```
$sql = 'SELECT
        access_level, access_name
    FROM
        cms_access_levels
    ORDER BY
        access_name ASC';
$result = mysql_query($sql, $db) or die(mysql_error($db));

$privileges = array();
$limit = mysql_num_rows($result);
while ($row = mysql_fetch_assoc($result)) {
    $privileges[$row['access_level']] = $row['access_name'];
}
mysql_free_result($result);
```

You use the $limit value when you begin to iterate through the list of permissions. Note that you start the for loop with a starting value of 1, as opposed to 0. PHP arrays usually start their numeric indexes with 0, but you overrode this behavior by assigning the indexes with the permissions' IDs. You start with 1 because there is no ID 0. Also, you must use <= in your condition in this case, to make sure you process every permission.

```php
for($i = 1; $i <= $limit; $i++) {
    . . .
}
```

Alternatively, you could have used a foreach loop, for example:

```php
foreach ($privileges as $id => $privilege)
```

During each iteration of the loop, you query the database for the users who have a particular permission.

```php
$sql = 'SELECT
        user_id, name
    FROM
        cms_users
    WHERE
        access_level = ' . $i . '
    ORDER BY
        name ASC';
$result = mysql_query($sql, $db) or die(mysql_error($db));
```

If no records are returned, then there are no users with the given permission, and you output a message to alert the user of that fact.

```php
if (mysql_num_rows($result) == 0) {
    echo '<p><strong>There are no ' . $privileges[$i] . ' accounts ' .
        'registered.</strong></p>';
}
```

Otherwise, you list the users. A user cannot modify his or her own record from this list, so his or her name is shown as plaintext, not as a link (the user can modify his or her account from the control panel). All other users' names are displayed as links that point to the cms_user_account.php page.

```php
else {
    echo '<ul>';
    while ($row = mysql_fetch_assoc($result)) {
        if ($_SESSION['user_id'] == $row['user_id']) {
            echo '<li>' . htmlspecialchars($row['name']) . '</li>';
        } else {
            echo '<li><a href="cms_user_account.php?user_id=' .
                $row['user_id'] . '">' . htmlspecialchars($row['name']) .
                '</a></li>';
        }
    }
    echo '</ul>';
}
```

And, of course, statements that include `cms_header.inc.php` and `cms_footer.inc.php` bookend your script so that the output is a complete HTML page.

Article Publishing

So far, you have a large set of scripts to manage your users' accounts, but nothing that would put your application squarely into the CMS category. It's time to change that. Now you will be creating the pages that allow you to create, review, read, and comment on articles. On to the articles!

Creating an Article

In your first step toward having content, you're going to create the page that allows you to actually write out the articles and save them to the database.

1. Create a new file, and name it `cms_compose.php`:

```php
<?php
require 'db.inc.php';
include 'cms_header.inc.php';

$db = mysql_connect(MYSQL_HOST, MYSQL_USER, MYSQL_PASSWORD) or
    die ('Unable to connect. Check your connection parameters.');

mysql_select_db(MYSQL_DB, $db) or die(mysql_error($db));

$action = (isset($_GET['action'])) ? $_GET['action'] : '';
$article_id = (isset($_GET['article_id']) && ctype_digit($_GET['article_
id'])) ?
    $_GET['article_id'] : '' ;

$title = (isset($_POST['title'])) ? $_POST['title'] : '' ;
$article_text = (isset($_POST['article_text'])) ? $_POST['article_text'] : '' ;
$user_id = (isset($_POST['user_id'])) ? $_POST['user_id'] : '' ;

if ($action == 'edit' && !empty($article_id)) {
    $sql = 'SELECT
            title, article_text, user_id
        FROM
            cms_articles
        WHERE
            article_id = ' . $article_id;
    $result = mysql_query($sql, $db) or die(mysql_error($db));

    $row = mysql_fetch_array($result);
```

```php
      extract($row);
      mysql_free_result($result);
  }
?>
<h2>Compose Article</h2>
<form method="post" action="cms_transact_article.php">
 <table>
  <tr>
   <td><label for="title">Title:</label></td>
   <td><input type="text" name="title" id="title" maxlength="255"
     value="<?php echo htmlspecialchars($title); ?>"/></td>
  </tr><tr>
   <td><label for="article_text">Text:</label></td>
   <td><textarea name="article_text" name="article_text" rows="10"
     cols="60"><?php echo htmlspecialchars($article_text); ?></textarea></td>
  </tr><tr>
   <td> </td>
   <td>
<?php
if ($_SESSION['access_level'] < 2) {
    echo '<input type="hidden" name="user_id" value="' . $user_id . '"/>';
}

if (empty($article_id)) {
    echo '<input type="submit" name="action" "value="Submit New Article"/>';
} else {
    echo '<input type="hidden" name="article_id" value="' . $article_id . '"/>';
    echo '<input type="submit" name="action" "value="Save Changes"/>';
}
?>
   </td>
  </tr>
 </table>
</form>
<?php
require_once 'cms_footer.inc.php';
?>
```

2. Click the Compose link to load `cms_compose.php` (see Figure 13-7).

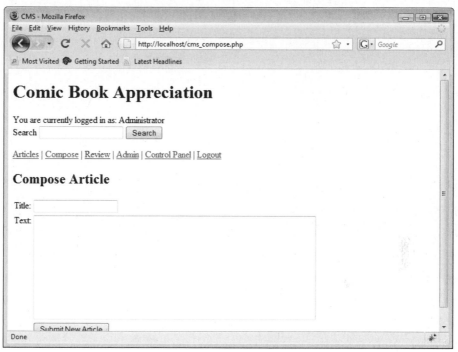

Figure 13-7

3. Enter a title and some text for the article. When you are done, click Submit New Article. You will be taken back to the index page, but there will still be no article; the article you just wrote is pending review.

How It Works

You just wrote `cms_compose.php`, the page where you and your users can create new articles. First, you accept and filter any incoming values:

```
$action = (isset($_GET['action'])) ? $_GET['action'] : '';
$article_id = (isset($_GET['article_id']) && ctype_digit($_GET['article_id'])) ?
    $_GET['article_id'] : '' ;

$title = (isset($_POST['title'])) ? $_POST['title'] : '' ;
$article_text = (isset($_POST['article_text'])) ? $_POST['article_text'] : '' ;
$user_id = (isset($_POST['user_id'])) ? $_POST['user_id'] : '' ;
```

If the user is editing an article, `action=edit` and the article ID will be passed along in the URL string, so `$action` will contain the value `'edit'`, and `$article_id` will contain the ID of the article. You may retrieve the existing article from the `cms_articles` table.

```php
if ($action == 'edit' && !empty($article_id)) {
    $sql = 'SELECT
            title, article_text, user_id
        FROM
            cms_articles
        WHERE
            article_id = ' . $article_id;
    $result = mysql_query($sql, $db) or die(mysql_error($db));

    $row = mysql_fetch_array($result);
    extract($row);
    mysql_free_result($result);
}
```

Then you display the form that is used to enter or edit an article. Towards the end of the form, you check the value of `$_SESSION['access_level']` and include a hidden field with the author's user ID, if the access level is less than 2 (the viewer is a normal user). Also, you display the appropriate submit button and the `article_id` if it is being edited or if it is a new article. The author's user ID is passed if the original author is editing his or her own document. The article ID must be carried over to the transaction page if an existing article is being modified.

```php
<h2>Compose Article</h2>
<form method="post" action="cms_transact_article.php">
 <table>
  <tr>
   <td><label for="title">Title:</label></td>
   <td><input type="text" name="title" id="title" maxlength="255"
     value="<?php echo htmlspecialchars($title); ?>"/></td>
  </tr><tr>
   <td><label for="article_text">Text:</label></td>
   <td><textarea name="article_text" name="article_text" rows="10"
     cols="60"><?php echo htmlspecialchars($article_text); ?></textarea></td>
  </tr><tr>
   <td> </td>
   <td>
<?php
if ($_SESSION['access_level'] < 2) {
    echo '<input type="hidden" name="user_id" value="' . $user_id . '"/>';
}

if (empty($article_id)) {
    echo '<input type="submit" name="action" "value="Submit New Article"/>';
} else {
    echo '<input type="hidden" name="article_id" value="' . $article_id . '"/>';
```

```
        echo '<input type="submit" name="action" "value="Save Changes"/>';
}
?>
    </td>
   </tr>
  </table>
</form>
```

If you've looked around your web site, you might have noticed that the article you just created doesn't show up yet. That's because you've set up a review system wherein an administrator or moderator must approve an article before it is published for the public to view. This sort of control is found on many CMS-based sites on the web, and it's a good way to keep an eye on quality and duplicate stories.

Try It Out   **Reviewing New Articles**

In this exercise, you'll create the reviewing system that lets you approve your articles.

1.   Create cms_pending.php:

```
<?php
require 'db.inc.php';
include 'cms_header.inc.php';

$db = mysql_connect(MYSQL_HOST, MYSQL_USER, MYSQL_PASSWORD) or
    die ('Unable to connect. Check your connection parameters.');

mysql_select_db(MYSQL_DB, $db) or die(mysql_error($db));

echo '<h2>Article Availability</h2>';

echo '<h3>Pending Articles</h3>';
$sql = 'SELECT
        article_id, title, UNIX_TIMESTAMP(submit_date) AS submit_date
    FROM
        cms_articles
    WHERE
        is_published = FALSE
    ORDER BY
        title ASC';
$result = mysql_query($sql, $db) or die(mysql_error($db));

if (mysql_num_rows($result) == 0) {
    echo '<p><strong>No pending articles available.</strong></p>';
```

```php
    } else {
        echo '<ul>';
        while ($row = mysql_fetch_array($result)) {
            echo '<li><a href="cms_review_article.php?article_id=' .
                $row['article_id'] . '">' . htmlspecialchars($row['title']) .
                '</a> (' . date('F j, Y', $row['submit_date']) . ')</li>';
        }
        echo '</ul>';
    }
    mysql_free_result($result);

    echo '<h3>Published Articles</h3>';
    $sql = 'SELECT
            article_id, title, UNIX_TIMESTAMP(publish_date) AS publish_date
        FROM
            cms_articles
        WHERE
            is_published = TRUE
        ORDER BY
            title ASC';
    $result = mysql_query($sql, $db) or die(mysql_error($db));

    if (mysql_num_rows($result) == 0) {
        echo '<p><strong>No published articles available.</strong></p>';
    } else {
        echo '<ul>';
        while ($row = mysql_fetch_array($result)) {
            echo '<li><a href="cms_review_article.php?article_id=' .
                $row['article_id'] . '">' . htmlspecialchars($row['title']) .
                '</a> (' . date('F j, Y', $row['publish_date']) . ')</li>';
        }
        echo '</ul>';
    }
    mysql_free_result($result);

    include 'cms_footer.inc.php';
    ?>
```

2. Next, create `cms_review_article.php`:

```php
    <?php
    require 'db.inc.php';
    require 'cms_output_functions.inc.php';
    include 'cms_header.inc.php';

    $db = mysql_connect(MYSQL_HOST, MYSQL_USER, MYSQL_PASSWORD) or
        die ('Unable to connect. Check your connection parameters.');

    mysql_select_db(MYSQL_DB, $db) or die(mysql_error($db));

    $article_id = (isset($_GET['article_id']) && ctype_digit($_GET['article_
    id'])) ?
```

```php
        $_GET['article_id'] : '';

echo '<h2>Article Review</h2>';
output_story($db, $article_id);

$sql = 'SELECT
        is_published, UNIX_TIMESTAMP(publish_date) AS publish_date,
access_level
    FROM
        cms_articles a INNER JOIN cms_users u ON a.user_id = u.user_id
    WHERE
        article_id = ' . $article_id;
$result = mysql_query($sql, $db) or die(mysql_error());

$row = mysql_fetch_array($result);
extract($row);
mysql_free_result($result);

if (!empty($date_published) and $is_published) {
    echo '<h4>Published: ' . date('l F j, Y H:i', $date_published) . '</h4>';
}
?>

<form method="post" action="cms_transact_article.php">
 <div>
  <input type="submit" name="action" value="Edit"/>
<?php
if ($access_level > 1 || $_SESSION['access_level'] > 1) {
    if ($is_published) {
        echo '<input type="submit" name="action" value="Retract"/> ';
    } else {
        echo '<input type="submit" name="action" value="Publish"/> ';
        echo '<input type="submit" name="action" value="Delete"/> ';
    }
}
?>
  <input type="hidden" name="article_id" value="<?php echo $article_id; ?>"/>
 </div>
</form>
<?php
include 'cms_footer.inc.php';
?>
```

3. Click the Review link. The Review page `cms_pending.php` loads (see Figure 13-8), with a list of all pending and published articles. Right now, there is only one pending article, which is the one you just wrote.

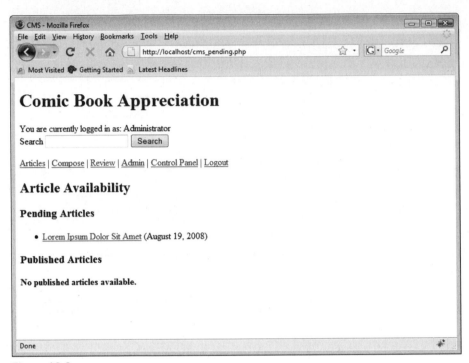

Figure 13-8

4. Click the article. You will be taken to `cms_review_article.php`. It should look similar to Figure 13-9. You have the option to edit, publish, or delete the article.

Figure 13-9

5. Click the Publish button. You will be taken back to `cms_pending.php`, and the article will now be listed under Published Articles.

6. Click the Articles link, and you will be taken back to the index page. This time, the article should appear on the page (see Figure 13-10).

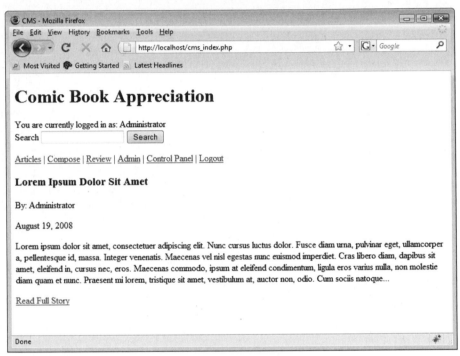

Figure 13-10

How It Works

You wrote two scripts in this section, `cms_pending.php` and `cms_review_article.php`. Hopefully, you are beginning to see just how easy it is to build up the interface and tie all the functionality together, with the heavy-duty work delegated to the transaction files.

The `cms_pending.php` script generates a page to list the articles that are pending approval and articles that have been published. You first generate this SQL query to fetch a list of pending articles:

```
$sql = 'SELECT
        article_id, title, UNIX_TIMESTAMP(submit_date) AS submit_date
    FROM
        cms_articles
    WHERE
        is_published = FALSE
    ORDER BY
        title ASC';
$result = mysql_query($sql, $db) or die(mysql_error($db));
```

You then check `mysql_num_rows()` to determine the number of records that the query returned. If no records were returned, then you display a message stating there are no pending articles available. Otherwise, you loop through the list of articles that is returned from the database, and you display the title of each as a link to `cms_review_article.php`.

```
if (mysql_num_rows($result) == 0) {
    echo '<p><strong>No pending articles available.</strong></p>';
} else {
    echo '<ul>';
    while ($row = mysql_fetch_array($result)) {
        echo '<li><a href=" cms_review_article.php?article_id=' .
            $row['article_id'] . '">' . htmlspecialchars($row['title']) .
            '</a> (' . date('F j, Y', $row['submit_date']) . ')</li>';
    }
    echo '</ul>';
}
```

The same process is followed to retrieve the list of published articles, though the query and the message that is displayed if no articles are returned have been modified accordingly.

```
$sql = 'SELECT
        article_id, title, UNIX_TIMESTAMP(publish_date) AS publish_date
    FROM
        cms_articles
    WHERE
        is_published = TRUE
    ORDER BY
        title ASC';
$result = mysql_query($sql, $db) or die(mysql_error($db));

if (mysql_num_rows($result) == 0) {
    echo '<p><strong>No published articles available.</strong></p>';
} else {
    echo '<ul>';
    while ($row = mysql_fetch_array($result)) {
        echo '<li><a href=" cms_review_article.php?article_id=' .
            $row['article_id'] . '">' . htmlspecialchars($row['title']) .
            '</a> (' . date('F j, Y', $row['publish_date']) . ')</li>';
    }
    echo '</ul>';
}
```

The whole purpose of the `cms_review_article.php` script is to present the article for review by the administrator. First, you display the title of the page, and then you use the `output_story()` function to display the article on the page.

```
echo '<h2>Article Review</h2>';
output_story($db, $article_id);
```

It is important to note that you passed only two variables to the function `output_story()`, even though `output_story()` takes three arguments. PHP automatically used the default value because you did not specify the optional third parameter, which you should recall is FALSE. (If there were no default value assigned when you first wrote `output_story()`, then attempting to call the function with only the two arguments would result in a PHP warning telling you that you are missing an argument. Providing default arguments when you are writing your functions makes them more flexible and easier to use.)

You also want to display additional data about the document, such as when it was published. You used this SQL statement to retrieve the additional information:

```
$sql = 'SELECT
        is_published, UNIX_TIMESTAMP(publish_date) AS publish_date, access_
level
    FROM
        cms_articles a INNER JOIN cms_users u ON a.user_id = u.user_id
    WHERE
        article_id = ' . $article_id;
$result = mysql_query($sql, $db) or die(mysql_error());
```

Yes, output_story() retrieves this data too, but if you modified output_story() so that articles did not display their author or publish date, you would still want the information displayed on this review page. This is why you repeat this tiny bit of functionality here.

If the document is published, then the administrator has an option to retract the article. If it is still pending, then the administrator can publish it. Only moderators and admins are allowed to retract, publish, and delete an article, and an article may only be deleted if it is pending.

```
<form method="post" action="cms_transact_article.php">
 <div>
  <input type="submit" name="action" value="Edit"/>
<?php
if ($access_level > 1 || $_SESSION['access_level'] > 1) {
    if ($is_published) {
        echo '<input type="submit" name="action" value="Retract"/> ';
    } else {
        echo '<input type="submit" name="action" value="Publish"/> ';
        echo '<input type="submit" name="action" value="Delete"/> ';
    }
}
?>
  <input type="hidden" name="article_id" value="<?php echo $article_id; ?>"/>
 </div>
</form>
```

Try It Out   Article Pages

So you've created an article, reviewed it, and published it. Now it's time to give the public a way to view the article and provide feedback. It's time to write cms_view_article.php and cms_comment.php, both of which are relatively short scripts.

1. Create `cms_view_article.php`:

```php
<?php
require 'db.inc.php';
require 'cms_output_functions.inc.php';

$db = mysql_connect(MYSQL_HOST, MYSQL_USER, MYSQL_PASSWORD) or
    die ('Unable to connect. Check your connection parameters.');

mysql_select_db(MYSQL_DB, $db) or die(mysql_error($db));

include 'cms_header.inc.php';
output_story($db, $_GET['article_id']);
show_comments($db, $_GET['article_id'], TRUE);
include 'cms_footer.inc.php';
?>
```

2. Now, create `cms_comment.php`:

```php
<?php
require 'db.inc.php';
require 'cms_output_functions.inc.php';
include 'cms_header.inc.php';

$db = mysql_connect(MYSQL_HOST, MYSQL_USER, MYSQL_PASSWORD) or
    die ('Unable to connect. Check your connection parameters.');

mysql_select_db(MYSQL_DB, $db) or die(mysql_error($db));

$article_id = (isset($_GET['article_id']) && ctype_digit($_GET['article_
id'])) ?
    $_GET['article_id'] : '';

output_story($db, $article_id);
?>
<h3>Add a comment</h3>
<form method="post" action="cms_transact_article.php">
 <div>
   <label for="comment_text">Comment:</label><br/>
   <textarea id="comment_text" name="comment_text" rows="10"
   cols="60"></textarea><br/>
   <input type="submit" name="action" value="Submit Comment" />
   <input type="hidden" name="article_id" value="<?php echo $article_id; ?>" />
 </div>
</form>
<?php
show_comments($db, $article_id, FALSE);
include 'cms_footer.inc.php';
?>
```

3. Go back to the index by clicking the Articles link. Click the Read Full Story link below the snippet of the article you want to view. The full article should appear, complete with a link to add comments.

How It Works

The first page, `cms_view_article.php`, is very short, yet it illustrates the nature of included files and functions wonderfully.

As you can see, there is no content displayed directly with `cms_view_article.php`. It simply includes the necessary files and calls the `output_story()` and `show_comments()` functions from `cms_output_functions.inc.php` to display the article and all of its comments.

```php
<?php
require 'db.inc.php';
require 'cms_output_functions.inc.php';

$db = mysql_connect(MYSQL_HOST, MYSQL_USER, MYSQL_PASSWORD) or
    die ('Unable to connect. Check your connection parameters.');

mysql_select_db(MYSQL_DB, $db) or die(mysql_error($db));

include 'cms_header.inc.php';
output_story($db, $_GET['article_id']);
show_comments($db, $_GET['article_id'], TRUE);
include 'cms_footer.inc.php';
?>
```

You may notice that you don't worry about the situation in which an article is not passed. As it stands, if you load `cms_view_article.php` without the "`article_id`" parameter in the URL, you will simply get a page that consists of the site title, search, and a menu (all included in `cms_header.inc.php`). The rest will be blank. If that's the desired result, then that's fine. You may decide to redirect the user back to the home page if `$_GET['article_id']` is empty. If you do, don't forget to include `cms_http_functions.inc.php` and use `redirect()` *before* including `cms_header.inc.php`.

The most important feature of `cms_comment.php` is the HTML form it produces to let readers enter their comments on an article. It has a `textarea` element to accept the comment, a submit button, and a hidden input field to pass the article's ID.

```html
<form method="post" action="cms_transact_article.php">
  <div>
    <label for="comment_text">Comment:</label><br/>
    <textarea id="comment_text" name="comment_text" rows="10"
     cols="60"></textarea><br/>
    <input type="submit" name="action" value="Submit Comment" />
    <input type="hidden" name="article_id" value="<?php echo $article_id; ?>"
 />
  </div>
</form>
```

And that's it! That last one was a doozy, huh? Hardly! Because you planned well and wrote most of the CMS's functional code up front, these scripts are getting easier. Stay with us — you only need to write a couple more short scripts to finish off your application.

Additional CMS Features

So far, you've created a system to create and manage users and publish articles, but there are a couple of additional features that can help make your CMS even better. What you're going to add now is the ability for users to update their information and the ability to search published articles by keyword.

User Control Panel

In this exercise, you're going to create a page to allow users to maintain their own information.

1. Enter the following code, and save it as `cms_cpanel.php`:

```php
<?php
require 'db.inc.php';
require 'cms_output_functions.inc.php';
include 'cms_header.inc.php';

$db = mysql_connect(MYSQL_HOST, MYSQL_USER, MYSQL_PASSWORD) or
    die ('Unable to connect. Check your connection parameters.');


mysql_select_db(MYSQL_DB, $db) or die(mysql_error($db));

$sql = 'SELECT
        email, name
    FROM
        cms_users
    WHERE
        user_id=' . $_SESSION['user_id'];
$result = mysql_query($sql, $db) or die(mysql_error($db));

$row = mysql_fetch_array($result);
extract($row);
mysql_free_result($result);
?>
<h2>User Info</h2>
<form method="post" action="cms_transact_user.php">
 <table>
  <tr>
   <td><label for="name">Full Name:</label></td>
   <td><input type="text" id="name" name="name" maxlength="100"
     value="<?php echo htmlspecialchars($name); ?>"/></td>
  </tr><tr>
   <td><label for="email">Email Address:</label></td>
   <td><input type="text" id="email" name="email" maxlength="100"
     value="<?php echo htmlspecialchars($email); ?>"/></td>
  </tr><tr>
   <td> </td>
   <td><input type="submit" name="action" value="Change my info"/></td>
  </tr>
 </table>
</form>
```

```php
<?php
echo '<h2>Pending Articles</h2>';

$sql = 'SELECT
        article_id, UNIX_TIMESTAMP(submit_date) AS submit_date, title
    FROM
        cms_articles
    WHERE
        is_published = FALSE AND
        user_id = ' . $_SESSION['user_id'] . '
    ORDER BY
        submit_date ASC';
$result = mysql_query($sql, $db) or die(mysql_error($db));

if (mysql_num_rows($result) == 0) {
    echo '<p><strong>There are currently no pending articles.</strong></p>';
} else {
    echo '<ul>';
    while ($row = mysql_fetch_array($result)) {
        echo '<li><a href="cms_review_article.php?article_id=' .
            $row['article_id'] . '">' . htmlspecialchars($row['title']) .
            '</a> (submitted ' . date('F j, Y', $row['submit_date']) .
            ')</li>';
    }
    echo '</ul>';
}
mysql_free_result($result);

echo '<h2>Published Articles</h2>';

$sql = 'SELECT
        article_id, UNIX_TIMESTAMP(publish_date) AS publish_date, title
    FROM
        cms_articles
    WHERE
        is_published = TRUE AND
        user_id = ' . $_SESSION['user_id'] . '
    ORDER BY
        publish_date ASC';
$result = mysql_query($sql, $db) or die(mysql_error($db));

if (mysql_num_rows($result) == 0) {
    echo '<p><strong>There are currently no published articles.</strong></p>';
} else {
    echo '<ul>';
    while ($row = mysql_fetch_array($result)) {
        echo '<li><a href="cms_review_article.php?article_id=' .
            $row['article_id'] . '">' . htmlspecialchars($row['title']) .
            '</a> (published ' . date('F j, Y', $row['publish_date']) .
            ')</li>';
    }
    echo '</ul>';
}
```

```
mysql_free_result($result);

include 'cms_footer.inc.php';
?>
```

2. Click the navigation link to go to the Control Panel page. You should see a screen similar to the one shown in Figure 13-11. Here you can change your user information (username and e-mail), and see what articles you have written for the site.

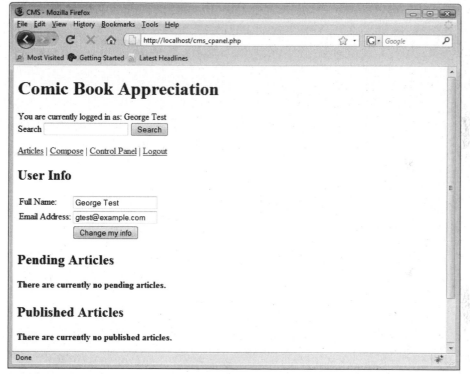

Figure 13-11

How It Works

The Control Panel page, cms_cpanel.php, is used to allow users to change their usernames and e-mail addresses. They can also see all of the articles they have written, categorized by whether they are pending or have been published.

You first go out to the database and retrieve the user's e-mail address and name from the cms_users table.

```
$sql = 'SELECT
        email, name
    FROM
        cms_users
```

```
    WHERE
        user_id=' . $_SESSION['user_id'];
$result = mysql_query($sql, $db) or die(mysql_error($db));

$row = mysql_fetch_array($result);
extract($row);
mysql_free_result($result);
```

The form to let the user edit his or her information uses the `post` method. When the submit button is clicked, it will post the name and e-mail address to `cms_transact_user.php` for processing. The rest of the form is standard HTML with some PHP statements mixed in to populate the fields with the values from the database.

```
<form method="post" action="cms_transact_user.php">
 <table>
  <tr>
   <td><label for="name">Full Name:</label></td>
   <td><input type="text" id="name" name="name" maxlength="100"
     value="<?php echo htmlspecialchars($name); ?>"/></td>
  </tr><tr>
   <td><label for="email">Email Address:</label></td>
   <td><input type="text" id="email" name="email" maxlength="100"
     value="<?php echo htmlspecialchars($email); ?>"/></td>
  </tr><tr>
   <td> </td>
   <td><input type="submit" name="action" value="Change my info"/></td>
  </tr>
 </table>
</form>
```

Next, you display pending and published articles. Time to drop back into using PHP, where you query the database to retrieve the pending articles written by this user, ordered by the date they were submitted:

```
$sql = 'SELECT
        article_id, UNIX_TIMESTAMP(submit_date) AS submit_date, title
    FROM
        cms_articles
    WHERE
        is_published = FALSE AND
        user_id = ' . $_SESSION['user_id'] . '
    ORDER BY
        submit_date ASC';
$result = mysql_query($sql, $db) or die(mysql_error($db));
```

You handle the contingency that there may not be any pending articles, in which case you output an appropriate message. Otherwise, you loop through the pending articles and display the titles as links to `cms_reviewarticle.php`.

```
if (mysql_num_rows($result) == 0) {
    echo '<p><strong>There are currently no pending articles.</strong></p>';
} else {
    echo '<ul>';
    while ($row = mysql_fetch_array($result)) {
        echo '<li><a href="cms_review_article.php?article_id=' .
            $row['article_id'] . '">' . htmlspecialchars($row['title']) .
            '</a> (submitted ' . date('F j, Y', $row['submit_date']) .
            ')</li>';
    }
    echo '</ul>';
}
mysql_free_result($result);
```

This next section of code, which displays the published articles, is almost identical to the code used to display pending articles, though this time the selection is where is_published is TRUE, and the results are ordered by the article's publication date.

```
$sql = 'SELECT
        article_id, UNIX_TIMESTAMP(publish_date) AS publish_date, title
    FROM
        cms_articles
    WHERE
        is_published = TRUE AND
        user_id = ' . $_SESSION['user_id'] . '
    ORDER BY
        publish_date ASC';
$result = mysql_query($sql, $db) or die(mysql_error($db));

if (mysql_num_rows($result) == 0) {
    echo '<p><strong>There are currently no published articles.</strong></p>';
} else {
    echo '<ul>';
    while ($row = mysql_fetch_array($result)) {
        echo '<li><a href="cms_review_article.php?article_id=' .
            $row['article_id'] . '">' . htmlspecialchars($row['title']) .
            '</a> (published ' . date('F j, Y', $row['publish_date']) .
            ')</li>';
    }
    echo '</ul>';
}
mysql_free_result($result);
```

Try It Out   Search

The last feature you are going to add is a simple search feature. Using the power of the full-text searching capabilities of MySQL, you can easily put a keyword search field on each page and show the results here.

1. Create `cms_search.php`:

```php
<?php
require 'db.inc.php';
require 'cms_output_functions.inc.php';

$db = mysql_connect(MYSQL_HOST, MYSQL_USER, MYSQL_PASSWORD) or
    die ('Unable to connect. Check your connection parameters.');

mysql_select_db(MYSQL_DB, $db) or die(mysql_error($db));

include 'cms_header.inc.php';

$search = (isset($_GET['search'])) ? $_GET['search'] : '';

$sql = 'SELECT
        article_id
    FROM
        cms_articles
    WHERE
        MATCH (title, article_text) AGAINST ("' .
            mysql_real_escape_string($search, $db) . '" IN BOOLEAN MODE)
    ORDER BY
        MATCH (title, article_text) AGAINST ("' .
            mysql_real_escape_string($search, $db) . '" IN BOOLEAN MODE)
DESC';
$result = mysql_query($sql, $db) or die(mysql_error($db));

if (mysql_num_rows($result) == 0) {
    echo '<p><strong>No articles found that match the search terms.</strong></p>';
} else {
    while ($row = mysql_fetch_array($result)) {
        output_story($db, $row['article_id'], TRUE);
    }
}
mysql_free_result($result);

include 'cms_footer.inc.php';
?>
```

2. On any page with a search box on the top, enter a word that existed in the article you created. Once you submit the form, `cms_search.php` will appear, and any matches should be shown.

How It Works

In the following SQL statement, you'll notice the MATCH and AGAINST keywords. This is the syntax MySQL uses to perform a full-text search in those fields. They must be full-text indexed fields in order to perform this search, which you specified when you created the table in db_ch13.php.

```
$sql = 'SELECT
        article_id
    FROM
        cms_articles
    WHERE
        MATCH (title, article_text) AGAINST ("' .
            mysql_real_escape_string($search, $db) . '" IN BOOLEAN MODE)
    ORDER BY
        MATCH (title, article_text) AGAINST ("' .
            mysql_real_escape_string($search, $db) . '" IN BOOLEAN MODE) DESC';
$result = mysql_query($sql, $db) or die(mysql_error($db));
```

If you don't find a match, you output a message saying that no articles were found matching the search terms. Otherwise, you loop through the results and display a preview of each article, using output_story():

```
if (mysql_num_rows($result) == 0) {
    echo '<p><strong>No articles found that match the search terms
.</strong></p>';
} else {
    while ($row = mysql_fetch_array($result)) {
        output_story($db, $row['article_id'], TRUE);
    }
}
```

Summary

We hope this application has given you some insight into the separation of content and design, as well as the importance of organizing your applications. Because of the way the application was designed, you can easily modify the look and feel of the application, by either directly altering your header and footer files or using a CSS file to set up different styles. This won't matter to your users; they will still be able to enter articles without ever having to worry about what the article will look like on the web when it's published.

We also hope that you understand the importance of updating your site often enough to draw users back again and again. By adding an application like this to your site, and allowing users to add content for you, you create a dynamically changing site with fresh information. Just think about all the ways you could implement such a design:

❑   Create a message board. (This is examined in more detail in Chapter 16.)

❑   Add a daily comic. Perhaps you have an artist who can draw you a comic every day. You could create an application that allows him or her to upload comic strips and allows users to comment on them.

❑ Compile photo journals. A while back, there was a project in which photographers went all over the world, and in a 24-hour period, they took their pictures and uploaded the digital images. People in the central office typed up descriptions and allowed people to view them online. It was a very ambitious project and a perfect example of a CMS application.

The bottom line is that if you have content that you want to be able to update on a regular basis, you definitely want to implement a CMS application. And now, you have the basic tools to build one on your own!

Perhaps you should send your users an e-mail to tell them of your improved functionality. You'll do that in Chapter 14.

Exercises

Now that you have the basic workings of a CMS application, see how you might accomplish the following tasks:

1. **Find out about the author:** Authors of articles might want the readers to know a little more about them. Add the ability to enter extra fields in a user's profile, and provide a link on the article's full-view page to the author's information.

2. **Notify the author:** Authors might want to be automatically notified when their stories have been approved. Add an e-mail notification upon approval, and give users the ability to toggle their notification on and off.

Mailing Lists

Ah, yes … mailing lists. Two small and innocent words that never meant anyone harm. That is, until someone decided to put the two together, and junk mail was born. But mailing lists are used for more than just junk mail or spam. After all, how are you going to receive your *Quilting Monthly* newsletter unless your name and address are on a mailing list?

In a world of e-mail communication, a mailing list is the perfect way for you to communicate with all of your users about your new web site. Maybe you want to send out a monthly newsletter or just send out important announcements. Whatever the reason, you will occasionally need to send e-mails to many people, and you will need a relatively easy way to do so when that time comes. Do not fret, because we plan on helping you with just that in this chapter.

Specifically, this chapter discusses the following:

❑ Creating a mailing list

❑ Administering a mailing list

❑ Spam

❑ Opt-in and opt-out

What Do You Want to Send Today?

Before you actually create a mailing list, you should have something that you intend to send to a large number of your users. Here are a few possibilities:

❑ **Web site notifications:** These are important tidbits of information about your web site. For example, you would want to let your users know you've improved the level of security for online transactions on your site.

❑ **Newsletters:** If you had a family web site, and wanted to let your whole family know about a new addition to your family, such as the birth of a child, you could send them a newsletter.

❑ **Important announcements:** Our site will be down for 5 days. Sorry for the inconvenience. We'll let you know when it is back up.

❑ **Advertising:** Perhaps you've partnered with an online comic book store to offer deals on rare comics to your members.

Once you know what you want to say, you format the information you wish to share, using plaintext or HTML. Then you e-mail this information to *every* member of your web site who has subscribed to receive messages from you.

In this chapter's project, you are going to send out two different e-mails: web site change notifications and a newsletter. The former will be sent to all members of the web site. The latter will be sent only to those who subscribe to the newsletter.

In Chapter 11, you saw how to easily send HTML e-mails and wrapped this functionality up in its own class. Reusing existing code is a great way to be a more efficient programmer, so you will do that in this chapter. You can also e-mail links to an online version of the HTML you are sending, so that those with text-only e-mail clients can see your message in all its glory as well.

Coding the Administration Application

The first thing you're going to do is create an administration page where you can add and remove mailing lists. There are a few scripts that need to be written here because they will all rely on one another. Hey — you're the one who wanted to write some code, so let's get cracking!

Try It Out   Preparing the Database

First, you're going to create the file that will build the necessary tables in the database for your mailing list application.

1. Enter the following code, save it as db_ch14.php on your server, and load it in your browser:

```php
<?php
require 'db.inc.php';

$db = mysql_connect(MYSQL_HOST, MYSQL_USER, MYSQL_PASSWORD) or
    die ('Unable to connect. Check your connection parameters.');

mysql_select_db(MYSQL_DB, $db) or die(mysql_error($db));

$query = 'CREATE TABLE IF NOT EXISTS ml_lists (
        ml_id     INTEGER UNSIGNED NOT NULL AUTO_INCREMENT,
        listname VARCHAR(100)      NOT NULL,

        PRIMARY KEY (ml_id)
    )
    ENGINE=MyISAM';
mysql_query($query, $db) or die(mysql_error($db));

$query = 'CREATE TABLE IF NOT EXISTS ml_users (
```

```
            user_id    INTEGER UNSIGNED NOT NULL AUTO_INCREMENT,
            first_name VARCHAR(20)       NOT NULL,
            last_name  VARCHAR(20)       NOT NULL,
            email      VARCHAR(100)      NOT NULL,

            PRIMARY KEY (user_id)
        )
        ENGINE=MyISAM';
    mysql_query($query, $db) or die(mysql_error($db));

    $query = 'CREATE TABLE IF NOT EXISTS ml_subscriptions (
            ml_id    INTEGER UNSIGNED NOT NULL,
            user_id  INTEGER UNSIGNED NOT NULL,
            pending BOOLEAN            NOT NULL DEFAULT TRUE,

            PRIMARY KEY (ml_id, user_id)
        )
        ENGINE=MyISAM';
    mysql_query($query, $db) or die(mysql_error($db));

    echo 'Success!';
    ?>
```

2. When you run db_ch14.php in your browser, it should display "Success!" indicating that the database tables were created.

How It Works

You can see that several tables are created in this script. In fact, your database should now have three new tables in it for the mailing list application. The first table is named ml_lists and will store the names of the different mailing lists you set up.

Fieldname	Type	Description of What It Stores
ml_id	INTEGER UNSIGNED	A unique ID assigned to a mailing list. This will auto-increment and is the table's primary key.
listname	VARCHAR(100)	The name of the mailing list.

The next table is ml_users and contains the list of subscribers to your mailing lists:

Fieldname	Type	Description of What It Stores
user_id	INTEGER UNSIGNED	A unique ID assigned to each subscriber. This will auto-increment and is the table's primary key.
first_name	VARCHAR(20)	Subscriber's first name.
last_name	VARCHAR(20)	Subscriber's last name.
Email	VARCHAR(100)	Subscriber's e-mail address.

The final table you create is called `ml_subscriptions` and links the subscribers to the mailing lists they subscribe to:

Fieldname	Type	Description of What It Stores
ml_id	INTEGER UNSIGNED	The ID of the list that the individual has subscribed to. This is a foreign key that references ml_lists.
user_id	DATETIME	The ID of the subscriber. This is a foreign key that references ml_users.
pending	BOOLEAN	Whether the subscription is pending.

As long as all three tables are created (or already exist), you will see "Done" echoed to the screen. Otherwise, you will see an error message.

Try It Out   **Mailing List Administration**

Next, you will create the admin page where the administrator can create, delete, and rename mailing lists.

1. Create the following code, and save it as `ml_admin.php`:

```php
<?php
require 'db.inc.php';

$db = mysql_connect(MYSQL_HOST, MYSQL_USER, MYSQL_PASSWORD) or
    die ('Unable to connect. Check your connection parameters.');

mysql_select_db(MYSQL_DB, $db) or die(mysql_error($db));
?>
<html>
 <head>
  <title>Mailing List Administration</title>
  <style type="text/css">
   td { vertical-align: top; }
  </style>
 </head>
 <body>
  <h1>Mailing List Administration</h1>
  <form method="post" action="ml_admin_transact.php">
   <p><label for="listname">Add Mailing List:</label><br />
    <input type="text" id="listname" name="listname" maxlength="100" />
    <input type="submit" name="action" value="Add New Mailing List" />
   </p>
<?php
$query = 'SELECT
```

```
        ml_id, listname
    FROM
        ml_lists
    ORDER BY
        listname ASC';
$result = mysql_query($query, $db) or die(mysql_error($db));

if (mysql_num_rows($result) > 0) {
    echo '<p><label for="ml_id">Delete Mailing List:</label><br />';
    echo '<select name="ml_id" id="ml_id">';
    while ($row = mysql_fetch_array($result)) {
        echo '<option value="' . $row['ml_id'] . '">' . $row['listname'] .
            '</option>';
    }
    echo '</select>';
    echo '<input type="submit" name="action" value="Delete ' .
        'Mailing List" />';
    echo '</p>';
}
mysql_free_result($result);
?>
  </form>
  <p><a href="ml_quick_msg.php">Send a quick message to users.</a></p>
 </body>
</html>
```

2. The administrator needs the ability to send e-mails to the members of various mailing lists. Otherwise, what was the point of creating the mailing lists in the first place? Enter the following code, and save it as ml_quick_msg.php:

```
<?php
require 'db.inc.php';

$db = mysql_connect(MYSQL_HOST, MYSQL_USER, MYSQL_PASSWORD) or
    die ('Unable to connect. Check your connection parameters.');

mysql_select_db(MYSQL_DB, $db) or die(mysql_error($db));
?>
<html>
 <head>
  <title>Send Message</title>
  <style type="text/css">
   td { vertical-align: top; }
  </style>
 </head>
 <body>
  <h1>Send Message</h1>
  <form method="post" action="ml_admin_transact.php">
   <table>
    <tr>
     <td><label for="ml_id">Mailing List:</label></td>
     <td><select name="ml_id" id="ml_id">
       <option value="all">All</option>
```

```php
<?php
$query = 'SELECT ml_id, listname FROM ml_lists ORDER BY listname';
$result = mysql_query($query, $db) or die(mysql_error($db));

while ($row = mysql_fetch_array($result)) {
    echo '<option value="' . $row['ml_id'] . '">' . $row['listname'] .
        '</option>';
}
mysql_free_result($result);
?>
        </select></td>
      </tr><tr>
       <td><label for="subject">Subject:</label></td>
       <td><input type="text" name="subject" id="subject"/></td>
      </tr><tr>
       <td><label for="message">Message:</label></td>
       <td><textarea name="message" id="message" rows="10"
         cols="60"></textarea></td>
      </tr><tr>
       <td> </td>
       <td><input type="submit" name="action" value="Send Message"/></td>
      </tr><tr>
     </table>
    </form>
    <p><a href="ml_admin.php">Back to mailing list administration.</a></p>
   </body>
</html>
```

3. This next script should look a bit familiar. If you remember, this is exactly the same `SimpleMail` class you used in Chapter 11. In case you've lost it, here is the code for `class.SimpleMail.php` again.

```php
<?php
class SimpleMail
{
    private $toAddress;
    private $CCAddress;
    private $BCCAddress;
    private $fromAddress;
    private $subject;
    private $sendText;
    private $textBody;
    private $sendHTML;
    private $HTMLBody;

    public function __construct() {
        $this->toAddress = '';
        $this->CCAddress = '';
        $this->BCCAddress = '';
        $this->fromAddress = '';
        $this->subject = '';
        $this->sendText = true;
```

```
        $this->textBody = '';
        $this->sendHTML = false;
        $this->HTMLBody = '';
    }

    public function setToAddress($value) {
        $this->toAddress = $value;
    }

    public function setCCAddress($value) {
        $this->CCAddress = $value;
    }

    public function setBCCAddress($value) {
        $this->BCCAddress = $value;
    }

    public function setFromAddress($value) {
        $this->fromAddress = $value;
    }

    public function setSubject($value) {
        $this->subject = $value;
    }

    public function setSendText($value) {
        $this->sendText = $value;
    }

    public function setTextBody($value) {
        $this->sendText = true;
        $this->textBody = $value;
    }

    public function setSendHTML($value) {
        $this->sendHTML = $value;
    }

    public function setHTMLBody($value) {
        $this->sendHTML = true;
        $this->HTMLBody = $value;
    }

    public function send($to = null, $subject = null, $message = null,
        $headers = null) {

        $success = false;
        if (!is_null($to) && !is_null($subject) && !is_null($message)) {
            $success = mail($to, $subject, $message, $headers);
            return $success;
        } else {
            $headers = array();
            if (!empty($this->fromAddress)) {
```

```php
            $headers[] = 'From: ' . $this->fromAddress;
        }

        if (!empty($this->CCAddress)) {
            $headers[] = 'CC: ' . $this->CCAddress;
        }

        if (!empty($this->BCCAddress)) {
            $headers[] = 'BCC: ' . $this->BCCAddress;
        }

        if ($this->sendText && !$this->sendHTML) {
            $message = $this->textBody;
        } elseif (!$this->sendText && $this->sendHTML) {
            $headers[] = 'MIME-Version: 1.0';
            $headers[] = 'Content-type: text/html; charset="iso-8859-1"';
            $headers[] = 'Content-Transfer-Encoding: 7bit';
            $message = $this->HTMLBody;
        } elseif ($this->sendText && $this->sendHTML) {
            $boundary = '==MP_Bound_xyccr948x==';
            $headers[] = 'MIME-Version: 1.0';
            $headers[] = 'Content-type: multipart/alternative;
boundary="' .
                $boundary . '"';

            $message = 'This is a Multipart Message in MIME format.'
. "\n";

            $message .= '--' . $boundary . "\n";
            $message .= 'Content-type: text/plain; charset="iso-8859
-1"' .
                "\n";
            $message .= 'Content-Transfer-Encoding: 7bit' . "\n\n";
            $message .= $this->textBody  . "\n";
            $message .= '--' . $boundary . "\n";

            $message .= 'Content-type: text/html; charset="iso-8859-1"'
. "\n";
            $message .= 'Content-Transfer-Encoding: 7bit' . "\n\n";
            $message .= $this->HTMLBody  . "\n";
            $message .= '--' . $boundary . '--';
        }

        $success = mail($this->toAddress, $this->subject, $message,
            join("\r\n", $headers));
        return $success;
        }
    }
}
?>
```

4. There is one last script to enter for the administration portion of the mailing list application. When an administrator clicks a button, you need to have a page that handles the transactions. Enter the following, and save it as `ml_admin_transact.php`:

```php
<?php
require 'db.inc.php';
require 'class.SimpleMail.php';

$db = mysql_connect(MYSQL_HOST, MYSQL_USER, MYSQL_PASSWORD) or
    die ('Unable to connect. Check your connection parameters.');

mysql_select_db(MYSQL_DB, $db) or die(mysql_error($db));

$action = (isset($_REQUEST['action'])) ? $_REQUEST['action'] : '';

switch ($action) {
case 'Subscribe':
    $email = (isset($_POST['email'])) ? $_POST['email'] : '';
    $query = 'SELECT
            user_id
        FROM
            ml_users
        WHERE
            email="' . mysql_real_escape_string($email, $db) . '"';
    $result = mysql_query($query, $db) or die(mysql_error($db));

    if (mysql_num_rows($result) > 0) {
        $row = mysql_fetch_assoc($result);
        $user_id = $row['user_id'];
    } else {
        $first_name = (isset($_POST['first_name'])) ?
            $_POST['first_name'] : '';
        $last_name = (isset($_POST['last_name'])) ?
            $_POST['last_name'] : '';

        $query = 'INSERT INTO ml_users
                (first_name, last_name, email)
            VALUES
                ("' . mysql_real_escape_string($first_name, $db) . '", ' .
                '"' . mysql_real_escape_string($last_name, $db) . '", ' .
                '"' . mysql_real_escape_string($email, $db) . '")';
        mysql_query($query, $db);
        $user_id = mysql_insert_id($db);
    }
    mysql_free_result($result);

    foreach ($_POST['ml_id'] as $ml_id) {
        if (ctype_digit($ml_id)) {
            $query = 'INSERT INTO ml_subscriptions
                    (user_id, ml_id, pending)
                VALUES
                    (' . $user_id . ', ' . $ml_id . ', TRUE)';
```

```
                mysql_query($query, $db);

                $query = 'SELECT listname FROM ml_lists WHERE ml_id = ' .
                    $ml_id;
                $result = mysql_query($query, $db);

                $row = mysql_fetch_assoc($result);
                $listname = $row['listname'];

                $message = 'Hello ' . $first_name . "\n" .
                $message .= 'Our records indicate that you have subscribed ' .
                    'to the ' . $listname . ' mailing list.' . "\n\n";
                $message .= 'If you did not subscribe, please accept our ' .
                    'apologies. You will not be subscribed if you do ' .
                    'not visit the confirmation URL.' . "\n\n";
                $message .= 'If you subscribed, please confirm this by ' .
                    'visiting the following URL: ' .
                    'http://www.example.com/ml_user_transact.php?user_id=' .
                    $user_id . '&ml_id=' . $ml_id . '&action=confirm';

                $mail = new SimpleMail();
                $mail->setToAddress($email);
                $mail->setFromAddress('list@example.com');
                $mail->setSubject('Mailing list confirmation');
                $mail->setTextBody($message);
                $mail->send();
                unset($mail);
            }
        }
        header('Location: ml_thanks.php?user_id=' . $user_id . '&ml_id=' .
            $ml_id . '&type=c');
        break;

    case 'confirm':
        $user_id = (isset($_GET['user_id'])) ? $_GET['user_id'] : '';
        $ml_id = (isset($_GET['ml_id'])) ? $_GET['ml_id'] : '';

        if (!empty($user_id) && !empty($ml_id)) {
            $query = 'UPDATE ml_subscriptions
                SET
                    pending = FALSE
                WHERE
                    user_id = ' . $user_id . ' AND
                    ml_id = ' . $ml_id;
            mysql_query($query, $db);

            $query = 'SELECT
                    listname
                FROM
                    ml_lists
                WHERE
                    ml_id = ' . $ml_id;
```

```php
        $result = mysql_query($query, $db);

        $row = mysql_fetch_assoc($result);
        $listname = $row['listname'];
        mysql_free_result($result);

        $query = 'SELECT
                first_name, email
            FROM
                ml_users
            WHERE
                user_id = ' . $user_id;
        $result = mysql_query($query, $db);

        $row = mysql_fetch_assoc($result);
        $first_name = $row['first_name'];
        $email = $row['email'];
        mysql_free_result($result);

        $message = 'Hello ' . $first_name . ',' . "\n";
        $message .= 'Thank you for subscribing to the ' . $listname .
            ' mailing list.  Welcome!' . "\n\n";
        $message .= 'If you did not subscribe, please accept our ' .
            'apologies.  You can remove' . "\n";
        $message .= 'this subscription immediately by visiting the ' .
            'following URL:' . "\n";
        $message .= 'http://www.example.com/ml_remove.php?user_id=' .
            $user_id . '&ml_id=' . $ml_id;

        $mail = new SimpleMail();
        $mail->setToAddress($email);
        $mail->setFromAddress('list@example.com');
        $mail->setSubject('Mailing list subscription confirmed');
        $mail->setTextBody($message);
        $mail->send();

    header('Location: ml_thanks.php?user_id=' . $user_id . '&ml_id=' .
        $ml_id);
    } else {
        header('Location: ml_user.php');
    }
    break;

case 'Remove':
    $email = (isset($_POST['email'])) ? $_POST['email'] : '';
    if (!empty($email)) {
        $query = 'SELECT
                user_id
            FROM
                ml_users
            WHERE
                email="' . $email . '"';
```

```
        $result = mysql_query($query, $db) or die(mysql_error($db));

        if (mysql_num_rows($result)) {
            $row = mysql_fetch_assoc($result);
            $user_id = $row['user_id'];
        header('Location: ml_remove.php?user_id=' . $user_id .
            '&ml_id=' . $ml_id);
        break;
        }
        header('Location: ml_user.php');
    }
  break;
}
?>
```

5. The first page of the mailing list application you want to take a look at is the Mailing List Administration page. To view it, load `ml_admin.php` in your browser. As you can see in Figure 14-1, you can create a new mailing list or send a quick message to users. You will also be able to delete mailing lists from this page after they have been created. Feel free to create a couple of new mailing lists. Go crazy, have fun, get wacky.

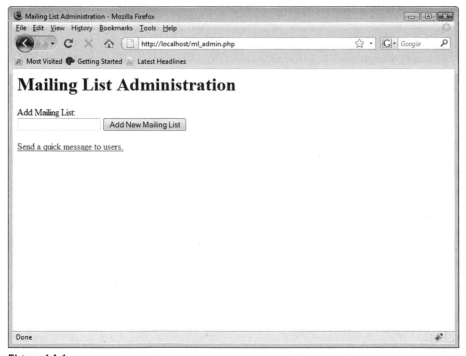

Figure 14-1

6. Click the link at the bottom of the page to send a message to your users. A new page appears where you can compose a new message and send it either to a single mailing list or to the users of all the mailing lists, as shown in Figure 14-2. Since you just created these pages, you don't have any users yet. You can compose a message, but it won't go to anyone. You need to create the user pages, which you'll do shortly.

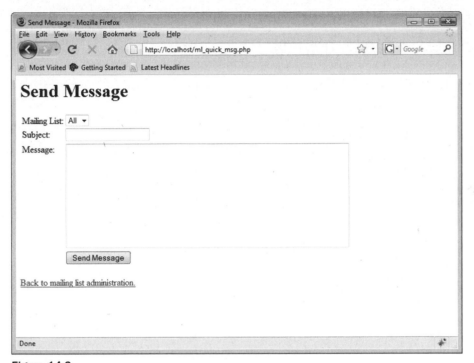

Figure 14-2

How It Works

A common practice is to post a form back to itself, and you certainly could have done that here. In fact, you have done this in earlier projects in this book. When your page contains data that needs to be inserted into a database, however, you need to think twice about a self-posting form. If the user were to refresh or reload the page, all of your database functions would run again, and that could be disastrous. You could end up with duplicate data or delete records you didn't mean to delete.

To minimize that probability, you post to a separate script called ml_admin_transact.php. This page handles all of the necessary database transactions, and then directs you back to the page from which you came. No harm will come to your database if the user reloads the page at that point.

To accommodate having several forms post their information to a central transaction script, all of your submit buttons have the same name, "action," but each has a different value. The transaction script can check the value of the $_POST['action'] variable to see which button was pressed and perform the appropriate actions.

In `ml_admin.php`, you present a form that collects information to be sent to `ml_admin_transact`
`.php`. The first portion of the form is used to create new mailing lists, and is basic HTML because it is
always visible.

```
<form method="post" action="ml_admin_transact.php">
 <p><label for="listname">Add Mailing List:</label><br />
  <input type="text" id="listname" name="listname" maxlength="100" />
  <input type="submit" name="action" value="Add New Mailing List" />
 </p>
```

The second portion of the form allows you to delete a mailing list, and should only be shown if there
are mailing lists available to delete. You first query the database for a list of mailing lists, and if
`mysql_num_rows()` returns a value larger than 0, you display a `select` element populated with the
lists. Each `option` displays the list's name and uses the list's ID as its value.

```
<?php
$query = 'SELECT
        ml_id, listname
     FROM
        ml_lists
     ORDER BY
        listname ASC';
$result = mysql_query($query, $db) or die(mysql_error($db));

if (mysql_num_rows($result) > 0) {
    echo '<p><label for="ml_id">Delete Mailing List:</label><br />';
    echo '<select name="ml_id" id="ml_id">';
    while ($row = mysql_fetch_array($result)) {
        echo '<option value="' . $row['ml_id'] . '">' . $row['listname'] .
            '</option>';
    }
    echo '</select>';
    echo '<input type="submit" name="action" value="Delete ' .
        'Mailing List" />';
    echo '</p>';
}
mysql_free_result($result);
?>
  </form>
```

Most of `ml_quick_msg.php` is HTML, and the PHP code that is used is practically identical to the
code used to build the select in `ml_admin.php`.

```
<form method="post" action="ml_admin_transact.php">
 <table>
  <tr>
   <td><label for="ml_id">Mailing List:</label></td>
   <td><select name="ml_id" id="ml_id">
     <option value="all">All</option>
<?php
$query = 'SELECT ml_id, listname FROM ml_lists ORDER BY listname';
```

```
$result = mysql_query($query, $db) or die(mysql_error($db));

while ($row = mysql_fetch_array($result)) {
    echo '<option value="' . $row['ml_id'] . '">' . $row['listname'] .
        '</option>';
}
mysql_free_result($result);
?>
    </select></td>
  </tr><tr>
   <td><label for="subject">Subject:</label></td>
   <td><input type="text" name="subject" id="subject"/></td>
  </tr><tr>
   <td><label for="message">Message:</label></td>
   <td><textarea name="message" id="message" rows="10"
     cols="60"></textarea></td>
  </tr><tr>
   <td> </td>
   <td><input type="submit" name="action" value="Send Message"/></td>
  </tr><tr>
 </table>
</form>
```

Finally, you come to the real workhorse of the mailing list administrator application, admin_ transact.php. This page is the one to which you post your forms; it will process the information, update the database tables, and send out e-mails as required. It uses the SimpleMail class from Chapter 11 to send e-mail. If you are scratching your head and trying to remember exactly how the class works, then now would be a good time to take a break and review class.SimpleMail.php.

```
require 'class.SimpleMail.php';
```

Did the user click an "action" button? You filter the incoming value of $_POST['action'] and then act on the value accordingly, using a switch statement. Depending on which button was clicked, you're going to perform one of three actions: create a new mailing list, delete an old mailing list, or send a message to the users subscribed to a list.

```
$action = (isset($_POST['action'])) ? $_POST['action'] : '';

switch ($action) {
case 'Add New Mailing List':
    ...
    break;

case 'Delete Mailing List':
    ...
    break;

case 'Send Message':
    ...
    break;
}
```

To add a new mailing list, you filter the incoming list name and insert a new record into the ml_lists table.

```
case 'Add New Mailing List':
    $listname = isset($_POST['listname']) ? $_POST['listname'] : '';
    if (!empty($listname)) {
        $query = 'INSERT INTO ml_lists
                (listname)
            VALUES
                ("' . mysql_real_escape_string($listname, $db) . '")';
        mysql_query($query, $db) or die(mysql_error($db));
    }
    break;
```

Deleting a mailing list is only slightly more complex. Not only must you delete the mailing list itself, but you must also delete any subscriptions to the list.

```
case 'Delete Mailing List':
    $ml_id = isset($_POST['ml_id']) ? $_POST['ml_id'] : '';
    if (ctype_digit($ml_id)) {
        $query = 'DELETE FROM ml_lists WHERE ml_id=' . $ml_id;
        mysql_query($query, $db) or die(mysql_error($db));

        $query = 'DELETE FROM ml_subscriptions WHERE ml_id=' . $ml_id;
        mysql_query($query, $db) or die(mysql_error($db));
    }
    break;
```

The form in ml_quick_msg.php posts the mailing list as the mailing list's ID, which — while great for ml_admin_transact.php — isn't of much use to the subscriber. When you send a message, you want to let the user know which mailing list you are referring to. If the mailing list ID is 'all' instead of a number, you want to reflect that as well:

```
case 'Send Message':
    $ml_id = isset($_POST['ml_id']) ? $_POST['ml_id'] : '';
    $subject = isset($_POST['subject']) ? $_POST['subject'] : '';
    $message = isset($_POST['message']) ? $_POST['message'] : '';

    if ($ml_id == 'all') {
        $listname = 'Master';
    } else if (ctype_digit($ml_id)) {
        $query = 'SELECT
                listname
            FROM
                ml_lists
            WHERE
                ml_id=' . $ml_id;
        $result = mysql_query($query, $db) or die(mysql_error($db));
        $row = mysql_fetch_assoc($result);
        $listname = $row['listname'];
        mysql_free_result($result);
    } else {
        break;
    }
```

What follows is a more complicated SQL statement than you've written thus far, but not too difficult. What's happening here is that you are grabbing the e-mails, first names, and user IDs from the `ml_users` table where the mailing list ID (`ml_id`) matches their user ID in the `ml_subscriptions` table. You do this by using the `INNER JOIN` command in SQL. You also don't want to send any e-mails to those that are awaiting subscription confirmation, so select only those where `pending = FALSE`.

If the administrator did not choose `'all'` in the select list, you must limit your selection to the specific users that are subscribed to the mailing list the administrator selected. You do this by adding on the `AND` condition.

```
$query = 'SELECT DISTINCT
        u.user_id, u.first_name, u.email
    FROM
        ml_users u INNER JOIN ml_subscriptions s ON
            u.user_id = s.user_id
    WHERE
        s.pending = FALSE';
if ($ml_id != 'all') {
    $query .= ' AND s.ml_id = ' . $ml_id;
}
$result = mysql_query($query, $db) or die(mysql_error($db));
```

Finally, you iterate through the returned records with a while loop. Within the loop, you append a footer to the message that will be sent out, explaining how the user can unsubscribe from the mailing list, if he or she wants to. Then you create a new instance of the `SimpleMail` class and set the relevant options, and then the message can be sent on its way.

Notice that you are looping through *each* e-mail address you have and sending an e-mail to each one, using the `send()` method. It is important to note that the page will not finish loading until it has sent every e-mail. This works fine if you have a few e-mail addresses (a few hundred or less). It has the added benefit of allowing you to personalize each e-mail.

If you need to send to more people and don't want to deal with the long wait time, we recommend putting all of your e-mail addresses in the BCC: field of the mail. You can't personalize the e-mail, but the page will load much faster.

```
while ($row = mysql_fetch_assoc($result)) {

    $footer = "\n\n" . '--------------' . "\n";
    if (ctype_digit($ml_id)) {
        $footer .= 'You are receiving this message as a member ' .
            'of the ' . $listname . "\n";
        $footer .= 'mailing list. If you have received this ' .
            'email in error or would like to' . "\n";
        $footer .= 'remove your name from this mailing list, ' .
            'please visit the following URL:' . "\n";
        $footer .= 'http://www.example.com/ml_remove.php?user_id=' .
            $row['user_id'] . "&ml=" . $ml_id;
    } else {
        $footer .= 'You are receiving this email because you ' .
            'subscribed to one or more' . "\n";
        $footer .= 'mailing lists. Visit the following URL to ' .
            'change your subscriptions:' . "\n";
```

```
            $footer .= 'http://www.example.com/ml_user.php?user_id=' .
                $row['user_id'];
        }

    $mail = new SimpleMail();

    $mail->setToAddress($row['email']);
    $mail->setFromAddress('list@example.com');
    $mail->setSubject($subject);
    $mail->setTextBody($message . $footer);

    $mail->send();
    }
    mysql_free_result($result);
    break;
```

After the page is done with its transactions, it redirects the user to the ml_admin.php page.

```
header('Location: ml_admin.php');
```

Sign Me Up!

Now it's time to look at the other half of the application, the Mailing List sign-up form. This is the page your users will use to sign up for any of the mailing lists that you have created. This portion of the application consists of ml_user.php, ml_user_transact.php, ml_thanks.php, and ml_remove.php.

Try It Out   Mailing List Signup

The first task in coding this portion of the application is to create the scripts necessary to sign up subscribers. You will be coding ml_user.php, ml_user_transact.php, and ml_transact.php. You will code ml_remove.php later.

1. Enter the following code in your editor, and save it as ml_user.php:

```
<?php
require 'db.inc.php';

$db = mysql_connect(MYSQL_HOST, MYSQL_USER, MYSQL_PASSWORD) or
    die ('Unable to connect. Check your connection parameters.');

mysql_select_db(MYSQL_DB, $db) or die(mysql_error($db));

$user_id = (isset($_GET['user_id']) && ctype_digit($_GET['user_id'])) ?
    $_GET['user_id'] : '';

$first_name = '';
```

```php
$last_name = '';
$email = '';
$ml_ids = array();

if (!empty($user_id)) {
    $query = 'SELECT
            first_name, last_name, email
        FROM
            ml_users
        WHERE
            user_id = ' . $user_id;
    $result = mysql_query($query, $db) or die(mysql_error($db));
    if (mysql_num_rows($result) > 0) {
        $row = mysql_fetch_assoc($result);
        extract($row);
    }
    mysql_free_result($result);

    $query = 'SELECT ml_id FROM ml_subscriptions WHERE user_id = ' . $user_id;
    $result = mysql_query($query, $db) or die(mysql_error($db));
    while ($row = mysql_fetch_assoc($result)) {
        $ml_ids[] = $row['ml_id'];
    }
    mysql_free_result($result);
}
?>
<html>
 <head>
  <title>Mailing List Signup</title>
 </head>
 <body>
  <h1>Sign up for Mailing List:</h1>
  <form method="post" action="ml_user_transact.php">
   <table>
    <tr>
     <td><label for="email">Email Address:</label></td>
     <td><input type="text" name="email" id="email" value="<?php echo
$email; ?>"/>
     </td>
    </tr>
   </table>
   <p>If you aren't currently a member, please provide your name:</p>
   <table>
    <tr>
     <td><label for="first_name">First Name:</label></td>
     <td><input type="text" name="first_name" id="first_name"
       value="<?php echo $first_name; ?>"/></td>
    </tr><tr>
     <td><label for="last_name">Last Name:</label></td>
     <td><input type="text" name="last_name" id="last_name"
       value="<?php echo $last_name; ?>"/></td>
    </tr>
   </table>
```

```
   <p>Select the mailing lists you want to receive:</p>
   <p>
   <select name="ml_id[]" multiple="multiple">
<?php
$query = 'SELECT
       ml_id, listname
   FROM
       ml_lists
   ORDER BY
       listname ASC';
$result = mysql_query($query, $db) or die(mysql_error($db));

print_r($ml_ids);
while ($row = mysql_fetch_array($result)) {
    if (in_array($row['ml_id'], $ml_ids)) {
        echo '<option value="' . $row['ml_id'] . '" selected="selected">';
    } else {
        echo '<option value="' . $row['ml_id'] . '">';
    }
    echo $row['listname'] . '</option>';
}
mysql_free_result($result);
?>
   </select>
   </p>
   <p><input type="submit" name="action" value="Subscribe" /></p>
  </form>
 </body>
</html>
```

2. Enter the transaction page by entering the following and saving it as `ml_user_transact`
    `.php`:

```
<?php
require 'db.inc.php';
require 'class.SimpleMail.php';

$db = mysql_connect(MYSQL_HOST, MYSQL_USER, MYSQL_PASSWORD) or
    die ('Unable to connect. Check your connection parameters.');

mysql_select_db(MYSQL_DB, $db) or die(mysql_error($db));

$action = (isset($_REQUEST['action'])) ? $_REQUEST['action'] : '';

switch ($action) {
case 'Subscribe':
    $email = (isset($_POST['email'])) ? $_POST['email'] : '';
    $query = 'SELECT
            user_id
        FROM
            ml_users
```

```
    WHERE
        email="' . mysql_real_escape_string($email, $db) . '"';
$result = mysql_query($query, $db) or die(mysql_error($db));

if (mysql_num_rows($result) > 0) {
    $row = mysql_fetch_assoc($result);
    $user_id = $row['user_id'];
} else {
    $first_name = (isset($_POST['first_name'])) ?
        $_POST['first_name'] : '';
    $last_name = (isset($_POST['last_name'])) ?
        $_POST['last_name'] : '';

    $query = 'INSERT INTO ml_users
            (first_name, last_name, email)
        VALUES
            ("' . mysql_real_escape_string($first_name, $db) . '", ' .
            '"' . mysql_real_escape_string($last_name, $db) . '", ' .
            '"' . mysql_real_escape_string($email, $db) . '")';
    mysql_query($query, $db);
    $user_id = mysql_insert_id($db);
}
mysql_free_result($result);

foreach ($_POST['ml_id'] as $ml_id) {
    if (ctype_digit($ml_id)) {
        $query = 'INSERT INTO ml_subscriptions
                (user_id, ml_id, pending)
            VALUES
                (' . $user_id . ', ' . $ml_id . ', TRUE)';
        mysql_query($query, $db);

        $query = 'SELECT listname FROM ml_lists WHERE ml_id = ' .
            $ml_id;
        $result = mysql_query($query, $db);

        $row = mysql_fetch_assoc($result);
        $listname = $row['listname'];

        $message = 'Hello ' . $first_name . "\n" .
        $message .= 'Our records indicate that you have subscribed ' .
            'to the ' . $listname . ' mailing list.' . "\n\n";
        $message .= 'If you did not subscribe, please accept our ' .
            'apologies. You will not be subscribed if you do ' .
            'not visit the confirmation URL.' . "\n\n";
        $message .= 'If you subscribed, please confirm this by ' .
            'visiting the following URL: ' .
            'http://example.com/ml_user_transact.php?user_id=' .
            $user_id . '&ml_id=' . $ml_id . '&action=confirm';

        $mail = new SimpleMail();
```

```
                    $mail->setToAddress($email);
                    $mail->setFromAddress('list@example.com');
                    $mail->setSubject('Mailing list confirmation');
                    $mail->setTextBody($message);
                    $mail->send();
                    unset($mail);
                }
        }
        header('Location: ml_thanks.php?user_id=' . $user_id . '&ml_id=' .
            $ml_id . '&type=c');
        break;

    case 'confirm':
        $user_id = (isset($_GET['user_id'])) ? $_GET['user_id'] : '';
        $ml_id = (isset($_GET['ml_id'])) ? $_GET['ml_id'] : '';

        if (!empty($user_id) && !empty($ml_id)) {
            $query = 'UPDATE ml_subscriptions
                SET
                    pending = FALSE
                WHERE
                    user_id = ' . $user_id . ' AND
                    ml_id = ' . $ml_list;
            mysql_query($query, $db);

            $query = 'SELECT
                    listname
                FROM
                    ml_lists
                WHERE
                    ml_id = ' . $ml_id;
            $result = mysql_query($query, $db);

            $row = mysql_fetch_assoc($result);
            $listname = $row['listname'];
            mysql_free_result($result);

            $query = 'SELECT
                    first_name, email
                FROM
                    ml_users
                WHERE
                    user_id = ' . $user_id;
            $result = mysql_query($query, $db);

            $row = mysql_fetch_assoc($result);
            $first_name = $row['first_name'];
            $email = $row['email'];
            mysql_free_result($result);

            $message = 'Hello ' . $first_name . ',' . "\n";
```

```php
    $message .= 'Thank you for subscribing to the ' . $listname .
        ' mailing list.  Welcome!' . "\n\n";
    $message .= 'If you did not subscribe, please accept our ' .
        'apologies.  You can remove' . "\n";
    $message .= 'this subscription immediately by visiting the ' .
        'following URL:' . "\n";
    $message .= 'http://example.com/ml_remove.php?user_id=' .
        $user_id . '&ml_id=' . $ml_id;

    $mail = new SimpleMail();
    $mail->setToAddress($email);
    $mail->setFromAddress('list@example.com');
    $mail->setSubject('Mailing list subscription confirmed');
    $mail->setTextBody($message);
    $mail->send();

    header('Location: ml_thanks.php?user_id=' . $user_id . '&ml_id=' .
        $ml_id . '&type=s');
    } else {
        header('Location: ml_user.php');
    }
    break;
}
?>
```

3. You may have noticed when entering the last script that you are redirecting your users to a page called ml_thanks.php. It would probably be a good idea to create that page now, by entering the following code and saving it as ml_thanks.php:

```php
<html>
 <head>
  <title>Thank You</title>
 </head>
 <body>
<?php
require 'db.inc.php';

$db = mysql_connect(MYSQL_HOST, MYSQL_USER, MYSQL_PASSWORD) or
    die ('Unable to connect. Check your connection parameters.');

mysql_select_db(MYSQL_DB, $db) or die(mysql_error($db));

$user_id = (isset($_GET['user_id'])) ? $_GET['user_id'] : '';
$ml_id = (isset($_GET['ml_id'])) ? $_GET['ml_id'] : '';
$type = (isset($_GET['type'])) ? $_GET['type'] : '';

if (empty($user_id)) {
    die('No user id available.');
}
```

```php
$query = 'SELECT first_name, email FROM ml_users WHERE user_id = ' .
    $user_id;
$result = mysql_query($query, $db) or die(mysql_error());

if (mysql_num_rows($result) > 0) {
    $row = mysql_fetch_assoc($result);
    $first_name = $row['first_name'];
    $email = $row['email'];
} else {
    die('No match for user id.');
}
mysql_free_result($result);

if (empty($ml_id)) {
    die('No mailing list id available.');
}
$query = 'SELECT listname FROM ml_lists WHERE ml_id = ' . $ml_id;
$result = mysql_query($query, $db) or die(mysql_error());

if (mysql_num_rows($result)) {
    $row = mysql_fetch_assoc($result);
    $listname = $row['listname'];
} else {
    die ('No match for mailing list id');
}
mysql_free_result($result);

if ($type == 'c') {
    echo '<h1>Thank You ' . $first_name . '</h1>';
    echo '<p>A confirmation for subscribing to the ' . $listname .
' mailing list ' .
        'has been sent to ' . $email . '.</p>';
} else {
    echo '<h1>Thank You ' . $first_name . '</h1>';
    echo '<p>Thank you for subscribing to the ' . $listname . '
mailing list.</p>';
}
?>
 </body>
</html>
```

4. Open your browser, and open `ml_user.php`. You should see a form that looks very much like the one in Figure 14-3.

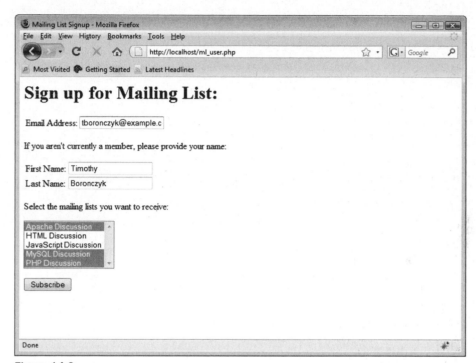

Figure 14-3

5. Enter your e-mail address and your first and last name, choose one or more mailing lists to subscribe to, and click Subscribe.

    You should see a Thank You screen (shown in Figure 14-4) and receive a confirmation e-mail at the e-mail address you supplied.

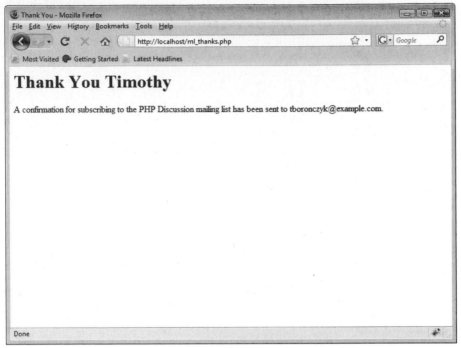

Figure 14-4

6. Open the confirmation e-mail. There will be a link at the bottom (or a non-linked URL, if you are using a text e-mail client).

7. Click the link, and it takes you back to the Thank You page, this time thanking you for confirming your subscription. You will get another e-mail informing you about your subscription, with a link that allows you to remove yourself from the mailing list. Don't click that link just yet!

8. Open `ml_admin.php`, and then click the link at the bottom, "Send a quick message to users."

9. In the Quick Message page, choose a mailing list that you just subscribed to in the previous steps, and enter a subject. Then type a quick message.

10. Click Send Message.

11. Open your e-mail client again, and read the message you should have received.

How It Works

Excellent job! Now that you've written and tested your code, it's time for us to explain how it all works. Typically, ml_user.php will display a blank form. Occasionally, you may want the fields to be populated with the subscriber's information, and so you pass the user ID of the subscriber along in the URL. ml_user.php will use the ID to look up the information in the database and pre-populate the form's fields.

You filter the incoming user ID (if it appears in the URL) and initialize the variables that are used in displaying the form to blank values:

```
$user_id = (isset($_GET['user_id']) && ctype_digit($_GET['user_id'])) ?
    $_GET['user_id'] : '';

$first_name = '';
$last_name = '';
$email = '';
$ml_ids = array();
```

If a user's ID has been supplied, then you retrieve the information from the database and populate the variables you just initialized:

```
if (!empty($user_id)) {
    $query = 'SELECT
            first_name, last_name, email
        FROM
            ml_users
        WHERE
            user_id = ' . $user_id;
    $result = mysql_query($query, $db) or die(mysql_error($db));
    if (mysql_num_rows($result) > 0) {
        $row = mysql_fetch_assoc($result);
        extract($row);
    }
    mysql_free_result($result);

    $query = 'SELECT ml_id FROM ml_subscriptions WHERE user_id = ' .
$user_id;
    $result = mysql_query($query, $db) or die(mysql_error($db));
    while ($row = mysql_fetch_assoc($result)) {
        $ml_ids[] = $row['ml_id'];
    }
    mysql_free_result($result);
}
```

Displaying the fields to collect the subscriber's e-mail address, first name, and last name is pretty straightforward. You output the variables' contents for the field's value attributes, so if a user ID has been provided, then the fields will appear pre-populated. Since the variables were initialized with blank default values, the fields will be empty if no valid user ID has been received.

You need to again query the database when you display the select field. You retrieve all the IDs and names of the mailing lists, and then iterate through them to generate the select's options. During each run through the loop, you check the current record's ml_id to see if the user is subscribed to it, and if so, then you set the option as selected, so all of the lists the user is subscribed to will be selected when the form is pre-populated.

```
<select name="ml_id[]" multiple="multiple">
<?php
$query = 'SELECT
        ml_id, listname
    FROM
        ml_lists
    ORDER BY
        listname ASC';
$result = mysql_query($query, $db) or die(mysql_error($db));

print_r($ml_ids);
while ($row = mysql_fetch_array($result)) {
    if (in_array($row['ml_id'], $ml_ids)) {
        echo '<option value="' . $row['ml_id'] . '" selected="selected">';
    } else {
        echo '<option value="' . $row['ml_id'] . '">';
    }
    echo $row['listname'] . '</option>';
}
mysql_free_result($result);
?>
    </select>
```

The ml_thanks.php is almost not worth mentioning because its PHP code is something you should already be familiar with at this point. It accepts the subscriber's user ID (user_id), the ID of the mailing list he or she subscribed to (ml_id), and the type of thank you message it should display (type) from the URL. After filtering them, the page displays the appropriate thank you message to the subscriber.

The real action happens in ml_user_transact.php, which handles creating and updating subscribers' records in the database.

You filter the incoming value of $_REQUEST['action'] and then act on the value accordingly, using a switch statement. Depending on which action is requested, you either subscribe a user to a mailing list or confirm a user's subscription.

```
$action = (isset($_REQUEST['action'])) ? $_REQUEST['action'] : '';

switch ($action) {
case 'Subscribe':
    ...
    break;

case 'confirm':
    ...
    break;
}
```

If the user was sent to ml_user_transact.php because he or she clicked the Subscribe button of ml_user.php's form, you subscribe him or her to the appropriate lists. A number of things have to be done for this to happen. First, you must look up the e-mail address that was provided, to see if the user already exists in the `ml_user` table and retrieve the user's ID. If the user doesn't exist, then you create a new record for the user, including his or her first and last name. Once a record is created, then you use `mysql_insert_id()` to retrieve the user's ID.

```
case 'Subscribe':
    $email = (isset($_POST['email'])) ? $_POST['email'] : '';
    $query = 'SELECT
            user_id
        FROM
            ml_users
        WHERE
            email="' . mysql_real_escape_string($email, $db) . '"';
    $result = mysql_query($query, $db) or die(mysql_error($db));

    if (mysql_num_rows($result) > 0) {
        $row = mysql_fetch_assoc($result);
        $user_id = $row['user_id'];
    } else {
        $first_name = (isset($_POST['first_name'])) ?
            $_POST['first_name'] : '';
        $last_name = (isset($_POST['last_name'])) ?
            $_POST['last_name'] : '';

        $query = 'INSERT INTO ml_users
                (first_name, last_name, email)
            VALUES
                ("' . mysql_real_escape_string($first_name, $db) . '", ' .
                '"' . mysql_real_escape_string($last_name, $db) . '", ' .
                '"' . mysql_real_escape_string($email, $db) . '")';
        mysql_query($query, $db);
        $user_id = mysql_insert_id($db);
    }
    mysql_free_result($result);
```

Then you loop through each mailing list the user wants to subscribe to, and create an entry in the `ml_subscriptions` table that links the user's ID to the list's ID. The record's status is also set to pending at this point, with `pending` set to `TRUE`.

You send the new user an e-mail informing him or her of the new subscription, using the `SimpleMail` class from Chapter 11. The subscription will not be active until the user visits a link you provide in the e-mail for the user to confirm the subscription.

```
foreach ($_POST['ml_id'] as $ml_id) {
    if (ctype_digit($ml_id)) {
        $query = 'INSERT INTO ml_subscriptions
                (user_id, ml_id, pending)
            VALUES
                (' . $user_id . ', ' . $ml_id . ', TRUE)';
        mysql_query($query, $db);

        $query = 'SELECT listname FROM ml_lists WHERE ml_id = ' .
            $ml_id;
```

```
            $result = mysql_query($query, $db);

            $row = mysql_fetch_assoc($result);
            $listname = $row['listname'];

            $message = 'Hello ' . $first_name . "\n" .
            $message .= 'Our records indicate that you have subscribed ' .
                'to the ' . $listname . ' mailing list.' . "\n\n";
            $message .= 'If you did not subscribe, please accept our ' .
                'apologies. You will not be subscribed if you do ' .
                'not visit the confirmation URL.' . "\n\n";
            $message .= 'If you subscribed, please confirm this by ' .
                'visiting the following URL: ' .
                'http://www.example.com/ml_user_transact.php?user_id=' .
                $user_id . '&ml_id=' . $ml_id . '&action=confirm';

            $mail = new SimpleMail();
            $mail->setToAddress($email);
            $mail->setFromAddress('list@example.com');
            $mail->setSubject('Mailing list confirmation');
            $mail->setTextBody($message);
            $mail->send();
            unset($mail);
        }
    }
    header('Location: ml_thanks.php?user_id=' . $user_id . '&ml_id=' .
        $ml_id . '&type=c');
```

When the user visits the link you provided in the confirmation e-mail, he or she should be taken to ml_user_transact.php, and the "confirm" branch of the switch statement is executed. Here is where you validate the incoming user ID and list ID and update the user's records in the ml_subscriptions table, so the subscription is no longer marked pending. You then retrieve the user's first name and e-mail address, to send another e-mail to inform him or her of the subscription's change in status.

```
    case 'confirm':
        $user_id = (isset($_GET['user_id'])) ? $_GET['user_id'] : '';
        $ml_id = (isset($_GET['ml_id'])) ? $_GET['ml_id'] : '';

        if (!empty($user_id) && !empty($ml_id)) {
            $query = 'UPDATE ml_subscriptions
                SET
                    pending = FALSE
                WHERE
                    user_id = ' . $user_id . ' AND
                    ml_id = ' . $ml_id;
            mysql_query($query, $db);

            $query = 'SELECT
                    listname
```

```
            FROM
                ml_lists
            WHERE
                ml_id = ' . $ml_id;
        $result = mysql_query($query, $db);

        $row = mysql_fetch_assoc($result);
        $listname = $row['listname'];
        mysql_free_result($result);

        $query = 'SELECT
                first_name, email
            FROM
                ml_users
            WHERE
                user_id = ' . $user_id;
        $result = mysql_query($query, $db);

        $row = mysql_fetch_assoc($result);
        $first_name = $row['first_name'];
        $email = $row['email'];
        mysql_free_result($result);

        $message = 'Hello ' . $first_name . ',' . "\n";
        $message .= 'Thank you for subscribing to the ' . $listname .
            ' mailing list.  Welcome!' . "\n\n";
        $message .= 'If you did not subscribe, please accept our ' .
            'apologies.  You can remove' . "\n";
        $message .= 'this subscription immediately by visiting the ' .
            'following URL:' . "\n";
        $message .= 'http://www.example.com/ml_remove.php?user_id=' .
            $user_id . '&ml_id=' . $ml_id;

        $mail = new SimpleMail();
        $mail->setToAddress($email);
        $mail->setFromAddress('list@example.com');
        $mail->setSubject('Mailing list subscription confirmed');
        $mail->setTextBody($message);
        $mail->send();

header('Location: ml_thanks.php?user_id=' . $user_id . '&ml_id=' .
    $ml_id);
} else {
    header('Location: ml_user.php');
}
break;
```

Now that you've given users the ability to add themselves to your mailing lists, you need to give them the ability to remove themselves, if they want. The e-mails that you send have a link allowing your users to remove themselves from the mailing lists, if they so desire.

1.   Enter this code, and save it as `ml_remove.php`:

```php
<html>
 <head>
  <title>Remove Subscription</title>
 </head>
 <body>
  <h1>Remove Subscription</h1>
<?php
require 'db.inc.php';

$db = mysql_connect(MYSQL_HOST, MYSQL_USER, MYSQL_PASSWORD) or
    die ('Unable to connect. Check your connection parameters.');

mysql_select_db(MYSQL_DB, $db) or die(mysql_error($db));

$user_id = (isset($_GET['user_id']) && ctype_digit($_GET['user_id'])) ?
    $_GET['user_id'] : -1;

$ml_id = (isset($_GET['ml_id']) && ctype_digit($_GET['ml_id'])) ?
    $_GET['ml_id'] : -1;

if (empty($user_id) || empty($ml_id)) {
    die('Incorrect parameters passed.');
}
$query = 'DELETE FROM ml_subscriptions WHERE user_id = ' . $user_id . '
    AND ml_id = ' . $ml_id;
mysql_query($query, $db) or die(mysql_error());

$query = 'SELECT listname FROM ml_lists WHERE ml_id = ' . $ml_id;
$result = mysql_query($query, $db) or die(mysql_error($db));
if (mysql_num_rows($result) == 0) {
    die('Unknown list.');
}
$row = mysql_fetch_array($result);
$listname = $row['listname'];
mysql_free_result($result);

echo '<p>You have been removed from the ' . $listname . ' mailing list</p>';
echo '<p><a href="ml_user.php?user_id=' . $user_id . '">Return to Mailing ' .
    'List Signup page.</a></p>';
?>
 </body>
</html>
```

2. Go back to the e-mail you sent yourself earlier, and find the link at the bottom of it. Click it to remove yourself from the mailing list. You should see the Removal page, as shown in Figure 14-5. If you send another message to that mailing list, then that message should not be sent to your e-mail address.

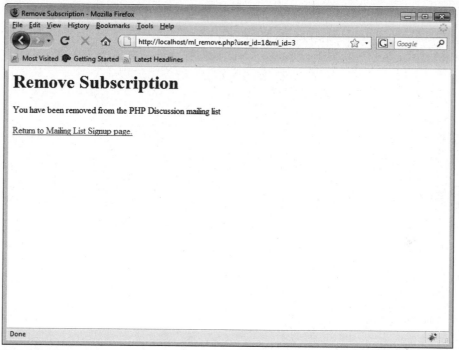

Figure 14-5

How It Works

Users can remove themselves from a mailing list by following the link at the bottom of any e-mail they receive from the list. The link directs the user to the ml_remove.php page, which requires two parameters, the user's ID and the mailing list's ID, to be supplied in the URL.

You take in and filter the user's ID and the list's ID, and then use them in a DELETE query against the ml_subscriptions table, to remove the user's subscription.

```
$user_id = (isset($_GET['user_id']) && ctype_digit($_GET['user_id'])) ?
    $_GET['user_id'] : -1;

$ml_id = (isset($_GET['ml_id']) && ctype_digit($_GET['ml_id'])) ?
    $_GET['ml_id'] : -1;

if (empty($user_id) || empty($ml_id)) {
    die('Incorrect parameters passed.');
}
$query = 'DELETE FROM ml_subscriptions WHERE user_id = ' . $user_id . '
    AND ml_id = ' . $ml_id;
mysql_query($query, $db) or die(mysql_error());
```

Afterwards, you retrieve the name of the mailing list from the `ml_lists` table and use it to display a message telling the user that the removal has taken place.

```
$query = 'SELECT listname FROM ml_lists WHERE ml_id = ' . $ml_id;
$result = mysql_query($query, $db) or die(mysql_error($db));
if (mysql_num_rows($result) == 0) {
    die('Unknown list.');
}
$row = mysql_fetch_array($result);
$listname = $row['listname'];
mysql_free_result($result);

echo '<p>You have been removed from the ' . $listname . ' mailing list</p>';
echo '<p><a href="ml_user.php?user_id=' . $user_id . '">Return to Mailing ' .
    'List Signup page.</a></p>';
```

Mailing List Ethics

You should know about a couple of ethical issues when dealing with the world of mailing lists, namely spam and opt-in/opt-out. This section represents our personal soap box for airing our opinions about them. Although these are our opinions, however, you may want to pay close attention.

A Word about Spam

With the advent of the computer, mailing lists have been brought to a whole new level. Now you can be (and no doubt are) told on a daily basis that Sally really wants you to visit her web site, and that a little blue pill will solve all of your personal problems. Yes, occasionally an e-mail sits in your inbox informing you of new job postings, new posts on PHPBuilder.com, or tour dates for Jimmy Buffett. But we think you know what mailing lists are primarily used for: spam!

For those of you just crawling out of a suspended animation chamber, *spam* is a term used to describe a shotgun approach to advertising. You simply send your e-mail advertisement to as many people as you possibly can, in the hopes that a certain small percentage of them will actually respond.

What is our point? SPAM is a luncheon meat. You spell it in all capital letters, and you enjoy it on your sandwiches. Spam, on the other hand isn't so tasty. It's another name for unsolicited commercial e-mail. It is spelled in all lowercase, and we shun it.

The bottom line: Don't use mailing lists to send spam. Your mother would be *very* disappointed.

Opt-In versus Opt-Out

You may have heard the terms opt-in and opt-out before. What do they mean? To most of your users, probably not much. Users simply answer the questions on your registration, read the fine print, and click the Submit button. However, you aren't a user anymore — at least, not on your own site. You are the administrator. You need to understand the difference between opt-in and opt-out because it may mean the difference between annoyance and acceptance from your users.

Opt-in and opt-out are fancy ways of asking, "What is the default choice for your users?" Opt-in means the user is not currently scheduled to receive a specific newsletter, but he or she may *opt* to subscribe. Obviously, opt-out is the opposite — your user will automatically receive notifications unless he or she *opts* to remove him- or herself from that mailing list.

Why the difference? As the administrator, you may sometimes have to walk a fine line between satisfying your advertisers (the ones that might be giving you money to keep your site alive) and your users (the ones visiting your site, keeping your advertisers happy by driving up the number of hits). If an advertiser pays you enough, you might agree to automatically send advertisements from that company unless the user explicitly chooses not to receive them (opt-out).

However, you might have a newsletter you send once per week that contains, for example, details of comic conventions throughout the country (or even the world). Not all visitors to your site will be interested in that, but if any are, they can subscribe to the newsletter so they will always be notified (opt-in).

As we mentioned, you walk a fine line when choosing between the two. Because this is a new web site for you, the decision might not be that difficult. But as your site grows, interest increases, and companies want to advertise with you, you'll need to make these important decisions. For now, we suggest you make all mailing lists opt-in, with the exception of important site announcements.

Summary

You have just created a nice, relatively simple mailing list subscription application. You have the ability to create new mailing lists, delete old ones, and send e-mails to multiple recipients. Users can subscribe to and unsubscribe from any mailing lists, and you added a step for confirmation to help stamp out abuse.

We hope you come away from this chapter with an understanding of the difference between good, informative mass e-mails and spam.

Mailing lists are good. Spam is bad. Any questions? Good. Next, we'll take a look at how to sell your SPAM collection on your web site.

Exercises

1. **Hide your users' addresses:** Modify the send message functionality to send the e-mails to your users, using the BCC: e-mail field, instead of the usual To: field.

2. **Reduce sending:** Modify the send message functionality to send e-mails to your users in groups of 10. That is, every e-mail that is sent should be sent to 10 users at a time (when possible), instead of one e-mail per user.

3. **Let the administrator know:** Add functionality to send an e-mail to an administrator when new users confirm their subscription to the mailing list.

4. **Clean up any leftovers:** Add functionality to the administration page to allow an admin to purge the database of any subscriptions that haven't yet been confirmed.

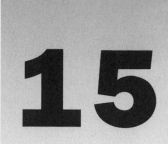

Online Stores

Some of us cringe when we hear the word "e-commerce" and the phrase "selling over the Internet." Perhaps we've had a bad experience ourselves, or the thought of opening an online store is just too overwhelming. Even though this is the part of the book that all geeks out there probably dread reading, we're here to show you that e-commerce is nothing to fear and that pretty much anyone can do it.

However, the fact that anyone can do it doesn't mean it's always done the right way. Done the wrong way, your site can look downright cheesy. Done the right way, your site can look professional and inviting and become an excellent resource for your visitors and potential customers. There are definite guidelines for selling things over the web, and we want to make sure you do things the right way.

Selling things from your web site can not only put some extra cash in your pocket, but it can enhance your relationship with your web site visitors as well, even if e-commerce is not your site's primary function. In the case of your comic book fan site, offering pertinent items can make your site more interactive and interesting. It can bring in new visitors who may not have known about your site before, and keep visitors coming back to see what new items you have for sale. True comic book fans will appreciate the niche of items you are providing, especially if some of the items are unique or hard to come by.

This chapter discusses the following:

- ❑   Creating a simple shopping-cart script.
- ❑   Ideas to improve your script.
- ❑   The basics of e-commerce.

Adding E-Commerce to the Comic Book Fan Site

The time has come to incorporate an e-commerce section into your Comic Book Appreciation fan site. You will need a few things to get started:

❑ Something to sell.

❑ Some mechanism for your customers to pick what they want to buy.

❑ Some way for your customers to pay for what they want to buy.

❑ Some process to get the merchandise to your customers.

Let's break it down and talk about each of these things individually. The first two we can help you with, but the second two are really beyond a general discussion and outside the scope of this book.

Something to Sell

Before you can sell something, you have to have something to sell. Retailers spend millions of dollars a year researching what will sell, what won't, what the hottest trends are, and what the latest technology has to offer. All that being said, your ideas for products will probably come from one or more of the following categories:

❑ **Your own knowledge:** You will most likely know what your customers want, based on your knowledge of the focus of your web site. For example, if you have a site for collectors of old tractors, then you probably know what products would appeal to your typical customer because *you* are the typical customer.

❑ **Something you yourself couldn't easily find:** You also may have been looking for a specific product or group of products, only to find that they did not exist on one particular site until you created it and pulled them all together. (For example, one of this book's authors created www.giftsforengineers.com to be a compilation of products that appeal to engineers.)

❑ **Your own inventions:** Another item you might sell from your site is a new invention or design you have created. Many budding artists and inventors sell their wares on the web, where they can reach a multitude of potential buyers.

❑ **Promotion of your site:** Many other web sites offer promotional items for sale that tout the URL of their site. This acts as a win-win for both parties; the customers can proclaim their support for a cool site, and the site makes a few bucks and gets its name out there for all to see.

So whether you're reinventing the wheel, selling specific types of wheels, taking a bunch of wheels and putting them together, or just selling wheels with your name on them, you must create a product base.

You will be selling items from a few different categories at your CBA site. To spice things up a bit, we decided it would be great to have some fun with this:

❑ T-shirts, bumper stickers, and coffee mugs with the CBA logo.

❑ Superhero suits with customizable color schemes and monogrammed torso letters.

❑ Two different types of grappling hooks for all our superheroes' needs.

You will be expanding on these products later and adding them to your product catalog.

A Shopping Cart

Now that you know what you are going to sell, you need some way for your customers to choose the specific products they want to buy. This involves a shopping cart. You can hook yourself up with ready-made shopping-cart software, or you can use a cart straight from a programming script, such as PHP. Because we're on this topic, we may as well talk a little bit about the pros and cons of each.

Shopping-Cart Software

Numerous shopping-cart software packages are available that can easily hook your customers up and make it easy for them to pick what they want. These software packages can also take care of things such as security, complex product option selection, maintaining customer information, and keeping track of previously placed orders. The price of these packages ranges from free to very expensive.

An example of shopping-cart software is Cart32. Available at `www.cart32.com`, this is a widely used shopping-cart program that provides numerous configuration options. Features include web-based administration of your cart and pending/sent orders, the ability to use your own database or theirs to store product and customer information, automatic credit card processing and e-mail confirmations, complex product options and discount structures, online tracking through the major shipping carriers for your customers to track their orders, inventory management, and customization of the look of your cart. Many web-hosting companies have chosen Cart32 as the cart they offer their customers.

This type of shopping cart application is popular because it enables you to get your store up and running with relative ease, and because it takes care of the security issues for you.

Your Own Cart Software Code

The largest problem you face whenever you depend on someone else to supply a portion of your site is that you are at the mercy of their service, their servers, and their software. If a third party is hosting your shopping cart for you, when the provider is experiencing downtime, so may your site. If their servers catch a virus or are affected by malware, it can affect you and your customers, too. Plus, there may be a function you need that the third party does not offer, or the cost to activate it may be prohibitive for your fledgling web site. Whatever your reason, you may want to code your own shopping-cart application.

You'll start with a very simple shopping-cart system that will consist of several files:

❏ `db_ch15-1.php` creates the main tables in the database for this application.

❏ `db_ch15-2.php` populates the tables with initial product information.

❏ `ecomm_shop.php` displays the inventory for your store by listing the available products.

❏ `ecomm_view_product.php` retrieves detailed information about a single product.

❏ `ecomm_update_cart.php` adds, deletes, or changes quantities of a product in the shopping cart.

❏ `ecomm_view_cart.php` displays the contents of the shopping cart.

❏ `ecomm_checkout.php` is the first step in the checkout process; this is where the customer enters billing and shipping information.

❑ ecomm_checkout2.php is the second step in the checkout process; this is where customers verify the accuracy of their orders.

❑ ecomm_checkout3.php is the final step of the checkout process, where the customer actually sends the order to you, and receives an order number and confirmation. The information is put into the database and deleted from the temporary table, a customer number is assigned (if it's a new customer), and an order number is assigned, as well. E-mail confirmations are sent to the customer and to you.

Try It Out   Defining the Database and Tables

In this exercise, you'll create a run-once script that creates the database tables for this chapter's project.

1. Open your text editor, and type the following code:

```php
<?php
require 'db.inc.php';

$db = mysql_connect(MYSQL_HOST, MYSQL_USER, MYSQL_PASSWORD) or
    die ('Unable to connect. Check your connection parameters.');
mysql_select_db(MYSQL_DB, $db) or die(mysql_error($db));

// define the products table
$query = 'CREATE TABLE IF NOT EXISTS ecomm_products (
        product_code  CHAR(5)       NOT NULL,
        name          VARCHAR(100)  NOT NULL,
        description   MEDIUMTEXT,
        price         DEC(6,2)      NOT NULL,

        PRIMARY KEY(product_code)
    )
    ENGINE=MyISAM';
mysql_query($query, $db) or die(mysql_error($db));

// define the customers table
$query = 'CREATE TABLE IF NOT EXISTS ecomm_customers (
        customer_id INTEGER UNSIGNED NOT NULL AUTO_INCREMENT,
        first_name  VARCHAR(20)      NOT NULL,
        last_name   VARCHAR(20)      NOT NULL,
        address_1   VARCHAR(50)      NOT NULL,
        address_2   VARCHAR(50),
        city        VARCHAR (20)     NOT NULL,
        state       CHAR(2)          NOT NULL,
        zip_code    CHAR(5)          NOT NULL,
        phone       CHAR(12)         NOT NULL,
        email       VARCHAR(100)     NOT NULL,

        PRIMARY KEY (customer_id)
    )
    ENGINE=MyISAM';
mysql_query($query, $db) or die(mysql_error($db));

// define the general order table
```

```
$query = 'CREATE TABLE IF NOT EXISTS ecomm_orders (
        order_id                INTEGER UNSIGNED NOT NULL AUTO_INCREMENT,
        order_date              DATE             NOT NULL,
        customer_id             INTEGER UNSIGNED NOT NULL,
        cost_subtotal           DEC(7,2)         NOT NULL,
        cost_shipping           DEC (6,2),
        cost_tax                DEC(6,2),
        cost_total              DEC(7,2)         NOT NULL,
        shipping_first_name     VARCHAR(20)      NOT NULL,
        shipping_last_name      VARCHAR(20)      NOT NULL,
        shipping_address_1      VARCHAR(50)      NOT NULL,
        shipping_address_2      VARCHAR(50),
        shipping_city           VARCHAR (20)     NOT NULL,
        shipping_state          CHAR(2)          NOT NULL,
        shipping_zip_code       CHAR(5)          NOT NULL,
        shipping_phone          CHAR(12)         NOT NULL,
        shipping_email          VARCHAR(100)     NOT NULL,

        PRIMARY KEY(order_id),
        FOREIGN KEY (customer_id) REFERENCES ecomm_customers(customer_id)
    )
    ENGINE=MyISAM';
mysql_query($query, $db) or die(mysql_error($db));

// define the order details table
$query = 'CREATE TABLE IF NOT EXISTS ecomm_order_details (
        order_id    INTEGER UNSIGNED NOT NULL,
        order_qty   INTEGER UNSIGNED NOT NULL,
        product_code CHAR(5)         NOT NULL,

        FOREIGN KEY (order_id) REFERENCES ecomm_orders(order_id),
        FOREIGN KEY (product_code) REFERENCES ecomm_products(product_code)
    )
    ENGINE=MyISAM';
mysql_query($query, $db) or die(mysql_error($db));

$query = 'CREATE TABLE IF NOT EXISTS ecomm_temp_cart (
        session      CHAR(50)        NOT NULL,
        product_code CHAR(5)         NOT NULL,
        qty          INTEGER UNSIGNED NOT NULL,

        PRIMARY KEY (session, product_code),
        FOREIGN KEY (product_code) REFERENCES ecomm_products(product_code)
    )
    ENGINE=MyISAM';
mysql_query($query, $db) or die(mysql_error($db));

echo 'Success!';
?>
```

2. Save this as `db_ch15-1.php`.

3. Run the file from your browser. You should get confirmation that the database and all the tables have been successfully created.

How It Works

You can see that several things are accomplished in this script. Your database now has four new e-commerce tables in it. The first table is named `ecomm_products` and will contain the list of products available on your site:

Fieldname	Type	Description of What It Stores
products_code	CHAR(5)	An individual product code assigned to each product. This is the table's primary key.
name	VARCHAR(100)	A brief title for the product, such as "Fashionable CBA Logo T-shirt."
description	MEDIUMTEXT	A longer description you can use on the individual page for that product. May contain HTML code.
price	DEC(6,2)	The price of the product up to 999.99.

The next table is named `ecomm_customers` and contains the list of customers and their information:

Fieldname	Type	Description of What It Stores
customer_id	INTEGER UNSIGNED	A unique ID assigned to each customer. This will auto-increment and is the table's primary key.
first_name	VARCHAR(20)	Customer's first name.
last_name	VARCHAR(20)	Customer's last name.
address_1	VARCHAR(50)	Customer's address line 1.
address_2	VARCHAR(50)	Customer's address line 2 (can be left empty).
city	VARCHAR(20)	Customer's city.
state	CHAR(2)	Customer's state.
zip_code	CHAR(5)	Customer's zip code.
phone	CHAR(12)	Customer's phone number (in xxx-xxx-xxxx format).
email	VARCHAR(100)	Customer's e-mail address.

The next table you create is called `ecomm_orders` and contains the main order information:

Fieldname	Type	Description of What It Stores
order_id	INTEGER UNSIGNED	The individual number assigned to each order. This will auto-increment and is the table's primary key.
order_date	DATETIME	Date the order was placed.
customer_id	INT(6)	The customer ID of the customer who placed the order. This is a foreign key that references `ecomm_customers`.
cost_subtotal	DEC(7,2)	Subtotal of the order before tax and shipping, up to 9,999.99.
subtotal_shipping	DEC(6,2)	Shipping costs for the order, up to 999.99.
cost_tax	DEC(6,2)	Tax on the order, up to 999.99.
cost_total	DEC(7,2)	Total of the order, up to 9999.99.
shipping_first_name	VARCHAR(20)	First name of the shipping contact for this order.
shipping_last_name	VARCHAR(20)	Last name of the shipping contact.
shipping_address_1	VARCHAR(50)	Shipping contact's address line 1.
shipping_address_2	VARCHAR(50)	Shipping contact's address line 2 (can be left empty).
shipping_city	VARCHAR(20)	Shipping contact's city.
shipping_state	CHAR(2)	Shipping contact's state.
shipping_zip_code	CHAR(5)	Shipping contact's zip code.
shipping_phone	CHAR(12)	Shipping contact's phone number (in xxx-xxx-xxxx format).
shipping_email	VARCHAR(100)	Shipping contact's e-mail address.

The fourth table is named `ecomm_order_details` and contains a detailed list of the products in each order:

Fieldname	Type	Description of What It Stores
order_id	INTEGER UNSIGNED	The ID of the order this information belongs to. This is a foreign key that references `ecomm_orders`.
order_qty	INTEGER UNSIGNED	How many of the item the customer wants.
product_code	CHAR(5)	The product associated with this order. This is a foreign key that references `ecomm_products`.

The fifth and final table is named `ecomm_temp_cart` and is used to temporarily store the shopping cart's product list while the customer is browsing:

Fieldname	Type	Description of What It Stores
session	INTEGER UNSIGNED	The customer's session identifier.
product_code	CHAR(5)	The product associated with this order. This is a foreign key that references `ecomm_products`.
qty	INTEGER UNSIGNED	How many of the item the customer wants.

You now have a mechanism set up so that you can store all your products, customers, and the information associated with the orders they place.

You may be wondering why the temporary information is stored in the database. Certainly the list of shopping-cart items can be stored as `$_SESSION` variables or in cookies, but storing the information in the database lets you keep track of orders that customers never complete — information that would be lost if it were stored in the user's session or in cookies. This is commonly called shopping-cart abandonment, and it is considered one of the major obstacles e-commerce ventures face. Data in this temporary cart can really help you glean information about your customers, such as:

❑ **Percentage of potential sales:** You can gauge what percentage of visitors or potential customers are abandoning their carts. If it's exceedingly high, then your checkout procedure may be too complicated or convoluted for them to finish the process, or perhaps your shipping costs are not made clear up-front, and people are forced into faking their shopping carts to determine shipping costs.

❑ **Analysis of Stock:** You can track any trends in the items that are consistently being put in the cart before abandonment. If the same items are found to be abandoned, then perhaps there is something wrong with your checkout procedure for these items, the shipping costs are exceedingly high, or the price for the item itself is too high based on your competitors' rates. This would require greater analysis of the cost of the flagged items to ensure that you're being competitive.

❑ **Periods of use:** You can track any trends in when your customers are leaving items in the cart. If you find that a large number of customers are abandoning their carts during your web site or server maintenance, perhaps the workload on the server is causing your site to load slowly, and your customers are losing patience and leaving their carts. In this instance, you would want to schedule such maintenance for a time when your site has the fewest shoppers online. As you can see, what people *don't* buy can be just as informative as what they *do* buy.

By understanding these key concepts and where to glean this information, you can find a large amount of helpful tracking information. You should use this table as a reference when trying to enhance sales of your product or services. Many professionals use this table to help them better their site, their services, and their products and company overall.

The type of person shopping also factors into this equation. For example, younger (and generally more naïve) shoppers are likely to quickly click through your offerings and either impulsively make a purchase or abandon the process at the last moment, from fear of committing to a purchase they may know little about. Then there are older shoppers, who are generally wiser. This potential base of customers is more likely to try to verify the legitimacy of your site and comparison-shop, which contributes to a large amount of abandonment.

If a potential buyer is trying to find out any hidden costs along the way, he or she is likely to find two other competitors online and move through the entire shopping process, to find the true and final cost, then select the one that is the cheapest and most reputable — and abandon the rest.

Try It Out   Adding Your Products

Now that you have a set of tables set up in your database, you need to populate them with some information. In this exercise, you'll do just that.

1. Open your text editor, and type the following program:

```php
<?php
require 'db.inc.php';

$db = mysql_connect(MYSQL_HOST, MYSQL_USER, MYSQL_PASSWORD) or
    die ('Unable to connect. Check your connection parameters.');
mysql_select_db(MYSQL_DB, $db) or die(mysql_error($db));


$query = 'INSERT INTO ecomm_products
        (product_code, name, description, price)
    VALUES
        ("00001",
        "CBA Logo T-shirt",
        "This T-shirt will show off your CBA connection. Our t-shirts are ' .
        'all made of high quality and 100% preshrunk cotton.",
        17.95),
        ("00002",
        "CBA Bumper Sticker",
        "Let the world know you are a proud supporter of the CBA web site ' .
        'with this colorful bumper sticker.",
```

```
                    5.95),
                    ("00003",
                    "CBA Coffee Mug",
                    "With the CBA logo looking back at you over your morning cup of ' .
                    'coffee, you are sure to have a great start to your day. Our mugs ' .
                    'are microwave and dishwasher safe.",
                    8.95),
                    ("00004",
                    "Superhero Body Suit",
                    "We have a complete selection of colors and sizes for you to choose ' .
                    'from. This body suit is sleek, stylish, and won\'t hinder either ' .
                    'your crime-fighting skills or evil scheming abilities. We also ' .
                    'offer your choice in monogrammed letter applique.",
                    99.95),
                    ("00005",
                    "Small Grappling Hook",
                    "This specialized hook will get you out of the tightest places. ' .
                    'Specially designed for portability and stealth, please be aware ' .
                    'that this hook does come with a weight limit.",
                    139.95),
                    ("00006",
                    "Large Grappling Hook",
                    "For all your heavy-duty building-to-building swinging needs, this ' .
                    'large version of our grappling hook will safely transport you ' .
                    'throughout the city. Please be advised however that at 50 pounds ' .
                    'this is hardly the hook to use if you are a lightweight.",
                    199.95)';
  mysql_query($query, $db) or die(mysql_error($db));

  echo 'Success!';
  ?>
```

2. Save it as db_ch15-2.php.

3. Open the file in your browser. You should see confirmation that the products were successfully loaded into the table.

How It Works

You inserted each of your products into the ecomm_products table. Notice that, although you assigned sequential numbers as your products' product code, they are string values, and you are not using the auto-increment feature. This is because you may wish to assign product numbers based on category, distributor/manufacturer, or another numbering scheme in the real world. These product codes may include letters and numbers.

If you had no errors and your query didn't cause the script to die, you should have seen the success message displayed, and your products should now be in the database.

Try It Out   **Creating the Store Home Page**

In this exercise, you'll create the home page that all users will see when they start to shop at your site. The home page is responsible for listing all the available products you have for sale. Unfortunately, we can't give you the image files through this book, but you can download them from the book's companion web site, or you can create your own.

1.   Open your text editor, and save the following as `ecomm_shop.php`.

```php
<html>
 <head>
  <title>Comic Book Appreciation Site Product List</title>
  <style type="text/css">
   th { background-color: #999;}
   td { vertical-align: top; }
   .odd_row { background-color: #EEE; }
   .even_row { background-color: #FFF; }
  </style>
 </head>
 <body>
  <h1>Comic Book Appreciation Store</h1>
  <p><a href="ecomm_view_cart.php">View Cart</a></p>
  <p>Thanks for visiting our site! Please see our list of awesome products
below, and click on the link for more information:</p>
  <table style="width:75%;">
<?php
require 'db.inc.php';

$db = mysql_connect(MYSQL_HOST, MYSQL_USER, MYSQL_PASSWORD) or
    die ('Unable to connect. Check your connection parameters.');

mysql_select_db(MYSQL_DB, $db) or die(mysql_error($db));

$query = 'SELECT
        product_code, name, price
    FROM
        ecomm_products
    ORDER BY
        product_code ASC';
$result = mysql_query($query, $db)or die(mysql_error($db));

$odd = true;
while ($row = mysql_fetch_array($result)) {
    echo ($odd == true) ? '<tr class="odd_row">' : '<tr class="even_row">';
    $odd = !$odd;
    extract($row);
    echo '<td style="text-align: center; width:100px;"><a href="' .
        'ecomm_view_product.php?product_code=' . $product_code .
        '"><img src="images/' . $product_code .'_t.jpg" alt="' . $name .
        '"/></a></td>';
    echo '<td><a href="ecomm_view_product.php?product_code=' . $product_code .
        '">' . $name . '</a></td>';
```

```
        echo '<td style="text-align: right;"><a href="ecomm_view_product.php?' .
             'product_code=' . $product_code . '">' . $price . '</a></td>';
        echo '</tr>';
    }
?>
  </table>
 </body>
</html>
```

2. Your screen should now look like Figure 15-1.

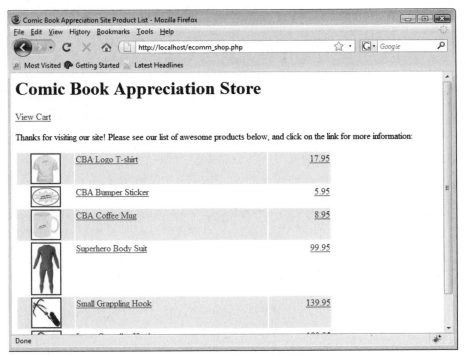

Figure 15-1

How It Works

After querying the database to retrieve a list of products, you present the results in a table. Each row displays a thumbnail image, the name of the product, and its price. Each element is also a link for the customer to click, to view the product's details. You haven't written `ecomm_view_product.php` yet, so these links are a dead end for now, but you will code that script in the next section.

```
$query = 'SELECT
        product_code, name, price
    FROM
        ecomm_products
    ORDER BY
        product_code ASC';
```

```php
$result = mysql_query($query, $db)or die(mysql_error($db));

$odd = true;
while ($row = mysql_fetch_array($result)) {
    echo ($odd == true) ? '<tr class="odd_row">' : '<tr class="even_row">';
    $odd = !$odd;
    extract($row);
    echo '<td style="text-align: center; width:100px;"><a href="' .
        'ecomm_view_product.php?product_code=' . $product_code .
        '"><img src="images/' . $product_code .'_t.jpg" alt="' . $name .
        '"/></a></td>';
    echo '<td><a href="ecomm_view_product.php?product_code=' . $product_code .
        '">' . $name . '</a></td>';
    echo '<td style="text-align: right;"><a href="ecomm_view_product.php?' .
        'product_code=' . $product_code . '">' . $price . '</a></td>';
    echo '</tr>';
}
```

We are storing the product's images in an `images` folder for this project, though you can store them elsewhere, if you would like. The filename for the image is the same as the item's product code, and thumbnail versions include the suffix _t.

Try It Out   **Viewing the Products**

A site with dead-end links is never a good thing, especially in this case, when the user is looking for more information about the product. You are now going to create the page that displays the details of each product.

1. Enter this code in your text editor, then save this file as `ecomm_view_product.php`.

```php
<?php
session_start();

require 'db.inc.php';

$db = mysql_connect(MYSQL_HOST, MYSQL_USER, MYSQL_PASSWORD) or
    die ('Unable to connect. Check your connection parameters.');
mysql_select_db(MYSQL_DB, $db) or die(mysql_error($db));

$product_code = isset($_GET['product_code']) ? $_GET['product_code'] : '';

$query = 'SELECT
        name, description, price
    FROM
        ecomm_products
    WHERE
        product_code = "' . mysql_real_escape_string($product_code, $db) .
 . '"';
$result = mysql_query($query, $db)or die(mysql_error($db));

if (mysql_num_rows($result) != 1) {
```

```php
      header('Location: ecomm_shop.php');
      mysql_free_result($result);
      mysql_close($db);
      exit();
}
$row = mysql_fetch_assoc($result);
extract($row);
?>
<html>
 <head>
  <title><?php echo $name; ?></title>
  <style type="text/css">
   th { background-color: #999;}
   td { vertical-align: top; }
   .odd_row { background-color: #EEE; }
   .even_row { background-color: #FFF; }
  </style>
 </head>
 <body>
  <h1>Comic Book Appreciation Store</h1>
  <p><a href="ecomm_view_cart.php">View Cart</a></p>
  <h2><?php echo $name; ?></h2>
  <table>
   <tr>
    <td rowspan="4"><img src="images/<?php echo $product_code; ?>.jpg"
      alt="<?php echo $name; ?>"/></td>
    <td><?php echo $description; ?></td>
   </tr><tr>
    <td><strong>Product Code:</strong> <?php echo $product_code; ?></td>
   </tr><tr>
    <td><strong>Price:</strong> $<?php echo $price; ?></td>
   </tr><tr>
    <td>
     <form method="post" action="ecomm_update_cart.php">
      <div>
       <input type="hidden" name="product_code"
        value="<?php echo $product_code; ?>"/>
       <label for="qty">Quantity: </label>
<?php
echo '<input type="hidden" name="redirect" value="ecomm_view_product.php?' .
    'product_code=' . $product_code . '"/>';

$session = session_id();
$query = 'SELECT
      qty
    FROM
      ecomm_temp_cart
    WHERE
      session = "' . $session . '" AND
      product_code = "' . $product_code . '"';
$result = mysql_query($query, $db)or die(mysql_error($db));

if (mysql_num_rows($result) > 0) {
    $row = mysql_fetch_assoc($result);
```

```
      extract($row);
} else {
    $qty = 0;
}
mysql_free_result($result);

echo '<input type="text" name="qty" id="qty" size="2" maxlength="2" value="' .
    $qty . '"/>';

if ($qty > 0) {
    echo '<input type="submit" name="submit" value="Change Qty"/>';
} else {
    echo '<input type="submit" name="submit" value="Add to Cart"/>';
}
?>
      </div>
    </form>
   </td>
  </tr>
 </table>
 <hr/>
 <p><a href="ecomm_shop.php"><< Back to main page</a></p>
</body>
</html>
```

2. Open the `ecomm_shop.php` script in your browser, and then click on any of the elements in the row for the Superhero Body Suit. Your screen should look like that shown in Figure 15-2.

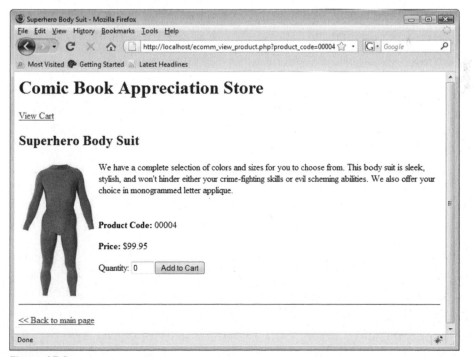

Figure 15-2

How It Works

First, you call the `session_start()` function because you will be accessing the session information for the customer. Then, you use the `product_id` value passed in the query string to retrieve the product information from the `ecomm_products` table. If an erroneous `product_id` has been provided and there is no matching product in the database, then you redirect the customer back to the `ecomm_shop.php` page.

```php
$product_code = isset($_GET['product_code']) ? $_GET['product_code'] : '';

$query = 'SELECT
        name, description, price
    FROM
        ecomm_products
    WHERE
        product_code = "' . mysql_real_escape_string($product_code, $db) .
'"';
$result = mysql_query($query, $db)or die(mysql_error($db));

if (mysql_num_rows($result) != 1) {
    header('Location: ecomm_shop.php');
    mysql_free_result($result);
    mysql_close($db);
    exit();
}
$row = mysql_fetch_assoc($result);
```

You display the product's information in the form of a table with pretty much the standard mix of PHP and HTML you've grown accustomed to using throughout this book. Things get interesting again when it comes time to display the quantity field, for the customer to add the product to his or her shopping cart.

First you query the `ecomm_temp_cart` table, using the customer's session ID. The session ID is retrieved by calling PHP's `session_id()` function. Your goal is to find out if the customer has already placed this item in the shopping cart, and if so, in what quantity.

```php
$session = session_id();
$query = 'SELECT
        qty
    FROM
        ecomm_temp_cart
    WHERE
        session = "' . $session . '" AND
        product_code = "' . $product_code . '"';
$result = mysql_query($query, $db)or die(mysql_error($db));

if (mysql_num_rows($result) > 0) {
    $row = mysql_fetch_assoc($result);
    extract($row);
} else {
    $qty = 0;
}
mysql_free_result($result);
```

Armed with this information, you can now display the quantity field in an appropriate manner.

```
echo '<input type="text" name="qty" id="qty" size="2" maxlength="2"
value="' .
    $qty . '"/>';

if ($qty > 0) {
    echo '<input type="submit" name="submit" value="Change Qty"/>';
} else {
    echo '<input type="submit" name="submit" value="Add to Cart"/>';
}
```

The form `element` that the quantity field and action button are part of posts its information to
ecomm_update_cart.php. It sends the product code, the desired quantity, the action to be performed
on the cart, and a redirect location where the customer should be sent next.

Try It Out   **Adding, Changing, and Deleting Items in the Cart**

In this exercise, you'll write the script that updates the contents of the cart. It is responsible for
handling the addition of items, updating/removing items, and clearing out the entire contents of the
shopping cart.

1.   Type in this code, and save it as ecomm_update_cart.php:

```
<?php
require 'db.inc.php';

$db = mysql_connect(MYSQL_HOST, MYSQL_USER, MYSQL_PASSWORD) or
    die ('Unable to connect. Check your connection parameters.');
mysql_select_db(MYSQL_DB, $db) or die(mysql_error($db));

session_start();
$session = session_id();

$qty = (isset($_POST['qty']) && ctype_digit($_POST['qty'])) ? $_POST['qty'] : 0;
$product_code = (isset($_POST['product_code'])) ? $_POST['product_code'] : '';
$action = (isset($_POST['submit'])) ? $_POST['submit'] : '';
$redirect = (isset($_POST['redirect'])) ? $_POST['redirect'] : 'ecomm_shop
.php';

switch ($action) {
case 'Add to Cart':
    if (!empty($product_code) && $qty > 0) {
        $query = 'INSERT INTO ecomm_temp_cart
                (session, product_code, qty)
            VALUES
                ("' . $session . '", "' .
                mysql_real_escape_string($product_code, $db) . '", ' . $qty . ')';
```

```
            mysql_query($query, $db) or die(mysql_error($db));
        }
        header('Location: ' . $redirect);
        exit();
        break;

    case 'Change Qty':
        if (!empty($product_code)) {
            if ($qty > 0) {
                $query = 'UPDATE ecomm_temp_cart
                    SET
                        qty = ' . $qty . '
                    WHERE
                        session = "' . $session . '" AND
                        product_code = "' .
                        mysql_real_escape_string($product_code, $db) . '"';
            } else {
                $query = 'DELETE FROM ecomm_temp_cart
                    WHERE
                        session = "' . $session . '" AND
                        product_code = "' .
                        mysql_real_escape_string($product_code, $db) . '"';
            }
            mysql_query($query, $db) or die(mysql_error($db));
        }
        header('Location: ' . $redirect);
        exit();
        break;

    case 'Empty Cart':
        $query = 'DELETE FROM ecomm_temp_cart
            WHERE
                session = "' . $session . '"';
        mysql_query($query, $db) or die(mysql_error($db));
        header('Location: ' . $redirect);
        exit();
        break;
}
?>
```

2. Go back to the product description page of the Superhero Body Suit. Enter a number in the quantity field, and add the product to your cart. You will be redirected to the same page, but this time the field will reflect the quantity of suits you've just added to your cart.

3. Change the quantity to zero, and click the button that is now labeled "Change Qty," to remove the suits from your shopping cart.

How It Works

All of the code to manage your shopping cart is contained in one file, ecomm_update_cart.php. The correct course of action is determined by the value of action as posted from the previous form. First, you retrieve the user's session ID, and then you filter the incoming values:

```
session_start();
$session = session_id();

$qty = (isset($_POST['qty']) && ctype_digit($_POST['qty'])) ? $_POST['qty'] : 0;
$product_code = (isset($_POST['product_code'])) ? $_POST['product_code'] : '';
$action = (isset($_POST['submit'])) ? $_POST['submit'] : '';
$redirect = (isset($_POST['redirect'])) ? $_POST['redirect'] : 'ecomm_shop
.php';
```

The first case of the switch statement handles adding products to the ecomm_temp_cart table
for the user. Afterwards, it redirects the user to the page specified in $redirect (which should be
ecomm_view_product.php).

```
case 'Add to Cart':
    if (!empty($product_code) && $qty > 0) {
        $query = 'INSERT INTO ecomm_temp_cart
                (session, product_code, qty)
            VALUES
                ("' . $session . '", "' .
                mysql_real_escape_string($product_code, $db) . '", ' . $qty
. ')';
        mysql_query($query, $db) or die(mysql_error($db));
    }
    header('Location: ' . $redirect);
    exit();
    break;
```

The next case is responsible for changing the quantity of an item in the cart. If the value of $qty is
greater than 0, then you send an UPDATE query to MySQL. If the value of $qty is 0, then the product's
record in ecomm_temp_cart should be removed, so you issue a DELETE query.

```
case 'Change Qty':
    if (!empty($product_code)) {
        if ($qty > 0) {
            $query = 'UPDATE ecomm_temp_cart
                SET
                    qty = ' . $qty . '
                WHERE
                    session = "' . $session . '" AND
                    product_code = "' .
                    mysql_real_escape_string($product_code, $db) . '"';
        } else {
            $query = 'DELETE FROM ecomm_temp_cart
                WHERE
                    session = "' . $session . '" AND
                    product_code = "' .
                    mysql_real_escape_string($product_code, $db) . '"';
        }
        mysql_query($query, $db) or die(mysql_error($db));
    }
    header('Location: ' . $redirect);
    exit();
    break;
```

The final case in the `switch` statement handles the event in which the customer is emptying his or her shopping cart entirely. You do this by sending a DELETE query to delete all records in the ecomm_temp_cart that have the user's session ID.

```
case 'Empty Cart':
    $query = 'DELETE FROM ecomm_temp_cart
        WHERE
            session = "' . $session . '"';
    mysql_query($query, $db) or die(mysql_error($db));
    header('Location: ' . $redirect);
    exit();
    break;
```

<hr />

Try It Out   Viewing the Shopping Cart

In this exercise, you'll create the page to view the contents of the shopping cart.

1. Same drill as usual . . . enter this code, and save it as `ecomm_view_cart.php`:

```php
<?php
session_start();
require 'db.inc.php';
?>
<html>
 <head>
  <title>Here is Your Shopping Cart!</title>
  <style type="text/css">
   th { background-color: #999;}
   td { vertical-align: top; }
   .odd_row { background-color: #EEE; }
   .even_row { background-color: #FFF; }
  </style>
 </head>
 <body>
  <h1>Comic Book Appreciation Store</h1>
<?php
$db = mysql_connect(MYSQL_HOST, MYSQL_USER, MYSQL_PASSWORD) or
    die ('Unable to connect. Check your connection parameters.');

mysql_select_db(MYSQL_DB, $db) or die(mysql_error($db));

$session = session_id();

$query = 'SELECT
        t.product_code, qty,
        name, description, price
```

```
    FROM
        ecomm_temp_cart t JOIN ecomm_products p ON
            t.product_code = p.product_code
    WHERE
        session = "' . $session . '"
    ORDER BY
        t.product_code ASC';
$result = mysql_query($query, $db) or die (mysql_error($db));

$rows = mysql_num_rows($result);
if ($rows == 1) {
    echo '<p>You currently have 1 product in your cart.</p>';
} else {
    echo '<p>You currently have ' . $rows . ' products in your cart.</p>';
}

if ($rows > 0) {
?>
  <table style="width: 75%;">
   <tr>
    <th style="width: 100px;"> </th><th>Item Name</th><th>Quantity</th>
    <th>Price Each</th><th>Extended Price</th>
   </tr>
<?php
    $total = 0;
    $odd = true;
    while ($row = mysql_fetch_array($result)) {
        echo ($odd == true) ? '<tr class="odd_row">' : '<tr class="even_
row">';
        $odd = !$odd;
        extract($row);
?>
    <td style="text-align:center;"><a href="ecomm_view_product.php?product_
code=<?php
      echo $product_code; ?>"><img src="images/<?php echo $product_code;
?>_t.jpg"
        alt="<?php echo $name; ?>"/></a></td>
    <td><a href="ecomm_view_product.php?product_code=<?php echo
$product_code;
?>"><?php
      echo $name; ?></a></td>
    <td>
     <form method="post" action="ecomm_update_cart.php">
      <div>
       <input type="text" name="qty" maxlength="2" size="2"
       value="<?php echo $qty; ?>"/>
       <input type="hidden" name="product_code"
       value="<?php echo $product_code; ?>"/>
```

```
                <input type="hidden" name="redirect" value="ecomm_view_cart.php"/>
                <input type="submit" name="submit" value="Change Qty"/>
            </div>
          </form>
        </td>
        <td style="text-align: right;"> $<?php echo $price; ?></td>
        <td style="text-align: right;"> $<?php echo number_format
($price * $qty, 2); ?>
        </td>
      </tr>
<?php
        $total = $total + $price * $qty;
      }
?>
  </table>
  <p>Your total before shipping is:
    <strong>$<?php echo number_format($total, 2); ?></strong></p>
  <form method="post" action="ecomm_checkout.php">
    <div>
      <input type="submit" name="submit" value="Proceed to Checkout"
        style="font-weight: bold;"/>
    </div>
  </form>
  <form method="post" action="ecomm_update_cart.php">
    <div>
      <input type="hidden" name="redirect" value="ecomm_shop.php"/>
      <input type="submit" name="submit" value="Empty Cart"/>
    </div>
  </form>
<?php
}
?>
  <hr/>
  <p><a href="ecomm_shop.php"><< Back to main page</a></p>
 </body>
</html>
```

2. Add a few items to your shopping cart, as before, and then click the View Cart link. What you see should resemble Figure 15-3.

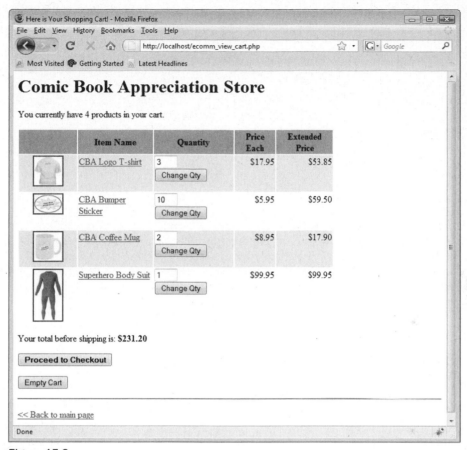

Figure 15-3

How It Works

You retrieve the contents of the customer's shopping cart by querying the ecomm_temp_cart table with the session ID. Only the product code is stored in the ecomm_temp_cart table, so you use a JOIN against the ecomm_products table to retrieve the name, description, and price of the products in the cart as well.

```
$session = session_id();

$query = 'SELECT
        t.product_code, qty,
        name, description, price
    FROM
        ecomm_temp_cart t JOIN ecomm_products p ON
            t.product_code = p.product_code
    WHERE
        session = "' . $session . '"
    ORDER BY
        t.product_code ASC';
$result = mysql_query($query, $db) or die (mysql_error($db));
```

You want to display the number of items in the cart, but you should not simply write code like this to do it:

```
$rows = mysql_num_rows($result);
echo '<p>You have ' . $rows . ' products in your cart.</p>';
```

Why? If the customer is only purchasing one product, then you wouldn't be showing the information in proper English. You could remedy this by changing it to say "product(s)," but it is more professional to use the singular when there is one product, and the plural when there are none or more than one. Luckily, this isn't too difficult and requires just a simple check.

```
if ($rows == 1) {
    echo '<p>You currently have 1 product in your cart.</p>';
} else {
    echo '<p>You currently have ' . $rows . ' products in your cart.</p>';
}
```

If there are items in the cart, then you display them as a table in a manner very similar to the way you did in `ecomm_shop.php`. This table, however, has a quantity column, which the customer can use to see how many of the product are being purchased, and to update the quantity. You also keep a tally of the total price of the items as you loop through the cart's contents.

```
<table style="width: 75%;">
 <tr>
  <th style="width: 100px;"> </th><th>Item Name</th><th>Quantity</th>
  <th>Price Each</th><th>Extended Price</th>
 </tr>
<?php
    $total = 0;
    $odd = true;
    while ($row = mysql_fetch_array($result)) {
        echo ($odd == true) ? '<tr class="odd_row">' : '<tr class="even_
row">';
        $odd = !$odd;
        extract($row);
?>
   <td style="text-align:center;"><a href="ecomm_view_product.php?product_
code=<?php
     echo $product_code; ?>"><img src="images/<?php echo $product_code; ?>_t.
jpg"
      alt="<?php echo $name; ?>"/></a></td>
   <td><a href="ecomm_view_product.php?product_code=<?php echo $product_code;
?>"><?php
     echo $name; ?></a></td>
   <td>
    <form method="post" action="ecomm_update_cart.php">
     <div>
      <input type="text" name="qty" maxlength="2" size="2"
       value="<?php echo $qty; ?>"/>
      <input type="hidden" name="product_code"
       value="<?php echo $product_code; ?>"/>
      <input type="hidden" name="redirect" value="ecomm_view_cart.php"/>
```

```
        <input type="submit" name="submit" value="Change Qty"/>
      </div>
    </form>
  </td>
  <td style="text-align: right;"> $<?php echo $price; ?></td>
  <td style="text-align: right;"> $<?php echo number_format($price * $qty, 2);
?>
  </td>
 </tr>
<?php
        $total = $total + $price * $qty;
    }
?>
</table>
```

The total cost that the customer has accumulated is then displayed after the table.

```
<p>Your total before shipping is:
 <strong>$<?php echo number_format($total, 2); ?></strong></p>
```

You used the `number_format()` function to format the total cost (and earlier in the while loop to format the extended price). The function formats a number by inserting grouping separators. It accepts the number and, optionally, how many digits to preserve after the decimal place, and what characters to use as the decimal point and thousands separator.

Finally, you provided buttons for the visitor to continue forward in the checkout process or empty out his or her shopping cart completely. You want to offer the ability for customers to empty the cart as a convenience, because setting each quantity to 0 and submitting it would be tedious, if there were a large number of items in the cart. But you don't want them to accidentally delete the cart's contents when they really intend to continue checking out, so you made the checkout button's text bold, as an extra visual cue.

```
<form method="post" action="ecomm_checkout.php">
 <div>
  <input type="submit" name="submit" value="Proceed to Checkout"
   style="font-weight: bold;"/>
 </div>
</form>
<form method="post" action="ecomm_update_cart.php">
 <div>
  <input type="hidden" name="redirect" value="ecomm_shop.php"/>
  <input type="submit" name="submit" value="Empty Cart"/>
 </div>
</form>
```

Try It Out Checking Out

The checkout process consists of three steps. You will code three files, one for each step. We're warning you in advance that there will be a lot of typing, so we hope you have your fingers ready. But the logic in the script is pretty straightforward.

1. As usual, enter this code, and then save it as `ecomm_checkout.php`:

```php
<?php
session_start();
?>
<html>
 <body>
  <title>Checkout Step 1 of 3</title>
  <style type="text/css">
   th { background-color: #999;}
   td { vertical-align: top; }
   .odd_row { background-color: #EEE; }
   .even_row { background-color: #FFF; }
  </style>
  <script type="text/javascript">

window.onload = function() {
    // assign toggle_shipping_visibility to same_info checkbox
    var c = document.getElementById('same_info');
    c.onchange = toggle_shipping_visibility;
}

function toggle_shipping_visibility() {
    var c = document.getElementById('same_info');
    var t = document.getElementById('shipping_table');

    // update shipping table's visibility
    t.style.display = (c.checked) ? 'none' : '';
}
  </script>
 </head>
 <body>
  <h1>Comic Book Appreciation Store</h1>
  <h2>Order Checkout</h2>
  <ol>
   <li><strong>Enter Billing and Shipping Information</strong></li>
   <li>Verify Accuracy of Order Information and Send Order</li>
   <li>Order Confirmation and Receipt</li>
  </ol>
  <form method="post" action="ecomm_checkout2.php">
   <table>
    <tr>
     <td>
      <table>
       <tr>
        <th colspan="2">Billing Information</th>
       </tr><tr>
```

```
      <td><label for="first_name">First Name:</label></td>
      <td><input type="text" id="first_name" name="first_name" size="20"
        maxlength="20"/></td>
    </tr><tr>
      <td><label for="last_name">Last Name:</label></td>
      <td><input type="text" id="last_name" name="last_name" size="20"
        maxlength="20"/></td>
    </tr><tr>
      <td><label for="address_1">Billing Address:</label></td>
      <td><input type="text" id="address_1" name="address_1" size="30"
        maxlength="50"/></td>
    </tr><tr>
      <td> </td>
      <td><input type="text" id="address_2" name="address_2" size="30"
        maxlength="50"/></td>
    </tr><tr>
      <td><label for="city">City:</label></td>
      <td><input type="text" id="city" name="city" size="20"
        maxlength="20"/></td>
    </tr><tr>
      <td><label for="state">State:</label></td>
      <td><input type="text" id="state" name="state" size="2"
        maxlength="2"/></td>
    </tr><tr>
      <td><label for="zip_code">Zip Code:</label></td>
      <td><input type="text" id="zip_code" name="zip_code" size="5"
        maxlength="5"/></td>
    </tr><tr>
      <td><label for="phone">Phone Number:</label></td>
      <td><input type="text" id="phone" name="phone" size="10"
        maxlength="10"/></td>
    </tr><tr>
      <td><label for="email">Email Address:</label></td>
      <td><input type="text" id="email" name="email" size="30"
        maxlength="100"/>
      </td>
    </tr><tr>
      <td colspan="2" style="text-align: center;">
       <input type="checkbox" id="same_info" name="same_info"
        checked="checked"/>
       <label for="same_info">Shipping information is same as billing
</label>
      </td>
    </tr>
   </table>
  </td>
  <td>
   <table id="shipping_table" style="display:none;">
    <tr>
     <th colspan="2">Shipping Information</th>
    </tr><tr>
     <td><label for="shipping_first_name">First Name:</label></td>
     <td><input type="text" id="shipping_first_name"
       name="shipping_first_name" size="20" maxlength="20"/></td>
```

```
          </tr><tr>
            <td><label for="shipping_last_name">Last Name:</label></td>
            <td><input type="text" id="shipping_last_name"
              name="shipping_last_name" size="20" maxlength="20"/></td>
          </tr><tr>
            <td><label for="shipping_address_1">Shipping Address:</label></td>
            <td><input type="text" id="shipping_address_1" name="shipping_
address_1"
              size="30" maxlength="50"/></td>
          </tr><tr>
            <td> </td>
            <td><input type="text" id="shipping_address_2" name="shipping_
address_2"
              size="30" maxlength="50"/></td>
          </tr><tr>
            <td><label for="shipping_city">City:</label></td>
            <td><input type="text" id="shipping_city" name="shipping_city"
size="20"
              maxlength="20"/></td>
          </tr><tr>
            <td><label for="shipping_state">State:</label></td>
            <td><input type="text" id="shipping_state" name="shipping_state"
size="2"
              maxlength="2"/></td>
          </tr><tr>
            <td><label for="shipping_zip_code">Zip Code:</label></td>
            <td><input type="text" id="shipping_zip_code" name="shipping_zip_
code"
              size="5" maxlength="5"/></td>
          </tr><tr>
            <td><label for="shipping_phone">Phone Number:</label></td>
            <td><input type="text" id="shipping_phone" name="shipping_phone"
              size="10" maxlength="10"/></td>
          </tr><tr>
            <td><label for="shipping_email">Email Address:</label></td>
            <td><input type="text" id="shipping_email" name="shipping_email"
              size="30" maxlength="100"/>
            </td>
          </tr>
        </table>
      </td>
    </tr><tr>
      <td colspan="2">
        <input type="submit" value="Proceed to Next Step"/>
      </td>
    <tr>
    </table>
  </form>
 </body>
</html>
```

2. Now, enter this code, and save it as `ecomm_checkout2.php`:

```php
<?php
session_start();
require 'db.inc.php';

$db = mysql_connect(MYSQL_HOST, MYSQL_USER, MYSQL_PASSWORD) or
    die ('Unable to connect. Check your connection parameters.');

mysql_select_db(MYSQL_DB, $db) or die(mysql_error($db));

$session = session_id();

if (isset($_POST['same_info'])) {
    $_POST['shipping_first_name'] = $_POST['first_name'];
    $_POST['shipping_last_name'] = $_POST['last_name'];
    $_POST['shipping_address_1'] = $_POST['address_1'];
    $_POST['shipping_address_2'] = $_POST['address_2'];
    $_POST['shipping_city'] = $_POST['city'];
    $_POST['shipping_state'] = $_POST['state'];
    $_POST['shipping_zip_code'] = $_POST['zip_code'];
    $_POST['shipping_phone'] = $_POST['phone'];
    $_POST['shipping_email'] = $_POST['email'];
}
?>
<html>
 <body>
  <title>Checkout Step 2 of 3</title>
  <style type="text/css">
   th { background-color: #999;}
   td { vertical-align: top; }
   .odd_row { background-color: #EEE; }
   .even_row { background-color: #FFF; }
  </style>
 </head>
 <body>
  <h1>Comic Book Appreciation Store</h1>
  <h2>Order Checkout</h2>
  <ol>
   <li>Enter Billing and Shipping Information</li>
   <li><strong>Verify Accuracy of Order Information and Send Order</strong>
</li>
   <li>Order Confirmation and Receipt</li>
  </ol>
   <table style="width: 75%;">
    <tr>
     <th style="width: 100px;"> </th><th>Item Name</th><th>Quantity</th>
     <th>Price Each</th><th>Extended Price</th>
    </tr>
<?php
$query = 'SELECT
        t.product_code, qty,
        name, description, price
    FROM
```

```
                ecomm_temp_cart t JOIN ecomm_products p ON
                    t.product_code = p.product_code
        WHERE
            session = "' . $session . '"
        ORDER BY
            t.product_code ASC';
$results = mysql_query($query, $db) or die (mysql_error($db));

$rows = mysql_num_rows($results);

$total = 0;
$odd = true;
while ($row = mysql_fetch_array($results)) {
    echo ($odd == true) ? '<tr class="odd_row">' : '<tr class="even_row">';
    $odd = !$odd;
    extract($row);
?>
    <td style="text-align:center;">
     <img src="images/<?php echo $product_code; ?>_t.jpg"
     alt="<?php echo $name; ?>"/>
    </td>
    <td><?php echo $name; ?></td>
    <td><?php echo $qty; ?></td>
    <td style="text-align: right;">$<?php echo $price; ?></td>
    <td style="text-align: right;">$<?php echo number_format
($price * $qty, 2);?>
    </td>
    </tr>
<?php
    $total = $total + $price * $qty;
}
?>
    </table>
    <p>Your total before shipping and tax is:
    <strong>$<?php echo number_format($total, 2); ?></strong></p>
    <table>
     <tr>
      <td>
       <table>
        <tr>
         <th colspan="2">Billing Information</th>
        </tr><tr>
         <td>First Name:</td>
         <td><?php echo htmlspecialchars($_POST['first_name']);?></td>
        </tr><tr>
         <td>Last Name:</td>
         <td><?php echo htmlspecialchars($_POST['last_name']);?></td>
        </tr><tr>
         <td>Billing Address:</td>
         <td><?php echo htmlspecialchars($_POST['address_1']);?></td>
        </tr><tr>
         <td> </td>
         <td><?php echo htmlspecialchars($_POST['address_2']);?></td>
        </tr><tr>
```

```
            <td>City:</td>
            <td><?php echo htmlspecialchars($_POST['city']);?></td>
        </tr><tr>
            <td>State:</td>
            <td><?php echo htmlspecialchars($_POST['state']);?></td>
        </tr><tr>
            <td>Zip Code:</td>
            <td><?php echo htmlspecialchars($_POST['zip_code']);?></td>
        </tr><tr>
            <td>Phone Number:</td>
            <td><?php echo htmlspecialchars($_POST['phone']);?></td>
        </tr><tr>
            <td>Email Address:</td>
            <td><?php echo htmlspecialchars($_POST['email']);?></td>
            </td>
        </tr><tr>
            <td colspan="2" style="text-align: center;">
<?php
if (isset($_POST['same_info'])) {
    echo 'Shipping information is same as billing.';
}
?>
            </td>
        </tr>
        </table>
      </td>
        <td>
<?php
if (!isset($_POST['same_info'])) {
?>
        <table>
        <tr>
        <th colspan="2">Shipping Information</th>
        </tr><tr>
        <td>First Name:</td>
        <td><?php echo htmlspecialchars($_POST['shipping_first_name']);?></td>
        </tr><tr>
        <td>Last Name:</td>
        <td><?php echo htmlspecialchars($_POST['shipping_last_name']);?></td>
        </tr><tr>
        <td>Billing Address:</td>
        <td><?php echo htmlspecialchars($_POST['shipping_address_1']);?></td>
        </tr><tr>
        <td> </td>
        <td><?php echo htmlspecialchars($_POST['shipping_address_2']);?></td>
        </tr><tr>
        <td>City:</td>
        <td><?php echo htmlspecialchars($_POST['shipping_city']);?></td>
        </tr><tr>
        <td>State:</td>
        <td><?php echo htmlspecialchars($_POST['shipping_state']);?></td>
        </tr><tr>
        <td>Zip Code:</td>
```

```
          <td><?php echo htmlspecialchars($_POST['shipping_zip_code']);?></td>
        </tr><tr>
        <td>Phone Number:</td>
        <td><?php echo htmlspecialchars($_POST['shipping_phone']);?></td>
        </tr><tr>
        <td>Email Address:</td>
        <td><?php echo htmlspecialchars($_POST['shipping_email']);?></td>
        </td>
        </tr>
      </table>
<?php
}
?>
    </td>
   </tr>
  </table>
  <form method="post" action="ecomm_checkout3.php">
   <div>
    <input type="submit" name="submit" value="Process Order"/>
    <input type="hidden" name="first_name"
     value="<?php echo htmlspecialchars($_POST['first_name']);?>"/>
    <input type="hidden" name="last_name"
     value="<?php echo htmlspecialchars($_POST['last_name']);?>"/>
    <input type="hidden" name="address_1"
     value="<?php echo htmlspecialchars($_POST['address_1']);?>"/>
    <input type="hidden" name="address_2"
     value="<?php echo htmlspecialchars($_POST['address_2']);?>"/>
    <input type="hidden" name="city"
     value="<?php echo htmlspecialchars($_POST['city']);?>"/>
    <input type="hidden" name="state"
     value="<?php echo htmlspecialchars($_POST['state']);?>"/>
    <input type="hidden" name="zip_code"
     value="<?php echo htmlspecialchars($_POST['zip_code']);?>"/>
    <input type="hidden" name="phone"
     value="<?php echo htmlspecialchars($_POST['phone']);?>"/>
    <input type="hidden" name="email"
     value="<?php echo htmlspecialchars($_POST['email']);?>"/>
    <input type="hidden" name="shipping_first_name"
     value="<?php echo htmlspecialchars($_POST['shipping_first_name']);?>"/>
    <input type="hidden" name="shipping_last_name"
     value="<?php echo htmlspecialchars($_POST['shipping_last_name']);?>"/>
    <input type="hidden" name="shipping_address_1"
     value="<?php echo htmlspecialchars($_POST['shipping_address_1']);?>"/>
    <input type="hidden" name="shipping_address_2"
     value="<?php echo htmlspecialchars($_POST['shipping_address_2']);?>"/>
    <input type="hidden" name="shipping_city"
     value="<?php echo htmlspecialchars($_POST['shipping_city']);?>"/>
    <input type="hidden" name="shipping_state"
     value="<?php echo htmlspecialchars($_POST['shipping_state']);?>"/>
    <input type="hidden" name="shipping_zip_code"
```

```
              value="<?php echo htmlspecialchars($_POST['shipping_zip_code']);?>"/>
        <input type="hidden" name="shipping_phone"
          value="<?php echo htmlspecialchars($_POST['shipping_phone']);?>"/>
        <input type="hidden" name="shipping_email"
          value="<?php echo htmlspecialchars($_POST['shipping_email']);?>"/>
      </div>
    </form>
  </body>
</html>
```

3. Enter the third code file, and save it as `ecomm_checkout3.php`:

```php
<?php
session_start();
require 'db.inc.php';

$db = mysql_connect(MYSQL_HOST, MYSQL_USER, MYSQL_PASSWORD) or
    die ('Unable to connect. Check your connection parameters.');

mysql_select_db(MYSQL_DB, $db) or die(mysql_error($db));

$now = date('Y-m-d H:i:s');
$session = session_id();

$first_name = $_POST['first_name'];
$last_name = $_POST['last_name'];
$address_1 = $_POST['address_1'];
$address_2 = $_POST['address_2'];
$city = $_POST['city'];
$state = $_POST['state'];
$zip_code = $_POST['zip_code'];
$phone = $_POST['phone'];
$email = $_POST['email'];

$shipping_first_name = $_POST['shipping_first_name'];
$shipping_last_name = $_POST['shipping_last_name'];
$shipping_address_1 = $_POST['shipping_address_1'];
$shipping_address_2 = $_POST['shipping_address_2'];
$shipping_city = $_POST['shipping_city'];
$shipping_state = $_POST['shipping_state'];
$shipping_zip_code = $_POST['shipping_zip_code'];
$shipping_phone = $_POST['shipping_phone'];
$shipping_email = $_POST['shipping_email'];

// assign customer id to new customer, or find existing customer id
$query = 'SELECT
        customer_id
    FROM
        ecomm_customers
```

537

```
    WHERE
        first_name = "' . mysql_real_escape_string($first_name, $db) . '" AND
        last_name = "' . mysql_real_escape_string($last_name, $db) . '" AND
        address_1 = "' . mysql_real_escape_string($address_1, $db) . '" AND
        address_2 = "' . mysql_real_escape_string($address_2, $db) . '" AND
        city = "' . mysql_real_escape_string($city, $db) . '" AND
        state = "' . mysql_real_escape_string($state, $db) . '" AND
        zip_code = "' . mysql_real_escape_string($zip_code, $db) . '" AND
        phone = "' . mysql_real_escape_string($phone, $db) . '" AND
        email = "' . mysql_real_escape_string($email, $db) . '"';
$result = mysql_query($query, $db) or (mysql_error($db));

if (mysql_num_rows($result) > 0) {
    $row = mysql_fetch_assoc($result);
    extract($row);
} else {
    $query = 'INSERT INTO ecomm_customers
            (customer_id, first_name, last_name, address_1, address_2, city,
            state, zip_code, phone, email)
        VALUES
            (NULL,
            "' . mysql_real_escape_string($first_name, $db) . '",
            "' . mysql_real_escape_string($last_name, $db) . '",
            "' . mysql_real_escape_string($address_1, $db) . '",
            "' . mysql_real_escape_string($address_2, $db) . '",
            "' . mysql_real_escape_string($city, $db) . '",
            "' . mysql_real_escape_string($state, $db) . '",
            "' . mysql_real_escape_string($zip_code, $db) . '",
            "' . mysql_real_escape_string($phone, $db) . '",
            "' . mysql_real_escape_string($email, $db) . '")';
    mysql_query($query, $db) or (mysql_error($db));
    $customer_id = mysql_insert_id();
}
mysql_free_result($result);

// start order entry
$query = 'INSERT into ecomm_orders
        (order_id, order_date, customer_id, cost_subtotal, cost_total,
        shipping_first_name, shipping_last_name, shipping_address_1,
        shipping_address_2, shipping_city, shipping_state, shipping_zip_code,
        shipping_phone, shipping_email)
    VALUES
            (NULL,
            "' . $now . '",
            ' . $customer_id . ',
            0.00,
            0.00,
            "' . mysql_real_escape_string($shipping_first_name, $db) . '",
            "' . mysql_real_escape_string($shipping_last_name, $db) . '",
            "' . mysql_real_escape_string($shipping_address_1, $db) . '",
            "' . mysql_real_escape_string($shipping_address_2, $db) . '",
            "' . mysql_real_escape_string($shipping_city, $db) . '",
            "' . mysql_real_escape_string($shipping_state, $db) . '",
```

```php
                    "' . mysql_real_escape_string($shipping_zip_code, $db) . '",
                    "' . mysql_real_escape_string($shipping_phone, $db) . '",
                    "' . mysql_real_escape_string($shipping_email, $db) . '")';
    mysql_query($query, $db) or (mysql_error($db));
    $order_id = mysql_insert_id();

// Move order information from ecomm_temp_cart into ecomm_order_details
$query = 'INSERT INTO ecomm_order_details
    (order_id, order_qty, product_code)
SELECT
    ' . $order_id . ', qty, product_code
FROM
    ecomm_temp_cart
WHERE
    session = "' . $session . '"';
mysql_query($query, $db) or (mysql_error($db));

$query = 'DELETE FROM ecomm_temp_cart WHERE session = "' . $session . '"';
mysql_query($query, $db) or (mysql_error($db));

// retrieve subtotal
$query = 'SELECT
        SUM(price * order_qty) AS cost_subtotal
    FROM
        ecomm_order_details d JOIN ecomm_products p ON
            d.product_code = p.product_code
    WHERE
        order_id = ' . $order_id;
$result = mysql_query($query, $db) or (mysql_error($db));
$row = mysql_fetch_assoc($result);
extract($row);

// calculate shipping, tax and total costs
$cost_shipping = round($cost_subtotal * 0.25, 2);
$cost_tax = round($cost_subtotal * 0.1, 2);
$cost_total = $cost_subtotal + $cost_shipping + $cost_tax;

// upate costs in ecomm_orders
$query = 'UPDATE ecomm_orders
    SET
        cost_subtotal = ' . $cost_subtotal . ',
        cost_shipping = ' . $cost_shipping . ',
        cost_tax = ' . $cost_tax . ',
        cost_total = ' . $cost_total . '
    WHERE
        order_id = ' . $order_id;
mysql_query($query, $db) or (mysql_error($db));

ob_start();
?>
```

```html
<html>
 <head>
  <title>Order Confirmation</title>
  <style type="text/css">
   th { background-color: #999;}
   td { vertical-align: top; }
   .odd_row { background-color: #EEE; }
   .even_row { background-color: #FFF; }
  </style>
 </head>
 <body>
<?php
$html_head = ob_get_contents();
ob_clean();
?>
  <p>Here is a recap of your order:</p>
  <p>Order Date: <?php echo $now; ?></p>
  <p>Order Number: <?php echo $order_id; ?></p>
  <table>
   <tr>
    <td>
     <table>
      <tr>
       <th colspan="2">Billing Information</th>
      </tr><tr>
       <td>First Name:</td>
       <td><?php echo htmlspecialchars($first_name);?></td>
      </tr><tr>
       <td>Last Name:</td>
       <td><?php echo htmlspecialchars($last_name);?></td>
      </tr><tr>
       <td>Billing Address:</td>
       <td><?php echo htmlspecialchars($address_1);?></td>
      </tr><tr>
       <td> </td>
       <td><?php echo htmlspecialchars($address_2);?></td>
      </tr><tr>
       <td>City:</td>
       <td><?php echo htmlspecialchars($city);?></td>
      </tr><tr>
       <td>State:</td>
       <td><?php echo htmlspecialchars($state);?></td>
      </tr><tr>
       <td>Zip Code:</td>
       <td><?php echo htmlspecialchars($zip_code);?></td>
      </tr><tr>
       <td>Phone Number:</td>
       <td><?php echo htmlspecialchars($phone);?></td>
      </tr><tr>
       <td>Email Address:</td>
       <td><?php echo htmlspecialchars($email);?></td>
      </td>
```

```
        </tr>
       </table>
      </td>
      <td>
       <table>
        <tr>
         <th colspan="2">Shipping Information</th>
        </tr><tr>
         <td>First Name:</td>
         <td><?php echo htmlspecialchars($shipping_first_name);?></td>
        </tr><tr>
         <td>Last Name:</td>
         <td><?php echo htmlspecialchars($shipping_last_name);?></td>
        </tr><tr>
         <td>Billing Address:</td>
         <td><?php echo htmlspecialchars($shipping_address_1);?></td>
        </tr><tr>
         <td> </td>
         <td><?php echo htmlspecialchars($shipping_address_2);?></td>
        </tr><tr>
         <td>City:</td>
         <td><?php echo htmlspecialchars($shipping_city);?></td>
        </tr><tr>
         <td>State:</td>
         <td><?php echo htmlspecialchars($shipping_state);?></td>
        </tr><tr>
         <td>Zip Code:</td>
         <td><?php echo htmlspecialchars($shipping_zip_code);?></td>
        </tr><tr>
         <td>Phone Number:</td>
         <td><?php echo htmlspecialchars($shipping_phone);?></td>
        </tr><tr>
         <td>Email Address:</td>
         <td><?php echo htmlspecialchars($shipping_email);?></td>
        </tr>
       </table>
      </td>
     </tr>
    </table>
    <table style="width: 75%;">
     <tr>
      <th>Item Code</th><th>Item Name</th><th>Quantity</th><th>Price Each</th>
      <th>Extended Price</th>
     </tr>
<?php
$query = 'SELECT
        p.product_code, order_qty, name, description, price
```

```
        FROM
            ecomm_order_details d JOIN ecomm_products p ON
                d.product_code = p.product_code
        WHERE
            order_id = "' . $order_id . '"
        ORDER BY
            p.product_code ASC';
$result = mysql_query($query, $db) or die (mysql_error($db));

$rows = mysql_num_rows($result);

$total = 0;
$odd = true;
while ($row = mysql_fetch_array($result)) {
    echo ($odd == true) ? '<tr class="odd_row">' : '<tr class="even_row">';
    $odd = !$odd;
    extract($row);
?>
    <td><?php echo $product_code; ?></td>
    <td><?php echo $name; ?></td>
    <td><?php echo $order_qty; ?></td>
    <td style="text-align: right;">$<?php echo $price; ?></td>
    <td style="text-align: right;">$<?php
      echo number_format($price * $order_qty, 2);?>
    </td>
  </tr>
<?php
}
?>
  </table>
  <p>Shipping: $<?php echo number_format($cost_subtotal, 2); ?></p>
  <p>Tax: $<?php echo number_format($cost_tax, 2); ?></p>
  <p><strong>Total Cost: $<?php echo number_format($cost_total, 2); ?>
</strong></p>
 </body>
</html>
<?php
$html_body = ob_get_clean();

// display the page
echo $html_head;
?>
<h1>Comic Book Appreciation Store</h1>
<h2>Order Checkout</h2>
<ol>
 <li>Enter Billing and Shipping Information</li>
 <li>Verify Accuracy of Order Information and Send Order</li>
 <li><strong>Order Confirmation and Receipt<strong></li>
</ol>
<h3>A copy of this order has been emailed to you for your records.</h3>
<?php
```

```
echo $html_body;

// send email
$headers = array();
$headers[] = 'MIME-Version: 1.0';
$headers[] = 'Content-type: text/html; charset="iso-8859-1"';
$headers[] = 'Content-Transfer-Encoding: 7bit';
$headers[] = 'From: <store@example.com>';
$headers[] = 'Bcc: <store@example.com>';

mail($email, "Order Confirmation", $html_head . $html_body,
    join("\r\n", $headers));
?>
```

4. Now to test it out. Enter the site and place a few items in your shopping cart. Then choose to check out. You should see something that looks like Figure 15-4.

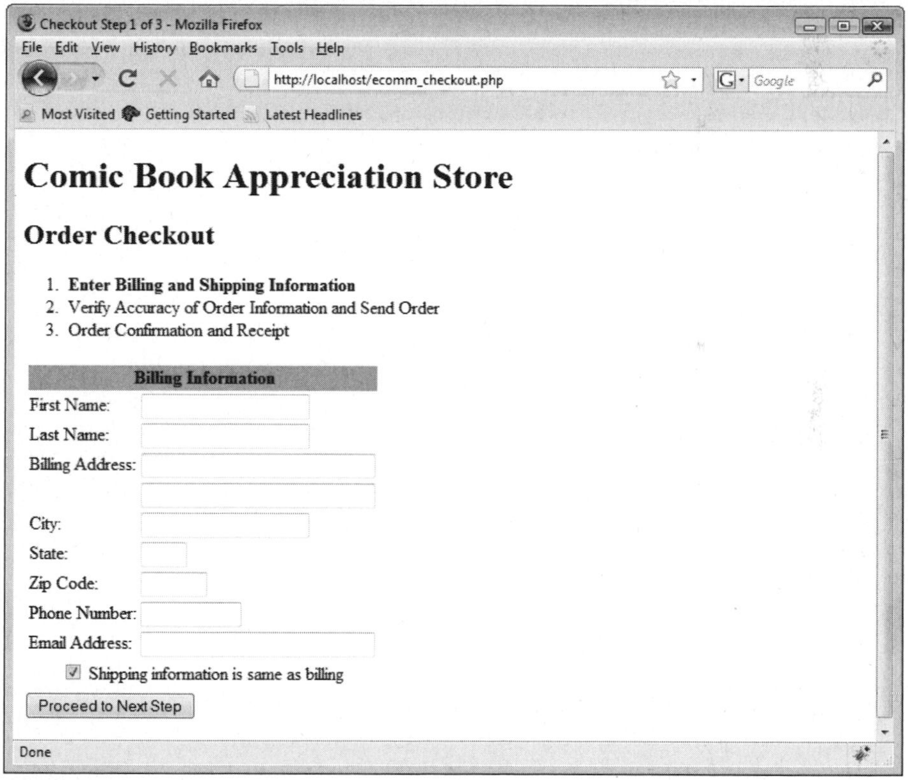

Figure 15-4

5. Enter your billing information, and click the button to proceed to the next step of the checkout process. Your screen should resemble Figure 15-5.

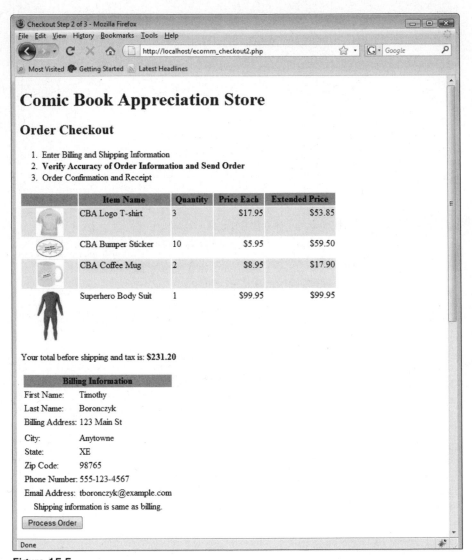

Figure 15-5

6. Finally, click the Process Order button. Your screen should resemble Figure 15-6.

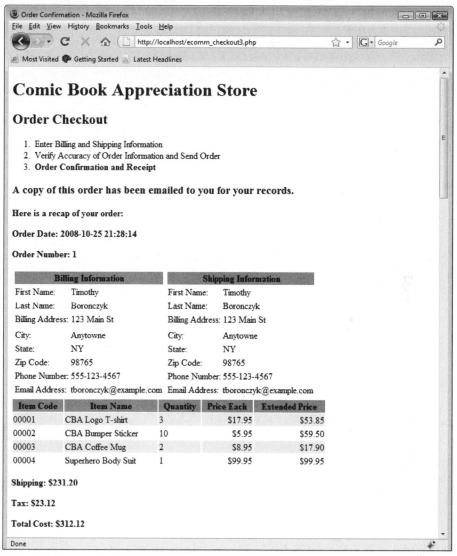

Figure 15-6

How It Works

As you can see, checkout is a three-step process. First, you allow the customer to enter his or her billing and shipping information. Then, you present the information back to the customer, along with the contents of the shopping cart, for review. The final step performs some database manipulation and sends an e-mail to both the customer and to you, as confirmation for the order.

Taking a closer look at `ecomm_checkout.php`, you see it is your basic web form which collects the billing and shipping information and then posts the data to `ecomm_checkout2.php`. This is the first step in the checkout process. While you could display the form fields for both the billing and shipping areas side by side, the shipping fields aren't necessary unless the addresses are different. A little bit of

JavaScript can be tied to the check-box button; if the customer wishes to use a shipping address that is different from the billing address, the shipping area can be displayed. Otherwise, it remains hidden.

```
window.onload = function() {
    // assign toggle_shipping_visibility to same_info checkbox
    var c = document.getElementById('same_info');
    c.onchange = toggle_shipping_visibility;
}

function toggle_shipping_visibility() {
    var c = document.getElementById('same_info');
    var t = document.getElementById('shipping_table');

    // update shipping table's visibility
    t.style.display = (c.checked) ? 'none' : '';
}
```

`ecomm_checkout2.php` accepts the incoming posted data, presents it back for review, and inserts it into a form full of hidden fields. To make sure all the data is passed along to the next step, you check to see if `$_POST['same_info']` is set. This means the shipping information (if any) that was sent should be disregarded and set the same as the billing information.

```
if (isset($_POST['same_info'])) {
    $_POST['shipping_first_name'] = $_POST['first_name'];
    $_POST['shipping_last_name'] = $_POST['last_name'];
    $_POST['shipping_address_1'] = $_POST['address_1'];
    $_POST['shipping_address_2'] = $_POST['address_2'];
    $_POST['shipping_city'] = $_POST['city'];
    $_POST['shipping_state'] = $_POST['state'];
    $_POST['shipping_zip_code'] = $_POST['zip_code'];
    $_POST['shipping_phone'] = $_POST['phone'];
    $_POST['shipping_email'] = $_POST['email'];
}
```

The information is placed in a form of hidden fields, so when the customers click the Process Order button, they are really posting the data to the final step.

```
<form method="post" action="ecomm_checkout3.php">
 <div>
  <input type="submit" name="submit" value="Process Order"/>
  <input type="hidden" name="first_name"
   value="<?php echo htmlspecialchars($_POST['first_name']);?>"/>
  <input type="hidden" name="last_name"
   value="<?php echo htmlspecialchars($_POST['last_name']);?>"/>
  <input type="hidden" name="address_1"
   value="<?php echo htmlspecialchars($_POST['address_1']);?>"/>
  <input type="hidden" name="address_2"
   value="<?php echo htmlspecialchars($_POST['address_2']);?>"/>
  <input type="hidden" name="city"
   value="<?php echo htmlspecialchars($_POST['city']);?>"/>
  <input type="hidden" name="state"
```

```
       value="<?php echo htmlspecialchars($_POST['state']);?>"/>
     <input type="hidden" name="zip_code"
      value="<?php echo htmlspecialchars($_POST['zip_code']);?>"/>
     <input type="hidden" name="phone"
      value="<?php echo htmlspecialchars($_POST['phone']);?>"/>
     <input type="hidden" name="email"
      value="<?php echo htmlspecialchars($_POST['email']);?>"/>
     <input type="hidden" name="shipping_first_name"
      value="<?php echo htmlspecialchars($_POST['shipping_first_name']);?>"/>
     <input type="hidden" name="shipping_last_name"
      value="<?php echo htmlspecialchars($_POST['shipping_last_name']);?>"/>
     <input type="hidden" name="shipping_address_1"
      value="<?php echo htmlspecialchars($_POST['shipping_address_1']);?>"/>
     <input type="hidden" name="shipping_address_2"
      value="<?php echo htmlspecialchars($_POST['shipping_address_2']);?>"/>
     <input type="hidden" name="shipping_city"
      value="<?php echo htmlspecialchars($_POST['shipping_city']);?>"/>
     <input type="hidden" name="shipping_state"
      value="<?php echo htmlspecialchars($_POST['shipping_state']);?>"/>
     <input type="hidden" name="shipping_zip_code"
      value="<?php echo htmlspecialchars($_POST['shipping_zip_code']);?>"/>
     <input type="hidden" name="shipping_phone"
      value="<?php echo htmlspecialchars($_POST['shipping_phone']);?>"/>
     <input type="hidden" name="shipping_email"
      value="<?php echo htmlspecialchars($_POST['shipping_email']);?>"/>
   </div>
 </form>
```

The `ecomm_checkout3.php` script contains the most complex logic of the three checkout scripts, but you will find it is understandable if you patiently work your way through it. The first major task is to assign the incoming data and some other important information (such as the current timestamp and the user's session ID) to the variables that will be used throughout the script.

```
$now = date('Y-m-d H:i:s');
$session = session_id();

$first_name = $_POST['first_name'];
$last_name = $_POST['last_name'];
$address_1 = $_POST['address_1'];
$address_2 = $_POST['address_2'];
$city = $_POST['city'];
$state = $_POST['state'];
$zip_code = $_POST['zip_code'];
$phone = $_POST['phone'];
$email = $_POST['email'];

$shipping_first_name = $_POST['shipping_first_name'];
$shipping_last_name = $_POST['shipping_last_name'];
$shipping_address_1 = $_POST['shipping_address_1'];
$shipping_address_2 = $_POST['shipping_address_2'];
$shipping_city = $_POST['shipping_city'];
```

```
    $shipping_state = $_POST['shipping_state'];
    $shipping_zip_code = $_POST['shipping_zip_code'];
    $shipping_phone = $_POST['shipping_phone'];
    $shipping_email = $_POST['shipping_email'];
```

Then you need to retrieve the customer's ID from the ecomm_customers database. In the case of an existing customer, the ID can be retrieved with a SELECT statement. If the customer is new, then he or she will not have an ID already stored in the database, so the information needs to be added and a new ID generated.

```
$query = 'SELECT
        customer_id
    FROM
        ecomm_customers
    WHERE
        first_name = "' . mysql_real_escape_string($first_name, $db) . '" AND
        last_name = "' . mysql_real_escape_string($last_name, $db) . '" AND
        address_1 = "' . mysql_real_escape_string($address_1, $db) . '" AND
        address_2 = "' . mysql_real_escape_string($address_2, $db) . '" AND
        city = "' . mysql_real_escape_string($city, $db) . '" AND
        state = "' . mysql_real_escape_string($state, $db) . '" AND
        zip_code = "' . mysql_real_escape_string($zip_code, $db) . '" AND
        phone = "' . mysql_real_escape_string($phone, $db) . '" AND
        email = "' . mysql_real_escape_string($email, $db) . '"';
$result = mysql_query($query, $db) or (mysql_error($db));

echo mysql_num_rows($result);
if (mysql_num_rows($result) > 0) {
    $row = mysql_fetch_assoc($result);
    extract($row);
} else {
    $query = 'INSERT INTO ecomm_customers
            (customer_id, first_name, last_name, address_1, address_2, city,
            state, zip_code, phone, email)
        VALUES
            (NULL,
            "' . mysql_real_escape_string($first_name, $db) . '",
            "' . mysql_real_escape_string($last_name, $db) . '",
            "' . mysql_real_escape_string($address_1, $db) . '",
            "' . mysql_real_escape_string($address_2, $db) . '",
            "' . mysql_real_escape_string($city, $db) . '",
            "' . mysql_real_escape_string($state, $db) . '",
            "' . mysql_real_escape_string($zip_code, $db) . '",
            "' . mysql_real_escape_string($phone, $db) . '",
            "' . mysql_real_escape_string($email, $db) . '")';
    mysql_query($query, $db) or (mysql_error($db));
    echo $query;
    $customer_id = mysql_insert_id();
}
mysql_free_result($result);
```

With the customer's valid ID now known, you begin the process of actually storing the order in the database. First, you insert the shipping information into the ecomm_orders table. This creates the record and generates the order's ID, which you need to transfer the shopping cart's contents into the ecomm_order_details table. You come back later to insert the cost values after you transfer the order details.

```
$query = 'INSERT into ecomm_orders
        (order_id, order_date, customer_id, cost_subtotal, cost_total,
        shipping_first_name, shipping_last_name, shipping_address_1,
        shipping_address_2, shipping_city, shipping_state, shipping_zip_code,
        shipping_phone, shipping_email)
    VALUES
            (NULL,
            "' . $now . '",
            ' . $customer_id . ',
            0.00,
            0.00,
            "' . mysql_real_escape_string($shipping_first_name, $db) . '",
            "' . mysql_real_escape_string($shipping_last_name, $db) . '",
            "' . mysql_real_escape_string($shipping_address_1, $db) . '",
            "' . mysql_real_escape_string($shipping_address_2, $db) . '",
            "' . mysql_real_escape_string($shipping_city, $db) . '",
            "' . mysql_real_escape_string($shipping_state, $db) . '",
            "' . mysql_real_escape_string($shipping_zip_code, $db) . '",
            "' . mysql_real_escape_string($shipping_phone, $db) . '",
            "' . mysql_real_escape_string($shipping_email, $db) . '")';
    mysql_query($query, $db) or (mysql_error($db));
    $order_id = mysql_insert_id();
```

An INSERT SELECT statement is used to transfer the values from the temp table to the ecomm_order_details table.

```
$query = 'INSERT INTO ecomm_order_details
    (order_id, order_qty, product_code)
SELECT
    ' . $order_id . ', qty, product_code
FROM
    ecomm_temp_cart
WHERE
    session = "' . $session . '"';
mysql_query($query, $db) or (mysql_error($db));
```

Instead of returning the information retrieved with the SELECT statement to PHP, the script passes the values directly into an INSERT statement and adds them to the table. You can add a clause after the SELECT portion of the statement to instruct MySQL how to handle cases where a duplicate value might be inserted into a column that requires all unique values (a primary key, for example), though that clause is not necessary for your purposes here. The syntax for an INSERT SELECT statement is:

```
INSERT [IGNORE] INTO tbl_name
    [(col_name,...)]
SELECT ...
    [ ON DUPLICATE KEY UPDATE col_name=expr, ... ]
```

After the products have been transferred from the ecomm_temp_cart table to the ecomm_order_details table, they are removed from ecomm_temp_cart.

```
$query = 'DELETE FROM ecomm_temp_cart WHERE session = "' . $session . '"';
mysql_query($query, $db) or (mysql_error($db));
```

The product information is now stored permanently in the details table and associated with the appropriate order. You now need to determine the cost of the purchase and then go back to update the record in `ecomm_orders` with that information. MySQL's SUM() function adds the values of a column together and is used to determine the purchase subtotal.

```
$query = 'SELECT
        SUM(price * order_qty) AS cost_subtotal
    FROM
        ecomm_order_details d JOIN ecomm_products p ON
            d.product_code = p.product_code
    WHERE
        order_id = ' . $order_id;
$result = mysql_query($query, $db) or (mysql_error($db));
$row = mysql_fetch_assoc($result);
extract($row);
```

For the sake of simplicity, we just use 25% of the subtotal as the cost of shipping, and 10% as the tax rate. Your values would be different, depending on your delivery arrangements and the municipality in which you live.

```
$cost_shipping = round($cost_subtotal * 0.25, 2);
$cost_tax = round($cost_subtotal * 0.1, 2);
$cost_total = $cost_subtotal + $cost_shipping + $cost_tax;
```

The order record in the `ecomm_orders` table is then updated with the order's costs.

```
$query = 'UPDATE ecomm_orders
    SET
        cost_subtotal = ' . $cost_subtotal . ',
        cost_shipping = ' . $cost_shipping . ',
        cost_tax = ' . $cost_tax . ',
        cost_total = ' . $cost_total . '
    WHERE
        order_id = ' . $order_id;
mysql_query($query, $db) or (mysql_error($db));
```

The script finishes off by generating a confirmation to display and send to you and your customer by e-mail.

```
$headers = array();
$headers[] = 'MIME-Version: 1.0';
$headers[] = 'Content-type: text/html; charset="iso-8859-1"';
$headers[] = 'Content-Transfer-Encoding: 7bit';
$headers[] = 'From: <store@example.com>';
$headers[] = 'Bcc: <store@example.com>';

mail($email, "Order Confirmation", $html_head . $html_body,
    join("\r\n", $headers));
```

E-Commerce, Any Way You Slice It

As we mentioned before, you can integrate e-commerce into your site the right way, or you can do it the wrong way. To prevent yourself from looking like a complete idiot and virtually ensuring the failure of your venture into e-commerce, we highly recommend doing things the right way! Good word of mouth travels slowly, but we all know how quickly bad word of mouth spreads. Also, with so many millions of web sites out there competing for consumers' attention, you undoubtedly want to elevate yours above the rest.

Here are a few things to remember about some of the more challenging characteristics of your potential customers:

❑ **Your customers are impatient.** They don't want to have to wait for your pages to load or for answers to their questions. They are busy people, just like you, and if they don't find what they need right away, they will leave your site and go somewhere else.

❑ **Your customers are distrustful.** Who wants their personal information strewn about all over the web? You certainly don't, and your customers don't either. They don't want their credit card number to be used by every geek in your office, and they don't want to give you tons of money and never see the product they purchased. They don't want to order from you one week and have you go bankrupt the next.

❑ **Your customers want a lot for a little.** In this age of web site competition, when people can compare prices on virtually any product with just a few mouse clicks, customers are striving to get the best deal they can. But they also appreciate the value-added services of a high-quality web site.

❑ **Your customers are generally lazy.** They don't want to have to put any effort into finding the right product on your site or figuring out what you're trying to say or what your policies are. They don't want to work at trying to get the checkout process to work, and they don't want to have to filter through pages and pages of text to glean information. Make things clear and easy to find.

❑ **Your customers aren't very forgiving.** You basically have one chance to make a good first impression on your customers. Nothing can eliminate a sale (and future sales for that matter) faster than a bad experience. Whether it is something minor such as spelling mistakes and broken images on your site or something major such as selling faulty merchandise, your customers are likely to remember something bad a lot longer than something good. They will also be more likely to share a bad experience than a good one.

❑ **Your customers may not be as technically savvy as you are.** Yes, there are actually people out there who still use dial-up with 56K. There are people out there who still use 14-inch monitors, and there are people out there who have never made an online purchase in their lives. Remember these people, and don't leave them behind totally when designing your site. If you do, you are alienating a huge percentage of the population.

Don't worry: Satisfying e-commerce customers is not hard, but a little effort can really go a long way. We've included some general guidelines to follow. After reading them, you may think, "Well, duh, no kidding," but you'd be surprised at how many big, well-known companies don't follow them.

Information Is Everything

Your customers have to get as much information as possible about your product, because they can't actually see, feel, touch, or smell what you have to offer. Your site is your window to your customers, and they have to depend on what you're telling them to make their purchasing decision. Whatever blanks you leave in your product description, policies, company history, or checkout process will have to be filled in by the customer's imagination. While that may be good in certain circumstances, you do not want your customers to make incorrect assumptions that leave them dissatisfied after the fact, or for their uncertainty to prevent the sale altogether.

Besides textual information, graphics are a very important part of the sale. There is a fine balance between adding too many graphics to your site, which causes your potential patrons to wait longer than they need to, and providing enough high-quality pictures so they can actually see what they're getting.

Importance of Trust

Let's talk for a minute about trust over the web. We all know that most of the proclaimed 14-year-old females in those online chat rooms are really 40-year-old guys sitting in their living rooms. Things are not always as they seem in the online world, and because of that, as an e-commerce retailer, you are at a disadvantage over those with a physical storefront and salespeople. And then there's the old saying "caveat emptor" ("buyer beware"), which goes along with any purchase/sales transaction. Trust must be established, and it certainly is an uphill battle. If you're an established business already and you have spent years building product or brand-name recognition, don't think that switching to e-commerce will be so easy. Yes, if your business has an established reputation, you may have an easier time than some unknown entity, like "Joe's House of Beauty," but people still want to know what they're getting and to be assured that they're not going to get ripped off.

Privacy Policy

Users want to know that their personal information will not be sold and they won't end up on 47 spam e-mail lists. They also want to make sure they won't be on an annoying telemarketing phone list or receive junk snail mail. The only way they can be assured that this won't happen is if you provide a clear and concise privacy policy in an easy-to-find place on your site.

Return Policy

Returns are a sometimes overlooked part of a company's e-commerce venture. There have to be processes in place for accepting returns and shipping out replacement merchandise or issuing credits in exchange. Your users need to know what your return policy is, what your requirements are for accepting returns, and how returns will be handled once they reach your warehouse (or basement).

If you are a relatively or completely unknown entity, you may want to consider providing a 100 percent money back guarantee or something similar, to try to build trust with your potential customers. You may get burned once or twice on this, and it may require more work from you, but overall it can be a very beneficial asset to you, especially if your customers are riding the fence on a potential purchase. It also motivates you to provide the best product or service you can, because you obviously don't want to lose 100 percent of a sale!

Whatever you decide, you should think long and hard about how you want to handle returned merchandise and then make sure your customers understand your decisions, in order to avoid potentially messy misunderstandings later on.

Warm Bodies

In this age of technology, sometimes it's nice just to talk to an actual living, breathing person who can answer your questions or help you find what you are looking for. If you can manage this in your e-commerce environment, it is another great feature that will undoubtedly pay for itself in those "on the fence" purchasing decisions. You can provide personal customer service in a few ways:

❑ Give your customers a phone number (preferably a toll-free number) where they can contact your customer service staff (or just you, if you're a one-person show).

❑ Offer online customer service chat for your customers, where you can address customer questions or concerns without having to pay someone to wait for the phone to ring.

❑ Provide a customer service e-mail address for questions and problems. Although this isn't the optimal solution, because many people don't want to wait for answers to their questions, at least this gives customers an outlet to vent their frustrations and then move on to something else. It also gives you a chance to prepare a proper reply and respond accordingly.

Secure Credit Card Processing

Nothing will make your customers feel better than knowing their credit card information is safe and won't get stolen along the way. Make sure you are using a secure encryption method to transfer sensitive information, such as SSL certificates, a commonly used standard security technology for establishing an encrypted link between a web server and a browser. This technology will make sure your customers understand how safe their transaction and personal information is. It's a good idea not to get too technical; just explain the security process in layman's terms.

If it's possible, it's a good idea to have a third party such as VeriSign verify that your site is secure, and prominently display its seal somewhere on your site.

Professional Look

You want to make sure your e-commerce site doesn't look amateurish and that it appears as professional as possible. A professional appearance is oftentimes equated with credibility in the minds of your customers, and it helps to build that elusive trusting relationship.

Here are some ways to improve the look of your site:

❑ Spend some time viewing other e-commerce sites. What do you personally like about them? What don't you like? By emulating the big guys, you can look big, too.

❑ Invest in a few web site design books, or do some online research. Numerous articles and books have been written on the topic, and you may as well not reinvent the wheel.

❑ If you use a template of some sort, please, please, please do yourself a favor and make sure you remove all generic instances. We've seen sites with a title bar that reads "Insert Description Here." This is not a good look … trust us.

❑ *Spell check* your document. Spell checkers are available in nearly all text editors, so spelling mistakes are pretty much unacceptable and can really undermine your professional look.

Easy Navigation

You want to make sure your customers are able to move around your site and find what they need. Remember the rule from earlier in this section: They do not want to work too hard. Make it easy, or they will lose interest and go somewhere else.

Common Links

Make sure you have clear links to every area of your site, and put the common links near the top where they can be seen easily. Common links include a customer's shopping cart, customer service, and user login.

Search Function

You should give your customers a way to easily find what they're looking for. An accurate and quick search engine is essential to accomplish this. There are many ways to add this feature to your site, either through coding it by hand in PHP or hooking up with third-party software. Another way to improve your search engine is to make sure you include misspellings and not-so-common terms, to give your customers the best results possible.

Typical Design

It's been long enough now that most people are accustomed to seeing navigation links either at the top or to the left side of a page. By keeping with this general scheme, you can ensure that your customers will know where to look to find what they need.

Competitive Pricing

If you are selling items that are available from other sources, it's important to remember that your store can easily be compared with numerous other stores selling the same thing. If your prices are way out of line, your customers will get a good chuckle and then promptly click back to their Google search. Do your research, and make sure you are in line with similar products being sold on the web. Not all customers base their decision solely on price, but they definitely don't want to be taken for a ride, unless you have a Lamborghini Diablo, and that's a different story.

Appropriate Merchandise

Only a handful of stores on the web can get away with carrying a wide range of unrelated products, and — no offense — chances are you aren't one of them. Be sure you are carrying items that are related to your overall site and to each other, or you will confuse your customers and detract from your look and focus.

Timely Delivery

In this world of "overnight this" and "immediately download that," it is no longer acceptable to ask for six to eight weeks to deliver your merchandise to your customers. The only exception is if you are creating something custom made, or if your customers are preordering something that hasn't been officially released yet. The typical lead time for standard products to ship to a customer is roughly two to three business days. If you can do better than that, your customers will be happy, and if not, you need to make sure your customers realize it will take longer, and give them an explanation.

It is also important to provide numerous shipping options to your customers and let them decide how quickly they need your products and how much they are willing to spend to get them faster.

Communication

Because you are isolated from your customers, communication is essential to building strong relationships. Your customers want to know that you received their order, when the order is ready to ship, and when it ships. They appreciate getting a tracking number so they can see where their package is every step of the way. Some companies even track each outgoing package and let their customers know when they think the package has been delivered, in case there are any misunderstandings. All of this can be communicated via e-mail. Your customers will definitely appreciate being kept in the loop and knowing that their order has not been lost somewhere along the order fulfillment and delivery chain.

Customer Feedback

The online world presents an interesting dilemma for e-commerce retailers, in that you must operate your store in a bubble. You can't tell what your customers are thinking or how they react to your site. You only know you're relatively successful if you have sales, and relatively unsuccessful if you don't. Figuring out which of our rules you're breaking can be a tricky endeavor. That's when your customer feedback can make or break you.

You always want to give your customers an outlet to express their concerns or problems, and it can give you a warm fuzzy feeling to get some positive feedback once in a while. To encourage your customers to provide you with feedback, you should do two things:

❑ Give them an incentive to complete a survey or provide some sort of feedback. Free shipping, a discount on their next order, or a special gift of some sort are a few good possibilities.

❑ Make it easy for your customers to complete a survey, but make sure it provides you with valuable feedback. Don't just ask for their comments; ask them to rate certain areas of your site. Also, don't give customers 100 questions; keep it to a maximum of 20. After that, people lose interest, and the special gift isn't worth it.

By sticking to the preceding guidelines and advice, you will increase the quality and quantity of your customer feedback and increase your ability to tap into one of your most valuable resources.

Summary

Now that you have the know-how to add e-commerce to your site, you should feel comfortable making your site as competitive and professional as any other site out there. You should be able to set up a simple shopping cart, and, with time, you will be able to continue to add features to really enhance your cart and your site in general. E-commerce concepts aren't difficult to comprehend, and by following the simple guidelines we've outlined, you will soon be well on your way. Although e-commerce retailers don't typically enjoy overnight success, adding e-commerce to your site can really augment what you're currently doing and may grow to something big over time.

Exercises

We know we're not perfect, so before you start naming all the things we didn't accomplish in our shopping-cart scripts, we'll save you the trouble and list some of them for you. As a matter of fact, we did these things on purpose because we wanted to give you some homework.

Here are the things you can work on, and hints are in Appendix A in case you want some help:

1.   **Allow for tax:** Many states require that you charge sales tax on the orders shipped to the state where you have a physical presence, and some states require sales tax on all online orders. Set your code to check for customers in your own state, and add the appropriate sales tax to those orders only.

2.   **Allow for inventory control:** Your shopping-cart script can keep track of how many items you have in stock and display that to your customers. You can also show an "out of stock" message to your customers, letting them know that a particular item is temporarily out of stock, but still available for purchase if they like.

3.   **Show your customers your most popular items:** Which of your items are purchased the most? If an item is in the top five on your bestseller list, show a "bestseller" icon in the description of that item.

Other things you can add to your shopping-cart script include:

❑   **Allow for options:** You may have noticed that you didn't let your customers pick the size of their T-shirt, or the size and color of their Superhero Body Suit. Alter the codes to allow for these options.

❑   **Allow for payment:** Because of copyright issues, we weren't able to actually hook you up with PayPal or one of the other payment processors available. Decide how you want to accept payment, and then alter the code accordingly.

❑   **Check for mistakes:** We have not included any mechanism to check for required fields or for mismatched types (such as a bogus e-mail address). Add these checks in your code.

❑   **Perform a cart-abandonment analysis:** Numerous studies have shown that online shoppers abandon their carts roughly 75 percent of the time. How does your site stack up?

❑   **Make add-on purchase recommendations:** Once customers place an item in their cart, you might make suggestions for related items or items that other customers have bought in addition to the current item.

❑   **Allow for registering, login, and order tracking:** Some customers like to check the status of their orders.

Creating a Bulletin Board System

People are social beings and don't like to be isolated. Throughout our brief history as civilized human beings, we have consistently tried to maintain some sort of connection to others, whether it be the family unit, clans, chess clubs, or AA meetings. With the advent of the computer, many geeks found themselves shut in a room for long periods of time, becoming the modern equivalent of the social outcast. (How many of us have joked about not knowing what the sun looks like?) The development of the electronic bulletin board made it possible for computer geeks to communicate and once again take part in the social aspect of humanity — without ever having to look at each other's faces.

The bulletin board system, or BBS for short, is an electronic meeting area, also referred to as a *forum*. A traditional forum is a gathering place where people can meet and discuss different topics, and that is a very apt definition for a BBS. However, we want to expand upon it a little further, for use in the computer world. By our definition (and the way we'll use it in this chapter), a forum is a way to talk to other people with a common interest. A bulletin board is the location in which the forum exists, and a bulletin board may house multiple forums. You might visit a book-based BBS to find different forums for science fiction, nonfiction, authors, and more.

Your Bulletin Board

No doubt, you have visited many bulletin boards by now and are aware of the different features they have to offer. Some of them have many bells and whistles and are very slick programs. PHPBB and Vbulletin are two of those very nice, full-featured applications. You have probably seen some very simple boards out there, too. Some are nothing more than a couple of input boxes for a message subject and body with no authentication.

In this chapter, you are going to create a bulletin board system. Once you create your BBS, it will be up to you to create any type of forums within it that you like. Yours will not have quite the feature set of the likes of Vbulletin or PHPBB (unless you are ambitious and decide to expand the application you write), but you will have to put in a few nice expanded features. This is the last application of the book, after all, and we wouldn't let you get away with building something small!

Here is a list of some of the more prominent features of the bulletin board you will build:

- **User authentication:** You want to keep track of who is posting what. You will allow anonymous access to read posts, but this application will require users to log in before they can post their own messages and participate in a discussion.

- **Search:** This is the key feature of any good board, in our opinion. Searching allows users to see if their questions have already been answered, as well as enabling people to find discussions they're interested in.

- **Regular expressions:** We include BBcodes in the application. If you have never seen them, these are special formatting codes that give users limited ability to format and add styles to their posts. For example, placing [b] and [/b] around words will make them bold (for example, [b]some words[/b] will become **some words**). You will be using regular expressions to implement this feature.

- **Pagination:** You don't want to have 328 posts on a single page. Such a page is too long for users to easily read, and it may take a while for web browsers to render such a page. You will be creating a pagination function to avoid this.

You will add a few more bells and whistles in addition to these features, but we won't spoil the surprise yet. We want to give you plenty of "ooh," "aah," and "you're a genius!" moments later.

There are many screens involved in this application. Since you have probably seen a bulletin board application before, it wouldn't make sense for us to show you each and every screen as we describe the application. We'll show you screenshots of just some of the more important screens.

Preparing the Database

This is a large application — the biggest in the book. It consists of about 1,850 lines of code. Are you scared yet? Don't be. The hardest part is the typing, because we will explain everything along the way. But the first thing you will need to do is create the database tables used by the bulletin board application.

Try It Out   **Preparing the Database**

There's a lot of work to be done, so do your typing finger warmups, settle in and get comfortable, and let's get started!

1. Open your favorite editor. Enter the following code as db_ch16.php:

```
<?php
require 'db.inc.php';

$db = mysql_connect(MYSQL_HOST, MYSQL_USER, MYSQL_PASSWORD) or
    die ('Unable to connect. Check your connection parameters.');

mysql_select_db(MYSQL_DB, $db) or die(mysql_error($db));
```

```
$sql = 'CREATE TABLE IF NOT EXISTS frm_access_levels (
        access_lvl    TINYINT UNSIGNED NOT NULL AUTO_INCREMENT,
        access_name   VARCHAR(50)      NOT NULL,

        PRIMARY KEY (access_lvl)
    )
    ENGINE=MyISAM';
mysql_query($sql, $db) or die(mysql_error($db));

$sql = 'INSERT IGNORE INTO frm_access_levels
        (access_lvl, access_name)
    VALUES
        (1, "User"),
        (2, "Moderator"),
        (3, "Administrator")';
mysql_query($sql, $db) or die(mysql_error($db));

$sql = 'CREATE TABLE IF NOT EXISTS frm_admin (
        id       INTEGER UNSIGNED NOT NULL AUTO_INCREMENT,
        title    VARCHAR(100)     NOT NULL DEFAULT "",
        value    VARCHAR(255)     NOT NULL DEFAULT "",
        constant VARCHAR(100)     NOT NULL DEFAULT "",

        PRIMARY KEY (id)
    )
    ENGINE=MyISAM';
mysql_query($sql, $db) or die(mysql_error($db));

$sql = 'INSERT IGNORE INTO frm_admin
        (id, title, value, constant)
    VALUES
        (NULL, "Board Title", "Comic Book Appreciation Forums", "title"),
        (NULL, "Board Description", "The place to discuss your favorite ' .
        'comic books, movies and more!", "description"),
        (NULL, "Admin Email", "admin@example.com", "admin_email"),
        (NULL, "Copyright", "&copy; Comic Book Appreciation, Inc.  All ' .
        'rights reserved.", "copyright"),
        (NULL, "Board Titlebar", "CBA Forums", "titlebar"),
        (NULL, "Pagination Limit", "10", "pageLimit"),
        (NULL, "Pagination Range", "7", "pageRange")';
mysql_query($sql, $db) or die(mysql_error($db));

$sql = 'CREATE TABLE IF NOT EXISTS frm_bbcode (
        id          INTEGER UNSIGNED NOT NULL AUTO_INCREMENT,
        template    VARCHAR(255)     NOT NULL DEFAULT "",
        replacement VARCHAR(255)     NOT NULL DEFAULT "",

        PRIMARY KEY (id)
    )
    ENGINE=MyISAM';
mysql_query($sql, $db) or die(mysql_error($db));
```

```
$sql = 'CREATE TABLE IF NOT EXISTS frm_forum (
        id              INTEGER UNSIGNED NOT NULL AUTO_INCREMENT,
        forum_name      VARCHAR(100)    NOT NULL DEFAULT "",
        forum_desc      VARCHAR(255)    NOT NULL DEFAULT "",
        forum_moderator INTEGER UNSIGNED NOT NULL DEFAULT 0,

        PRIMARY KEY (id)
    )
    ENGINE=MyISAM';
mysql_query($sql, $db) or die(mysql_error($db));

$sql = 'INSERT IGNORE INTO frm_forum
        (id, forum_name, forum_desc, forum_moderator)
    VALUES
        (NULL, "New Forum", "This is the initial forum created when ' .
        'installing the database.  Change the name and the ' .
        'description after installation.", 1)';
mysql_query($sql, $db) or die(mysql_error($db));

$sql = 'CREATE TABLE IF NOT EXISTS frm_post_count (
        user_id    INTEGER UNSIGNED NOT NULL DEFAULT 0,
        post_count INTEGER UNSIGNED NOT NULL DEFAULT 0,

        PRIMARY KEY (user_id)
    )
    ENGINE=MyISAM';
mysql_query($sql, $db) or die(mysql_error($db));

$sql = 'INSERT INTO frm_post_count VALUES (1, 1)';
mysql_query($sql, $db) or die(mysql_error($db));

$sql = 'CREATE TABLE IF NOT EXISTS frm_posts (
        id              INTEGER UNSIGNED NOT NULL AUTO_INCREMENT,
        topic_id        INTEGER UNSIGNED NOT NULL DEFAULT 0,
        forum_id        INTEGER UNSIGNED NOT NULL DEFAULT 0,
        author_id       INTEGER UNSIGNED NOT NULL DEFAULT 0,
        update_id       INTEGER UNSIGNED NOT NULL DEFAULT 0,
        date_posted DATETIME            NOT NULL DEFAULT "0000-00-00 00:00:00",
        date_updated DATETIME,
        subject     VARCHAR(100)    NOT NULL DEFAULT "",
        body        MEDIUMTEXT,

        PRIMARY KEY (id),
        INDEX (forum_id, topic_id, author_id, date_posted),
        FULLTEXT INDEX (subject, body)
    )
    ENGINE=MyISAM';
mysql_query($sql, $db) or die(mysql_error($db));

$sql = 'INSERT IGNORE INTO frm_posts
        (id, topic_id, forum_id, author_id, update_id, date_posted,
        date_updated, subject, body)
    VALUES
```

```
              (1, 0, 1, 1, 0, "' . date('Y-m-d H:i:s') . '", 0, "Welcome",
         "Welcome to your new Bulletin Board System.  Do not forget to ' .
         'change your admin password after installation.  Have fun!")';
mysql_query($sql, $db) or die(mysql_error($db));


$sql = 'CREATE TABLE IF NOT EXISTS frm_users (
         id           INTEGER UNSIGNED NOT NULL AUTO_INCREMENT,
         email        VARCHAR(100)     NOT NULL UNIQUE,
         password     CHAR(41)         NOT NULL,
         name         VARCHAR(100)     NOT NULL,
         access_lvl   TINYINT UNSIGNED NOT NULL DEFAULT 1,
         signature    VARCHAR(255),
         date_joined  DATETIME         NOT NULL,
         last_login   DATETIME,

         PRIMARY KEY (id)
)
ENGINE=MyISAM';
mysql_query($sql, $db) or die(mysql_error($db));

$sql = 'INSERT IGNORE INTO frm_users
         (id, name, email, password, access_lvl, signature,
         date_joined, last_login)
     VALUES
         (1, "Administrator", "admin@example.com", PASSWORD("secret"),
         3, "", "' . date('Y-m-d H:i:s') . '", NULL)';
mysql_query($sql, $db) or die(mysql_error($db));
?>

<html>
 <head>
  <title>Forum Tables Created</title>
 </head>
 <body>
 <h1>Comic Book Appreciation Forums</h1>
 <p>The following forum tables have been created:</p>
 <ul>
  <li>frm_admin</li>
  <li>frm_access_levels</li>
  <li>frm_admin</li>
  <li>frm_bbcode</li>
  <li>frm_form</li>
  <li>frm_post_count</li>
  <li>frm_posts</li>
  <li>frm_users</li>
 </ul>
 <p><a href="frm_login.php">Log In</a> to the site now.</p>
 </body>
</html>
```

2. Load db_ch16.php in your browser. If all goes well, you should see a page that resembles Figure 16-1.

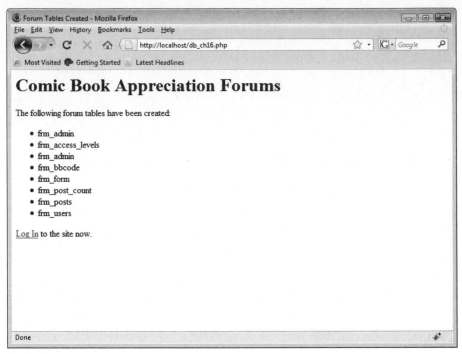

Figure 16-1

How It Works

The script creates the seven tables used by the bulletin board application. The first table is named `frm_access_levels` and is used to store access permission:

Fieldname	Type	Description of What It Stores
access_lvl	TINYINT UNSIGNED	Unique ID. Column is the primary key and auto-increments.
access_name	VARCHAR(50)	Descriptive name of permission.

The second table is `frm_admin`, which holds a handful of configuration parameters for the application:

Fieldname	Type	Description of What It Stores
id	INTEGER UNSIGNED	Unique ID. Column is the primary key and auto-increments.
title	VARCHAR(100)	Descriptive name of the parameter.
value	VARCHAR(255)	The parameter's setting.
constant	VARCHAR(100)	The parameter's name when referenced by a script.

The next table you create is called `frm_bbcode` and contains the patterns and replacements to support BBCode markup:

Fieldname	Type	Description of What It Stores
id	INTEGER UNSIGNED	Unique ID. Column is the primary key and auto-increments.
template	VARCHAR(255)	The regular expression for which to search.
replacement	VARCHAR(255)	The replacement text.

The fourth table is named `frm_forum` and contains the list of forums:

Fieldname	Type	Description of What It Stores
id	INTEGER UNSIGNED	Unique ID. Column is the primary key and auto-increments.
forum_name	VARCHAR(100)	The name of the forum.
forum_desc	VARCHAR(255)	A description of the forum.
forum_moderator	INTEGER UNSIGNED	The user ID of the forum's moderator. Foreign key that references `frm_user.id`.

The next table is `frm_post_count` and will hold the number of messages each user has posted:

Fieldname	Type	Description of What It Stores
user_id	INTEGER UNSIGNED	References `frm_user.id`.
post_count	INTEGER UNSIGNED	The number of posts the user has made.

The sixth table is `frm_posts` and will hold the discussion messages posted to the forums:

Fieldname	Type	Description of What It Stores
id	INTEGER UNSIGNED	Unique ID. Column is the primary key and auto-increments.
topic_id	INTEGER UNSIGNED	The ID of the parent post, if any.
forum_id	INTEGER UNSIGNED	The forum ID to which the post belongs.
author_id	INTEGER UNSIGNED	User ID of user who posted the message. Foreign key that references `frm_user.id`.

(continued)

Fieldname	Type	Description of What It Stores
update_id	INTEGER UNSIGNED	User ID of user who last updated the post. Foreign key that references frm_user.id.
date_posted	DATETIME	The date the post was made.
date_updated	DATETIME	The date the post was last updated.
subject	VARCHAR(100)	The subject of the message.
body	MEDIUMTEXT	The text of the message.

The final table is frm_users and stores the forum's registered users:

Fieldname	Type	Description of What It Stores
user_id	INTEGER UNSIGNED	Unique ID. Column is the primary key and auto-increments.
name	VARCHAR(50)	The user's name.
email	VARCHAR(100)	The user's e-mail address.
password	CHAR(41)	The user's password.
access_lvl	TINYINT UNSIGNED	The permission level the user has.
Signature	VARCHAR(255)	The user's signature to be appended at the end of his or her posts.
last_login	DATETIME	The date and time when the user last logged in.
date_joined	DATETIME	The date and time when the user joined.

After creating each table, you insert into it any records you may need initially. You now have the tables set up in the database and the necessary entries you will need to start to build your bulletin board application.

Reusable Code

The next thing you need to do is create the support files that will be included in your forum scripts. If you experience a sense of déjà vu, that's because some of the code here is similar to the reusable functions you wrote in Chapter 13.

Try It Out   **Creating Reusable Scripts**

In this exercise, the reusable scripts you are creating don't have any standalone purpose. Even though they don't show anything on the screen, you must pay careful attention when typing them, because they form part of the backbone of your application.

1.   Create `frm_output_functions.inc.php`. This file contains most of the major functions that the board uses.

```php
<?php
function msg_box($message, $title, $destination = 'frm_index.php') {
    $msg = '<div>';
    $msg .= '<h2>' . $title . '</h2>';
    $msg .= '<p>' . $message . '</p>';
    $msg .= '<p><a href="' . $destination . '">Yes</a> <a href=
"frm_index.php">' .
        'No</a></p>';
    $msg .= '</div>';
    return $msg;
}

function get_forum($db, $id) {
    $sql = 'SELECT
            forum_name as name, forum_desc as description,
            forum_moderator as moderator
        FROM
            frm_forum
        WHERE id = ' . $id;
    $result = mysql_query($sql, $db) or die(mysql_error($db));
    $row = mysql_fetch_assoc($result);
    mysql_free_result($result);
    return $row;
}

function get_forum_id($db, $topic_id) {
    $sql - 'SELECT forum_id FROM frm_posts WHERE id = ' . $topic_id;
    $result = mysql_query($sql, $db) or die(mysql_error($db));
    $row = mysql_fetch_assoc($result);
    $retVal = $row['forum_id'];
    mysql_free_result($result);
    return $retVal;
}

function breadcrumb($db, $id, $get_from = 'F') {
    $separator = ' &middot; ';
    if ($get_from == 'P') {
        $sql = 'SELECT forum_id, subject FROM frm_posts WHERE id = ' . $id;
        $result = mysql_query($sql, $db) or die(mysql_error($db));
        $row = mysql_fetch_array($result);
        $id = $row['forum_id'];
        $topic = $row['subject'];
        mysql_free_result($result);
```

```
    }
    $row = get_forum($db, $id);

    $bcrumb = '<a href="frm_index.php">Home</a>' . $separator;
    switch ($get_from) {
    case 'P':
        $bcrumb .= '<a href="frm_view_forum.php?f=' . $id . '">'
. $row['name'] .
            '</a>' . $separator . $topic;
        break;

    case 'F':
        $bcrumb .= $row['name'];
        break;
    }
    return '<h2>' . $bcrumb . '</h2>';
}

function show_topic($db, $topic_id, $user_id, $limit = 25) {

    echo breadcrumb($db, $topic_id, 'P');

    if (isset($_GET['page'])) {
        $page = $_GET['page'];
    } else {
        $page = 1;
    }

    $start = ($page - 1) * $limit;

    if (isset($_SESSION['user_id'])) {
        echo topic_reply_bar($db, $topic_id, get_forum_id($db, $topic_id));
    }

    $sql = 'SELECT SQL_CALC_FOUND_ROWS
            p.id, p.subject, p.body, p.date_posted, p.date_updated,
            u.name as author, u.id as author_id, u.signature as sig,
            c.post_count as postcount, p.forum_id as forum_id,
            f.forum_moderator as moderator, p.update_id, u2.name
as updated_by
        FROM
            frm_forum f JOIN frm_posts p ON f.id = p.forum_id
            JOIN frm_users u ON u.id = p.author_id
            LEFT JOIN frm_users u2 ON u2.id = p.update_id
            LEFT JOIN frm_post_count c ON u.id = c.user_id
        WHERE
            p.topic_id = ' . $topic_id . ' OR
            p.id = ' . $topic_id . ' '
```

```
        ORDER BY
            p.topic_id, p.date_posted
        LIMIT ' . $start . ', ' . $limit;
    $result = mysql_query($sql, $db) or die(mysql_error($db));

    $page_links = paginate($db, $limit);
    if (mysql_num_rows($result) == 0) {
        $msg = "There are currently no posts.  Would you " .
                "like to be the first person to create a thread?";
        $title = "No Posts...";
        $dest = "frm_compose.php?forumid=" . $forum_id;
        echo msg_box($msg, $title, $dest);
    } else {
        echo '<table style="width: 80%;">';
        echo '<tr>';
        echo '<th>Author</th>';
        echo '<th style="width: 85%;">Post</th>';
        echo '</tr>';
        $rowclass = '';
        while ($row = mysql_fetch_array($result)) {
            $lastupdate = '';
            $editlink = '';
            $dellink = '';
            $replylink = ' ';
            $pcount = '';
            $pdate = '';
            $sig = '';
            $body = $row['body'];
            if (isset($_SESSION['user_id'])) {
                $replylink = '<a href="frm_compose.php?forumid=' .
                    $row['forum_id'] . '&topicid=' . $topic_id .'&reid=' .
                    $row['id'] . '">REPLY</a> ';
            } else {
                $replylink = '';
            }
            if ($row['update_id'] > 0) {
                $lastupdate = '<p>Last updated: ' . $row['date_updated'] .
                    ' by ' . $row['updated_by'] . '</p>';
            }
            if ($user_id == $row['author_id'] ||
                $user_id == $row['moderator'] ||
                (isset($_SESSION['access_lvl']) && $_SESSION
['access_lvl'] > 2)) {
                $editlink = '<a href="frm_compose.php?a=edit&post=' .
                    $row['id'] . '">EDIT</a> ';
                $dellink = '<a href="frm_transact_affirm.php?' .
                    'action=deletepost&id=' . $row['id'] . '">DELETE</a> ';
            }
            $pcount = '<br/>Posts: ' . ($row['postcount'] == '' ? 0 :
                $row['postcount']);
            $pdate = $row['date_posted'];
            $sig = (($row['sig'] != '') ? '<p class="sig">' .
```

```
                    bbcode($db, nl2br($row['sig']))) : '') . '</p>';
            $rowclass = ($rowclass == 'odd_row') ? 'even_row' : 'odd_row';
            echo '<tr class="' . $rowclass . '">';
            echo '<td>' . $row['author'];
            echo $pcount;
            echo '</td><td><p>';
            if (isset($_SESSION['user_id']) &&
                $_SESSION['last_login'] < $row['date_posted']) {
                echo NEWPOST . ' ';
            }
            if (isset($_GET['page'])) {
                $pagelink = '&page=' . $_GET['page'];
            } else {
                $pagelink = '';
            }
            echo '<a name="post' . $row['id'] . '" href="frm_view
_topic.php?t=' .
                $topic_id . $pagelink . '#post' . $row['id'] . '">' .
 POSTLINK .
                '</a>';
            if (isset($row['subject'])) {
                echo ' <strong>' . $row['subject'] . '</strong>';
            }
            echo '</p><p>' . bbcode($db, nl2br(htmlspecialchars
($body))) . '</p>';
            echo $sig;
            echo $lastupdate;
            echo '</td>';
            echo '</tr><tr class="' . $rowclass . '">';
            echo '<td>' . $pdate . '</td>';
            echo '<td style="text-align: right;">';
            echo $replylink;
            echo $editlink;
            echo $dellink;
            echo '</td></tr>';
        }
        echo '</table>';
        echo $pagelink;
        echo '<p>' . NEWPOST . ' = New Post     ';
        echo POSTLINK . ' = Post link (use to bookmark)</p>';
    }
}

function isParent($page) {
    return (strpos($_SERVER['PHP_SELF'], $page) !== false);
}

function topic_reply_bar($db, $topic_id, $forum_id) {
    $html = '<p>';
```

```
        if ($topic_id > 0) {
            $html .= '<a href="frm_compose.php?forumid=' .
$forum_id . '&topicid=' .
                $topic_id . '&reid=' . $topic_id . '">Reply to Thread</a>';
        }
        if ($forum_id > 0) {
            $html .= ' <a href="frm_compose.php?forumid=' . $forum_id . '">' .
                'New Thread</a>';
        }
        $html .= '</p>';
        return $html;
}

function user_option_list($db, $level) {
    $sql = 'SELECT
                id, name, access_lvl
            FROM
                frm_users
            WHERE
                access_lvl = ' . $level . '
            ORDER BY
                name';
    $result = mysql_query($sql) or die(mysql_error($db));

    while ($row = mysql_fetch_array($result)) {
        echo '<option value="' . $row['id'] . '">' .
            htmlspecialchars($row['name']) . '</option>';
    }
    mysql_free_result($result);
}

function paginate($db, $limit = 10) {
    global $admin;

    $sql = 'SELECT FOUND_ROWS();';
    $result = mysql_query($sql, $db) or die(mysql_error($db));
    $row = mysql_fetch_array($result);
    $numrows = $row[0];
    $pagelinks = '<p>';
    if ($numrows > $limit) {
        if(isset($_GET['page'])){
            $page = $_GET['page'];
        } else {
            $page = 1;
        }
        $currpage = $_SERVER['PHP_SELF'] . '?' . $_SERVER['QUERY_STRING'];
        $currpage = str_replace('&page=' . $page, '', $currpage);

        if($page == 1) {
            $pagelinks .= '&lt; PREV';
```

```
        } else {
            $pageprev = $page - 1;
            $pagelinks .= '<a href="' . $currpage . '&page=' . $pageprev .
                '">&lt; PREV</a>';
        }

        $numofpages = ceil($numrows / $limit);
        $range = $admin['pageRange']['value'];
        if ($range == '' or $range == 0) {
            $range = 7;
        }
        $lrange = max(1, $page - (($range - 1) / 2));
        $rrange = min($numofpages, $page + (($range - 1) / 2));
        if (($rrange - $lrange) < ($range - 1)) {
            if ($lrange == 1) {
                $rrange = min($lrange + ($range - 1), $numofpages);
            } else {
                $lrange = max($rrange - ($range - 1), 0);
            }
        }

        if ($lrange > 1) {
            $pagelinks .= '..';
        } else {
            $pagelinks .= '  ';
        }
        for($i = 1; $i <= $numofpages; $i++) {
            if ($i == $page) {
                $pagelinks .= $i;
            } else {
                if ($lrange <= $i and $i <= $rrange) {
                    $pagelinks .= '<a href="' . $currpage . '&page=' . $i .
                        '">' . $i . '</a>';
                }
            }
        }
        if ($rrange < $numofpages) {
            $pagelinks .= '..';
        } else {
            $pagelinks .= '  ';
        }

        if(($numrows - ($limit * $page)) > 0) {
            $pagenext = $page + 1;
            $pagelinks .= '<a href="' . $currpage . '&page=' . $pagenext .
                '">NEXT &gt;</a>';
        } else {
            $pagelinks .= 'NEXT &gt;';
        }
    } else {
        $pagelinks .= '&lt; PREV  NEXT &gt;  ';
    }
$pagelinks .= '</p>';
```

```
            return $pagelinks;
    }

    function bbcode($db, $data) {
        $sql = 'SELECT
                template, replacement
            FROM
                frm_bbcode';
        $result = mysql_query($sql, $db) or die(mysql_error($db));
        if (mysql_num_rows($result) > 0) {
            while($row = mysql_fetch_array($result)) {
                $bbcode['tpl'][] = '/' .
                    html_entity_decode($row['template'], ENT_QUOTES). '/i';
                $bbcode['rep'][] = html_entity_decode($row['replacement'],
                    ENT_QUOTES);
            }
            $data1 = preg_replace($bbcode['tpl'], $bbcode['rep'], $data);
            $count = 1;
            while (($data1 != $data) and ($count < 4)) {
                $count++;
                $data = $data1;
                $data1 = preg_replace($bbcode['tpl'], $bbcode['rep'], $data);
            }
        }
        return $data;
    }
?>
```

2. Create `frm_config.inc.php`. This sets up any constants or variables you may need in the application. It loads admin settings and BBcode patterns into arrays to be used by the board.

```
<?php
$sql = 'SELECT * FROM frm_admin';
$result = mysql_query($sql, $db) or die(mysql_error($db));

while ($row = mysql_fetch_array($result)) {
    $admin[$row['constant']]['title'] = $row['title'];
    $admin[$row['constant']]['value'] = $row['value'];
}
mysql_free_result($result);

$sql = 'SELECT * FROM frm_bbcode';
$result = mysql_query($sql, $db) or die(mysql_error($db));

while ($row = mysql_fetch_array($result)) {
    $bbcode[$row['id']]['template'] = $row['template'];
    $bbcode[$row['id']]['replacement'] = $row['replacement'];
}
mysql_free_result($result);

define('NEWPOST', '&raquo;');
define('POSTLINK', '&diams;');
?>
```

3. Create `frm_header.inc.php`. This goes at the top of each page that gets displayed.

```php
<?php
session_start();
require 'db.inc.php';
require 'frm_output_functions.inc.php';

$db = mysql_connect(MYSQL_HOST, MYSQL_USER, MYSQL_PASSWORD) or
    die ('Unable to connect. Check your connection parameters.');

mysql_select_db(MYSQL_DB, $db) or die(mysql_error($db));

require 'frm_config.inc.php';

$title = $admin['titlebar']['value'];
if (isset($pageTitle) and $pageTitle != '') {
    $title .= ' :: ' . $pageTitle;
}
if (isset($_SESSION['user_id'])) {
    $userid = $_SESSION['user_id'];
} else {
    $userid = null;
}
if (isset($_SESSION['access_lvl'])) {
    $access_lvl = $_SESSION['access_lvl'];
} else {
    $access_lvl = null;
}
if (isset($_SESSION['name'])) {
    $username = $_SESSION['name'];
} else {
    $username = null;
}
?>
<html>
 <head>
  <title><?php echo $title; ?></title>
  <style type="text/css">
   th { background-color: #999;}
   td { vertical-align: top; }
   .odd_row { background-color: #EEE; }
   .even_row { background-color: #FFF; }
  </style>
 </head>
 <body>
  <h1><?php echo $admin['title']['value']; ?></h1>
  <h2><?php echo $admin['description']['value']; ?></h2>
<?php
if (isset($_SESSION['name'])) {
    echo '<p>Welcome, ' . $_SESSION['name'] . '</p>';
}
```

```
?>
  <form method="get" action="frm_search.php">
   <div>
    <input type="text" name="keywords"
<?php
if (isset($_GET['keywords'])) {
    echo 'value="' . htmlspecialchars($_GET['keywords']) . '" ';
 }
?>
/>
    <input type="submit" value="Search"/>
   </div>
  </form>
<?php
echo '<p><a href="frm_index.php">Home</a>';
if (!isset($_SESSION['user_id'])) {
    echo ' | <a href="frm_login.php">Log In</a>';
    echo ' | <a href="frm_useraccount.php">Register</a>';
} else {
    echo ' | <a href="frm_transact_user.php?action=Logout">';
    echo "Log out " . $_SESSION['name'] . "</a>";
    if ($_SESSION['access_lvl'] > 2) {
        echo ' | <a href="frm_admin.php">Admin</a>';
    }
    echo ' | <a href="frm_useraccount.php">Profile</a>';
}
echo '</p>';
?>
```

4. Enter `frm_footer.inc.php`, which places a footer at the bottom of each page that gets displayed:

```
<p><?php echo $admin['copyright']['value']; ?></p>
 </body>
</html>
```

How It Works

Most of the code in these scripts should be pretty understandable, by this point. You've seen functions like `trim_body)_` before in similar functionality in Chapter 13's content management system (CMS) application. Let's look, however, at some of the more powerful functionality that `frm_output_ functions.inc.php` gives you.

Pagination

If you are not familiar with pagination, then we suggest you do a quick search — for anything — on your favorite search engine. No matter what you search for, most likely you'll have a large number of links returned in response to your query. You should see some links somewhere that will take you to more pages of search results, with the option of clicking next, previous, or a specific numbered page. That, my friend, is pagination, and we are going to teach you how to do it for your own pages.

When paginating your data, there are a few things you should have. The first, of course, is a large set of data that you can't display on one page. You also need to know how many rows of data you will display per page, and how many total records you have in your result set. You also need to know how many pages you will have access to at one time. For example, if you had 40 pages of data to display, you might want to show links only for pages 1 through 10, or 12 through 21, and so forth. This is called the *range*.

Take a look at show_topic() in frm_output_functions.inc.php. It's quite lengthy, so we'll highlight for you the relevant code lines that affect pagination.

```
function show_topic($db, $topic_id, $user_id, $limit = 25) {
...
    if (isset($_GET['page'])) {
        $page = $_GET['page'];
    } else {
        $page = 1;
    }

    $start = ($page - 1) * $limit;
```

In a calling page, you pass in a number equaling the maximum number of records per page you want to display. If you don't pass a page parameter in the URL to the web page, you assume you are on page 1. Otherwise, you will be setting page to the value passed to you in the URL. By knowing the page and the limit (number of posts per page), you can calculate your $start value (which will be used by the LIMIT statement in the SQL statement used to retrieve rows). For example, if you are on page 3, and your limit is 25 posts per page, then the third page will display rows 51 through 75.

Here is the SQL statement for returning posts. It may be long, but thankfully it is not overly complex. It is simply four tables joined by the JOIN statement. Please note the first line and the last line of the SQL statement:

```
$sql = 'SELECT SQL_CALC_FOUND_ROWS
        p.id, p.subject, p.body, p.date_posted, p.date_updated,
        u.name as author, u.id as author_id, u.signature as sig,
        c.post_count as postcount, p.forum_id as forum_id,
        f.forum_moderator as moderator, p.update_id, u2.name as updated_by
    FROM
        frm_forum f JOIN frm_posts p ON f.id = p.forum_id
        JOIN frm_users u ON u.id = p.author_id
        LEFT JOIN frm_users u2 ON u2.id = p.update_id
        LEFT JOIN frm_post_count c ON u.id = c.user_id
    WHERE
        p.topic_id = ' . $topic_id . ' OR
        p.id = ' . $topic_id . '
    ORDER BY
         p.topic_id, p.date_posted
    LIMIT ' . $start . ', ' . $limit;
$result = mysql_query($sql, $db) or die(mysql_error($db));

$page_links = paginate($db, $limit);
```

This query will return a maximum of the number of rows in $limit. The problem is, you need to know how many rows *would have been returned* if LIMIT had not been used. You could execute the query again without the LIMIT clause and retrieve the number of rows returned, but it turns out that isn't necessary. MySQL provides the SQL_CALC_FOUND_ROWS command as a means for you to find out. In the first line, immediately following SELECT, you use the SQL command SQL_CALC_FOUND_ROWS. This doesn't do anything to the query directly, but does allow you to subsequently run the SQL command:

```
$sql = "SELECT FOUND_ROWS();";
```

The MySQL function FOUND_ROWS() returns the number of rows that SQL_CALC_FOUND_ROWS found. SQL_CALC_FOUND_ROWS makes the SELECT query take slightly longer to execute, but it is still more efficient than running the query a second time to find out how many rows would have been returned if you had not used a LIMIT clause.

After you have your numbers, it's time to create the page links. Take a look at the paginate() function in the same file:

```
function paginate($db, $limit = 10) {
    global $admin;

    $sql = 'SELECT FOUND_ROWS();';
    $result = mysql_query($sql, $db) or die(mysql_error($db));
    $row = mysql_fetch_array($result);
    $numrows = $row[0];
    $pagelinks = '<p>';
    if ($numrows > $limit) {
        if(isset($_GET['page'])){
            $page = $_GET['page'];
        } else {
            $page = 1;
        }
...
    } else {
        $pagelinks .= '&lt; PREV  NEXT &gt;  ';
    }
    $pagelinks .= '</p>';
    return $pagelinks;
}
```

The paginate function takes a $limit parameter, which, if it is not passed in to the function, you set to a default value of 10. In order for the code to access the forum configuration variables, such as range and limit, $admin must be declared global because the scope of PHP's execution is now in the function. Otherwise, you would not be able to access the configuration.

As you can see, because you used SELECT FOUND_ROWS(), $numrows contains the number of rows your query returns. As long as the number of rows is larger than your limit, you'll generate the pagination links. Otherwise, you'll just display inactive links.

Next, you grab the page variable, if it is set. If not, then you set $page to 1. Then you determine whether the <PREV link should be active or not. Obviously if you are on page 1, there is no previous

page, and the link should not be active. Otherwise, the previous page is one less than the number of the current page:

```
if($page == 1) {
    $pagelinks .= '&lt; PREV';
} else {
    $pageprev = $page - 1;
    $pagelinks .= '<a href="' . $currpage . '&page=' . $pageprev .
        '">&lt; PREV</a>';
}
```

The next chunk of code does a little bit of math. The number of pages is determined by dividing the total number of rows returned by your previous SELECT FOUND_ROWS() query by the number of posts per page ($numrows divided by $limit) and rounding up.

The range is grabbed from $admin['pagerange']['value'] and stored in $range. If it's not available, then $range defaults to 7. This value determines how many pages are accessible via a link at the bottom of the page. For example, if the range is 5, there are 13 pages, and you are currently viewing page 6, you will have access to pages 4, 5, 6, 7, and 8:

```
< PREV .. [4] [5] 6 [7] [8] .. NEXT >
```

The ".." shows you that there are more pages in that direction (either before or after).

```
$numofpages = ceil($numrows / $limit);
$range = $admin['pageRange']['value'];
if ($range == '' or $range == 0) {
    $range = 7;
}
```

The next few lines determine what range of pages to show you. In the previous example, if the $range is 5, but you are viewing page 2 out of 13 pages, the code should be smart enough to allow you access to pages 1 through 5:

```
< PREV  [1] 2 [3] [4] [5] .. NEXT >
```

As you can see, you are viewing page 2, you can get to pages 1 through 5 directly, and there are more pages past 5. The piece of logic that determines which pages are available is the following:

```
$lrange = max(1, $page - (($range - 1) / 2));
$rrange = min($numofpages, $page + (($range - 1) / 2));
if (($rrange - $lrange) < ($range - 1)) {
    if ($lrange == 1) {
        $rrange = min($lrange + ($range - 1), $numofpages);
    } else {
        $lrange = max($rrange - ($range - 1), 0);
    }
}
```

Then, the next part of the code renders the space between PREV and NEXT. If the lower range is higher than 1, you put .. in to show that more pages can be accessed by clicking <PREV. Then, use the $lrange and $rrange values to build the page number links. If the link corresponds to the current page, don't

make it a link. Next, if the high end of the range of pages is lower than the total number of pages available, you put in the .. to show that more pages can be accessed by clicking NEXT>.

```
if ($lrange > 1) {
    $pagelinks .= '..';
} else {
    $pagelinks .= '  ';
}
for($i = 1; $i <= $numofpages; $i++) {
    if ($i == $page) {
        $pagelinks .= $i;
    } else {
        if ($lrange <= $i and $i <= $rrange) {
            $pagelinks .= '<a href="' . $currpage . '&page=' . $i .
                '">' . $i . '</a>';
        }
    }
}
if ($rrange < $numofpages) {
    $pagelinks .= '..';
} else {
    $pagelinks .= '  ';
}
```

The last part of the code renders NEXT> as an active or inactive link, depending on whether or not you are looking at the last post of the thread, as it doesn't make sense to go beyond the last page. Doing this is relatively simple:

```
if(($numrows - ($limit * $page)) > 0) {
    $pagenext = $page + 1;
    $pagelinks .= '<a href="' . $currpage . '&page=' . $pagenext .
        '">NEXT &gt;</a>';
} else {
    $pagelinks .= 'NEXT &gt;';
}
} else {
    $pagelinks .= '&lt; PREV  NEXT &gt;  ';
}
```

Voilà! You have a terrific, customizable, dynamically built pagination function. Your code generates simple text links for the pages. However, you can easily take the logic presented here and modify the code to implement CSS styles, images, or whatever else tickles your creative fancy.

Breadcrumbs

Once upon a time, there were two little children named Hansel and Gretel. They didn't want to get lost in the forest, so the story goes. So Hansel got the bright idea of dropping crumbs of bread along the path so that they could find their way back. Birds ate the bread, the kids got lost, and then they stumbled upon a house made out of gingerbread and candy (yum!). The little old lady who owned the house wasn't too keen on the idea of children eating holes through her walls, and so she enslaved them. Hansel got fat eating German chocolates and candies while sitting in a cage, and Gretel was forced to do chores. Then one day they stuffed the little old lady in an oven and ran home. The end.

Exactly how Hansel and Gretel found their way home remains a mystery to us, since the birds ate the breadcrumbs marking the trail, and that's how they got lost in the first place! But aside from that, Hansel had the right idea. By leaving some sort of trail behind them, they should have been able to navigate out of any dark forest.

Some time ago, search engines came along, and some of them gave us the ability to find web sites based on categories. Because there are so many sites out there that are very specialized, some of them might be in a sub-sub-sub-subcategory. For example, say you wanted to view some sites in the Yahoo! directory about PHP. You click the Computers and Internet category. Hmmm. Next, click Software, then Internet, World Wide Web, Servers (ah, we're getting close), Server Side Scripting, and (yes, finally!) PHP. Now that you have reached this page, wouldn't it be nice to remember how you got here? If you look near the top of the screen, you should see something that looks like this:

```
Directory > Computers and Internet > Software > Internet >
    World Wide Web > Servers >Server Side Scripting > PHP
```

It is a map of categories and subcategories telling you exactly how to get to the category you are looking at. Someone (probably a fan of gingerbread houses, but don't quote us on that) saw this "map" and decided to call it a breadcrumb list. The name has stuck.

The truth is, breadcrumbs are very helpful, and they make a lot of sense for a bulletin board forum. They can give you a map from the post you are reading to the thread it was in, to the forum the thread was in, to the category the forum was in, and to the home page. By clicking on any part of the breadcrumb trail, you can easily navigate to another part of the site. Perhaps one would look like this:

```
Home > Comic Book Movies > Spider-Man > This movie rocked! > I agree
```

You have implemented breadcrumbs for this application, and we will explain to you how it was done. You could implement a breadcrumb system in many different ways (such as by folder structure). This is just one way, and it is relatively simple.

The function itself takes two arguments, $id and $getfrom. The argument $getfrom will either be F for forum or P for post. There is no one standard separator for crumbs. Some people use >, but we like to use a bullet or dot. You can use whichever HTML entity you like:

```
function breadcrumb($db, $id, $get_from = 'F') {
    $separator = ' &middot; ';
```

If you are in a post, then you want your breadcrumb to include a link to the forum, along with a nonlinked indication of what thread you are in. You pass in the topic_id to retrieve the right topic and get the forum_id from that topic and put it into the $id field. You also extract the name of the topic.

```
if ($get_from == 'P') {
    $sql = 'SELECT forum_id, subject FROM frm_posts WHERE id = ' . $id;
    $result = mysql_query($sql, $db) or die(mysql_error($db));
    $row = mysql_fetch_array($result);
    $id = $row['forum_id'];
    $topic = $row['subject'];
    mysql_free_result($result);
}
```

Next, you call `get_forum()` with the `$id` that is now a `forum_id`. It returns a row that contains the name and description of the forum. You don't currently use the description, but you could use it as `alt` or `title` attributes for the breadcrumb, if you wanted to.

```
$row = get_forum($db, $id);
```

At this point, you begin building the breadcrumb in the variable `$bcrumb`. `Home` is always first, and then the separator. Next is either a link to the forum (if looking at a post), or simply the forum listed without a link. Next comes the thread title for the post you are looking at.

```
    $bcrumb = '<a href="frm_index.php">Home</a>' . $separator;
    switch ($get_from) {
    case 'P':
        $bcrumb .= '<a href="frm_view_forum.php?f=' . $id . '">'
. $row['name'] .
            '</a>' . $separator . $topic;
        break;

    case 'F':
        $bcrumb .= $row['name'];
        break;
    }
    return '<h2>' . $bcrumb . '</h2>';
}
```

As we said before, this breadcrumb is not that difficult or complex, but we are sure that, armed with all of the PHP knowledge you now have from reading this book, you could easily come up with a very impressive breadcrumb function!

Next, take a look at your `frm_header.inc.php` file. There isn't much new to see here, but it gives us a chance to discuss authentication with you for a moment.

A Last Look at User Authentication

The Comic Book Appreciation board uses user authentication, but it is by no means totally secure. For a board application, it is probably secure enough. If this were human resources data containing sensitive information, you might want to make it a bit more secure. This book does not attempt to help you create a virtual Fort Knox. If you have such a need, we strongly suggest you look for a good book on security, and perhaps look at a few online resources. A good start is www.w3.org/Security/Faq/.

Take a look at your security model, and see where there might be some places to improve it a bit. If you look at most of the PHP pages that make up the application, you see that you check for a user's access level before displaying certain items. For example, examine `frm_header.inc.php`.

Because `frm_header.inc.php` is included at the top of almost every web page, you do most of your user authentication there. By checking for the existence of the `user_id` session variable, you know the user is logged in. By checking if `access_lvl` is greater than 2, you know whether the user has administrator access. This allows you to customize the main menu according to the user's login status and his or her access level. It also allows you to address the user by name.

```
if (isset($_SESSION['name'])) {
    echo '<p>Welcome, ' . $_SESSION['name'] . '</p>';
}
...
echo '<p><a href="frm_index.php">Home</a>';
if (!isset($_SESSION['user_id'])) {
    echo ' | <a href="frm_login.php">Log In</a>';
    echo ' | <a href="frm_useraccount.php">Register</a>';
} else {
    echo ' | <a href="frm_transact_user.php?action=Logout">';
    echo "Log out " . $_SESSION['name'] . "</a>";
    if ($_SESSION['access_lvl'] > 2) {
        echo ' | <a href="frm_admin.php">Admin</a>';
    }
    echo ' | <a href="frm_useraccount.php">Profile</a>';
}
echo '</p>';
```

If users are not logged in, you give them links to log in or register as a new user. If they are logged in, they can log out or view their profile. If they are administrators, they will have access to the admin functions.

Transaction Pages

The next group of files you're going to create is the transaction pages. Like the reusable scripts just covered, they don't have anything pretty to show the end user, but they drive a large portion of the behind-the-scenes board operations.

Try It Out   **Admin Transactions**

The first file is responsible for all transactions related to the general administration of the board — things like creating new forums, changing the board options, text substitutions, and so on.

1. Create `frm_transact_admin.php`, the first of four transaction pages. Admin forms post to this page, which manipulates the data and then redirects the user to another page. Transaction pages do not send any data to the client unless there is an error.

```
<?php
require 'db.inc.php';
require 'frm_output_functions.inc.php';

$db = mysql_connect(MYSQL_HOST, MYSQL_USER, MYSQL_PASSWORD) or
    die ('Unable to connect. Check your connection parameters.');

mysql_select_db(MYSQL_DB, $db) or die(mysql_error($db));

if (isset($_REQUEST['action'])) {
    switch ($_REQUEST['action']) {
```

```
    case 'Add Forum':
        if (isset($_POST['forumname']) && $_POST['forumname'] != '' &&
            isset($_POST['forumdesc']) && $_POST['forumdesc'] != '') {
            $sql = 'INSERT IGNORE INTO frm_forum
                    (id, forum_name, forum_desc, forum_moderator)
                VALUES
                    (NULL, "' . htmlspecialchars($_POST['forumname'],
ENT_QUOTES) .
                    '", "' . htmlspecialchars($_POST['forumdesc'],
ENT_QUOTES) .
                    '", ' . $_POST['forummod'][0] . ')';
            mysql_query($sql, $db) or die(mysql_error($db));
        }
        header('Location: frm_admin.php?option=forums');
        exit();
        break;

    case 'Edit Forum':
        if (isset($_POST['forumname']) && $_POST['forumname'] != '' &&
            isset($_POST['forumdesc']) && $_POST['forumdesc'] != '') {
            $sql = 'UPDATE frm_forum SET
                    forum_name = "' . $_POST['forumname'] . '",
                    forum_desc = "' . $_POST['forumdesc'] . '".
                    forum_moderator = ' . $_POST['forummod'][0] . '
                WHERE
                    id = ' . $_POST['forum_id'];
            mysql_query($sql, $db) or die(mysql_error($db));
        }
        header('Location: frm_admin.php?option=forums');
        exit();
        break;

    case 'Modify User':
        header('Location: frm_useraccount.php?user=' .
$_POST['userlist'][0]);
        exit();
        break;

    case 'Update':
        foreach ($_POST as $key => $value) {
            if ($key != 'action') {
                $sql = 'UPDATE frm_admin SET
                    value="' . $value . '"
                WHERE
                    constant = "' . $key . '"';
                mysql_query($sql, $db) or die(mysql_error($db));
            }
        }
        header('Location: frm_admin.php');
        exit();
        break;
```

```
    case 'deleteForum':
        $sql = 'DELETE FROM frm_forum WHERE id=' . $_GET['f'];
        mysql_query($sql, $db) or die(mysql_error($db));

        $sql = 'DELETE FROM forum_posts WHERE forum_id=' . $_GET['f'];
        mysql_query($sql, $db) or die(mysql_error($db));

        header('Location: frm_admin.php?option=forums');
        exit();
        break;

    case 'Add New':
        $sql = 'INSERT INTO frm_bbcode
                (id, template, replacement)
            VALUES
                (NULL, "' . htmlentities($_POST['bbcode-tnew'],
ENT_QUOTES) . '",
                "' . htmlentities($_POST['bbcode-rnew'],ENT_QUOTES) . '")';
        mysql_query($sql, $db) or die(mysql_error($db));
        header('Location: frm_admin.php?option=bbcode');
        exit();
        break;

    case 'deleteBBCode':
        if (isset($_GET['b'])) {
            $bbcodeid = $_GET['b'];
            $sql = 'DELETE FROM frm_bbcode WHERE id=' . $bbcodeid;
            mysql_query($sql, $db) or die(mysql_error($db));
        }
        header('Location: frm_admin.php?option=bbcode');
        exit();
        break;

    case 'Update BBCodes':
        foreach($_POST as $key => $value) {
            if (substr($key, 0, 7) == 'bbcode_') {
                $bbid = str_replace('bbcode_', '', $key);
                if (substr($bbid, 0, 1) == 't') {
                    $col = 'template';
                } else {
                    $col = 'replacement';
                }
                $id = substr($bbid, 1);
                $sql = 'UPDATE frm_bbcode SET ' .
                    $col . ' = "' . htmlentities($value, ENT_QUOTES) . '"
                    WHERE
                        id = ' . $id;
                mysql_query($sql, $db) or die(mysql_error($db));
            }
        }
        header('Location: frm_admin.php?option=bbcode');
```

```
        exit();
        break;

    default:
        header('Location: frm_index.php');
    }
} else {
    header('Location: frm_index.php');
}
?>
```

How It Works

At this point, none of the code in `frm_transact_admin.php` should be unfamiliar to you. As seen before in previous chapters, this script determines what action is to be performed in the database, executes a corresponding query, then redirects the user to the appropriate page.

One of the more important things to remember from this page is the actions it handles, as shown here:

```
switch ($_REQUEST['action']) {
case 'Add Forum':
    ...

case 'Edit Forum':
    ...

case 'Modify User':
    ...

case 'Update':
    ...

case 'deleteForum':
    ...

case 'Add New':
    ...

case 'deleteBBCode':
    ...

case 'Update BBCodes':
    ...

default:
    ...
}
```

You probably already understand how the `switch` statement works, so the key thing to keep in mind is the different cases this specific switch processes. Remembering where a certain action takes place can help you more quickly find and diagnose problems when they occur.

Try It Out **Post Transactions**

The next transaction file controls all transactions related to forum posts — creating, editing, replying, and so on.

1. Enter `frm_transact_post.php`, the second of four transaction pages:

```php
<?php
session_start();
require 'db.inc.php';
require 'frm_output_functions.inc.php';

$db = mysql_connect(MYSQL_HOST, MYSQL_USER, MYSQL_PASSWORD) or
    die ('Unable to connect. Check your connection parameters.');

mysql_select_db(MYSQL_DB, $db) or die(mysql_error($db));

if (isset($_REQUEST['action'])) {
    switch (strtoupper($_REQUEST['action'])) {
    case 'SUBMIT NEW POST':
        if (isset($_POST['subject']) && isset($_POST['body']) &&
            isset($_SESSION['user_id'])) {
            $sql = 'INSERT INTO frm_posts
                    (id, topic_id, forum_id, author_id, update_id,
date_posted,
                    date_updated, subject, body)
                VALUES (
                    NULL, ' . $_POST['topic_id'] . ', ' .
                    $_POST['forum_id'] . ', ' . $_SESSION['user_id'] . ', 0,
                    "' . date('Y-m-d H:i:s') . '", 0,
                    "' . $_POST['subject'] . '", "' . $_POST['body'] . '")';
            mysql_query($sql, $db) or die(mysql_error($db));
            $postid = mysql_insert_id();

            $sql = 'INSERT IGNORE INTO frm_post_count
                    (user_id, post_count)
                VALUES (' . $_SESSION['user_id'] . ',0)';
            mysql_query($sql, $db) or die(mysql_error($db));

            $sql = 'UPDATE frm_post_count SET
                    post_count = post_count + 1
                WHERE
                    user_id = ' . $_SESSION['user_id'];
            mysql_query($sql, $db) or die(mysql_error($db));
        }
        $topicid = ($_POST['topic_id'] == 0) ? $postid : $_POST['topic_id'];
        header('Location: frm_view_topic.php?t=' . $topicid . '#post'
. $postid);
        exit();
        break;
```

```
        case 'NEW TOPIC':
            header('Location: frm_compose.php?f=' . $_POST['forum_id']);
            exit();
            break;

        case 'EDIT':
            header('Location: frm_compose.php?a=edit&post=' . $_POST['topic_id']);
            exit();
            break;

        case 'SAVE CHANGES':
            if (isset($_POST['subject']) && isset($_POST['body'])) {
                $sql = 'UPDATE frm_posts SET
                        subject = "' . $_POST['subject'] . '",
                        update_id = ' . $_SESSION['user_id'] . ',
                        body = "' . $_POST['body'] . '",
                        date_updated = "' . date('Y-m-d H:i:s') . '"
                    WHERE
                        id = ' . $_POST['post'];
                if (isset($_POST['author_id'])) {
                    $sql .= ' AND author_id = ' . $_POST['author_id'];
                }
                mysql_query($sql, $db) or die(mysql_error($db));
            }
            $redirID = ($_POST['topic_id'] == 0) ? $_POST['post'] :
$_POST['topic_id'];
            header('Location: frm_view_topic.php?t=' . $redirID);
            exit();
            break;

        case 'DELETE':
            if ($_REQUEST['post']) {
                $sql = 'DELETE FROM frm_posts WHERE id = ' . $_REQUEST['post'];
                mysql_query($sql, $db) or die(mysql_error($db));
            }
            header('Location: ' . $_REQUEST['r']);
            exit();
            break;
    }
} else {
    header('Location: frm_index.php');
}
?>
```

How It Works

Like the previous example, most of this is familiar by now. It's good practice to keep in mind what actions this transaction page performs. One bit of code worth noting is the addition of a new post.

```
case 'SUBMIT NEW POST':
    if (isset($_POST['subject']) && isset($_POST['body']) &&
        isset($_SESSION['user_id'])) {
        $sql = 'INSERT INTO frm_posts
                    (id, topic_id, forum_id, author_id, update_id, date_posted,
                    date_updated, subject, body)
            VALUES (
                NULL, ' . $_POST['topic_id'] . ', ' .
                $_POST['forum_id'] . ', ' . $_SESSION['user_id'] . ', 0,
                "' . date('Y-m-d H:i:s') . '", 0,
                "' . $_POST['subject'] . '", "' . $_POST['body'] . '")';
        mysql_query($sql, $db) or die(mysql_error($db));
        $postid = mysql_insert_id();

        $sql = 'INSERT IGNORE INTO frm_post_count
                    (user_id, post_count)
            VALUES (' . $_SESSION['user_id'] . ',0)';
        mysql_query($sql, $db) or die(mysql_error($db));

        $sql = 'UPDATE frm_post_count SET
                    post_count = post_count + 1
            WHERE
                    user_id = ' . $_SESSION['user_id'];
        mysql_query($sql, $db) or die(mysql_error($db));
    }
    $topicid = ($_POST['topic_id'] == 0) ? $postid : $_POST['topic_id'];
    header('Location: frm_view_topic.php?t=' . $topicid . '#post' . $postid);
    exit();
    break;
```

Note how you first insert the post into the frm_posts table, then proceed to update the post count for the user. In this case, you add the user into the frm_post_count table, in case he or she doesn't yet exist there, and follow up by incrementing the user's post count by one.

Try It Out   User Transactions

Now you're going to create the file responsible for all user-related transactions. Any time a user is created or modified in the system, the database changes are performed here.

1. Create frm_transact_user.php, the third of four transaction pages. This one handles functions related to the users, such as logging in.

```php
<?php
session_start();
require 'db.inc.php';

$db = mysql_connect(MYSQL_HOST, MYSQL_USER, MYSQL_PASSWORD) or
    die ('Unable to connect. Check your connection parameters.');

mysql_select_db(MYSQL_DB, $db) or die(mysql_error($db));
```

```php
if (isset($_REQUEST['action'])) {
    switch ($_REQUEST['action']) {
    case 'Login':
        if (isset($_POST['email']) && isset($_POST['passwd'])) {
            $sql = 'SELECT
                    id, access_lvl, name, last_login
                FROM
                    frm_users
                WHERE
                    email = "' . $_POST['email'] . '" AND
                    password = "' . $_POST['passwd'] . '"';
            $result = mysql_query($sql, $db) or die(mysql_error($db));
            if ($row = mysql_fetch_array($result)) {
                $_SESSION['user_id'] = $row['id'];
                $_SESSION['access_lvl'] = $row['access_lvl'];
                $_SESSION['name'] = $row['name'];
                $_SESSION['last_login'] = $row['last_login'];
                $sql = 'UPDATE frm_users SET
                        last_login = "' . date('Y-m-d H:i:s') . '"
                    WHERE
                        id = ' . $row['id'];
                mysql_query($sql, $db) or die(mysql_error($db));
            }
        }
        header('Location: frm_index.php');
        exit();
        break;

    case 'Logout':
        session_unset();
        session_destroy();
        header('Location: frm_index.php');
        exit();
        break;

    case 'Create Account':
        if (isset($_POST['name']) && isset($_POST['email']) &&
            isset($_POST['passwd']) && isset($_POST['passwd2']) &&
            $_POST['passwd'] == $_POST['passwd2']) {
            $sql = 'INSERT INTO frm_users
                    (email, name, password, date_joined, last_login)
                VALUES
                    ("' . $_POST['email'] . '", "' . $_POST['name'] . '",
                    "' . $_POST['passwd'] . '", "' . date('Y-m-d H:i:s') . '",
                    "' . date('Y-m-d H:i:s') . '")';
            mysql_query($sql, $db) or die(mysql_error($db));

            $_SESSION['user_id'] = mysql_insert_id($db);
            $_SESSION['access_lvl'] = 1;
            $_SESSION['name'] = $_POST['name'];
            $_SESSION['login_time'] = date('Y-m-d H:i:s');
```

```
            }
        header('Location: frm_index.php');
        exit();
        break;

    case 'Modify Account':
        if (isset($_POST['name']) && isset($_POST['email']) &&
            isset($_POST['accesslvl']) && isset($_POST['userid'])) {
            $sql = 'UPDATE frm_users SET
                    email = "' . $_POST['email'] . '",
                    name = "' . $_POST['name'] . '",
                    access_lvl = ' . $_POST['accesslvl'] . ',
                    signature = "' . $_POST['signature'] . '"
                WHERE
                    id = ' . $_POST['userid'];
            mysql_query($sql, $db) or die(mysql_error($db));
        }
        header('Location: frm_admin.php');
        exit();
        break;

    case 'Edit Account':
        if (isset($_POST['name']) && isset($_POST['email']) &&
            isset($_POST['accesslvl']) && isset($_POST['userid'])) {
            $chg_pw = FALSE;
            if (!empty($_POST['oldpasswd'])) {
                $sql = 'SELECT
                        passwd
                    FROM
                        frm_users
                    WHERE
                        id = ' . $_POST['userid'];
                $result = mysql_query($sql, $db) or die(mysql_error($db));
                if ($row = mysql_fetch_array($result)) {
                    if ($row['passwd'] == $_POST['oldpasswd'] &&
                        isset($_POST['passwd']) && isset($_POST['passwd2']) &&
                        $_POST['passwd'] == $_POST['passwd2']) {
                        $chg_pw = TRUE;
                    } else {
                        header('Location: frm_useraccount
.php?error=nopassedit');
                        exit();
                        break;
                    }
                }
            }
            $sql = 'UPDATE frm_users SET
                    email = "' . $_POST['email'] . '",
                    name="' . $_POST['name'] . '",
                    access_lvl = ' . $_POST['accesslvl'] . ',
                    signature = "' . $_POST['signature'] . '"';
```

```
                    if ($chg_pw) {
                        $sql .= '", passwd = "' . $_POST['passwd'] . '"';
                    }
                $sql .= ' WHERE id=' . $_POST['userid'];
                mysql_query($sql, $db) or die(mysql_error($db));
            }
        header('Location: frm_useraccount.php?blah=' . $_POST['userid']);
        break;

    case 'Send my reminder!':
        if (isset($_POST['email'])) {
            $sql = 'SELECT
                        passwd
                    FROM
                        frm_users
                    WHERE
                        email="' . $_POST['email'] . '"';

            $result = mysql_query($sql, $db) or die(mysql_error($db));

            if (mysql_num_rows($result)) {
                $row = mysql_fetch_array($result);

                $headers = 'From: admin@yoursite.com' . "\r\n";
                $subject = 'Comic site password reminder';
                $body = 'Just a reminder, your password for the ' .
                    'Comic Book Appreciation site is: ' . $row
['passwd'] ."\n\n";
                $body .= 'You can use this to log in at http://' .
                    $_SERVER['HTTP_HOST'] . dirname($_SERVER['PHP_SELF']) .
                    '/frm_login.php?e=' . $_POST['email'];

                mail($_POST['email'], $subject, $body, $headers);
            }
        }
        header('Location: frm_login.php');
        break;
    }
}
?>
```

How It Works

Like its predecessors, this transaction page follows the familiar "determine action, query database, return" pattern. Most of the action processing is pretty straightforward, with the exception of the account edit action. Let's take a look at that specific case.

```
case 'Edit Account':
    if (isset($_POST['name']) && isset($_POST['email']) &&
        isset($_POST['accesslvl']) && isset($_POST['userid'])) {
```

This time instead of passing a simple query to the database, you must do some preliminary checks. The script first checks to see if users have elected to change their password:

```
$chg_pw = FALSE;
if (!empty($_POST['oldpasswd'])) {
```

If this condition is met, then the script checks the old password in the database to see if a change has truly been made. If not, the user is redirected back to the account edit page, and an error is flagged.

```
$sql = 'SELECT
        passwd
    FROM
        frm_users
    WHERE
        id = ' . $_POST['userid'];
$result = mysql_query($sql, $db) or die(mysql_error($db));
if ($row = mysql_fetch_array($result)) {
    if ($row['passwd'] == $_POST['oldpasswd'] &&
        isset($_POST['passwd']) && isset($_POST['passwd2']) &&
        $_POST['passwd'] == $_POST['passwd2']) {
        $chg_pw = TRUE;
    } else {
        header('Location: frm_useraccount.php?error=nopassedit');
        exit();
        break;
    }
}
}
```

Then, the account is finally updated.

```
$sql = 'UPDATE frm_users SET
        email = "' . $_POST['email'] . '",
        name="' . $_POST['name'] . '",
        access_lvl = ' . $_POST['accesslvl'] . ',
        signature = "' . $_POST['signature'] . '"';
    if ($chg_pw) {
        $sql .= '", passwd = "' . $_POST['passwd'] . '"';
    }
    $sql .= ' WHERE id=' . $_POST['userid'];
    mysql_query($sql, $db) or die(mysql_error($db));
}
header('Location: frm_useraccount.php?blah=' . $_POST['userid']);
break;
```

The rest of the actions should be pretty self-explanatory. All actions update the database with appropriate information, with the exception of the last case, where a reminder e-mail is sent to users if they have forgotten their password.

Removal Transactions

The last transaction page covers situations where forums or posts need to be deleted.

1. Create `frm_transact_affirm.php`. This is the only so-called transaction page that *does* send data to the client. If a function requires confirmation, the user is sent here and redirected forward.

```php
<?php
require 'frm_header.inc.php';
?>
<script type="text/javascript">
function deletePost(id, redir) {
    if (id > 0) {
        window.location = 'frm_transact_post.php?action=delete&post=' +
            id + '&r=' + redir;
    } else {
        history.back();
    }
}

function deleteForum(id) {
    if (id > 0) {
        window.location = 'frm_transact_admin.php?action=deleteForum&f
=' + id;
    } else {
        history.back();
    }
}
</script>
<?php
switch (strtoupper($_REQUEST['action'])) {
case 'DELETEPOST':
    $sql = 'SELECT
            id, topic_id, forum_id, subject
        FROM
            frm_posts
        WHERE
            id = ' . $_REQUEST['id'];
    $result = mysql_query($sql, $db) or die(mysql_error($db));
    $row = mysql_fetch_array($result);
    if ($row['topic_id'] > 0) {
        $msg = 'Are you sure you wish to delete the post<br/>' .
            '<em>' . $row['subject'] . '</em>?';
        $redir = htmlspecialchars('frm_view_topic.php?t=' . $row[
'topic_id']);
    } else {
        $msg = 'If you delete this post, all replies will be deleted as well. ' .
        'Are you sure you wish to delete the entire thread<br/>' .
        '<em>' . $row['subject'] . '</em>?';
```

```
                    $redir = htmlspecialchars('frm_view_forum.php?f='
. $row['forum_id']);
        }
        echo '<div>';
        echo '<h2>DELETE POST?</h2>';
        echo '<p>' . $msg . '</p>';
        echo '<p><a href="#" onclick="deletePost(' . $row['id'] . ', \'' .
            $redir . '\'); return false;">Yes</a> ' .
            '<a href="#" onclick="history.back(); return false;">No</a></p>';
        echo '</div>';
        break;

case 'DELETEFORUM':
    $sql = 'SELECT
                forum_name
            FROM
                frm_forum
            WHERE
                id=' . $_REQUEST['f'];
    $result = mysql_query($sql, $db) or die(mysql_error($db));
    $row = mysql_fetch_array($result);
    echo '<div>';
    echo '<h2>DELETE Forum?</h2>';
    echo '<p>If you delete this forum, all topics and replies will ' .
        'be deleted as well.  Are you sure you wish to delete ' .
        'the entire forum<br/><em>' . $row['forum_name'] . '</em>?</p>';
    echo '<p><a href="#" onclick="deleteForum(' . $_REQUEST['f'] .
        '); return false;">Yes</a> <a href="#" ' .
        'onclick="history.back(); return false;">No</a></p>';
    echo '</div>';
}
require_once 'footer.php';
?>
```

How It Works

An exception to the previous group of transaction pages, this script actually generates output to which the user can respond. The `switch()` statement determines which text to display:

```
switch (strtoupper($_REQUEST['action'])) {
case 'DELETEPOST':
    ...

case 'DELETEFORUM':
    ...
}
```

Each of the options outputs two buttons, one to confirm the action and one to go back. If users choose to confirm, the button calls a bit of client-side JavaScript code to redirect them to the proper transaction page:

```
function deletePost(id, redir) {
    if (id > 0) {
        window.location = 'frm_transact_post.php?action=delete&post=' +
            id + '&r=' + redir;
    } else {
```

```
            history.back();
        }
    }

    function deleteForum(id) {
        if (id > 0) {
            window.location = 'frm_transact_admin.php?action=deleteForum&f=' + id;
        } else {
            history.back();
        }
    }
```

Account Functionality

The next section of your bulletin board application deals with general account functionality. Here, you'll give users the ability to create their own account, request a forgotten password, and administer other users. Let's continue.

Try It Out   **Initial Login**

The first thing you need to do is create the pages that allow users to create their account and log in to the site.

1. Enter `frm_login.php`, the login page.

```php
<?php include 'frm_header.inc.php'; ?>
<h1>Member Login</h1>
<form method="post" action="frm_transact_user.php">
 <table>
  <tr>
   <td><label for="email">Email Address:</label></td>
   <td><input type="text" id="email" name="email" maxlength="100"/></td>
  </tr><tr>
   <td><label for="passwd">Password:</label></td>
   <td><input type="password" id="passwd" name="passwd" maxlength="20"/></td>
  </tr><tr>
   <td> </td>
   <td><input type="submit" class="submit" name="action" value="Login"/></td>
  </tr>
 </table>
</form>
<p>Not a member yet? <a href="frm_useraccount.php">Create a new account!</a></p>
<p><a href="frm_forgotpass.php">Forgot your password?</a></p>
<?php include 'frm_footer.inc.php'; ?>
```

2. Create `frm_index.php`, the home page. This is the page users will first see when they view the board.

```php
<?php
require 'frm_header.inc.php';

$sql = 'SELECT
        f.id as id, f.forum_name as forum, f.forum_desc as description,
        COUNT(forum_id) as threads, u.name as moderator
    FROM
        frm_forum f LEFT JOIN frm_posts p ON f.id = p.forum_id AND
p.topic_id = 0
        LEFT JOIN frm_users u ON f.forum_moderator = u.id
    GROUP BY
        f.id';
$result = mysql_query($sql, $db) or die(mysql_error($db) . $sql);

if (mysql_num_rows($result) == 0) {
  echo '<h2>There are currently no forums to view.</h2>';
} else {
?>
<table>
 <tr>
  <th>Forum</th>
  <th>Threads</th>
  <th>Moderator</th>
 </tr>
<?php
    $odd = true;
    while ($row = mysql_fetch_array($result)) {
        echo ($odd == true) ? '<tr class="odd_row">' : '<tr class=
"even_row">';
        $odd = !$odd;
        echo '<td><a href="frm_view_forum.php?f=' . $row['id'] . '">' .
            $row['forum'] . '</a><br/>' . $row['description'] . '</td>';
        echo '<td style="text-align: center;">' . $row['threads'] . '</td>';
        echo '<td>' . $row['moderator'] . '</td>';
        echo '</tr>';
    }
    echo '</table>';
}

require 'frm_footer.inc.php';
?>
```

3. Create `frm_forgotpass.php`. This page is displayed if the user forgets his or her password.

```php
<?php include 'frm_header.inc.php'; ?>
<h2>Email Password Reminder</h2>
<p>Forgot your password? Just enter your email address, and we'll email
you a new one!</p>
<form method="post" action="frm_transact_user.php">
 <div>
  <label for="email">Email Address:</label>
  <input type="text" id="email" name="email" maxlength="100"/>
  <input type="submit" name="action" value="Send my reminder!"/>
 </div>
</form>
<?php include 'frm_footer.inc.php'; ?>
```

4. Load `frm_login.php` in your browser. You are taken to the login page. Observe the link at the bottom of the login screen, "Forgot your password?" A user who cannot remember his or her password can click this link and enter the e-mail address submitted when the account was created. If he or she is verified to be a valid user, the password will be sent to the e-mail address given. You can try this out yourself if you like, assuming you are using a legitimate e-mail address (and not the admin@example.com default).

5. Enter your password, and click the Login button. You should now see the home page of the CBA board application (see Figure 16-2).

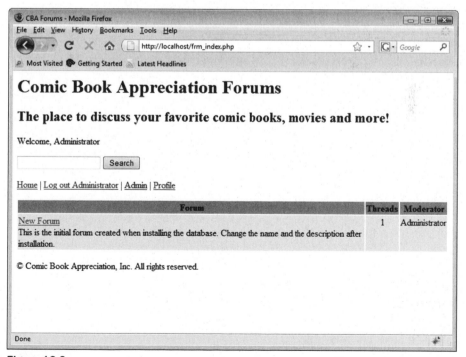

Figure 16-2

You are now logged in as the administrator of the CBA board application. As the administrator, you have complete control of your application. Three other roles apply to the board: Moderator, User, and Anonymous. Technically "Anonymous" isn't really a role, but if you are not logged in, the system does not know who you are and treats you as "Anonymous."

How It Works

You may have noticed that `frm_login.php` and `frm_forgotpass.php` are similar to the corresponding files in Chapter 13. Since they are pretty much just HTML, we'll skip those for now, and talk about your home page, `frm_index.php`.

At the start of the file, you include your standard three reusable scripts and then proceed to query the database. This time you use a three-table JOIN to retrieve a list of all the available forums, the number of threads per forum, and the name of the moderator for each.

```
$sql = 'SELECT
        f.id as id, f.forum_name as forum, f.forum_desc as description,
        COUNT(forum_id) as threads, u.name as moderator
    FROM
        frm_forum f LEFT JOIN frm_posts p ON f.id = p.forum_id AND p.topic_id
= 0
        LEFT JOIN frm_users u ON f.forum_moderator = u.id
    GROUP BY
        f.id';
$result = mysql_query($sql, $db) or die(mysql_error($db) . $sql);
```

The rest of the script is all output. You check if any forums are found, and if so, you generate a table with links to each forum.

```
if (mysql_num_rows($result) == 0) {
  echo '<h2>There are currently no forums to view.</h2>';
} else {
?>
<table>
 <tr>
  <th>Forum</th>
  <th>Threads</th>
  <th>Moderator</th>
 </tr>
<?php
    $odd = true;
    while ($row = mysql_fetch_array($result)) {
        echo ($odd == true) ? '<tr class="odd_row">' : '<tr class=
"even_row">';
        $odd = !$odd;
        echo '<td><a href="frm_view_forum.php?f=' . $row['id'] . '">' .
            $row['forum'] . '</a><br/>' . $row['description'] . '</td>';
        echo '<td style="text-align: center;">' . $row['threads'] . '</td>';
        echo '<td>' . $row['moderator'] . '</td>';
        echo '</tr>';
    }
    echo '</table>';
}
```

Try It Out   **User Management**

The next thing you are going to do is create the pages that allow the admin to control board settings and create user accounts.

1.   Enter `frm_admin.php`. This is the page used to edit different board attributes, user information, forums, and more.

```php
<?php
require_once 'header.php';
?>
<script type="text/javascript">
function delBBCode(id) {
    window.location = 'frm_transact_admin.php?action=deleteBBCode&b=' + id;
}
function delForum(id) {
    window.location = 'frm_transact_affirm.php?action=deleteForum&f=' + id;
}
</script>
<?php
$sql = 'SELECT
        access_lvl, access_name
    FROM
        frm_access_levels
    ORDER BY
        access_lvl DESC';
$result = mysql_query($sql, $db) or die(mysql_error($db));

while ($row = mysql_fetch_array($result)) {
    $a_users[$row['access_lvl']] = $row['access_name'];
}

$menuoption = 'boardadmin';
if (isset($_GET['option'])) $menuoption = $_GET['option'];

$menuItems = array(
    'boardadmin' => 'Board Admin',
    'edituser' => 'Users',
    'forums' => 'Forums',
    'bbcode' => 'BBcode');
echo '<p>|';
foreach ($menuItems as $key => $value) {
    if ($menuoption != $key) {
        echo '<a href="' . $_SERVER['PHP_SELF'] . '?option=' . $key. '">';
    }
    echo ' ' . $value . ' ';
    if ($menuoption != $key) {
        echo '</a>';
    }
    echo '|';
```

```
}
echo '</p>';

switch ($menuoption) {
case 'boardadmin':
?>
<h2>Board Administration</h2>
<form method="post" action="frm_transact_admin.php">
 <table>
  <tr>
   <th>title</th>
   <th>Value</th>
   <th>Parameter</th>
  </tr>
<?php
    foreach ($admin as $key => $value) {
        echo '<tr>';
        echo '<td>' . $value['title'] . '</td>';
        echo '<td><input type="text" name="' . $key . '" value="' .
           $value['value'] . '" size="60" /></td>';
        echo '<td>' . $key . '</td>';
        echo '</tr>';
    }
?>
 </table>
 <p><input type="submit" name="action" id="Update" value="Update" /></p>
</form>
<?php
    break;

case 'edituser':
?>
<h2>User Administration</h2>
    <div id="users">
<form action="frm_transact_admin.php" method="post">
 <div>
  <label for="userlist">Please select a user to manage:</label>
  <select id="userlist" name="userlist[]">
<?php
    foreach ($a_users as $key => $value) {
        echo '<optgroup label="' . $value . '">' . user_option_list
($db, $key) .
           '</optgroup>';
    }
  ?>
  </select>
  <input type="submit" name="action" value="Modify User"/>
 </div>
</form>
<?php
    break;

case 'forums':
?>
```

```
<h2>Forum Administration</h2>
<table>
 <tr><th colspan="3">Forum</th></tr>
<?php
    $sql = 'SELECT
            id, forum_name, forum_desc
        FROM
            frm_forum';
    $result = mysql_query($sql, $db) or die(mysql_error($db));
    while ($row = mysql_fetch_array($result)) {
        echo '<tr>';
        echo '<td>' . $row['forum_name'] . '<br/>' . $row['forum_desc']
. '</td>';
        echo '<td><a href="frm_edit_forum.php?forum=' .$row['id'] .
            '">Edit</a></td>';
        echo '<td><a href="#" onclick="delForum('. $row['id'] .
            '); return false;">Delete</a></td>';
        echo '</tr>';
    }
?>
</table>
<p><a href="frm_edit_forum.php">New Forum</a></p>
<?php
    break;

case 'bbcode':
  ?>
<h2>BBcode Administration</h2>
<form method="post" action="frm_transact_admin.php">
 <table>
  <tr>
   <th>Template</th>
   <th>Replacement</th>
   <th>Action</th>
  </tr>
<?php
    if (isset($bbcode)) {
        foreach ($bbcode as $key => $value) {
            echo '<tr>';
            echo '<td><input type="text" name="bbcode_t' . $key . '" value="' .
                $value['template'] . '" size="32"/></td>';
            echo '<td><input type="text" name="bbcode_r' . $key . '" value="' .
                $value['replacement'] . '" size="32"/></td>';
            echo '<td><input type="button" name="action" id="DelBBCode" ' .
                'value="Delete" onclick="delBBCode(' . $key .
                '); return false;"/></td>';
            echo '</tr>';
        }
    }
?>
  <tr>
   <td><input type="text" name="bbcode-tnew" size="32"/></td>
   <td><input type="text" name="bbcode-rnew" size="32"/></td>
```

```
    <td><input type="submit" name="action" id="AddBBCode" value=
"Add New"/></td>
  </tr>
 </table>
 <p><input type="submit" name="action" id="Update" value="Update BBCodes"/></p>
</form>
  <?php
    break;
}

require_once 'frm_footer.inc.php';
?>
```

2. Create `frm_useraccount.php`. Users access this page to edit their own profiles.

```php
<?php
require_once 'frm_header.inc.php';

$userid = $username = $useremail = $password = $accesslvl = '';
$mode = 'Create';
if (isset($_SESSION['user_id'])) {
    $userid = $_SESSION['user_id'];
    $mode = 'Edit';
    if (isset($_GET['user'])) {
        if ($_SESSION['user_id'] == $_GET['user'] || $_SESSION
['access_lvl'] > 2) {
            $userid = $_GET['user'];
            $mode = 'Modify';
        }
    }
    $sql = 'SELECT
            name, email, access_lvl, signature
        FROM
            frm_users
        WHERE
            id = ' . $userid;
    $result = mysql_query($sql, $db) or die(mysql_error($db));

    $row = mysql_fetch_array($result);
    $username = $row['name'];
    $useremail = $row['email'];
    $accesslvl = $row['access_lvl'];
    $signature = $row['signature'];
}

echo '<h2>' . $mode  . ' Account</h2>';
?>
<form method="post" action="frm_transact_user.php">
 <p>Full name:<br />
  <input type="text" name="name" maxlength="100"
   value="<?php echo htmlspecialchars($username); ?>"/></p>
 <p>Email Address:<br />
  <input type="text" name="email" maxlength="255"
```

```php
    value="<?php echo htmlspecialchars($useremail); ?>"/></p>
<?php

if ($mode == 'Modify') {
    echo '<div><fieldset>';
    echo '   <legend>Access Level</legend>';

    $sql = 'SELECT
               access_lvl, access_name
           FROM
               frm_access_levels
           ORDER BY
               access_lvl DESC';
    $result = mysql_query($sql, $db) or die(mysql_error($db));

    while ($row = mysql_fetch_array($result)) {
        echo '<input type="radio" id="acl_' . $row['access_lvl'] .
            '" name="accesslvl" value="' . $row['access_lvl'] . '" ';
        if ($row['access_lvl'] == $accesslvl) {
            echo 'checked="checked"';
        }
        echo '/>' . $row['access_name'] . '<br/>';
    }
    echo '</fieldset></div>';
}
if ($mode != 'Modify') {
    echo '<div id="passwords">';
}
if ($mode == 'Edit') {
    if (isset($_GET['error']) && $_GET['error'] == 'nopassedit') {
        echo '<strong>Could not modify passwords. Please try again
.</strong><br/>';
    }
?>
 <p>Old Password:<br/>
  <input type="password" id="oldpasswd" name="oldpasswd" maxlength="50" /></p>
<?php
}
if ($mode != 'Modify') {
?>
 <p>New Password:<br/>
  <input type="password" id="passwd" name="passwd" maxlength="50" /></p>
 <p>Password Verification:<br/>
  <input type="password" id="passwd2" name="passwd2" maxlength="50"/></p>
<?php
}
if ($mode != 'Modify') {
    echo '</div>';
}
if ($mode != 'Create') {
?>
 <p>Signature:<br/>
  <textarea name="signature" id="signature" cols="60" rows="5"><?php
    echo $signature; ?></textarea></p>
```

```php
<?php
}
?>
 <p><input type="submit" name="action" value="<?php echo $mode; ?>
Account"></p>
<?php
if ($mode == 'Edit') {
?>
 <input type="hidden" name="accesslvl" value="<?php echo $accesslvl; ?>" />
<?php
}
?>
 <input type="hidden" name="userid" value="<?php echo $userid; ?>"/>
</form>
<?php
require_once 'frm_footer.inc.php';
?>
```

3. You are going to create a couple of new user identities to demonstrate the difference between the various roles.

Log out, and click Register. You should see a screen similar to the one shown in Figure 16-3.

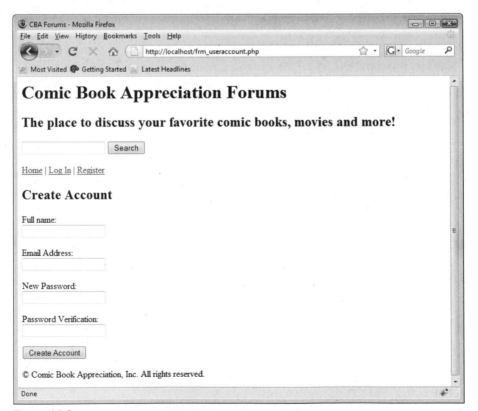

Figure 16-3

4. Enter a name. This name will be used for display purposes.

5. Enter your e-mail address.

6. Enter your password twice for verification.

7. Click the Create Account button.

    Your account will be created, and you will be automatically logged in with your new account.

8. Repeat steps 3 through 7 to create one more account.

9. Log out, and then log back in with your original admin account.

10. Now that you are logged in as the site administrator, you should see a menu item called Admin. Click it.

11. Click Users in the Administration menu.

    This displays the User Administration screen; from here, you can select a user from the drop-down menu and edit user details.

12. Choose one of the user profiles you created in step 7, and click Modify User. You should see a page similar to Figure 16-4. From this page, you can modify a user's name, access level, and signature.

Figure 16-4

13.   Change the user's access level to Moderator, and click Modify Account.

How It Works

Let's begin by looking at `frm_useraccount.php`. At the beginning of the file, you check the user's credentials stored in your session variables. If the user is an admin, then the form is set up to allow the admin to change his or her access level.

```
$mode = 'Create';
if (isset($_SESSION['user_id'])) {
    $userid = $_SESSION['user_id'];
    $mode = 'Edit';
    if (isset($_GET['user'])) {
        if ($_SESSION['user_id'] == $_GET['user'] || $_SESSION[
'access_lvl'] > 2) {
            $userid = $_GET['user'];
            $mode = 'Modify';
        }
    }
    $sql = 'SELECT
            name, email, access_lvl, signature
        FROM
            frm_users
        WHERE
            id = ' . $userid;
    $result = mysql_query($sql, $db) or die(mysql_error($db));

    $row = mysql_fetch_array($result);
    $username = $row['name'];
    $useremail = $row['email'];
    $accesslvl = $row['access_lvl'];
    $signature = $row['signature'];
}
```

Later down in the page, the determined mode toggles whether or not the Access Level controls will be displayed.

```
if ($mode == 'Modify') {
    echo '<div><fieldset>';
    echo '  <legend>Access Level</legend>';

    $sql = 'SELECT
            access_lvl, access_name
        FROM
            frm_access_levels
        ORDER BY
            access_lvl DESC';
    $result = mysql_query($sql, $db) or die(mysql_error($db));

    while ($row = mysql_fetch_array($result)) {
        echo '<input type="radio" id="acl_' . $row['access_lvl'] .
```

```
                '" name="accesslvl" value="' . $row['access_lvl'] . '" ';
            if ($row['access_lvl'] == $accesslvl) {
                echo 'checked="checked"';
            }
            echo '/>' . $row['access_name'] . '<br/>';
        }
        echo '</fieldset></div>';
    }
```

The rest of the page simply finishes out the form. Let's move on to `frm_admin.php`.

You may have noticed sections of code in `frm_admin.php` that involve forum settings, BBcode settings, and more. We're going to ignore those for now to talk about the User Administration portion of the admin area, instead. We promise that we'll touch back on those other functions later in this chapter.

User Administration

On the User Administration page, the first thing you need to do is gather up all of the access levels, along with their names. That is done with the following code in `frm_admin.php`, which results in a numerical array of access levels:

```
$sql = 'SELECT
        access_lvl, access_name
    FROM
        frm_access_levels
    ORDER BY
        access_lvl DESC';
$result = mysql_query($sql, $db) or die(mysql_error($db));

while ($row = mysql_fetch_array($result)) {
    $a_users[$row['access_lvl']] = $row['access_name'];
}
```

Next, under the `edituser` case of your `switch()`, you create an HTML select field, dynamically building up the options. By looping through the access level array you just created, you can also use the `optgroup` tag to categorize the select list by access level.

```
    <select id="userlist" name="userlist[]">
<?php
    foreach ($a_users as $key => $value) {
        echo '<optgroup label="' . $value . '">' . user_option_list
($db, $key) .
            '</optgroup>';
    }
?>
    </select>
```

Note that you create the list of users by calling the `user_option_list()` function. This function resides in `frm_output_functions.inc.php` and is called once for each access level. A list of `option` tags is output, each containing the appropriate user information.

```
function user_option_list($db, $level) {
    $sql = 'SELECT
            id, name, access_lvl
        FROM
            frm_users
        WHERE
            access_lvl = ' . $level . '
        ORDER BY
            name';
    $result = mysql_query($sql) or die(mysql_error($db));

    while ($row = mysql_fetch_array($result)) {
        echo '<option value="' . $row['id'] . '">' .
            htmlspecialchars($row['name']) . '</option>';
    }
    mysql_free_result($result);
}
```

That's really all there is to it. When the appropriate user is chosen, his or her ID is passed on to the `frm_transact_admin.php` transaction page, where the admin user is redirected to the `frm_useraccount.php` page for that user.

Forum Functionality

The last section of this application covers the actual forum-specific functionality. Up until now, everything — with the exception of some functions and transaction pages — has been pretty generic, and could really be used for almost any type of member-driven Web site. Now, we're getting to the fun stuff, the reason for this chapter.

Try It Out   Editing Board Settings

The first thing you need to do is customize your bulletin board to your liking.

1.   Enter `frm_edit_forum.php`, which is used to edit forum details:

```
<?php
if (isset($_GET['forum'])) {
    $action = 'Edit';
} else {
    $action = 'Add';
}
$pageTitle = $action . 'Forum';
require_once 'frm_header.inc.php';

$forum = 0;
$fname = '';
$fdesc = '';
$fmod = '';
$userid = 0;
```

```php
if (isset($_GET['forum'])) {
    $forum = $_GET['forum'];
    $sql = 'SELECT
            forum_name, forum_desc, u.name, u.id
        FROM
            frm_forum f LEFT JOIN frm_users u ON f.forum_moderator = u.id
        WHERE
            f.id = ' . $forum;
    $result = mysql_query($sql, $db) or die(mysql_error($db));
    if ($row = mysql_fetch_array($result)) {
        $fname = $row['forum_name'];
        $fdesc = $row['forum_desc'];
        $fmod = $row['name'];
        $userid = $row['id'];
    }
}
echo '<h2>' . $action . 'forum</h2>';
?>
<form action="frm_transact_admin.php" method="post">
 <table>
  <tr>
   <th colspan="2">General Forum Settings</th>
  </tr><tr>
   <td>Forum Name</td>
   <td><input type="text" name="forumname" value="<?php echo $fname; ?>"/></td>
  </tr><tr>
   <td>Forum Description</td>
   <td><input type="text" name="forumdesc" size="75" value="<?php
   echo $fdesc; ?>"/></td>
  </tr><tr>
   <td>Forum Moderator</td>
   <td><select id="moderator" name="forummod[]">
     <option value="0">unmoderated</option>
<?php
$sql = 'SELECT
        id, name
    FROM
        frm_users
    WHERE
        access_lvl > 1';
$result = mysql_query($sql, $db) or die(mysql_error($db));
while ($row = mysql_fetch_array($result)) {
    echo '<option value="' . $row['id'] . '"';
    if ($userid == $row['id']) {
        echo ' selected="selected"';
    }
    echo '>' . $row['name'] . '</option>';
}
?>
   </select>
  </td>
 </tr><tr>
```

```
      <td colspan="2">
        <input type="hidden" name="forum_id" value="<?php echo $forum; ?>" />
        <input type="submit" name="action" value="<?php echo $action; ?> Forum" />
      </td>
    </tr>
  </table>
</form>
<?php require_once 'frm_footer.inc.php'; ?>
```

2. Click the Admin link from the navigation menu. This brings you to the administration page, as shown in Figure 16-5. The values in the fields you now see are used in the application. For instance, the first field, Board Title, is "Comic Book Appreciation Forums."

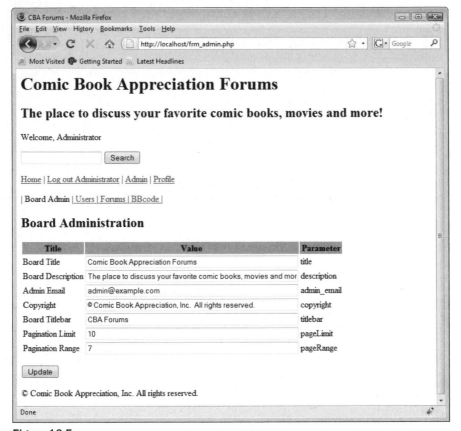

Figure 16-5

3. Edit the Board Title field to read "Comic Book Appreciation Bulletin Board," and click Update. The title at the top of the page should change accordingly.

4. Complete the other fields in the administration page:

- ❏ Board Description
- ❏ Admin Email
- ❏ Copyright
- ❏ Board Titlebar

Most of those should be fairly self-explanatory. The last two fields control how many posts you see on one page and how many pages you have access to at one time.

5. Change Pagination Limit to 3, and click the Update button.

6. Now, click Forums in the Administration menu. You should see a list of the forums available for your board. If this is your initial installation, you will have only one forum — called New Forum. You can edit this forum, delete it, or create a new forum. Feel free to create as many forums as you want. Note that when creating or editing a forum, you can choose a moderator. The user's account you edited earlier is now available as a choice in the Moderator field.

7. Click BBcodes in the Administration menu.

You will see a form where you can enter a "template" and "replacement." This allows you to designate words or phrases that will be replaced by different words or phrases. For instance, you can enter the phrase "very hard" in the template field, and "cats and dogs" in the replacement field. Once you click the Add New button, these will be added to the database. Note that the real power of this page is in the use of regular expressions. If you are not familiar with regular expressions, we explain how they work in the "How It Works" section.

8. Enter the following template and replacement values exactly as they are shown. Remember to click Add New after entering each one:

Template	Replacement
`\[url\]([^[]+?)\[\/url\]`	`<a href="$1" target="_blank">$1</a>`
`\[img\]([^[]+?)\[\/img\]`	`<img src="$1">`
`\[i\]([^[]+?)\[\/i\]`	`<i>$1</i>`
`\[b\]([^[]+?)\[\/b\]`	`<b>$1</b>`
`\[u\]([^[]+?)\[\/u\]`	`<u>$1</u>`
`\[url=([^]]+?)\]`	`<a href="$1" target="_blank">`
`\[\/url\]`	`</a>`
`very hard`	`cats and dogs`

That's it for the administration functions. There are not too many, but we are sure you will think of many things to add, down the road.

How It Works

That brings you back to the `frm_admin.php` page. You were able to get here by clicking the Admin link, which is available only if you are logged in as the administrator. So far, so good. What if the user attempts to access the `frm_admin.php` page directly?

Try it yourself. Load `frm_index.php` in your browser, and then make sure you are logged out. Once you are logged out, load `frm_admin.php` by typing it directly in the address bar of your browser. It should load with no problem. Now, edit one of the fields on the main admin page. Again, nothing is stopping you. Indeed, when you click the Update button, the data will be saved.

But wait ... you are not logged in! How is this possible? Simple. You have not checked the user's credentials once he or she got into the page.

Just as you are responsible for checking IDs in your bar in case underage patrons slip in, you are responsible for the users' access to your entire site. If you don't want certain people to access a page, you not only have to bar access to any link loading the page, but kick them off the page if they are successful in loading it.

Fortunately, this is easy to do. At the top of your page, simply check their credentials (those are up to you — do they need a certain access level? do they just need to be logged in?), and then redirect them to another page if they don't pass (`shameonyou.php` or simply back to `frm_index.php`).

You can do other things to make your site more secure. Most are way beyond the scope of this book. A look at the W3C security FAQ link we gave you earlier should help you, if you are interested in learning more about security. Just don't ever think you are "secure enough" if you haven't considered the risk of unauthorized access.

While you are still visiting `frm_admin.php`, let's take a closer look at it.

The file `frm_admin.php` is set up in four different areas: Board Administration, User Administration, Forum Admininistration, and BBcode Administration. A lot is going on in this page. You've already seen User Administration, so we'll tackle the other three areas one at a time. First let's look at Board Administration.

Board Administration

Looking at the code, you will see that you simply build your table of fields by looping through the array called `$admin` that has the board configuration values.

```
foreach ($admin as $key => $value) {
    echo '<tr>';
    echo '<td>' . $value['title'] . '</td>';
    echo '<td><input type="text" name="' . $key . '" value="' .
    $value['value'] . '" size="60" /></td>';
    echo '<td>' . $key . '</td>';
    echo '</tr>';
}
```

The array `$admin` is associative. The key is a unique identifier for the data, which is associated with a value and a title. For example, the title bar's title is Board Titlebar, and the value is CBA Forums. It is represented in the `$admin` array as follows:

```
$admin['titlebar']['title'] = 'Board Titlebar'
$admin['titlebar']['value'] = 'CBA Forums'
```

By looping through the `$admin` array, you can extract each piece of data and use it to build your form. But the question is, where is `$admin` populated? It is certainly not created anywhere in `frm_admin.php`.

If you look at the top of `frm_admin.php`, you'll notice that `frm_header.inc.php` is included. The array is not built in `frm_header.inc.php` either, but looking at the top of `frm_header.inc.php` you will notice another included file, `frm_config.inc.php`. A quick look into `frm_config.inc.php` uncovers the fact that `$admin` is loaded there. Note that `$bbcode` is also being built. You'll see that used shortly.

```
$sql = 'SELECT * FROM frm_admin';
$result = mysql_query($sql, $db) or die(mysql_error($db));

while ($row = mysql_fetch_array($result)) {
    $admin[$row['constant']]['title'] = $row['title'];
    $admin[$row['constant']]['value'] = $row['value'];
}
mysql_free_result($result);

$sql = 'SELECT * FROM frm_bbcode';
$result = mysql_query($sql, $db) or die(mysql_error($db));

while ($row = mysql_fetch_array($result)) {
    $bbcode[$row['id']]['template'] = $row['template'];
    $bbcode[$row['id']]['replacement'] = $row['replacement'];
}
mysql_free_result($result);
```

Notice that `$admin` and `$bbcode` are built by looping through the entire admin and BBcode table. This is important because it illustrates how the Board Administration page contains every piece of data contained in the admin table. These values are available, and are used, throughout the application. For example, `frm_header.inc.php` uses some of the `$admin` data:

```
$title = $admin['titlebar']['value'];
...
  <title><?php echo $title; ?></title>
...
  <h1><?php echo $admin['title']['value']; ?></h1>
<h2><?php echo $admin['description']['value']; ?></h2>
```

You may also notice the lack of any way to add or delete admin values. There is a good reason for this. The `$admin` values are available at the code level. Because of this, you don't want to be able to delete a value that the code is relying on. You also don't need to create new values, because the code wouldn't use the new values in any case.

However, you may find the need to create a new row of data in the admin table to be used in your board application. For example, suppose you are using a style sheet to alter the appearance of the application. Perhaps you want the ability to dynamically change the style sheet used by changing a value in the admin page, rather than by editing the `frm_eader.php` file.

The good news is that once you add a new row of data to the admin table, it is automatically detected by the Board Administration page and displayed. The bottom line? If you feel you need a new, administrator-controlled value in your application, simply add the appropriate row of data to your admin table, and access it in your code, using the `$admin['key']['value']` and `$admin['key']['title']` syntax.

Forum Administration

Forum Administration is pretty straightforward. You look up all of the forums in the forum table and then list them with their descriptions, plus a link for editing and a link for deleting. Choosing delete takes the administrator to `frm_ransact-affirm.php`, which prompts the user for confirmation before deleting the forum. This is a safety precaution, because deleting a forum results in the deletion of all posts within that forum as well. We leave it to you to explore `frm_transact-affirm.php` on your own, as it is a fairly self-explanatory page, and by now you should have no problem figuring out how it works.

BBcode Administration

In step 8 of the previous "Try It Out" section, you entered a few strange patterns in the BBcode Administration page. These patterns are regular expressions, which were first discussed in Chapter 8. We will clear up the mystery of those values for you, if you're having trouble deciphering them, and show you how they work. Before we do that, however, let's look at how BBcodes are implemented. Once you see where the replacements take place, we will look at the actual patterns.

If you take a look at the `show_topic()` function defined in `frm_output_functions.inc.php`, you'll see a line that looks like this:

```
echo '</p><p>' . bbcode($db, nl2br(htmlspecialchars($body))) . '</p>';
```

The variable `$body` contains the text you want to display on the screen. However, before you do that, you have a couple of cleanup tasks to perform. First, you want to convert (and not render) any HTML that might exist in the form to the HTML equivalents, so that the HTML is displayed in the body as it was entered. This will prevent malicious users from inputting HTML that can break your page. The function `htmlspecialchars()` performs this conversion for you.

Once all of the necessary characters in the HTML have been converted to their HTML entity equivalents, you want to replace each newline of the body text with `<br/>` tags so that all of the paragraphs in the post don't run together. PHP has a handy tool for that, too: the `nl2br()` function.

Finally, you perform all of the replacements you have set up on the BBcode Administration page. That is accomplished using the function `bbcode()`, which runs through each of the target/replacement pairs in the BBcode database, replacing any relevant text in the body. It does this recursively for a max of four iterations until no more matches are found.

```php
function bbcode($db, $data) {
    $sql = 'SELECT
            template, replacement
        FROM
            frm_bbcode';
    $result = mysql_query($sql, $db) or die(mysql_error($db));
    if (mysql_num_rows($result) > 0) {
        while($row = mysql_fetch_array($result)) {
            $bbcode['tpl'][] = '/' .
                html_entity_decode($row['template'], ENT_QUOTES). '/i';
            $bbcode['rep'][] = html_entity_decode($row['replacement'],
                ENT_QUOTES);
        }
        $data1 = preg_replace($bbcode['tpl'], $bbcode['rep'], $data);
        $count = 1;
        while (($data1 != $data) and ($count < 4)) {
            $count++;
            $data = $data1;
            $data1 = preg_replace($bbcode['tpl'], $bbcode['rep'], $data);
        }
    }
    return $data;
}
```

Because regular expressions (or regex) use many odd characters in the pattern, before storing the data in your table you use `htmlentities()` to convert the data into something MySQL can safely store. For that reason, when retrieving the data, you must perform `html_entity_decode()`. Also note the use of the *i* modifier after the right-hand modifier. This specifies that you do not care about upper- or lowercase matching. If you want to respect case when matching a pattern, simply remove this modifier.

As you can see from the code, `$row['template']` contains the regex pattern. The array variable `$row['replacement']` contains the replacement pattern. Now, let's look at some of the pattern/replacement pairs you entered earlier:

Pattern	Replacement	Explanation
very hard	cats and dogs	This is a very simple replacement, using a literal pattern match. It replaces the words "very hard" with the words "cats and dogs" in any post or signature. You will see evidence of this in one of your posts.
\[\/url\]	</a>	Replaces any instance of [/url] in the body with </a>. Note that the opening and closing square brackets and the forward slash have special meaning in a regexp, so they must be delimited to show that you want to match them literally.
\[b\]([^[]+?) \[\/b\]	$1	Now we're getting into some interesting stuff. This pattern matches [b]some text here[/b] and replaces it with some text here.

The last pattern deserves a bit of explanation, because it introduces a couple of new concepts. The parentheses are there so you can use what we call *back references*. Note the $1 in the replacement pattern. This tells the function: "Take whatever you found in the first set of parentheses and put it here." If you had a more complex pattern with a second set of parentheses, you would refer to the data matched within those parentheses using $2. A third set of parenthesis would map to $3, and so forth.

Within those parentheses, you are matching any character at all *except* a left square bracket. The + tells the expression to match from 1 to any number of those characters. If you wanted the expression to match 0 or more, you would instead use *.

The ? can be very confusing, especially if you're not familiar with regular expressions. Because it is immediately preceded by a quantifier (+), it does not mean 0 characters or 1 character as it usually does. In this case, it is telling the regex not to be greedy. What do we mean by "greedy"? Let's look at the following text example:

```
Hello, [b]George[/b], how are [b]you[/b] doing today?
```

If you ran the regex pattern \[b\]([^[]+)\[\/b\] against that text (note the lack of ?), the regex would be greedy and match the maximum-sized pattern it could find, by default. The result is that the preceding text would be altered like so:

```
Hello, <b>George[/b], how are [b]you</b> doing today?
```

This isn't good in this particular case, because you are only trying to style "George" and "you" in boldface. You use the ? in your pattern after the + to tell the regex pattern to be *ungreedy*, so that it finds the smallest matches. By adding in the ?, you get the result you really intended.

```
Hello, <b>George</b>, how are <b>you</b> doing today?
```

We know regular expressions can be a bit confusing. Take the time to learn them, though. If you understand them well, they can be your biggest ally. You will be surprised at the sort of patterns you can match with regex.

Try It Out   Using the Board

The final thing you're going to do is use the board as a normal user would. You're going to create a new post, view it, and reply to it.

1. Create frm_view_forum.php, which displays all of the threads (topics) for a forum:

```php
<?php
if (!isset($_GET['f'])) {
    header('Location: frm_index.php');
}

require_once 'frm_header.inc.php';

$forumid = $_GET['f'];
$forum = get_forum($db, $forumid);
```

```
echo breadcrumb($db, $forumid, 'F');
if (isset($_GET['page'])) {
    $page = $_GET['page'];
} else {
    $page = 1;
}
$limit = $admin['pageLimit']['value'];
if ($limit == '') {
    $limit = 25;
}
$start = ($page - 1) * $admin['pageLimit']['value'];

$sql = 'CREATE TEMPORARY TABLE tmp (
        topic_id INTEGER UNSIGNED NOT NULL DEFAULT 0,
        postdate DATETIME NOT NULL
    )';
mysql_query($sql, $db) or die(mysql_error($db));

$sql = 'LOCK TABLES frm_users READ, frm_posts READ';
mysql_query($sql, $db) or die(mysql_error($db));

$sql = 'INSERT INTO tmp SELECT
        topic_id, MAX(date_posted)
    FROM
        frm_posts
    WHERE
        forum_id = ' . $forumid . ' AND topic_id > 0
    GROUP BY
        topic_id';
mysql_query($sql, $db) or die(mysql_error($db));

$sql = 'UNLOCK TABLES';
mysql_query($sql, $db) or die(mysql_error($db));

$sql = 'SELECT SQL_CALC_FOUND_ROWS
        t.id as topic_id, t.subject as t_subject, u.name as t_author,
        COUNT(p.id) as numreplies, t.date_posted as t_posted,
        tmp.postdate as re_posted
    FROM
        frm_users u JOIN frm_posts t ON t.author_id = u.id
        LEFT JOIN tmp ON t.id = tmp.topic_id
        LEFT JOIN frm_posts p ON p.topic_id = t.id
    WHERE
        t.forum_id = ' . $forumid . ' AND t.topic_id = 0
    GROUP BY
        t.id
    ORDER BY
        re_posted DESC
    LIMIT ' . $start . ', ' . $limit;
$result = mysql_query($sql, $db) or die(mysql_error($db));
```

```php
$numrows = mysql_num_rows($result);
if ($numrows == 0) {
    $msg = 'There are currently no posts.  Would you like to be the first ' .
        'person to create a thread?';
    $title = 'Welcome to ' . $forum['name'];
    $dest = 'frm_compose.php?forumid=' . $forumid;
    echo msg_box($msg, $title, $dest);
} else {
    if (isset($_SESSION['user_id'])) {
        echo topic_reply_bar($db, 0, $_GET['f']);
    }
}
?>
<table style="width: 80%;">
 <tr>
  <th style="width: 50%;">Thread</th>
  <th>Author</th>
  <th>Replies</th>
  <th>Last Post</th>
 </tr>
<?php
    $rowclass = '';
    while ($row = mysql_fetch_array($result)) {
        $rowclass = ($rowclass == 'odd_row') ? 'even_row' : 'odd_row';
        if ($row['re_posted'] == '') {
            $lastpost = $row['t_posted'];
        } else {
            $lastpost = $row['re_posted'];
        }
        if (isset($_SESSION['user_id']) && $_SESSION['last_login']
< $lastpost) {
            $newpost = true;
        } else {
            $newpost = false;
        }
        echo '<tr class="' . $rowclass . '">';
        echo '<td>' . (($newpost) ? NEWPOST . ' ' : '') .
            '<a href="frm_view_topic.php?t=' . $row['topic_id'] . '">' .
            $row['t_subject'] . '</a></td>';
        echo '<td>' . $row['t_author'] . '</td>';
        echo '<td>' . $row['numreplies'] . '</td>';
        echo '<td>' . $lastpost . '</td>';
        echo '</tr>';
    }
    echo '</table>';
    echo paginate($db, $limit);
    echo '<p>' . NEWPOST . ' = New Post(s)</p>';
}
$sql = 'DROP TABLE tmp';
mysql_query($sql, $db) or die(mysql_error($db));

require_once 'frm_footer.inc.php';
?>
```

2. Create `frm_view_topic.php`, which displays all of the posts in a thread:

```php
<?php
if (!isset($_GET['t'])) {
    header('Location: frm_index.php');
}

require_once 'frm_header.inc.php';

$topicid = $_GET['t'];
$limit = $admin['pageLimit']['value'];

$user_id = (isset($_SESSION['user_id'])) ? $_SESSION['user_id'] : 0;
show_topic($db, $topicid, $user_id);

require_once 'frm_footer.inc.php';
?>
```

3. Enter `frm_compose.php`, the form used to enter the subject and body of a post:

```php
<?php
require_once 'frm_header.inc.php';

$subject = '';
if (isset($_GET['topicid'])) {
    $topicid = $_GET['topicid'];
} else {
    $topicid = '';
}
if (isset($_GET['forumid'])) {
    $forumid = $_GET['forumid'];
} else {
    $forumid = '';
}
if (isset($_GET['reid'])) {
    $reid = $_GET['reid'];
}
$body = '';
$post = '';
$authorid = isset($_SESSION['user_id']) ? $_SESSION['user_id'] : null;
$edit_mode = FALSE;

if (isset($_GET['a']) && $_GET['a'] == 'edit' && isset($_GET['post']) &&
    $_GET['post']) {
    $edit_mode = TRUE;
}

if (!isset($_SESSION['user_id'])) {
    echo '<p><strong>You must be logged in to post.  Please ' .
        '<a href="frm_login.php">Log in</a> before posting a message
.</strong>' .
        '</p>';
```

```
    } else if ($edit_mode && $_SESSION['user_id'] != $authorid) {
        echo '<p><strong>You are not authorized to edit this post. Please
contact ' .
           'your administrator.</strong></p>';
    } else {
        if ($edit_mode) {
            $sql = 'SELECT
                    topic_id, forum_id, author_id, subject, body
               FROM
                    frm_posts p JOIN frm_forum f ON p.forum_id = f.id
               WHERE p.id = ' . $_GET['post'];
            $result = mysql_query($sql, $db) or die(mysql_error($db));

            $row = mysql_fetch_array($result);

            $post = $_GET['post'];
            $topicid = $row['topic_id'];
            $forumid = $row['forum_id'];
            $authorid = $row['author_id'];
            $subject = $row['subject'];
            $body = $row['body'];
        } else {

            if ($topicid == '') {
                $topicid = 0;
                $topicname = 'New Topic';
            } else {
                if ($reid != '') {
                $sql = 'SELECT
                        subject
                   FROM
                        frm_posts
                   WHERE
                        id = ' . $reid;
                $result = mysql_query($sql, $db) or die(mysql_error($db));
                if (mysql_num_rows($result) > 0) {
                    $row = mysql_fetch_array($result);
                    $re = preg_replace('/(re: )/i', '', $row['subject']);
                }
            }
            $sql = 'SELECT
                    subject
               FROM
                    frm_posts
               WHERE
                    id = ' . $topicid . ' AND topic_id = 0 AND
                    forum_id = ' . $forumid;
            $result = mysql_query($sql, $db) or die(mysql_error($db));
            if (mysql_num_rows($result) > 0) {
                $row = mysql_fetch_array($result);
                $topicname = 'Reply to <em>' . $row['subject'] . '</em>';
                $subject = ($re == '') ? '' : 'Re: ' . $re;
            } else {
                $topicname = 'Reply';
```

```
            $topicid = 0;
        }
    }
}

if ($forumid == '' || $forumid == 0) {
    $forumid = 1;
}
$sql = 'SELECT
        forum_name
    FROM
        frm_forum
    WHERE id = ' . $forumid;
$result = mysql_query($sql, $db) or die(mysql_error($db));
$row = mysql_fetch_array($result);
$forumname = $row['forum_name'];
?>

<h2><?php echo ($edit_mode) ? 'Edit Post' : $forumname . ': '
. $topicname; ?></h2>
<form method="post" action="frm_transact_post.php">
 <p>Subject:<br/>
  <input type="text" name="subject" maxlength="255"
   value="<?php echo $subject; ?>"/></p>
 <p>Body:<br/>
  <textarea name="body" rows="10" cols="60"><?php echo $body; ?>
</textarea></p>
<p><input type="submit" name="action" value="<?php
 echo ($edit_mode) ? 'Save Changes' : 'Submit New Post'; ?>" />
 <input type="hidden" name="post" value="<?php echo $post; ?>">
 <input type="hidden" name="topic_id" value="<?php echo $topicid; ?>">
 <input type="hidden" name="forum_id" value="<?php echo $forumid; ?>">
 <input type="hidden" name="author_id" value="<?php echo $authorid; ?>"></p>
</form>
<?php
}
require_once 'footer.php';
?>
```

4. Create `frm_search.php`, which displays the user's search results:

```
<?php
require_once 'frm_header.inc.php';

echo '<h2>Search Results</h2>';

if (isset($_GET['keywords'])) {
    $sql = 'SELECT
            id, topic_id, subject, MATCH (subject, body) AGAINST ("' .
            $_GET['keywords'] . '") AS score
        FROM
            frm_posts
        WHERE
```

```
                    MATCH (subject, body) AGAINST ("' . $_GET['keywords'] . '")
            ORDER BY
                score DESC';
    $result = mysql_query($sql, $db) or die(mysql_error($db));

    if (mysql_num_rows($result) == 0) {
    echo '<p>No articles found that match the search term(s) <strong>' .
        $_GET['keywords'] . '</strong></p>';
    } else {
        echo '<ol>';
        while ($row = mysql_fetch_array($result)) {
            $topicid = ($row['topic_id'] == 0) ? $row['id'] : $row['topic_id'];
            echo '<li><a href="frm_view_topic.php?t=' . $topicid . '#post' .
                $row['id'] . '">' . $row['subject'] . '</a><br/>' .
                'relevance: ' . $row['score'] . '</li>';
        }
        echo '</ol>';
    }
}

require_once 'frm_footer.inc.php';
?>
```

5. Click the Home item on the main menu. You should now see a screen similar to Figure 16-6. If you did not make any changes to the forums, there will be just one forum, called "New Forum." If you did make changes, you should see your forums listed here.

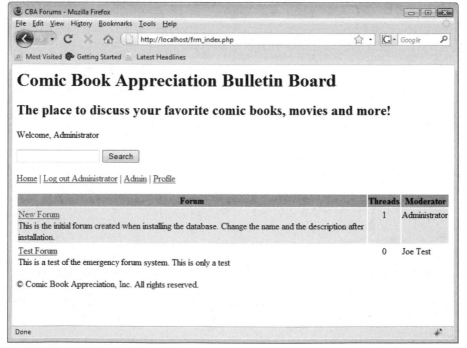

Figure 16-6

6.   Click a forum on the page.

7.   If you are prompted to create a new thread, click "yes." Otherwise, click New Thread.

8.   Enter any subject you like, and any text in the body. Somewhere in the body field, include the phrase "It was raining very hard today."

9.   When you are done, click the Submit New Post button. You should now see your post on the screen, as shown in Figure 16-7. Note that although you typed "very hard" in your post, it now reads "cats and dogs." That is the BBcode tool at work. We'll look at that in more detail in the "How It Works" section that follows.

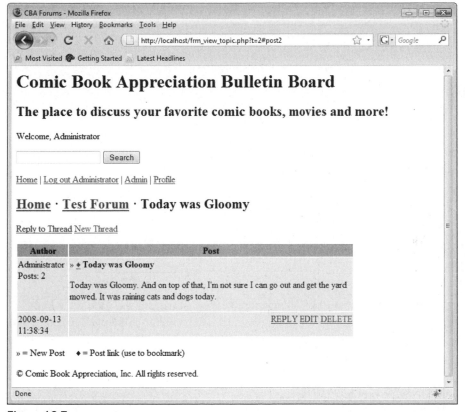

Figure 16-7

10.   Click Reply to Thread, and repeat steps 8 and 9 to create at least three more posts. After creating the last post, note that the Next/Prev buttons become available at the bottom of the thread. Because you changed your Pagination Limit to 3 in the steps, you can see only three posts on this page. You can see that you can click the number 2, or click "Next," and it will take you to the next (up to 3) posts.

11. Let's look at one more function, Search. Up at the top of the screen, you should see a text box with a button labeled Search. Enter the word "raining," and click the Search button.

12. If you followed step 8 in the previous series of steps, you should see at least one document returned in the search results, as shown in Figure 16-8.

Figure 16-8

That's just about it for the bulletin board application. It's not overly complex, but it does have a few useful features, as we promised it would. When you are done with this chapter (and the book), you should be armed with enough knowledge to add your own ideas to this and the other applications.

How It Works

By now, most of the code in this section should be easy for you to understand. The steps involved in creating a post, editing a post, replying to a post, and displaying a forum or post have been covered in similar applications in the previous chapters — the basics of that process being: collect information from the user, store it in a database, and display the information based on user request. Since we've covered this kind of behavior before, let's talk about something a little more powerful, searching.

Searching

A bulletin board would not be worth much in the long run unless you had the ability to search for old posts. Visit any bulletin board you might be familiar with, and most likely you will find a search function there.

There are many types of searches. The simplest requires that you enter text into an input field, and when you click the Search button, the script looks for any of the text you entered. That is the search we created for this application. Searches can get very complicated, too. You might want to search posts by the date they were entered, or by author. You might want to find a range of dates. You might even want to be able to designate how the result page is sorted. These capabilities are not currently available in the CBA forums, but feel free to beef up your search if you feel ambitious enough.

The actual search mechanism is fairly simple, and we quickly introduced it in Chapter 13. You have a single text field with a Search button that submits your form. The frm_search.php page captures the search term, and builds a relatively simple SQL statement that is designed to return matching rows. You then simply iterate through those rows and display the data on the screen. It's not that much different from displaying a forum or thread on the page. The only real difference is the SQL statement.

```
$sql = 'SELECT
        id, topic_id, subject, MATCH (subject, body) AGAINST ("' .
        $_GET['keywords'] . '") AS score
    FROM
        frm_posts
    WHERE
        MATCH (subject, body) AGAINST ("' . $_GET['keywords'] . '")
    ORDER BY
        score DESC';
$result = mysql_query($sql, $db) or die(mysql_error($db));
```

The bulk of the work of the search happens in the database. It stands to reason, then, that the more efficient and well-built your database is, the faster your data will be retrieved. To maximize the efficiency, you create an index for the fields to be searched. In this case, you index the subject and body columns of your frm_posts table. You can see how this works in the appropriate CREATE TABLE query in db_ch16.php:

```
$sql = 'CREATE TABLE IF NOT EXISTS frm_posts (
        id           INTEGER UNSIGNED NOT NULL AUTO_INCREMENT,
        topic_id     INTEGER UNSIGNED NOT NULL DEFAULT 0,
        forum_id     INTEGER UNSIGNED NOT NULL DEFAULT 0,
        author_id    INTEGER UNSIGNED NOT NULL DEFAULT 0,
        update_id    INTEGER UNSIGNED NOT NULL DEFAULT 0,
        date_posted  DATETIME         NOT NULL DEFAULT "0000-00-00 00:00:00",
        date_updated DATETIME,
        subject      VARCHAR(100)     NOT NULL DEFAULT "",
        body         MEDIUMTEXT,

        PRIMARY KEY (id),
        INDEX (forum_id, topic_id, author_id, date_posted),
        FULLTEXT INDEX (subject, body)
    )
    ENGINE=MyISAM';
mysql_query($sql, $db) or die(mysql_error($db));
```

Note that after creating each of the columns, you set the primary key, an index, and a full-text index. Primary keys were discussed in Chapter 10. These help you create and track unique records. An index makes searching for rows much faster, and as you can see, you have created an index on `forum_id`, `topic_id`, `author_id`, and `date_posted`. A full-text index is set for the `subject` and `body` columns, which allows you to quickly find records using `MATCH`.

Let's take a look at the SQL statement that does the actual search. Assume you are looking for the word "Board."

```
SELECT
    id, topic_id, subject, MATCH (subject, body) AGAINST ("Board") AS score
FROM
    frm_posts
WHERE
    MATCH (subject, body) AGAINST ("Board")
ORDER BY
    score DESC
```

To understand how this returns records, you must understand the `MATCH` command. `MATCH` returns a score value that rates how relevant the match was for each and every row in the table. According to the MySQL manual, it is based on the "number of words in the row, the number of unique words in that row, the total number of words in the collection, and the number of documents (rows) that contain a particular word."

Note that the same `MATCH` command is used twice. Fortunately, the MySQL optimizer caches the results of the `MATCH` command the first time it is run and will not run it twice. Because the `MATCH` command returns a zero (0) for rows that do not match at all, putting `MATCH` in the `WHERE` clause prevents those rows from returning. If you do not put in the `WHERE` clause, all rows in the table will be returned, and they will not be sorted.

Using `MATCH` in the `WHERE` clause causes the rows to be returned sorted by relevance. This is not intuitive to all users, however, so we like to put in `ORDER BY score DESC` just for good measure, although it is not required.

Afterthoughts

Congratulations! You have just completed the creation of a fully functioning bulletin board system. It is more powerful than some of the simpler ones you'll find, but it is certainly not the most complex. You could still do many things to this application that could really make it sing, if you were so inclined.

What else could you add to this application? Perhaps you have a few ideas already, based on what you have seen on other forums. If you need some ideas, here is a short list to get you started:

❑ **Avatars:** Allow your users to upload (or choose from your site) a small image that can be placed under their username.

❑ **Smilies:** Most forums will replace smilies with a graphical representation of some sort. Create some smilies yourself, or find good ones on the Internet that are not copyrighted, store them in an images folder on your web site, and use regular expressions to replace smilies with the appropriate images.

❑ **User profiles:** Allow users to add more information to their profiles, such as hobbies, location, age, gender, and so on. Also allow them to add their AIM, Yahoo! IM, and MSN IDs. Make their username into a link that allows other users to contact them via e-mail or Instant Messenger. Make sure you include a check box to allow users to hide their e-mail address if they want to.

❑ **Quoting:** What is a forum without the ability to quote relevant text? Allow users to quote all or part of a post. We leave it up to you to figure out how to implement this.

❑ **Polls:** A very popular option, polls allow users to post a short questionnaire for their peers to answer. Install a poll option when posting a new topic, and display a graph of the results at the top of the thread.

Summary

Now you have created a community where your visitors can hang their hats and stay a while. Combine this with all of the other applications you have built, and you should no doubt have a very cool, integrated web site up and running in no time! Congratulations on making it this far. This chapter was long, with a lot of code. Most of it was not overly difficult; indeed, most of the code was stuff you did in other chapters. But we hope that by the time you have finished this chapter, you will feel comfortable creating a web site from the ground up, using PHP and MySQL installed on an Apache server.

Exercises

If you would like to test out how much you have learned from this chapter, take the time to do these small exercises. Not only will they help you learn, they will allow you to add some extra features to your bulletin board application.

1. Add code to `frm_admin.php` to prevent unauthorized users from loading the page. Redirect them back to `frm_index.php`.

2. Create a regular expression that recognizes an e-mail address in a post and turns it into a link.

3. Add a bit of code to the pagination function to allow the user to go to the first page or last page. For example, if there are 14 pages, and the user is on page 8, and the range is 7, it should look something like this:

```
<PREV [1] .. [5] [6] [7] 8 [9] [10] [11] .. [14] NEXT >
```

Using Log Files to Improve Your Site

The cool thing about being a web developer is that sometimes you get to act like Big Brother and keep close watch on what your visitors are doing. Although it may seem voyeuristic to some, analyzing what goes on at your site can give you valuable information that will enable you to make your site better. To perform this analysis, you have to first gather the data necessary for the analysis, and to do that you need a log.

A *log* is a simply a text file saved on your server. It is updated by a logging application on the server every time something happens, such as when a particular file is requested by someone or when an error occurs. When the event happens, a line of text is appended to the end of the file, essentially "logging in" the activity. Here are three basic types of logs:

❑   Access Logs track every hit on your web server.

❑   Error Logs track every error or warning.

❑   Custom Logs track whatever information you tell them to.

Some examples of the types of information you can glean from logs include:

❑   What IP addresses your visitors are using so you can get a geographical location for your most common visitors; this may help with geographical demographic research.

❑   What browsers your visitors are using, either just for your own curiosity or so you can make sure you don't implement any special browser-specific rendering features on your site that only a small portion of your viewership would be able to take advantage of.

❑   What times and days your visitors are visiting, so you can schedule maintenance during slow times or special promotional events during busier times.

❑   What pages are the most popular on your site, so you can gauge the success or failure of certain pages and prune your web site of any dead weight.

❑ Whether the volume of your traffic is increasing, so you can determine if your site is either becoming more well known or stagnating itself into oblivion.

❑ If you're using user authentication on your site, what users are logging in when, and what their activity is, so you can see who your MVPs are and perhaps offer them special web site features (or maybe a beer at the local bar).

As you may have guessed, this chapter is all about logs. It will cover the following:

❑ What logs look like and what information they contain.

❑ Where you can find them on your system.

❑ What resources exist that you can use to help analyze the data.

❑ How you can use the information to improve your site.

Locating Your Logs

Log files are in different locations depending on what program created them and what their function is. Most are available in a folder outside the scope of your web site so that users don't have access to them.

Apache

Apache keeps access logs and error logs. If Apache has been installed on your server following the instructions in Chapter 1 (or Appendix I), the default location is `C:\Program Files\Apache Software Foundation\Apache2.2\logs` (or `/usr/local/apache/logs` on Linux).

A typical access log entry looks like this:

```
127.01.0.1 - - [29/Sep/2008:12:08:35 -0400] "GET /index.php?xyz=123 HTTP/1.1"
200 4069 "http://www.example.com/cms/index.php" "Mozilla/5.0 (Windows; U;
Windows NT 5.1; en-US; rv:1.8.1.14) Gecko/20080404 Firefox/2.0.0.14"
```

All of this information is on one line of the log and is built by Apache according to the `LogFormat` directive in the `mod_log_config` module. The typical configuration looks like this:

```
LogFormat "%h %l %u %t \"%r\" %>s %b" common
```

The config string that built the line you saw from the log file used the *combined format* and looks like this:

```
LogFormat "%h %l %u %t \"%r\" %>s %b \"%{Referer}i\" \"%{User-agent}i\""
    combined
```

Although the `LogFormat` directive is beyond the scope of this book, we will list each parameter here so that you can understand what each piece of the log is and how it's broken down:

❑ **%h (127.0.0.1):** The address of the client currently accessing your server. This can be an IP address or a hostname.

❑ **%l (-):** The RFC 1413 identity of the client. This is usually a hyphen (-) to indicate that Apache was not able to obtain the information.

❏ **%u (-):** The username of the client. This is set if the page is using HTTP User Authentication. Otherwise, you see a hyphen (-).

❏ **%t ([29/Sep/2008:12:08:35 -0400]):** The date and time the client accessed your server.

   ❏ The format for this is as follows: [day/month/year:hour:minute:second zone]

   ❏ day = 2 digits

   ❏ month = 3 letters

   ❏ year = 4 digits

   ❏ hour = 2 digits

   ❏ minute = 2 digits

   ❏ second = 2 digits

   ❏ zone = ('+' | '-') 4 digits

❏ **\@@dp%r\@@dp (@@GET /index.php?xyz=123 HTTP/1.1@@dp):** The request line from the client. This is wrapped in quotes, which have to be escaped. This is actually multiple information, which could be built using other parameters:

   ❏ %m (request method), in this case, GET

   ❏ %U (URL), in this case, /index.php

   ❏ %q (query string), in this case, ?xyz=123

   ❏ %H (protocol), in this case, HTTP/1.1

   ❏ \@@dp%m %U%p %H\@@dp is the functional equivalent of \@@dp%r\@@dp

❏ **%>s (200):** The status code sent back to the client. In this case, because it starts with a "2," we know it was a successful request.

❏ **%b (4069):** The size of the object returned to the client in bytes (not including headers). If no content is returned, the value is hyphen (-), or "0" if %B is used.

❏ **\@@dp%{Referer}i\@@dp (@@dphttp://www.yexample.com/cms/index.php@@dp):** The address of the page the client came from. This is useful for compiling information about where your users heard about your web site.

❏ **\@@dp%{User-agent}i\@@dp (@@Mozilla/5.0 (Windows; U; Windows NT 5.1; en-US; rv:1.8.1.14) Gecko/20080404 Firefox/2.0.0.14@@dp):** User-Agent HTTP request header information. This is the information the client's browser sends about itself. This is very useful for determining how many people are using certain browsers.

If the preceding information looks like Greek to you, don't worry. There are ways of getting the information without understanding any programming, and methods of reading the information to build statistics, charts, graphs, and other things that are much easier to read. We'll share those methods with you shortly.

The information in the error log is pretty self-explanatory. It is free-form and descriptive, but typically most error logs capture the date and time, the error severity, the client IP address, the error message, and the object the client was requesting.

Here is what the typical error log entry looks like:

```
[Mon Sep 29 11:18:35 2008] [error] [client 69.129.21.24] File does not exist:
/svr/apache/example.com/www/public_files/index.htm
```

Because the error message is also contained in the Apache access log, it makes more sense to pull the data out of the access log. For example, the preceding error will show up in the access log with access code 404.

PHP

PHP also keeps a log of errors for you, but as we discussed in Chapter 1, the default setting for this feature is set to "off" in your php.ini file. You have to turn it on to enable error logging, which we highly recommend doing. Also, don't forget to tell your php.ini file where you want the error log to be saved.

The typical error log entry looks like this:

```
[Mon Sep 29 15:08:12 2008] PHP Parse error:  parse error, unexpected '}' in
C:\Program Files\Apache Software Foundation\Apache2.2\htdocs\example.php on
line 14
```

As in the other logs we have looked at, the logs themselves are relatively straightforward, and their purpose is to keep track of all of the errors that occurred when your PHP pages were being accessed.

In the preceding example, you can see that there was a parse error in the file example.php on line 14, which merits attention. Anyone attempting to see the contents of this file will see only the parse error until it is fixed.

A regular check of the PHP error log should be on your "to-do" list, just to make sure there aren't any errors in your code.

MySQL

As if that's not enough, MySQL also logs queries and errors that pertain to database transactions. By default, the error log is stored as hostname.err in the data directory (this is true under both Windows and UNIX). You can specify where the error log is saved by issuing the following command from the command prompt when starting the MySQL server:

```
mysqld --log-error[=filename].
```

Here is a typical entry in the error log:

```
080929  0:28:02  InnoDB: Started
MySql: ready for connections.
Version: '5.0.51b'  socket: ''  port: 3306
```

This lets you know that the MySQL server started successfully, what version is currently running, and what socket and port it is configured for. It also gives you the date and time that the server began running (in the first line). You should know that on Windows, you cannot access this log while the server is running; you need to stop the server to open this file.

MySQL also allows you to view every query that is sent to the server. To specify where the general query log is located, you would type the following command when starting the MySQL server:

```
mysqld --log[=file]
```

Again, by default, this file will be stored in the data directory with the name `hostname.log` file, unless you specify otherwise. An entry in the general query log looks like this:

```
 /usr/local/mysql/libexec/mysqld, Version: 5.0.51b-log, started with:
Tcp port: 3306  Unix socket: /tmp/mysql.sock
Time                 Id Command     Argument
080929 21:33:34       1 Connect     buzzly_comic@localhost on
              1 Init DB       buzzly_comicsite
              1 Query         SELECT * FROM forum_admin
              1 Query         SELECT * FROM forum_bbcode
              1 Quit
080929 21:33:50       2 Connect     buzzly_comic@localhost on
              2 Init DB       buzzly_comicsite
              2 Query         SELECT id,access_lvl,name,last_login FROM
forum_users
WHERE email='admin@yoursite.com' AND passwd='admin'
              2 Query         UPDATE forum_users SET last_login =
'2008-09-29
21:33:50'
WHERE id = 1
              2 Quit
              3 Connect     buzzly_comic@localhost on
              3 Init DB       buzzly_comicsite
              3 Query         SELECT * FROM forum_admin
              3 Query         SELECT * FROM forum_bbcode
```

If you are interested in seeing only the queries that changed data, you should view the binary log file instead of the general query file.

This file is also saved by default in your "data" directory, with the filename of `hostname-bin` unless you specify otherwise. You activate this log by typing the following at the command prompt:

```
mysqld --log-bin[=file_name]
```

An entry in the binary log looks like this:

```
# at 4
#080929 21:29:46 server id 1  log pos 4        Start: binlog v 3, server v
5.0.51b-
log created 080929 21:29:46 at startup
# at 79
#080929 21:33:50 server id 1  log_pos 79 Query        thread_id=2  exec_time=0
error_code=0
use buzzly_comicsite;
SET TIMESTAMP=1068431630;
UPDATE forum_users SET last_login = '2008-09-29 21:33:50' WHERE id = 1;
# at 196
#080929 21:34:52 server id 1  log_pos 196       Query        thread_id=8
exec_time=0
error_code=0
SET TIMESTAMP=1068431692;
UPDATE forum_users SET email='admin@yoursite.com', name='Admin', access_lvl=3,
signature='Testing, testing, 123.'  WHERE id=1;
```

Unlike the other logs in this chapter that you can access with WordPad or Notepad, you must access the binary log using the `mysqlbinlog` utility. At the command prompt, you would type **mysqlbinlog** to see the parameters for this software. Your screen will look something like the one shown in Figure 17-1.

Figure 17-1

As you can see, there are many parameters you can set to glean the specific information you are looking for.

Analyzing Your Log Data

Numerous software programs are available that live to help you make sense of this gobbledygook. Although you could write your own log analysis application, there's no real reason to when there are so many alternatives available. We'll describe some of them in this section. Note that most of these programs are used for analyzing web server activity and not MySQL or PHP logs.

Webalizer

You can find Webalizer at `www.webalizer.com`, and it is a proud part of the wonderful open source community we talked about in Chapter 1. It provides reports in an easy-to-read HTML format with pretty charts and such that can be read by just about anyone, including the higher-ups. Its main purpose is to produce reports on server activity, most specifically Apache. If you set your Apache config files to do DNS server lookups, then your reports with Webalizer will show those instead of simple IP addresses. This program is also known for its incredible speed, as it can process 10,000 records in a matter of one second.

You can see a sample screenshot in Figure 17-2, also available at the Webalizer web site.

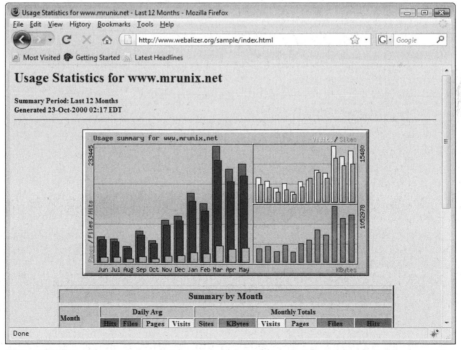

Figure 17-2

Analog

Another open source contender for helping you make sense of your log files is Analog, which you can find at www.analog.cx. Although it's a little rough around the edges, it's still a powerful tool that can be customized to show what you want to see. By using the add-on, Report Magic (available at www.reportmagic.org), you can generate all kinds of fancy 3-D charts and graphs and really impress your superiors.

You can see a sample screenshot in Figure 17-3, also available at the Analog web site.

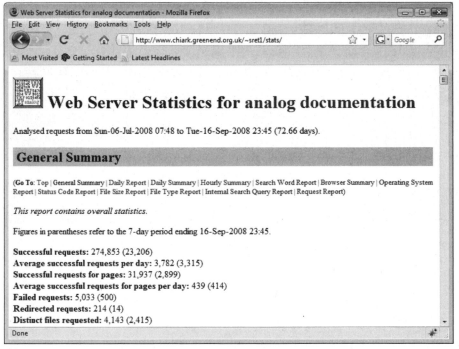

Figure 17-3

AWStats

Another of our open source buddies, AWStats can be found at http://awstats.sourceforge.net. Unlike some of the other open source stats programs, AWStats can track the number of unique visitors, entry and exit pages, search engines and keywords used to find the site, and browser details of each visitor, such as version and screen size.

AWStats also allows the web administrator to set up customized reports for tracking something of specific interest for his or her specific needs, which is a welcome addition to this software package.

You can see a sample screenshot in Figure 17-4, also available at the AWStats web site.

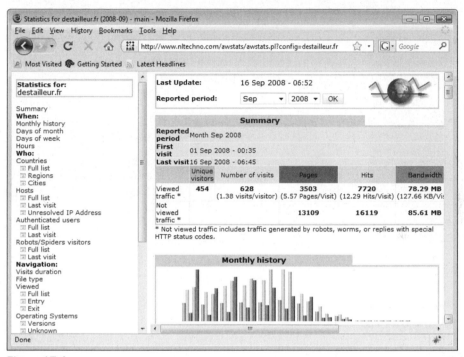

Figure 17-4

HTTP Analyze

One more stats program for you to investigate is HTTP Analyze, which you can find at www.http-analyze.org. Another open source favorite, this program works on any log file that is in the NCSA Common Logfile Format or W3C Extended File Format, and thus works great with Apache. It should be noted that HTTP Analyze is supported by both UNIX and Windows systems. It also provides several different options for viewing data, all in HTML and easy-to-read formats.

You can see a sample screenshot in Figure 17-5, also available at the HTTP Analyze web site.

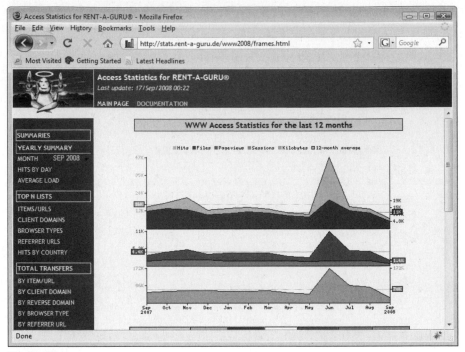

Figure 17-5

Google Analytics

You can take advantage of Google's never-ending thirst for data by signing up for Google Analytics at www.google.com/analytics and have access to some pretty impressive reporting utilities for your web site. Unlike the previous offerings mentioned in this chapter, Google Analytics doesn't parse your server's log files. Instead, when you sign up for an account you are given custom tracking code you must insert into the pages you want to monitor. But after that, Google does the rest! It incorporates their Adsense program exceptionally well (why wouldn't they?), and you can see how successful your campaigns are. Figure 17-6 shows a sample screenshot.

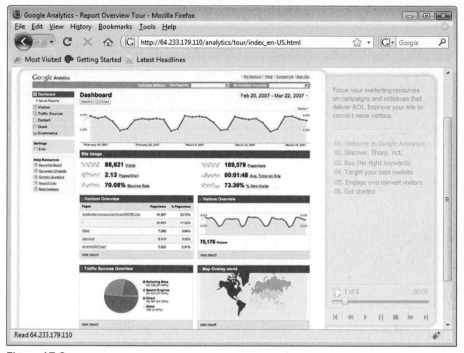

Figure 17-6

Putting the Analysis to Work

So now you have all these beautiful reports, and you go to your boss and proudly display your charts and graphs and expect a big pat on the back. But what happens when she says to you, "So what does it all mean?"

Let's talk a minute about what the reports mean to you, so you have a nice, neat, witty response prepared.

Earlier in the chapter, we touched on how using the stats can help you improve your site. Your logs are, in many cases, your only source of feedback from your visitors. You can't know what you're doing right or wrong without any feedback, so as your only tangible evidence, these stats are really quite valuable. There are several different areas you probably want to pay attention to, depending on the specific needs of your site.

Site Health

Your error logs and Apache server logs (specifically the 404 errors) can be crucial in ensuring that your site is completely functional and has no broken links. This can be especially true if you have a large site with a lot of intertwined links and pages; it would be virtually impossible for you to manually test each link on each page of your site. Broken links can be frustrating for the user, and if it is a link to a crucial portion of your site, can have adverse affects on your site performance.

User Preferences and Information

You can't please all of the people all of the time, but you can certainly try. You care about what your users like, so you obviously want to tailor your site to the most common visitor and try to minimize the number of visitors who won't have the optimal viewing experience. You want to know what percentage of visitors are using which browsers so that you can be sure to test your site against the browsers that are most popular with your audience. You also care about how many unique and not-so-unique visitors are coming to your site so that you can tell if your site is gaining a new following, while maintaining its current one. You also want to know what screen size they are using, so you can again tailor the look of your site to be the best it can be for the most visitors.

Number of Hits and Page Views

Remember, a "hit" is any request made to the server, whereas a "page view" is a request for a page (such as an HTML or PHP page). Hits can consist of images, sound files, or anything that requires activity from the server. This number doesn't really give you an accurate count of how many people are viewing a page, so you typically go by page views.

You want to see which pages get the most page views, and which are the most popular so that if you need to make something known about your site, you can make sure that it appears on those pages. For example, say that you have a new product to promote — if no one ever visits the "new products" page, it won't do you much good to only post it there. If the home page of your site is the most popular, you want to also post that information on that page, so you make sure that everybody who visits your site knows about your new product.

You also want to be able to look at the pages that are doing well and compare them with the pages that aren't doing so well. Is the content of both pages clear and concise? What is it about the popular pages that makes them so great? Can you make your losers closer to the winners in page design, content, or positioning?

Trends over Time

It's rewarding to see your site become more popular as time goes on, but it creates a big pit in your stomach if things are going downhill. Tracking popularity over time can help you discern if interest in your site is waning, or if the site is perhaps more popular around certain seasons of the year. If your site sells golf equipment and you notice a dip in page views during the winter months, obviously you don't have much to worry about, because your business is a seasonal business and this dip is understandable. Perhaps you notice that during the winter months your average visitor is coming from Florida (makes sense, eh?). Perhaps you can work with Marketing to develop an advertising strategy tailored to the loyal Floridians during those months.

Referring Sites

If you can discern where people are finding your site, you will have a very valuable resource at your disposal. Are the search engines actually working in your favor? What keywords are people using to reach your site? Do you fare better with certain search engines than others? Are you getting referred from other, non-directory sites?

Perhaps you have a site that sells bowling equipment, and you notice through your stats that the Professional Bowlers Association has your site listed on its own site as a resource for its visitors, and has referred the majority of your visitors. Perhaps then you decide you want to offer a special discount to PBA members as a "thank you." Increasing your web site traffic can be as simple as getting yourself listed on as many other sites as possible. Not only will it help people see you, but it will also help increase your listing in search engines such as Google that take into account criteria such as how many other places your web site is listed.

Summary

You should now feel comfortable looking at log files to benefit your site and your skills as a professional web developer. You can choose to massage the data based on a program you have written yourself, or you may choose to utilize numerous other resources out there to provide you with fancy reports that let you know what is going on with your site. By paying attention to trends and popular pages in your site, you can get a better feel for who your visitors really are. This, in turn, enables you to continually improve your site.

At the very least, you will be able to speak intelligently to your boss when she asks "So what's going on with our web site?"

Troubleshooting

Nothing is more frustrating than thinking you have all your t's crossed and your i's dotted only to have your program produce completely perplexing and unwanted results and blow up on you with a string of errors that you do not understand.

You may find comfort in knowing that many developers experience the same types of obstacles. With this chapter, we hope to shed light on some problems you may encounter and suggest a few troubleshooting strategies.

Installation Troubleshooting

Suppose you are trying to access either PHP, MySQL, or Apache, and you are running into problems. Perhaps for some reason they are not playing well with one another, and you are getting strange errors. Things aren't working the way they should be, based on the installation instructions.

Many times, commonly seen errors or obstacles will be discussed on the web sites for each of the AMP components. The web sites also provide detailed instructions for the particular system you are using, and we encourage you to read through them carefully to double-check yourself. Make sure you follow the instructions exactly.

If while configuring PHP you receive an error that tells you that the server can't find a specific library, we recommend you check the following:

❑   Verify that the correct paths have been specified in your configure commands.

❑   Make sure you've actually installed the library and any of its dependencies on your machine.

❑   Make sure you've restarted the Apache web server after making any changes in your php .ini or httpd.conf files (changes in .htaccess files normally do not require a restart).

Parse Errors

We're sure you've seen this many times:

```
Parse error: parse error, expecting '','' or '';'' in /foo/public_html/forum/
index.php on line 25
```

Oh no, it's the dreaded parse error! These are quite common even for experienced programmers. One or two parse errors will undoubtedly slip through, even with the best color-coded PHP text editors to help check your syntax. While these can be very frustrating, they are usually the simplest errors to fix because they are commonly caused by mistakes in your syntax instead of your logic. Check for any missing semicolons, missing commas, or misplaced quotation marks.

Cleanup on Line 26 . . . Oops, I Mean 94

When PHP displays a parse error, it includes a line number, which provides your first clue for solving the mystery. However, sometimes the line number can be misleading. In fact, at times the mistake will have occurred in a place several lines preceding the one identified by the server as the culprit.

Take a missing semicolon, for example; without the semicolon to signify to the server that the statement has come to an end, the server will continue to string subsequent lines together. It may not realize there is a problem until several lines later, and it will then issue a parse error on the wrong line. Likewise, similar behavior can result when a missing quotation mark or parenthesis is the culprit. Let's look at the following lines of code as an example (we have added line numbers to prove our point):

```
1 <?php
2 $greeting1="aloha";
3 $greeting2="bon jour";
4 $greeting3="hola"
5 $greeting4="good morning";
6 ?>
```

When you run this test, the error you get is as follows:

```
Parse error: parse error, unexpected T_VARIABLE in C:\Program Files\Apache
Software Foundation\Apache2.2\htdocs\error.php on line 5
```

For our purposes here, we named the above script error.php, and you can see that line 5 is referenced when line 4 was actually the line with the error in it. Because we neglected to use a semicolon at the end of line 4, line 5 was seen as a continuation of line 4, and PHP became quite confused.

Elementary, My Dear Watson!

Sometimes the simplest answer is the right answer. Make sure you check to see that you've done all of the following:

- ❏ Each statement ends with a semicolon.
- ❏ All opening quotes, parentheses, and braces are matched with closing ones.
- ❏ All single and double quotation marks are nested and/or escaped properly.

You will greatly decrease the risk of introducing parse errors if you get into the habit of checking your syntax regularly as you write your code. You may want to use an editor that is familiar with PHP and can color-code your programs as you write them. Syntax highlighting makes it much easier to recognize when you have misspelled a function name or forgotten to close your quotes. We've provided a matrix comparing various text editors, some of which support syntax highlighting, in Appendix F.

Empty Variables

You've just built a large page that collects 50 fields of information from your users. There are no parse errors. You fill in the form online and click on the submit button. The next page loads just as it should. The only problem is that none of the variables seem to have been passed on to the new form!

This actually happens quite often. The first possible cause is that you are expecting your values to be posted, but you forgot to use `method="post"` on your form. By default, forms use the `get` method.

How do you solve this? Check the address of your second page. Are there variables in the query string? If so, then you've inadvertently used the GET method, and you need to go back and change your method to POST. Mystery solved.

Consistent and Valid Variable Names

First, you should make sure that your variable names are appropriate and valid according to the naming rules, as outlined in Chapter 2. Make sure you aren't beginning any variable name with a number, or trying to use a predefined variable for your variable name, such as `$php_errormsg`. You can find a complete list in the PHP manual, at `www.php.net/manual/en/reserved.variables.php`.

Also, check the case you are using when referencing variables, because variable names are case-sensitive. The same holds true for database and table names. Make sure you are referencing them correctly and consistently, and be sure to change all the instances of the variable name if you make a change to a variable name after the fact.

It is easier to maintain consistent variable names if you pick a naming convention and stick with it throughout your scripts. This ties into the discussion in Chapter 2 regarding good coding practices.

Open a New Browser

Sometimes if you are working with sessions and you are in the testing phase of your scripts, there may be an extraneous session setting hanging out there that could be preventing you from obtaining the desired results and altering your variable values.

You can clear all session variables (provided you haven't changed your config files, as we discussed in Chapter 2) by simply closing the web browser and opening a new one.

"Headers Already Sent" Error

You may encounter an error message that looks like this:

```
Warning: Cannot modify header information - headers already sent by (output
started at C:\Program Files\Apache Software Foundation\Apache2.2\htdocs\
headererror.php:1) in C:\Program Files\Apache Software Foundation\Apache2.2\
htdocs\headererror.php on line 2
```

This is a common error when working with sessions and cookies. It can occur if you try to set them after you have sent HTML code to the server. The server has to deal with sessions and cookies before any HTML output is sent to the browser, which means that these lines must be the first in the code before any HTML code or `echo` statement. If you have even a trailing leading space before your first `<?php` line of code, you will see this error.

If you need to set cookie or session variables within the body of your code, you need to rethink your logic to accommodate this limitation. As we discussed in Chapter 2, those variables need to be addressed at the beginning of your code for them to be parsed correctly by the PHP server.

Ways exist to get around this error, using the output buffer to suppress these errors. The output buffer is used to store all HTML output in a buffer until you are ready to send it to the browser. The function `ob_start()` is used to begin the output-buffering process, and `ob_end_flush()` will send all of the stored HTML output to the browser, empty the buffer, and end the output-storing process. This will let you cheat the system and store session and cookie variables in the body of the code, as well as allow you to use the `header()` function in the body of the code. For example, this snippet of code uses the output buffer to suppress our error. In the following example, the `header.php` file contains the connection variables to connect to the MySQL database, as well as some HTML code that is common to all the pages in our site.

```php
<?php
ob_start()
include 'header.php';
//perform a mysql query to determine which page the user is supposed to see;

if ($userage < 18) {
    header('Location: child.php');
} else {
    header('Location: adult.php');
}
ob_end_flush();
?>
```

Without the use of the `ob_start()` and `ob_end_flush()` functions, we would have gotten the "headers already sent" error when we tried to redirect our user. This is because of the HTML code that is in the `header.php` file. You can see that the logic is flawed somewhat because we should keep our connection variables in a separate file, away from the HTML code, but it's not such a fatal design flaw that our web site shouldn't function. We can thus cheat the system.

Although this is not recommended for beginners because it is more important for you to learn to code well and according to the rules, this can be a useful set of functions for a more experienced programmer. If you would like to learn more about the output buffer functions, you can find a complete list of them in Appendix C, or visit www.php.net.

Sometimes, the problem may not even be in the same script that's generating this type of error. If you have extra whitespace after the closing ?> in an included file, that might cause a problem as well. Some people prefer to omit the ?> at the end of include files. Many times, extra space is inserted by hitting the Tab key or spacebar unnecessarily.

General Debugging Tips

Even the most difficult of errors can be worked out with a bit of focus and patience. After all, it's just code and is nothing to be afraid of. Following are a few tips for general debugging purposes that can help you out of many sticky spots.

Use echo

Occasionally you might want to read the server's mind and see what it thinks is going on. One way to do this is to display the contents of variables periodically in your code. This will let you verify that the server is parsing everything correctly.

You can use echo in a step-by-step process as you follow the path of your variable, to see how the server is treating the value throughout the code. This process would help, for example, if you wanted to perform a complex mathematical equation on a variable's value, and all you could tell from your output was that you were getting the wrong answer. You need to find out at what point the breakdown occurs, so you insert echo statements throughout each step of the equation to verify the accuracy of your calculation as it runs through the equation. You will then see the value of the variable as it changes.

The echo command can also be useful in if statements, foreach statements, functions, and so on, to ensure that these loops are being called or processed correctly.

Here's a simple example to illustrate how echo can help you. Let's assume you have the following script:

```php
<?php
$curr_var = 0;

while ($curr_var < 20) {
    $abc = 2 * $curr_var;
    $curr_var ++;
}
echo $abc;
?>
```

By running this code in your browser, you get the number 38. What if you were expecting to get the number 40, or you wanted to check to see if your $abc variable was right? You could echo out the variable as it was processed, to see how the program was working, thus:

```php
<?php
$curr_var = 0;

while ($curr_var < 20) {
    $abc = 2 * $curr_var;
    $curr_var ++;

    // debug line
    echo $curr_var . '<br/>';
}
echo $abc;
?>
```

You now see the numbers 1 through 20, plus your original answer of 38. It is easier for you to see that, although the $curr_var goes to 20, it processes the answer only 19 times, and so you get the answer of 38. Therefore, you should change the while statement as follows:

```php
while ($curr_var <= 20) {
```

Now your while statement will process when $curr_var = 20, and you get a result of 40 at the end. Use the comments as a reminder to yourself to delete the debugging lines when you have solved the problem, to avoid unwanted output to your browser when your page goes live.

Remember that arrays and object references, although they are variables, behave a little differently when you try to display them. If you echo an array, for example, all you will see on the screen is Array(). To view the contents of an array, use the print_r() function instead of echo. print_r() will print out every member of an array, even with multidimensional arrays. In the case of object references, print_r() will display all members of the object. A similar function you may want to use is var_dump().

Divide and Conquer

Another good way to tackle a huge problem is to break it down into baby steps and test each one to make sure you are getting the correct result every step of the way. One small mistake in the beginning of a complex block of statements can have a snowball effect and completely alter your results at the end. By checking each step one by one, you can iron out those small bugs and can eventually get the intended results. Sometimes it may be helpful to comment out a section of code to see how the script runs without it, or to isolate a particularly troublesome section.

Test, Test, Test!

Many coders test their program out on their own system, and as long as it works for them with their settings, they assume they are home free. You should test your code using every different environment available to you in an effort to be thorough: different browsers, different preferences, different computer systems, and so on. If you have the opportunity and know-how, you should even try to hack through your own system to look for security holes that might be exploited by someone a little less kind than you.

Debug with Xdebug

PHP has a large selection of introspective functions to help you with debugging, such as `var_dump()` and `print_r()`. But there is also Xdebug, a powerful extension for PHP that adds additional debugging and profiling functions. Xdebug lets you view stack traces (the path PHP took through various functions to get to a certain point) and code coverage information, and even provides the ability to debug your scripts interactively with any debugging client that understands the DBGp protocol.

As we stated previously, Xdebug is an extension and is not available as part of PHP by default. You must install and configure it properly before Xdebug's functions are available to you. You can find out more at the Xdebug web site, `www.xdebug.org`.

Where to Go for Help

Fortunately, the PHP, Apache, and MySQL user communities are quite vibrant. Numerous sources are available online to help guide you through the murky waters when the going gets tough. We have mentioned some of these numerous times throughout this book, but here they are again, one more time.

www.wrox.com

This book is specifically designed to provide help online in a companion web site, so if you encounter trouble we strongly encourage you to check out the book's sister site at `www.wrox.com`.

PHPBuilder.com

Many PHP help web sites are out there, but our personal favorite tends to be PHPBuilder.com. At this site, you can find numerous articles, archives, snippets of useful code, and, most importantly, a well-developed and very helpful online community of fellow coders from all over the world, with all levels of competency, to assist you as quickly as they can. We have yet to find such a tight-knit and friendly community elsewhere, and we encourage you to post your questions in their forums.

If you are lucky, you might find one of the authors of this book lurking around at PHPBuilder.com. We are all regular contributors, and some of us are moderators.

Source Web Sites

You will see this time and time again, but as with the other advice, we can't stress it enough. If you have a question about virtually anything, chances are the answer can be found at a source web site. Each of these web sites provides a very comprehensive manual that encompasses basically all known information about the software at hand.

To refresh your memory, here they are:

❑ **PHP:** www.php.net (Useful hint: If you are looking for help with a function, such as echo, you can simply type www.php.net/echo in your browser, and it takes you directly to the echo page. How nifty is that?)

PHP also provides the manual in a Microsoft Windows Help format (CHM), which is very useful for Windows users. You can download the manual from the php.net web site and install it on your local machine.

❑ **Apache:** httpd.apache.org

❑ **MySQL:** www.mysql.com

Search and Rescue

If you're experiencing problems with a script, chances are you aren't the first to experience the same obstacles. Use your favorite search engine to scour the Internet for articles, discussion forum posts, tutorials, or anything that discusses the problems you're having. This can be a very quick and easy way to keep from reinventing the wheel.

IRC Channels

You may require immediate assistance with your dilemma or question, and the IRC resource may be your solution. Many PHP IRC channels are out there; #php and #phphelp on the quakenet network are good ones.

Summary

Errors will happen. The important thing to do when you encounter them is to not get discouraged, and to patiently and methodically traverse your code to find the culprit. We hope the tips we have provided in this chapter will help you trudge through the slush and muck of debugging and working out the errors in your programs, when you have having difficulty.

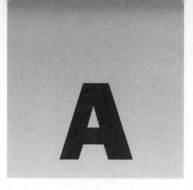

Answers to Exercises

This appendix supplies answers to the exercises you were given at the end of most of the chapters you read. Keep in mind that, as is always the case in programming, there is more than one way to solve a problem, and these are just recommendations. If you were able to accomplish the given task some other way, then congratulate yourself (and why not even treat yourself to a movie?). You're well on your way to becoming a truly diverse programmer!

Chapter 2

1. Go back to your `date.php` file, and, instead of displaying only the number of days in the current month, add a few lines that say:

The month is _____.

There are _____ days in this month.

There are _____ months left in the current year.

A. Your `date.php` file should look like something like this:

```
<html>
 <head>
  <title>How many days in this month?</title>
 </head>
 <body>
<?php
date_default_timezone_set('America/New_York');

$month_name = date('F');
echo '<p>The month is ' . $month_name . '.</p>';

echo '<p>There are ';
$month = date('n');
if ($month ==  1) { echo '31'; }
if ($month ==  2) { echo '28 (unless it\'s a leap year)'; }
if ($month ==  3) { echo '31'; }
```

```
if ($month ==  4) { echo '30'; }
if ($month ==  5) { echo '31'; }
if ($month ==  6) { echo '30'; }
if ($month ==  7) { echo '31'; }
if ($month ==  8) { echo '31'; }
if ($month ==  9) { echo '30'; }
if ($month == 10) { echo '31'; }
if ($month == 11) { echo '30'; }
if ($month == 12) { echo '31'; }
echo ' days in this month.</p>';

$months_left = 12 - $month;
echo '<p>There are ' . $months_left . ' months left in the year.</p>';
?>
 </body>
</html>
```

2. On your movie web site, write a file that displays the following line at the bottom center of every page of your site, with a link to your e-mail address.

This site developed by: ENTER YOUR NAME HERE.

A. The files of your movie site should all include these lines near the bottom of the script:

```
<?php
include 'footer.php';
?>
```

Then you need to create the file footer.php, which consists of these lines:

```
<div style="text-align: center">
 This site developed by: <a href="mailto:jdoe@example.com">John Doe</a>
</div>
```

3. Write a program that displays a different message, based on the time of day. For example, have the site display "Good Morning!" if it is accessed in the morning.

A. Your program should include lines that resemble something like this:

```
<html>
 <head>
  <title>Greeting</title>
 </head>
 <body>
<?php
date_default_timezone_set('America/New_York');

if (date('G') >= 5 && date('G') <= 11) {
    echo '<h1>Good Morning!</h1>';
}
else if (date('G') >= 12 && date('G') <= 18) {
    echo '<h1>Good Afternoon!</h1>';
}
```

```
else if (date('G') >= 19 && date('G') <= 4) {
    echo '<h1>Good Evening!</h1>';
}
?>
 </body>
</html>
```

4. Write a program that formats a block of text (to be input by the user) based on preferences chosen by the user. Give your user options for color of text, font choice, and size. Display the output on a new page.

A. First you would display a form to your users, possibly on the login page, such as this:

```
<table>
 <tr>
  <td><label for="font">Select Font:</label></td>
  <td><select id="font" name="font">
    <option value="Verdana">Verdana</option>
    <option value="Arial">Arial</option>
    <option value="Times New Roman">Times New Roman</option>
   </select>
  </td>
 </tr><tr>
  <td><label for="size">Select Size:</label></td>
  <td><select id="size" name="size">
    <option value="10px">10px</option>
    <option value="12px">12px</option>
    <option value="16px">16px</option>
    <option value="20px">20px</option>
   </select>
  </td>
 </tr><tr>
  <td><label for="color">Select Color:</label></td>
  <td><select id="size" name="size">
    <option value="black">black</option>
    <option value="green">green</option>
    <option value="purple">purple</option>
    <option value="red">red</option>
   </select>
  </td>
 </tr>
</form>
```

Store the received values in your session variables. You would add something like this to whatever the first script is that processes the form:

```
$_SESSION['font']=$_POST['font'];
$_SESSION['size']=$_POST['size'];
$_SESSION['color']=$_POST['color'];
```

Then, every time you had text that needed to be styled, you could output your session variables' value, like this:

```
<p <?php
echo ' style="font-family: ' . $_SESSION['font'] . '; ';
echo 'font-size: ' . $_SESSION['size'] . '; ';
echo 'color: ' . $_SESSION['color'] ';" ';
?> >Text to display</p>
```

As you can see, this would be quite tedious to type everywhere you had a lot of text that should be styled, so perhaps you would prefer putting this information in an include file, or using a separate CSS file.

5. In the program you created in step 4, allow your users the option of saving the information for the next time they visit. If they choose "yes," save the information in a cookie.

A. You would add a line like this to the end of your font preference form:

```
<input type="checkbox" id="save_prefs" name="save_prefs"/>
<label for="save_prefs">Save these preferences for the next time you log
 in.</label>
```

Then at the very beginning of the script that processes the incoming form data, you would add a statement that looks something like this:

```
if (isset($_POST['save_prefs'])) {
    setcookie('font', $_POST['font'], time() + 60);
    setcookie('size', $_POST['size'], time() + 60);
    setcookie('color', $_POST['color'], time () + 60);
}
```

Instead of accessing those variables through the session later when you need them, you would access them through the cookie like this:

```
echo $_COOKIE['font'];
```

6. Using functions, write a program that keeps track of how many times a visitor has loaded the page.

A. Your program would resemble this code:

```
<?php
function display_times($num) {
    echo '<h1>You have viewed this page ' . $num . ' time(s).</h1>';
}

// get the cookie value and add 1 to it for this visit
$num_times = 1;
if (isset($_COOKIE['num_times'])) {
    $num_times = $_COOKIE['num_times'] + 1;
}

// set the value back to the cookie for the next time
setcookie('num_times', $num_times, time() + 60);
```

```
?>
<html>
 <head>
  <title>Viewed Times</title>
 </head>
 <body>
<?php display_times($num_times); ?>
 </body>
</html>
```

Chapter 3

1.   Create a PHP program that prints the lead actor and director for each movie in the database.

A.   Your program should look something like this:

```php
<?php
function get_people_fullname($db, $people_id) {
    $query = 'SELECT
            people_fullname
        FROM
            people
        WHERE
            people_id = ' . $people_id;
    $result = mysql_query($query, $db) or die(mysql_error($db));
    $row = mysql_fetch_assoc($result);
    return $row['people_fullname'];
}

$db = mysql_connect('localhost', 'bp6am', 'bp6ampass') or
    die ('Unable to connect. Check your connection parameters.');

mysql_select_db('moviesite', $db) or die(mysql_error($db));
?>
<html>
 <head>
  <title>Movie Info</title>
 </head>
 <body>
  <table border="1">
   <tr>
    <th>Movie Name</th>
    <th>Lead Actor</th>
    <th>Director</th>
   </tr>
<?php
//get the movies
$query = 'SELECT
        movie_name, movie_leadactor, movie_director
    FROM
        movie';
```

```
$result = mysql_query($query, $db) or die(mysql_error($db));

while ($row = mysql_fetch_assoc($result)) {
    //call our functions to get specific info
    $actor_name = get_people_fullname($db, $row['movie_leadactor']);
    $director_name = get_people_fullname($db, $row['movie_director']);

    //show table row
    echo '<tr>';
    echo '<td>' . $row['movie_name'] . '</td>';
    echo '<td>' . $actor_name . '</td>';
    echo '<td>' . $director_name . '</td>';
    echo '</tr>';
}
?>
  </table>
 </body>
</html>
```

2. Pick only comedies from the movie table, and show the movie name and the year it was produced. Sort the list alphabetically.

A. Your code should look something like this:

```
<?php
$db = mysql_connect('localhost', 'bp6am', 'bp6ampass') or
    die ('Unable to connect. Check your connection parameters.');

mysql_select_db('moviesite', $db) or die(mysql_error($db));
?>
<html>
 <head>
  <title>Comedy Movies</title>
 </head>
 <body>
  <table border="1">
   <tr>
    <th>Movie Name</th>
    <th>Year</th>
   </tr>
<?php
// get the movie_type for comedies
$query = 'SELECT
        movietype_id
    FROM
        movietype
    WHERE
        movietype_label = "Comedy"';
$result = mysql_query($query, $db) or die(mysql_error($db));
$row = mysql_fetch_assoc($result);

//get the movies
$query = 'SELECT
        movie_name, movie_year
```

```
    FROM
        movie
    WHERE
        movie_type = ' . $row['movietype_id'] . '
    ORDER BY
        movie_name';
$result = mysql_query($query, $db) or die(mysql_error($db));

while ($row = mysql_fetch_assoc($result)) {

    //show table row
    echo '<tr>';
    echo '<td>' . $row['movie_name'] . '</td>';
    echo '<td>' . $row['movie_year'] . '</td>';
    echo '</tr>';
}
?>
  </table>
 </body>
</html>
```

3. Show each movie in the database on its own page, and give the user links in a "page 1, page 2, page 3" –type navigation system. Hint: Use LIMIT to control which movie is on which page.

A. Although you could do this many ways, a simple way is to manipulate the LIMIT clause in your SELECT statement and pass an offset value through the URL:

```
<?php
$db = mysql_connect('localhost', 'bp6am', 'bp6ampass') or
    die ('Unable to connect. Check your connection parameters.');

mysql_select_db('moviesite', $db) or die(mysql_error($db));

//get our starting point for the query from the URL
if (isset($_GET['offset'])) {
    $offset = $_GET['offset'];
} else {
    $offset = 0;
}

//get the movie
$query = 'SELECT
        movie_name, movie_year
    FROM
        movie
    ORDER BY
        movie_name
    LIMIT ' . $offset . ', 1';
$result = mysql_query($query, $db) or die(mysql_error($db));
$row = mysql_fetch_assoc($result);
?>
<html>
 <head>
  <title><?php echo $row['movie_name']; ?></title>
```

```
 </head>
 <body>
  <table border="1">
   <tr>
    <th>Movie Name</th>
    <th>Year</th>
   </tr><tr>
    <td><?php echo $row['movie_name']; ?></td>
    <td><?php echo $row['movie_year']; ?></td>
   </tr>
  </table>
  <p>
   <a href="page.php?offset=0">Page 1</a>,
   <a href="page.php?offset=1">Page 2</a>,
   <a href="page.php?offset=2">Page 3</a>
  </p>
 </body>
</html>
```

Chapter 4

1. Add an entry in the top table of your movie_details.php file that shows the average rating given by reviewers.

A. First you need to add the display in your movie_details.php file, as follows:

```
// display the information
echo <<<ENDHTML
<html>
 <head>
  <title>Details and Reviews for: $movie_name</title>
 </head>
 <body>
  <div style="text-align: center;">
   <h2>$movie_name</h2>
   <h3><em>Details</em></h3>
   <table cellpadding="2" cellspacing="2"
    style="width: 70%; margin-left: auto; margin-right: auto;">
    <tr>
     <td><strong>Title</strong></strong></td>
     <td>$movie_name</td>
     <td><strong>Release Year</strong></strong></td>
     <td>$movie_year</td>
    </tr><tr>
     <td><strong>Movie Director</strong></td>
     <td>$movie_director</td>
     <td><strong>Cost</strong></td>
     <td>$$movie_cost<td/>
    </tr><tr>
     <td><strong>Lead Actor</strong></td>
     <td>$movie_leadactor</td>
     <td><strong>Takings</strong></td>
```

```
        <td>$$movie_takings<td/>
      </tr><tr>
        <td><strong>Running Time</strong></td>
        <td>$movie_running_time</td>
        <td><strong>Health</strong></td>
        <td>$movie_health<td/>
      </tr><tr>
        <td> </td>
        <td> </td>
        <td><strong>Average Review</strong></td>
        <td>$average_review<td/>
      </tr>
    </table>
ENDHTML;
```

Then you can create a function to determine the number of total reviews and calculate the average. These lines would go near the top of your movie_details.php file where the rest of the functions are defined.

```
function get_avg_review($db, $movie_id) {
    $query ='SELECT
                review_rating
            FROM
                reviews
            WHERE
                review_movie_id = ' . $movie_id;
    $result = mysql_query($query, $db);
    $total_reviews = mysql_num_rows($result);

    $current = 0;
    while ($row = mysql_fetch_assoc($result)) {
        $current = $current + $row['review_rating'];
    }

    return $current / $total_reviews;
}
```

Then call the function when you get the main information for the movie by adding the following lines to movie_details.php:

```
$movie_health        = calculate_differences($row['movie_takings'],
                         $row['movie_cost']);
$average_review      = get_avg_review($db, $_GET['movie_id']);
$average_review      = round($average_review, 2);
```

2. Change each column heading of the reviews table in your movie_details.php to a link that allows the user to sort by that column (i.e., the user would click on "Date" to sort all the reviews by date).

A. You need to change your movie_details.php file as follows:

```
if (isset($_GET['sort'])) {
    $sort = $_GET['sort'];
} else {
    $sort = 'review_date';
```

```
    }

    // retrieve reviews for this movie
    $query = 'SELECT
                review_movie_id, review_date, reviewer_name, review_comment,
                review_rating
            FROM
                reviews
            WHERE
                review_movie_id = ' . $_GET['movie_id'] . '
            ORDER BY
                ' . $sort . ' ASC';

    $result = mysql_query($query, $db) or die(mysql_error($db));

    // display the reviews
    $mid = $_GET['movie_id'];
    echo <<< ENDHTML
        <h3><em>Reviews</em></h3>
        <table cellpadding="2" cellspacing="2"
         style="width: 90%; margin-left: auto; margin-right: auto;">
          <tr>
            <th style="width: 7em;">
              <a href="movie_details.php?movie_id=$mid&sort=review_date">Date</a>
    </th>
            <th style="width: 10em;">
              <a href="movie_details.php?movie_id=$mid&sort=reviewer_name">Reviewer
    </a></th>
            <th>
              <a href="movie_details.php?movie_id=$mid&sort=review_comment">Comments
    </a></th>
            <th style="width: 5em;">
              <a href="movie_details.php?movie_id=$mid&sort=review_rating">Rating</a>
    </th>
          </tr>
    ENDHTML;
```

3. Alternate the background colors of each row in the review table of your movie_details.php file to make them easier to read. Hint: Odd-numbered rows would have a background of one color, even-numbered rows would have a background of another color.

A. Your movie_details.php file will need these lines added in or changed:

```
    $odd = true;
    while ($row = mysql_fetch_assoc($result))
    {
        $date = $row['review_date'];
        $name = $row['reviewer_name'];
        $comment = $row['review_comment'];
        $rating = generate_ratings($row['review_rating']);

        if ($odd) {
            echo '<tr style="background-color: #EEEEEE;">';
```

```
    } else {
        echo '<tr style="background-color: #FFFFFF;">';
    }
    echo <<<ENDHTML
      <td style="vertical-align:top; text-align: center;">$date</td>
      <td style="vertical-align:top;">$name</td>
      <td style="vertical-align:top;">$comment</td>
      <td style="vertical-align:top;">$rating</td>
    </tr>
ENDHTML;
    $odd = !$odd;
}
```

Chapter 5

1. Create a form and processing page that let you choose a rating (stars, thumbs up, number from 1 to 5, whatever) and provide comments for a movie.

A. All that's needed for this exercise is a simple HTML form, something similar to the following:

```
<form method="post" action="showratings.php">
 <table>
  <tr>
   <td>Movie title: </td>
   <td><input type="text" name="movie"></td>
  </tr><tr>
   <td>Rating: </td>
   <td>
<?php
for ($i = 1; $i <= 5; $i++) {
    echo '<input type="radio" name="rating" value="' . $i . '"> ' . $i .
'<br/>';
}
?>
   </td>
  </tr><tr>
   <td>Comments: </td>
   <td><textarea name="comments" cols="40" rows="10"></textarea></td>
  </tr>
 </table>
</form>
```

2. Create a form with several text input boxes that allow you to populate the options of a select field on a subsequent page.

A. This exercise takes the form of two pages. The first provides the form to enter the options, and the latter shows the result. First, the form on the input page:

```
<form method="post" action="showratings.php">
 <table>
  <tr>
   <td>Select options: </td>
```

```
        <td>
    <?php
    for ($i = 0; $i < 5; $i++) {
        echo '<input type="text" name="sval[' . $i . ']" /><br/>';
    }
    ?>
        </td>
      </tr>
     </table>
    </form>
```

And then, on the second page:

```
    <select>
    <?php
    for ($i = 0; $i < 5; $i++) {
        echo '<option value="' . $_POST['sval'][$i] . '">' . $_POST['sval'][$i] .
            '</option>';
    }
    ?>
    </select>
```

3. Create a calculator form that takes two numbers and calculates their sum.

A. This exercise is easily handled using a few form fields and some basic arithmetic:

```
<?php
$num1 = (isset($_POST['num1'])) ? $_POST['num1'] : null;
$num2 = (isset($_POST['num2'])) ? $_POST['num2'] : null;
$operator = (isset($_POST['operator'])) ? $_POST['operator'] : '+';
?>
<form method="post" action="#">
 <div>
  <input type="text" name="num1" size="3" value="<?php echo $num1; ?>" />
  <select name="operator">
   <option value="+"
    <?php if ($operator == '+') { echo 'selected="selected"'; } ?>>+</option>
   <option value="-"
    <?php if ($operator == '-') { echo 'selected="selected"'; } ?>>-</option>
   <option value="*"
    <?php if ($operator == '*') { echo 'selected="selected"'; } ?>>&times;
</option>
   <option value="/"
    <?php if ($operator == '/') { echo 'selected="selected"'; } ?>>&divide;
</option>
  </select>
  <input type="text" name="num2" size="3" value="<?php echo $num2; ?>" />
  <input type="submit" value="=" />
  <strong>
<?php
if (!is_null($num1) && !is_null($num2)) {
    if ($operator == '+') {
        echo $num1 + $num2;
    } else if ($operator == '-') {
```

```
        echo $num1 - $num2;
    } else if ($operator == '*') {
        echo $num1 * $num2;
    } else if ($operator == '/') {
        echo $num1 / $num2;
    } else {
        echo 'UNKNOWN';
    }
}
?>
  </strong>
 </div>
</form>
```

Chapter 6

1. Create the edit/delete code for the `people` table. Use the movie code as an example.

A. One possible solution is as follows. Change `commit.php` as highlighted:

```php
<?php
//connect to MySQL
$db = mysql_connect('localhost', 'bp6am', 'bp6ampass') or
    die ('Unable to connect. Check your connection parameters.');

//make sure our recently created database is the active one
mysql_select_db('moviesite', $db) or die(mysql_error($db));
?>
<html>
 <head>
  <title>Commit</title>
 </head>
 <body>
<?php
switch ($_GET['action']) {
case 'add':
    switch ($_GET['type']) {
    case 'movie':
        $query = 'INSERT INTO movie
                (movie_name, movie_year, movie_type, movie_leadactor,
                movie_director)
            VALUES
                ("' . $_POST['movie_name'] . '",
                ' . $_POST['movie_year'] . ',
                ' . $_POST['movie_type'] . ',
                ' . $_POST['movie_leadactor'] . ',
                ' . $_POST['movie_director'] . ')';
        break;
    case 'people':
        $query = 'INSERT INTO people
                (people_fullname, people_isactor, people_isdirector)
            VALUES
                ("' . $_POST['people_name'] . '",
```

```
                            ' . $_POST['people_isactor'] . ',
                            ' . $_POST['people_isdirector'] . ')';
                break;
        }
        break;
    case 'edit':
        switch ($_GET['type']) {
        case 'movie':
            $query = 'UPDATE movie SET
                    movie_name = "' . $_POST['movie_name'] . '",
                    movie_year = ' . $_POST['movie_year'] . ',
                    movie_type = ' . $_POST['movie_type'] . ',
                    movie_leadactor = ' . $_POST['movie_leadactor'] . ',
                    movie_director = ' . $_POST['movie_director'] . '
                WHERE
                    movie_id = ' . $_POST['movie_id'];
            break;
        case 'people':
            $query = 'UPDATE people SET
                    people_fullname = "' . $_POST['people_fullname'] . '",
                    people_isactor = "' . $_POST['people_isactor'] . '",
                    people_isdirector = "' . $_POST['people_isdirector'] . '"
                WHERE
                    people_id = ' . $_GET['id'];
            break;
        }
        break;
    }

    if (isset($query)) {
        $result = mysql_query($query, $db) or die(mysql_error($db));
    }
    ?>
      <p>Done!</p>
     </body>
    </html>
```

Chapter 7

1. Create a site called "A Virtual Vacation." Offer different backgrounds that people can superimpose photos of themselves on, and let them send virtual postcards to their friends and family.

A. Your code would need to include a background/upload page and a result page. We cover sending e-mail postcards in Chapter 11, so you can simply use the scripts from that chapter and insert your newly created postcard.

This code comes with some caveats; of course, you don't have access to the sample image files we've used, and you will have to alter your code a bit based on the sizes of your images. Also, we haven't stored our images in any database, and we've only allowed for JPG images to be uploaded. Keeping those things in mind, your background/upload page should look something like this (we named our file vacation.html):

```html
<html>
 <head>
  <title>Go on a Virtual Vacation!</title>
 </head>
 <body>
  <form method="post" action="upload_image.php" enctype="multipart/
form-data">
   <table>
    <tr>
     <td><label for="image_caption">Image Name or Caption</label><br/>
      <em>Example: Wish you were here!</em></td>
     <td><input id="image_caption" name="image_caption" type="text"
      size="55"/></td>
    </tr><tr>
     <td><label for="image_username">Your Name:</label></td>
     <td><input id="image_username" name="image_username" type="text"
      size="15"></td>
    </tr><tr>
     <td><label for="image_filename">Upload Image:</label></td>
     <td><input id="image_filename" name="image_filename" type="file" /></td>
    </tr>
   </table>
   <p><em>Acceptable image formats include: JPG/JPEG</em></p>
   <p>Select your destination:</p>
   <table>
    </tr><tr>
     <td><input type="radio" id="destination_1" name="destination"
      value="beach" /></td>
     <td><label for="destination_1"><img src="images/beach.jpg"></label></td>
    </tr><tr>
     <td><input type="radio" id="destination_2" name="destination"
      value="golfcourse" /></td>
     <td><label for="destination_2"><img src="images/golfcourse.jpg">
</label></td>
    </tr><tr>
     <td><input type="radio" id="destination_3" name="destination"
      value="mountains" /></td>
     <td><label for="destination_3"><img src="images/mountains.jpg"></label>
</td>
    </tr>
   </table>
   <p style="text-align: center">
    <input type="submit" name="Submit" value="Submit" />
    <input type="reset" value="Clear Form" /></p>
  </form>
 </body>
</html>
```

Then we have a page that processes the photos and merges them together, called upload_image.php.

```php
<?php
// filter incoming variables
$image_caption = (isset($_POST['image_caption'])) ? $_POST['image_caption'] :
'';
$image_username = (isset($_POST['image_username'])) ? $_POST['image_
username'] :
    'Anonymous';
$destination = $_POST['destination'];
$image_tempname = $_FILES['image_filename']['name'];
$today = date('Y-m-d');

//change this path to match your images directory
$dir ='C:/Program Files/Apache Software Foundation/Apache2.2/htdocs/images';

$image_name = $dir . $image_tempname;

if (move_uploaded_file($_FILES['image_filename']['tmp_name'], $image_name))
{
    //get info about the image being uploaded
    list($width, $height, $type, $attr) = getimagesize($image_name);

    if ($type != IMAGETYPE_JPEG) {
        echo '<p><strong>Sorry, but the file you uploaded was not a JPG ' .
            'file.<br/>Please hit your back button and try again.</strong></p>';
    } else {
        //image is acceptable; ok to proceed
        $dest_image_name = $dir . $destination . '.jpg';

        $image = imagecreatefromjpeg($image_name);
        list($width2, $height2, $type2, $attr2) = getimagesize($dest_image_
name);

        $image2 = imagecreatefromjpeg($dest_image_name);
        imagecopymerge($image2, $image, 0,0,0, 0, $width, $height, 100);
    }

    header('Content-type:image/jpeg');
    imagejpeg($image2);
}
?>
```

2. Have a page on your site with funny photographs or cartoons, and allow your users to write the captions for them. Place the text in a speech bubble that is appropriately sized, based on the length of the caption they submit.

A. First, you need to have the page that gathers the input from the user:

```html
<html>
 <head>
  <title>Write your own caption!</title>
 </head>
 <body>
  <h1>Write Your Own Caption!</h1>
  <img src="images/cartoon.jpg" alt="captionless cartoon"/>
```

```
    <form method="post" action="caption.php">
     <table>
      <tr>
       <td><label for="image_caption">Write a caption for the cartoon:
</label><br/>
         <em>Example: You talkin' to me?</em></td>
        <td><input id="image_caption" name="image_caption" type="text"
          size="25" maxlength="25" /></td>
      </tr><tr>
        <td> </td>
        <td><input type="submit" value="Send my Caption"/></td>
      </tr>
     </table>
    </form>
   </body>
  </html>
```

Then you need to put the text in the bubble. We are using a simple ellipse shape that will stretch to fit how long the text is. You can use the following code:

```php
<?php
$image_filename = 'images/cartoon.jpg';
$image_caption = (isset($_POST['image_caption'])) ? $_POST['image_caption'] :
' ';
$length = strlen($image_caption);

$image = imagecreatefromjpeg($image_filename);

//draw a white ellipse based on string length
$white = imagecolorallocate($image, 0xFF, 0xFF, 0xFF);

// the center point for the bubble on our cartoon is at coordinates 134, 14
// alter these values for your specific image if necessary
$e_x = 134;
$e_y = 14;

// assume each character is 10px plus 10px on either side of the string for
// extra cushion.
$e_width=($length * 10) + 20;
$ellipse = imagefilledellipse($image, $e_x, $e_y, $e_width, 25, $white);

//get starting point for text
$x = $e_x - (($length * 10) / 2) - 10;
$y = $e_y + 5;

//place the text in the bubble
imagettftext($image, 12, 0, $x, $y, 0, 'arial.ttf', $image_caption);

header('Content-type: image/jpeg');
imagejpeg($image);
?>
```

You could also have used `imagettfbbox()` to perform a similar task. We didn't cover this in Chapter 7, so you might want to refer to the manual at www.php.net/imagettfbbox for more information on this function.

3. Create a page for kids where they can choose different heads, bodies, and tails from animals and put them together to make a new creation and a new image. Or, create a virtual paper doll site where kids can place different outfits on a model and then save the images they create.

A. Although there are many ways to do this, we will have four separate pages: one for picking the head, one for picking the midsection, one for picking the behind/tail, and one for putting them all together and outputting our final result. We could easily create these images by taking stock photos of animals, resizing them so they are the same size, and then cutting them into three sections, using an image-processing program such as Photoshop or GIMP (or heck, we can even do this using PHP, right?). When we have our sections all ready to go, our first page, `animal1.html`, will look something like this:

```
<html>
 <head>
  <title>Create your very own animal!</title>
 </head>
 <body>
  <p>First, you must pick a head for your new animal.</p>
  <form method="post" action="animal2.php">
   <table>
    <tr>
     <td><input id="head_1" name="head" type="radio" value="cowhead" /></td>
     <td><label for="head_1"><img src="images/cowhead.jpg" /></label></td>
    </tr><tr>
     <td><input id="head_2" name="head" type="radio" value="elephanthead" /></td>
     <td><label for="head_2"><img src="images/elephanthead.jpg" /></label></td>
    </tr><tr>
     <td><input id="head_3" name="head" type="radio" value="giraffhead" /></td>
     <td><label for="head_3"><img src="images/giraffhead.jpg" /></label></td>
    </tr><tr>
     <td><input id="head_4" name="head" type="radio" value="pighead" /></td>
     <td><label for="head_4"><img src="images/pighead.jpg" /></label></td>
    </tr><tr>
     <td> </td>
     <td><input type="submit" name="Submit" value="Pick a Body ->" /></td>
    </tr>
   </table>
  </form>
 </body>
</html>
```

Our next file, `animal2.php`, looks like this:

```
<html>
 <head>
  <title>Create your very own animal!</title>
 </head>
 <body>
  <p>Second, you must pick a body for your new animal.</p>
  <form method="post" action="animal3.php">
```

```
   <table>
    <tr>
     <td><input id="body_1" name="body" type="radio" value="cowbody" /></td>
     <td><label for="body_1"><img src="images/cowbody.jpg" /></label></td>
    </tr><tr>
     <td><input id="body_2" name="body" type="radio" value="elephantbody" /></td>
     <td><label for="body_2"><img src="images/elephantbody.jpg" /></label></td>
    </tr><tr>
     <td><input id="body_3" name="body" type="radio" value="giraffbody" /></td>
     <td><label for="body_3"><img src="images/giraffbody.jpg" /></label></td>
    </tr><tr>
     <td><input id="body_3" name="body" type="radio" value="pigbody" /></td>
     <td><label for="body_3"><img src="images/pigbody.jpg" /></label></td>
    </tr><tr>
     <td> </td>
     <td><input type="hidden" name="head" value="<?php echo $_POST['head'];
?>" />
       <input type="submit" name="Submit" value="Pick a Tail ->" /></td>
    </tr>
   </table>
  </form>
 </body>
</html>
```

And our next file, `animal3.php`, looks like this:

```
<html>
 <head>
  <title>Create your very own animal!</title>
 </head>
 <body>
  <p>Finally, you must pick a tail for your new animal.</p>
  <form method="post" action="animal4.php">
   <table>
    <tr>
     <td><input id="tail_1" name="tail" type="radio" value="cowtail" /></td>
     <td><label for="tail_1"><img src="images/cowtail.jpg" /></label></td>
    </tr><tr>
     <td><input id="tail_2" name="tail" type="radio" value="elephanttail" /></td>
     <td><label for="tail_2"><img src="images/elephanttail.jpg" /></label></td>
    </tr><tr>
     <td><input id="tail_3" name="tail" type="radio" value="girafftail" /></td>
     <td><label for="tail_3"><img src="images/girafftail.jpg" /></label></td>
    </tr><tr>
     <td><input id="tail_3" name="tail" type="radio" value="pigtail" /></td>
     <td><label for="tail_3"><img src="images/pigtail.jpg" /></label></td>
    </tr><tr>
     <td> </td>
     <td><input type="hidden" name="head" value="<?php echo $_POST['head'];
?>" />
       <input type="hidden" name="tail" value="<?php echo $_POST['tail'];
?>" />
       <input type="submit" name="Submit" value="Make the Animal!" /></td>
    </tr>
```

```
      </table>
    </form>
  </body>
</html>
```

And finally, the file that combines the three images, our `animal4.php` file:

```php
<?php
$head = $_POST['head'];
$body = $_POST['body'];
$tail = $_POST['tail'];

$image_dir='images/';

$head_image = imagecreatefromjpeg($image_dir . $head . '.jpg');
$body_image = imagecreatefromjpeg($image_dir . $body . '.jpg');
$tail_image = imagecreatefromjpeg($image_dir . $tail . '.jpg');

// Our images are 100px x 200px and were chopped horizontally.
$new_animal = imagecreatetruecolor(300, 200);

//merge the head
imagecopymerge($new_animal, $head_image, 0, 0, 0, 0, 100, 200, 100);

//now merge in the body
imagecopymerge($new_animal, $body_image, 100,0, 0, 0, 100, 200, 100);

//and finally the tail
imagecopymerge($new_animal, $tail_image, 200, 0, 0, 0, 100, 200, 100);


header('Content-type: image/jpeg');
imagejpeg($new_animal);
?>
```

Chapter 8

1. Add validation to the code that adds and edits people records.

A. In `commit.php`, add or change the lines highlighted below:

```php
switch ($_GET['action']) {
case 'add':
    switch ($_GET['type']) {
    case 'movie':
        $error = array();
...
        break;
    case 'people':
        $error = array();
        $people_name = trim($_POST['people_name']);
        if (empty($people_name)) {
```

```
                    $error[] = urlencode('Please enter a name!');
                }
                if (empty($_POST['people_isactor']) &&
                    empty($_POST['people_isdirector'])) {
                    $error[] = urlencode('Please specify if the person is an actor ' .
                        'or a director!');
                }
                if (empty($error)) {
                    $query = 'INSERT INTO people
                            (people_fullname, people_isactor, people_isdirector)
                        VALUES
                            ("' . $people_name . '",
                            ' . $_POST['people_isactor'] . ',
                            ' . $_POST['people_isdirector'] . ')';
                }
                break;
        }
        break;
case 'edit':
    switch ($_GET['type']) {
    case 'movie':
        $error = array();
...
        break;

    case 'people':
        $error = array();
        $people_name = trim($_POST['people_name']);
        if (empty($people_name)) {
            $error[] = urlencode('Please enter a name!');
        }
        if (empty($_POST['people_isactor']) &&
            empty($_POST['people_isdirector'])) {
            $error[] = urlencode('Please specify if the person is an actor ' .
                'or a director!');
        }
        if (empty($error)) {
            $query = 'UPDATE people SET
                    people_fullname = "' . $people_name . '",
                    people_isactor = "' . $_POST['people_isactor'] . '",
                    people_isdirector = "' . $_POST['people_isdirector'] . '"
                WHERE
                    people_id = ' . $_GET['id'];
        }
        break;
    }
    break;
```

2. Write and test a regular expression pattern to validate an e-mail address.

A. This is not the only answer, but it gets the job done:

```
/[\w\-]+(\.[\w\-]+)*@[\w\-]+(\.[\w\-]+)+/
```

Chapter 9

In Chapter 9, you were shown three short snippets of code and asked to spot the errors and figure out how to fix them. Then you were asked to create a little error-catching script to catch the errors.

1.

```php
<?php
$query = "SELECT * FROM table_name " .
        "WHERE name = '" . $_POST['name'] . "';"
$result = mysql_query($result)
  or die(mysql_error());
?>
```

A. Parse error from lack of semicolon at the end of the statement; the semicolon there is for the SQL statement. The correct code is:

```php
<?php
$query = "SELECT * FROM table_name " .
        "WHERE name = '" . $_POST['name'] . "'";
$result = mysql_query($result)
  or die(mysql_error());
?>
```

2.

```php
<?
if ($_POST['first_name'] = "Jethro") {
echo "Your name is " . $_POST['first_name'];
}
?>
```

A. You always need to check equality with double equals (==), not single equals (=). A single equals sign is for setting a variable equal to a value. The correct code is:

```php
<?php
if ($_POST['first_name'] == "Jethro") {
  echo "Your name is " . $_POST['first_name'];
}
?>
```

3.

```php
<?
$full_name = $_POST['mrmiss'] ". " $_POST['first_name'] " " $_POST['last_name'];
?>
```

A. This is missing concatenation operators between the variables and the strings. Here is the correct code:

```php
<?php
$full_name = $_POST['mrmiss'] . ". " . $_POST['first_name'] . " " .
    $_POST['last_name'];
?>
```

Chapter 10

1. Add a "costume description" field to the character record, and provide a way to modify the costume description.

A. The three main tasks you need to accomplish in this exercise are to modify the database to hold the costume descriptions, modify the character edit page to provide a character description field, and modify the transaction page to process the extra field.

Start by adding a field to the `comic_character` table in your database with a SQL statement similar to the following:

```sql
ALTER TABLE comic_character
    ADD COLUMN costume VARCHAR(255);
```

Then, modify `edit_character.php`, adding or modifying the lines highlighted below:

```php
<?php
require 'db.inc.php';

$db = mysql_connect(MYSQL_HOST, MYSQL_USER, MYSQL_PASSWORD) or
    die ('Unable to connect. Check your connection parameters.');
mysql_select_db(MYSQL_DB, $db) or die(mysql_error($db));

$action = 'Add';

$character = array('alias' => '',
                   'real_name' => '',
                   'alignment' => 'good',
                   'costume' => '',
                   'address' => '',
                   'city' => '',
                   'state' => '',
                   'zipcode_id' => '');
$character_powers = array();
$rivalries = array();

// validate incoming character id value
$character_id = (isset($_GET['id']) && ctype_digit($_GET['id'])) ?
    $_GET['id'] : 0;

// retrieve information about the requested character
```

```
if ($character_id != 0) {
    $query = 'SELECT
            c.alias, c.real_name, c.alignment, c.costume,
            l.address, z.city, z.state, z.zipcode_id
        FROM
            comic_character c, comic_lair l, comic_zipcode z
        WHERE
            z.zipcode_id = l.zipcode_id AND
            c.lair_id = l.lair_id AND
            c.character_id = ' . $character_id;
    $result = mysql_query($query, $db) or die (mysql_error($db));
...
    </tr><tr>
     <td>Alignment:</td>
     <td><input type="radio" name="alignment" value="good"
       <?php echo ($character['alignment']=='good') ? 'checked="checked"' :
'';
       ?>/> Good<br/>
      <input type="radio" name="alignment" value="evil"
       <?php echo ($character['alignment']=='evil') ? 'checked="checked"' : '';
       ?>/> Evil
     </td>
    </tr><tr>
     <td>Costume Description:</td>
     <td><input type="text" name="costume" size="40" maxlength="255"
       value="<?php echo $character['costume'];?>"></td>
    </tr><tr>
     <td>Rivalries:<br/><small><em>CTRL-click to select multiple enemies</em>
      </small>
     </td>
```

Finally, in `char_transact.php`, we change the following:

```
case 'Add Character':

    // escape incoming values to protect database
    $alias = mysql_real_escape_string($_POST['alias'], $db);
    $real_name = mysql_real_escape_string($_POST['real_name'], $db);
    $address = mysql_real_escape_string($_POST['address'], $db);
    $city = mysql_real_escape_string($_POST['city'], $db);
    $state = mysql_real_escape_string($_POST['state'], $db);
    $zipcode_id = mysql_real_escape_string($_POST['zipcode_id'], $db);
    $alignment = ($_POST['alignment'] == 'good') ? 'good' : 'evil';
    $costume = mysql_real_escape_string($_POST['costume'], $db);
...
    $query = 'INSERT INTO comic_character
            (character_id, alias, real_name, lair_id, alignment, costume)
        VALUES
            (NULL, "' . $alias . '", "' . $real_name . '", ' .
            $lair_id . ', "' . $alignment . '", "' . $costume . '")';
    mysql_query($query, $db) or die (mysql_error($db));
...
```

```
case 'Edit Character':

    // escape incoming values to protect database
    $character_id = (int)$_POST['character_id'];
    $alias = mysql_real_escape_string($_POST['alias'], $db);
    $real_name = mysql_real_escape_string($_POST['real_name'], $db);
    $address = mysql_real_escape_string($_POST['address'], $db);
    $city = mysql_real_escape_string($_POST['city'], $db);
    $state = mysql_real_escape_string($_POST['state'], $db);
    $zipcode_id = mysql_real_escape_string($_POST['zipcode_id'], $db);
    $alignment = ($_POST['alignment'] == 'good') ? 'good' : 'evil';
    $costume = mysql_real_escape_string($_POST['costume'], $db);

...

    $query = 'UPDATE comic_lair l, comic_character c
        SET
            l.zipcode_id = ' . $zipcode_id . ',
            l.address = "' . $address . '",
            c.real_name = "' . $real_name . '",
            c.alias = "' . $alias . '",
            c.alignment = "' . $alignment . '",
            c.costume = "' . $costume . '"
    WHERE
        c.character_id = ' . $character_id . ' AND
        c.lair_id = l.lair_id';
    mysql_query($query, $db) or die (mysql_error($db));
```

2. Modify the character listing to display the characters' locations alongside their powers.

A. This time, you only need to modify the charlist.php file. You're going to change the initial queries to return additional fields, and add those fields to the table display as highlighted below:

```
// select list of charaters for table
$query = 'SELECT
        c.character_id, c.alias, c.real_name, c.alignment, z.city, z.state
    FROM
        comic_character c JOIN comic_lair l ON c.lair_id = l.lair_id
        JOIN comic_zipcode z ON l.zipcode_id = z.zipcode_id
    ORDER BY c.' . $order[$o];
$result = mysql_query($query, $db) or die (mysql_error($db));
...
        // select list of powers for this character
        $query2 = 'SELECT
                power
            FROM
                comic_power p
                JOIN comic_character_power cp
                    ON p.power_id = cp.power_id
            WHERE
                cp.character_id = ' . $row['character_id'] . '
            ORDER BY
                power ASC';
```

```
$result2 = mysql_query($query2, $db) or die (mysql_error($db));

if (mysql_num_rows($result2) > 0) {
    $powers = array();
    while ($row2 = mysql_fetch_assoc($result2)) {
        $powers[] = $row2['power'];
    }
    echo '<td>' . implode(', ', $powers) . '</td>';
} else {
    echo '<td>none</td>';
}
mysql_free_result($result2);

echo '<td>' . $row['city'] . ', ' . $row['state'] . '</td>';
```

Chapter 11

1. Create code to send a message to an e-mail account, and blind carbon copy (BCC) yourself or another account.

A. This one is surprisingly short. You can send a BCC message by adding a mail header. All you need is something similar to the following:

```
$to = 'youremail@example.com';
$subject = 'Testing email';
$message = 'This is testing Bcc fields.';

$bcc = 'secret@example.com';
$headers = 'BCC: ' . $bcc . "\r\n";

mail($to, $subject, $message, $headers);
```

2. Create a simple web form that e-mails comments or suggestions to an account of your choosing.

A. For this exercise, you can create two files: one that provides a form for user entry of the required fields and another to send the actual e-mail. The web form should include something similar to the following:

```
<form action="sendcomments.php" method="post">
 <div>
  <p>Please provide your comments or suggestions to help make our site
better!</p>
  <textarea name="comments" cols="40" rows="10"></textarea>
 </div>
</form>
```

And the processing page should be similar to this code:

```
$to = 'youremail@example.com';
$subject = 'Comments from Web Site';
$message = 'The following comments were entered: ' . $_POST['comments'];
mail($to, $subject, $message);
```

Chapter 12

1. Create a hidden area that is only displayed to users who are logged in with your system.

A. You might be expecting to see a simplified PHP login/session example here, but we're going to go a different route. Instead, we're going to revisit the simple, yet effective, solution of using .htaccess directives.

Create a directory of your choosing, and create a .htaccess file within it:

```
AuthType Basic
AuthUserFile "C:\Program Files\Apache Software Foundation\Apache2.2\hiddenauth"
AuthName "Restricted"
<LIMIT GET POST>
    require valid-user
</LIMIT>
```

Then, create a user entry with the htpasswd command.

```
htpasswd -c "C:\Program Files\Apache Software Foundation\Apache2.2\
hiddenauth" john
```

2. Use cookies to retain some information for 30 minutes, dependent on logged-in users.

A. Here's one example of how this might be done:

```
session_start();

if ($_SESSION['user_logged']) {
    setcookie('testcookie', 'cows say moo', time() + 60 * 30);
}
```

3. Create a system where only certain users have certain options, dependent on their user level.

A. This exercise is actually a common component of many web sites that use access levels to control what a user sees. For example, here's a sample navigation menu that presents the "Create News" link to users with access level 1 or higher, and the "Site Administration" link to users with access level 2 or higher:

```
<ul>
 <li><a href="index.php">Home</a></li>
 <li><a href="news.php">News</a></li>
 <li><a href="contact.php">Contact Us</a></li>
<?php
if ($_SESSION['access_level'] > 0) {
    echo '<li><a href="createnews.php">Create News</a></li>';
}
if ($_SESSION['access_level'] > 1) {
    echo '<li><a href="admin.php">Site Administration</a></li>';
}
?>
</ul>
```

Chapter 13

1. **Find out about the author:** Authors of articles might want the readers to know a little more about them. Add the ability to enter extra fields in a user's profile, and provide a link on the article's full-view page to the author's information.

A. We've covered adding a new field to a form and the corresponding database table before, so that should be familiar by now. Once the user form and database tables are modified to allow the extra information, you need to create a link in the `output_story()` function, which is contained in `cms_output_functions.inc.php`:

```php
function output_story($db, $article_id, $preview_only = FALSE) {
    if (empty($article_id)) {
        return;
    }
    $sql = 'SELECT
            a.user_id, name, is_published, title, article_text,
            UNIX_TIMESTAMP(submit_date) AS submit_date,
            UNIX_TIMESTAMP(publish_date) AS publish_date
        FROM
            cms_articles a JOIN cms_users u ON a.user_id = u.user_id
        WHERE
            article_id = ' . $article_id;
    $result = mysql_query($sql, $db) or die(mysql_error($db));

    if ($row = mysql_fetch_assoc($result)) {
        extract($row);
        echo '<h2>' . htmlspecialchars($title) . '</h2>';
        echo '<p>By: <a href="author_info.php?id=' . $user_id . '">' .
            htmlspecialchars($name) . '</a></p>';
        echo '<p>';
```

The link we added would pull up a page listing the author's profile. Constructing such a profile page is a matter of a SELECT query and outputting the results to the browser.

2. **Notify the author:** Authors might want to be automatically notified when their stories have been approved. Add an e-mail notification upon approval, and give users the ability to toggle their notification on and off.

A. For this exercise, you'll need to make some modifications to the `cms_transact_article.php` page similar to the following highlighted lines:

```php
case 'Publish':
    $article_id = (isset($_POST['article_id'])) ? $_POST['article_id'] : '';
    if (!empty($article_id)) {
        $sql = 'SELECT
                email
            FROM
                cms_users u JOIN cms_articles a ON u.user_id = a.user_id
            WHERE
                a.article_id = " . $article_id;
        $result = mysql_query($sql, $db);
```

```
        $row = mysql_query($sql, $db) or die(mysql_error($db));

        mail($row['email'], 'Article approved',
            'Your article has been approved!');

        $sql = 'UPDATE cms_articles SET
                is_published = TRUE,
                publish_date = "' . date('Y-m-d H:i:s') . '"
            WHERE
                article_id = ' . $article_id;
        mysql_query($sql, $db) or die(mysql_error($db));
    }
    redirect('pending.php');
    break;
```

Chapter 14

1. **Hide your users' addresses:** Modify the send message functionality to send the e-mails to your users, using the BCC: e-mail field, instead of the usual To: field.

A. Modify the following highlighted lines inside the "Send Message" case in `ml_admin_transact.php`:

```
$mail = new SimpleMail();

$mail->setToAddress('list@example.com');
$mail->setFromAddress('list@example.com');
$mail->sendBCCAddress($row['email']);
$mail->setSubject($subject);
$mail->setTextBody($message . $footer);

$mail->send();
```

2. **Reduce sending:** Modify the send message functionality to send e-mails to your users in groups of 10. That is, every e-mail that is sent should be sent to 10 users at a time (when possible), instead of 1 e-mail per user.

A. One possible solution requires editing the "Send Message" case in `ml_admin_transact.php`, as highlighted:

```
$maillimit = 10;
$mailcount = 0;
$to = '';
while ($row = mysql_fetch_assoc($result)) {
    $mailcount = $mailcount + 1;

    $footer = "\n\n" . '--------------' . "\n";
    if (ctype_digit($ml_id)) {
        $footer .= 'You are receiving this message as a member ' .
            'of the ' . $listname . "\n";
        $footer .= 'mailing list. If you have received this ' .
            'email in error or would like to' . "\n";
```

```
        $footer .= 'remove your name from this mailing list, ' .
            'please visit the following URL:' . "\n";
        $footer .= 'http://www.example.com/ml_remove.php?user_id=' .
            $row['user_id'] . "&ml=" . $ml_id;
    } else {
        $footer .= 'You are receiving this email because you ' .
            'subscribed to one or more' . "\n";
        $footer .= 'mailing lists. Visit the following URL to ' .
            'change your subscriptions:' . "\n";
        $footer .= 'http://www.example.com/ml_user.php?user_id=' .
            $row['user_id'];
    }
```

```
    if ($mailcount == $maillimit) {
        mail($to, $subject, $message . $footer)
        $mailcount = 0;
        $to = '';
    } else {
        $to .= $row['email'] . ', ';
    }
```
```
}
```

3. **Let the administrator know:** Add functionality to send an e-mail to an administrator when new users confirm their subscription to the mailing list.

A. Add code to `ml_user_transact.php`, similar to the following:

```
$mail = new SimpleMail();
$mail->setToAddress($email);
$mail->setFromAddress('list@example.com');
$mail->setSubject('Mailing list subscription confirmed');
$mail->setTextBody($message);
$mail->send();
```

```
$mail = new SimpleMail();
$mail->setToAddress('admin@example.com');
$mail->setFromAddress('list@example.com');
$mail->setSubject('Mailing list subscription confirmed');
$mail->setTextBody($first_name . 'just subscribed to ' . $listname . '.');
$mail->send();
```

```
header('Location: ml_thanks.php?user_id=' . $user_id . '&ml_id=' .
    $ml_id);
```

4. **Clean up any leftovers:** Add functionality to the administration page to allow an admin to purge the database of any subscriptions that haven't yet been confirmed.

A. The first step in this exercise is to add a link on the admin page to a new page you'll create, for example:

```
<a href="ml_purge.php">Purge unconfirmed users</a>
```

Then, create the processing page (ml_purge.php):

```php
<?php
require 'db.inc.php';

$db = mysql_connect(MYSQL_HOST, MYSQL_USER, MYSQL_PASSWORD) or
    die ('Unable to connect. Check your connection parameters.');

mysql_select_db(MYSQL_DB, $db) or die(mysql_error($db));

$sql = 'DELETE FROM ml_subscriptions WHERE pending = 1`;
mysql_query($sql, $db) or die(mysql_error($db));

echo 'Records successfully purged.';
?>
```

Chapter 15

1. **Allow for tax:** Many states require that you charge sales tax on the orders shipped to the state where you have a physical presence, and some states require sales tax on all online orders. Set your code to check for customers in your own state and add the appropriate sales tax to those orders only.

A. Because you allowed for a sales tax field already in the main order table, this requires an `if` statement in the next-to-last step of the order, where everything is processed. You will also change your "total" to "subtotal." Locate the following lines of code in `ecomm_checkout2.php`, and make your changes as highlighted below.

```php
$subtotal = 0;
$odd = true;
while ($row = mysql_fetch_array($results)) {
    echo ($odd == true) ? '<tr class="odd_row">' : '<tr class="even_row">';
    $odd = !$odd;
    extract($row);
?>
    <td style="text-align:center;">
     <img src="images/<?php echo $product_code; ?>_t.jpg"
      alt="<?php echo $name; ?>"/>
    </td>
    <td><?php echo $name; ?></td>
    <td><?php echo $qty; ?></td>
    <td style="text-align: right;">$<?php echo $price; ?></td>
    <td style="text-align: right;">$<?php echo number_format($price *
$qty, 2);?>

    </td>
    </tr>
<?php
    $subtotal = $subtotal + $price * $qty;
}
?>
```

```
    </table>
    <p>Your subtotal before shipping and tax is:
    <strong>$<?php echo number_format($subtotal, 2); ?></strong></p>
    <p>Your total is:
    <strong>$<?php
$tax_state = 'CA';

if ($_POST['state'])) == $tax_state) {
    $tax_rate = 0.07;
} else {
    $tax_rate = 0.00;
}

$tax = $subtotal * $tax_rate;
$total = $subtotal + $tax;
```

```
echo number_format($total, 2); ?></strong></p>
    <table>
     <tr>
      <td>
       <table>
        <tr>
         <th colspan="2">Billing Information</th>
...
     <input type="hidden" name="shipping_email"
       value="<?php echo htmlspecialchars($_POST['shipping_email']);?>"/>
     <input type="hidden" name="tax_rate" value="<?php echo $tax_rate;?>"/>
    </div>
    </form>
 </body>
</html>
```

Then, you also need to change your ecomm_checkout3.php as highlighted below:

```
$now = date('Y-m-d H:i:s');
$session = session_id();

$first_name = $_POST['first_name'];
$last_name = $_POST['last_name'];
$address_1 = $_POST['address_1'];
$address_2 = $_POST['address_2'];
$city = $_POST['city'];
$state = $_POST['state'];
$zip_code = $_POST['zip_code'];
$phone = $_POST['phone'];
$email = $_POST['email'];

$shipping_first_name = $_POST['shipping_first_name'];
$shipping_last_name = $_POST['shipping_last_name'];
$shipping_address_1 = $_POST['shipping_address_1'];
$shipping_address_2 = $_POST['shipping_address_2'];
$shipping_city = $_POST['shipping_city'];
$shipping_state = $_POST['shipping_state'];
$shipping_zip_code = $_POST['shipping_zip_code'];
```

```
$shipping_phone = $_POST['shipping_phone'];
$shipping_email = $_POST['shipping_email'];

$tax_rate = $_POST['tax_rate'];

...
// calculate shipping, tax and total costs
$cost_shipping = round($cost_subtotal * 0.25, 2);

$cost_tax = round($tax_rate * $cost_subtotal, 2);

$cost_total = $cost_subtotal + $cost_shipping + $cost_tax;
```

2. **Allow for inventory control:** Your shopping-cart script can keep track of how many items you have in stock and display that to your customers. You can also show an "out of stock" message to your customers, letting them know that a particular item is temporarily out of stock but still available for purchase if they like.

A. First, you need to alter your products table structure to include a field for "on-hand" quantity. Then you can keep track of how many you have in stock by altering this field as necessary.

```
ALTER TABLE ecomm_products
    ADD COLUMN qty_onhand INTEGER UNSIGNED NOT NULL DEFAULT 0;
```

To show the in-stock quantity on the products detail page, you could make the following changes to the `ecomm_view_product.php` file:

```
$query = 'SELECT
        name, description, price, qty_onhand
    FROM
        ecomm_products
    WHERE
        product_code = "' . mysql_real_escape_string($product_code, $db) .
'"';
$result = mysql_query($query, $db)or die(mysql_error($db));
...
<h2><?php echo $name; ?></h2>
<table>
 <tr>
   <td rowspan="5"><img src="images/<?php echo $product_code; ?>.jpg"

    alt="<?php echo $name; ?>"/></td>
  <td><?php echo $description; ?></td>
 </tr><tr>
   <td><strong>Product Code:</strong> <?php echo $product_code; ?></td>

   </tr><tr>
    <td><strong>Qty in Stock:</strong>
<?php
if ($qty_onhand < 1) {
    echo '<strong style="color: red;">This product is currently out of
stock.' .
        '</strong>';
```

```
} else {
    echo $qty_onhand;
}
?>
  </td>
 </tr><tr>
  <td><strong>Price:</strong> $<?php echo $price; ?></td>
 </tr><tr>
```

Then, to keep an accurate count of how many items you have in stock, you want to change the quantity-on-hand field when any items are sold. You need to make the following change to the final step in your checkout process. Edit your ecomm_checkout3.php as follows:

```
while ($row = mysql_fetch_array($result)) {
    echo ($odd == true) ? '<tr class="odd_row">' : '<tr class="even_row">';
    $odd = !$odd;
    extract($row);
?>
    <td><?php echo $product_code; ?></td>
    <td><?php echo $name; ?></td>
    <td><?php echo $order_qty; ?></td>
    <td style="text-align: right;">$<?php echo $price; ?></td>
    <td style="text-align: right;">$<?php
     echo number_format($price * $order_qty, 2);?>
    </td>
  </tr>
<?php
    $query = 'UPDATE ecomm_products SET
            qty_onhand = qty_onhand - ' . $order_qty . '
        WHERE
            product_code = ' . $product_code;
    mysql_query($query, $db) or die(mysql_error($db));
}
?>
```

3. **Show your customers your most popular items:** Which of your items are purchased the most? If an item is in the top five on your bestseller list, show a "bestseller" icon in the description of that item.

A. There are several ways to do this, but probably the simplest way is to add another field to your products table that will keep a master count of the total quantity sold:

```
ALTER TABLE ecomm_products
    ADD COLUMN total_qty_sold INTEGER UNSIGNED NOT NULL DEFAULT 0;
```

You want to check for a bestselling item when you show your product details, so you alter ecomm_view_product.php as follows:

```
function is_bestseller($db, $product_code) {
    $query = SELECT
            product_code
        FROM
            ecomm_products
```

```
        ORDER BY
            total_qty_sold DESC
        LIMIT 5`;
    $result = mysql_query($query, $db) or die(mysql_error($db));
    $retVal = false;
    while ($row = mysql_fetch_assoc($result)) {
        if ($product_code == $row['product_code']) {
            $retVal = true;
        }
    }
    mysql_free_result($result);
    return $retVal;
}
...
<h2>
<?php
echo $name;
if (is_bestseller($db, $product_code)) {
    echo '<img src="images/bestseller.jpg" alt="Best Seller!"/>';
}
?>
</h2>
<table>
 <tr>
   <td rowspan="4"><img src="images/<?php echo $product_code; ?>.jpg"
   alt="<?php echo $name; ?>"/></td>
  <td><?php echo $description; ?></td>
 </tr><tr>
```

Then, just as you did with the inventory count, you would alter your ecomm_checkout3.php file to update the total number sold with the customer's current order information, as follows:

```
$total = 0;
$odd = true;
while ($row = mysql_fetch_array($result)) {
    echo ($odd == true) ? '<tr class="odd_row">' : '<tr class="even_row">';
    $odd = !$odd;
    extract($row);
?>
    <td><?php echo $product_code; ?></td>
    <td><?php echo $name; ?></td>
    <td><?php echo $order_qty; ?></td>
    <td style="text-align: right;">$<?php echo $price; ?></td>
    <td style="text-align: right;">$<?php
     echo number_format($price * $order_qty, 2);?>
    </td>
    </tr>
<?php
```

```
$query = 'UPDATE ecomm_products SET
        total_qty_sold = total_qty_sold + ' . $order_qty . '
    WHERE
        product_code = ' . $product_code;
    mysql_query($query, $db) or die(mysql_error($db));
}
?>
```

Chapter 16

1. Add code to `frm_admin.php` to prevent unauthorized users from loading the page. Redirect them back to `frm_index.php`.

A. This block of code should go at the top of `frm_admin.php`:

```
<?php
session_start();
if ($_SESSION['access_lvl'] < 3) {
header ('Location: frm_index.php');
}
?>
```

2. Create a regular expression that recognizes an e-mail address in a post and turns it into a link.

A. This is not the only answer, but it gets the job done:

```
/[\w\-]+(\.[\w\-]+)*@[\w\-]+(\.[\w\-]+)+/
```

3. Add a bit of code to the pagination function to allow the user to go to the first page or last page. For example, if there are 14 pages, and the user is on page 8, and the range is 7, it should look something like this:

```
<PREV [1] .. [5] [6] [7] 8 [9] [10] [11] .. [14] NEXT >
```

A. Replace the appropriate lines of code with the following code snippets:

```
if ($lrange > 1) {
    $pagelinks .= '<a href="' . $currpage . '&page=1">[1]</a> .. ';
} else {
    $pagelinks .= '  ';
}

if ($rrange < $numofpages) {
    $pagelinks .= ' .. <a href="' . $currpage . '&page=' . $numofpages .
    '">[' . $numofpages . ']</a>';
} else {
    $pagelinks .= '  ';
}
```

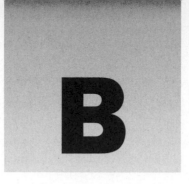

PHP Quick Reference

This appendix lists some quick PHP reference notes for your use. Consider the information in this appendix to be your "cheat sheet" to the topics covered throughout this book. For complete information on PHP's syntax, see www.php.net/manual/en/langref.php.

Marking PHP Code

Sections of PHP code start with <?php and end with ?>. An example of this syntax is:

```php
<?php
// enter lines of code, make sure they end with a semicolon;
?>
```

You can also use <script language="PHP"> </script> to delimit your code, but the above syntax is more convenient.

Displaying to Browser

The echo and print constructs are used to display text in a browser:

```php
echo 'Enter text here';    // echo text
echo $variable;            // echo values
echo '<br/>';              // echo HTML text
```

Comments

It's always a good idea to comment your code. PHP gives you two ways to do so:

```
// This is a single line comment that runs to the end of the line.
/* This is a multiple line comment and
   can
   span
   multiple
   lines. */
```

Variables

Variables are named references to locations in memory. Variable names start with $. Legal variable names consist of numbers, letters, and the underscore character but cannot start with a number.

```
$MyVariable            // valid
$1stVariable           // invalid (cannot start with a number)
$variable_1            // valid
```

To assign a value to a variable, use the following syntax:

```
$variable_1 = 123;
$variable_2 = 'value';
```

Passing Variables

You can pass variables among pages in your Web site in three ways: through a URL, through sessions, and through a form.

Through a URL

To pass a variable through a URL, use the following format:

```
http://www.example.com?variable1=value&variable2=value
```

Through Sessions

To pass a variable through a session, use the following PHP code:

```
session_start();                      // starts session handling
$_SESSION['var_name1'] = value;  // sets values for the entire session
$_SESSION['var_name2'] = value;
```

session_start() must be used in every script that sets or accesses session variables. It must be called before any output is sent to the browser.

Through a Form

A form element's `action` attribute must reference the PHP script that will parse the variables:

```
<form action="process.php">
```

The variables can be referenced from the `$_POST` and `$_GET` arrays, depending on the form element's method:

```
$value = $_POST['varname'];      // this is how you will access the
                                 // values from a form with method="post"
$value = $_GET['varname'];       // this is how you will access the
                                 // values from a form with method="get"
```

Strings

A string is a set of characters delimited by quotation marks. Either single quotation marks or double quotation marks can be used, but PHP treats these differently. Variables that appear within double-quoted strings will be interpolated. Variables within single-quoted strings will not be.

```
$var = 42;
echo "The answer to life, the universe and everything is: $var.";
// The answer to life, the universe and everything is 42.
echo 'The answer to life, the universe and everything is: $var.';
// The answer to life, the universe and everything is $var.
```

\ is used to escape characters within strings:

```
echo '<a href="link.php">Don\'t Click on Me!</a>';
```

Two strings can be joined together with the . operator:

```
$piece_1 = 'Hello';
$piece_2 = 'World';
echo $piece_1 . ' ' . $piece_2;   // Hello World
```

if Statements

`if` statements are used to mark sections of code that should be executed only if a given condition is true:

```
if (condition)
    // execute this one statement if true;
if (true condition) {
    // execute statement 1;
    // execute statement 2;
    // execute statement 3;
}
```

else Statements

`if`/`else` statements branch code depending on whether a condition is true or false:

```php
if (condition)
    //execute this statement if true;
else
    //execute this statement false;
if (condition) {
    // execute statement 1;
    // execute statement 2;
    // execute statement 3;
} else {
    // execute statement 4;
    // execute statement 5;
    // execute statement 6;
}
```

The ternary operator (`?:`) is a shorthand notation for simple `if`/`else` statements:

```php
$var = (true) ? 'value 1' : 'value 2';
```

is the same as:

```php
if (true) {
    $var = 'value 1';
} else {
    $var = 'value 2';
}
```

Nested if Statements

You can nest `if` statements:

```php
if (condition A) {
    if (condition B) {
        // execute this statement if A and B are true;
    }
    else if (condition C) {
        // execute this statement if A and C are true;
    } else {
        // execute this statement if A is true and B and C are false;
    }
}
```

Including a File

To include PHP code from another file, use one of the following statements:

```
include 'header.php';        // include file header.php (PHP will continue
                             // processing even if file is not found
include_once 'header.php';   // ensure file header.php is only included once
                                even if
                             // attempt to include same file again later in
                             // processing
require 'header.php';        // include file header.php (PHP will terminate
                                with
                             // error if file is not found
require_once 'header.php';   // ensure file header.php is only included once
                                even if
                             // attempt to include same file again later
```

Arrays

An array is a collection of data represented by the same variable name but accessible by indexes. Indexes can be either numeric or strings.

```
$name = array('first_name' => 'Joe', 'last_name' => 'Shmoe');
echo $name['first_name'];
```

If no keys are required, you can set the values for an array like this and let PHP automatically assign numeric keys starting at 0:

```
$flavors = array('blue raspberry', 'root beer', 'pineapple');
echo $flavor[0];
```

New elements can be added to an array after it is defined:

```
$states = array();
$states['AL'] = 'Alabama';
$states['AK'] = 'Alaska';
$states['AZ'] = 'Arizona';
...
```

Loops

PHP has numerous looping structures to repeat the execution of a block of code: while, do/while, for, and foreach.

while

You can execute a section of code repeatedly while a given condition is true, with a `while` statement:

```php
$n = 0;
while ($n < 10) {
    // these lines will execute while the value of $n is
    // less than 10
    echo $n . '<br />';
    $n = $n + 1;
}
echo $n;
```

do/while

You can execute a section of code repeatedly while a given condition is true, with a `do/while` statement. Unlike a `while` statement, the loop is guaranteed to run at least once because the condition is not tested until the end of the block:

```php
$n = 0;
do {
    // these lines will execute while the value of $n is
    // less than 10
    echo $n . '<br />';
    $n = $n + 1;
} while ($n < 10);
```

for

You can execute a block of code a specified number of times with the `for` statement:

```php
for ($n = 0; $n < 10; $n = $n + 1) {
    // this will execute while the value of $n is
    // less than 10
    echo $n . '<br/>';
}
```

foreach

You can apply the same block of code to each value in a given array with the `foreach` statement:

```php
foreach ($arrayvalue as $currentvalue) {
    // this will execute as long as there is a value in $arrayvalue
    echo $currentvalue . '<br/>';
}
```

In addition to each value in the array, you can also identify the index or key:

```php
foreach ($arrayvalue as $currentkey => $currentvalue) {
    // this will execute as long as there is a value in $arrayvalue
    echo $currentkey . ':' . currentvalue . '<br/>';
}
```

Functions

You can create and call functions using the following syntax:

```
function funcname()      // defines the function
{
    // line of php code;
    // line of php code;
}
funcname();      // calls the function to execute
```

Values can be passed in and returned from functions:

```
function add($value1, $value2)      // add two numbers together
{
    $value3 = $value1 + $value2;
    return $value3;
}
$val = funcname(1, 1);      // $val = 2
```

Classes

You can define new objects and use its methods using the following syntax:

```
class ClassName()      // class definition
{
    public  $var1;      // property with public access
    private $var2;      // property with private access

    // constructor method
    public function __construct() {
        // code to initialize object goes here
    }

    // public method
    public function setFoo($value) {
        // properties and methods are accessed inside the class
        // using $this->
        $this->var2 = $value;
    }

    // private method
    private function bar() {
        // more code goes here
    }

    // destructor method
    public function __destruct() {
        // clean up code goes here
    }
}
```

```php
$c = new ClassName();        // create a new instance of the object

$c->var1 = 42;               // properties and methods are accessed using ->
$c->setFoo('Hello World');
```

Namespaces

Namespaces are one of the more recent additions to PHP's syntax (added in version 5.3) and help prevent name clashing. Namespaces can contain class, constant, and function definitions. Namespaces are declared with the namespace keyword at the beginning of a file:

```php
namespace MyProject\Foo\Bar;
function fizz() {
    // ...
}
```

When using functions and classes that are defined within a namespace, they can be referenced by their full name:

```php
$var = MyProject::Foo::Bar::fizz();
```

Namespaces can be imported with the use keyword:

```php
use MyProject\Foo\Bar;
$var = fizz();
```

Namespaces can be aliased with use/as:

```php
use MyProject\Foo\Bar as my;
$var = my\fizz();
```

Using MySQL

This is the basic sequence for connecting to a MySQL database, executing a SELECT query and displaying the results:

```php
// connect to MySQL
$db = mysql_connect('localhost', 'username', 'password') or
    die ('Unable to connect. Check your connection parameters.');

// select the correct database
mysql_select_db('database', $db) or die(mysql_error($db));

// query the database
$query = 'SELECT column1, column2 FROM table ORDER BY column1 ASC';
$result = mysql_query($query, $db) or die (mysql_error($db));
```

```php
// check if any rows were returned
if (mysql_num_rows($result) > 0) {

    // cycle through the returned records
    while ($row = mysql_fetch_assoc($result)) {
        echo 'column1: ' . $row['column1'] . '<br/>';
        echo 'column2: ' . $row['column2'] . '<br/>';
    }
}

// free the result resource
mysql_free_result($result);

// disconnect from MySQL

mysql_close($db);
```

PHP6 Functions

For your convenience, we have listed many (but not all) of PHP's functions in this appendix to serve as a quick reference. PHP has numerous other functions available to you, and you can find a complete listing in the manual at its web site, www.php.net/manual/en/funcref.php. Each table presented here lists the function's signature in a format similar to that used in the official PHP documentation and a brief description of what the function does. Functions that are deprecated and should no longer be used are not listed here.

Please note that some functions are designed to work only on Linux, and some only on Windows. If you encounter otherwise unexplained errors in your code, we recommend checking the function's documentation to ensure that it is available and fully compatible with your platform.

Apache/PHP Functions

PHP Function	Description
bool apache_child_terminate(void)	Stop the Apache server from running after the PHP script has been executed.
array apache_get_modules(void)	Return an array of loaded Apache modules.
string apache_get_version(void)	Return the version of Apache that is currently running.
string apache_getenv(string $variable[, bool $walk_to_top])	Return an Apache subprocess environment variable as specified by $variable.
object apache_lookup_uri(string $filename)	Return information about the URI in $filename as an object.

PHP Function	Description
`string apache_note(string $notename[, string $ value])`	Return or set values in the Apache notes tables.
`array apache_request_headers(void)`	Return all HTTP headers as an associative array.
`array apache_response_headers(void)`	Return all HTTP response headers as an associative array.
`bool apache_setenv(string $variable, $value[, bool $walk_to_top])`	Set an Apache subprocess environment variable.
`int ascii2ebcdic(string $string)`	Convert an ASCII-coded string to EBCDIC (only available on EBCDIC-based operating systems).
`int ebcdic2ascii(string $string)`	Convert an EBCDIC-coded string to ASCII (only available on EBCDIC-based operating systems).
`array getallheaders()`	Return all HTTP request headers as an associative array.
`bool virtual(string $filename)`	Perform an Apache subrequest, useful for including the output of CGI scripts or `.shtml` files.

Array Functions

Function	Description
`array array([mixed $...])`	Create an array of values.
`array array_change_key_case(array $array[, int $case])`	Convert the keys in an array to either all uppercase or all lowercase. The default is lowercase.
`array array_chunk(array $array, int $size[, bool $keep_keys])`	Split an array into specifically sized chunks.
`array array_combine(array $keys, array $values)`	Combine two arrays with equal number of keys and values, using the values from one array as keys and the other's as values.
`array array_count_values(array $array)`	Return an associative array of values as keys and their count as values.

Function	Description
`array array_diff(array $array1, array $array2[, array $...])`	Return the values from the first array that do not appear in subsequent arrays. Opposite of `array_intersect()`.
`array array_diff_assoc(array $array1, array $array2[, array $...])`	Return the values from the first array that do not appear in subsequent arrays, taking key values into account.
`array array_diff_key(array $array1, array $array2[, array $...])`	Return the keys from the first array that do not appear in subsequent arrays.
`array array_diff_uassoc(array $array1, array $array2[, array $...], string $function_name)`	Return the keys from the first array that do not appear in subsequent arrays. Use supplied callback function to compare keys, instead of PHP's internal algorithm.
`array array_diff_ukey(array $array1, array $array2[, array $...], string $function_name)`	Return the keys from the first array that do not appear in subsequent arrays. Use supplied callback function to compare keys, instead of PHP's internal algorithm.
`array array_fill(int $start, int $count, mixed $value)`	Return an array filled with $value.
`array array_fill_keys(array $keys, mixed $value)`	Return an array filled with $value, using values of the $keys array as keys.
`array array_filter(array $array[, string $function_name])`	Return an array of values filtered by $function_name. If the callback function returns true, then the current value from $array is returned into the result array. Array keys are preserved.
`array array_flip(array $array)`	Flip an array's values and keys and return the result as an array.
`array array_intersect(array $array1, array $array2[, array $...])`	Return the values from the first array that appear in subsequent arrays. Opposite of `array_diff()`.
`array array_intersect_assoc(array $array1, array $array2[, array $...])`	Return the values from the first array that appear in subsequent arrays. Unlike `array_intersect()`, this function takes key values into account.
`array array_intersect_key(array $array1, array $array2[, array $...])`	Return the keys from the first array that appear in subsequent arrays.

Function	Description
`array array_intersect_uassoc(array $array1, array $array2[, array $...], string $function_name)`	Return the keys from the first array that appear in subsequent arrays. Use supplied callback function to compare keys, instead of PHP's internal algorithm.
`array array_intersect_ukey(array $array1, array $array2[, array $...], string $function_name)`	Return the keys from the first array that appear in subsequent arrays. Use supplied callback function to compare keys, instead of PHP's internal algorithm.
`bool array_key_exists(mixed $key, array $array)`	Verify whether a key exists in an array.
`array array_keys(array $array [, mixed $search [, bool $strict]])`	Return keys of array $array as an array. If $search is provided, then only those keys containing those values will be returned.
`array array_map(string $function_name, array $array1[, array $...])`	Return an array containing elements from the supplied arrays that fit the applied criterion.
`array array_merge(array $array1[, $array2[, array $...]])`	Merge arrays together and return the results as an array. If two arrays have the same associative keys, then the later array will overwrite an earlier key. If two arrays have the same numeric keys, then the array will be appended instead of overwritten.
`array array_merge_recursive(array $array1[, arrary $...])`	Similar to `array_merge()`, but the values of the arrays are appended.
`bool array_multisort(array $array [, mixed $parameter[, mixed $...]])`	Sort either a complex multidimensional array or several arrays at one time. Numeric keys will be reindexed, but associative keys will be maintained.
`array array_pad(array $array, int $pad_size, mixed $pad_value)`	Return a copy of an array padded to size $pad_size with $pad_value.
`mixed array_pop(array &$array)`	Shorten an array by popping and returning its last value. Opposite of `array_push(.)`.
`number array_product(array $array)`	Return the product of an array's values.
`int array_push(array &$array, mixed $variable[, mixed $...])`	Extend an array by pushing variables on to its end, and return the new size of the array. Opposite of `array_pop()`.
`mixed array_rand(array $array[, int $number])`	Return a random key from an array (an array of random keys is returned if more than one value is requested).

Function	Description
`mixed array_reduce(array $array, string $function_name)`	Reduce an array to a single function, using a supplied callback function.
`array array_reverse(array $array[, bool $preserve_keys])`	Return an array with its elements in reverse order.
`mixed array_search(mixed $search, array $array[, bool $strict])`	Search an array for the given value, and return the key if it is found.
`mixed array_shift(array &$array)`	Similar to `array_pop()`, except that this shortens an array by returning its first value. Opposite of `array_unshift()`.
`array array_slice(array $array, int $offset[, int $length[, bool $preserve_keys]])`	Return a subset of the original array.
`array array_splice(array &$array, int $offset[, int $length[, mixed $new_values]])`	Remove a section of an array and replace it with new values.
`number array_sum(array $array)`	Calculate the sum of the values in an array.
`array array_udiff(array $array1, array $array2[, array $...], string $function_name)`	Return the values from the first array that do not appear in subsequent arrays, using the provided callback function to perform the comparison.
`array array_udiff_assoc(arrays $array1, array $array2[, array $...], string $function_name)`	Return values from the first array that do not appear in subsequent arrays, using the provided callback function to perform the comparison. Unlike `array_udiff()`, the array's keys are used in the comparison.
`array array_udiff_assoc(arrays $array1, array $array2[, array $...], string $value_compare, string $key_compare)`	Return the values from the first array that do not appear in subsequent arrays, using the provided callback functions to perform the comparison (`$data_compare` is used to compare values, and `$key_compare` is used to compare keys).
`array array_uintersect(array $array1, array $array2[, array $...], string $function_name)`	Return the intersection of arrays through a user-defined callback function.
`array array_uintersect_assoc(array $array1, array $array2[, array $...], string $function_name)`	Return the intersection of arrays with additional index checks, using the provided callback function to perform the comparison.

Function	Description
`array array_uintersect_uassoc(array $array1, array $array2[, array $...], string $value_compare, string $key_compare)`	Return the intersection of arrays with additional index checks, using the provided callback functions to perform the comparison ($data_compare is used to compare values, and $key_compare is used to compare keys).
`array array_unique(array $array)`	Return a copy of an array excluding any duplicate values.
`mixed array_unshift(array &$array, mixed $variable[, mixed $...])`	Similar to `array_push ()` except that this adds values to the beginning of an array. Opposite of `array_unshift()`.
`array array_values(array $array)`	Return a numerically indexed array of the values from an array.
`bool array_walk(array $array, string $function_name[, mixed $parameter])`	Apply a named function to every value in an array.
`bool array_walk_recursive(array $array, string $function_name[, mixed $parameter])`	Apply a named function recursively to every value in an array.
`bool arsort(array &$array[, int $sort_flags])`	Sort an array in descending order, while maintaining the key/value relationship.
`bool asort(array &$array[, int $sort_flags])`	Sort an array in ascending order, while maintaining the key/value relationship.
`array compact(mixed $variable[, mixed $...])`	Merge variables into an associative array. Opposite of `extract()`.
`int count(mixed $array[, int $mode])`	Return the number of values in an array or the number of properties in an object.
`mixed current(array &$array)`	Return the current value in an array.
`array each(array &$array)`	Return the current key and value pair of an array, and advance the array's internal pointer.
`mixed end(array &$array)`	Advance an array's internal pointer to the end of an array, and return the array's last value.
`int extract(array $array[, int $extract_type[, string $prefix]])`	Import values from an associative array into the symbol table. The $extract_type option provides directions if there is a conflict.
`bool in_array(mixed $search, array $haystack[, bool $strict])`	Return whether a specified value exists in an array.
`mixed key(array &$array)`	Return the key for the current value in an array.

Function	Description
`bool krsort(array &$array[, int $sort_flags])`	Sort an array in reverse order by keys, maintaining the key/value relationship.
`bool ksort(array &$array[, int $sort_flags])`	Sort an array by keys, maintaining the key/value relationship.
`void list(mixed $variable[, mixed $...])`	Assign a list of variables in an operation as if they were an array.
`bool natcasesort(array &$array)`	Sort an array using case-insensitive "natural ordering."
`bool natsort(array &$array)`	Sort an array using case-sensitive "natural ordering."
`mixed next(array &$array)`	Similar to `current()` but advances an array's internal pointer.
`mixed pos(array &$array)`	Alias for `current()`.
`mixed prev(array &$array)`	Return the previous value in an array. Opposite of `next()`.
`array range(mixed $low, mixed $high[, int $step])`	Create an array of integers or characters between the named parameters.
`mixed reset(array &$array)`	Set an array's internal pointer to the first element, and return its value.
`bool rsort(array &$array[, int $sort_flags])`	Sort an array in descending order. Opposite of `sort()`.
`bool shuffle(array &$array)`	Shuffle the elements of an array in random order.
`int sizeof(mixed $array[, int $mode])`	Alias for `count()`.
`bool sort(array &$array[, int $sort_flags])`	Sort an array in ascending order.
`bool uasort(array &$array, .string $function_name)`	Sort an array, maintaining the key/value relationship. Use supplied callback function to compare values, instead of PHP's internal algorithm.
`bool uksort(array &$array, .string $function_name)`	Sort the keys of an array. Use supplied callback function to compare keys, instead of PHP's internal algorithm.
`bool usort(array &$array, string $function_name)`	Sort an array. Use supplied callback function to compare values, instead of PHP's internal algorithm.

Date and Time Functions

Function signatures marked with a * are available when running on Windows by default, but must be explicitly enabled when running on Linux by compiling PHP with --enable-calendar.

Function	Description
`int cal_days_in_month(int $calendar, int $month, int $year)*`	Return the number of days in the given month.
`array cal_from_jd($int julian_day, int $calendar)*`	Convert a Julian day count to the date of a specified calendar.
`array cal_info([int $calendar])*`	Return an array containing information about the named calendar.
`int cal_to_jd(int $calendar, int $month, int $day, int $year)*`	Convert a specified calendar date to a Julian day count.
`bool checkdate(int $month, int $day, int $year)`	Validate a given date.
`string date(string $format[, int $timestamp])`	Return a formatted date based on the provided format string (see the following table for available formatting specifiers). The default is the current UNIX timestamp, if `$timestamp` is not provided.
`void date_add(DateTime $object[, DateInterval $object])`	Add the given `DateInterval` object to the given `DateTime` object.
`DateTime date_create(string $time[, DateTimeZone $timezone])`	Create a new `DateTime` object. The object-oriented equivalent of this function is `new DateTime(string $time[, DateTimeZone $timezone])`.
`void date_date_set(DateTime $object, int $year, int $month, int $day)`	Set the date of a `DateTime` object. The object-oriented equivalent of this function is `DateTime::setDate(int $year, int $month, int $day)`.
`string date_default_timezone_get(void)`	Return the current default time zone string.
`bool date_default_timezone_set(string $timezone)`	Set the current default time zone.
`string date_format(DateTime $object, string $format)`	Return a formatted string value of a `DateTime` object based on the provided format string (see the following table for available formatting specifiers). The object-oriented equivalent of this function is `DateTime::format(string $format)`.

Function	Description
`void date_isodate_set(DateTime $object, int $year, int $week[, int $day])`	Set the ISO date of a `DateTime` object. The object-oriented equivalent of this function is `DateTime::setISODate(int $year, int $week[, int $day])`.
`void date_modify(DateTime $object, string $offset)`	Modify the value of a `DateTime` object. The object-oriented equivalent of this function is `DateTime::modify(string $offset)`.
`int date_offset_get(DateTime $object)`	Return the offset for daylight savings for a `DateTime` object. The object-oriented equivalent of this function is `DateTime::getOffset(void)`.
`array date_parse(string $date)`	Return an associative array representation of a parsed date.
`void date_sub(DateTime $object[, DateInterval $object])`	Subtract the given `DateInterval` object from the given `DateTime` object.
`array date_sun_info(int $timestamp, float $latitude, float $longitude)`	Return an associative array with sunrise, sunset, and twilight start/end details.
`string date_sunrise(int $timestamp[, int $format [, float $latitude[, float $longitude[, float $zenith[, float $gmt_offset]]]]])`	Return the sunrise time for a given date and location.
`string date_sunset(int $timestamp[, int $format [, float $latitude[, float $longitude[, float $zenith[, float $gmt_offset]]]]])`	Return the sunset time for a given date and location.
`void date_time_set(DateTime $object, int $hour, int $minutes[, int $seconds])`	Set the time value of a `DateTime` object. The object-oriented equivalent of this function is `DateTime::setTime(int $hour, int $minutes[, int $seconds])`.
`DateTimeZone date_timezone_get(DateTime $object)`	Return the `DateTime` object's time zone as a `DateTimeZone` object. The object-oriented equivalent of this function is `DateTime::getTimezone(void)`.
`void date_timezone_set(DateTime $object, DateTimeZone $timezone)`	Set the time zone of a `DateTime` object. The object-oriented equivalent of this function is `DateTime::setTimezone(DateTimeZone $timezone)`.

Function	Description
int easter_date([int $year])*	Return the UNIX timestamp of midnight on Easter for the given year. The default is the current year, if $year is not provided.
int easter_days([int $year])*	Return the number of days between March 21 and Easter in the given year. The default is the current year, if $year is not provided.
int frenchtojd(int $month, int $day, int $year)*	Convert a French Republican calendar date to a Julian day count.
array getdate([int $timestamp])	Return an associative array representation of a timestamp. The default is the current local time, if a timestamp is not provided.
mixed gettimeofday([bool $return_float])	Return an associative array or float representation of the current time.
string gmdate(string $format[, int $timestamp])	Similar to date() but returns the formatted date in Greenwich Mean Time.
int gmtmktime([int $hour[, int $minutes[, int $seconds[, int $month[, int $day[, int $year[, int $is_dst]]]]]]])	Similar to mktime() but returns the UNIX timestamp in Greenwich Mean Time.
string gmtstrftime(string $format [, int $timestamp])	Similar to gmtstrftime() but returns the formatted date in Greenwich Mean Time.
int gregoriantojd(int $month, int $day, int $year)*	Convert a Gregorian calendar date to a Julian day count.
int idate(string $format[, int $timestamp])	Return a date/time as an integer. The default is the current UNIX timestamp, if $timestamp is not provided.
mixed jddayofweek(int $julian_day[, int $mode])*	Return the day of week of a Julian day count in the format based on the specified mode.
string jdmonthname(int $julian_day, int $mode)*	Return the month of a Julian day count in the format based on the specified mode.
string jdtofrench(int $julian_day)*	Convert a Julian day count to a French Republican calendar date.
string jdtogregorian(int $julian_day)*	Convert a Julian day count to a Gregorian calendar date.
string jdtojewish(int $julian_day[, bool $hebrew[, int $fl]])*	Convert a Julian day count to a Jewish calendar date.

Function	Description
`string jdtojulian(int $julian_day)*`	Convert a Julian day count to a Julian calendar date.
`int jdtounix(int $julian_day)*`	Convert a Julian day count to a UNIX timestamp.
`int jewishtojd(int $month, int $day, int $year)*`	Convert a Jewish calendar date to a Julian day count.
`int juliantojd(int $month, int $day, int $year)*`	Convert a Julian calendar date to a Julian day count.
`array localtime([int $timestamp[, bool $is_associative])`	Return the local time as an array.
`mixed microtime([bool $return_float])`	Return the current UNIX timestamp with microseconds.
`int mktime([int $hour[, int $minutes[, int $seconds[, int $month[, int $day[, int $year[, int $is_dst]]]]]]])`	Return the UNIX timestamp for a date. The default is the current UNIX timestamp, if the parameters are not provided.
`string strftime(string $format [, int $timestamp])`	Return a formatted date based on the current locale settings. The default is the current UNIX timestamp, if `$timestamp` is not provided.
`int strtotime(string $time[, int $timestamp])`	Convert a US English time/date format into a UNIX timestamp. The default is the current UNIX timestamp, if `$timestamp` is not provided.
`int time(void)`	Return the current UNIX timestamp.
`array timezone_abbreviations_list(void)`	Return an array with information about all known time zones. The object-oriented equivalent of this function is `DateTimeZone::listAbbreviations(void)`.
`array timezone_identifiers_list(void)`	Return an array of all known time zone identifiers. The object-oriented equivalent of this function is `DateTimeZone::listIdentifiers(void)`.
`string timezone_name_from_abbr(string $abbreviation[, int $gmt_offset[, int $is_dst]])`	Return the time zone name of an abbreviation.
`string timezone_name_get(DateTimeZone $object)`	Return the time zone name of a `DateTimeZone` object. The object-oriented equivalent of this function is `DateTimeZone::getName(void)`.

Function	Description
int timezone_offset_get(DateTimeZone $object, DateTime $object)	Return the offset from Greenwich Mean Time of a DateTimeZone object. The object-oriented equivalent of this function is DateTimeZone::getOffset(DateTime $object).
DateTimeZone timezone_open(string $timezone)	Return a new DateTimeZone object. The object-oriented equivalent of this function is new DateTimeZone(string $timezone).
array timezone_transitions_get(DateTimeZone $object)	Return an array of all transitions for a DateTimeZone object. The object-oriented equivalent of this function is DateTimeZone::getTransitions(void).
int unixtojd([int $timestamp])*	Convert a UNIX timestamp to a Julian day count. The default is the current UNIX timestamp, if $timestamp is not provided.

Date and Time Formatting Codes

The following codes can be used in conjunction with date()*,* date_format()*, and* gmdate()*. See* www.php.net/strftime *for formatting specifiers used with* strftime() *and* gmstrftime()*. For formatting specifiers recognized by* idate()*, see* www.php.net/idate.

Format Character	Description	What Is Returned
Month		
F	Unabbreviated month name	January through December
M	Abbreviated month name	Jan through Dec
m	Month in numeric format as 2 digits with leading zeros	01 through 12
n	Month in numeric format without leading zeros	1 through 12
t	The number of days in the month	28 through 31
Day		
D	Abbreviated day of the week	Mon through Sun
d	Day of the month as 2 digits with leading zeros	01 to 31

Format Character	Description	What Is Returned
j	Day of the month without leading zeros	1 to 31
l (lowercase L)	Unabbreviated day of the week	Sunday through Saturday
N	Day of the week in numeric format (ISO-8601)	1 through 7 (1 is Sunday)
S	English ordinal suffix for the day of the month	st, nd, rd, or th
w	Day of the week in numeric format	0 through 6 (0 is Sunday)
z	Day of the year in numeric format	0 through 366
Year		
L	Whether the year is a leap year	1 if it is a leap year, 0 if it is not
o	ISO-8601 year number (this generally returns the same value as Y, except when W belongs to the previous or next year and that year is used instead)	example: 2009, 2010, etc.
Y	Year in numeric format as 4 digits	example: 2009, 2010, etc.
y	Year in numeric format as 2 digits	example: 09, 10, etc.
Week		
W	Week number of year (weeks start on Monday, ISO-8601)	1 through 52
Time		
A	Uppercase ante meridian and post meridian.	AM or PM
a	Lowercase ante meridian and post meridian	am or pm
B	Swatch Internet time	000 through 999
G	Hour in 24-hour format without leading zeros	0 through 23
g	Hour in 12-hour format without leading zeros	1 through 12

Format Character	Description	What Is Returned
H	Hour in 24-hour format as 2 digits with leading zeros	00 through 23
h	Hour in 12-hour format as 2 digits with leading zeros	01 through 12
i	Minutes as 2 digits with leading zeros	00 to 59
s	Seconds as 2 digits with leading zeros	00 through 59
u	Milliseconds	example: 012345
Time Zone		
e	Time zone identifier	example: America/New_York
I (capital i)	Indicates if date is in daylight saving time	1 if DST, 0 if it is not
O	Difference from Greenwich Mean Time in hours	example: −0500
P	Difference from Greenwich Mean Time formatted with colon	example: −05:00
T	Abbreviated time zone identifier	example: EST
Z	Time zone offset as seconds (west of UTC is negative, east of UTC is positive)	−43200 through 43200
Full Date and Time		
c	ISO8601 formatted date	example: 2009-02-04T00:50:06-05:00
r	RFC 822 formatted date	example: Wed, 04 Feb 2009 00:50:06 -0500
U	Seconds since the UNIX Epoch (January 1 1970 00:00:00 GMT)	example: 1233726606

Directory and File Functions

*Function signatures marked with a * are not available when running on Windows.*

Function	Description
`string basename(string $path[, string $suffix])`	Return the filename portion of a path, optionally trimming the filename's suffix if it matches `$suffix`.
`bool chdir(string $directory)`	Change PHP's current working directory.
`bool chgrp(string $filename, mixed $group)`	Change a file's group association.
`bool chroot(string $directory) *`	Chroot PHP to a directory.
`bool chmod(string $filename, int $mode)`	Change a file's permissions.
`bool chown(string $filename, mixed $user)`	Change a file's owner.
`void clearstatcache(void)`	Clear the file status cache.
`void closedir([resource $directory])`	Close the directory stream.
`bool copy(string $source, string $destination[, resource $context])`	Copy a file.
`Directory dir(string $)`	Return a directory iterator object.
`string dirname(string $path)`	Return the directory name component listed in the named path.
`float disk_free_space(string $directory)`	Return the amount of free space left in bytes on the filesystem or disk partition.
`float disk_total_space(string $directory)`	Return the amount of total space in bytes on the filesystem or disk partition.
`float diskfreespace(string $directory)`	Alias for `disk_free_space()`.
`string getcwd(void)`	Return the current working directory.
`bool fclose(resource $handle)`	Close an open file.
`bool feof([resource $handle])`	Verify whether the end of the file has been reached.

Appendix C: PHP6 Functions

Function	Description
`bool fflush(resource $handle)`	Force a write of all buffered output to an open file.
`string fgetc(resource $handle)`	Return a character from an open file.
`array fgetcsv(resource $handle[, int $length[, string $delimiter[, string $quote[, string $escape]]]])`	Parse a line of an open CSV file, and return it as an array.
`string fgets(resource $handle[, int $length])`	Return a line of up to ($length - 1) from an open file.
`string fgetss(resource $handle[, int $length[, string $allowed_tags]])`	Similar to fgets() but also strips any HTML and PHP tags from the data.
`array file(string $filename[, int $flags[, resource $context]])`	Return the entire contents of a file as an array, with each line as an element of the array.
`bool file_exists(string $filename)`	Verify whether a file exists.
`string file_get_contents(string $filename[, int $flags[, resource $context[, $offset[, int $maxlen]]]])`	Read the entire contents of a file into a string.
`string file_put_contents(string $filename, mixed $data[, int $flags[, resource $context]])`	Write the contents of a string to a file.
`int fileatime(string $filename)`	Return the UNIX timestamp of when a file was last accessed.
`int filectime(string $filename)`	Return the UNIX timestamp of when a file was last changed.
`int filegroup(string $filename)`	Return the owner group of a file (use `posix_getgrgid()` to resolve it to the group name).
`int fileinode(string $filename)`	Return a file's inode number.
`int filemtime(string $filename)`	Return the UNIX timestamp of when a file was modified.
`int fileowner(string $filename)`	Return the user id of the owner of a file (use `posix_getpwuid()` to resolve it to the username).
`int fileperms(string $filename)`	Return the permissions associated with a file.

Function	Description
`int filesize(string $filename)`	Return the size of a file.
`string filetype(string $filename)`	Return the file type of the named file.
`bool flock(resource $handle, int $operation[, int &$block])`	Lock or unlock a file. `$operation` may be `LOCK_SH` to set a shared lock for reading, `LOCK_EX` to set an exclusive lock for writing, and `LOCK_UN` to release a lock.
`bool fnmatch(string $pattern, string $string[, int $flags])`*	Return whether a string matches the shell wildcard pattern.
`resource fopen(string $filename, string $mode[, bool $use_include_path[, resource $context]])`	Open a resource handle to a file.
`int fpassthru(resource $handle)`	Output all remaining data from the open file.
`int fputcsv(resource $handle, array $fields[, string $delimiter[, string $quote]])`	Write an array as a CSV formatted line to a file.
`int fputs(resource $handle, string $string[, int $length])`	Alias for `fwrite()`.
`string fread(resource $handle, int $length)`	Return a string of the indicated length from an open file.
`mixed fscanf(resource $handle, string $format[, mixed &$ ...])`	Parse input read from a file, based on the provided formatting specifiers.
`int fseek(resource $handle, int $offset[, int $start])`	Move the file pointer in an open file.
`array fstat(resource $handle)`	Return information about an open file.
`int ftell(resource $handle)`	Return the current position of the open file pointer.
`bool ftruncate(resource $handle, int $length)`	Truncate an open file to the given length.
`int fwrite(resource $handle, string $string[, int $length])`	Write the contents of `$string` to a file.
`array glob(string $string[, int $flags])`	Return an array containing file and directory names that match the given pattern.
`bool is_dir(string $filename)`	Verify whether a file is a directory.

Function	Description
`bool is_executable(string $filename)`	Verify whether a file is an executable.
`bool is_file(string $filename)`	Verify whether a file is a regular file.
`bool is_link(string $filename)`	Verify whether a file is a symbolic link.
`bool is_readable(string $filename)`	Verify whether a file is readable.
`bool is_writable(string $filename)`	Alias for `is_writeable()`.
`bool is_writeable(string $filename)`	Verify whether a file is writeable.
`bool is_uploaded_file(string $filename)`	Verify whether a file was uploaded using HTTP POST.
`bool is_writeable(string $filename)`	Verify whether a file is writeable.
`bool link(string $target, string $link)`*	Create a new hard link.
`int linkinfo(string $path)`*	Return the `st_dev` field of the UNIX C `stat` structure returned by the `lstat` system call.
`array lstat(string $filename)`	Return information about a file or symbolic link.
`bool mkdir(string $pathname[, int $mode[, bool $recursive[, resource $context]]])`	Create a directory.
`bool move_uploaded_file(string $filename, string $destination)`	Move an uploaded file to a new location.
`resource opendir(string $path[, resource $context])`	Open a directory stream resource.
`array parse_ini_file(string $filename[, bool $process_sections])`	Return an array built from information in the provided INI configuration file.
`mixed pathinfo(string $path[, int $options])`	Return information about a path.
`string readdir([resource $directory])`	Return the name of the next file from the directory.
`int readfile(filename[, usepath])`	Read the named file.
`string readlink(string $path)`*	Return the target of a symbolic link.

Function	Description
`string realpath(string $path)`	Return an absolute pathname.
`bool rename(string $old_name, string $new_name[, resource $context])`	Rename a file.
`bool rewind(resource $handle)`	Move the pointer to the beginning of a file stream.
`void rewinddir([resource $directory])`	Reset the directory stream to the beginning of the directory.
`bool rmdir(string $directory[, resource $context])`	Delete a directory.
`array scandir(string $directory[, int $sort_order[, resource $context]])`	Return an array containing the names of files and directories in `$directory`.
`int set_file_buffer(resource $stream, int $buffer)`	Alias of `stream_set_write_buffer()`.
`array stat(string $filename)`	Return information about a file.
`bool symlink(string $target, string $link)*`	Create a symbolic link.
`string tempnam(string $directory, string $prefix)`	Create a temporary file in the named directory.
`resource tmpfile(void)`	Create a temporary file.
`bool touch(string $filename[, int $time[, int $atime]])`	Set the access and modification time of a file.
`int umask(int $mask)`	Modify the current umask.
`bool unlink(string $filename[, resource $context])`	Delete a file.

Error-Handling and Logging Functions

Function	Description
`bool closelog(void)`	Close the connection to the system logger opened by `openlog()`.
`array debug_backtrace([bool $provide_object])`	Generate a backtrace and return the information as an array.
`void debug_print_backtrace(void)`	Generate and display a backtrace.
`void define_syslog_variables(void)`	Initialize all constants used by syslog functions.
`array error_get_last(void)`	Return an array containing information about the last error that occurred.
`bool error_log(string $message[, int $message_type[, string $destination[, string $extra_headers]]])`	Write an error message to the web server's log, send an e-mail, or post to a file, depending on `$message_type` and `$destination`.
`int error_reporting([int $level])`	Set the `error_reporting` directive at run time for the duration of the script's execution, and return the directive's previous value.
`bool openlog(string $msg_prefix, int $option, int $facility)`	Open a connection to the system logger. See also `syslog()`.
`bool restore_error_handler(void)`	Restore the default error-handling behavior.
`bool restore_exception_handler(void)`	Restore the default exception-handling behavior.
`bool syslog(int $priority, string $message)`	Write a log message to the system logger (syslog in Linux and Event Log in Windows).
`mixed set_error_handler(string $function_name[, int $error_types])`	Override the default error-handling behavior with a user-defined callback function.
`mixed set_exception_handler(string $function_name)`	Override the default exception-handling behavior with a user-defined callback function.
`bool trigger_error(string $error_message[, int $error_type])`	Generate a user-level error, warning, or notice message.
`bool user_error(string $error_message[, int $error_type])`	Alias for `trigger_error()`.

Function- and Object-Handling Functions

Function	Description
`mixed call_user_func(string $function_name[, mixed $parameter, [mixed $...]])`	Call the named user-defined function.
`mixed call_user_func_array(string $function_name[, array $parameters])`	Call the named user-defined function, passing the indexed array to it as the function's parameters.
`bool class_exists(string $class_name[, bool $autoload])`	Verify whether a class has been defined.
`string create_function(string $parameters, string $code)`	Create an unnamed function.
`mixed func_get_arg(int $offset)`	Return an item from a function's argument list.
`array func_get_args(void)`	Return an array containing the values from a function's argument list.
`int func_num_args(void)`	Return the number of arguments in a function's argument list.
`bool function_exists(string $function_name)`	Verify whether a function is defined.
`string get_class(object $object)`	Return the class name of an object.
`array get_class_methods(mixed $class)`	Return an array containing the method names of an object or class name.
`array get_class_vars(string $class_name)`	Return an array of the names of a class's default properties.
`array get_declared_classes(void)`	Return an array containing the names of all the defined classes.
`array get_declared_interfaces(void)`	Return an array containing the names of all the defined interfaces.
`array get_defined_functions(void)`	Return a multidimensional array containing the names of all the defined functions.
`array get_object_vars(object $object)`	Return an array containing the names of an object's public properties.
`string get_parent_class(mixed $class)`	Return the name of a class or object's parent class.

Function	Description
`bool interface_exists(string $interface_name[, bool $autoload)`	Verify whether an interface has been defined.
`bool is_subclass_of(mixed $class, string $class_name)`	Verify whether an object or class has `$class_name` as one of its parents.
`bool method_exists(object $object, string $method_name)`	Verify whether a method is defined.
`bool property_exists(mixed $class, string $property_name)`	Verify whether a property is defined.
`void register_shutdown_ function(string $function_name[, mixed $parameter[, mixed $...]])`	Register a function to be executed when the script has finished processing.
`bool register_tick_function(string $function_name[, mixed $parameter[, mixed $...]])`	Register a function for execution upon every tick.
`void unregister_tick_ function(string $function_name)`	Unregister a function previously registered with `register_tick_function()`.

Image Functions

Function	Description
`int exif_imagetype(string $filename)`	Return the type of an image file.
`array exif_read_data(string $filename)`	Return the EXIF headers from a JPEG or TIFF image.
`string exif_thumbnail(string $filename[, int &$width[, int &$height[, int &$type]]].)`	Read the embedded thumbnail image within a JPEG or TIFF image file.
`array gd_info(void)`	Return information about the currently installed GD library.
`array getimagesize(string $filename, [array &$image_info])`	Return the size of an image file.
`string image_type_to_extension(int $image_type[, bool $include_dot])`	Return the file extension for an image type.
`string image_type_to_mime_type(int $image_type)`	Return the MIME type for an image type.

Function	Description
`bool image2wbmp(resource $image[, string $filename[, int $threshold]])`	Output a WBMP image directly to a browser, or save to disk if a filename is provided.
`bool imagealphablending(resource $image, bool $mode)`	Set the blending mode for an image.
`bool imageantialias(resource $image, bool $value)`	Set whether antialiasing should be on and off for an image.
`bool imagearc(resource $image, int $cx, int $cy, int $width, int $height, int $start, int $end, int $color)`	Draw a partial ellipse based on the given attributes to an image.
`bool imagechar(resource $image, int $font, int $x, int $y, character $c, int $color)`	Write a character at the given position horizontally to an image.
`bool imagecharup(resource $image, int $font, int $x, int $y, character $c, int $color)`	Write a character at the given position vertically to an image.
`int imagecolorallocate(resource $image, int $red, int $green, int $blue)`	Allocate a color to be used in an image, and return the color's identifier.
`int imagecolorallocatealpha(resource $image, int $red, int $green, int $blue, int $alpha)`	Similar to `imagecolorallocate()` with the addition of transparency.
`int imagecolorat(resource $image, int $x, int $y)`	Return the index of the color of the pixel at the named coordinates in an image.
`int imagecolorclosest(resource $image, int $red, int $green, int $blue)`	Return the index of the closest color in the palette of an image.
`int imagecolorclosestalpha(resource $image, int $red, int $green, int $blue, int $alpha)`	Similar to `imagecolorclosest()` with the addition of transparency.
`int imagecolorclosesthwb(resource $image, int $red, int $green, int $blue)`	Similar to `imagecolorclosest()` with the addition of considering hue, whiteness, and blackness.
`bool imagecolordeallocate(resource $image, int $red, int $green, int $blue)`	Free a color allocated with `imagecolorallocate()` or `imagecolorallocatealpha()`.
`int imagecolorexact(resource $image, int $red, int $green, int $blue)`	Return the exact color in the palette of an image.

Function	Description
`int imagecolorexactalpha(resource $image, int $red, int $green, int $blue, int $alpha)`	Similar to `imagecolorexact()` with the addition of transparency.
`bool imagecolormatch(resource $image1, resource $image2)`	Force the colors of a palette image to more closely match a true color.
`int imagecolorresolve(resource $image1, int $red, int $green, int $blue)`	Return either the index of the exact color or the closest color available in the palette of an image.
`int imagecolorresolvealpha(resource $image1, int $red, int $green, int $blue, int $alpha)`	Similar to `imagecolorresolve()` with the addition of transparency.
`void imagecolorset(resource $image, int $index, int $red, int $green, int $blue)`	Set the color at a given palette index of an image.
`array imagecolorsforindex(resource $image, int $index)`	Return an array with the red, blue, and green values of a color at the specified index of an image.
`int imagecolorstotal(resource $image)`	Return the number of available colors in an image's palette.
`int imagecolortransparent(resource $image [, int $color])`	Set a color as transparent in an image.
`bool imageconvolution(resource $image, array $matrix, float $div, float $offset)`	Apply a 3×3 convolution matrix to an image.
`bool imagecopy(resource $destination_image, resource $source_image, int $dest_x, int $dest_y, int $src_x, int $src_y, int $src_width, int $src_height)`	Copy part of an image onto another image.
`bool imagecopymerge(resource $destination_file, resource $source_image, int $dest_x, int $dest_y, int $src_x, int $src_y, int $src_width, int src_height, int $alpha)`	Similar to `imagecopy()` with the addition of transparency.
`bool imagecopymergegray(resource $destination_file, resource $source_image, int $dest_x, int $dest_y, int $src_x, int $src_y, int $src_width, int src_height, int $alpha)`	Similar to `imagecopymerge()` except that it copies image in grayscale.

Function	Description
`bool imagecopyresampled(resource $destination_file, resource $source_name, int $dest_x, int $dest_y, int $src_x, int $src_y, int $dest_width, int $dest_height, int $src_width, int $src_height)`	Similar to `imagecopyresized()` with the addition of resampling.
`bool imagecopyresized(resource $destination_file, resource $source_name, int $dest_x, int $dest_y, int $src_x, int $src_y, int $dest_width, int $dest_height, int $src_width, int $src_height)`	Copy and resize an image onto another image.
`resource imagecreate(int $width, int $height)`	Create a new palette-based image of the given size.
`resource imagecreatefromgd2(string $filename)`	Create a new image from a GD2 file.
`resource imagecreatefromgd2part(string $filename, int $x, int $y, int $width, int $height)`	Create a new image from a part of a GD2 file.
`resource imagecreatefromgd(string $filename)`	Create a new image from a GD file.
`resource imagecreatefromgif(string $filename)`	Create a new image from a GIF file.
`resource imagecreatefromjpeg(string $filename)`	Create a new image from a JPEG or JPG file.
`resource imagecreatefrompng(string $filename)`	Create a new image from a PNG file.
`resource imagecreatefromstring(string $stream_data)`	Create a new image from an image stream.
`resource imagecreatefromwbmp(string $filename)`	Create a new image from a WBMP file.
`resource imagecreatefromxbm(string $filename)`	Create a new image from an XBM file.
`resource imagecreatefromxpm(string $filename)`	Create a new image from an XPM file.
`resource imagecreatetruecolor(int $width, int $height)`	Create a new true-color–based image of the given size.

Appendix C: PHP6 Functions

Function	Description
`bool imagedestroy(resource $image)`	Free an image resource from memory.
`bool imageellipse(resource $image, int $cx, int $cy, int $width, int $height, int $color)`	Draw an ellipse based on the given attributes to an image.
`bool imagefill(resource $image, int $x, int $y, int $color)`	Flood-fill an entire image with one color.
`bool imagefilledarc(resource $image, int $cx, int $cy, int $width, int $height, int $start, int $end, int $color, int $style)`	Draw a filled partial ellipse based on the given attributes to an image.
`bool imagefilledellipse(resource $image, int $cx, int $cy, int $width, int $height, int $color)`	Draw a filled ellipse based on the given attributes to an image.
`bool imagefilledpolygon(resource $image, array $points, int $num_points, int $color)`	Draw a filled polygon based on the given attributes to an image.
`bool imagefilledrectangle(resource $image, int $x1, int $y1, int $x2, int $y2, int $color)`	Draw a filled rectangle based on the given attributes to an image.
`bool imagefilltoborder(resource $image, int $x, int $y, int $border_color, int $color)`	Flood-fill an image with a color, and then outline it with a border color.
`bool imagefilter(resource $image, int $filter_type[, int $filter_arg[, int $...]])`	Apply a filter to an image.
`int imagefontheight(int $font)`	Return the height of a character in pixels for a given font.
`int imagefontwidth(int $font)`	Return the width of a character in pixels for a given font.
`array imageftbbox(float $size, float $angle, string $font, string $text[, array $extra])`	Return an array with elements representing points of the text's bounding box.
`array imagefttext(resource $image, float $size, float $angle, int $x, int $y, int $color, string $font, string $text[, array $extra])`	Write a string of text at the given position to an image.

Function	Description
`bool imagegammacorrect(resource $image, float $input_gamma, float $output_gamma)`	Correct the gamma levels of a GD image.
`bool imagegd2(resource $image[, string $filename[, int $chunk_size[, $type]]])`	Output a GD2 image directly to a browser, or save to disk if a filename is provided.
`bool imagegd(resource $image[, string $filename])`	Output a GD image directly to a browser, or save to disk if a filename is provided.
`bool imagegif(resource $image [, string $filename])`	Output a GIF image directly to a browser, or save to disk if a filename is provided.
`resource imagegrabscreen(void)`	Return a screenshot of the whole screen. This function is only available on Windows, and the Apache service must be allowed to interact with the desktop.
`resource imagegrabwindow(int $window, int $client_area)`	Return a screenshot of a window. This function is only available on Windows, and the Apache service must be allowed to interact with the desktop.
`int imageinterlace(resource $image[, int $value])`	Set whether interlacing should be on or off for an image.
`bool imageistruecolor(resource $image)`	Return whether an image is true-color.
`bool imagejpeg(resource $image[, string $filename[, itn $quality]])`	Output a JPEG image directly to a browser, or save to disk if a filename is provided.
`bool imagelayereffect(resource $image, int $effect)`	Set the alpha blending flag to use the bundled layering effects.
`bool imageline(resource $image, int $x1, int $y1, int $x2, int $y2, int $color)`	Draw a solid line based on the given attributes to an image.
`int imageloadfont(string $filename)`	Load a font.
`void imagepallettecopy(resource $destination_image, resource $source_image)`	Copy a color palette.
`bool imagepng(resource $image[, string $filename[, int $quality[, int $filters]]])`	Output a PNG image directly to a browser, or save to disk if a filename is provided.
`bool imagepolygon(resource $image, array $points, int $num_points, int $color)`	Draw a polygon based on the given attributes to an image.

Function	Description
`array imagepsbbox(string $text, resource $font, int $size[, int $space, int $width, float $angle])`	Return an array with elements representing points of the text's bounding box, using a PostScript font.
`bool imagepsencodefont(resource $font_index, string $encoding_file)`	Change the character-encoding vector for a PostScript font.
`bool imagepsextendfont(resource $font_index, float $value)`	Extend or condense a PostScript font.
`bool imagepsfreefont(resource $font_index)`	Free a PostScript font resource from memory.
`resource imagepsloadfont(string $filename)`	Load a PostScript font.
`bool imagepsslantfont(resource $font_index, float $slant)`	Slant a PostScript font.
`array imagepstext(resource $image, string $text, resource $font_index, int $size, int $foreground_color, int $background_color, int $x, int $y[, int $space[, tint $width[, float $angle[, int $antialias_steps]]]])`	Write a string of text at the given position to an image using a PostScript font.
`bool imagerectangle(resource $image, int $x1, int $y1, int $x2, int $y2, int $color)`	Draw a rectangle based on the given attributes to an image.
`resource imagerotate(resource $image, float $angle, int $color[, int $ignore_transparent])`	Rotate an image.
`bool imagesavealpha(resource $image, bool $value)`	Set the flag to save with the image's alpha information.
`bool imagesetbrush(resource $image, resource $brush)`	Set the brush used for line drawing functions.
`bool imagesetpixel(resource $image, int $x, int $y, int $color)`	Set the color of a pixel in an image.
`bool imagesetstyle(resource $image, array $style)`	Set the line style for line-drawing functions.
`bool imagesetthickness(resource $image, int $thickness)`	Set the line thickness for line-drawing functions.
`bool imagesettile(resource $image, resource $tile_image)`	Set the tile image for use with fill functions.

Function	Description
`bool imagestring(resource $image, int $font, int $x, int $y, string $string, int $color)`	Write a string of text horizontally at the given position.
`bool imagestringup(resource $image, int $font, int $x, int $y, string $string, int $color)`	Write a string of text vertically at the given position.
`int imagesx(resource $image)`	Return the width of an image.
`int imagesy(resource $image)`	Return the height of an image.
`bool imagetruecolortopallette(resource $image, bool $dither, int $max_colors)`	Convert a true-color image to a color palette.
`array imagettfbbox(float $size, float $angle, string $fontname, string $text)`	Draw a text box using the named TrueType font and based on the named parameters.
`array imagettftext(resource $image, float $size, float $angle, int $x, int $y, int $color, string $fontname, string $text)`	Write a string of text at the given position to an image, using a True-Type font.
`int imagetypes(void)`	Return the supported image types as a bit-field.
`bool imagewbmp(resource $image[, string $filename[, int $foreground]])`	Output a WBMP image directly to a browser, or save to disk if a filename is provided.
`bool imagexbm(resource $image[, string $filename[, int $foreground]])`	Output an XBM image directly to a browser, or save to disk if a filename is provided.
`mixed iptcembed(string $data, string $filename[, int $spool])`	Embed binary IPTC data into a JPEG file.
`array iptcparse(string $block)`	Return an array of a parsed IPTC block indexed by tag markers.
`bool jpeg2wbmp(string $jpeg_filename, string $wbmp_filename, int $height, int $width, int $threshold)`	Convert a JPEG image to a WBMP image.
`bool png2wbmp(string $png_filename, string $wbmp_filename, int $height, int $width, int $threshold)`	Convert a PNG image to a WBMP image.
`array read_exif_data(string $filename)`	Alias for `exif_read_data()`.

Network, Mail, and HTTP Functions

Function	Description
bool checkdnsrr(string $host[, string $type])	Check DNS records for a given IP address or hostname.
bool dns_check_record(string $host [, string $type])	Alias for checkdnsrr().
bool dns_get_mx(string $hostname, array &$mxhosts[, array &$weight])	Alias for getmxrr().
array dns_get_record(string $hostname [, int $type, array &$authns, array &$addtl])	Return an array of DNS resource record information for a given hostname.
resource fsockopen(string $hostname[, int $port[, int &$errno[, string &$errstr [, float $timeout]]]])	Open a socket connection.
string gethostbyaddr(string $ip_address)	Return the hostname associated with an IP address.
string gethostbyname(string $hostname)	Return the IP address associated with a hostname.
array gethostbynamel(string $hostname)	Return an array of IP addresses associated with a hostname.
bool getmxrr(string $hostname, array &$mxhosts[, array &$weight])	Retrieve DNS MX records for a given hostname.
void header(string $string[, bool $replace[, int $ response_code]])	Output a raw HTTP header. header() must be called before any other output has been sent from the script.
array headers_list(void)	Return an array containing the headers that will be sent.
bool headers_sent(string &$file[, int &$line])	Verify whether HTTP headers have already been sent.
string inet_ntop(string $in_addr)	Return a human-readable IP address from a IPv4 or IPv6 packed address.
string inet_pton(string $address)	Return a packed IP address from a human-readable address.
int ip2long(string $ip_address)	Return an integer from a string representation of an IPv4 IP address.
string long2ip(int $proper_address)	Return a string representation of an IPv4 address from an integer.

Function	Description
`bool mail(string $to, string $subject, string $message[, string $headers[, string $ parameters]])`	Send an e-mail message.
`resource pfsockopen(string $hostname[, int $port[, int &$errno[, string &$errstr[, float $timeout]]]])`	Open a persistent socket connection.
`bool setcookie(string $name[, string $value[, int $expire[, string $path[, string $domain[, bool $secure[, bool $http_only]]]]]])`	Send a cookie to be sent to the user along with the rest of the HTTP headers based on the provided parameters. The cookie's value will be urlencoded.
`bool setrawcookie(string $name[, string $value[, int $expire[, string $path[, string $domain[, bool $secure[, bool $http_only]]]]]])`	Similar to `setcookie()`, but the cookie's value will not be urlencoded.

Mathematical Functions

Function	Description
`number abs(number $number)`	Return the absolute value of a number.
`float acos(float $value)`	Return the arc cosine in radians of a value.
`float acosh(float $value)`	Return the inverse hyperbolic cosine of a value.
`float asin(float $value)`	Return the arc sine in radians of a value.
`float asinh(float $value)`	Return the inverse hyperbolic sine of a value.
`float atan(float $value)`	Return the arc tangent in radians of a value.
`float atan2(float $y, float $x)`	Return the arc tangent of x and y in radians.
`float atanh(float $value)`	Return the inverse hyperbolic tangent of a value.
`string base_convert(string $number, int $start_base, $end_base)`	Convert a number between two arbitrary bases.
`number bindec(string $value)`	Convert a binary number represented as a string to a decimal. Opposite of `bindec()`.
`float ceil(float $value)`	Return the next highest integer by rounding the value upwards.

Function	Description
`float cos(float $value)`	Return the cosine in radians of a value.
`float cosh(float $value)`	Return the hyperbolic cosine of a value.
`string decbin(int $number)`	Convert a decimal number to a binary string representation. Opposite of `bindec()`.
`string dechex(int $number)`	Convert a decimal number to its hexadecimal representation. Opposite of `hexdec()`.
`string decoct(int $number)`	Convert a decimal number to its octal representation. Opposite of `octdec()`.
`float deg2rad(float $number)`	Convert a number from degrees to radians. Opposite of `rad2deg()`.
`float exp(float $value)`	Return the value of e raised to the power of `$value`.
`float expm1(float $value)`	Return the value of `exp($value)` - 1. The return value is computed by PHP in a way that is accurate even when `$value` is near zero.
`float floor(float $value)`	Return the next lowest integer by rounding the value downwards.
`float fmod(float $x, float $y)`	Return the floating-point remainder of the division of two numbers.
`int getrandmax(void)`	Return the maximum random value possible `rand()` could return.
`number hexdec(string $number)`	Convert a hexadecimal value to a decimal. Opposite of `dechex()`.
`float hypot(float $x, float $y)`	Return the length of the hypotenuse of a right-angle triangle.
`bool is_finite(float $number)`	Return whether a value is a finite number.
`bool is_infinite(float $number)`	Return whether a value is an infinite number.
`bool is_nan(float $value)`	Return whether a value is truly a number.
`float lcg_value(void)`	Return a pseudorandom number between 0 and 1. Combined linear congruential generator.
`float log(float $value[, float $base])`	Return the natural logarithm of a value.

Function	Description
`float log10(float $value)`	Return the base 10 logarithm of a value.
`float log1p(float $value)`	Return the value of `log(1 + $value)`. The return value is computed by PHP in a way that is accurate even when `$value` is near zero.
`mixed max(mixed $value1[, mixed $value2[, mixed $...]])`	Return the highest value from the supplied values.
`mixed min(mixed $value1[, mixed $value2[, mixed $...]])`	Return the lowest value from the supplied values.
`int mt_getrandmax(void)`	Return the maximum random value possible `mt_rand()` could return.
`int mt_rand([int $min, int $max])`	Return a random number. PHP uses a Mersenne Twister to generate the random value.
`number octdec(string $number)`	Convert an octal number to its decimal representation. Opposite of `decoct()`.
`float pi(void)`	Return the approximate value of pi.
`number pow(number $value, number $exponent)`	Return a number raised to the power of the given exponent.
`float rad2deg(float $number)`	Convert a number from radians to degrees. Opposite of `deg2rad()`.
`int rand([int $min, int $max])`	Return a random number.
`float round(float $number[, int $precision])`	Return a value rounded to the requested precision.
`float sin(float $value)`	Return the sine in radians of a value.
`float sinh(float $value)`	Return the hyperbolic sine of a value.
`float sqrt(float $value)`	Return the square root of a value.
`float tan(float $value)`	Return the tangent in radians of a value.
`float tanh(float $value)`	Return the hyperbolic tangent of a value.

MySQL Functions

Function	Description
`int mysql_affected_rows([resource $db])`	Return the number of records affected by the previous query.
`string mysql_client_encoding([resource $db])`	Return the character set used by the current database connection.
`bool mysql_close([resource $db])`	Close the active database connection.
`resource mysql_connect([string $host[, string $username[, string $password[, bool $new_link[, int $flags]]]]])`	Open a connection to the database server based on the named parameters. See also `mysql_pconnect()`.
`bool mysql_create_db(string $name[, resource $db])`	Create a new database schema.
`bool mysql_data_seek(resource $db, int $row_number)`	Move the internal pointer to a specific row in the result set.
`string mysql_db_name(resource $result, int $row[, mixed $field])`	Return the database name from the result set returned by `mysql_list_dbs()`.
`resource mysql_db_query(string $database, string $query[, resource $db])`	Return the result set after executing a query on the named database.
`int mysql_errno([resource $db])`	Return the error number generated by the previous query.
`string mysql_error([resource $db])`	Return the error message generated by the previous query.
`array mysql_fetch_array(resource $result[, int $type])`	Return a row of data from a result set as an associative array, numeric array, or both.
`array mysql_fetch_assoc(resource $result)`	Return an associative array of data from a result set.
`object mysql_fetch_field(resource $result[, int $field])`	Return column information from a result set as an object.
`array mysql_fetch_lengths(resource $result)`	Return an array with the lengths of each field in a result set.
`object mysql_fetch_object(resource $result[, string $class[, array $parameters]])`	Return a row of data from a result set as an object.

Function	Description
`array mysql_fetch_row(resource $result)`	Return a row of data from a result set as a numeric array.
`string mysql_field_flags(resource $result, int $field)`	Return the flag associated with a field in a result set.
`int mysql_field_len(resource $result, int $field)`	Return the length of a field in a result set.
`string mysql_field_name(resource $result, int $field)`	Return the name of a field in a result set.
`bool mysql_field_seek(resource $result, int $field)`	Move the internal pointer to a specific field offset.
`string mysql_field_table(resource $result, int $field)`	Return the name of the table in which a field is defined.
`string mysql_field_type(resource $result, int $field)`	Return the type of a field in a result set.
`bool mysql_free_result(resource $result)`	Free memory used by a result set from a previous query.
`string mysql_get_client_info(void)`	Return the MySQL client information.
`string mysql_get_host_info([resource $db])`	Return information about the server host.
`int mysql_get_proto_info[resource $db])`	Return the MySQL protocol.
`string mysql_get_server_info([resource $db])`	Return information about the server.
`string mysql_info([resource $db])`	Get information about the previous query.
`int mysql_insert_id([resource $db])`	Return the value of the most recently inserted `auto_increment` field.
`resource mysql_list_dbs([resource $db])`	Return a list of the databases available on the MySQL server.
`resource mysql_list_processes([resource $db])`	List the MySQL processes.
`int mysql_num_fields(resource $result)`	Return the number of fields in a row of the result set.

Function	Description
`int mysql_num_rows(resource $result)`	Return the number of rows in the result set.
`resource mysql_pconnect([string $host[, string $username[, string $password[, bool $new_link[, int $flags]]]]])`	Open a persistent connection to the database server based on the named parameters. See also `mysql_connect()`.
`bool mysql_ping([resource $db])`	Ping the server to verify the connection is working properly.
`resource mysql_query(string $query[, resource $db])`	Return a result set after executing a query.
`string mysql_real_escape_string(string $string[, resource $db])`	Return an escaped string to be used in a query.
`string mysql_result(resource $result, int $row[, mixed $field])`	Obtain the data located in the named field/row of the results.
`bool mysql_select_db(string $database[, resource $db])`	Select the active database.
`bool mysql_set_charset(string $charset[, resource $db])`	Set the default character set for the current database connection.
`string mysql_stat([resource $db])`	Return the MySQL server's status.
`int mysql_thread_id([resource $db])`	Return current connection thread ID.
`resource mysql_unbuffered_query(string $query[, resource $db])`	Return a result resource after executing a query. The result set is unbuffered.

Output Buffer Functions

Function	Description
`void flush(void)`	Flush the contents of the output buffer.
`void ob_clean(void)`	Discard the contents of the output buffer.
`bool ob_end_flush(void)`	Output the buffer's contents and disable output buffering.
`bool ob_end_clean(void)`	Flush the output buffer's contents and destroy output buffering.
`void ob_flush(void)`	Flush the contents of the output buffer. Does not destroy the buffer.
`string ob_get_clean(void)`	Return the contents of the output buffer and destroy the buffer.
`string ob_get_contents(void)`	Return the contents of the output buffer.
`int ob_get_length(void)`	Return the length of the content in the output buffer.
`int ob_get_level(void)`	Return the nesting level of the current output buffer.
`array ob_get_status([bool $full_status])`	Return the status of either the current output buffer or all active output buffers.
`string ob_gzhandler(string $buffer, int $mode)`	Callback function for `ob_start()` to compress the output buffer.
`void ob_implicit_flush([int $flag])`	Set implicit flushing of the buffer on and off.
`array ob_list_handlers(void)`	Return an array listing all output handlers being used.
`bool ob_start(string $function_name[, int $chunk_size[, bool $erase]])`	Enable output buffering.
`bool output_add_rewrite_var(string $variable, string $value)`	Add values to a URL. `output_add_rewrite_var()` will implicitly start output buffering, if it is not already active.
`bool output_reset_rewrite_vars(void)`	Reset a URL and remove any values added to it by `output_add_rewrite_var()`.

PHP Data Object (PDO) Database Interface

Function	Description
`PDO PDO::__construct(string $dsn[, string $username[, string $password [, array $driver_options]]])`	Create an instance of a `PDO` object representing a connection to a database.
`bool PDO::beginTransaction(void)`	Initiate a database transaction.
`bool PDO::commit(void)`	Commit a database transaction.
`string PDO::errorCode(void)`	Return the error code generated by the previous query.
`array PDO::errorInfo(void)`	Return an array of error information generated by the previous query.
`int PDO::exec(string $query)`	Return the number of affected rows after executing a database query.
`mixed PDO::getAttribute(int $attribute)`	Return the value of a database connection attribute.
`array PDO::getAvailableDrivers(void)`	Return an array of all currently available PDO drivers.
`string PDO::lastInsertId([string $name])`	Return the value of the most recently inserted `auto_increment` field or sequence ID.
`PDOStatement PDO:: prepare(string$query[, array $driver_ options])`	Return a `PDOStatement` object representing a database query prepared for execution.
`PDOStatement PDO::query(string $query)`	Return a `PDOStatement` object after executing a database query.
`string PDO::quote(string $string[, int $parameter_type])`	Return a string quoted for use in a database query.
`bool PDO::rollBack(void)`	Roll back a database transaction.
`bool PDO::setAttribute(int $attribute, mixed $value)`	Set the value of a PDO attribute.
`bool PDOStatement::bindColumn(mixed $column, mixed &$parameters[, int $type[, int $max_length[, mixed $driver_options]]])`	Bind a database column to a PHP variable.
`bool PDOStatement::bindParam(mixed $parameter, mixed &$variable[, int $data_type[, int $length[, mixed $driver_options]]])`	Bind a parameter to a PHP variable.

Function	Description
`bool PDOStatement::bindValue(mixed $parameter, mixed $value[, int $data_type])`	Bind a value to a PHP variable.
`bool PDOStatement::closeCursor(void)`	Close the result set's cursor to enable a query to be executed again.
`bool PDOStatement::columnCount(void)`	Return the number of columns in a result set.
`string PDOStatement::errorCode(void)`	Return the error code generated by the previous action on the result set.
`array PDOStatement::errorInfo(void)`	Return an array of error information generated by the previous action on the result set.
`bool PDOStatement::execute([array $parameters])`	Execute a prepared statement.
`mixed PDOStatement::fetch([int $mode [, int $cursor_orientation[, int $offset]]])`	Return the next row from a result set.
`array PDOStatement::fetchAll([int $mode [, int $index[, array $arguments]]])`	Return an array of all rows from a result set.
`string PDOStatement::fetchColumn([int $index])`	Return a single column from the next row of a result set.
`mixed PDOStatement::fetchObject([string $class_name[, array $arguments]])`	Return the next row from a result set as an object.
`mixed PDOStatement::getAttribute(int $attribute)`	Return the value of a statement attribute.
`array PDOStatement::getColumnMeta(int $column)`	Return an array of metadata information for a column in a result set.
`bool PDOStatement::nextRowset(void)`	Move the cursor to the next row in the result set.
`int PDOStatement::rowCount(void)`	Return the number of rows in a result set.
`bool PDOStatement::setAttribute(int $attribute , mixed $value)`	Set a statement attribute.
`bool PDOStatement::setFetchMode(int $mode)`	Set the statement's fetch mode.

PDO Fetch Mode Constants

Constant	Description
PDO::FETCH_ASSOC	Return the results as an associative array.
PDO::FETCH_BOTH	Return the results as an array indexed by both column name and numeric values. This is the default behavior, if no other mode is specified.
PDO::FETCH_BOUND	Assign the result's values back to the PHP variables to which they were bound.
PDO::FETCH_CLASS	Return a new instance of a class with the results mapped to the object's properties.
PDO::FETCH_CLASSTYPE	Can be combined with PDO::FETCH_CLASS, and the name of the class will be determined by the value of the first column in the result set.
PDO::FETCH_INTO	Update an existing object with values from the result set.
PDO::FETCH_LAZY	Combination of PDO::FETCH_BOTH and PDO::FETCH_OBJ.
PDO::FETCH_NUM	Return the results as a numerically indexed array.
PDO::FETCH_OBJ	Return an anonymous object with the results mapped to the object's properties.

PHP Configuration Information

Function	Description
bool assert(mixed $assertion)	Return whether an assertion is false. If $assertion is given a string, then it will be evaluated as PHP code.
mixed assert_options(int $option,[mixed $value])	Set or return an assert flag.
bool extension_loaded(string $extension_name)	Return whether an extension library is loaded.
string get_cfg_var(string $option)	Return the value of a configuration option.
string get_current_user(void)	Return the owner of the PHP script.

Function	Description
array get_defined_constants([mixed $categorize])	Return an array with the available defined constants and their values.
array get_extension_funcs(string $module)	Return an array of the function names made available by a module.
string get_include_path(void)	Return the current include path as specified by the include_path configuration option.
array get_included_files(void)	Return an array of filenames of included or required files.
bool get_loaded_extensions([bool $zend_extension])	Return an array of the compiled and loaded modules available.
array get_required_files(void)	Alias for get_included_files().
string getenv(string $variable)	Return the value of an environment variable.
int getlastmod(void)	Return when the current page was last modified.
int getmygid(void)	Return the group ID of the current script.
int getmyinode(void)	Return the inode of the current script.
int getmypid(void)	Return the process ID of the current PHP process.
int getmyuid(void)	Return the user ID of the owner of the current PHP script.
array getopt(string $options[, array $longopts])	Return an array of options and their arguments from the command-line argument list.
array getrusage([int $who])	Return the current resource usage.
string ini_alter(string $option, string $value)	Alias for ini_set().
array ini_get_all([string $extension[, bool $details]])	Return all php.ini configuration options.
string ini_get(string $option)	Return the current value of a php.ini option.
string ini_restore(string $option)	Restore the original value of a php.ini option.
string ini_set(string $option, string $value)	Set a php.ini option.

Function	Description
`int memory_get_peak_usage([bool $real_usage])`	Return the peak amount of memory allocated by PHP in bytes.
`int memory_get_usage(([bool $real_usage])`	Return the amount of memory allocated by PHP in bytes.
`string php_ini_loaded_file(void)`	Return a path to the active `php.ini` file.
`string php_ini_scanned_files(void)`	Return a list of ini files parsed from an additional directory.
`string php_logo_guid(void)`	Return an ID which can be used to display the PHP logo.
`string php_sapi_name(void)`	Return the type of interface between the web server and PHP.
`string php_uname([string $mode])`	Return information about the operating system on which PHP is running.
`bool phpcredits([int $section])`	Output the credits list for PHP.
`bool phpinfo([int $section])`	Output information about the current environment and PHP configuration.
`string phpversion([string $extension])`	Return the version string of PHP.
`bool putenv(string $setting)`	Set the value of an environment variable.
`void restore_include_path(void)`	Restore the `include_path` configuration option.
`string set_include_path(string $path)`	Set the `include_path` configuration option.
`void set_time_limit(int $seconds)`	Set the maximum amount of time a PHP script can run.
`string sys_get_temp_dir(void)`	Return the directory path used to store temporary files.
`mixed version_compare(string $version1, string $version2[, string $operator])`	Compare two PHP version numbers.
`string zend_logo_guid(void)`	Return an ID which can be used to display the Zend logo.
`string zend_version(void)`	Return the version of the Zend engine.

Process and Program Execution Functions

Function	Description
string escapeshellarg(string $arg)	Return an escaped string to be used as an argument in a shell command.
string escapeshelllcmd(string $command)	Return an escaped shell command.
string exec(string $command[, array &$output[, int $return_value]])	Execute a command and return the last line of its result.
void passthru(string $command[, int &$return_value])	Execute a command, and output the raw output directly to the browser.
int pclose(resource $handle)	Close a process file pointer.
resource popen(string $command, string $mode)	Open a process file pointer.
int proc_close(resource $process)	Close a process opened by proc_open().
array proc_get_status(resource $process)	Return information about a process opened by proc_open().
bool proc_nice(int $priority)	Change the priority of the current process.
resource proc_open(string $command, array $descriptor_spec, array &$pipes[, string $directory[, array $env[, array $options]]])	Execute a command, and open file pointers for input/output.
bool proc_terminate(resource $process[, int $signal])	Terminate a process opened by proc_open().
string shell_exec(string $command)	Execute a command through the shell, and return the complete output as a string.
string system(string $command[, int &$return_value])	Execute an external command, and display the output.

Session Functions

Function	Description
`int session_cache_expire([int $expire])`	Return or set the cache expiration time in minutes.
`string session_cache_limiter([string $cache_limiter])`	Return or set the cache limiter.
`void session_commit(void)`	Alias for `session_write_close()`.
`bool session_decode(string $data)`	Decode session data.
`bool session_destroy(void)`	Destroy session data.
`string session_encode(void)`	Return encoded session data as a string.
`array session_get_cookie_params(void)`	Return an array with the session cookie's configuration information.
`string session_id([string $id])`	Return or set the session ID.
`bool session_is_registered(string $variable)`	Return whether a variable has been registered in the current session.
`string session_module_name([string $module])`	Return or set the session module.
`string session_name([string $name])`	Return or set the session name.
`bool session_regenerate_id([bool $delete_old])`	Generate a new session ID for the current session, maintaining session variables and their contents.
`bool session_register(mixed $name[, mixed $...])`	Register variables with the current session.
`string session_save_path([string $path])`	Return or set the path where session data is saved.
`void session_set_cookie_params(int $lifetime[, string $path[, string $domain[, bool $secure[, bool $http_only]]]])`	Set the session cookie's configuration information.
`bool session_set_save_handler(string $open_function, string $close_function, string $read_function, string $write_function, string $destroy_function, string $gc_function)`	Set user-level callback functions to handle session storage, and override PHP's default session storage mechanism.

Function	Description
`bool session_start(void)`	Start a new session.
`bool session_unregister(string $name)`	Unregister session variables.
`void session_unset(void)`	Delete all session variables.
`void session_write_close(void)`	Save all session variables, and end the current session.

SimpleXML Functions

Function	Description
`SimpleXMLElement simplexml_import_dom(DOMNode $node[, string $class_name])`	Retrieve a `SimpleXMLElement` object from a DOM node.
`SimpleXMLElement simplexml_load_file(string $filename[, string $class_name[, int $options[, string $namespace[, bool $is_prefix]]]])`	Load an XML file into a `SimpleXMLElement` object.
`SimpleXMLElement simplexml_load_string(string $data[, string $class_name[, int $options [, string $namespace [,bool $is_prefix]]]])`	Load an XML string into a `SimpleXMLElement` object.
`SimpleXMLElement SimpleXMLElement::__construct(string $data [, int $options[, bool $is_url[, string $namespace[, bool $is_prefix]]]])`	Create a new instance of a `SimpleXMLElement` object.
`void SimpleXMLElement::addAttribute(string $name, string $value[, string $namespace])`	Add an attribute to an XML node.
`SimpleXMLElement SimpleXMLElement::addChild(string $name, string $value[, string $namespace])`	Add a child element to an XML node.
`mixed SimpleXMLElement::asXML([string $filename])`	Return an XML string representation of a `SimpleXML` element.
`SimpleXMLElement SimpleXMLElement::attributes([string $namespace[, bool $is_prefix]])`	Return the attributes of an element.

Function	Description
`SimpleXMLElement SimpleXMLElement::children([string $namespace[, bool $is_prefix]])`	Return the children of an element.
`array SimpleXMLElement::getDocNamespaces([bool $is_recursive])`	Return an array of namespaces declared in the XML document
`string SimpleXMLElement::getName(void)`	Return the name of an element.
`array SimpleXMLElement::getNamespaces([bool $is_recursive])`	Return an array of namespaces.
`bool SimpleXMLElement::registerXPathNamespace(string $prefix, string $namespace)`	Create a prefix/namespace context for an XPath query.
`array SimpleXMLElement::xpath(string $path)`	Return an array of `SimpleXMLElement` objects that match an XPath query.

String Functions

Function signatures marked with a * are not available when running on Windows.

Function	Description
`string addcslashes(string $string, string $character_list)`	Return a string with slashes added before named characters in a string.
`string addslashes(string $string)`	Return a string with slashes added to quote characters in a string.
`string bin2hex(string $string)`	Convert a string from binary to ASCII hexadecimal format.
`string chop(string $string[, string $character_list])`	Alias for `rtrim()`.
`string chr(int ascii)`	Return the character equivalent of a given ASCII code.
`string chunk_split(string $string[, int $length[, string $end]])`	Return a string with `$end` inserted every `$length` characters.
`string convert_cyr_string(string $string, string $from_set, $to_set)`	Convert a string from one Cyrillic character set to another.
`string convert_uudecode(string $string)`	Return a decoded string previously encoded by `convert_uuencode()`.

Function	Description
`string convert_uuencode(string $string)`	Return a string encoded using the uuencode algorithm.
`mixed count_chars(string $string[, int mode])`	Count the number of occurrences of each character in a string.
`int crc32(string $string)`	Return the cyclic redundancy checksum of a string.
`string crypt(string $string[, string $salt])`	Return a one-way encrypted string using a DES-based algorithm.
`void echo(string $string1[, string $...])`	Output a string.
`array explode(string $separator, string $string[, int $limit])`	Separate a string by a string. Opposite of `implode()`.
`int fprintf(resource $handle, string $format[, mixed $args[, mixed $...]])`	Output a formatted string.
`array get_html_translation_ table([int $table[, int $quote_ styles]])`	Return a translation table used by `htmlspecialchars()` and `htmlentities()`.
`string hebrev(string $string[, int $max_ per_line])`	Return a string of visual text converted from logical Hebrew text.
`string hebrevc(string $string [, int $max_ per_line]])`	Return a string of visual text with newlines converted from Hebrew text.
`string html_entity_decode(string $string[, int $quote style[, string $charset]])`	Return a string with HTML entities converted into their applicable characters. Opposite of `htmlentities()`.
`string htmlentities(string $[, int $quote_style[, string $charset[, bool $double_encode]]])`	Return a string with characters converted into HTML entities.
`string htmlspecialchars (string $[, int $quote_style[, string $charset[, bool $double_encode]]])`	Return a string with special characters converted into HTML entities.
`string htmlspecialchars_ decode(string $string[, int $quote_ style])`	Return a string with all HTML entities converted to characters.
`string implode(string $delimiter, array $pieces)`	Return a string of array elements joined by the specified delimiter. Opposite of `explode()`.

741

Appendix C: PHP6 Functions

Function	Description
string join(string $delimiter, array $pieces)	Alias for implode().
string lcfirst(string $string)	Return a string with the first character lowercased.
int levenshtein(string $string1, string string2[, int $insert_cost, int $replace_cost, int $delete_cost])	Return the Levenshtein distance between the two strings.
array localeconv(void)	Return an array of local monetary and numeric formatting information.
string ltrim(string $string[, string $character_list])	Return a string with leading spaces removed.
string md5_file(string $filename[, bool $raw_output])	Return the MD5 hash of a file.
string md5(string $string[, bool $raw_output])	Return the MD5 hash of a string.
string metaphone(string $string[, int $phones])	Return the metaphone key of a string.
string money_format(string $format, float $number) *	Return a string representing a number formatted as currency.
string nl_langinfo(int $item)	Return specific information about the local language and numeric/monetary formatting.
string nl2br(string $string[, bool $is_xhtml])	Return a string with all line breaks replaced with .
string number_format(float $number[, int $decimal_places[, string $decimal_point, string thousands_sep]])	Return a string representing a formatted number.
int ord(string $character)	Return the ASCII code of a character. Opposite of chr().
string pack(string $format[, mixed $arg1[, mixed $...]])	Return a binary string of packed data.
void parse_str(string $string[, array &$array])	Parse a string into variables.
array preg_grep(string $pattern, array $input[, int $flags])	Return an array with elements that match a regular expression pattern.

Function	Description
`int preg_error(void)`	Return the error code from the last regular expression.
`int preg_match(string $pattern, string $string, [array &$matches[, int $flags[, int $offset]]])`	Perform a regular expression match.
`int preg_match_all(string $pattern, string $string, array &$matches, int $flags[, int $offset]]])`	Perform a global regular expression match.
`string preg_quote(string $string[, string $delimiter])`	Return a string with escaped regular expression metacharacters.
`mixed preg_replace(mixed $pattern, mixed $replacement, mixed $subject[, int $limit[, int &$count]])`	Perform a regular expression search and replace.
`mixed preg_replace_callback(mixed $pattern, string $function_name, mixed $subject, [, int $limit[, int &$count]])`	Perform a regular expression search and replace, using a callback function to perform the replacement.
`array preg_split(string $pattern, string $subject[, int $limit[, int $flags]])`	Split a string by a regular expression.
`int print(string $string)`	Output a string. Always returns 1.
`int printf(string $format[, mixed $arg1[, mixed $...]])`	Output a formatted string.
`string quoted_printable_decode(string $string)`	Return an 8-bit string converted from a quoted-printable string.
`string quoted_printable_encode(string $string)`	Return a quoted-printable string converted from an 8-bit string.
`string quotemeta(string $string)`	Return a string with metacharacters escaped.
`string rtrim(string $string[, string $character_list])`	Return a string with trailing spaces removed.
`string setlocale(int $category, string $locale[, string $...])` or `string setlocale(int $category, array $locale)`	Set the locale information for a category of functions.

Function	Description
`string sha1_file(string $filename[, bool $raw_output])`	Return the sha1 hash of a file.
`string sha1(string $string[, bool $raw_output])`	Return the sha1 hash of a string.
`int similar_text(string $string1, string $string2[, float &$percent])`	Return the similarity between two strings.
`string soundex(string $string)`	Return the soundex key of a string.
`string sprintf(string $format[, mixed $args[, mixed $...]])`	Return a formatted string.
`string sscanf(string $string, string $format[, mixed &$var1[, mixed &$...]])`	Parse input from a formatted string.
`array str_getcsv(string $input[, string $delimiter[, string $quote[, string $escape]]])`	Parse a string as a CSV record, and return it as an array.
`string str_ireplace(mixed $search, mixed $replace, mixed $subject[, int &$count])`	Case-insensitive version of `str_replace()`.
`string str_pad(string $string, int $pad_length[, string $pad_string[, int $pad_type]]`	Return a string padded to the desired length, using another string.
`string str_repeat(string $string, int $multiplier)`	Return a string built by repeating another string the desired number of times.
`mixed str_replace(mixed $search, mixed $replace, mixed $subject[, int $count])`	Return a string with one expression replaced by another and, optionally, the number of changes made.
`string str_rot13(string $string)`	Return a ROT13 encoded string.
`string str_shuffle(string $string)`	Return a randomly shuffled string.
`array str_split(string $string[, int $split_length])`	Return an array from a string with each element part of the string.
`mixed str_word_count(string $string[, int $format[, string $character_list]])`	Return information about words in a string.
`int strcasecmp(string $string1, string $string2)`	Perform a case-insensitive comparison between two strings.

Function	Description
`string strchr(string $haystack[, mixed $search[, bool $before_search])`	Alias for `strstr()`.
`int strcmp(string $string1, string $string2)`	Similar to `strcasecmp()`, except that comparison is case-sensitive.
`int strcoll(string $string1, string $tring2)`	Compare two strings based on the locale.
`int strcspn(string $string1, string $string2[, int $start[, int $length])`	Return the number of characters at the beginning of `$string1` that do not match `$string2`. Opposite of `strspn()`.
`string strip_tags(string $string[, string $allowed_tags])`	Return a string with HTML and PHP tags removed.
`string stripcslashes(string $string)`	Return a string with slashes removed.
`int stripos(string $haystack[, string $search[, int $offset]])`	Similar to `strpos()` except is case-insensitive.
`string stripslashes(string $string)`	Return a string with escaped slashes removed.
`string stristr(string $haystack, mixed $search[, bool $before_search])`	Similar to `strstr()` except is case-insensitive.
`int strlen(string $string)`	Return the length of a string.
`int strnatcasecmp(string $string1, string $string2)`	Similar to `strnatcmp()` except is case-insensitive.
`int strnatcmp(string $string1, string $string2)`	Compare two strings using a "natural order" algorithm.
`int strncasecmp(string $string1, string $string2, int $length)`	Similar to `strncmp()` except is case-insensitive.
`int strncmp(string $string1, string $string2, int $length)`	Compare the first number of characters of two strings.
`string strpbrk(string $string, string $character_list)`	Return a portion of a string starting from the characters found in `$character_list`.
`int strpos(string $hastack, string $search[, int $offset])`	Return the position of the first occurrence of a string within another string.
`string strrchr(string $haystack, mixed $search)`	Return the position of the last occurrence of a string within another string.
`string strrev(string $string)`	Return a reversed string.

Function	Description
`int strripos(string $haystack, string $search[, int $offset])`	Similar to `strpos()` except is case-insensitive.
`int strrpos(string $haystack, string $search[, int $offset])`	Return the position of the last occurrence of a string within another string.
`int strspn(string $string1, string $string2[, int $start[, int $length]])`	Return the number of characters at the beginning of a string that match another string2. The opposite of `strcspn()`.
`string strstr(string $haystack, string $search [, bool $before_search])`	Find the first occurrence of a string within another string.
`string strtok(string $string, string $delimiter)`	Split a string into tokens.
`string strtolower(string $string)`	Return a lowercased string.
`string strtoupper(string $string)`	Return an uppercased string.
`string strtr(string $string, string $from, string $to)` or `string strtr(string $string, array $replace_pairs)`	Return a string with translated characters.
`int substr(string $string1, int $start [, int $length])`	Return a portion of a string.
`int substr_compare(string $string1, string $string2, int $offset[, int $length[, bool $case_insensitive]])`	Compare two strings from a given offset, with the option of case-insensitivity.
`int substr_count(string $haystack, string $string[, int $offset[, int $length]])`	Return the number of occurrences of a string appearing within another string.
`mixed substr_replace(mixed $string, string $replacement, int $start[, int $length])`	Replace text within a string.
`string trim(string $string[, string $character_list])`	Return a string with extra space removed from its beginning and end.
`string ucfirst(string $string)`	Return a string with the first character uppercased.

Function	Description
`string ucwords(string $string)`	Return a string with the first character of each word uppercased.
`array unpack(string $format, string $data)`	Return an array of unpacked binary data. Opposite of `pack()`.
`int vfprintf(resource $handle, string $format, array $arguments)`	Write a formatted string to a stream.
`int vprintf(string $format, array $arguments)`	Output a formatted string.
`string vsprintf(string $format, array $arguments)`	Return a formatted string.
`string wordwrap(string $string[, int $width[, string $break[, bool $cut]]])`	Return a string wrapped at the specified column.

String-Formatting Codes

The following codes can be used in conjunction with `*printf()` *and* `*scanf()` *functions.*

Format Character	Description
%	A literal percent sign character.
b	Format a value as a binary number.
c	Format a value as a character.
d	Format a value as a signed integer.
e	Format a value as a number in scientific notation.
F	Format a value as a non–locale aware floating-point number.
f	Format a value as a locale-aware floating-point number.
o	Format a value as an octal number.
s	Format a value as a string.
u	Format a value as an unsigned integer.
X	Format a value as an uppercase hexidecimal number.
x	Format a value as a lowercase hexadecimal number.

URL Functions

Function	Description
`string base64_decode(string $data)`	Return a decoded MIME base64 encoded string. Opposite of `base64_encode()`.
`string base64_encode(string $data)`	Return a MIME base64 encoded string.
`array get_headers(string $url[, int $format])`	Return an array of all headers sent by the server in response to an HTTP request.
`array get_meta_tags(string $filename[, bool $use_include_path)`	Return an array of all meta-tag information extracted from a file.
`string http_build_query(array $data[, string $prefix[, string $separator]])`	Return a URL-encoded query string.
`mixed parse_url(string $url[, int $component])`	Return the components of a parsed URL.
`string rawurldecode(string $url)`	Return a decoded URL-encoded string. Opposite of `rawurlencode()`.
`string rawurlencode(string $url)`	Return a URL-encoded string according to RFC-1738.
`string urldecode(string $url)`	Return a decoded URL-encoded string. Opposite of `rawurlencode()`.
`string urlencode(string $url)`	Return a URL-encoded string.

Variable Functions

Function	Description
float doubleval(mixed $var)	Alias for floatval().
bool empty(mixed $var)	Verifies whether a variable is empty or has a value that evaluates to zero (empty string, null, false, etc.).
float floatval(mixed $var)	Return the value of a variable as a float.
array get_defined_vars(void)	Return a list of all the defined variables in a script as an array.
string get_resource_type(resource $handle)	Return the resource type of a handle.
string gettype(mixed $var)	Return the type of the variable's value.
int intval(mixed $var[, int $base])	Return the value of a variable as an integer.
bool is_array(mixed $var)	Verify whether the value of a variable is an array.
bool is_binary(mixed $var)	Verify whether the value of a variable is a native binary string.
bool is_bool(mixed $var)	Verify whether the value of a variable is Boolean.
bool is_buffer(mixed $var)	Verify whether the value of a variable is a native Unicode or binary string.
bool is_callable(mixed $var[, bool $syntax_only[, string &$callable_name]])	Verify whether the value of a variable is callable as a function.
bool is_double(mixed $var)	Alias for is_float().
bool is_float(mixed $var)	Verify whether the value of a variable is a float.
bool is_int(mixed $var)	Verify whether the value of a variable is an integer.
bool is_integer(mixed $var)	Alias for is_int().
bool is_long(mixed $var)	Alias for is_int().
bool is_null(mixed $var)	Verify whether the value of a variable is null.
bool is_numeric(mixed $var)	Verify whether the value of a variable is a number or a numeric string.
bool is_object(mixed $var)	Verify whether the value of a variable is an object.

Function	Description
`bool is_real(mixed $var)`	Alias for `is_float()`.
`bool is_resource(mixed $var)`	Verify whether the value of a variable is a resource.
`bool is_scalar(mixed $var)`	Verify whether the value of a variable is a scalar (integer, float, string, or Boolean).
`bool is_string(mixed $var)`	Verify whether the value of a variable is a string.
`bool is_unicode(mixed $var)`	Verify whether the value of a variable is a Unicode string.
`bool isset(mixed $var[, mixed $var[, $...]])`	Verify whether a variable has been assigned a value.
`mixed print_r(mixed $expression[, bool $return])`	Output human-readable information about a variable.
`string serialize(mixed $value)`	Return a representation of a variable suitable for storage without losing its type and structure.
`bool settype(mixed &$var, string $type)`	Set the type of a variable.
`string strval(mixed $var)`	Return the string value of a variable.
`mixed unserialize(string $str)`	Return a PHP value from a serialized version.
`void unset(mixed $var[, mixed $var[, mixed $var]])`	Delete a variable.
`void var_dump(mixed $expression[, mixed $expression[, $...]])`	Output information about an expression.
`mixed var_export(mixed $expression[, bool $return])`	Output or return a parsable string representation of a variable.

Miscellaneous Functions

*Function signatures marked with a * are not available when running on Windows.*

Function	Description
`void __halt_compiler(void)`	Halt the execution of the PHP compiler.
`int connection_aborted(void)`	Return whether the client connection has been aborted.
`int connection_status(void)`	Return the connection status.
`mixed constant(string $name)`	Return the value of a constant.
`bool define(string $name, mixed $value[, bool $case_insensitive])`	Define a constant.
`bool defined(string $name)`	Return whether a constant exists.
`void die([mixed $status])`	Alias for `exit()`.
`mixed eval(string $string)`	Evaluate a string as PHP code.
`void exit([mixed $status])`	Terminate execution of the script.
`mixed get_browser([string $user_agent[, bool $return_array])`	Return an object with information about a browser. Information will be returned as an array if `$return_array` is true. Relies on `browscap.ini`.
`mixed highlight_file(string $filename[, bool $return])`	Output the syntax-highlighted source PHP file. The source will be returned as a string instead if `$return` is true.
`mixed highlight_string(string $string[, bool $return])`	Output a syntax-highlighted string of PHP code. The string will be returned instead if `$return` is true.
`int ignore_user_abort([bool $value])`	Set whether a script should continue executing after the user aborts the connection.
`string php_strip_whitespace(string $filename)`	Return the source code of a file with comments and whitespace removed.
`mixed show_source(string $filename)`	Alias for `highlight_file()`.
`int sleep(int $seconds)`	Pause execution of the script for a specified number of seconds.

Function	Description
array sys_getloadavg(void) *	Return an array with the system's load averages over the last 1, 5, and 15 minutes.
mixed time_nanosleep(int $seconds, int $nanoseconds) *	Pause execution of the script for a specified number of seconds and nanoseconds.
bool time_sleep_until(float $timestamp) *	Pause execution of the script until a specified time.
string uniqid($prefix[, bool $entropy])	Return a unique ID based on the current time and named prefix.
void usleep(int $microseconds)	Pause execution of the script for a specified number of microseconds.

MySQL Data Types

This appendix contains a listing of data types that are available in MySQL. Visit `http://dev.mysql.com/doc/refman/5.1/en/data-type-overview.html` for a complete discussion on each data type.

Numeric Data Types

MySQL Field Type	Description
`BIGINT[(m)] [UNSIGNED]`	Numeric field that stores integers from −9,223,372,036,854,775,808 to 9,223,372,036,854,775,807. m represents the maximum display width. Adding the `UNSIGNED` parameter allows storage of 0 to 18,446,744,073,709,551,615.
`BIT[(m)]`	Bit-type field. m represents the optional number of bits per value.
`BOOL, BOOLEAN`	Synonym for `TINYINT(1)`. A value of 0 represents false, and nonzero values represent true.
`DEC`	Synonym for `DECIMAL`.
`DECIMAL[(m[,d])] [UNSIGNED]`	A fixed-point numeric field that can store decimals. m represents the total number of displayed digits. d represents how many digits follow the decimal point. `UNSIGNED` allows only positive numbers to be stored.

MySQL Field Type	Description
DOUBLE[(m,d)] [UNSIGNED]	A double-precision floating-point number that stores values from $-1.7976931348623157E+308$ to $-2.2250738585072014E-308$, 0, and $2.2250738585072014E-308$ to $1.7976931348623157E+308$. m represents the total number of displayed digits. d represents how many digits follow the decimal point. UNSIGNED allows only positive numbers to be stored.
DOUBLE PRECISION[(m,d)] [UNSIGNED]	Synonym for DOUBLE.
FIXED	Synonym for DECIMAL.
FLOAT[(m,d)] [UNSIGNED]	A single-precision floating-point number that stores values from $-3.402823466E+38$ to $-1.175494351E-38$, 0, and $1.175494351E-38$ to $3.402823466E+38$. m represents the total number of displayed digits. d represents how many digits follow the decimal point. UNSIGNED allows only positive numbers to be stored.
INT[(m)] [UNSIGNED]	Numeric field that stores integers from $-2,147,483,648$ to $2,147,483,647$. m represents the maximum display width. Adding the UNSIGNED parameter allows storage of 0 to 4,294,967,295.
INTEGER[(m)] [UNSIGNED]	Synonym for INT.
MEDIUMINT[(m)] [UNSIGNED]	Numeric field that stores integers from $-8,388,608$ to 8,388,607. m represents the maximum display width. Adding the UNSIGNED parameter allows storage of 0 to 16,777,215.
NUMERIC	Synonym for DECIMAL.
SMALLINT[(m)] [UNSIGNED]	Numeric field that stores integers from $-32,768$ to 32,767. m represents the maximum display width. Adding the UNSIGNED parameter allows storage of 0 to 65,535.
REAL[(m,d)] [UNSIGNED]	Synonym for DOUBLE. (Note: If REAL_AS_FLOAT mode is enabled, then REAL is a synonym for FLOAT.)
TINYINT[(m)] [UNSIGNED]	Numeric field that stores integers from -128 to 127. m represents the maximum display width. Adding the UNSIGNED parameter allows storage of 0 to 255.

Date and Time Data Types

MySQL Field Type	Description
DATE	Stores a date as YYYY-MM-DD from 1000-01-01 to 9999-12-31.
DATETIME	Stores both a date and time as YYYY-MM-DD HH:MM:SS from 1000-01-01 00:00:00 to 9999-12-31 23:59:59.
TIMESTAMP	Stores a UNIX Epoch timestamp as YYYY-MM-DD HH:MM:SS from 1970-01-01 00:00:01 to 2038-01-09 03:14:07.
TIME	Stores a time as HH:MM:SS from −838:59:59 to 838:59:59.
YEAR[(2|4)]	Stores a year as either YY or YYYY, depending on whether two- or four-digit format is specified (default is four-digit). The range is from 1901 to 2155 in four-digit format, and from 70 to 69, representing years from 1970 to 2069, in two-digit format.

String Data Types

MySQL Field Type	Description
BINARY[(m)]	Stores fixed-length binary byte strings. m represents the length in bits.
BLOB[(m)]	Stores binary byte strings. m represents the length in bytes from 0 to 65,535.
[NATIONAL] CHAR[(m)]	Synonym for CHARACTER.
CHAR BYTE[(m)]	Synonym for BINARY.
[NATIONAL] CHARACTER[(m)]	Stores a fixed-length character string that is right-padded with spaces. m represents the length in characters from 0 to 255.
[NATIONAL] CHARACTER VARYING[(m)]	Stores a variable-length character string. m represents the length in characters from 0 to 65,535.
ENUM('value1', 'value2', ...)	Stores a string value. Allows only specified values to be stored in the field (up to a maximum of 65,535 different values).
LONGBLOB	Stores binary byte strings. m represents the length in bytes from 0 to 4,294,967,295 (4GB).

MySQL Field Type	Description
LONGTEXT	Stores a variable-length character string. m represents the length in characters from 0 to 4,294,967,295 (4GB).
MEDIUMBLOB	Stores binary byte strings. m represents the length in bytes from 0 to 16,777,215.
MEDIUMTEXT	Stores a variable-length character string. m represents the length in characters from 0 to 16,777,215.
NCHAR[(m)]	Synonym for NATIONAL CHARACTER.
NVCHAR[(m)]	Synonym for NATIONAL CHARACTER VARYING.
SET('value1', 'value2', ...)	Stores a set of string values from the specified list values (up to a maximum of 64 members).
TEXT[(m)]	Stores a variable-length character string. m represents the length in characters from 0 to 65,535.
TINYBLOB	Stores binary byte strings. m represents the length in bytes from 0 to 255.
TINYTEXT	Stores a variable-length character string. m represents the length in characters from 0 to 255.
VARBINARY[(m)]	Stores variable-length binary byte strings. m represents the length in bits.
[NATIONAL] VARCHAR[(m)]	Synonym for CHARACTER VARYING.

Spatial Data Formats

Spatial data is beyond the scope of this book. See http://dev.mysql.com/doc/refman/5.1/en/supported-spatial-data-formats.html for more information on the standard spatial formats used by MySQL.

MySQL Quick Reference

This appendix lists some quick reference notes for your use. These topics are covered in more depth in Chapter 3 and on the MySQL web site at www.mysql.com.

Database Manipulation Commands

Use the following commands to create and make changes to your database and tables.

Command	What It Does
`CREATE DATABASE [IF NOT EXISTS] db_name`	Creates a database
`CREATE TABLE [IF NOT EXISTS] tbl_ name (col1 col_type, col2 col_ type, ...)`	Creates a table
`ALTER TABLE tbl_name ADD col col_ type [AFTER col], ...`	Adds a new column to a table in the database
`ALTER TABLE tbl_name MODIFY col new_col_type, ...`	Changes columns' type definitions
`ALTER TABLE tbl_name CHANGE old_ col new_col new_col_type, ...`	Changes columns' names and type definitions
`ALTER TABLE tbl_name DROP col, ...`	Removes columns from a table in the database
`RENAME TABLE old_tbl_name TO new_ tbl_name`	Renames a table in the database

Command	What It Does
INSERT [IGNORE] INTO tbl_name [(col1, col2,...)] VALUES (value1, value2, ...)	Inserts a row into a table
UPDATE [IGNORE] tbl_name SET col1=value1, col2=value2, ... WHERE condition [ORDER BY ...] [LIMIT count]	Modifies information already stored in the table
DELETE [IGNORE] FROM tbl_name WHERE condition [ORDER BY ...] [LIMIT count]	Deletes information from the table
TRUNCATE TABLE tbl_name	Deletes all information from the table
DROP TABLE [IF EXISTS] tbl_name	Deletes a table from the database
DROP DATABASE [IF EXISTS] db_name	Deletes a database

Retrieving Data from the Database

You can access the data stored in your tables with the following statement:

```
SELECT col1[, col2, . . .] FROM tbl_name [WHERE condition] [ORDER BY col
[ASC|DESC]] [LIMIT offset, num_rows]
```

You can use * to retrieve all columns in a table:

```
SELECT * FROM tbl_name
```

Condition Clauses

Use the following conditions in conjunction with the SELECT statement:

```
col = value
col > value
col < value
col >= value
col <= value
col != value    - not equal to
col <> value
col BETWEEN value1 AND value2
col NOT BETWEEN value1 AND value2
col LIKE value
col NOT LIKE value
col IS NULL
col IS NOT NULL
col IN (value1, value2, value3, . . .)
col NOT IN (value1, value2, value3, . . .)
```

MySQL supports wildcard matching. Use to match a single character. Use % to match zero or more characters.

Selecting from Multiple Tables

You can retrieve information from two or more tables at once by using JOINs. MySQL supports the following syntax variations:

```
SELECT
    table1.col1, table1.col2, table2.col1, table2.col2
FROM
    table1, table2
WHERE
    table1.col1 = table2.col1
```

or

```
SELECT
    table1.col1, table1.col2, table2.col1, table2.col2
FROM
    table1 JOIN table2 ON table1.col1 = table2.col1
```

Sorting the Results

You can sort the results of the SELECT query by using the ORDER BY clause (and the optional ascending or descending qualifier):

```
SELECT * FROM table WHERE col1 = value1 ORDER BY col2 [ASC|DESC]
```

Limiting the Results

If you would like to limit the results returned from your query, you can do so with a LIMIT clause:

```
SELECT * FROM table WHERE col1 = value1 LIMIT [offset,] row_count
```

Comparison of Text Editors

Many software programs are available that you can use to enter all your code. They each have different features, some that you might view as better than others, depending on your needs and personal preferences. We've put together the following chart to help you compare apples with apples. It lists some of the more popular editors alphabetically and compares them against some common text editor features.

Many of these editors provide similar features, so your decision really depends on your budget, your needs, and how comfortable you are with each user interface.

You can read more about features not listed here, because many of these editors provide other unique benefits. We encourage you to visit the following web sites to download these programs and/or to get more information about them:

- ❏ **Dreamweaver CS3:** www.adobe.com/products/dreamweaver/
- ❏ **EditPlus:** www.editplus.com
- ❏ **Geany:** www.geany.org
- ❏ **HTML-Kit:** www.chami.com/html-kit/
- ❏ **jEdit:** www.jedit.org
- ❏ **Notepad:** www.microsoft.com
- ❏ **PhpED:** www.nusphere.com
- ❏ **PHPEdit:** www.waterproof.fr
- ❏ **TextPad:** www.textpad.com
- ❏ **UltraEdit-32:** www.ultraedit.com
- ❏ **WordPad:** www.microsoft.com
- ❏ **Zend Studio:** www.zend.com

Appendix F: Comparison of Text Editors

Editor	Highlighted Syntax	Spell Checker	Built-in FTP Access	Line Numbers	Word Wrap	PHP Code Auto-Completion	WYSIWYG Web Design Editor
Dreamweaver CS3	✓	✓	✓	✓	✓	✓	✓
EditPlus	✓	✓	✓	✓	✓		
Geany	✓			✓	✓	✓	
HTML-Kit Tools	✓	✓	✓	✓	✓	✓	✓
jEdit	✓		✓	✓	✓	✓	
Notepad					✓		
PhpED	✓	✓	✓	✓	✓	✓	
PHPEdit	✓		✓	✓	✓	✓	
TextPad		✓		✓	✓		
UltraEdit-32	✓	✓	✓	✓	✓	✓	
WordPad					✓		
Zend Studio	✓		✓	✓	✓	✓	

Database Connectivity	Content Preview	Multiple Undo/Redo	Search and Replace	Code Folding	PHP Debugging	CVS/ Subversion Integration	Price
✓	✓	✓	✓	✓		✓	$399
	✓	✓	✓	✓			$30
		✓	✓	✓			Free
	✓	✓	✓	✓			$65
			✓	✓			Free
			✓				Free
✓	✓	✓	✓	✓	✓	✓	$299
✓			✓		✓	✓	$90
		✓	✓				$33
✓	✓	✓	✓	✓			$49.95
			✓				Free
✓	✓	✓	✓	✓	✓	✓	$349

Choosing a Third-Party Host

Many people like to run their own servers out of their homes or offices, and that is a feasible solution for hosting, if you have the time and network resources. But sometimes hosting your own web site can lead to more problems than it's worth. You need to think about backup power, keeping security holes patched, performing regular maintenance and upgrades, and many other issues. And keep in mind that not only do you need to have a web server running, but you also need to have something to manage your domain records as well, a Domain Name System (DNS) server.

With third-party hosting solutions, you can have trained IT professionals who make sure your web server stays up and running 24 hours a day, at an affordable price. It's their job to make sure your site is secure and always available for viewing.

Hosting Options

If you decide to have a third party host your site, you have many options to choose from when making your hosting choice. Here are a few criteria to look at when you select a host:

- ❑ **Supported languages:** PHP, JAVA, CGI, ASP
- ❑ **Supported databases:** MySQL, PostgreSQL, MS SQL
- ❑ **Server control:** super user (su) or root access
- ❑ **Server access:** Such as FTP and SSH
- ❑ **Configuration ability:** Web server settings/configurations, cron jobs, `.htaccess` support
- ❑ **Administration GUIs:** E-mail, database, user setup
- ❑ **Bandwidth usage:** Web site, e-mail, streaming media, database connections
- ❑ **Price:** Based on features, contract time, and other criteria

Keep in mind that you aren't likely to have every combination and possibility with every host, so it's important that you research your prospective hosts to make a well-thought-out decision before jumping into a long-term contract. To that end, let's get into a little more detail about each of these topics.

Supported Languages

Obviously, we're assuming you want to use PHP (you did buy this book, after all), but there are other languages you may need to use. There may be a time when another language, such as Perl, Python, or even Java, is better suited for your needs than PHP. For example, perhaps you have to accomplish something a client already has set up at a different host or server, using a different programming language. It is nice to at least have the option of using the existing code, rather than spending the time and money to redevelop the application in PHP.

Supported Databases

Again, because this book is geared toward MySQL, we assume you will probably be looking for a host that supports MySQL. However, you can use many other databases with PHP. Here are just some of the databases that PHP can work with:

- MySQL
- PostgreSQL
- MS SQL Server
- MS Access
- Firebird
- Sybase

PHP even comes with the embedded database SQLite enabled. Depending on your situation, you may want to choose a host that has more than one of these databases set up by default. Some larger companies, for example, are using MS SQL as their database, usually because they are using ASP.NET for programming. Should you need to convert any site to PHP, you will be glad to know that PHP can connect and work nicely with MS SQL as well.

Server Control and Access

Many hosts won't give a web developer full access or control over their hosted domain. We tend to shy away from those hosts, because you are more likely to run into problems with them when you want to do some custom configuration to the server.

Look into the type of access your host provides. Obviously, your host will give you FTP access so you can upload your files to the web server. Some hosts, however, will give you FTP access but nothing else. The problem is that you are likely to run into a situation in which you want to configure your server. For this, you will need SSH (Secure Shell) access to use the command line.

In fact, the ability to configure is often necessary when performing tasks that usually aren't offered by hosts by default. For example, consider .htaccess files. With .htaccess files, you can deny and allow access to certain files and directories, based on the users you allow using htpasswd. (See Chapter 12 for more information on .htaccess and htpasswd.)

Along with .htaccess, most hosts allow you to use cron jobs, but are not likely to set them up for you. Therefore, you need to remote into the server and edit the crontab file to enable you to run scheduled tasks. There are countless configuration settings that you might want to change, if your host allows you to configure them. Keep all this in mind when choosing your hosting solution.

Administration GUIs

Certain hosts offer a dministration graphical user interfaces, (GUIs) or user control panels, as a feature of their packages. A lot of people don't really care for GUIs, but when you don't have a choice — either because you don't have sufficient access to the server or you don't fully understand how to get things done at a command prompt — a point-and-click solution can be a wonderful tool.

The interface can be as simple as one that allows you to view information about the server, or it can be as complex as one that allows you to install applications and programming languages with the click of a button. Also, keep in mind that many control panels have utilities that allow clients to administer their own e-mail users. With such a feature, the client can simply log on to the control panel and set up and delete users as the need arises, rather than having to call you or the hosting company to set up an e-mail account.

Bandwidth and Site Usage

Bandwidth and site usage both can factor into the overall price of hosting. Hosting companies usually give out only so much bandwidth usage per site per month. There is usually a hefty charge if you go over that amount. Consider the following issues when looking into bandwidth:

- Web site traffic
- E-mail usage and storage
- Database connections
- Streaming media

If you have heavy activity in any or all of these areas, you might get billed for bandwidth overutilization before you know it. You need to consider how many people will visit your site on average. In addition, some hosts count e-mail usage in the end-of-the-month calculation used to tally your bill. Some hosts will even go so far as to monitor your FTP access and count that toward the total bandwidth used.

Database connections don't really relate to bandwidth usage, but hosts often limit the number of database connections you can make, as another way to control the number of people allowed to visit the site at one time.

Finally, streaming media is very heavy on bandwidth; should you plan to use it as a form of conveying information to the end users of your site, then your hosting bill could rise dramatically.

Pricing

You need to consider all the areas discussed so far when figuring out how much your host is worth to you. Look at the price per feature rather than the total price. You won't often get all the features you want for your site, but as long as you get most of them and you choose the host that has the lowest price per feature, then you will probably make a wise hosting choice.

Ask yourself how much a particular feature is worth to you, when using price to make your choice. Remember that some hosting companies require that you sign up for a full year and won't offer a refund if you decide the service isn't worth the money you are paying. You want to find a host that will allow you to choose either monthly, quarterly, or yearly hosting options. That way you don't have to wait a full year to leave if you're dissatisfied. Just keep in mind that when you choose a shorter option, such as monthly or quarterly, the host will often charge a little more than if you pay up front, or they may charge service setup fees that might be waived if you paid up front.

Making the Choice

When making your hosting decision, it's very important to consider the criteria outlined in this appendix. You really don't want to get stuck in a situation in which you are unhappy with the service you are receiving, or, worse yet, in which your paying client is disappointed with services you recommended.

The following is a list of 12 hosting options that we feel offer the best bang for your buck. You may want to consider them when making your decision:

- ❑ www.olm.net
- ❑ www.lunarpages.com
- ❑ www.jumpline.com
- ❑ www.startlogic.com
- ❑ www.ipowerweb.com
- ❑ www.midphase.com
- ❑ www.infinology.com
- ❑ www.powweb.com
- ❑ www.invision.net
- ❑ www.ait.com
- ❑ www.1and1.com
- ❑ www.websitesource.com

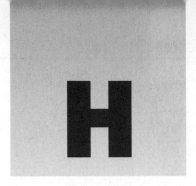

An Introduction to PHP Data Objects

PHP is a terrific programming language. It is relatively easy to learn, especially if you are already familiar with other programming languages. You can build some excellent interactive web pages that access databases, authenticate users, and provide dynamic, up-to-date content for your visitors in no time at all.

So, let's say you just finished creating your company's web site. It's perfect — users are being served up-to-the-minute content, and you have set up a complex content management system (CMS) that enables designated employees in the company to create new content. It's efficient, it's pretty, and you feel pretty darned good about it.

As you sit here thumbing through these final pages of the book and wondering what final nuggets of useful information we can share with you, we present you with a scenario: You have just finished a tough assignment assigned to you by your IT manager. She congratulates you on a job well done and engages you in general chit-chat — you know, the usual. As she gets up to leave, she stops in the doorway and casually mentions something that is about to completely overload your work schedule. . .

"Oh, by the way, the accounting department is switching to an Ingres database to support their accounting software. It's pretty slick. And since we'll be using Ingres in accounting, we've decided all of our databases should be standardized on Ingres throughout the rest of the company, for conformance. That's not going to be a problem, is it?"

Every developer has had something like this happen at one point or another, so you are not alone. One of the wonderful things about PHP is that it supports a very wide variety of different databases:

❑   dBase

❑   DB++

❑   FrontBase

- ❏ filePro
- ❏ Firebird/InterBase
- ❏ Informix
- ❏ IBM DB2 (IBM DB2, Cloudscape, and Apache Derby)
- ❏ Ingres Database (Ingres II)
- ❏ MaxDB
- ❏ mSQL
- ❏ Microsoft SQL Server
- ❏ MySQL
- ❏ Oracle OCI8
- ❏ Ovrimos SQL
- ❏ Paradox File Access
- ❏ PostgreSQL
- ❏ SQLite
- ❏ Sybase

That's quite an impressive list, isn't it? And there's a pretty good chance that if a new database were to come around, then someone would write functions that would enable PHP to work with it. Database integration has always been one of PHP's strong points.

However, the first point of contention here is that each database extension offers a different set of functions. `mysql_query()` is used to execute a database query against MySQL, but it cannot execute a query against Ingres II. When you change your back-end database solution, you must also update your code to use the appropriate functions.

The second point of contention is that most, but not all, of the extensions for the databases listed earlier follow the same general naming conventions for their functions. You would use the `ingres_query()` function to execute a query against Ingres II, but Oracle, for example, doesn't even have a `_query()` function. You have to use `ora_parse()` on the SQL statement and then run `ora_exec()`.

You must also consider that there may be some specific functions you are using in MySQL that have no equivalent function in your new database. Perhaps you are even using very specific SQL statements in MySQL that are not supported in other databases, or are executed in a different way. Flexibility and complexity often come along as a pair.

Wouldn't it be cool if there were a way to write your code more abstractly, so that when you run a function such as `get_query_results()`, it would be smart enough to know what type of database you are connecting to and perform all of the necessary steps to retrieve the data? That's what the PHP Data Objects (PDO) extension attempts to do — provide a seamless experience when using PHP to communicate across different databases. PDO provides a data-abstraction layer so that you can use the same set of functions to work with a database, regardless of what database back end your company is using.

That's great! So why didn't we share this with you sooner? The sad fact is that some hosting providers may not make PDO available to their customers. And while we strongly urge you to use the latest version of PHP for increased stability, security, and speed, many hosting companies still use older versions of PHP to support legacy applications. You will be trapped into using what is offered to you, unless you are hosting your own server.

It was only after much deliberation and discussion that we chose to continue showing you the mysql_* functions in this edition. PDO is the latest and the greatest, but mysql_* is the lowest common denominator, and we wanted to make this book relevant for the largest audience possible. We encourage you to learn both ways, to increase your knowledge of PHP, so that you can apply either solution depending on your needs. We also chose to present PDO to you towards the end of the book, after you've had some experience with objected-oriented programming, because PDO uses OOP syntax. So, let's take a good look at PDO requirements and get started using it.

PHP Data Objects (PDO) Requirements

First of all, you must be using at least PHP 5 to take advantage of PDO, because the extension depends on certain key features that aren't available in earlier versions of PHP. Any version of PHP before version 5 will not work. PDO is available as a separate extension for PHP 5.0, and has shipped in the default build of PHP starting with version 5.1. Of course, you'll be all set on this front if you're using version 6 (which we assume you are, since you're reading *Beginning PHP6, Apache, MySQL Web Development*).

Linux users shouldn't have to do anything out of the ordinary for PDO to be available, and Windows users just need to uncomment the extension=php_pdo.dll line in their php.ini, for PDO to be available. PDO also needs a database-specific driver for each type of database you plan on working with. This driver file allows the PDO extension to translate the PHP function calls to something more specific for the target database. For example, the PDO_MYSQL driver is used for a MySQL database, the PDO_INFORMIX driver is used for an Informix database, the PDO_OCI driver is used for an Oracle database, and so on. There is no specific PDO_INGRES driver, but you can access the Ingres II database via the PDO_ODBC driver. New drivers are being developed for different databases even as you read this, so for the most up-to-date list of drivers, you should visit http://www.php.net/pdo-drivers.

Your php.ini file should list the appropriate driver as an extension, regardless of your operating system platform. Complete instructions are available for installing drivers in the PHP online documentation.

Using PDO

With the core of PHP providing the internal mechanisms on which PDO relies, with PDO available as a PHP extension, and with the necessary driver file installed as an extension to translate common function calls to database-specific calls, you should be set and ready to start issuing those queries.

When you supplied a username, password, and hostname to connect to MySQL, you used the mysql_connect() function. You then supplied the name of the database you wanted to work with, using mysql_select_db(). All this information is gathered together when you are working with PDO instead of calling two functions. The database type, hostname, and database table set are formatted as a string called a Data Source Name (DSN). There are a few different ways to format a DSN, but here is probably the easiest way to accomplish it:

```
mysql:host=localhost;dbname=mywebapp
```

This DSN is used to establish a connection to a MySQL server running on the localhost, and you are connecting to a database named test. You pass the DSN, username, and password to the PDO constructor when you create a new instance of the object, like this:

```
$db = new PDO('mysql:host=localhost;dbname=mywebapp', 'dbuser', 'dbpassword');
```

You then prepare a statement to be sent to the database, using the prepare() method, which returns a PDOStatement object.

```
$query = 'SELECT * FROM users';
$stmt = $db->prepare($query);
```

The prepared query is sent to the database with the execute() method.

```
$stmt->execute();
```

So you've seen how relatively easy it is to use PDO to issue a query to a database, but the fun doesn't stop there. PDO also lets you prepare your SQL statements with placeholders and later bind data to them when you are ready to issue the query. This lets you think of your query more as a template that is prepared once by PDO and can be repeatedly run with different data, which is generally a more efficient approach than if you executed several statements sequentially that differed only in their data.

Another benefit (and perhaps more important feature) of working with prepared statements is that PDO will handle quoting and escaping of the parameters' data. This makes it much easier to protect your database against malicious input sneaking in.

When you prepare a statement, you can provide parameters as placeholders in your SQL. These parameters can either be represented with a ? or be explicitly named. Let's take a look at using ? as a placeholder in a query.

```
$query = 'INSERT INTO users
        (username, first_name, last_name, email)
    VALUES
        (?, ?, ?, ?)';
$stmt = $db->prepare($query);
$stmt->execute(array($username, $first_name, $last_name, $email));
```

The values that will replace the ? placeholders in the query are passed as an array to the execute() method. The values appear in the array in the same order in which they will replace the placeholders.

Named parameters can be used in a similar way, except that the names are used as keys in the array, so the order of the data elements is not as important. The parameter identifiers are prefixed with : in the query.

```
$query = 'INSERT INTO users
        (username, first_name, last_name, email)
    VALUES
        (:username, :first_name, :last_name, :email)';
$stmt = $db->prepare($query);
$stmt->execute(array(':username'   => $username,
                     ':first_name' => $first_name,
                     ':last_name'  => $last_name,
                     ':email'      => $email));
```

Compare these with how you would need to execute the same query using mysql_* functions, and you will see that PDO is more efficient, convenient, and flexible than the other database access extensions. It also makes your code more readable, which is a good thing, because it is then easier to debug and maintain.

```
$query = 'INSERT INTO users
        (username, first_name, last_name, email)
    VALUES
        ("' . mysql_real_escape_string($username, $db) . '",
        ("' . mysql_real_escape_string($first_name, $db) . '",
        ("' . mysql_real_escape_string($last_name, $db) . '",
        ("' . mysql_real_escape_string($email, $db) . '")';
$result = mysql_query($query, $db);
```

A PDOStatement is an interesting object, in that at first it represents a prepared statement. After you execute that statement, the object then represents the associated result set. You can call the statement's fetch() method to retrieve your results. Alternatively, you can use the fetchAll() method to retrieve all the records at one time as an array.

The PDOStatement object's fetch() and fetchAll() methods are more versatile than you may initially think. The methods accept arguments that affect how you access the results that are returned from the database. Both accept the following constants as an argument:

- ❏ PDO::FETCH_ASSOC returns the results as an associative array.

- ❏ PDO::FETCH_BOTH returns the results as an array indexed by both column name and numeric values. This is the default behavior, if no other mode is specified.

- ❏ PDO::FETCH_BOUND assigns the result's values back to the PHP variables to which they were bound.

- ❏ PDO::FETCH_CLASS returns a new instance of a class with the results mapped to the object's properties.

- ❏ PDO::FETCH_CLASSTYPE can be combined with PDO::FETCH_CLASS, and the name of the class will be determined by the value of the first column in the result set.

- ❏ PDO::FETCH_INTO updates an existing object with values from the result set.

- ❏ PDO::FETCH_LAZY is a combination of PDO::FETCH_BOTH and PDO::FETCH_OBJ.

- ❏ PDO::FETCH_NUM returns the results as a numerically indexed array.

- ❏ PDO::FETCH_OBJ returns an anonymous object with the results mapped to the object's properties.

```
while ($row = $stmt->fetch(PDO::FETCH_ASSOC)) {
    print_r($row);
}
```

Another useful method of the PDOStatement object is rowCount(). It is comparable to mysql_num_rows(), and returns the number of rows affected by an INSERT, UPDATE, or DELETE query or returned by a SELECT query.

```
$query = 'SELECT * FROM users';
$stmt = $db->prepare($query);
$stmt->execute();
echo 'There are ' . $stmt->rowCount() . ' users.';
```

You have seen several instances throughout this book where you want to retrieve the primary key of a record after you insert it into the database. For example, when you are creating a new user's record and want to associate various permissions with him or her but store the permissions in a separate table, you will often link them together by the user's ID. After you insert the user's information into a users table, you need to retrieve the new user ID so you can continue adding information in other tables. You employ the PDO object's lastInsertId() method for this, which is comparable to the mysql_insert_id() function.

```
$query = 'INSERT INTO users
        (username, first_name, last_name, email)
    VALUES
        (:username, :first_name, :last_name, :email)';
$stmt = $db->prepare($query);
$stmt->execute(array(':username'   => $username,
                     ':first_name' => $first_name,
                     ':last_name'  => $last_name,
                     ':email'      => $email));
$user_id = $db->lastInsertId();
$query = 'INSERT INTO addresses
        (user_id, address_1, address_2, city, state, zip_code)
    VALUES
        (:user_id, :address_1, :address_2, :city, :state, :zip_code)';
$stmt = $db->prepare($query);
$stmt->execute(array(':user_id'   => $user_id,
                     ':address_1' => $address_1,
                     ':address_2' => $address_2,
                     ':city'      => $city,
                     ':state'     => $state,
                     ':zip_code'  => $zip_code));
```

There is no method equivalent to `mysql_close()` to disconnect from the database with PDO. Instead, you simply set your reference to the PDO object to null. PHP will close the connection on your behalf when the reference is no longer needed.

```
$db = null;
```

You can find more information on PHP's PDO extension and its PDO and PDOStatement objects in the official documentation online at www.php.net/pdo.

Summary

Now that you know how to use PDO, you can go ahead and start writing your PHP applications using the PDO interface. So long as you keep your database queries themselves restricted to a subset of SQL commands that are supported by MySQL or any other database solution you choose — whether it be Sybase, Microsoft SQL Server, Oracle, Ingres II, or whatever other solution your company may throw your way — all you need to do is make sure you have the appropriate driver file listed as an extension, and you can avoid having to rewrite all of your PHP code. You won't even break a sweat when the IT manager informs you of the company's decision to switch everyone from Ingres II to PostgreSQL after the marketing department installs their new tracking system.

Each database understands its own unique dialect of SQL, and finding that subset of common keywords can be limiting. If your company has chosen to go with MySQL over PostgreSQL, or Ingres II over MySQL, it was probably for a reason. You will probably be writing queries that maximize your particular database's strengths and won't necessarily be directly compatible with other databases. Each of your queries will need to be reviewed when you change to another database. At least you won't have to rewrite your PHP code when you use PDO, though, and that's half the battle. Learning PDO will only make you a stronger developer and give you more options to choose from. Just remember its limitations, how you can use it with specific versions of PHP only, and how it's configured to work properly.

Installation and Configuration on Linux

In Chapter 1, you learned how to install and configure Apache, MySQL, and PHP on a Windows-based system, but the trio can run on other platforms as well! In fact, it is very popular to run AMP on Linux (many people add an L to AMP when running the applications on Linux, for the moniker LAMP). We felt it was just as important to provide you with installation instructions under Linux as well, but putting them in Chapter 1 would have been overwhelming, so we decided to present them separately in this appendix.

Installing Apache, MySQL, and PHP on Linux

After following these instructions, you will have successfully installed Apache, MySQL, and PHP on your Linux-based system. We cover compiling and installing the AMP components from source, even though other methods are available (such as apt-get and yum), because this method offers the most flexibility and works on nearly all UNIX-like systems. You should review each component's web site if you want more detailed installation instructions or information on other supported platforms.

- ❑ **Apache:** http://httpd.apache.org/docs/2.2/install.html
- ❑ **MySQL:** http://dev.mysql.com/doc/refman/5.1/en/installing-source.html
- ❑ **PHP:** http://www.php.net/manual/en/install.unix.php

Install MySQL

MySQL is the database that holds all the data to be accessed by your web site. Follow these steps to install it:

1. If there isn't a user on the system dedicated to running the mysql daemon (typically `mysql`), you'll need to create one. To do this, enter the following commands in a console:

    ```
    groupadd mysql
    useradd -r -g mysql mysql
    ```

2. Go to the MySQL web site at www.mysql.com, and click the Developer Zone tab. Then, click the Downloads link on the navigation bar just under the tabs.

3. Scroll down and click on the link for the latest General Availability version of MySQL.

4. Scroll down to the Source downloads section of the downloadable files, and click Pick a Mirror next to the Compressed GNU TAR (tar.gz) package.

5. Select the download from a nearby mirror, and the download will begin.

6. Open a console window, and change to the directory where you downloaded the tarball.

7. Extract the tarball, and change to the directory it creates:

    ```
    tar -vxzf mysql-5.0.51b.tar.gz
    cd mysql-5.0.51b
    ```

8. Next, configure the source:

    ```
    ./configure --prefix=/usr/local/mysql
    ```

    Using the `--prefix` switch tells the installer where to put the MySQL libraries and binaries after they're built. We recommend placing them in `/usr/local/mysql`, but you may choose to specify a different value, depending on your needs or your system's configuration. For a complete list of configuration options, run `./configure --help`.

9. Compile the source:

    ```
    make
    ```

10. Install the libraries and binaries. We use `sudo` to escalate our account's privileges, because superuser (root) privileges are needed for this step.

    ```
    sudo make install
    ```

11. Run the `mysql_install_db` script with elevated privileges to install the initial database:

    ```
    sudo scripts/mysql_install_db
    ```

12. Set the permissions on the installed files:

    ```
    sudo chown -R root /usr/local/mysql
    sudo chown -R mysql /usr/local/mysql/var
    sudo chgrp -R mysql /usr/local/mysql
    ```

13. It is advised to run MySQL with a configuration file in place. Five sample configuration files are included: `my-small.cnf`, `my-medium.cnf`, `my-large.cnf`, `my-huge.cnf`, and `my-innodb-heavy-4G.cnf`. Copy a suitable configuration file to `/etc/my.cnf`.

```
sudo cp support-files/my-medium.cnf /etc/my.cnf
```

MySQL looks in `/etc/my.cnf` for global configuration options. Any changes you wish to make to customize MySQL's configuration should be made in this file. You can also place a `my.cnf` file in the server's data directory (`/usr/local/mysql/var` in our setup) to supply server-specific configuration options, if you plan on having multiple instances running.

14. Add MySQL's `bin` directory to your `PATH` environment variable. This will allow you to run MySQL's utilities from the command line without having to explicitly type the full path each time. To temporarily set it, you can type:

```
PATH=$PATH:/usr/local/mysql/bin
```

You will need to edit the appropriate configuration file for your profile to make the setting permanent. Exactly how you do this is dependent upon which shell you use. Bash traditionally uses `.bashrc`, and C Shell/tcsh uses `.cshrc`.

15. Start the MySQL daemon:

```
sudo mysqld_safe --user=mysql &
```

You'll probably want to add the previous command to whatever facilities are available to automatically start the daemon at boot. This varies by OS, so you'll need to find out what works on your system. Here is one easy way to add this that works with most systems (but may not be the best way):

```
sudo echo '/usr/local/mysql/bin/mysqld_safe --user=mysql &' >> /etc/rc.local
```

Install Apache

Apache is responsible for serving your web pages generated by PHP. Follow these basic steps to install it:

1. If there isn't a user on the system dedicated to running the apache daemon (typically `nobody`, `apache`, or `www-data`), you'll need to create one. To do this, enter the following commands in a console:

```
groupadd www-data
useradd -r -g www-data
```

2. Go to `www.apache.org`, and click the HTTP Server link in the Apache Projects list. The Apache Software Foundation offers many different software packages, though this is the only one we are concerned with.

3. Click the Download link under the most recent version of Apache.

4. Click the Unix Source link for the tar.gz file.

If you experience problems downloading this file, you can try downloading from a different mirror site. Select an available mirror from the drop-down box near the top of the download page.

5.   Open a console window, and change to the directory where you downloaded the tarball.

6.   Extract the tarball, and change to the directory it creates:

```
tar -vxzf httpd-2.2.9.tar.gz
cd httpd-2.2.9
```

7.   Next, configure the source:

```
./configure --prefix=/usr/local/apache --enable-so
```

Using the `--prefix` switch tells the installer where to put the Apache server after it's built. We recommend placing it in `/usr/local/apache`, but you may choose to specify a different value, depending on your needs or your system's configuration. The `--enable-so` option configures Apache so it will support loadable modules (required later for PHP). For a complete list of configuration options, run `./configure --help`.

8.   Compile the source:

```
make
```

9.   Install the server. We use `sudo` to escalate our account's privileges, because superuser (root) privileges are needed for this step.

```
sudo make install
```

10.   Add Apache's `bin` directory to your `PATH` environment variable. This will allow you to run Apache and its utilities from the command line without having to explicitly type the full path each time. To temporarily set it, you can type:

```
PATH=$PATH:/usr/local/apache/bin
```

You will need to edit the appropriate configuration file for your profile to make the setting permanent. Exactly how you do this is dependent upon which shell you use. Bash traditionally uses `.bashrc`, and C Shell/tcsh uses `.cshrc`.

11.   Start the Apache daemon:

```
sudo apachectl start
```

12.   You'll probably want to add the previous command to whatever facilities are available to automatically start the daemon at boot. This varies by OS, so you'll need to find out what works on your system. Here is one easy way to add this that works with most systems (but may not be the best way):

```
sudo echo '/usr/local/apache/bin/apachectl start' >> /etc/rc.local
```

Install PHP

PHP is responsible for generating dynamic web pages with data from MySQL. Follow these steps to install PHP on your system:

1. Go to the PHP web site at www.php.net.

2. Click on the Download link to go to the site's downloads page.

3. Scroll down to the Complete Source Code section, and click on the appropriate link to download the latest tar.gz package.

4. Click any of the mirror sites to begin the download. If you have difficulties downloading from one mirror, try a different mirror that may be closer to you.

5. Open a console window, and change to the directory where you downloaded the tarball.

6. Extract the tarball, and change to the directory it creates:

```
tar -vxzf php-6.0.0.tar.gz
cd php-6.0.0
```

7. Configure the source:

```
./configure --with-apxs2=/usr/local/apache/bin/apxs --with-mysql=/usr/local/
mysql \
     --prefix=/usr/local/php
```

Using the `--prefix` switch tells the installer where to put the PHP server after it's built. We recommend placing it in /usr/local/php, but you may choose to specify a different value, depending on your needs or your system's configuration. The `--with-apxs2` option specifies the path to Apache's apxs tool. `--with-mysql` provides the path to your MySQL installation. If you did not install Apache to /usr/local/apache or MySQL to /usr/local/mysql, then you will need to change those values accordingly. There are numerous configuration options for PHP, and we would almost need a chapter just to describe them all! For a complete list of configuration options, run ./configure --help.

8. Compile the source:

```
make
```

9. Install PHP. We use sudo to escalate our account's privileges, because superuser (root) privileges are needed for this step.

```
sudo make install
```

10. It is advised to run PHP with a php.ini file. By default, the PHP installation provides two copies of the file with common configuration values: php.ini-dist and php.ini-recommended.

The php.ini-dist file is meant to be used for development purposes, while php.ini-recommended has additional security measures and should be used when your site goes live. Depending on your reason for using PHP, choose the php.ini file that best suits your needs.

For the purposes of this book, we are going to be using php.ini-dist. Feel free to switch to the php.ini-recommended file as your default once you are more familiar with how PHP behaves.

```
sudo cp php.ini-dist /usr/local/php/lib/php.ini
```

11. Add PHP's bin directory to your PATH environment variable. This will allow you to reference PHP and its utilities from the command line, if you ever want to, without having to explicitly type the full path each time. To temporarily set it, you can type:

```
PATH=$PATH:/usr/local/php/bin
```

You will need to edit the appropriate configuration file for your profile to make the setting permanent. Exactly how you do this is dependent upon which shell you use. Bash traditionally uses .bashrc, and C Shell/tcsh uses .cshrc.

Configuring Apache to Use PHP

Now that both Apache and PHP are installed, there are a few more customizable options that need to be adjusted. To configure Apache to recognize a PHP file as one that needs to be parsed with the PHP engine, you need to first locate the following lines in your httpd.conf file:

```
# AddType allows you to add to or override the MIME configuration
# file specified in TypesConfig for specific file types.
#
#AddType application/x-gzip .tgz
#
# AddEncoding allows you to have certain browsers uncompress
# information on the fly. Note: Not all browsers support this.
#
#AddEncoding x-compress .Z
#AddEncoding x-gzip .gz .tgz
#
# If the AddEncoding directives above are commented-out, then you
# probably should define those extensions to indicate media types:
#
AddType application/x-compress .Z
AddType application/x-gzip .gz .tgz
```

Then add the following lines:

```
AddType application/x-httpd-php .php
AddType application/x-httpd-php-source .phps
```

Next, you need to add the PHP module into your httpd.conf program so that Apache can properly coordinate with PHP to serve the dynamically generated pages PHP will produce. In your configuration file, locate the following lines:

```
# Dynamic Shared Object (DSO) Support
#
# To be able to use the functionality of a module which was built as a DSO you
# have to place corresponding `LoadModule' lines at this location so the
```

```
# directives contained in it are actually available _before_ they are used.
# Statically compiled modules (those listed by `httpd -l') do not need
# to be loaded here.
#
# Example:
# LoadModule foo_module modules/mod_foo.so
#
LoadModule actions_module modules/mod_actions.so
LoadModule alias_module modules/mod_alias.so
LoadModule asis_module modules/mod_asis.so
LoadModule auth_basic_module modules/mod_auth_basic.so
#LoadModule auth_digest_module modules/mod_auth_digest.so
...
#LoadModule usertrack_module modules/mod_usertrack.so
#LoadModule version_module modules/mod_version.so
#LoadModule vhost_alias_module modules/mod_vhost_alias.so
```

Add the following line:

```
LoadModule php6_module "libphp6.so"
```

Oh, and remember to restart Apache after you've saved your modifications to `httpd.conf`, or else Apache will not be aware of your changes! You can do this by calling `apachectl restart`.

Summary

You've installed and configured the Apache, MySQL, and PHP trio on your Linux system. Now you can proceed to Chapter 2 to get your hands dirty creating your movie review web site, as we begin discussing PHP code.

Index

FROM, 91
FrontBase, 769
full-featured error handler, 255–256
functions. *See also specific functions*
  array-sorting, 61
  ctype_*, 235, 236, 239
  customized, 55–59, 691
  defined, 55
  efficient code and, 55
  is_*, 235, 236, 239
  methods v., 351
  reference list, 695–752
    Apache/PHP, 695–696
    array, 696–701
    date/time, 702–706
    directory/file, 709–713
    error-handling, 714
    HTTP, 724–725
    image, 716–723
    logging, 714
    mail, 724–725
    mathematical, 33, 725–727
    miscellaneous, 751–752
    MySQL, 728–730
    network, 724–725
    object handling, 715–716
    online, 695
    output buffer, 731
    PDO database interface, 732–734
    PHP configuration information, 734–736
    process, 737
    program execution, 737
    session functions, 738–739
    SimpleXML, 739–740
    string, 740–747
    URL, 748
    variable, 749–750
  type-validating, 235

G

gallery.php, 214–215
Gaussian blur, 201
GD library, 175–177
  enabling, in PHP, 176
  image types and, 176
  online information, 177
  testing, 176–177
gd_info(), 176, 177
Geany, 762, 763

generate_ratings(), 128
generating errors, 250–252
GET method, 44, 134
$_GET superglobal array, 123, 127, 129
get_director(), 117, 124
getimageinfo(), 186
getimagesize(), 186
get_leadactor(), 117, 124
get_movietype(), 117, 124
gettor methods, 349
GIF, 176, 186
  IMAGETYPE_GIF, 186
  support, enabling, 176
global, 55
Google Analytics, 636–637
graphical user interfaces. *See GUIs*
Graphics Draw. *See GD Library*
grayscale, image in, 201
greater than (›), 50, 92
greater than or equal to (›=), 50, 92
GUIs (graphical user interfaces),
    administration, 767

H

handling errors. *See error handling*
hashing, 367
header(), 143–144
  problem code and, 144
  warning message and, 143
header.php, 53–54
'headers already sent' error, 40, 44, 143,
    644–645
headers, e-mail and, 323–325
Hello World, 26, 132, 135, 342
heredoc, 73, 110–114
  closing tag line, error and, 113
  syntax, 110–114
hits/page views, 638
hosting, 765
  third-party, 765–768
    administration GUIs, 767
    bandwidth usage, 767
    configuration ability, 767
    online companies (list), 768
    pricing, 768
    server access, 766–767
    server control, 766–767
    site usage, 767
    supported databases, 766

M